Developing Client/Server Applications with Oracle Developer/2000™

Paul Hipsley

SAMS PUBLISHING

201 West 103rd Street
Indianapolis, Indiana 46290

This book is dedicated to my family and friends.

FIRST EDITION

International Standard Book Number: 0-672-30852-5

Library of Congress Catalog Card Number: 95-70081

99 98 8 7 6 5

Interpretation of the printing code: the rightmost double-digit number is the year of the book's printing; the rightmost single-digit, the number of the book's printing. For example, a printing code of 96-1 shows that the first printing of the book occurred in 1996.

Composed in AGaramond and MCPdigital by Macmillan Computer Publishing

Printed in the United States of America

Publisher and President *Richard K. Swadley*
Acquisitions Manager *Greg Wiegand*
Development Manager *Dean Miller*
Managing Editor *Cindy Morrow*
Marketing Manager *Gregg Bushyeager*

Acquisitions Editor
Rosemarie Graham

Development Editor
Todd Bumbalough

Software Development Specialist
Steve Straiger

Production Editor
James Grass

Copy Editor
Joe Williams

Technical Reviewer
James Farmer
Stephen M. Tallon

Editorial Coordinator
Bill Whitmer

Technical Edit Coordinator
Lynette Quinn

Formatter
Frank Sinclair

Editorial Assistants
Sharon Cox
Andi Richter
Rhonda Tinch-Mize

Cover Designer
Tim Amrhein

Book Designer
Alyssa Yesh

Production Team Supervisor
Brad Chinn

Production
Carol Bowers, Georgianna Briggs, Michael Brumitt, Charlotte Clapp, Jeanne Clark, Louisa Klucznik, Ayanna Lacey, Kevin Laseau, Paula Lowell, Donna Martin, Casey Price, Nancy C. Price, Brian-Kent Proffitt, Erich J. Richter, SA Springer, Andrew Stone, Mark Walchle, Colleen Williams

Overview

Contents

Acknowledgments

I would like to acknowledge and thank the following people:

Rosemarie Graham, for her patience and guidance while I was writing this book.

Todd Bumbalough, for providing the opportunity to write this book.

Jim Grass, for his advice and help while editing this book.

Lori Windle, for a bit of editing and a lot of support.

Helen Middlemiss, for helping me get my paper in for CODA '95 where this book opportunity originated.

Peter Jensen, Steve Ehrlich, Joe Thomas, Dennis Moore, Steve Muench, Per Brondum, and Ivan Chong for providing opportunities with Oracle and supporting my work with the Oracle tools.

Ed Becker, for being a friend, business partner, and appreciating my style as well as my skills.

Paul Mannino and Sharon Kennedy, for giving me some of the best OJT I have ever had.

The CODA, and IOUW Paper Selection Committees, for providing opportunities to share my work with other Oracle developers.

Tony Ziemba, for publishing my first paid article in *Oracle Developer* magazine.

Albert Chen, for publishing my first article in the *Oracle Integrator.*

Larry Ellison, for giving me the inspiration to write and publish my first article, as well as for making an appearance in this book.

About the Author

Paul Hipsley has lived and worked as a consultant in the United States and Australia, and can be recognized for the following achievements as an Oracle developer:

- Authored a paper for the 1995 International Oracle User Week (IOUW) entitled, "Implementing Windows 95 Style Applications in Oracle Forms 4.5."
- Award-winning finalist in the Oracle Developer/2000 Programming Competition, CODA '95.
- Authored and presented a paper for CODA '95 entitled, "Oracle CDE2: The Next Generation…."
- Authored and presented two papers for the 1994 IOUW entitled, "Oracle Forms Floating Toolbar: A Reusable Date Field Tool," and "Integrating Oracle Forms 4 with WordPerfect 6.0 for Windows."
- Authored article in the premier edition of *Oracle Developer* entitled, "Highlight Items Dynamically in Oracle Forms Version 4.0."
- Award-winning finalist in the Oracle CDE Programming Competition, CODA '94.
- Authored article for the *Oracle Integrator* entitled "Implementing Objects in Oracle7."

Hipsley can be reached via e-mail at `hips@ozemail.com.au`.

Introduction

Oracle Developer/2000 is the next generation of development tools for Microsoft Windows applications development from Oracle Corporation. Oracle Developer/2000 leverages the power of Oracle7 and Microsoft Windows. Oracle7 is the most popular Relational Database Management System (RDBMS) in the world and Microsoft Windows is the most popular Graphical User Interface (GUI) in the world. The previous release of Oracle Developer/2000 was know as the Oracle Cooperative Development Environment (CDE). At times you may see or hear references to CDE2, which is now known as Oracle Developer/2000.

This book is intended to be of value to many different types of readers, including managers of Oracle client/server projects, individuals evaluating development tools, programmers who are new to the Oracle environment, experienced Oracle programmers who are new to the Windows development environment, and students interested in investing in their future careers in the Oracle application development job market.

It will serve you well as an introduction to Oracle Developer/2000, the Oracle7 RDBMS, OLE2 applications, and the integration of these components in a Windows environment. It also covers the development life cycle including project management, analysis, design, development, configuration, integration, and deployment. These are the major topics covered in this book, and the major components of many client/server management information system.

You will be provided with simple and practical examples and exercises that will reinforce the concepts and techniques being explained. And, while developing the examples and exercises throughout the book, you will be developing a completely integrated application system.

The completed system will utilize Oracle Forms, Oracle Reports, Oracle Graphics, Oracle Procedure Builder, Visual Basic Custom Controls, MS Word, MS Excel, MS ClipArt, bitmaps, icons, images, sounds, and video clips. All of the examples and exercises can be found on the companion CD-ROM included with this book.

This book is not intended to be a completely comprehensive reference guide to the Oracle database or the Oracle tools—that would require volumes of text and is already available in that form. Instead, this book summarizes and highlights, the most commonly used and significant features of the Oracle database and tools. It will quickly enable you to become familiar with the important concepts and the complete life cycle of an Oracle development project.

This book does not attempt to cover many other related topics including Oracle CASE, reverse engineering, migration of legacy systems or advanced features of SQL, PL/SQL, and the Oracle database and tools. The limits of scope are set with purpose and forethought, and for the benefit of the reader to quickly understand the significant components of an Oracle development project.

Part I—Starting the Project

Part I covers the motivation, initiation, organization, and analysis of a development project, and includes two chapters: "The Project Foundation," and "Analysis."

Part II—The Database

Part II contains four chapters on issues related to the development of a database, including "Logical Data Modeling," "Physical Database Design," "Building the Database," and "Populating the Database."

Part III—Oracle Developer/2000

Part III provides an overview of the common features of Oracle Developer/2000, as well as a review of the specific features and initial applications development with each tool. It contains five chapters, including "Introducing Oracle Developer/2000," "Introducing Oracle Forms," "Introducing Oracle Reports," "Introducing Oracle Graphics," and "Introducing Oracle Procedure Builder."

Part IV—Developing the System

Part IV contains four chapters that complete the development of the application system. These chapters include "Developing Oracle Forms Applications," "Developing Oracle Reports Applications," "Developing Oracle Graphics Applications," and "Integration and Deployment in the Windows Environment."

Part V—Appendixes

Part V contains eight appendixes that provide reference information on the Oracle Developer/2000 menus and properties. These appendixes compliment the chapters in Part III and Part IV.

I

Starting the Project

1

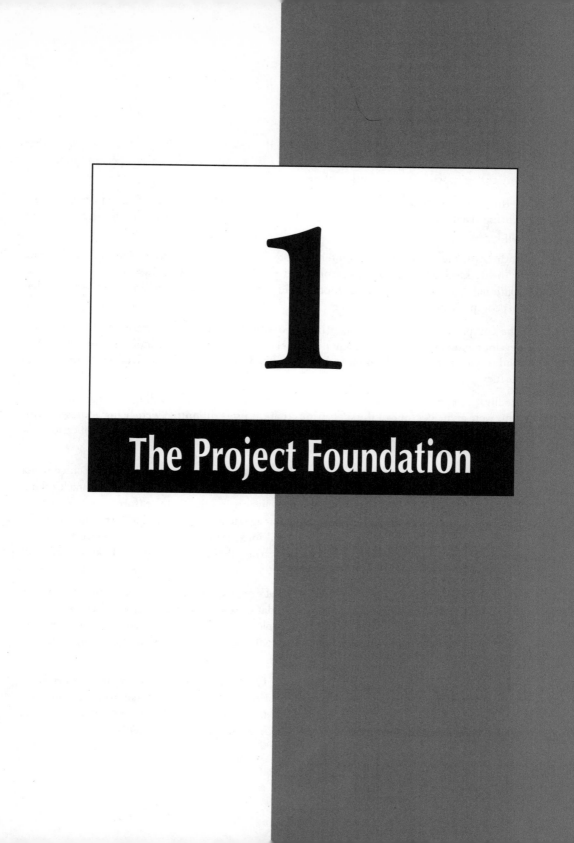

The Project Foundation

Introduction

The foundation of any project is management: the people who make the decisions about what to buy and what to do. It doesn't matter if it is a large corporation or a one-person shop; every project begins with the motivation of management to act.

In the project we will develop in this book, the company has many existing requirements and existing database applications. They also have a network and desktop applications for their employees.

In the past, the company has been reluctant to develop any new applications on the database or the desktop. This was based on some bad experiences and the advice of some experts that relational databases and development tools did not really provide what was advertised and what this company needed.

The company was patient and continued to keep an eye on the database and application-development markets. Management personnel read the magazines for independent reviews and made contacts with people in the industry who had a reputation for protecting the interests of business.

Finally, pressure started to mount from the user community. The feeling was that the old systems were archaic. None of the suggestions that the users submitted were being addressed with regard to systems development and leveraging the use of the network, desktop applications, or their laptop computers.

However, this company is not intimidated by pressure from anyone, and it only decided to act when it learned of some very promising software from Oracle Corporation. The Oracle7 database had been around for a few years and was delivering on the promise (formulated more than 25 years ago) of what a relational database management system could and should do. These capabilities included full declarative referential integrity, scalability, and support for storing objects of any type. Moreover, the company learned that there was even a desktop version of the Oracle7 database that ran on Windows.

The CEO always had a vision of a real RDBMS on each of his employees' laptops, a system that could be integrated with the corporate database on the main network server at headquarters. This database system would be capable of running the same applications that were developed for the stand-alone and online systems, using the same shared code and database structure.

In addition, the company had learned that the Oracle development tools were completely integrated with the database and were capable of providing the type of environment they had been looking for—one that could be seamlessly integrated with their desktop applications, that took advantage of the latest technology for GUI application development, and that included object-oriented features such as object classes and code reuse. And with Oracle, the company could develop applications with little or no coding. The code that was necessary could be shared and maintained in libraries and/or the database.

The company was interested but still not excited. As the CEO always said, nothing is certain until you prove it to yourself.

Therefore the company decided to invest a small amount of time from a few key personnel from the development department and the user community. A small team was formed from the most talented and interested people, people who had shared the CEO's vision of where their company could one day go.

The timing was right for such an effort—Oracle had started providing free 90-day trials for the database and the Oracle Developer/2000. Then the company learned that a book was available that detailed application development with Oracle7 and Oracle Developer/2000. A CD-ROM with Personal Oracle7 and Oracle Developer/2000 was included with the book. This book dealt with all of the things that the team had planned to do as soon as it had installed the database and tools.

The team planned to install the demonstration database and applications and then add a subset of their real requirements to the system. In doing this they would simulate their current system and create a prototype for future development projects. At the same time they would gain valuable experience working with the database, the tools, and a structured approach to applications development.

The team wanted its prototype to cover every aspect of the project life cycle, including:

- Management
- Analysis
- Data modeling
- Database design
- Construction of the database
- Loading data
- Training
- Developing the application system
- Integration with the desktop applications
- Configuring the environment
- Deploying the finished system on the network

This was going to be the foundation for future development projects in the company. At the same time, the team wanted to achieve all of this in as short a time period as possible.

The team worked through the project and followed the book as a guide. They were pleased at how easy the book had made everything—providing procedures, standards, and real-world experience in a practical explanation of how to develop an application system. And then there was the bonus of the CD-ROM, with the Oracle products and all the icons, bitmaps, toolbars, menus, and generalized library procedures.

When the team members were done with the project, they were happy to do the demonstration for the CEO, because they knew they had developed a working prototype that included all of the items on their list of goals. The welcome screen shown in Figure 1.1 was the first thing the CEO saw when the demo started.

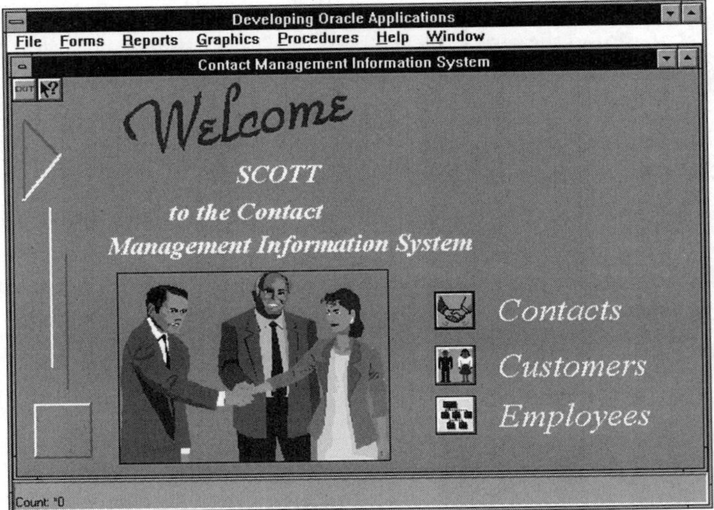

FIGURE 1.1.
The welcome screen—the application entry point.

A picture is worth a thousand words, and this picture was already saying that the system was looking good. The team pointed out that every feature in the system was available through the drop-down menus on this welcome screen, and it was noted that it also had a nice visual appeal. Then they did a quick review of some of the other features this screen demonstrated, such as iconic buttons, graphical boilerplate, and an embedded OLE2 object.

Someone in the back said: "It looks nice, but what does it do?" So the next thing the team did was review the main application that they had developed, the Contact Management application. (See Figure 1.2.)

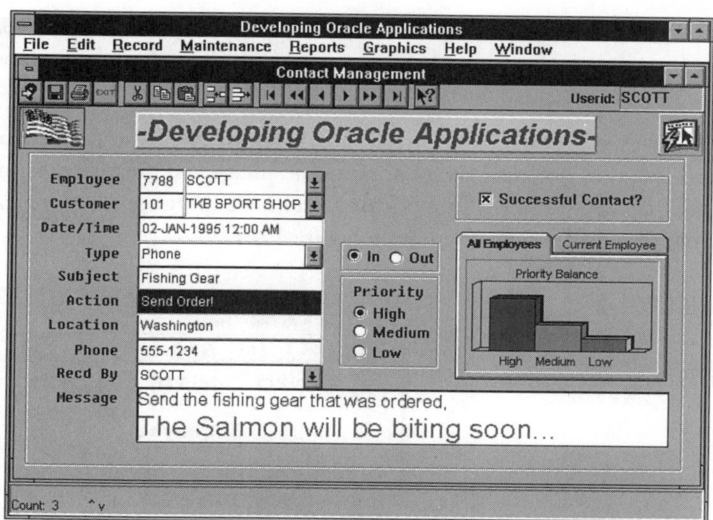

FIGURE 1.2.
The Contact Management application.

Here the team was able to point out the many features of Oracle Forms, such as custom menus, a standard toolbar, an embedded OLE2 object, images, Visual Basic Custom Controls, integration with Oracle Graphics, a list of values, radio groups, check boxes, three-dimensional boilerplate, and another OLE2 object that contained an MS Word document that was stored in the Oracle7 database.

From here the Salaries & Commissions report was selected from the Reports menu, and it appeared in the Reports Previewer. (See Figure 1.3.)

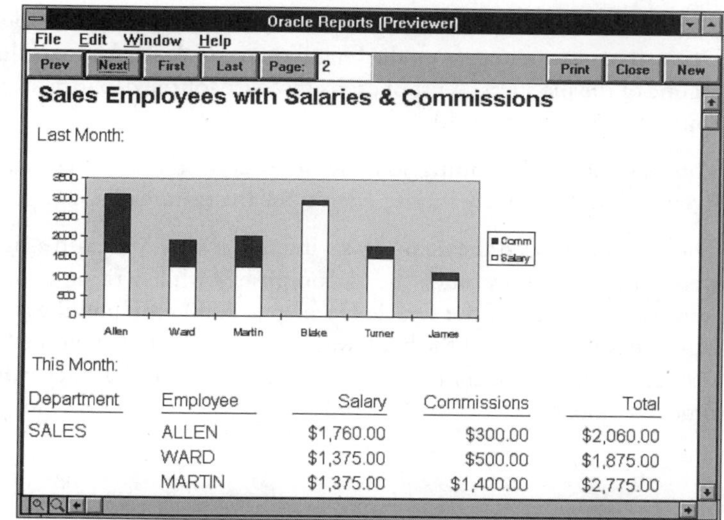

FIGURE 1.3.
Salaries & Commissions report with Excel link.

This was a simple report, but it did include a link to an Excel spreadsheet with a graph. They returned to the Contact Management application and clicked on the Exit button on the toolbar to go back to the Welcome screen.

Then they selected the Contact Totals report from the Reports menu. When the report appeared, they noticed that it contained an image and buttons next to the summary items. When they clicked on one of the buttons, another report appeared, revealing the details of the item that they had just selected. (See Figure 1.4.)

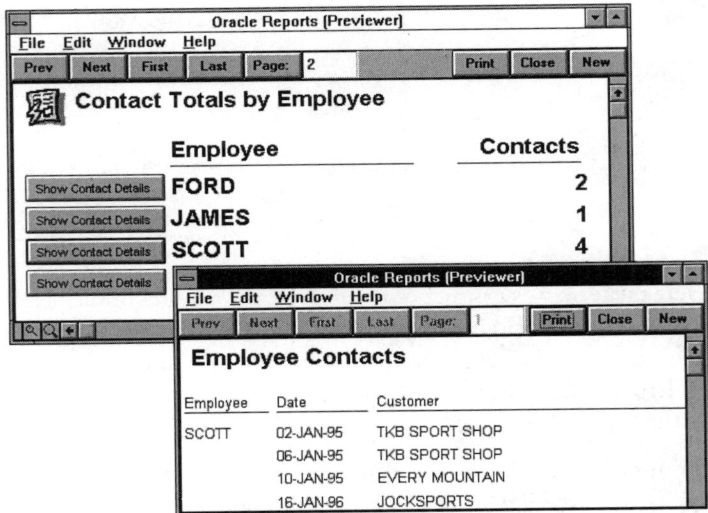

FIGURE 1.4.
The Employee Contact Totals drill-down report.

The demo was going well. They closed the drill-down report and selected the Employees by Department menu item from the Graphics menu. A pie chart was displayed. Then they clicked on one of the pie slices. A list of each employee for the department represented by the pie slice appeared. (See Figure 1.5.)

This was only the beginning, as there were many other features that were covered in the demo. Everyone was extremely impressed at what the team had accomplished.

The team concluded the demo by saying that it wasn't as hard as it looked and that even they were surprised at how much they accomplished while writing so little code. A lot of the credit went to the quality of the Oracle Developer/2000 tools and the strength of the Oracle7 database. They also said that the book was a great help and that without it they couldn't have done it so easily. The book contained a lot of tips and ideas that they would benefit from for a long time to come.

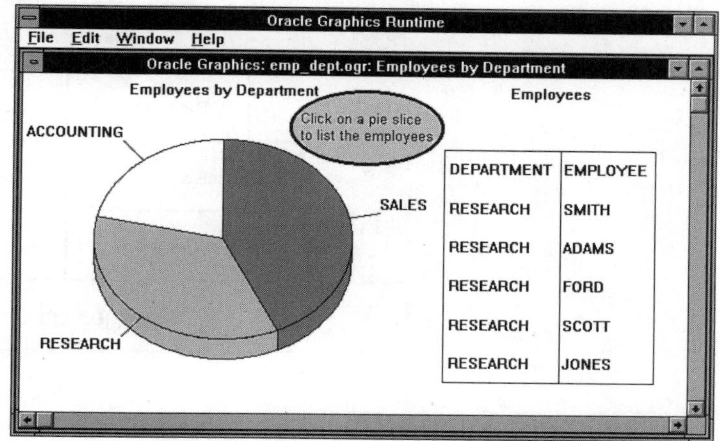

FIGURE 1.5.
An Oracle Graphics display of Employees by Department.

Wouldn't we all like to get the kind of results you just read? We can, with Oracle7, Oracle Developer/2000, and this book. But before we get into the details of developing applications with Oracle Developer/2000, we are going to review some of the basic principles behind a successful project, including:

- Management support
- Quality staff
- Network support
- Documented procedures
- Documented standards
- The network
- The database
- The development tools

After we have reviewed each of these topics in this chapter, we will go on to a chapter on analysis, then a section on the database, a section introducing Oracle Developer/2000, and the section where the application development is completed.

Foundation Overview

I would like to start off by describing the foundation of any client/server software development project, as illustrated in Figure 1.6. I will begin with an overview of each of the foundation layers. These layers are the components of success that must be in place prior to a project's initiation. Without a solid foundation from which the project is based, the entire project may falter regardless of the quality of the developers, the development tools, or the database.

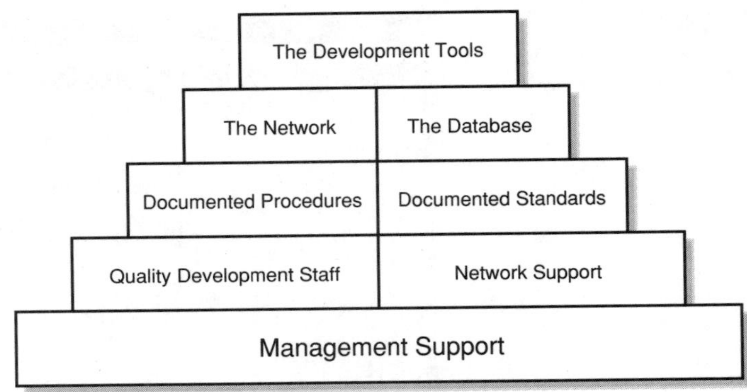

FIGURE 1.6.
The project foundation

Management Support

Management support must be the initial foundation layer of any software development project. From this foundation the project will be built. Just as in any engineering endeavor, a solid foundation capable of providing tremendous support will be critical. Each subsequent part that is to be constructed will be dependent on this initial foundation layer.

This is not intended to be a book on management; however, all too often, software development projects struggle because of breakdowns in the application of basic management principles.

Every successful project starts and ends with management support.

The Chain of Command

An integral component of a successful project is a clearly defined and consistently maintained chain of command, as represented by Figure 1.7. The larger the organization and the project, the more significant the chain of command becomes. All members of the team must understand and appreciate the division of roles and responsibilities. Clearly defined relationships between members of the organization will save considerable time and energy and will streamline communication.

Responsibility with Authority

Each person who is responsible for a task must have the authority to carry out that task. In addition, the chain of command must support each member of the organization, as appropriate, when issues arise that must be addressed outside any individual's level of authority.

FIGURE 1.7.
The chain-of-command diagram for the project.

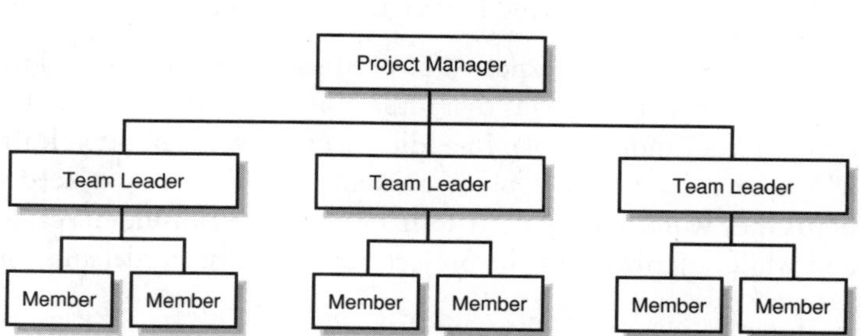

Quality Development Staff

The quality of the work is directly proportional to the quality of the people doing the work. Well-qualified workers with good work habits are much more likely to produce a good product. Workers with excellent knowledge of the products they are using as well as a commitment to follow an appropriate method for employing their skills are the kind of workers needed for a successful development project.

While this concept of excellent workers producing excellent products sounds quite reasonable, it is often very difficult to staff the project with the appropriate people. There are many reasons for the lack of proper project staffing, but the driving factors are availability and cost.

The following paragraphs detail an approach for combating this dilemma.

In-House Staff

As a general rule, it is best to use the resources that are available from in-house staff. These are usually the people who know the business side of things and are likely to be reasonably priced. In-house staff are also a good option when you will need them to maintain the system after development. You have an ideal situation if your staff are already skilled in the use of the development environment and have been productive for you in the past.

An existing worker who has proven herself is likely to relish the opportunity to be involved in a new development project or a conversion of the system she have been working with. If however, the existing staff lacks the appropriate skills for the environment you will be developing in, the use of consultants and trainers are certainly worth considering.

Consultants

The use of consultants can often provide a tremendous benefit to a project. These are people with the advanced skill sets required to work at a high level of productivity. Often the cost of hiring consultants inhibits management from selecting this option. However, there are many different factors that should be weighed prior to making this determination.

Consultants should be expected to produce at a much higher level and at a higher ratio than staff personnel. This means that often a single person, at twice the pay rate, could outperform two, three, or more people. In addition, employees can often learn a great deal when working with a consultant. Lastly, many consultants work on an as-needed basis and only bill for the hours they work. Hiring short-term or part-time consultants can significantly reduce the total cost while still providing the project with expertise, leadership, and a training source.

Training

Training is another valuable tool that can extend the skills of the in-house staff. Whether the training is formal or informal, in-house or out, developing the skills of the project team will provide dividends. Spreading the in-house knowledge around through informal brown-bag lunch sessions is a low-impact and high-results method. Individuals in the organization can alternate as the presenter of various training topics. Computer-based training and video training are a good way for some people to acquire knowledge and skills at their own pace. Formal training by a specialist in the field is usually the best place to start in the early days of project preparation. It is important to note, however, that once an individual receives training it will be most valuable and practical only if that person can return from the training and apply the knowledge and skills to workplace projects.

Network Support

The network support staff is just as important as the development staff. Network support will be required before, during, and after the development of the client/server system. The quality of support provided by the network engineers will be one of the keys to the success of the project. The very same issues that were covered in the discussion of the development staff pertain to the network support staff. Whenever possible and appropriate, use in-house staff. If the staff lacks the qualifications, consider bringing in network consultants and trainers. Network engineering consultants can be on call and available as needed. Training the existing staff is critical, whether the training be from a consultant, a specialist, or a fellow worker.

Documented Procedures

I cannot overemphasize the importance of having documented procedures in place during the initiation of a project. Too often, procedures are developed on the fly or after the fact. When this happens, it means that the opportunity to establish the procedures up front was lost. Much time and energy can be wasted by people who do not have a clear understanding of what to do or how to do it. The investment made in the initial stages of the project will pay dividends each day thereafter. Particular consideration should be given to any procedure that will be performed more than once. Instructions on how to manage files on the network file server or how to configure a PC for a developer are among the most commonly overlooked procedures, and yet they are two of the most important. The larger the project team, the more significant it is to define and document all of the procedures for the project.

Documented Standards

In the same vein as documenting procedures, it is extremely important that you develop and document standards for use by all project members. Developing standards early in the project cannot be taken lightly, as the cost of not having them can be a tremendous waste of resources. Selecting the appropriate tools and methods for analysis and development are part of this standard. The conventions and styles used during the project must be pre-defined. Do not allow any individual on the project to develop or implement his own standards outside of the project standards. Undocumented and unenforced standards can result in many inconsistencies and difficulties and therefore a less-valuable project. Again, the larger the project team, the more important it is to define and document all of the standards for the project.

The Network

Your client/server development project can only be successful if the network it is being developed for can support it. Whether you have a local-area network (LAN) or a wide-area network (WAN), many of the issues relating to the application system will hinge on the construction, performance, and maintenance of the network.

From a user's point of view, the system either works or it doesn't, and there is no value in blaming people after the fact if there are troubles. It is to everyone's advantage to be sure that the network operating system, the file server(s), the database server(s), the cable plant, and the computers being used as the client workstations are all capable of supporting the entire project.

Get good advise about what is required for what you are trying to accomplish. Consider a configuration that is easily upgradeable, so if more horsepower is needed, it can be added without significant interruption or loss of hardware or support.

Doing a prototype or pilot project is often a good source of discovery about various issues that might have gone unnoticed before. Issues such as coordination between the various groups within the organization, the division of authority, and participation in the planning and purchasing of network resources are the types of things that are sometimes overlooked until the network staff and the development staff learn that they must plan and work together.

The Database

The database will, of course, be one of the key components in the success of the project. Using a full-featured relational database management system such as Oracle7 is a sound choice for any project of any scope. Oracle7 is available on a tremendous number of platforms and is completely scaleable from the desktop to the largest systems in existence.

Oracle7 also provides support for declarative constraints, stored functions, procedures, and database triggers. In addition, Personal Oracle7 and the Workgroup Server/2000 products all include GUI DBA tools.

The Development Tools

Probably the most important thing for the developers are the development tools. But remember, the development tools become part of an overall development environment that is important to management and the user community as well. With good tools, good workers can do good work. Fortunately, Oracle Developer/2000 is an excellent development environment to work in and to deploy full-featured application systems. Few tools can provide the kind of robust applications with so little coding, as we will see as we work through this book.

Oracle Developer/2000 provides Oracle Forms, Oracle Reports, Oracle Graphics, and Oracle Procedure Builder all in one development environment. Each of these tools are integrated with the Oracle7 database, as well as with each other and any OLE2 compliant applications you may have on your network or your desktop. Numerous examples of integration between the Oracle Developer/2000 tools, the Oracle7 database, and OLE2 applications will be developed throughout this book.

Summary

Through a typical corporate scenario, this chapter introduced many of the topics and technical considerations that will be developed throughout this book. It also provided you with an introduction to some of the basic principles of application development and project management, including:

- Management support
- Building a quality staff
- Developing network support
- Documenting procedures
- Documenting standards
- The importance of the database
- The importance of the development tools

Now that we have discussed the project foundation and its principal components, we will continue on to the analysis of the project requirements.

2

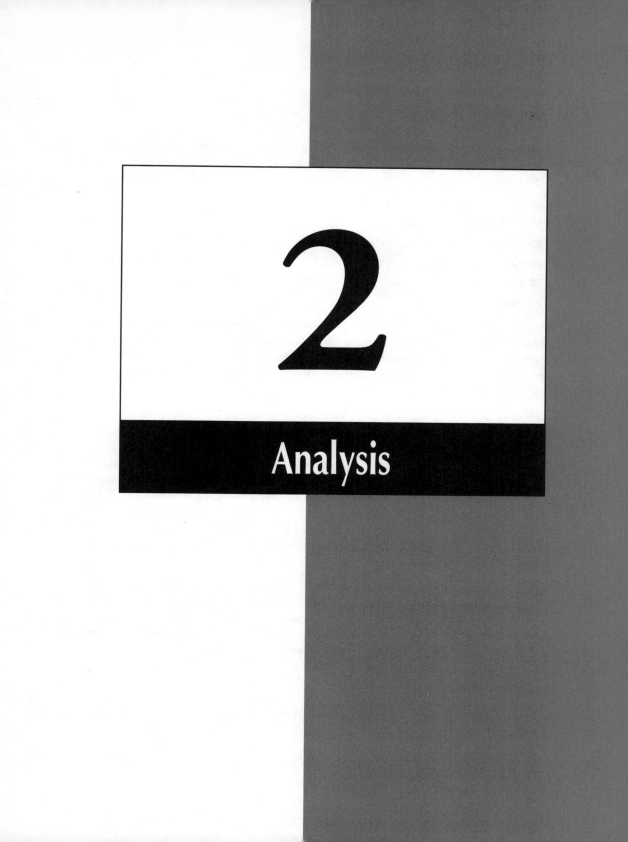

Analysis

Introduction

In order to succeed and to meet the expectations of management, every application-development project should begin with an analysis of the requirements and a clear list of goals. In this chapter we will review the following components of the planning process:

- Interviewing management and staff
- Project documentation
- Defining functional requirements
- Defining data requirements
- Configuration management
- Proposing a solution

We will begin by reviewing the topics to be addressed during the interviews with management and staff. These interviews will form the framework for the project. Then, using the guidelines from our interviews, we will complete the analysis phases of the project. This chapter concludes with an overview of the system configuration and a discussion on the benefits of early prototyping.

Interviews

One of the first things an application developer must do is interview management. This gets the management personnel involved immediately and provides the developer with some direction for the rest of the project. Management must define the scope of the project and identify key personnel, as well as determine the general requirements and limitations of the project. The developer should also obtain a list of goals, a list that includes bonus or optional items. The list of goals will allow the project to meet expectations, while the bonuses will allow the project to exceed those expectations.

After the management interview, the developer should interview the staff that were identified by management as the key personnel. They will become part of the project team. These staff members are sometimes referred to as user representatives. They will provide the detail requirements to support the general requirements from management. They may add further restraints, and they should also develop their own list of goals and bonus items.

Management

During the interview(s) with management, each of the following issues will be discussed, and the responses will be documented:

- The project scope
- Key personnel for the project team

- The general requirements
- The project restraints
- Goals
- Bonus items

The application that we will design in this book has been scoped as a fairly small project, because it will be the pilot project for the company and there is much interest in a timely appraisal of the outcome. It will be supported by a small team consisting of a manager, two staff members, and two developers.

From the management interview, we learn that the general project requirements include:

Following a structured approach
Writing the project documentation
Establishing standards and conventions
Creating Windows-style applications
Using standard menus and a standard toolbar
Integrating the project with the existing database
Developing usable applications
Storing OLE2 objects in the Oracle7 database
Loading data for testing and validation
Configuring the LAN and application environment

The project restraints include:

Keeping the impact on the existing system to a minimum
No immediate purchase of database or tools authorized

The list of goals includes:

Provide a single point of entry to the system
Show integration with desktop applications
Show integration with Oracle Developer/2000 tools
Use OLE2 as much as possible
Encourage self-training of current staff on tools
Use the capabilities of Oracle7 to the maximum extent
Complete the pilot project with current resources
Write very little code

The bonus items are:

Store different OLE2 objects in the same database column
Modify functional capabilities of applications at runtime
Develop objects to be used in future projects
Show integration with Visual Basic Custom Controls
Demonstrate applications functions that required no coding

As we proceed, we build on the information that was gathered from the management interview.

Staff

The management interviews provided a framework for the project. Next we will start to fill in the details by interviewing the staff members that were designated by management as key personnel for the project. We will be looking for specific requirements that amplify the general requirements we already have. During these interviews, we will discuss the process and the outcome of the previous interviews, then we will cover the following topics:

- Detailed requirements
- Additional project restraints
- Goals
- Additional bonus items

The detailed project requirements include:

Maintaining information on customers
Maintaining customer contact information
Maintaining our own lookup and validation data
Maintaining salary-increase percentages
Automatically calculating salary increases
Automatically updating annual salaries
Monitoring changes to employee salaries
Monitoring when a certain report is run
Highlighting sales people with high commissions
Listing all of the company's customers
Listing all of our employees in each department
Tracking contact priorities
Reviewing contact messages
Providing a graphical interface to employees in each department via point and click
Using standard menus and a standard toolbar

The additional restraints include:

Minimal time available to complete project
No Oracle expert on the team

The list of goals includes:

Develop a welcome screen
Show integration with Oracle Forms and Oracle Graphics
Show integration with Oracle Reports and Oracle Graphics

Use OLE2 to MS Word
Use OLE2 to MS Excel
Link to an MS Excel file from a report
Create a drill-down report
Create a drill-down graphics chart
Use object-orientation features such as property classes
Utilize declarative constraints in Oracle7
Create stored PL/SQL database objects
Create database triggers
Load various types of data in a variety of methods

The bonus items that were identified include:

Develop standard menus for the company
Develop a standard toolbar for the company
Utilize every type of declarative constraint in Oracle7
Utilize every type of stored PL/SQL database object
Enhance the visual appearance with various image types
Demonstrate multimedia capabilities, including sound and video

The project team even added a few additional restraints that pertained to themselves.

Documentation

The project documentation will be one of the most valuable assets to the project and the company. To support this valued asset, create a library, both physically (in the vicinity of the project team) and on the network. The project documentation library should include:

Functional requirements document
Data requirements document
Configuration management plan
Standards documents
The database administrator's guide
The Oracle documentation set
Developing Client/Server Applications with Oracle Developer/2000

and other documents you develop during the project. Many of these documents may be folders containing many related documents. Keep all documentation current and available. Appoint a librarian to manage the creation and maintenance of the library.

See the section on GUI styles and standards in Chapter 15, "Integration and Deployment in the Windows Environment," for some ideas on the types of things to consider for your standards documents.

Define Functional Requirements

During the process of defining the functional requirements for the project, we will identify and describe each function. We will indicate which functions are dependent on which other functions, and we will organize the functions so that we will be able to create a menu to navigate to all of the applications we develop. Then we will map each function to the data it requires and to the module that will be created to support it.

We will define high-level functions, supporting functions, and dependent functions. When we use the word "maintain" to describe a function, it means that function will automatically include the subordinate functions to insert, update, and delete.

Function Definition

Here we identify and describe each function. The high-level functions are described first, then the subordinate functions are described. Supporting functions reference their type in their description.

High-Level Function	*Description*
Forms	Any function that will be supported by creating a screen for data entry and update.
Reports	Any function that will be supported by creating a report.
Graphics	Any function that will be supported by creating a graphical display.
Procedures	Any function that will be supported by creating a SQL, or PL/SQL object.

Subordinate Function	*Description*
Contact Management	A form that will be used to maintain contact information and will also include graphical displays of priority summaries, as well as priority summaries for the current employee.
Maintain Customers	A form that will be used to maintain customer information.
Maintain Salary Increases	A form that will be used to maintain salary-increase percentages for each department and employee.
Maintain States	A form that will be used to maintain the lookup values for states.
List Customers	A report that will list all of the customers.
List Contact Messages	A report that will list all of the contact messages.

List Contact Priorities	A report that will summarize the number of overall contact priorities, as well as summarize the contact priorities for each employee. Each of the summaries will also be graphically displayed.
List Contact Totals	A report that will summarize the number of contacts by employee and provide drill-down to the contact details.
List Contacts by Employee	A report that will list each contact for a given employee.
List Employees by Department	A report that will list each department and their employees.
List Sales Employee Salaries and Commissions	A report that will include a graph from Excel, as well as the sales employees' salaries and commissions with the total.
Chart Contact Priorities	A graphical display that will summarize the overall contact priorities in a column chart.
Chart Contact Priorities by Employee	A graphical display that will summarize by employee the contact priorities for each employee in a column chart.
Chart Employee by Department	A graphical display that will summarize the number of employees in each department in a pie chart and list each of the employees in the selected department in a table chart.
Audit Reports	A graphical display that will list the priority reports that have been run in a table chart and automatically update itself every 20 seconds.
Chart Sales Employee Salaries and Commissions	A graphical display that will show the salaries and commissions of sales employees in a stacked bar chart, with commissions of more than $1,000 highlighted.
Annual Salary Increases	A procedure that will update the salaries of employees.
Calculate Salary Increases	A procedure that will calculate the salary increase for a given employee, using the increase percentages for the employee and his/her department.
Audit Reports	A procedure that will capture the date and userid when the priority report is run.
Audit Salary Increases	A procedure that will capture the date, old value, and new value, as well as the userid of the person who made the change, whenever an employees' salary is changed.

The high-level functions will become the menu for the application system, and each supporting function will become a menu item on that menu.

Functional Dependencies

Functional dependencies exist when one function requires the use of another function. We have several examples of this in our list of functions, as shown herein.

Dependent Function	*Required Function*
Contact Management	Chart Contact Priorities
	Chart Contact Priorities by Employee
List Contact Priorities	Chart Contact Priorities
	Chart Contact Priorities by Employee
	Audit Reports
List Contact Totals	List Contacts by Employee
Annual Salary Increases	Calculate Salary Increases

The Contact Management function requires the use of two graphical displays to show priority balance, and the List Contact Priorities function uses the same two displays as well as the Audit Reports procedure. The List Contact Totals function requires the use of List Contacts by Employee to provide the detail for the drill-down report. And finally, Annual Salary Increases requires Calculate Salary Increases to return the value of the new salary.

Function Hierarchy

Here we organize each of the functions and place them in a hierarchy to indicate their relative position in the system.

Function	*Subordinate Function*
Forms	Contact Management
	Maintain Customers
	Maintain Salary Increases by Department and Employee
	Maintain States
Reports	List Customers
	List Contact Messages
	List Contact Priorities
	List Contact Totals
	List Contacts by Employee
	List Employees by Department
	Sales Employee Salaries and Commissions
Graphics	Chart Contact Priorities
	Chart Contact Priorities by Employee
	Chart Employees by Department

	Audit Reports Sales Employee Salaries and Commissions
Procedures	Annual Salary Increases Calculate Salary Increases Audit Reports Audit Salary Increases

The high-level functions will become the menu for the application system, and each subordinate function will become a menu item on that menu.

Function-to-Module Mapping

The functions that we have defined are now mapped to a module name. The functions are grouped by function type, and the procedure functions are further detailed into either database trigger, database function, database procedure, or SQL script.

Form Functions	*Module Name*
Contact Management	contact
Maintain Customers	customer
Maintain Salary Increases by Department and Employee	dept_emp
Maintain States	state

Report Functions	*Module Name*
List Customers	customer
List Contact Messages	cont_msg
List Contact Priorities	priority
List Contact Totals	con_tot
List Contacts by Employee	econtot
List Employees by Department	dept_emp
Sales Employee Salaries and Commissions	sal_comm

Graphics Functions	*Module Name*
Chart Contact Priorities	priority
Chart Contact Priorities by Employee	priorite
Chart Employees by Department	dept_emp
Audit Reports	rpt_audit
Sales Employee Salaries and Commissions	sal_comm

Database Trigger Functions	*Module Name*
Audit Salary Increases	Emp_Audit

Database Procedure Functions	*Module Name*
Annual Salary Increases	annual_sal_update

Database Function Functions	*Module Name*
Calculate Salary Increases	sal_increase

SQL Script Functions	*Module Name*
Audit Reports	rptaudit

Function-to-Data Mapping

Each function will be mapped to the data required to support it. This is part of the analysis process that is dependent on the data model being defined. During the project, the definition of the functions and the data model can be done at the same time; but for purposes of organization in this book, the data model is defined in Chapter 3, "Logical Data Modeling." The details on function-to-data mapping can be found in the sections entitled "Function-to-Entity Mapping," and "Function-to-Attribute Mapping" in Chapter 3.

Business Rules

Business rules may be defined and supported through the data model and the Oracle7 database respectively. However, if a business rule is defined that must support a function and cannot be defined in the data model, it must be documented as part of the functional requirements. Then during the implementation of that function, the business rule can be enforced.

Define Data Requirements

Defining the data requirements for the project involves a review of the existing database and a review of each of the functions we will be supporting. During these reviews, we will determine which portion of the data that we require already exists and which portion of the data we require that we will need to add.

Review Existing Database

In reviewing the existing database structure, we find that the data we require for our departments, employees, and customers already exists. However, we notice that we will need to add the increase percentages for both the department and the employee. See Chapter 3 for the continuation of the data requirements against the existing database structures.

Review Functions

In reviewing each of our functions for the project, we notice that we will need to capture data on our customer contacts, the lookup and validation for states, report auditing, and auditing for salary changes. See Chapter 3 for the continuation of the new data requirements to support our functions.

Configuration Management

The early stages of the project are a good time to start preparing the configuration management plan. The configuration management plan should provide details on the LAN and application environment, including:

Directory structures to support the project
Creation of separate environments
Installation procedures
A standard configuration for the desktop
Information about the database and application servers.

Organize a Directory Structure

A well-organized directory structure to maintain the many files that will be created during the life of the project will be invaluable. I have provided details on setting up the appropriate directory structures for a project, and they can be found in the section "Setting up the Application Environment," in Chapter 15.

Establish Environments

You will need to establish separate application and database environments for this and any other projects. The creation and maintenance of a development, test, training, demonstration, and production environment is detailed in Chapter 15 in the sections entitled "Multiple Environments," "A Database for Each Environment," and "Application Installation." These sections in Chapter 15 will not only show you how to set up the environments, but also how to transparently connect to the appropriate database and how to easily install and use applications in the various environments.

Desktop Configuration

Setting up a standard desktop configuration will make things much easier for the user, the developers, and the LAN engineers. To see what is required for the client workstation for application deployment, see the section entitled "Application Deployment" in Chapter 15. For some tips on setting up the workstations for the developers and the users, see the section entitled "Memory, Disk Space, and Performance," also in Chapter 15.

Proposing a Solution

Once the goals and requirements have been identified for the project, you will want to propose a solution that will support it. The proposed solution should prove that the concept for the project is valid. Prototyping and the use of rapid application-development techniques can facilitate this end.

Proof of Concept

One approach to providing a workable solution for the project is to first prove that what has been conceived can be achieved. To prove that the technology exists to implement the system, the technology does what the vendors claim it will do and that the products will run on your system. There is no better way to prove that all of these things can be done than to try them yourself. Developing a prototype application is a good way to prove the concept is valid.

Prototype

Develop a prototype application by selecting a portion of the requirements for the system. Select functions to develop that will support each of the different types of goals to be achieved. Then demonstrate the functional and technical capabilities of the system by developing this prototype as quickly as possible. A prototype can be quickly developed using rapid application-development techniques.

Rapid Application Development

Rapid application development (RAD) is an approach that has value in these early stages of the project. RAD means a quick turnaround time to provide feedback to management and staff, as well as to support the proof of concept. The prototype can be developed quickly by eliminating some of the detail and presentation quality of the application. For example, if you are trying to quickly review the visual aspects of the application, such as buttons, icons, and toolbars, they don't have to actually *do* anything just yet. On the other hand, if you are trying to quickly develop a functional capability, it doesn't matter if every item is perfectly sized and aligned. Focus on completing the development cycle with the minimum of duplication and on developing functional capabilities that are independent of one another but may later be used in concert.

Summary

This chapter provided you with a review of the analysis process and its components, including:

- Interviewing management and staff
- Project documentation
- Defining functional requirements
- Defining data requirements
- Configuration management
- Proposing a solution

Now that we have completed this chapter on analysis, we will continue on to logical data modeling in Chapter 3.

II

The Database

3

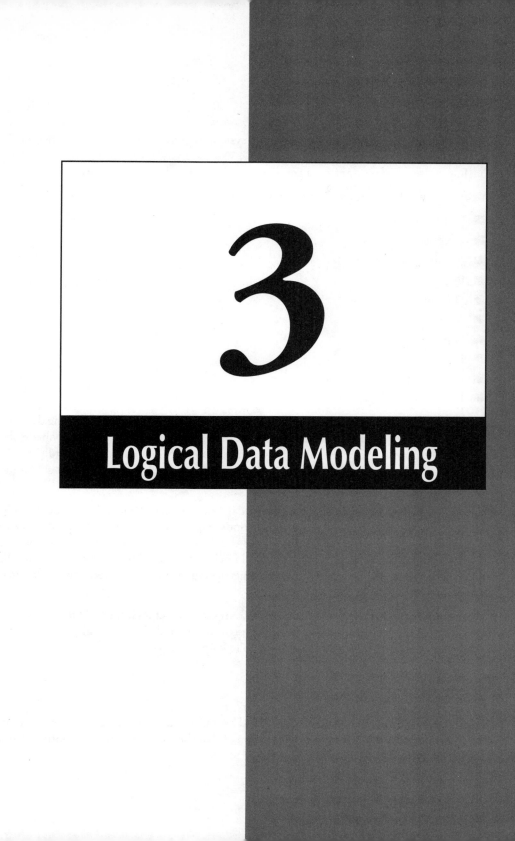

Logical Data Modeling

Introduction

After analysis of the users' functional, data, and systems requirements, the logical data model is defined to support these requirements. Whether you use a CASE tool or not, the logical data modeling process is important for a good database design and a successful project.

This chapter will review topics associated with logical data modeling, including:

- Normalization
- Integrity
- Naming conventions
- Entities
- Domains
- Attributes
- Unique identifiers
- Relations
- Entity/relationship diagrams
- Reviewing the logical data model

The logical data model is abstract. This means that the model is independent of the database, operating system, or hardware. It also means that the data model can include components that have been designed and implemented, as well as components that have not. In addition, this abstraction enables us to work on a data model that has been implemented without any immediate impact on the current implementation.

The creation of the database using the database definition language (DDL) is concrete. This means that the DDL is dependent on the vendor's implementation of the SQL language on the database. Even with the standardization of the SQL language, most database companies still use different syntax in their DDL. You will find much similarity, and the proprietary differences are eroding. But as in any computer language, there is a big difference to the compiler between *similar* and *identical*.

The physical database design is the transition from the abstract logical model to the concrete physical implementation. Physical database design, database definition, and population will be reviewed in their own respective chapters following this one.

Normalization

During the logical data modeling process, it will be important to understand a certain amount of relational theory and the practical application of that theory. The subjects of normalization and integrity are among the more significant components of relational theory for most database practitioners. In addition, it is necessary to understand the definition of entities, domains, attributes, unique identifiers, and relations.

We will review the three forms of normalization that are most commonly known and practiced. I will include a single statement of the form and a description of what it means.

1NF (first normal form): All entities have a primary key and no repeating groups.

All entities must be able to be uniquely identified by one or more attributes that will never be null. When more than one unique identifier exists, one of them must be nominated as the primary key. In addition, the same attribute cannot exist within the same entity more than once. If an attribute is repeated, it must be removed and associated with another entity.

2NF (second normal form): Complies with 1NF, and all attributes depend on the key.

All of the attributes associated with the entity must have a direct dependency on the primary key in order for their value to have meaning. If an attribute has meaning independent of the primary key, it must be removed and associated with another entity.

3NF (third normal form): Complies with 2NF, and no attributes are dependent on other attributes.

None of the attributes associated with the entity can have a dependency on another attribute. If an attribute has a dependency on another attribute, both attributes must be removed and associated with another entity.

Third normal form is generally the expected and accepted degree of normalization that is needed and useful to create a database without redundancy—that is, one that has integrity. You may hear the expression "the key, the whole key, and nothing but the key" used to describe third normal form.

Denormalization is the process of undoing some amount of the normalization process, and it is sometimes suggested for performance or ease of use.

A data model that is not normalized or is unnormalized is different than one that is denormalized. A data model that is not normalized may not have been normalized to begin with, while a data model that is denormalized was originally normalized.

CAUTION

Resist the temptation to denormalize. Do not compromise the integrity of the data model. If you do denormalize, be sure to document the impact on integrity and provide management for the restoration of the integrity in the physical design and implementation. For example, if you have redundant data, you could create a database trigger to update one of the columns from the other.

NOTE

This is the extent of normalization that can be covered within the scope of this book. For more information on normalization, refer to one of the many books available on relational databases.

Integrity

Integrity in a relational system means that the data will be consistent and reliable. There are four basic types of integrity found in a relational system:

- Entity
- Referential
- Column
- Business rules

A system has entity integrity when no entities can contain nulls in their primary key. Referential integrity exists when each foreign key references a primary key. Column integrity means that the values in the columns conform to the data type and format defined. Business-rule integrity means that anything and everything that the user defines as rules are enforced by the system.

The Oracle database provides declarative support for entity, referential, and column integrity, as well as support for business rules through the use of check constraints, database triggers, database functions, database procedures, and database packages. There are a variety of methods used during physical design and implementation to provide integrity, and we will explore them in the next several chapters.

This discussion was included in this chapter because the process of providing integrity begins in the logical data model.

Naming Conventions

Before we begin to define entities, domains, attributes, and relations, we will first discuss naming conventions. The purpose of establishing naming conventions is to create a consistent point of reference for the user community and the project staff. The names of all types of objects should be simple and meaningful. Avoid the use of jargon and acronyms unless they are very familiar and intuitive to everyone.

Using standard class words in attribute names is invaluable in creating a consistent convention. The following list is a good example of useful class words:

Amount
Code
Date
Description
Indicator
Id
Name
Number

Attributes may contain class words, but may need additional words for further clarification.

Create and maintain a list of all class words and standardized abbreviations to be used by the entire project. Make the list accessible to everyone, but appoint a custodian to manage the list.

If you are not using a CASE tool, create a table list for recording the words and abbreviations. For example, you can create a table as shown in Table 3.1.

Table 3.1. Abbreviations.

Word	*Abbreviation*
Commission	Comm
Customer	Cust
Department	Dept
Department Name	DName
Employee	Emp
Identifier	Id
Location	Loc
Manager	Mgr
Number	No
Order	Ord
Percentage	Pct
Received	Recd
Report	Rpt
Sales Representative	Rep
Salary	Sal

Abbreviations of entities should be used for short names, and abbreviations of attributes should be used for creating column names during physical design.

Entity names are singular; for example: employee, department, customer.

Entities

An entity is an object or thing of significance, and it is usually a noun. Entities should be given names that are singular, brief, and meaningful.

One of the first steps in modeling the logical database is to identify each of the entities that are needed to support the data requirements of the application system. You may have an existing system that is being extended to include additional functionality. Our application system includes the existing entities of customer, department, and employee. Yet it also requires the addition of new entities for contact, state, employee audit, and report audit.

Entities may be super-sets or sub-sets of other entities. A super-type is an entity that contains other entities called sub-types. And likewise, sub-types are contained within a super-type. Super-types contain attributes that are common, while sub-types contain attributes that are specific. For example, we could define the customer entity as a super-type with some basic attributes. Then, within the customer entity, define the entities government customer and commercial customer. Each of the sub-types would contain attributes that support and/or describe their respective entities.

NOTE

Super-types and sub-types can be implemented using one of three different methods. Each of these methods will be reviewed in Chapter 4, "Physical Database Design."

While identifying entities, it can be useful to associate a short name with each entity. Also, list any other names that the entities may have in a list of synonyms. For example, a customer is sometimes called a client, as shown in Table 3.2.

If you are not using a CASE tool, create a standard template for recording the entity names, short names, and synonyms. For example, you can create a simple table with the appropriate column headings, as shown in Table 3.2.

Table 3.2. Entities.

Entity	*Short Name*	*Synonyms*
Contact		
Customer	Cust	Client
Department	Dept	
Employee	Emp	
Employee Audit	Emp Audit	
Report Audit	Rpt Audit	
State		

NOTE

To provide management for time, which may be historical data or auditing information, you will need to add additional entities and attributes to the data model.

Domains

When several attributes share a common data type, length, and format, a single definition is created, called a domain. The domain is then associated with each attribute that it supports. Domains may also contain a range, or list of valid values. This use of domains will result in a more consistent definition of the data items in the system, and in some instances it will provide standard validation.

If you are not using a CASE tool, create a standard template for recording each domain. For example, you can create a simple table with column headings for the domain name, data type, length, format, and values, as shown in Table 3.3.

Table 3.3. Domains.

Domain	*Data Type*	*Length*	*Format*	*Values*
Amount	Number	7,2	$999,990.00	
Code	Character	2		
Date	Date	9	DD-MON-YY	
Id	Number	4		
Blob	Long Raw			
Name	Character	30		
Percent	Number	3	990	
Userid	Character	30		

Notice in Table 3.3 that at this time none of the domains are restricted to a given range or list of values.

TIP

Consider the data types and format masks supported by the system when defining your domains.

Notice the Employee Audit entity in Table 3.4 uses domains for every attribute.

Unique Identifiers

Every entity must be uniquely identified by one or more of its attributes. When no natural unique identifier exists, or the nominated UID could change value, create a sequence number for the primary key. Indicate which attributes comprise the unique identifier(s), as well as the primary key as shown in Table 3.4. Use a number to indicate the UID and a Y for the primary key. The number is used for the UID so that multiple UIDs in the same entity may be supported.

Attributes

An attribute describes the entity or provides information about the entity. After each of the entities has been defined, identify all of the attributes for each entity. Identify the data type, the maximum length, and whether or not a value is required for each entity.

Again, if you are not using a CASE tool, create a table, or spreadsheet to record all of the attributes associated with each entity. For example, Table 3.4 contains the entity, relation, attribute name, data type or domain, maximum length, value required, unique identifier, and primary key.

Table 3.4. Entities and attributes.

Entity Contact	*Relation*	*Attribute Name*	*Data Type or Domain*	*Max Len*	*Value Req'd*	*UID*	*PK*
	Employee				Yes	1	Y
	Customer				Yes	1	Y
		Contact Date	Date		Yes	1	Y
		Type	Character	5	Yes		
		Subject	Character	20			
		Action	Character	20			
		Location	Character	20			
		Phone	Character	20			
		Received By	Userid				
		Message	Blob				

Entity Contact	*Relation*	*Attribute Name*	*Data Type or Domain*	*Max Len*	*Value Req'd*	*UID*	*PK*
		Success	Character	1			
		Direction	Character	1			
		Priority	Character	1			

Entity Customer	*Relation*	*Attribute Name*	*Data Type or Domain*	*Max Len*	*Value Req'd*	*UID*	*PK*
		Id	Id		Yes	1	Y
		Name	Name				
		Address	Character	40			
		City	Character	30			
	State						
		Zip	Character	9			
		Area	Number	3			
		Phone	Character	9			
	Employee				Yes		
		Credit Limit	Number	9,2			
		Comments	Long				

Entity Department	*Relation*	*Attribute Name*	*Data Type or Domain*	*Max Len*	*Value Req'd*	*UID*	*PK*
		Number	Id		Yes	1	Y
		Name	Name				
		Location	Character	13			
		Increase	Percent				

Entity Employee	*Relation*	*Attribute Name*	*Data Type or Domain*	*Max Len*	*Value Req'd*	*UID*	*PK*
		Number	Id		Yes	1	Y
		Name	Name				
		Job	Character	9			
		Hire Date	Date				
		Salary	Amount				

continues

Table 3.4. continued

Entity Employee	*Relation*	*Attribute Name*	*Data Type or Domain*	*Max Len*	*Value Req'd*	*UID*	*PK*
		Commission Increase	Amount Percent				

Entitiy Employee Audit	*Relation*	*Attribute Name*	*Data Type or Domain*	*Max Len*	*Value Req'd*	*UID*	*PK*
	Employee				Yes	1	Y
		Change Date	Date		Yes	1	Y
		Old Salary	Amount				
		New Salary	Amount				
		Updated By	Userid				

Entity Report Audit	*Relation*	*Attribute Name*	*Data Type or Domain*	*Max Len*	*Value Req'd*	*UID*	*PK*
		Report	Character	8	Yes	1	Y
		Run By	Userid		Yes	1	Y
		Run	Date		Yes	1	Y

Entity State	*Relation*	*Attribute Name*	*Data Type or Domain*	*Max Len*	*Value Req'd*	*UID*	*PK*
		Code	Code		Yes	1	Y
		Name	Name		Yes		

NOTE

Notice in the contact, customer, and employee audit entities that the relations appear in the list. This method facilitates a better overall understanding of the entities and attributes without compromising the data model.

CAUTION

Foreign key columns are not attributes, just as calculations and derived data are not attributes. In fact, no columns are attributes. Columns only exist in the physical design and implementation of the database. Foreign key columns are represented in the logical data model as relations.

Relations

Relations describe how one entity is associated with another entity, and they should contain verbs. A relationship is the combination of two entities and two relations. There are five basic types of relationships:

- One-to-many
- Many-to-many
- One-to-one
- Mutually exclusive
- Recursive

The one-to-many relationship is the most common and represents the concept of the repeating group. The many-to-many relationship is common in the basic logical model, but it must be resolved to include an intersection entity for the detailed data model. The one-to-one relationship is very rare and usually not appropriate in a correct data model.

The occurrences of the entities in a relationship is sometimes called cardinality.

A mutually exclusive relationship exists when an entity has a relation to one entity, or another entity, but never to both entities. A recursive relationships exists when an entity has a relation to itself.

After defining the entities in the application system, define the relationships between them. There are several methods of defining relationships. Entity/relationship diagrams are very common, but they require the symbolic structure to be translated before the meaning of the diagram can be understood.

One alternative method is to use a sentence structure, as appears in Table 3.5. A sentence structure is usually an effective way to communicate to management and end-users, as well as members of the design team and development staff.

Table 3.5. E/R sentences.

Each	*Entity*	*May or Must*	*Relation*	*1 or Many*	*Entity*
Each	Contact	must	involve	1	Customer
Each	Contact	must	involve	1	Employee
Each	Contact	must	be received by	1	Employee
Each	Customer	may	be involved in	many	Contacts
Each	Customer	must	reside in	1	State
Each	Employee	may	be involved in	many	Contacts
Each	Employee	may	receive	many	Contacts
Each	Employee	may	be the subject of	many	Employee Audits
Each	Employee Audit	must	be auditing	1	Employee
Each	State	may	have	many	Customers

Each of the relationships will be implemented in the Oracle7 database using a reference constraint when we get to Chapter 5, "Building the Database."

Entity/Relationship Diagrams

Entity/relationship diagrams appear to the untrained eye as a bunch of boxes with names, lines with symbols, and verbs in-between. The key then for making effective use of E/R diagrams is training the people using them to understand the symbolic representation.

There are two common types of E/R diagrams: the basic E/R diagram and the detailed E/R diagram. The basic E/R diagram supports a high-level view of the data model and includes the major entities and their relations. It may contain many-to-many relationships and does not necessarily even have to show cardinality or optionality.

The detailed E/R diagram is the type of diagram you usually see that has been created using a CASE tool. It defines a much lower level of detail in the data model. Detailed E/R diagrams contain all entities and their relations. They have their many-to-many relationships resolved into intersection entities, and they must show cardinality and optionality. Some detailed E/R diagrams will even include the attribute(s) that have been nominated for the primary keys of the entities. You may even see the attribute list for each entity in a detailed E/R diagram.

NOTE

Not every entity has to be placed on a single detailed E/R diagram. In fact, it is quite common for larger systems to have many separate but related detailed E/R diagrams.

A mutually exclusive relationship is usually displayed in a detailed E/R diagram as an arc that crosses the lines of the two relations.

A recursive relationship is generally displayed in a detailed E/R diagram as a looping line that returns to the entity where it originated.

CAUTION

Entity/relationship diagrams may use different syntax, depending on the method or system being used. Also, E/R diagrams may be difficult for end users to understand because of their schematic nature, so be careful not to make them any more difficult to read than they already are.

TIP

Align the entities vertically and horizontally to create sight lines, use straight lines for the relationships, and use white space to avoid clutter. Be brief but meaningful when naming entities and relations. And include a legend in the data model documentation folder.

Review of the Logical Data Model

The user representatives should be reviewing the logical data model during the definition and at the conclusion of the process. The review should include all of the component parts of the model that were just reviewed in this chapter.

In addition, during initial review of the data model the entities should be mapped to the functions they support. Then, as the data model is completed, the entities and attributes should be mapped to the functions they support.

Function-to-Entity Mapping

The functions that were defined in Chapter 2, "Analysis," are listed here along with the supporting entities. The functions are grouped by function type.

The maintenance functions are shown in Table 3.6.

Table 3.6. Maintenance functions to entities.

Maintenance Function	*Entity*
Contact Management	Contact
	Customer
	Employee
Maintain Customers	Customer
	State
Maintain Salary Increases by Department and Employee	Department Employee
Maintain States	State

The report functions are shown in Table 3.7.

Table 3.7. Report functions to entities.

Report Function	*Entity*
List Customers	Customer
	State
List Contact Messages	Contact
	Customer
	Employee
List Contact Priorities	Contact
	Employee

Report Function	*Entity*
List Contact Totals	Contact Employee
List Contact by Employee	Employee Contact Customer
List Employees by Department	Department Employee
Sales Employee Salaries and Commissions	Department Employee

The chart functions are shown in Table 3.8.

Table 3.8. Chart functions to entities.

Chart Function	*Entity*
Chart Contact Priorities	Contact
Chart Contact Priorities by Employee	Contact Employee
Chart Employees by Department	Department Employee
Audit Reports	Report Audit
Sales Employee Salaries and Commissions	Employee

The PL/SQL functions are shown in Table 3.9.

Table 3.9. PL/SQL functions to entities.

PL/SQL Function	*Entity*
Audit Salary Increases	Employee Employee Audit
Audit Reports	Report Audit
Annual Salary Increases	Department Employee

Function-to-Attribute Mapping

The functions that were defined in Chapter 2 are again listed here along with the supporting entities and attributes. The functions are grouped by function type.

The maintenance functions are shown in Table 3.10.

Table 3.10. Maintenance functions to attributes.

Maintenance Function	*Entity*	*Attributes*
Contact Management	Contact	Contact Date
		Type
		Subject
		Action
		Location
		Phone
		Received By
		Message
		Success
		Direction
		Priority
	Customer	Name
	Employee	Name

Maintenance Function	*Entity*	*Attributes*
Maintain Customers	Customer	ID
		Name
		Address
		City
		ZIP
		Area
		Phone
		Comments
	State	Name
Maintain Salary Increases by Department and Employee	Department	Number
		Name
		Location
		Increase
	Employee	Number
		Name
		Job
		Increase
Maintain States	State	Code
		Name

Some of the attributes in the report functions are calculations. When the calculations involve attributes, the attributes are referenced.

The report functions are shown in Table 3.11.

Table 3.11. Report functions to attributes.

Report Function	*Entity*	*Attributes*
List Customers	Customer	City
		Name
		Phone
	State	Name

continues

Table 3.11. continued

Report Function	*Entity*	*Attributes*
List Contact Messages	Contact	Message
		Contact Date
	Customer	
	Name	
	Employee	Name
List Contact Priorities	Contact	Priority
	Employee	Name
List Contact Totals	Contact	(count)
	Employee	Name
List Contact by Employee	Employee	Name
	Contact	Contact Date
	Customer	Name
List Employees by Department	Department	Name
		Location
	Employee	Name
		Salary
		Commission
Sales Employee	Department	Name
Salaries and Commissions	Employee	Name
		Salary
		Commission
		(Salary+Commission)

The chart functions are shown in Table 3.12.

Table 3.12. Chart functions to attributes.

Chart Function	*Entity*	*Attributes*
Chart Contact Priorities	Contact	Priority
Chart Contact Priorities by Employee	Contact	Priority
Chart Employees by Department	Department	Name
	Employee	Name
Audit Reports	Report Audit	Report
		Run By
		Run Date
Sales Employee Salaries and Commissions	Employee	Name
		Salary
		Commission

The PL/SQL functions are shown in Table 3.13.

Table 3.13. PL/SQL functions to attributes.

PL/SQL Function	*Entity*	*Attributes*
Audit Salary Increases	Employee	Salary
	Employee Audit	Change Date
		Old Salary
		New Salary
		Updated By

continues

Table 3.13. PL/SQL functions to attributes.

PL/SQL Function	*Entity*	*Attributes*
Audit Reports	Report Audit	Report
		Run By
		Run Date
Annual Salary Increases	Department	Increase
	Employee	Increase
		Salary

Summary

This chapter reviewed the principles of logical data modeling, including:

- Normalization
- Integrity
- Naming conventions
- Entities
- Domains
- Attributes
- Unique identifiers
- Relations
- Entity/relationship diagrams
- Reviewing the logical data model

Now that we have reviewed logical data modeling, next we will examine physical database design.

4

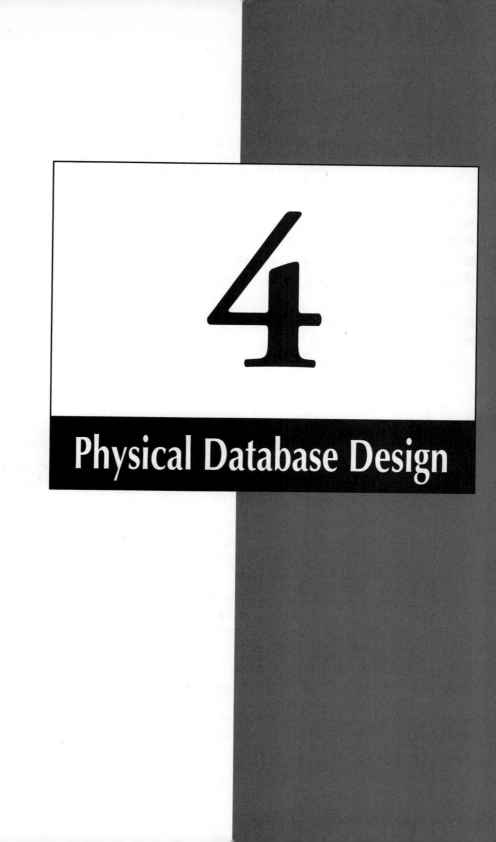

Physical Database Design

Introduction

After the logical data model is complete, physical database design can begin. The physical design process takes the information gathered in logical data modeling and maps the objects in the data model to objects in the physical model, including the following map processes:

- Entities to tables
- Attributes to columns
- Relations to foreign-key columns
- Primary keys to primary-key constraints
- UIDs to unique constraints
- Values required to not-null constraints
- Restricted values to check constraints
- Relations to reference constraints

As we progress through physical database design, we will establish the conventions that will be used for naming the physical objects. Then we will discuss views, indexes, and tablespaces. We will conclude this chapter by doing the module-to-table and module-to-column mapping.

Tables

Tables are defined by mapping the entities identified in the logical data model. We will document the definition of the exiting tables, as well as each of the new tables. The tables that already exist in the current system are Customer, Dept, and Emp.

We will add four additional tables to the existing system: the Contact table to keep track of employee and customer contact information, the Emp_Audit table to track changes to salaries, the Rpt_Audit table to monitor when reports have been run, and the State table to provide a database lookup for the Customer table.

To identify all of the tables and synonyms for the database, begin with the list of entities from the data model. Use the plural form of the entity name or the plural form of the short name as the table name. Replace the spaces with underscores. Base your decision about whether or not to use the short name on the general principle of keeping the table names brief and meaningful.

If the table already exists in the current system, keep the table name as it is, unless you are doing a complete make-over of the database. Be consistent in naming your tables. If the existing table names have not been pluralized, as in our example, then keep the new table names singular as well. At least this way the naming convention is consistent for the entire system.

Entity	*Table*	*Synonym*
Contact	Contact	Cont
Customer	Customer	Cust
		Client
Department	Dept	
Employee	Emp	
Employee Audit	Emp_Audit	EmpA
Report Audit	Rpt_Audit	RptA
State	State	St

If the short name is too brief, use the short name as a synonym. Make the Entity to Table and Synonym list accessible to everyone on the project, but appoint a custodian to manage the list.

Super-Type/Sub-Type Options

If the data model contains super-typed and sub-typed entities, you must choose which method will be used to implement them. There are three options:

- One table
- Separate sub-type tables
- A super-type table and separate sub-type tables

In the first method, a single table is defined for the super-type, and any specific attributes belonging to the sub-types must be added as columns to the super-type. Then an additional column is added to indicate the sub-type.

In the second method, a table is created for each sub-type, and the attributes belonging to the super-type are added as columns to each of the sub-type tables.

In the third method, tables are created for the super-type and sub-types, and an additional column is added to the super-type to indicate the sub-type. Then a single foreign-key column is added to the super-type.

CAUTION

Using the second and third methods means that a union must be used to access the complete set of data for the super-type. Also, you will not be able to directly insert, update, or delete data.

Mutually Exclusive Relationship Options

If the data model contains mutually exclusive relationships, you must choose which method will be used to implement them. There are two options:

- The generic
- The explicit

In the first method, the relation is added as a single foreign-key column, and an additional column is added to identify which relation the foreign key is associated with. In addition, each of the primary-key columns that map to the foreign-key column must have the same data type.

In the second method, each primary key is added as a foreign-key column.

> **NOTE**
>
> The generic implementation method for exclusive relationships is also the third implementation method for subtypes.

Data Types

Before defining the columns for our tables, we need to consider the data types that are supported by the database. Then we will map each of the domains and logical data types to their corresponding physical data types.

In addition, we will add to the list of domains from the logical data model to include existing physical implementations that are different and still need to be adhered to. For example, CreditLimit was in the Amount domain in the logical data model, but the existing physical implementation has a different precision. The same is true for CustId and DeptNo; that is, they were both in the Id domain, but their physical implementation is different.

Domain	*Logical Data Type*	*Physical Data Type*
Amount	Number	Number(7,2)
Blob	Long Raw	Long Raw
Code	Character	VarChar2(2)
CreditLimit	Number	Number(9,2)
CustId	Number	Number(6)
Date	Date	Date
DeptNo	Number	Number(2)
Id	Number	Number(4)
Name	Character	VarChar2(30)
Percent	Number	Number(3)
Userid	Character	VarChar2(30)

Another example of variation in the logical and physical data types exists when the version of the Oracle database is considered. Oracle6 uses the CHAR data type to support character data, and its maximum length is 255, whereas Oracle7 uses the VARCHAR2 data type, which has a maximum length of 2,000. A simple list of the mapping between the logical data type and the physical data type clarifies this issue.

Logical Data Type	*Physical Data Type*
Character	VarChar2
Long	Long
Number	Number

Columns

From the Entities and Attributes list created in logical data modeling and the relationships that we documented in the E/R Sentence table, we define the columns for our tables.

The process of naming columns is fairly straightforward. Use the attribute name for the column name, unless it is not brief enough, in which case you should use the list of abbreviations to create the appropriate name. Replace the spaces with underscores. For columns that will be created from relations, use the primary key column from the table being referenced, such as DeptNo in the Emp table. If this method does not create a brief and meaningful column name, then consider the following guidelines:

- Use the table name for codes, such as State in the Customer table
- Use the relation for recursive foreign-key columns, such as Mgr in the Emp table

The following is a list of each of the tables with the columns mapped from the attributes and relations:

Table Name	*Column Name*	*Data Type*	*Not Null*
Customer	CustId	Number(6)	Yes
	Name	VarChar2(45)	
	Address	VarChar2(40)	
	City	VarChar2(30)	
	State	VarChar2(2)	
	Zip	VarChar2(9)	
	Area	Number(3)	
	Phone	VarChar2(9)	
	RepId	Number(4)	Yes
	CreditLimit	Number(9,2)	
	Comments	Long	

Table Name	*Column Name*	*Data Type*	*Not Null*
Dept	DeptNo	Number(2)	Yes
	DName	VarChar2(14)	
	Loc	VarChar2(13)	
	Increase_Pct	Number(3)	

Table Name	*Column Name*	*Data Type*	*Not Null*
Emp	EmpNo	Number(4)	Yes
	EName	VarChar2(10)	
	Job	VarChar2(9)	
	Mgr	Number(4)	
	HireDate	Date	
	Sal	Number(7,2)	
	Comm	Number(7,2)	
	DeptNo	Number(2)	Yes
	Increase_Pct	Number(3)	

NOTE

Notice that the Increase_Pct columns have been added to the existing Dept and Emp tables.

Table Name	*Column Name*	*Data Type*	*Not Null*
Contact	EmpNo	Number(4)	Yes
	CustId	Number(6)	Yes
	Contact_Date	Date	Yes
	Type	VarChar2(5)	Yes
	Subject	VarChar2(20)	
	Action	VarChar2(20)	
	Location	VarChar2(20)	
	Phone	VarChar2(20)	
	Recd_By	VarChar2(30)	
	Message	Long Raw	
	Success	VarChar2(1)	
	Direction	VarChar2(1)	
	Priority	VarChar2(1)	

Table Name	*Column Name*	*Data Type*	*Not Null*
Emp_Audit	EmpNo	Number(4)	Yes
	Change_Date	Date	Yes

Table Name	Column Name	Data Type	Not Null
	Old_Sal	Number(7,2)	
	New_Sal	Number(7,2)	
	Updated_By	VarChar2(30)	

Table Name	Column Name	Data Type	Not Null
Rpt_Audit	EmpNo	VarChar2(8)	Yes
	Run_By	VarChar2(30)	Yes
	Date_Run	Date	Yes

Table Name	Column Name	Data Type	Not Null
State	Code	VarChar2(2)	Yes
	Name	VarChar2(30)	Yes

Naming Constraints

One of the most powerful features of Oracle7 is its capability to support declarative constraints. The proper identification, definition, and maintenance of declarative constraints is essential to the success of the project. Defining standard naming conventions for the constraints is therefore extremely important.

If you execute the following SQL select statement:

```
select constraint_type, table_name, constraint_name from user_constraints;
```

you will notice the different types of constraint names that exist on your database. There are likely to be constraints that have been system generated, constraints inserted for the Oracle demonstration database, and possibly the constraints defined for the tables in this book. The next thing you are likely to notice is that there doesn't seem to be any convention to the naming of these constraints. This list is an extract from the user_constraints table:

Type	*Table Name*	*Constraint Name*
P	CONTACT	CONT_PK_EMPNO_CUSTID_CONT_DATE
C	CONTACT	CONT_NN_EMPNO
R	CONTACT	CONT_FK_EMP_EMPNO
C	CUSTOMER	SYS_C00414
P	CUSTOMER	CUSTOMER_PRIMARY_KEY
C	CUSTOMER	CUSTID_ZERO
C	DEPT	SYS_C00407
P	DEPT	DEPT_PRIMARY_KEY
C	EMP	SYS_C00409
P	EMP	EMP_PRIMARY_KEY
R	EMP	EMP_SELF_KEY
R	EMP	EMP_FOREIGN_KEY

The following are the guidelines that are used for naming constraints in this book:

- The constraint name begins with the table name.
- If abbreviation is needed for the table name, use the short synonym.
- The table name is followed by the two-character constraint type, where primary key is PK, unique key is UK, foreign key is FK, not-null is NN, check range is CR, and check condition is CC.

> **NOTE**
>
> The system table contains constraint types for primary key (P), unique key (U), reference (R), and check (C). The two-character constraint types we are using add further clarification that is not possible with just the single character.

- When the constraint type is PK, UK, NN, CR, or CC, it is followed by the column(s) defined in the constraint.
- When the constraint type is FK, it is followed by the referenced table name and column(s) defined in the constraint.
- If abbreviation is needed following the constraint type, use the synonym for the table name or the abbreviation from the Abbreviation table for column names.
- If the abbreviation is not available from the Abbreviation table, create one and add it to the table.
- If abbreviation is required in any constraint name for a given table, the same abbreviation must be used for the second and subsequent references to the name that was abbreviated in the current constraint, as well as any other constraints for that table.

Now we will use examples to illustrate these points.

Primary Key and Unique

The conventions for naming primary-key and unique constraints are identical, with the exception of constraint type. Consider the following primary-key constraint:

Type	*Table Name*	*Constraint Name*
P	CONTACT	CONT_PK_EMPNO_CUSTID_CONT_DATE

The constraint type is P, for primary key. The constraint name is restricted to 30 characters. Therefore, we must abbreviate the table name using the synonym we defined earlier. The synonym is followed by the two-character constraint type. The primary-key constraint for this table is a multicolumn key, consisting of EMPNO, CUSTID, and CONTACT_DATE. The columns that define the primary key follow the two-character constraint type. Again, abbreviation was used for space consideration and consistency.

Check

The conventions for naming not-null, check-range, and check-condition constraints are identical, with the exception of constraint type. Consider the following not-null constraint:

Type	*Table Name*	*Constraint Name*
C	CONTACT	CONT_NN_EMPNO

The constraint type is C, for check. A previous abbreviation was used. Therefore, abbreviation is used again for the table name. The synonym is followed by the two-character constraint type. The column that is defined in the not-null constraint follows the two-character constraint type.

Reference

Consider the following reference constraint:

Type	*Table Name*	*Constraint Name*
R	CONTACT	CONT_FK_EMP_EMPNO

The constraint type is R, for reference. A previous abbreviation was used. Therefore, abbreviation is used again for the table name. The synonym is followed by the two-character constraint type. The table and column that is defined in the reference constraint follows the two-character constraint type.

TIP

Start with the longest constraint name first. The primary-key constraint name for a multicolumn key is usually the longest. This way, if abbreviation is needed, you can apply it to the subsequent constraint names as well.

The aim is to create meaningful names that will be unique. By using the method described here, you will achieve both of these goals.

Identifying Constraints

Now that we have a convention for naming constraints, we can define each of the constraints needed to support our data model.

Keep in mind that

- UIDs that are also PKs become primary-key constraints
- UIDs that are not also PKs become unique constraints

- Values Required become not-null constraints
- Restricted Values become check constraints
- Relations become reference constraints

Start by using the list of Entities and Attributes from our logical data model, and group the constraints by constraint type. In the next chapter we will create the constraints by table.

TIP

Using the list of Entities and Attributes will simplify the process of identifying constraints—especially since that lists includes, PKs, UIDs, Required Values, Domains, and Relations.

The existing constraints will be left unchanged for now. Once we can categorically verify that no reference exists anywhere in the system to any of the existing constraint names, we can change them to conform to our naming convention. Alternatively, once all the references have been discovered, a separate project could be initiated to change them (a project that is outside the scope of this book).

NOTE

Remember that one of the project requirements from Chapter 2, "Analysis," was to keep the impact on the exiting system to the minimum.

This is what the constraint names for the existing tables look like:

Type	*Table Name*	*Constraint Name*
C	CUSTOMER	SYS_C00414
P	CUSTOMER	CUSTOMER_PRIMARY_KEY
C	CUSTOMER	CUSTID_ZERO
P	DEPT	SYS_C00407
C	DEPT	DEPT_PRIMARY_KEY
C	EMP	SYS_C00409
C	EMP	SYS_C00410
P	EMP	EMP_PRIMARY_KEY
R	EMP	EMP_SELF_KEY
R	EMP	EMP_FOREIGN_KEY

This is what the new tables constraint names will look like:

Type	*Table Name*	*Constraint Name*
C	CONTACT	CONT_NN_EMPNO
C	CONTACT	CONT_NN_CUSTID
C	CONTACT	CONT_NN_CONTACT_DATE
C	CONTACT	CONT_NN_TYPE
P	CONTACT	CONT_PK_EMPNO_CUSTID_CONT_DATE
R	CONTACT	CONT_FK_EMP
R	CONTACT	CONT_FK_CUSTOMER
R	CUSTOMER	CUSTOMER_FK_STATE_CODE
C	EMP_AUDIT	EMP_AUDIT_NN_EMPNO
C	EMP_AUDIT	EMP_AUDIT_NN_CHANGE_DATE
P	EMP_AUDIT	EMP_AUDIT_PK_EMPNO_CHANGE_DATE
C	RPT_AUDIT	RPTA_NN_REPORT
C	RPT_AUDIT	RPTA_NN_RUN_BY
C	RPT_AUDIT	RPTA_NN_DATE_RUN
P	RPT_AUDIT	RPTA_PK_REPORT_RUN_BY_DATE_RUN
C	STATE	STATE_NN_CODE
C	STATE	STATE_NN_NAME
P	STATE	STATE_PK_CODE

Having seen where we are going may help put things in perspective, but we will still go through the process of identifying each constraint type for each table. We will review and document the constraint names for the existing tables, as well as the new ones.

Primary Key

Attributes that were unique identifiers and were nominated as primary keys will be assigned primary-key constraints. The existing tables with primary keys are as follows:

Table Name	*Column Name*	*Constraint Name*
Customer	CustId	Customer_PK_CustId
Dept	DeptNo	Dept_PK_DeptNo
Emp	EmpNo	Emp_PK_EmpNo

The new tables with primary keys are as follows:

Table Name	*Column Name*	*Constraint Name*
Contact	EmpNo CustId Contact_Date	Cont_PK_EmpNo_CustId_Cont_Date
Emp_Audit	EmpNo Change_Date	Emp_Audit_PK_EmpNo_Change_Date
Rpt_Audit	Report Run_By Date_Run	RptA_PK_Report_Run_By_Date_Run
State	Code	State_PK_Code

Unique

Attributes that were unique identifiers and were not nominated as primary keys will be assigned unique constraints. There are no existing tables with unique constraints. The new table with a unique constraint is as follows:

Table Name	*Column Name*	*Constraint Name*
State	Name	State_UK_Name

Not Null

Attributes that had values required will be assigned not-null column constraints. The existing tables with not-null constraints are as follows:

Table Name	*Column Name*	*Constraint Name*
Customer	CustId RepId	Customer_NN_CustId Customer_NN_RepId
Dept	DeptNo	Dept_NN_DeptNo
Emp	EmpNo DeptNo	Emp_NN_EmpNo Emp_NN_DeptNo

The new tables with not-null constraints are as follows:

Table Name	*Column Name*	*Constraint Name*
Contact	EmpNo	Cont_NN_EmpNo
	CustId	Cont_NN_CustId
	Contact_Date	Cont_NN_Cont_Date
	Type	Cont_NN_Type
Emp_Audit	EmpNo	Emp_Audit_NN_EmpNo
	Change_Date	Emp_Audit_NN_Change_Date
Rpt_Audit	Report	RptA_NN_Report
	Run_By	RptA_NN_Run_By
	Date_Run	RptA_NN_Date_Run
State	Code	State_NN_Code
	Name	State_NN_Name

Check Range

Attributes that have restricted values may be assigned check-range or check-condition column constraints. There are no new tables with check-range constraints. The existing table with a check-range constraint is as follows:

Table Name	*Column Name*	*Constraint Name*
Customer	RepId	Customer_CR_RepId

Check Condition

Again, attributes that have restricted values may be assigned check-range or check-condition column constraints. There are no existing tables with check-condition constraints. The new table with a check-condition constraint is as follows:

Table Name	*Column Name*	*Constraint Name*
Contact	Priority	Cont_CC_Priority

Reference

Relations become reference constraints. Reference constraints are often called foreign-key constraints and serve to enforce referential integrity. The existing tables with reference constraints are as follows:

Table Name	*Column Name*	*Constraint Name*
Customer	State	Customer_FK_State_Code
Emp	EmpNo DeptNo	Emp_FK_Emp_Mgr Emp_FK_Dept_DeptNo

The new tables with not-null constraints are as follows:

Table Name	*Column Name*	*Constraint Name*
Contact	EmpNo CustId	Cont_FK_Emp_EmpNo Cont_FK_Customer_CustId

For each reference constraint, you must choose a mode of cascade processing. Keep in mind that the first two options are declarative, and the first one is the default, while the last three will require the use of database triggers to implement. The five choices are as follows:

- Cascade Restrict
- Cascade Delete
- Cascade Null
- Cascade Default
- Cascade Update

Cascade Restrict means that no delete of the parent will be permitted while dependent children exist.

Cascade Delete means that all rows that are dependent on the reference will be deleted when the parent is deleted.

Cascade Null means that the value in the foreign-key column will be set to null when the parent is deleted.

Cascade Default means that the value in the foreign-key column will be set to a predetermined default value when the parent is deleted.

Cascade Update means that when the value in the parent is changed, the corresponding children will automatically be updated.

The first two can be defined declaritively, whereas the third and fourth require additional procedures and database triggers to implement.

Views

During the physical design process, you can define views. A view may be useful if, in reviewing the table and column requirements for the reports and displays, you discover a frequently used join condition. Views are sometimes thought of as stored queries. Views are documented as a special PL/SQL module type and mapped to the tables and columns that are used to create them.

Some developers might suggest that views are bad and create performance problems in the system. It is true that views are vulnerable to performance issues, but views are not inherently bad. For example, a view designed and built to support queries and/or reports may be very useful. They can standardize and simplify the use of several tables that are commonly used together.

When views are involved in performance problems, it is usually because an execution plan chosen by the optimizer is not optimal. This can happen when you are using a where clause against a view. This results in additions to the where clause of the total query. But, if the views are well designed and implemented, and these issues are understood and taken into consideration, views will not adversely affect performance.

Indexes

Indexes will automatically be created to support the unique and primary-key constraints. But, additional indexes may be needed to increase performance associated with querying on columns that are not already indexed. The appropriate use of additional indexes depends directly on the specific details of the system (and is therefore outside the scope of this book).

Tablespaces

During the physical design process you can begin to define the space requirements for the database. Depending on the size of the database and the physical characteristics of the database server, different approaches may be taken.

For smaller projects, the User Data tablespace can be used for tables and indexes. But for larger projects, the DBA is likely to create new tablespaces for the project tables, indexes, rollback segments, and redo logs. As with indexes, the appropriate use of tablespace depends directly on the specific details of the system and is therefore outside of the scope of this book.

Review of the Physical Database Design

The user representatives and project team should periodically review the physical database design, and the review should include all of the component parts reviewed in this chapter.

In addition, during the initial review of the physical database design, the tables should be mapped to the modules they support. Then, as the physical database design is completed, the tables and columns should be mapped to the modules they support.

Module-to-Table Mapping

The modules that were defined in Chapter 2 are listed here along with the supporting tables. The modules are grouped by module type.

Forms

Description	*Module Name*	*Table(s)*
Contact Management	contact	Contact Customer Emp
Maintain Customers	customer	Customer State
Maintain Salary Increases by Department and Employee	dept_emp	Dept Emp
Maintain States	state	State

Reports

Description	*Module Name*	*Table(s)*
List Customers	customer	Customer State
List Contact Messages	cont_msg	Contact Customer Emp
List Contact Priorities	priority	Contact Emp
List Contact Totals	con_tot	Contact Emp
List Contacts by Employee	econtot	Emp Contact Customer
List Employees by Department	dept_emp	Dept Emp

Sales Employee Salaries and Commissions	sal_comm	Dept Emp

Displays

Description	*Module Name*	*Table(s)*
Chart Contact Priorities	priority	Contact
Chart Contact Priorities by Employee	priorite	Contact Emp
Chart Employees by Department	dept_emp	Dept Emp
Audit Reports	rpt_audit	Rpt_Audit
Sales Employee Salaries and Commissions	sal_comm	Emp

Database Triggers

Description	*Module Name*	*Table(s)*
Audit Salary Increases	Emp_Audit	Emp Emp_Audit

Database Procedures

Description	*Module Name*	*Table(s)*
Annual Salary Increases	annual_sal_update	Dept Emp

SQL Scripts

Description	*Module Name*	*Table(s)*
Audit Reports	rptaudit	Report Audit

Views

Description	*Module Name*	*Table(s)*
Contact List	contlist	Contact Customer Emp

Module-to-Column Mapping

The modules that were defined in Chapter 2 are again listed here along with the supporting tables and columns. The modules are grouped by module type.

Forms *Description*	*Module Name*	*Table(s)*	*Column(s)*
Contact Management	contact	Contact	Contact_Date
			Type
			Subject
			Action
			Location
			Phone
			Received_By
			Message
			Success
			Direction
			Priority
		Customer	Name
		Emp	EName
Maintain Customers	customer	Customer	CustId
			Name
			Address
			City
			Zip
			Area
			Phone
			Comments
		State	Code
			Name
Maintain Salary Increases by Department and Employee	dept_emp	Dept	DeptNo
			DName
			Loc
			Increase_Pct
		Emp	EmpNo
			EName
			Job
			Increase_Pct
Maintain States	state	State	Code
			Name

Some of the columns in the reports are calculations. When the calculations involve columns, the columns are referenced.

Reports Description	*Module Name*	*Table(s)*	*Column(s)*
List Customers	customer	Customer	City
			Name
			Phone
		State	Name
List Contact Messages	cont_msg	Contact	Message
			Contact_Date
		Customer	Name
		Emp	EName
List Contact Priorities	priority	Contact	Priority
		Emp	EName
List Contact Totals	con_tot	Contact	(count)
		Emp	EName
List Contacts by Employee	econtots	Contact	Contact_Date
		Customer	Name
		Emp	EName
List Employees by Department	deptemp	Dept	DName
			Loc
		Emp	EName
			Sal
			Comm
Sales Employee Salaries and Commissions	sal_comm	Dept	DName
		Emp	EName
			Sal
			Comm
			(Sal+Comm)

Displays Description	*Module Name*	*Table(s)*	*Column(s)*
Chart Contact Priorities	priority	Contact	Priority

Displays Description	*Module Name*	*Table(s)*	*Column(s)*
Chart Contact Priorities by Employee	priorite	Contact	Priority
Chart Employees by Department	emp_dept	Dept Emp	DName EName
Audit Reports	rptaudit	Rpt_Audit	Report Run_By Run_Date
Sales Employee Salaries and Commissions	sal_comm	Emp	EName Sal Comm

Database Triggers Description	*Module Name*	*Table(s)*	*Column(s)*
Audit Salary Increases	Emp_Audit	Emp Emp_Audit	Sal EmpNo Change_Date Old_Sal New_Sal Updated_By

Database Procedures Description	*Module Name*	*Table(s)*	*Column(s)*
Annual Salary Increases	annual_sal_update	Dept Emp	Increase_Pct Increase_Pct Sal

SQL Scripts Description	*Module Name*	*Table(s)*	*Column(s)*
Audit Reports	rptaudit	Rpt_Audit	Report Run_By Run_Date

Views Description	*Module Name*	*Table(s)*	*Column(s)*
Contact List	contlist	Contact	Contact_Date
		Customer	Name
		Emp	EName

Summary

This chapter provided you with a review of physical database design, including the following map processes:

- Entities to tables
- Attributes to columns
- Relations to foreign-key columns
- Primary keys to primary-key constraints
- UIDs to unique constraints
- Values required to not-null constraints
- Restricted values to check constraints
- Relations to reference constraints

We established naming conventions for the physical objects. We discussed views, indexes, and tablespaces, and we concluded by doing the module-to-table and module-to-column mapping. Now that we have completed physical database design, next we will build the database.

5

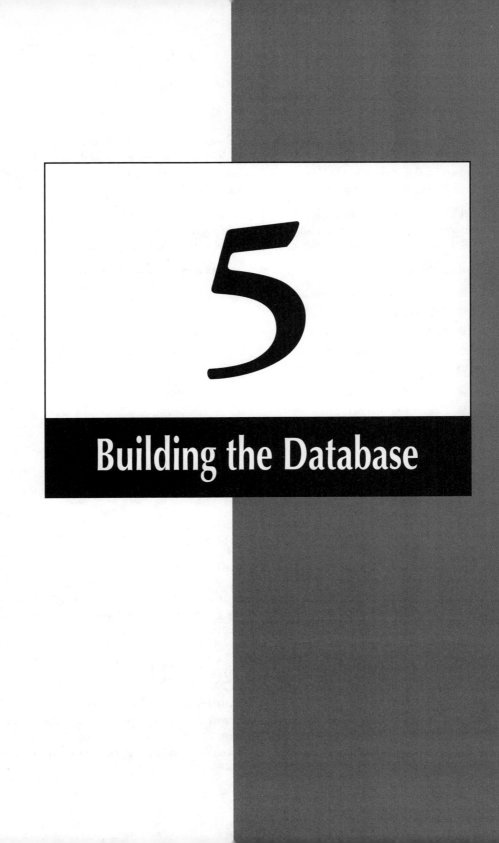

Building the Database

Introduction

After the physical database design is completed, the database can be built. The process of building the database involves taking the information gathered during the physical database design process and using it to create SQL Data Definition Language (DDL) scripts. The creation of the database using these scripts is the primary goal of this chapter.

In addition, we will review SQL Data Manipulation Language (DML). DML includes the SQL verbs `SELECT`, `INSERT`, `UPDATE`, and `DELETE`. Lastly we will look at SQL Data Control Language (DCL) including the `GRANT`, `REVOKE`, `DISABLE`, and `ENABLE` SQL commands.

During this chapter we will review the SQL scripts needed to do the following:

- Create tables with constraints
- Create a sequence
- Create a view
- Create synonyms for tables
- Create database triggers
- Create database functions, procedures, and packages
- Create a tablespace
- Create a user
- Alter tables to add columns and constraints
- Alter a tablespace
- Alter a user
- Drop database objects
- Select, insert, update, and delete
- Grant and revoke access
- Disable and enable constraints

As we go through this chapter, we review many of the SQL verbs and their usage. Specifically, we cover each of the database objects we create for this project. We cannot cover every SQL verb and its usage because that is outside the scope of this book.

Structured Query Language (SQL)

SQL is the ANSI (American National Standards Institute) standard relational database language. It is an extremely powerful language and provides verbs to support the definition, manipulation, and control of relational database objects. We review each of the following three component parts, as well as using the verbs they contain to build the database for this project:

- Data Definition Language (DDL)
- Data Manipulation Language (DML)
- Data Control Language (DCL)

DDL includes the SQL verbs `CREATE`, `ALTER`, `RENAME`, and `DROP` to define the database. DML includes the verbs `SELECT`, `INSERT`, `UPDATE`, and `DELETE` to manage data. DCL provides access to database objects via `GRANT`, `REVOKE`, `ENABLE`, and `DISABLE`.

Data Definition Language (DDL)

The Data Definition Language is the portion of SQL that is used to create, alter, rename, and drop database objects. DDL supports the creation and maintenance of the Oracle Data Dictionary. The dictionary contains the definition of every database object. Database objects include but are not limited to tables, sequences, views, synonyms, indexes, triggers, functions, procedures, packages, tablespaces, and users. For a complete list of all the database objects and SQL verbs, see the SQL Language Reference Manual.

CREATE

The `CREATE` verb is used to define database objects. We will create many tables, synonyms, and constraints. We will also create a sequence and a view. Then we will review and provide examples of the following `create` statements:

```
CREATE TRIGGER
CREATE FUNCTION
CREATE PROCEDURE
CREATE PACKAGE
CREATE PACKAGE BODY
CREATE TABLESPACE
CREATE USER
```

All of the constraints will be created in either the `CREATE TABLE` or `ALTER TABLE` scripts.

NOTE

I have included DEM7CMIS.SQL, and MAKECMIS.SQL in the \DEV2000\SQL directory of this book. DEM7CMIS.SQL includes an extract of the Oracle DEMOBLD7.SQL script and contains a subset of the Oracle demonstration database plus the CMIS database. If you already have the demonstration database installed, that's OK; you can run MAKECMIS.SQL to create just the CMIS database. If not, you can run DEM7CMIS.SQL. The exercise at the end of this chapter will create the demonstration database that we will be using throughout this project.

CREATE TABLE

`CREATE TABLE` is one of the most significant SQL statements, because it defines the structure of the data and the constraints on that data to the database management system. While all of the tables and constraints could have been created with `CREATE TABLE` statements, some of the constraints have been included in examples of the `ALTER TABLE` statement.

The DEMOTBLS.SQL script is an extract of the DEMOBLD7.SQL script and is shown in Figure 5.1.

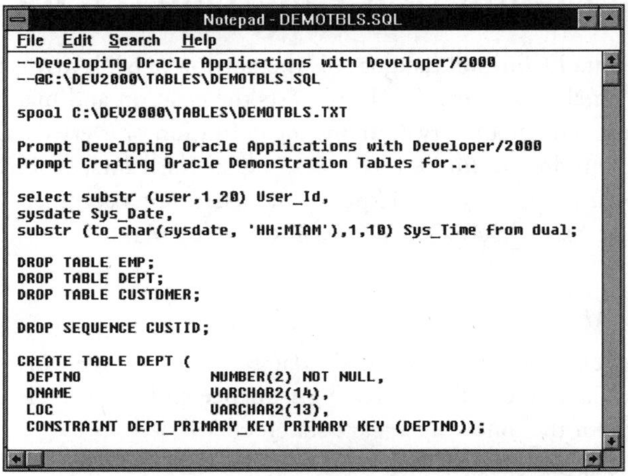

FIGURE 5.1.
The Build Oracle Demonstration Database script file, shown in Notepad.

```
Notepad - DEMOTBLS.SQL
File Edit Search Help
--Developing Oracle Applications with Developer/2000
--@C:\DEV2000\TABLES\DEMOTBLS.SQL

spool C:\DEV2000\TABLES\DEMOTBLS.TXT

Prompt Developing Oracle Applications with Developer/2000
Prompt Creating Oracle Demonstration Tables for...

select substr (user,1,20) User_Id,
sysdate Sys_Date,
substr (to_char(sysdate, 'HH:MIAM'),1,10) Sys_Time from dual;

DROP TABLE EMP;
DROP TABLE DEPT;
DROP TABLE CUSTOMER;

DROP SEQUENCE CUSTID;

CREATE TABLE DEPT (
 DEPTNO              NUMBER(2) NOT NULL,
 DNAME               VARCHAR2(14),
 LOC                 VARCHAR2(13),
 CONSTRAINT DEPT_PRIMARY_KEY PRIMARY KEY (DEPTNO));
```

Notice that a standard header appears at the top, and it includes a statement to spool the output to a text file. Also notice that the script drops the tables before creating them. Following are the `CREATE TABLE` statements for the portion of the Oracle demo database that we will be using:

```
CREATE TABLE DEPT (
        DEPTNO                  NUMBER(2) NOT NULL,
        DNAME                   VARCHAR2(14),
        LOC                     VARCHAR2(13),
CONSTRAINT DEPT_PRIMARY_KEY
PRIMARY KEY (DEPTNO));

CREATE TABLE EMP (
        EMPNO                   NUMBER(4) NOT NULL,
        ENAME                   VARCHAR2(10),
        JOB                     VARCHAR2(9),
        MGR                     NUMBER(4)
                                CONSTRAINT EMP_SELF_KEY
                                REFERENCES EMP (EMPNO),
        HIREDATE                DATE,
        SAL                     NUMBER(7,2),
        COMM                    NUMBER(7,2),
        DEPTNO                  NUMBER(2) NOT NULL,
```

```
CONSTRAINT EMP_FOREIGN_KEY FOREIGN KEY (DEPTNO) REFERENCES DEPT (DEPTNO),
CONSTRAINT EMP_PRIMARY_KEY PRIMARY KEY (EMPNO));

CREATE TABLE CUSTOMER (
 CUSTID                 NUMBER (6) NOT NULL,
 NAME                   VARCHAR2(45),
 ADDRESS                VARCHAR2(40),
 CITY                   VARCHAR2(30),
 STATE                  VARCHAR2(2),
 ZIP                    VARCHAR2(9),
 AREA                   NUMBER (3),
 PHONE                  VARCHAR2(9),
 REPID                  NUMBER (4) NOT NULL,
 CREDITLIMIT            NUMBER (9,2),
 COMMENTS               LONG,
 CONSTRAINT CUSTOMER_PRIMARY_KEY PRIMARY KEY (CUSTID),
 CONSTRAINT CUSTID_ZERO CHECK (CUSTID > 0));
```

Notice in all of the tables, we are using the Oracle7 character data type of VarChar2. Also, notice that the not-null column constraints are unnamed. This results in the system assigning a name to them. Lastly, notice the table-level constraints appear at the bottom of the CREATE TABLE statements.

These tables are created in the DEM7CMIS.SQL and MAKECMIS.SQL scripts, and they are the new tables that we require to implement our physical design:

```
CREATE TABLE CONTACT (
        EMPNO                   NUMBER(4)
                                CONSTRAINT CONT_NN_EMPNO NOT NULL,
        CUSTID                  NUMBER(6)
                                CONSTRAINT CONT_NN_CUSTID NOT NULL,
        CONTACT_DATE            DATE
                                CONSTRAINT CONT_NN_CONTACT_DATE NOT NULL,
        TYPE                    VARCHAR2(5)
                                CONSTRAINT CONT_NN_TYPE NOT NULL,
        SUBJECT                 VARCHAR2(20),
        ACTION                  VARCHAR2(20),
        LOCATION                VARCHAR2(20),
        PHONE                   VARCHAR2(20),
        RECD_BY                 VARCHAR2(30),
        MESSAGE                 LONG RAW,
        SUCCESS                 VARCHAR2(1),
        DIRECTION               VARCHAR2(1),
        PRIORITY                VARCHAR2(1),

CONSTRAINT CONT_FK_EMP_EMPNO
FOREIGN KEY (EMPNO) REFERENCES EMP (EMPNO),

CONSTRAINT CONT_FK_CUSTOMER_CUSTID
FOREIGN KEY (CUSTID) REFERENCES CUSTOMER (CUSTID),

CONSTRAINT CONT_PK_EMPNO_CUSTID_CONT_DATE
PRIMARY KEY (EMPNO, CUSTID, CONTACT_DATE));
```

The Contact table contains several constraints, including two reference constraints, named as FKs.

```
CREATE TABLE EMP_AUDIT (
        EMPNO                   NUMBER(4)
                                CONSTRAINT EMP_AUDIT_NN_EMPNO NOT NULL,
        CHANGE_DATE             DATE
                                CONSTRAINT EMP_AUDIT_NN_CHANGE_DATE NOT NULL,
        OLD_SAL                 NUMBER(7,2),
        NEW_SAL                 NUMBER(7,2),
        UPDATED_BY              VARCHAR2(30),

CONSTRAINT PK_EMPNO_CHANGE_DATE
PRIMARY KEY (EMPNO, CHANGE_DATE));
```

These tables will be created at the end of this chapter using SQL*Plus, but they can be created using any product that provides a SQL command line. For example, the `CREATE TABLE` statement for the EMP_AUDIT table appears in Figure 5.2, in the PL/SQL Interpreter window of Oracle Procedure Builder.

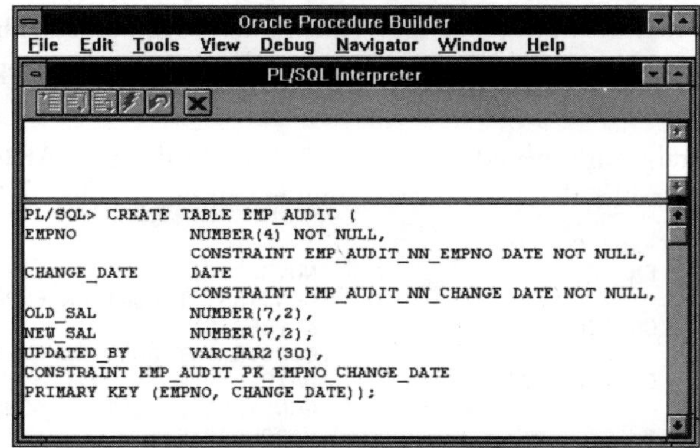

FIGURE 5.2.
The PL/SQL Interpreter in Oracle Procedure Builder being used to create the EMP_AUDIT table.

```
CREATE TABLE RPT_AUDIT (
        REPORT                  VARCHAR2(8)
                                CONSTRAINT RPTA_NN_REPORT NOT NULL,
        RUN_BY                  VARCHAR2(30)
                                CONSTRAINT RPTA_NN_RUN_BY NOT NULL,
        DATE_RUN                DATE
                                CONSTRAINT RPTA_NN_DATE_RUN NOT NULL,

CONSTRAINT RPTA_PK_REPORT_RUN_BY_RUN_DATE
PRIMARY KEY (REPORT, RUN_BY, DATE_RUN));
```

In addition to using the SQL command line for creating tables, Personal Oracle7 and the Workgroup Server/2000 database products provide a GUI tool for creating and maintaining database objects, called Oracle Object Manager.

Oracle Object Manager includes the Table Management dialog box and the Show Views dialog box for tables and views, respectively. Figure 5.3 shows the Table Management dialog box displaying the RPT_AUDIT table.

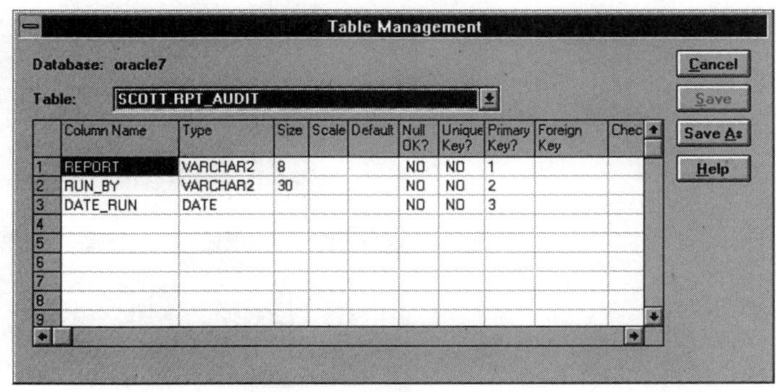

FIGURE 5.3.
The Table Management dialog box from Oracle Object Manager showing the RPT_AUDIT table.

```
CREATE TABLE STATE (
        CODE                            VARCHAR2(2)
                                        CONSTRAINT STATE_NN_CODE NOT NULL,
        NAME                            VARCHAR2(30)
                                        CONSTRAINT STATE_NN_NAME NOT NULL,

CONSTRAINT PK_STATE_CODE PRIMARY KEY (CODE));
```

You will again notice the column constraints in each of the new tables. But the constraints for the new tables all follow our naming conventions.

CREATE SEQUENCE

A sequence provides a system-generated number in sequential order. You can specify which number to start with and how much to increment the next number by. Here a sequence is created for the CUSTID in the Customer table:

```
CREATE SEQUENCE CUSTID
INCREMENT BY 1
START WITH 109
NOCACHE;
```

CREATE VIEW

A view is usually used to combine data from several different tables to provide an easier reference from queries and reports. We will create this view for contact lists.

```
CREATE VIEW CONTACT_LIST AS
        SELECT EMP.ENAME,
               CUSTOMER.NAME CNAME,
               CONTACT.CONTACT_DATE
        FROM EMP, CUSTOMER, CONTACT
        WHERE CONTACT.EMPNO = EMP.EMPNO
        AND CONTACT.CUSTID = CUSTOMER.CUSTID;
```

In Figure 5.4, the Show Views dialog box displays the CONTACT_LIST view from Oracle Object Manager.

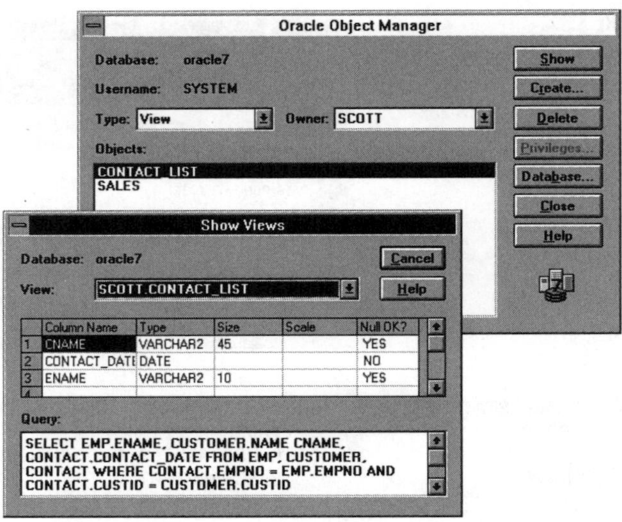

FIGURE 5.4.
The Show Views dialog box from Oracle Object Manager showing the CONTACT_LIST view.

CREATE SYNONYMS

Synonyms are created to provide additional names by which a table can be referenced. They are also used to facilitate access control. Both of these examples are demonstrated in this chapter. This is an example of the `CREATE` commands found in the CREATSYN.SQL file.

```
CREATE PUBLIC SYNONYM CONTACTS FOR SCOTT.CONTACT;
```

Figure 5.5 shows the CREATSYN.SQL script file.

Notepad - CREATSYN.SQL

File Edit Search Help

```
Prompt Developing Oracle Applications with Developer/2000
connect system/manager
Prompt Creating Public Synonyms as...

select substr (user,1,20) User_Id,
sysdate Sys_Date,
substr (to_char(sysdate, 'HH:MIAM'),1,10) Sys_Time from dual;

create public synonym contact          for SCOTT.contact;
create public synonym customer         for SCOTT.customer;
create public synonym dept             for SCOTT.dept;
create public synonym emp              for SCOTT.emp;
create public synonym emp_audit        for SCOTT.emp_audit;
create public synonym rpt_audit        for SCOTT.rpt_audit;
create public synonym state            for SCOTT.state;
create public synonym contacts         for SCOTT.contact;
create public synonym customers        for SCOTT.customer;
create public synonym departments      for SCOTT.dept;
create public synonym employees        for SCOTT.emp;
create public synonym employee_audits  for SCOTT.emp_audit;
create public synonym report_audits    for SCOTT.rpt_audit;
create public synonym states           for SCOTT.state;

Prompt Done Creating Public Synonyms.
```

FIGURE 5.5.
The Create Public Synonyms script file with plural names for the tables.

We chose to maintain consistency with the existing database and use the singular form of the entity name for the table name. Here we address this issue again by creating synonyms that are the plural form of the table names. In this way we can provide access to the data through the plural form of the table name while maintaining the existing convention.

Notice that we are connecting as system/manager in this script file. This is only OK for a demo, prototype, or other completely unsecured environment.

CAUTION

The use of the connect string in the script file is only done here for ease of use. It is not recommended, because it does not provide the necessary level of security required for a development project.

CREATE TRIGGER

Oracle7 supports the creation of database triggers. We have a functional requirement to capture auditing information on changes to employee salaries. To meet this requirement, we will create a database trigger on the Emp table that will insert a record into the Emp_Audit table whenever the salary is updated. This is what the `CREATE TRIGGER` statement would look like in SQL:

```
CREATE TRIGGER EMP_AUDIT
AFTER UPDATE OF SAL
ON EMP
FOR EACH ROW
DECLARE
        CUR_USER VARCHAR2(8);
        CUR_DATE DATE;
BEGIN
        SELECT USER, SYSDATE INTO CUR_USER, CUR_DATE FROM DUAL;
        INSERT INTO EMP_AUDIT
        VALUES (:OLD.EMPNO, CUR_DATE, :OLD.SAL, :NEW.SAL, CUR_USER);
END;
```

However, we are going to create this trigger using the GUI Database Trigger Editor in Chapter 11, "Introducing Oracle Procedure Builder." (See Figure 5.6.)

CREATE FUNCTION

Functions may be created as local program units in the each of the Developer/2000 tools, as we will see in later chapters of this book. The function shown in Figure 5.7 will be created as a local program unit in Chapter 11 and then later copied to the database without changing any of the code simply by dragging and dropping.

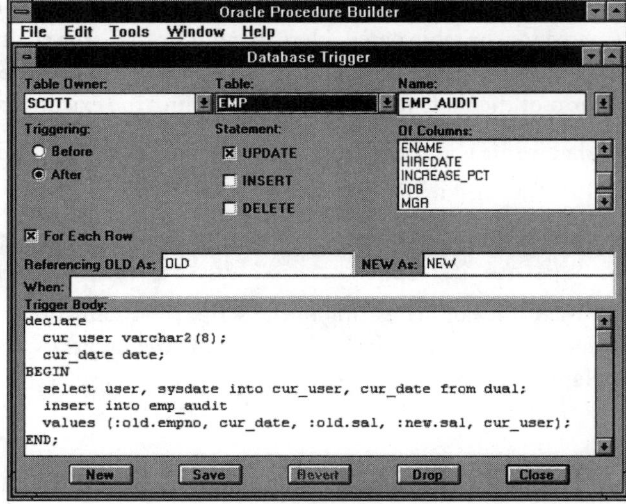

FIGURE 5.6.
The EMP_AUDIT *trigger in the Database Trigger Editor from Oracle Procedure Builder.*

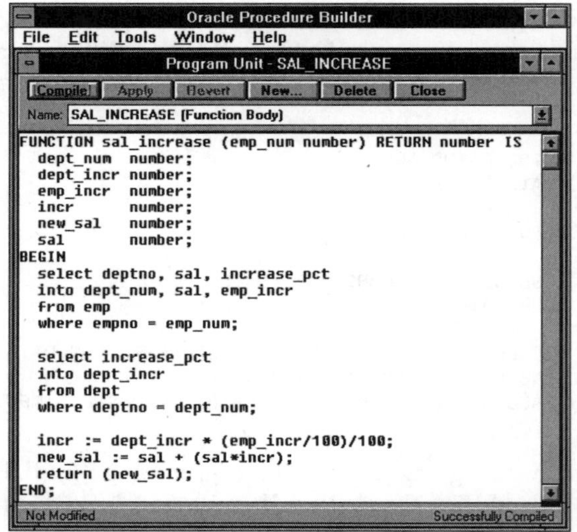

FIGURE 5.7.
The SAL_INCREASE *function in the Program Unit Editor from Oracle Procedure Builder.*

But functions may also be created in the Oracle7 database using the create function statement as we see here.

```
CREATE OR REPLACE FUNCTION
SAL_INCREASE (EMP_NUM NUMBER)
RETURN NUMBER
AS
        DEPT_NUM  NUMBER;
        DEPT_INCR NUMBER;
        EMP_INCR  NUMBER;
```

```
        INCR        NUMBER;
        NEW_SAL     NUMBER;
        SAL         NUMBER;
BEGIN
        SELECT DEPTNO, SAL, INCREASE_PCT
        INTO DEPT_NUM, SAL, EMP_INCR
        FROM EMP
        WHERE EMPNO = EMP_NUM;

        SELECT INCREASE_PCT INTO DEPT_INCR
        FROM DEPT
        WHERE DEPTNO = DEPT_NUM;

        INCR := DEPT_INCR * (EMP_INCR/100)/100;
        NEW_SAL := SAL + (SAL*INCR);
        RETURN (NEW_SAL);
END;
```

Notice this statement begins with `CREATE or REPLACE FUNCTION`. Not all database objects must be dropped before you can recreate them. This is an example of an object that may be replaced.

If you are using Oracle7.1 or higher, a function that is stored in the database is available to be used in SQL statements, as will be shown next in the `ANNUAL_SAL_UPDATE` procedure.

CREATE PROCEDURE

Procedures, like functions and triggers, may be created from the SQL command line as shown in Figure 5.8, where the `ANNUAL_SAL_UPDATE` procedure is created in SQL*Plus.

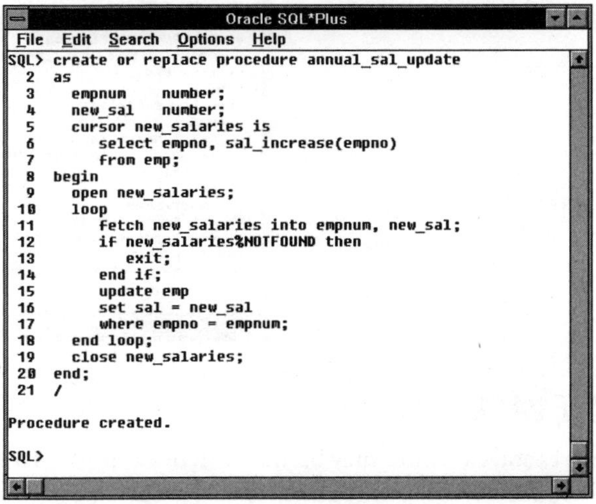

FIGURE 5.8.
The ANNUAL_SAL_UPDATE *procedure being created in SQL*Plus.*

```
Oracle SQL*Plus
File  Edit  Search  Options  Help
SQL> create or replace procedure annual_sal_update
  as
    empnum     number;
    new_sal    number;
    cursor new_salaries is
       select empno, sal_increase(empno)
       from emp;
  begin
    open new_salaries;
    loop
       fetch new_salaries into empnum, new_sal;
       if new_salaries%NOTFOUND then
          exit;
       end if;
       update emp
       set sal = new_sal
       where empno = empnum;
    end loop;
    close new_salaries;
  end;
  /

Procedure created.

SQL>
```

Notice that this procedure contains a `SELECT` statement that references the database function `SAL_INCREASES`.

```
CREATE OR REPLACE PROCEDURE ANNUAL_SAL_UPDATE
AS
        EMPNUM     NUMBER;
        NEW_SAL    NUMBER;
        CURSOR NEW_SALARIES IS
                SELECT EMPNO, SAL_INCREASE(EMPNO)
                FROM EMP;
BEGIN
        OPEN NEW_SALARIES;
        LOOP
                FETCH NEW_SALARIES INTO EMPNUM, NEW_SAL;
                IF NEW_SALARIES%NOTFOUND THEN
                        EXIT;
                END IF;
        UPDATE EMP
        SET SAL = NEW_SAL
        WHERE EMPNO = EMPNUM;
        END LOOP;
        CLOSE NEW_SALARIES;
END;
```

This database procedure will be created using the Stored Program Unit Editor in Chapter 11. (See Figure 5.9.)

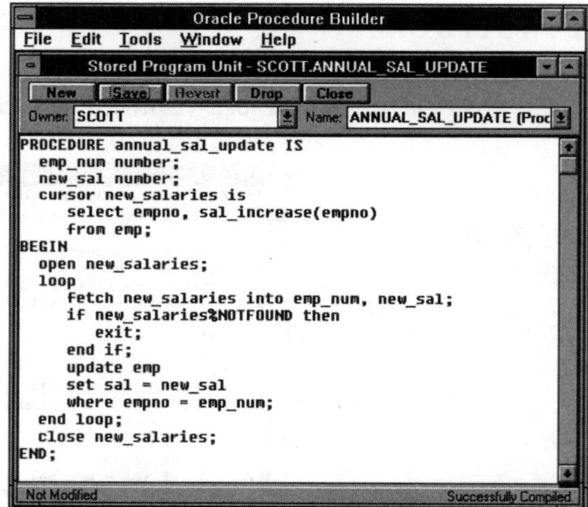

FIGURE 5.9.
The ANNUAL_SAL_UPDATE procedure compiled in the Stored Program Unit Editor of Oracle Procedure Builder.

CREATE PACKAGE

Procedures and functions may be also be defined inside of a package, using the `CREATE PACKAGE` statement. This is called the package specification, and an example is shown here in the `SAL_MGT` package.

```
CREATE OR REPLACE PACKAGE SAL_MGT AS
  PROCEDURE SAL_UPDATE;
  FUNCTION SAL_INCR (EMP_NUM NUMBER) RETURN NUMBER;
END SAL_MGT;
```

Notice that the package specification references the SAL_UPDATE procedure and the SAL_INCR function. Thus, in this example the function is contained within the package.

Here is another example that accomplishes the same thing, only in a different way. The package specification for SAL_MANAGEMENT shown here only references the ANNUAL_SAL_UPDATE procedure in the specification.

```
CREATE OR REPLACE PACKAGE SAL_MANAGEMENT AS
  PROCEDURE ANNUAL_SAL_UPDATE;
END SAL_MANAGEMENT;
```

This is because in the package body the SAL_INCREASE function is called from the database.

CREATE PACKAGE BODY

The package body contains the source code for the package. Notice here that the SAL_MGT package body contains the two program units SAL_UPDATE and SAL_INCR referenced in the SAL_MGT package.

```
CREATE OR REPLACE PACKAGE BODY SAL_MGT AS
PROCEDURE SAL_UPDATE IS
  EMPNUM    NUMBER;
  NEW_SAL   NUMBER;
  CURSOR NEW_SALARIES IS
     SELECT EMPNO
     FROM EMP;
BEGIN
  OPEN NEW_SALARIES;
  LOOP
     FETCH NEW_SALARIES INTO EMPNUM;
     IF NEW_SALARIES%NOTFOUND THEN
        EXIT;
     END IF;
     NEW_SAL := SAL_INCR(EMPNUM);
     UPDATE EMP
     SET SAL = NEW_SAL
     WHERE EMPNO = EMPNUM;
  END LOOP;
  CLOSE NEW_SALARIES;
END;
FUNCTION SAL_INCR (EMP_NUM NUMBER) RETURN NUMBER IS
  DEPT_NUM  NUMBER;
  DEPT_INCR NUMBER;
  EMP_INCR  NUMBER;
  INCR      NUMBER;
  NEW_SAL   NUMBER;
  SAL       NUMBER;
BEGIN
  SELECT DEPTNO, SAL, INCREASE_PCT
  INTO DEPT_NUM, SAL, EMP_INCR
  FROM EMP
  WHERE EMPNO = EMP_NUM;

  SELECT INCREASE_PCT INTO DEPT_INCR
  FROM DEPT
  WHERE DEPTNO = DEPT_NUM;
```

```
  INCR := DEPT_INCR * (EMP_INCR/100)/100;
  NEW_SAL := SAL + (SAL*INCR);
  RETURN (NEW_SAL);
END;
END SAL_MGT;
```

Notice here that the `SAL_MANAGEMENT` package body contains only one program unit, `ANNUAL_SAL_UPDATE`, as was referenced in the `SAL_MANAGEMENT` package.

```
CREATE OR REPLACE PACKAGE BODY SAL_MANAGEMENT AS
PROCEDURE ANNUAL_SAL_UPDATE IS
  EMPNUM    NUMBER;
  NEW_SAL   NUMBER;
  CURSOR NEW_SALARIES IS
     SELECT EMPNO, SAL_INCREASE(EMPNO)
     FROM EMP;
BEGIN
  OPEN NEW_SALARIES;
  LOOP
     FETCH NEW_SALARIES INTO EMPNUM, NEW_SAL;
     IF NEW_SALARIES%NOTFOUND THEN
        EXIT;
     END IF;
     UPDATE EMP
     SET SAL = NEW_SAL
     WHERE EMPNO = EMPNUM;
  END LOOP;
  CLOSE NEW_SALARIES;
END;
END SAL_MANAGEMENT;
```

Again this packaged procedure referenced `sal_increase`, a database function, in a `SELECT` statement.

CREATE TABLESPACE

You may want to physically separate the data in one project from the data in the rest of the system. This can be done using the `CREATE TABLESPACE` statement. In this example, a new 20MB tablespace is being created with the name CMIS.

```
CREATE TABLESPACE CMIS
DATAFILE 'C:\ORAWIN\DBS\TS_CMIS.ORA' SIZE 20M
DEFAULT STORAGE (INITIAL 10K NEXT 50K
MINEXTENTS 1 MAXEXTENTS 999
PCTINCREASE 10)
ONLINE
```

Once the new tablespace is created, the user(s) who will create the database objects can be altered to use this tablespace as their default, as will be seen in the "`Alter User`" section of this chapter.

CREATE USER

Each person who will be using the system should have their own Oracle user ID. This is an example of creating a new user.

```
CREATE USER LARRY IDENTIFIED BY ORACLE;
```

The user ID is LARRY, and the password is ORACLE.

ALTER

The ALTER verb is used to modify database objects. We will use ALTER TABLE to add columns to the existing Department and Employee tables. We will also use ALTER TABLE to add constraints to the Contact and State tables. Then we will use ALTER TABLESPACE to add more room the SYSTEM tablespace, and finally we will change the default tablespace for a user with alter user.

ALTER TABLE

This is an example of an ALTER TABLE statement. This statement adds the Increate_Pct column to the Dept table. It is an extract from the \DEV2000\ALTERS\DEPT.ALT file.

```
ALTER TABLE DEPT ADD
INCREASE_PCT NUMBER(3);
```

The DEPT.ALT script is shown in Figure 5.10.

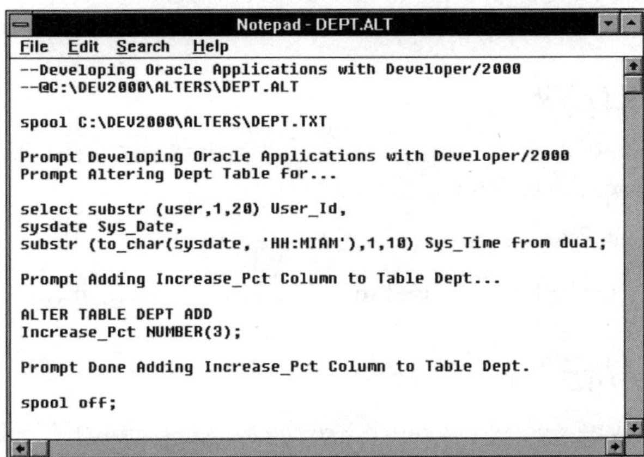

```
--Developing Oracle Applications with Developer/2000
--@C:\DEV2000\ALTERS\DEPT.ALT

spool C:\DEV2000\ALTERS\DEPT.TXT

Prompt Developing Oracle Applications with Developer/2000
Prompt Altering Dept Table for...

select substr (user,1,20) User_Id,
sysdate Sys_Date,
substr (to_char(sysdate, 'HH:MIAM'),1,10) Sys_Time from dual;

Prompt Adding Increase_Pct Column to Table Dept...

ALTER TABLE DEPT ADD
Increase_Pct NUMBER(3);

Prompt Done Adding Increase_Pct Column to Table Dept.

spool off;
```

FIGURE 5.10.
The Alter Department Table script file adding the INCREASE_PCT column.

This statement adds the Increate_Pct column to the Emp table just as we did for the Dept table. It is an extract from the \DEV2000\ALTERS\EMP.ALT file.

```
ALTER TABLE EMP ADD
INCREASE_PCT NUMBER(3);
```

The following statement adds a Check Condition constraint to the Contact table. It will ensure that only the low priority contacts may have a null subject. This is an extract from the \DEV2000\TABLES\CONTACT.TAB file.

```
ALTER TABLE CONTACT ADD
CONSTRAINT CONT_CC_PRIORITY
CHECK (PRIORITY = DECODE(SUBJECT, NULL, 'L'));
```

The following statement adds a Unique constraint to the State table for the Name column, so that two states won't have the same name. It is an extract from the \DEV2000\TABLES\STATE.TAB file.

```
ALTER TABLE STATE ADD
CONSTRAINT STATE_UK_NAME
UNIQUE (NAME);
```

Each of these `ALTER TABLE` statements will be run as part of the script to set up the database for the project at the end of this chapter.

ALTER TABLESPACE

This is an example of an `ALTER TABLESPACE` statement. This statement adds a physical datafile to increase the system tablespace:

```
ALTER TABLESPACE SYSTEM ADD DATAFILE 'C:\ORAWIN\DBS\TS_SYS.ORA' SIZE 10M REUSE;
```

Personal Oracle7 and the Oracle Workgroup/2000 Server products include a GUI tool called Database Expander to support this function.

ALTER USER

The following is an example of an `ALTER USER` statement. This statement changes the default tablespace for LARRY to CMIS.

```
ALTER USER LARRY DEFAULT TABLESPACE CMIS;
```

`alter user` can also be used to assign a password, by including the parameter `IDENTIFIED BY`.

RENAME

The `RENAME` verb works much like the `RENAME` command in DOS or the Rename function in File Manager. It simply changes the name of a database object from one name to another.

DROP

The `DROP` verb is used to remove database objects. `DROP` is usually used to clean up the environment just before creating objects in the database.

CAUTION

When you DROP a table, all of the rows in the table are deleted.

DROP TABLE

For each table in the Oracle demo script, as well as the CREATE TABLE scripts for this project, you will see a DROP TABLE statement before the table is created.

Each of the existing tables are dropped prior to creation:

```
DROP TABLE EMP;
DROP TABLE DEPT;
DROP TABLE CUSTOMER;
```

Each of these new tables are dropped prior to creation as well:

```
DROP TABLE CONTACT;
DROP TABLE EMP_AUDIT;
DROP TABLE RPT_AUDIT;
DROP TABLE STATE;
```

All of these tables are created in the "Create Table" section of this chapter.

DROP SEQUENCE

The Customer table uses a sequence for the key; therefore, to start the number off fresh, it is dropped first using the following statement, then later created:

```
DROP SEQUENCE CUSTID;
```

DROP VIEW

This is an example of the statement that will drop the CONTACT_INFO view:

```
DROP VIEW CONTACT_INFO;
```

DROP SYNONYM

Each synonym that we create can also be dropped. This is an example of the DROP commands found in the DROPSYN.SQL file:

```
DROP PUBLIC SYNONYM CONTACTS;
```

The DROPSYN.SQL script file is shown in Figure 5.11.

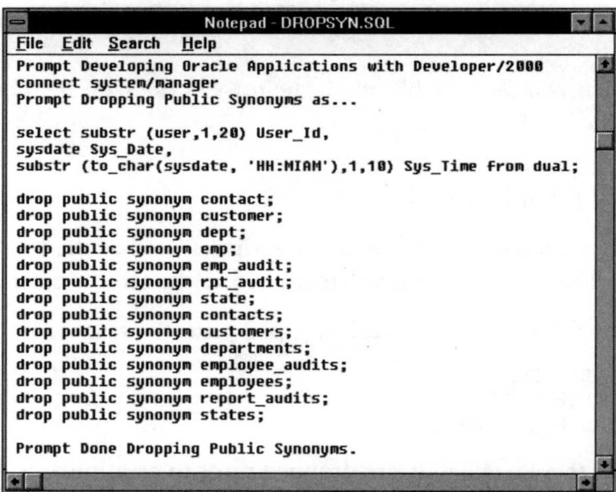
```
Prompt Developing Oracle Applications with Developer/2000
connect system/manager
Prompt Dropping Public Synonyms as...

select substr (user,1,20) User_Id,
sysdate Sys_Date,
substr (to_char(sysdate, 'HH:MIAM'),1,10) Sys_Time from dual;

drop public synonym contact;
drop public synonym customer;
drop public synonym dept;
drop public synonym emp;
drop public synonym emp_audit;
drop public synonym rpt_audit;
drop public synonym state;
drop public synonym contacts;
drop public synonym customers;
drop public synonym departments;
drop public synonym employee_audits;
drop public synonym employees;
drop public synonym report_audits;
drop public synonym states;

Prompt Done Dropping Public Synonyms.
```

FIGURE 5.11.
The `Drop Public Synonyms` *script file.*

Constraints

The constraints were added during the creation or alteration of the tables that they are associated with. If we had created all the tables with all the constraints using our naming conventions from the previous chapter, this is how they would look:

Type	*Table Name*	*Constraint Name*
C	CONTACT	CONT_NN_EMPNO
C	CONTACT	CONT_NN_CUSTID
C	CONTACT	CONT_NN_CONT_DATE
C	CONTACT	CONT_NN_TYPE
C	CONTACT	CONT_CC_PRIORITY
P	CONTACT	CONT_PK_EMPNO_CUSTID_CONT_DATE
R	CONTACT	CONT_FK_EMP_EMPNO
R	CONTACT	CONT_FK_CUSTOMER_CUSTID
C	CUSTOMER	CUSTOMER_NN_CUSTID
P	CUSTOMER	CUSTOMER_PK_CUSTID
C	CUSTOMER	CUSTOMER_CR_CUSTID
R	CUSTOMER	CUSTOMER_FK_STATE_CODE
C	CUSTOMER	CUSTOMER_NN_REPID
C	DEPT	DEPT_NN_DEPTNO
P	DEPT	DEPT_PK_DEPTNO

C	EMP	EMP_NN_EMPNO
P	EMP	EMP_PK_EMPNO
R	EMP	EMP_FK_EMP_MGR
C	EMP	EMP_NN_DEPTNO
R	EMP	EMP_FK_DEPT_DEPTNO
C	EMP_AUDIT	EMP_AUDIT_NN_EMPNO
C	EMP_AUDIT	EMP_AUDIT_NN_CHANGE_DATE
P	EMP_AUDIT	EMP_AUDIT_PK_EMPNO_CHANGE_DATE
C	RPT_AUDIT	RPTA_NN_REPORT
C	RPT_AUDIT	RPTA_NN_RUN_BY
C	RPT_AUDIT	RPTA_NN_DATE_RUN
P	RPT_AUDIT	RPTA_PK_REPORT_RUN_BY_DATE_RUN
C	STATE	STATE_NN_CODE
C	STATE	STATE_NN_NAME
P	STATE	STATE_PK_CODE

See if you can identify each constraint by reviewing the constraint name.

Data Manipulation Language (DML)

The Data Manipulation Language is the portion of SQL that is used to select, insert, update, and delete database objects. We have many requirements for the `select` statement throughout this book, and we will use the `insert` statement for recording audit information as well as populating the database. However, we won't need to use the `update` and `delete` statements from the SQL command line because our Oracle Forms applications will manage the updates and deletes as well as the inserts of our data for us.

SELECT

The `SELECT` statement is the most common of all the SQL verbs. We will use it often throughout the rest of this book. For example, we will be creating lists of values in our Oracle Forms applications and creating queries in our Oracle Reports and Oracle Graphics applications. The following is the `select` statement for the Oracle Graphics application that displays a chart of the priorities for all employees. It is used in Chapter 10, "Introducing Oracle Graphics."

```
SELECT COUNT (DECODE (PRIORITY, 'H', 'HIGH')) High,
       COUNT (DECODE (PRIORITY, 'M', 'MEDIUM')) Medium,
       COUNT (DECODE (PRIORITY, 'L', 'LOW')) Low
FROM CONTACT
```

This `select` statement is later modified in Chapter 14, "Developing Oracle Graphics Applications," to display priorities for specific employees.

```
SELECT COUNT (DECODE (PRIORITY, 'H', 'HIGH')) High,
        COUNT (DECODE (PRIORITY, 'M', 'MEDIUM')) Medium,
        COUNT (DECODE (PRIORITY, 'L', 'LOW')) Low
FROM CONTACT
WHERE EMPNO = :EMPLOYEE
```

Each of the other `select` statements that are needed to develop the applications for this project will be provided during the chapter exercises.

INSERT

The `INSERT` statement is used to add rows to a table. Here we are inserting a row into the Report Audit table to keep track of when the Priority report is being run:

```
DECLARE
        CUR_USER VARCHAR2(8);
        CUR_DATE DATE;
BEGIN
        SELECT USER, SYSDATE
        INTO CUR_USER, CUR_DATE
        FROM DUAL;
        INSERT INTO RPT_AUDIT
        VALUES ('Priority', CUR_USER, CUR_DATE);
END;
```

The `insert` statement is shown in Figure 5.12 and will be used in Chapter 13, "Developing Oracle Reports Applications." We will use the `insert` statement in the next chapter as well to populate the database.

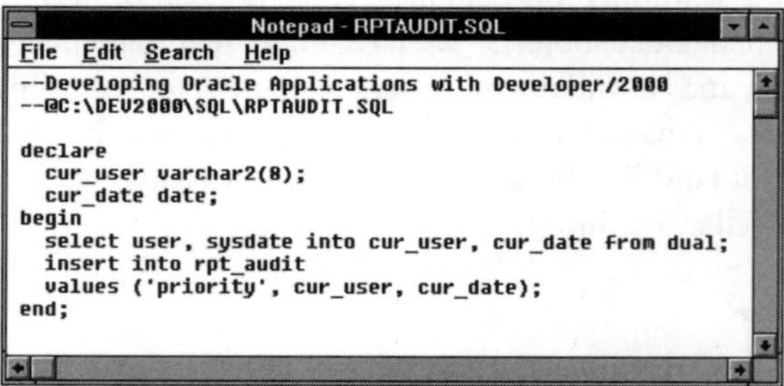
Notepad - RPTAUDIT.SQL
File Edit Search Help

```
--Developing Oracle Applications with Developer/2000
--@C:\DEV2000\SQL\RPTAUDIT.SQL

declare
  cur_user varchar2(8);
  cur_date date;
begin
  select user, sysdate into cur_user, cur_date from dual;
  insert into rpt_audit
  values ('priority', cur_user, cur_date);
end;
```

FIGURE 5.12.
An INSERT statement that will be used in a report trigger.

UPDATE

The following is an example of an `UPDATE` statement that increases SCOTTs' salary by 15 percent:

```
UPDATE EMP
SET SAL = SAL*1.15
WHERE EMPNO = 7788;
```

DELETE

The following is an example of a `DELETE` statement that removes SCOTT as an employee:

```
DELETE FROM EMP
WHERE EMPNO = 7788;
```

Data Control Language (DCL)

The Data Control Language is the portion of SQL that is used to grant, revoke, disable, and enable access to database objects.

GRANT

`GRANT` enables users to access database objects such as tables or even the database itself. the following is an example of providing a new user with access to the database and setting that user's password at the same time:

```
GRANT CONNECT, RESOURCE
TO HIPSLEY, IDENTIFIED BY HIPS;
```

The user ID is HIPSLEY, and the password is HIPS.

The following example provides access to the database to a existing user:

```
GRANT CONNECT, RESOURCE TO LARRY;
```

Notice the password was not assigned. The password for this user was set using the `create user` statement.

`grant` commands provide access control to tables, as illustrated by this example of the `grant` commands found in the GRANTS.SQL file:

```
GRANT SELECT ON CONTACT TO PUBLIC;
```

Figure 5.13 shows the GRANTS.SQL script file.

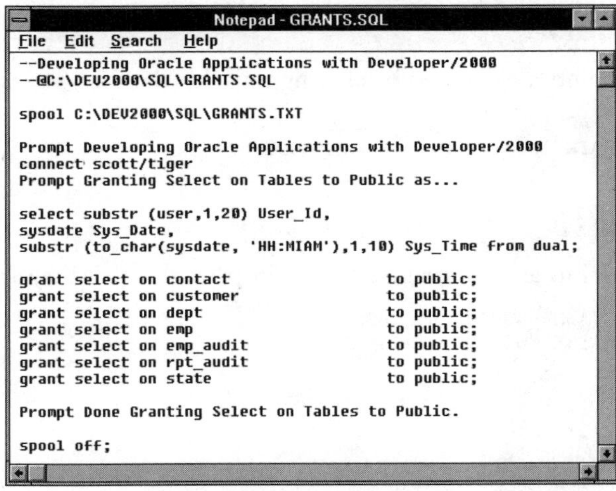

```
Notepad - GRANTS.SQL
File  Edit  Search  Help
--Developing Oracle Applications with Developer/2000
--@C:\DEV2000\SQL\GRANTS.SQL

spool C:\DEV2000\SQL\GRANTS.TXT

Prompt Developing Oracle Applications with Developer/2000
connect scott/tiger
Prompt Granting Select on Tables to Public as...

select substr (user,1,20) User_Id,
sysdate Sys_Date,
substr (to_char(sysdate, 'HH:MIAM'),1,10) Sys_Time from dual;

grant select on contact              to public;
grant select on customer             to public;
grant select on dept                 to public;
grant select on emp                  to public;
grant select on emp_audit            to public;
grant select on rpt_audit            to public;
grant select on state                to public;

Prompt Done Granting Select on Tables to Public.

spool off;
```

FIGURE 5.13.
A GRANT script that provides read access to the project tables.

REVOKE

REVOKE can be used to remove access to the database, or to remove the ability to insert, update, and delete a table, or to remove any access from any database object. Here access to connect to the database is being removed from SCOTT:

```
REVOKE CONNECT FROM SCOTT
```

revoke provides access control to tables, as shown in this example of the revoke commands found in the REVOKE.SQL file:

```
REVOKE SELECT ON CONTACT FROM PUBLIC;
```

Figure 5.14 shows the REVOKE.SQL script file.

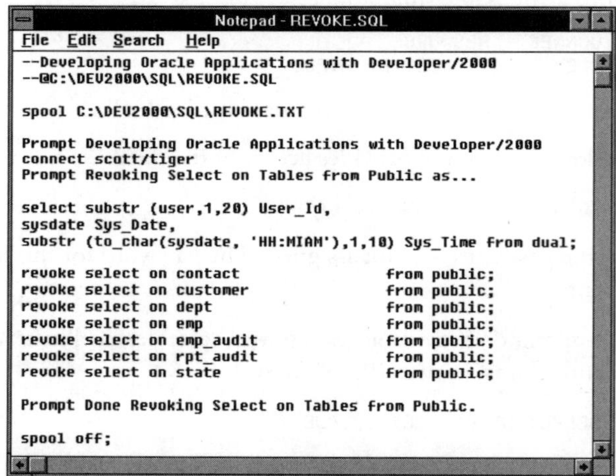

FIGURE 5.14.
A REVOKE script that removes access from the project tables.

DISABLE

Constraints are disabled by altering the table that they are associated with, as shown here:

```
ALTER TABLE CUSTOMER DISABLE
CONSTRAINT CUSTOMER_FK_STATE_CODE;
```

ENABLE

Constraints are also enabled by altering the table that they are associated with, as shown here:

```
ALTER TABLE CUSTOMER ENABLE
CONSTRAINT CUSTOMER_FK_STATE_CODE;
```

Exercise

The purpose of this exercise is to build the database for this project. It will give you hands-on experience with the material that has been covered in this chapter. Using SQL*Plus and the scripts provided with this book, you will create tables, synonyms, constraints, a sequence, and a view. Choose the exercise that is appropriate for your current system configuration.

Do the first exercise if you do not already have the Oracle Demonstration Database installed, or do the second exercise if you do. These SQL scripts assume that there are users already defined for SCOTT/TIGER and SYSTEM/MANAGER.

> **NOTE**
>
> Some of the database objects, such the database trigger, functions, procedures, and packages, are not in the create script and will not be created yet. This is because we will be creating them in Chapter 11 using the GUI tools.

Building the Oracle Demonstration and Project Databases

Follow these steps if you do not already have the Oracle Demonstration Database installed:

1. Start the Oracle7 database.
2. Launch SQL*Plus.
3. Connect to the Oracle database as SCOTT/TIGER.
4. Execute the create script by typing the following:
   ```
   start C:\DEV2000\SQL\DEM7CMIS.SQL
   ```
5. Review the DEM7CMIS.TXT file, to make sure there were no errors encountered.
6. If you find any errors in the text file, review them with the DBA.

Building the Project Database Only

Follow these steps if you already have the Oracle Demonstration Database installed:

1. Start the Oracle7 database.
2. Launch SQL*Plus.
3. Connect to the Oracle database as SCOTT/TIGER.
4. Execute the create script by typing the following:
   ```
   start C:\DEV2000\SQL\MAKECMIS.SQL
   ```
5. Review the MAKECMIS.TXT file, to make sure there were no errors encountered.
6. If you find any errors in the text file, review them with the DBA.

Summary

This chapter provided you with a overview of DDL, DML, and DCL, as well as the SQL commands needed to do the following:

- Create tables with constraints
- Create a sequence
- Create a view
- Create synonyms for tables
- Create database triggers
- Create database functions, procedures, and packages
- Create a tablespace
- Create a user
- Alter tables to add columns, and constraints
- Alter a tablespace
- Alter a user
- Drop database objects
- Select, insert, update, and delete
- Grant and revoke access
- Disable and enable constraints

We reviewed every database object type that will be used in this project—as well as a few other useful SQL statements that are not required for this project but will come in handy for larger projects. Now that we have built the database, we will populate it with lookup and sample data.

6

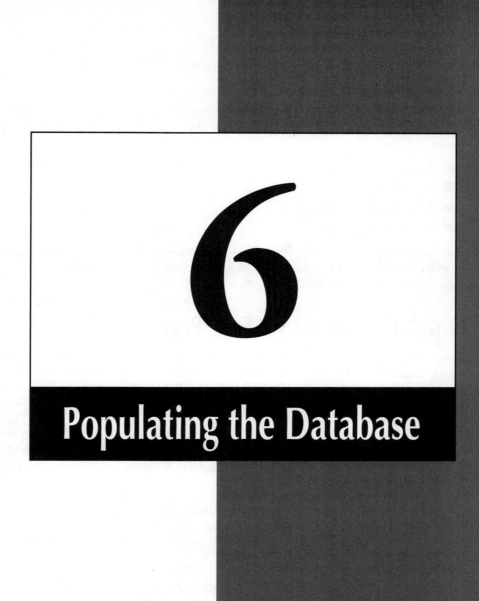

Populating the Database

Introduction

Now that the database has been built, we will populate the tables with the database lookups and some sample data. We will review a variety of methods that may be used to populate the database, including:

- The `INSERT INTO` command
- The `UPDATE` command
- The `LOAD DATA` command
- Using Oracle Forms

After we have reviewed each of the population methods, in the exercises at the end of this chapter, we will create the data for our database. We will be executing insert and update scripts from SQL*Plus as well as control files using SQL*Loader.

Populating Tables via SQL*Plus

As we saw in the previous chapter, SQL*Plus provides a SQL command-line interface to the Oracle database. Here we will again use SQL*Plus to run script files that insert and update our data.

INSERT INTO

The Oracle demo tables are populated via the `INSERT INTO` command in the DEMOBLD7.SQL script (or the DEM7CMIS.SQL script, depending on whether or not you have already installed the Oracle demo database).

These are the `INSERT` statements for the Department table:

```
INSERT INTO DEPT VALUES (10,'ACCOUNTING','NEW YORK');
INSERT INTO DEPT VALUES (20,'RESEARCH','DALLAS');
INSERT INTO DEPT VALUES (30,'SALES','CHICAGO');
INSERT INTO DEPT VALUES (40,'OPERATIONS','BOSTON');
```

These are the `INSERT` statements for the Employee table:

```
INSERT INTO EMP VALUES
(7839,'KING','PRESIDENT',NULL,'17-NOV-81',5000,NULL,10);
INSERT INTO EMP VALUES
(7698,'BLAKE','MANAGER',7839,'1-MAY-81',2850,NULL,30);
INSERT INTO EMP VALUES
(7782,'CLARK','MANAGER',7839,'9-JUN-81',2450,NULL,10);
INSERT INTO EMP VALUES
(7566,'JONES','MANAGER',7839,'2-APR-81',2975,NULL,20);
INSERT INTO EMP VALUES
(7654,'MARTIN','SALESMAN',7698,'28-SEP-81',1250,1400,30);
INSERT INTO EMP VALUES
(7499,'ALLEN','SALESMAN',7698,'20-FEB-81',1600,300,30);
```

```
INSERT INTO EMP VALUES
(7844,'TURNER','SALESMAN',7698,'8-SEP-81',1500,0,30);
INSERT INTO EMP VALUES
(7900,'JAMES','CLERK',7698,'3-DEC-81',950,NULL,30);
INSERT INTO EMP VALUES
(7521,'WARD','SALESMAN',7698,'22-FEB-81',1250,500,30);
INSERT INTO EMP VALUES
(7902,'FORD','ANALYST',7566,'3-DEC-81',3000,NULL,20);
INSERT INTO EMP VALUES
(7369,'SMITH','CLERK',7902,'17-DEC-80',800,NULL,20);
INSERT INTO EMP VALUES
(7788,'SCOTT','ANALYST',7566,'09-DEC-82',3000,NULL,20);
INSERT INTO EMP VALUES
(7876,'ADAMS','CLERK',7788,'12-JAN-83',1100,NULL,20);
INSERT INTO EMP VALUES
(7934,'MILLER','CLERK',7782,'23-JAN-82',1300,NULL,10);
```

The final table we are using for our project from the Oracle demo database is the Customer table, and these are the `INSERT` statements for that table:

```
INSERT INTO CUSTOMER
(ZIP, STATE, REPID, PHONE, NAME, CUSTID,
CREDITLIMIT, CITY, AREA, ADDRESS, COMMENTS)
VALUES ('96711', 'CA', '7844', '598-6609', 'JOCKSPORTS',
'100', '5000', 'BELMONT', '415', '345 VIEWRIDGE',
'Very friendly people to work with — sales rep likes to be called Mike.');

INSERT INTO CUSTOMER
(ZIP, STATE, REPID, PHONE, NAME, CUSTID,
CREDITLIMIT, CITY, AREA, ADDRESS, COMMENTS)
VALUES ('94061', 'CA', '7521', '368-1223', 'TKB SPORT SHOP',
'101', '10000', 'REDWOOD CITY', '415', '490 BOLI RD.',
'Rep called 5/8 about change in order - contact shipping.');

INSERT INTO CUSTOMER
(ZIP, STATE, REPID, PHONE, NAME, CUSTID,
CREDITLIMIT, CITY, AREA, ADDRESS, COMMENTS)
VALUES ('95133', 'CA', '7654', '644-3341', 'VOLLYRITE',
'102', '7000', 'BURLINGAME', '415', '9722 HAMILTON',
'Company doing heavy promotion beginning 10/89. Prepare for large orders
during[ic:ccc] winter.');

INSERT INTO CUSTOMER
(ZIP, STATE, REPID, PHONE, NAME, CUSTID,
CREDITLIMIT, CITY, AREA, ADDRESS, COMMENTS)
VALUES ('97544', 'CA', '7521', '677-9312', 'JUST TENNIS',
'103', '3000', 'BURLINGAME', '415', 'HILLVIEW MALL',
'Contact rep about new line of tennis rackets.');

INSERT INTO CUSTOMER
(ZIP, STATE, REPID, PHONE, NAME, CUSTID,
CREDITLIMIT, CITY, AREA, ADDRESS, COMMENTS)
VALUES ('93301', 'CA', '7499', '996-2323', 'EVERY MOUNTAIN',
'104', '10000', 'CUPERTINO', '408', '574 SURRY RD.',
'Customer with high market share (23%) due to aggressive advertising.');

INSERT INTO CUSTOMER
(ZIP, STATE, REPID, PHONE, NAME, CUSTID,
```

```
CREDITLIMIT, CITY, AREA, ADDRESS, COMMENTS)
VALUES ('91003', 'CA', '7844', '376-9966', 'K + T SPORTS',
'105', '5000', 'SANTA CLARA', '408', '3476 EL PASEO',
'Tends to order large amounts of merchandise at once. Accounting is
considering[ic:ccc] raising their credit limit. Usually pays on time.');

INSERT INTO CUSTOMER
(ZIP, STATE, REPID, PHONE, NAME, CUSTID,
CREDITLIMIT, CITY, AREA, ADDRESS, COMMENTS)
VALUES ('94301', 'CA', '7521', '364-9777', 'SHAPE UP',
'106', '6000', 'PALO ALTO', '415', '908 SEQUOIA',
'Support intensive. Orders small amounts (< 800) of merchandise at a time.');

INSERT INTO CUSTOMER
(ZIP, STATE, REPID, PHONE, NAME, CUSTID,
CREDITLIMIT, CITY, AREA, ADDRESS, COMMENTS)
VALUES ('93301', 'CA', '7499', '967-4398', 'WOMENS SPORTS',
'107', '10000', 'SUNNYVALE', '408', 'VALCO VILLAGE',
'First sporting goods store geared exclusively towards women. Unusual
promotion[ic:ccc]al style and very willing to take chances towards new products!');

INSERT INTO CUSTOMER
(ZIP, STATE, REPID, PHONE, NAME, CUSTID,
CREDITLIMIT, CITY, AREA, ADDRESS, COMMENTS)
VALUES ('55649', 'MN', '7844', '566-9123',
'NORTH WOODS HEALTH AND FITNESS SUPPLY CENTER', '108', '8000',
'HIBBING', '612', '98 LONE PINE WAY', '');
```

We will also be using the `INSERT INTO` statement to populate our project tables. The following are the `INSERT` statements for the State table. The State tables provides a database lookup for selection and validation in our Customer application that will be developed in Chapter 8, "Introducing Oracle Forms," and then modified to include a list of values in Chapter 12, "Developing Oracle Forms Applications."

```
INSERT INTO STATE VALUES ('AK','Alaska');
INSERT INTO STATE VALUES ('AL','Alabama');
INSERT INTO STATE VALUES ('AR','Arkansas');
INSERT INTO STATE VALUES ('AZ','Arizona');
INSERT INTO STATE VALUES ('CA','California');
INSERT INTO STATE VALUES ('CO','Colorado');
INSERT INTO STATE VALUES ('CT','Connecticut');
INSERT INTO STATE VALUES ('DC','Washington D.C.');
INSERT INTO STATE VALUES ('DE','Delaware');
INSERT INTO STATE VALUES ('FL','Florida');
INSERT INTO STATE VALUES ('GA','Georgia');
INSERT INTO STATE VALUES ('HI','Hawaii');
INSERT INTO STATE VALUES ('ID','Idaho');
INSERT INTO STATE VALUES ('IL','Illinois');
INSERT INTO STATE VALUES ('IN','Indiana');
INSERT INTO STATE VALUES ('IO','Iowa');
INSERT INTO STATE VALUES ('KA','Kansas');
INSERT INTO STATE VALUES ('KY','Kentucky');
INSERT INTO STATE VALUES ('LA','Louisiana');
INSERT INTO STATE VALUES ('MA','Massachusetts');
INSERT INTO STATE VALUES ('MD','Maryland');
INSERT INTO STATE VALUES ('ME','Maine');
```

```
INSERT INTO STATE VALUES ('MI','Michigan');
INSERT INTO STATE VALUES ('MN','Minnesota');
INSERT INTO STATE VALUES ('MO','Missouri');
INSERT INTO STATE VALUES ('MS','Mississippi');
INSERT INTO STATE VALUES ('MT','Montana');
INSERT INTO STATE VALUES ('NC','North Carolina');
INSERT INTO STATE VALUES ('ND','North Dakota');
INSERT INTO STATE VALUES ('NE','Nebraska');
INSERT INTO STATE VALUES ('NH','New Hampshire');
INSERT INTO STATE VALUES ('NJ','New Jersey');
INSERT INTO STATE VALUES ('NM','New Mexico');
INSERT INTO STATE VALUES ('NV','Nevada');
INSERT INTO STATE VALUES ('NY','New York');
INSERT INTO STATE VALUES ('OH','Ohio');
INSERT INTO STATE VALUES ('OK','Oklahoma');
INSERT INTO STATE VALUES ('OR','Oregon');
INSERT INTO STATE VALUES ('PA','Pennsylvania');
INSERT INTO STATE VALUES ('RI','Rhode Island');
INSERT INTO STATE VALUES ('SC','South Carolina');
INSERT INTO STATE VALUES ('SD','South Dakota');
INSERT INTO STATE VALUES ('TN','Tennessee');
INSERT INTO STATE VALUES ('TX','Texas');
INSERT INTO STATE VALUES ('UT','Utah');
INSERT INTO STATE VALUES ('VA','Virginia');
INSERT INTO STATE VALUES ('VT','Vermont');
INSERT INTO STATE VALUES ('WA','Washington');
INSERT INTO STATE VALUES ('WI','Wisconsin');
INSERT INTO STATE VALUES ('WV','West Virginia');
INSERT INTO STATE VALUES ('WY','Wyoming');
```

These are the `INSERT` statements for the Contact table. The sample data inserted here will be available through the Contact Management application that will be developed in Chapter 12.

```
INSERT INTO CONTACT VALUES
(7844, 104, '01-JAN-95', 'phone', 'Camping Gear', 'Ship', 'New York',
'555-1234', 'SCOTT', null, 'Y', 'I', 'M');
INSERT INTO CONTACT VALUES
(7788, 101, '02-JAN-95', 'phone', 'Fishing Gear', 'Wait', 'Washington',
'555-1234', 'SCOTT', null, 'Y', 'I', 'M');
INSERT INTO CONTACT VALUES
(7900, 106, '01-JAN-95', 'fax', 'Rowing Machine', 'Ship', 'Texas',
'555-3241', 'SCOTT', null, 'Y', 'I', 'H');
INSERT INTO CONTACT VALUES
(7902, 107, '02-JAN-95', 'phone', 'Cricket Ball', 'Order', 'Maryland',
'555-1212', 'SCOTT', null, 'Y', 'I', 'L');
INSERT INTO CONTACT VALUES
(7902, 107, '03-JAN-95', 'phone', '10 Speed Bike', Order', 'Maryland',
'555-1212', 'SCOTT', null, 'Y', 'I', 'H');
INSERT INTO CONTACT VALUES
(7788, 101, '06-JAN-95', 'phone', 'Tennis Gear', 'Send on Tuesday', 'Texas',
'555-1234', 'SCOTT', null, 'Y', 'I', 'H');
INSERT INTO CONTACT VALUES
(7788, 104, '10-JAN-95', 'fax', 'Car', 'Rental', 'Texas',
'555-1234', 'SCOTT', null, 'Y', 'I', 'M');
```

The data is inserted by executing the `INSERT` scripts using SQL*PLus, as shown in Figure 6.1.

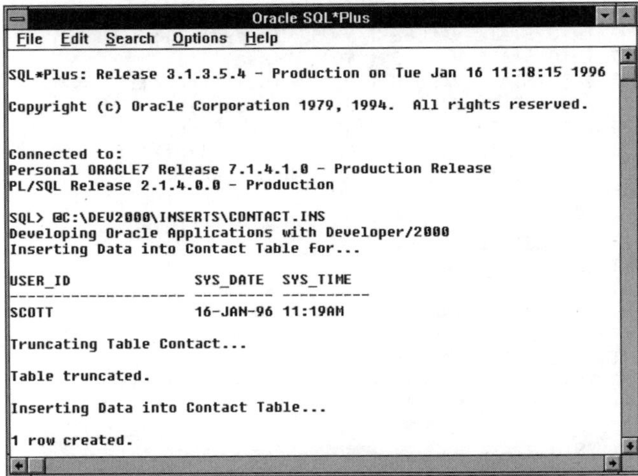
Oracle SQL*Plus
File Edit Search Options Help
SQL*Plus: Release 3.1.3.5.4 - Production on Tue Jan 16 11:18:15 1996
Copyright (c) Oracle Corporation 1979, 1994. All rights reserved.
Connected to:
Personal ORACLE7 Release 7.1.4.1.0 - Production Release
PL/SQL Release 2.1.4.0.0 - Production
SQL> @C:\DEV2000\INSERTS\CONTACT.INS
Developing Oracle Applications with Developer/2000
Inserting Data into Contact Table for...
USER_ID SYS_DATE SYS_TIME
SCOTT 16-JAN-96 11:19AM
Truncating Table Contact...
Table truncated.
Inserting Data into Contact Table...
1 row created.

FIGURE 6.1.
*SQL*Plus inserting data.*

This script is inserting the sample data into the Contact table. Notice that the table is truncated before the records are inserted. Truncating the table deletes any existing records from the table without having to drop the table.

UPDATE

To add data to an existing record, we use the `UPDATE` statement. Here we are populating the new column that was added to the Department and Employee tables for Increase_Pct. This is an example of the `UPDATE` statements that set the Increase_Pct to 100 for the Department and Employee tables.

```
UPDATE EMP
SET INCREASE_PCT = 100;

UPDATE DEPT
SET INCREASE_PCT = 100;
```

These `UPDATE` statements can be found in the \DEV2000\SQL\UPDATE.SQL file.

Populating Tables via SQL*Loader

Either the database administrator or you the developer (acting as an administrator) can use SQL*Loader to populate data into the Oracle tables. SQL*Loader is capable of loading a variety of file types. In the following examples, we are using a simple fixed-format ASCII file and a comma-delimited ASCII file.

Control Files

SQL*Loader uses a control file to determine the type and location of the data it will be loading. I have also provided examples of populating the State and Contact tables using SQL*Loader control files and ASCII data.

The State table control file looks like this:

```
LOAD DATA
INFILE "C:\DEV2000\DATA\STATE.DAT"
REPLACE
INTO TABLE STATE APPEND (
CODE                        POSITION(1:2) CHAR,
NAME                        POSITION(4:20) CHAR)
```

In Figure 6.2, the SQL*Loader dialog box is displayed, containing the username, password, database, control file, data file, and log file just prior to loading the data for the State table.

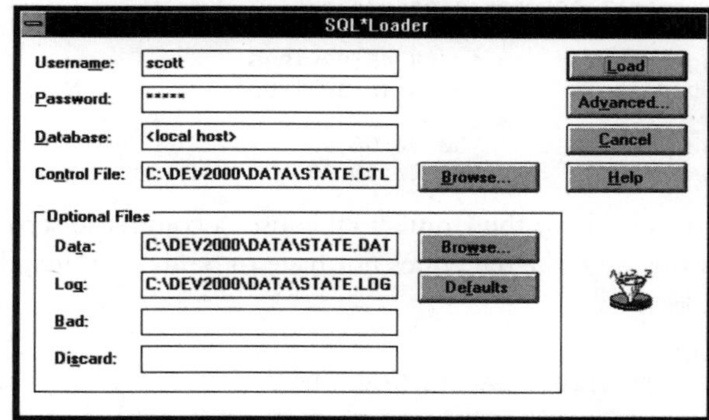

FIGURE 6.2.
*SQL*Loader identifying the data to load for the State table.*

During the load, a log file is created to record the results of the process. The log file for the State table from SQL*Loader is shown here:

```
SQL*Loader: Release 7.1.4.0.2 - Production on Tue Jan 16 08:46:28 1996
Copyright (c) Oracle Corporation 1979, 1994.  All rights reserved.

Control File:   C:\DEV2000\DATA\STATE.CTL
Data File:      C:\DEV2000\DATA\STATE.DAT
  Bad File:     C:\DEV2000\DATA\STATE.bad
  Discard File: C:\DEV2000\DATA\STATE.dsc
 (Allow all discards)

Number to load: ALL
Number to skip: 0
Errors allowed: 50
Bind array:     64 rows, maximum of 65024 bytes
Continuation:   none specified
Path used:      Conventional
```

```
Table STATE, loaded from every logical record.
Insert option in effect for this table: APPEND

   Column Name                  Position   Len  Term Encl Datatype
------------------------------ ---------- ----- ---- ---- ----------
CODE                                  1:2     2           CHARACTER
NAME                                 4:20    17           CHARACTER

Table STATE:
  51 Rows successfully loaded.
  0 Rows not loaded due to data errors.
  0 Rows not loaded because all WHEN clauses were failed.
  0 Rows not loaded because all fields were null.

Space allocated for bind array:                  1536 bytes(64 rows)
Space allocated for memory besides bind array:   41918 bytes

Total logical records skipped:          0
Total logical records read:            51
Total logical records rejected:         0
Total logical records discarded:        0

Run began on Tue Jan 16 08:46:28 1996
Run ended on Tue Jan 16 08:46:36 1996

Elapsed time was:     00:00:08.07
CPU time was:         00:00:00.00     (May not include ORACLE CPU time)
```

The control file for the Contact table uses a comma to separate the data values in the ASCII file. In this way, the data does not have to be fixed in length. The Contact table control file looks like this:

```
LOAD DATA
INFILE "C:\DEV2000\DATA\CONTACT.DAT"
REPLACE
INTO TABLE CONTACT APPEND
FIELDS TERMINATED BY ','
(EMPNO,
CUSTID,
CONTACT_DATE,
TYPE,
SUBJECT,
ACTION,
LOCATION,
PHONE,
RECD_BY,
MESSAGE,
SUCCESS,
DIRECTION,
PRIORITY)
```

Figure 6.3 shows the SQL*Loader Status dialog box, indicating that two records were loaded for the Contact table. You will also notice the SQL*Loader dialog box in the background.

FIGURE 6.3.
*The SQL*Loader Status dialog box indicating the number of records that were loaded for the Contact table.*

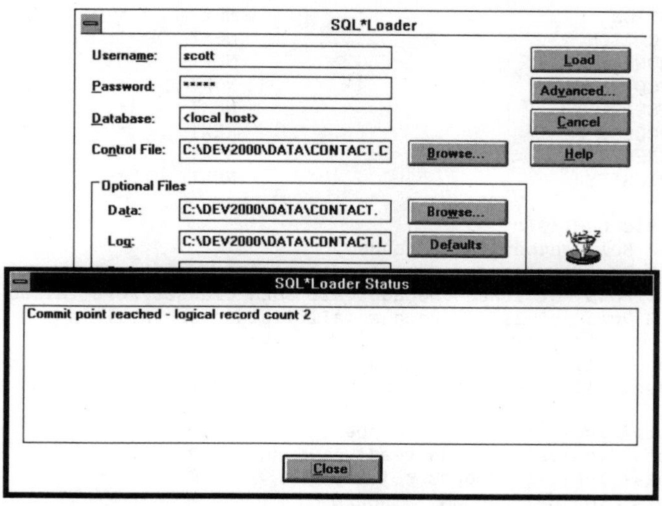

Again, during the load a log file is created to record the results of the process. The log file for the Contact table from SQL*Loader is shown here:

```
SQL*Loader: Release 7.1.4.0.2 - Production on Tue Jan 16 09:59:29 1996

Copyright (c) Oracle Corporation 1979, 1994.  All rights reserved.

Control File:   C:\DEV2000\DATA\CONTACT.CTL
Data File:      C:\DEV2000\DATA\CONTACT.DAT
  Bad File:     C:\DEV2000\DATA\CONTACT.bad
  Discard File: C:\DEV2000\DATA\CONTACT.dsc
 (Allow all discards)

Number to load: ALL
Number to skip: 0
Errors allowed: 50
Bind array:     64 rows, maximum of 65024 bytes
Continuation:   none specified
Path used:      Conventional

Table CONTACT, loaded from every logical record.
Insert option in effect for this table: APPEND

   Column Name                  Position   Len  Term Encl Datatype
------------------------------ ---------- ----- ---- ---- ---------
EMPNO                               FIRST     *   ,       CHARACTER
CUSTID                               NEXT     *   ,       CHARACTER
CONTACT_DATE                         NEXT     *   ,       CHARACTER
TYPE                                 NEXT     *   ,       CHARACTER
SUBJECT                              NEXT     *   ,       CHARACTER
```

```
ACTION                                NEXT     *    ,      CHARACTER
LOCATION                              NEXT     *    ,      CHARACTER
PHONE                                 NEXT     *    ,      CHARACTER
RECD_BY                               NEXT     *    ,      CHARACTER
MESSAGE                               NEXT     *    ,      CHARACTER
SUCCESS                               NEXT     *    ,      CHARACTER
DIRECTION                             NEXT     *    ,      CHARACTER
PRIORITY                              NEXT     *    ,      CHARACTER

Table CONTACT:
  2 Rows successfully loaded.
  0 Rows not loaded due to data errors.
  0 Rows not loaded because all WHEN clauses were failed.
  0 Rows not loaded because all fields were null.

Space allocated for bind array:                  64220 bytes(19 rows)
Space allocated for memory besides bind array:   110164 bytes

Total logical records skipped:          0
Total logical records read:             2
Total logical records rejected:         0
Total logical records discarded:        0

Run began on Tue Jan 16 09:59:29 1996
Run ended on Tue Jan 16 09:59:36 1996

Elapsed time was:      00:00:06.92
CPU time was:          00:00:00.00     (May not include ORACLE CPU time)
```

Notice in this log file that the Position and Length are calculated, wherein the first log file they were specified.

Populating Tables via Oracle Forms

Of course, using Oracle Forms applications is another method of populating tables in the database. The applications developed during the exercises in this book can be used to maintain the State, Customer, and Contact tables, for example.

Maintain State Table

In Chapter 12, we will develop a variety of forms applications, including the one shown in Figure 6.4, to maintain the State table.

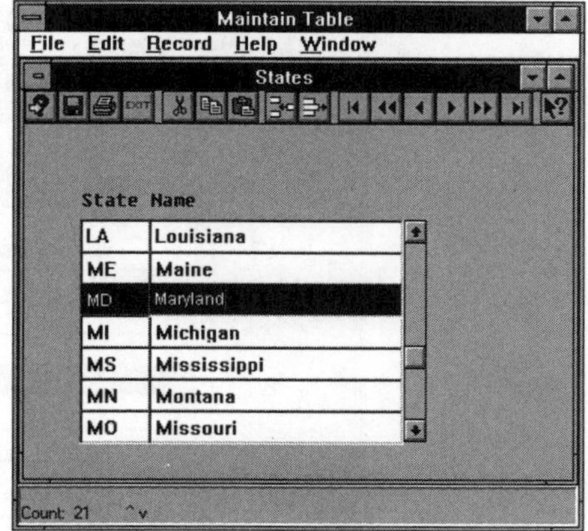

FIGURE 6.4.
The Maintain States forms application.

Customer

The Customer application that will be developed in Chapter 8 and then modified in Chapter 12 is shown in Figure 6.5. You may also notice the list of values button for the State column in this application.

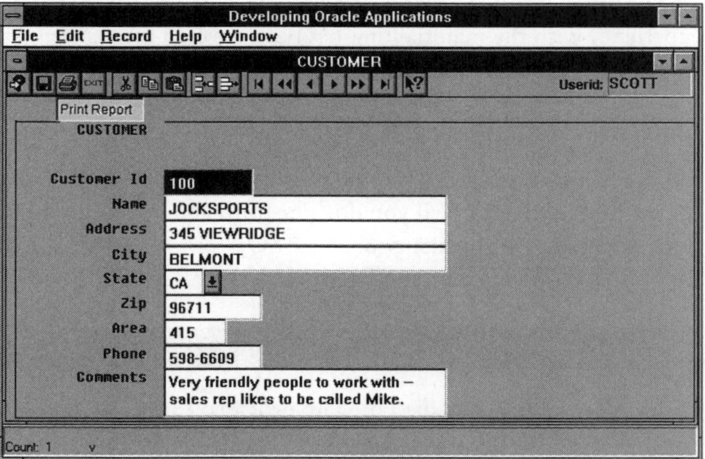

FIGURE 6.5.
The Customer forms application.

Contact Management

The Contact Management application that will be developed in Chapter 12 and enhanced throughout each of the subsequent chapters is illustrated in Figure 6.6. Notice also the references to the employee name and customer name in this application.

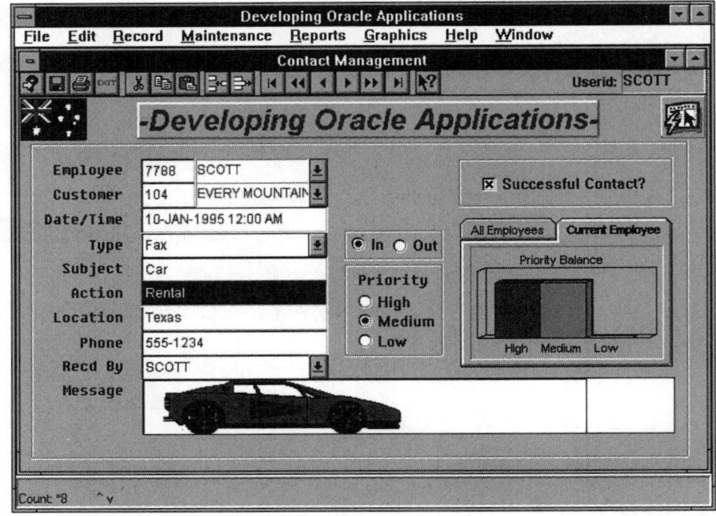

FIGURE 6.6.
The Contact Management application.

Exercise

The purpose of this exercise is populate the database for this project. It will give you hands-on experience with the material that has been covered in this chapter. You can create data for the Department, Employee, Customer, Contact, and State tables with the scripts provided with this book, using SQL*Plus. Choose the exercise that is appropriate for your current system configuration.

Do the first exercise if you do not already have the Oracle Demonstration Database installed, or do the second exercise if you do. The third and forth exercises are optional, and they can be done after either of the first two. These SQL scripts assume that there are users already defined for SCOTT/TIGER and SYSTEM/MANAGER.

NOTE

The control files and data files are provided for the SQL*Loader exercises; however, the data added during these exercises is not critical to the success of the remainder of this project. So if SQL*Loader is not available, you can safely skip the SQL*Loader exercises.

Populating the Oracle Demonstration and Project Databases

Follow these steps if you do not already have the Oracle Demonstration Database installed:

1. Start the Oracle7 database.
2. Launch SQL*Plus.
3. Connect to the Oracle database as SCOTT/TIGER.
4. Execute the create script by typing the following:
   `start C:\DEV2000\SQL\POPDEMO7.SQL`
5. Review the POPDEMO7.TXT file to make sure there were no errors encountered.
6. If you find any errors in the text file, review them with the DBA.

Populating the Project Database Only

Follow these steps if you already have the Oracle Demonstration Database installed:

1. Start the Oracle7 database.
2. Launch SQL*Plus.
3. Connect to the Oracle database as SCOTT/TIGER.
4. Execute the create script by typing the following:
   `start C:\DEV2000\SQL\POPCMIS.SQL`
5. Review the POPCMIS.TXT file to make sure there were no errors encountered.
6. If you find any errors in the text file, review them with the DBA.

Populating the State Table via SQL*Loader

Follow these steps if you want to populate the State table using SQL*Loader:

1. Launch SQL*Loader.
2. Enter the Username as SCOTT.
3. Enter the Password as TIGER.
4. Enter the Control File as \DEV2000\DATA\STATE.CTL.
5. Enter the Data File as \DEV2000\DATA\STATE.DAT.
6. Review the STATE.LOG file to make sure there were no errors encountered.
7. If you find any errors in the text file, review them with the DBA.

Populate the Contact Table via SQL*Loader

Follow these steps if you want to populate the Contact table using SQL*Loader:

1. Launch SQL*Loader.
2. Enter the Username as SCOTT.
3. Enter the Password as TIGER.
4. Enter the Control File as \DEV2000\DATA\CONTACT.CTL.
5. Enter the Data File as \DEV2000\DATA\CONTACT.DAT.
6. Review the CONTACT.LOG file to make sure there were no errors encountered.
7. If you find any errors in the text file, review them with the DBA.

Summary

This chapter provided you with a review of the various methods available to populate the database, including

- The `INSERT INTO` command
- The `UPDATE` command
- The `LOAD DATA` command
- Using Oracle Forms

Now that we have completed each of the database chapters, we will move on to the Oracle Developer/2000 tools. We will begin with an introduction to Oracle Developer/2000, and then review Oracle Forms, Oracle Reports, Oracle Graphics, and Oracle Procedure Builder separately.

III

Oracle Developer/2000

7

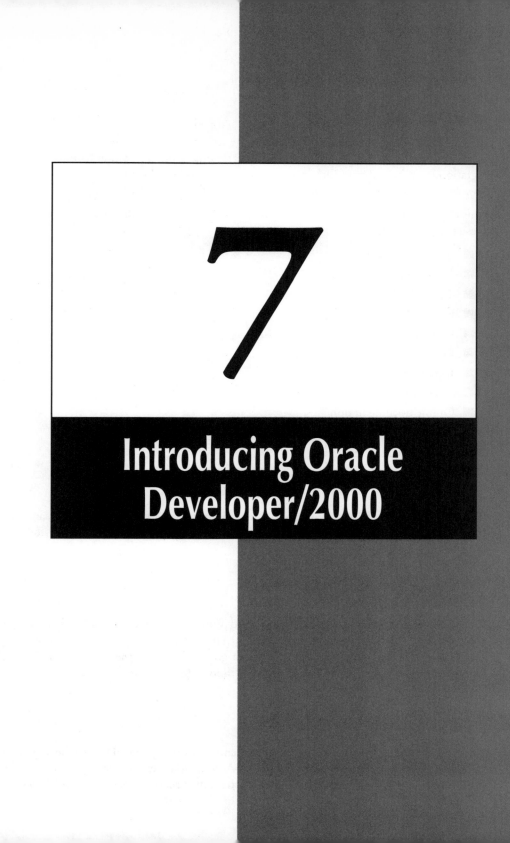

Introducing Oracle Developer/2000

Introduction

Oracle Developer/2000 represents the next generation of Oracle development tools, with improvements in the Designer interfaces, greater object orientation, enhanced product integration, and the ability of Oracle applications to act as OLE2 containers and servers. Oracle Developer/2000 is a complete, powerful, and open development environment.

This chapter will review many of the common features found in the Oracle Developer/2000 Designers, including:

- Windows interface
- Object Navigators
- Toolbars
- Properties
- Layout Editors
- PL/SQL editors
- Defaulting capabilities
- Interactive debuggers
- Online documentation
- Help
- Object-oriented features
- Product integration
- OLE2 support

The unique features of Oracle Forms 4.5, Oracle Reports 2.5, Oracle Graphics 2.5, and Oracle Procedure Builder 1.5 will be reviewed in their own respective chapters, which follow this chapter.

Windows Interface

Oracle Developer/2000 uses all of the standard Windows interface elements that you are already familiar with: resizable windows, pull-down menus, toolbars, point-and-click access, cut, copy, paste, dialog boxes, and so on. I will not go into detail on the basics of MS Windows here except to say that all of the standard Windows features are supported within Oracle Developer/2000.

Menus

There are a number of common menus and menu items that you will see whenever you open one of the Oracle Developer/2000 Designers. As you would expect, each product has a File, Edit, Window, and Help menu. In addition, each product also has a Navigator and Tools menu.

Additional menu items that are specific to the products will be covered in the following chapters. Menus will change dynamically as the context of the work you are doing changes. For example, the Navigator menu is replaced with View, Format, and Arrange as the Layout Editor becomes active. (Layout Editor menus will be reviewed in this chapter within the section on the Layout Editor.)

The following is a quick overview of the common menu items for the Oracle Developer/2000 Designers menus.

File

The File menu contains the usual New, Open, Close, Save, Save As, and Exit items. The function of each of the usual File menu items is self-explanatory, with the exception being that files can be opened from and saved to the file system or the database. The additional common File menu items found in Oracle Developer/2000 are as follows:

Menu Item	*Menu Description*
Revert	Undoes all of the changes made since the last save.
Compile	Compiles all of the code in the application.
Connect	Invokes the dialog box to connect to the database.
Disconnect	Disconnects from the database.

Edit

The Edit menu contains the standard items Undo, Cut, Copy, Paste, Clear, Duplicate, Search/Replace, Import, and Export. There are only a few additional Edit menu items that are product specific.

Tools

Each of the Tools menus contains Properties and Options items. In addition, all of the editors and all of the application-specific objects available for each product are found here.

Navigator

The Navigator menu provides support for manipulating the Object Navigator. The Object Navigator and the Navigator menu items are explained in detail following this overview of the menus.

Window

The Window menu contains all the standard Windows items and enables you to arrange the open windows or icons. The Windows menu also provides a numbered list of all the open windows in the application to simplify navigation from one open window to another.

Help

The Help menu provides access to the Microsoft Help facility implemented by Oracle Developer/2000. Help includes subject searching and hypertext links to related topics.

TIP

The use of the right mouse button for context-sensitive pop-up menus is supported throughout Oracle Developer/2000. Look for specific tips on pop-up menu usage in this and upcoming chapters.

Object Navigators

Oracle Developer/2000 includes many new improvements in the Designer interface. The most significant of which are the Object Navigators. The Object Navigators provide the developer with a hierarchical view of all of the objects in the application and in the database. The Object Navigators are implemented in a consistent manner in the Designers for Oracle Forms, Reports, Graphics, and Procedure Builder. (See Figure 7.1.)

FIGURE 7.1.
The Oracle Developer/2000 Object Navigators.

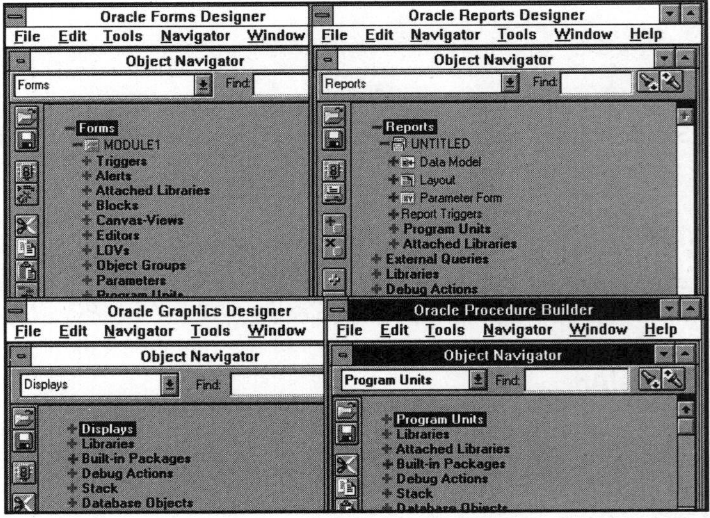

You will notice in Figure 7.1 that each Designer contains an Object Navigator window complete with an item identifier, a Find field, a toolbar, and a hierarchical view of each of their application's objects, as well as the database objects.

Once you have worked with the Navigators, you will immediately notice and appreciate the familiar outline style and an ease of use that closely resembles the functional capabilities of Windows File Manager. As in File Manager, each item is either a *node* or an *object*. A *node* is a heading identifying a group of *objects* of a specific type. Nodes and objects are presented in a hierarchical view with the ownership of the object and relative level in the hierarchy indicated by indentation.

Navigating the Hierarchy

Each node in the Object Navigator may be expanded or collapsed, and the nodes indicate whether or not they contain subordinate items with plus and minus symbols respectively. As can be seen in Figure 7.1, the form contains a module and the module contains triggers, alerts, and so on.

A single-click on the plus symbol expands the tree, revealing that object's hidden subordinate objects, while a single-click on the minus symbol collapses the tree, hiding that object's subordinate objects. A double-click will expand or collapse all subordinate objects. If the plus symbol is gray, it is an indication that subordinate items may be created but none currently exist. Double-click a gray plus symbol and an object of that type is automatically created. An object at the lowest level of the hierarchy is preceded by a bullet, indicating that no subordinate objects may be created belonging to this object.

TIP

The use of the arrow keys on the keyboard is also supported for navigating through the various levels of the hierarchy.

Iconic View of Objects

Within the Object Navigator, at the object level, icons are included to indicate that the object is of a particular type. For example, there are icons that indicate whether the object is a text item, a button, an image, a radio group, a checkbox, a chart, a trigger, a library, a window, a module, a table, a query, or one of many other object types. The example in Figure 7.2 shows a form with icons being displayed for triggers and the canvas-view.

Context-Sensitive Objects

In addition, the objects within the Object Navigator provide point-and-click navigation that is context-sensitive to the object type. For example, a single-click on an object sets the focus to that object and displays the Properties palette for that object, while a double-click on a trigger icon displays the PL/SQL Editor, a double-click on a canvas-view icon displays the Layout

Editor, and so on. The example in Figure 7.2 shows a form displaying the PL/SQL Editor that was invoked by double-clicking the trigger icon for the WHEN-NEW-FORMS-INSTANCE trigger.

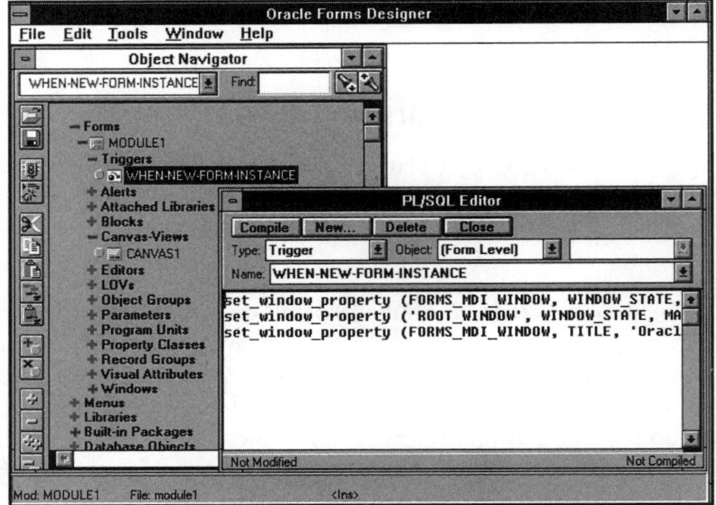

FIGURE 7.2.
The Oracle Forms 4.5 Object Navigator with Iconic Objects.

Synchronization

Another feature of the Object Navigator is the ability to synchronize with the Layout Editor. When synchronization is turned on, clicking an object in the Object Navigator selects that object in the Layout Editor. Likewise, the selection of an object in the Layout Editor also selects that object in the Object Navigator. Notice in Figure 7.3 that the PUSH_BUTTON1 item is selected in both the Object Navigator and the Layout Editor.

NOTE

Synchronization is selected by default.

TIP

You can turn off the synchronization between the Object Navigator and the Layout Editor from the Navigator menu.

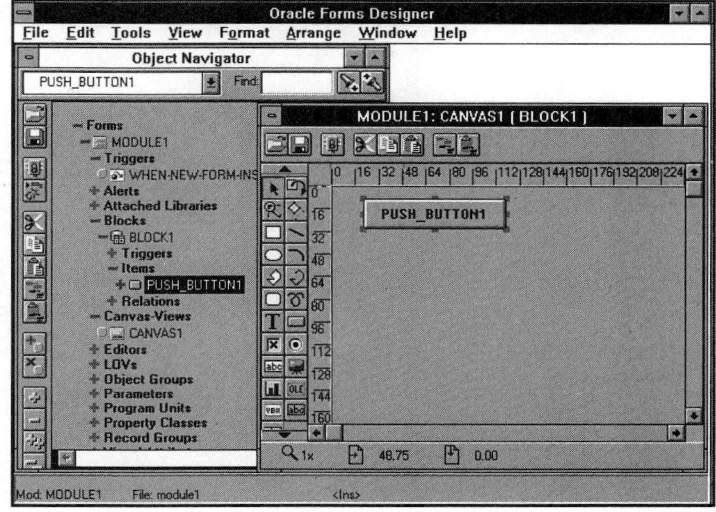

FIGURE 7.3.
The Oracle Forms 4.5 Object Navigator and the Layout Editor.

Point-and-Click, Drag-and-Drop

The features of the Object Navigator continue with the capability to select one or more objects in the hierarchy by shift-clicking for a range or control-clicking for multiple object selection, just as you would in any Windows application. In addition, drag-and-drop resequencing and reuse is supported, which makes moving or copying code and objects almost effortless. An extremely powerful feature of the Object Navigators is the ability to move procedures to and from the Oracle7 database and the application simply by dragging and dropping.

Searching the Hierarchy

Located at the top of the Object Navigator is a drop-down list to indicate the selected object and a Find field for searching forward or backward for a given character string. In Figure 7.4, the PUSH_BUTTON1 item is located by entering only a portion of the name in the Find field. Searching can be directed by entering a name or a portion of a name and clicking the Up or Down Search buttons located to the right of the Find field.

NOTE

Searching automatically begins as you enter characters in the Find field.

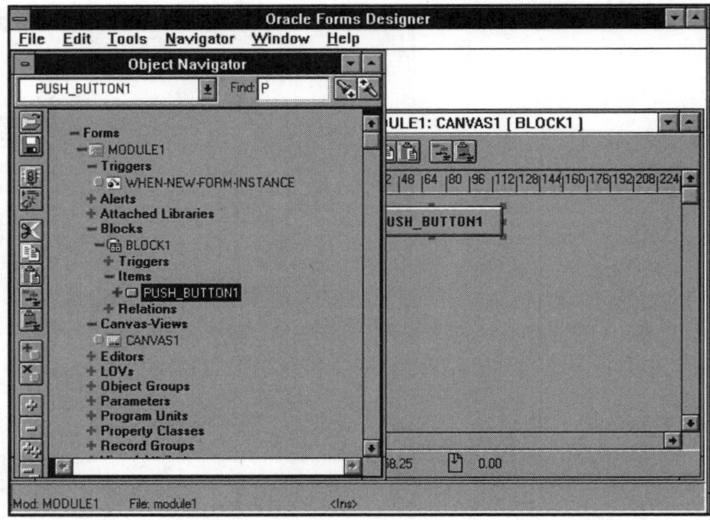

FIGURE 7.4.
Searching the hierarchy.

Multiple Object Navigators

The Object Navigator can be split either vertically or horizontally but not both vertically and horizontally at the same time. Once the Object Navigator is split, it may be split again. Each time the navigator is split, it reveals another navigator. (See Figure 7.5.) Each navigator can then be manipulated independently by using the scroll bars.

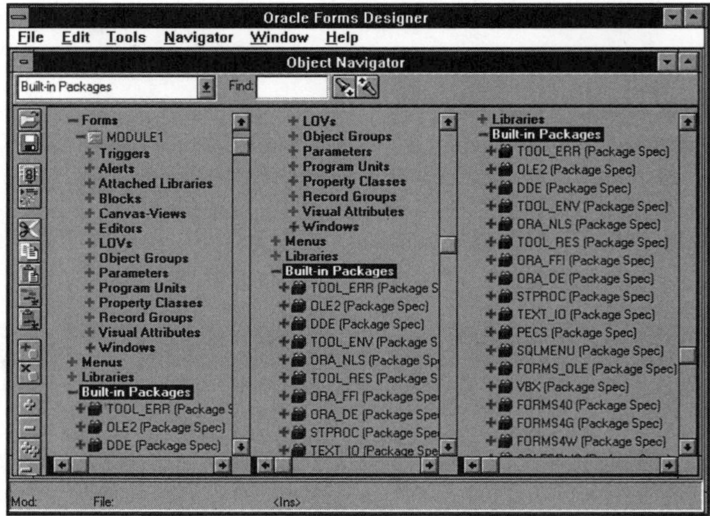

FIGURE 7.5.
Multiple Object Navigators.

Navigate Menu

Lastly, the Object Navigator is also supported from the menu. The common Navigator menu items are as follows:

Menu Item	*Menu Description*
Create	Creates an object of the type selected.
Delete	Deletes the object selected.
Expand	Expands the current branch one level.
Collapse	Collapses the current branch one level.
Expand All	Expands all branches under the current node.
Collapse All	Collapses all branches above the current node.
Mark	Marks an object to return to.
Goto Mark	Returns to the previously marked object.

As you can see, the Navigators are much more powerful than a simple outliner for your objects. They are a welcome improvement in productivity for all Oracle applications developers.

Toolbars

There is an iconic toolbar on the left side of the Object Navigator in each of the Oracle Developer/2000 Designers, which provides point-and-click access to many commonly performed operations. Figure 7.6 shows each of the Object Navigator toolbars.

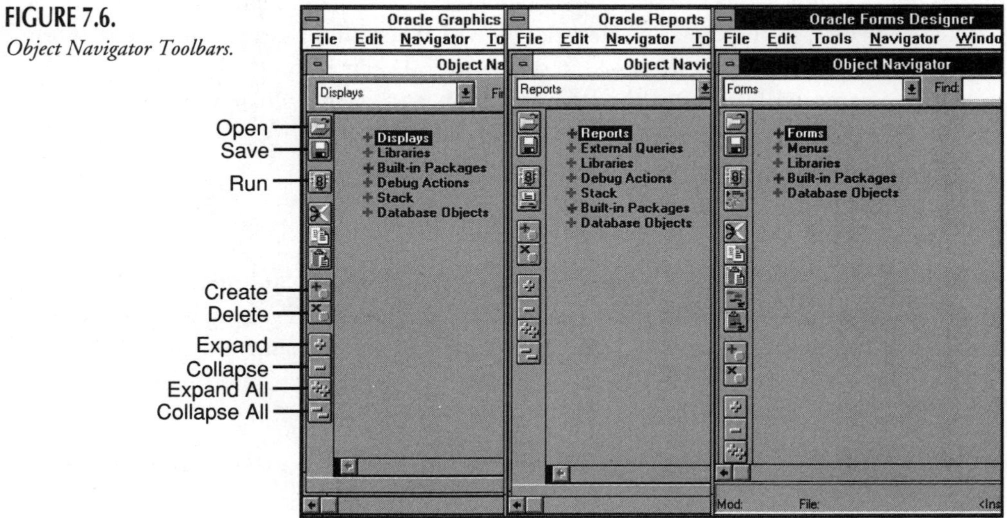

FIGURE 7.6.
Object Navigator Toolbars.

The following are the common items on the toolbars:

Button	*Description*
Open	Invokes the Open dialog box.
Save	Invokes the Save dialog box.
Run	Runs the current application.
Create	Creates an object of the type selected.
Delete	Deletes the object selected.
Expand	Expands the current branch one level.
Collapse	Collapses the current branch one level.
Expand All	Expands all branches under the current node.
Collapse All	Collapses all branches above the current node.

NOTE

Bubble Help is provided for all of the iconic buttons for each of the toolbars within Oracle Developer/2000.

As you can see in Figure 7.6, the toolbars are not identical, but they do share many common functions and they do present themselves in a consistent manner from within their respective Designers.

Oracle Forms, Reports, and Graphics also have toolbars to support their Layout Editors. The objects and activities associated with laying out a form, report, or graph differ to a significant degree. Therefore, the unique characteristics of the Layout Editor toolbars for Oracle Forms, Reports, and Graphics will be reviewed in the respective chapters for those applications. A review of the common features of the Layout Editors and their toolbars will follow the next section.

Properties

Each Oracle Developer/2000 Designer provides a way to review and modify the properties of any object within the application. The standard method for revealing the Properties for the currently selected object is to select the Properties menu item from the Tools menu.

In addition to navigating from the menus, you can find the properties for objects if you double-click each object's icon from within the Object Navigator.

TIP

You can change the name of any object by editing from within the Object Navigator. First select the name by clicking on it in the Object Navigator. Then go into edit mode by clicking again.

Now you can position your cursor with the arrow keys or with a single click. You can select the entire text by double-clicking. Once the cursor is positioned or the text you want to modify is highlighted, make the change.

The properties are displayed in forms with a Properties window. (See Figure 7.7.)

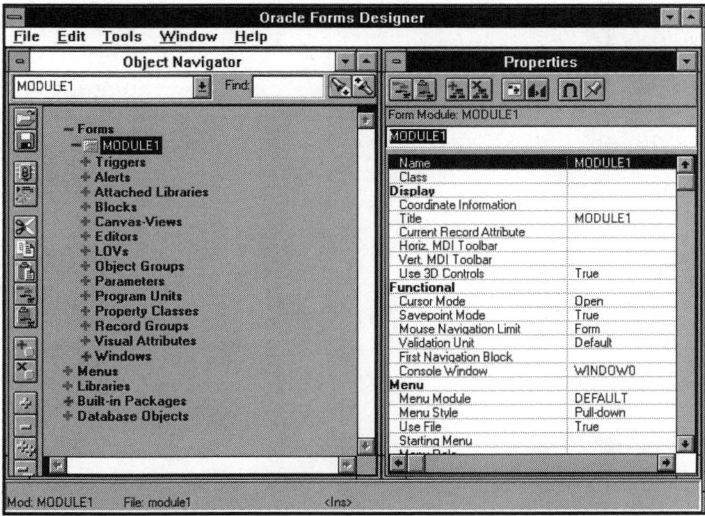

FIGURE 7.7.
Oracle Forms 4.5 Properties window.

Reports and graphics use property sheets, as shown in figures 7.8 and 7.9. In either case, the concept is the same. The obvious difference is in forms, where the Properties window can remain in view while you are working on the application. Chapter 8, "Introducing Oracle Forms," includes more information about the Forms Properties window.

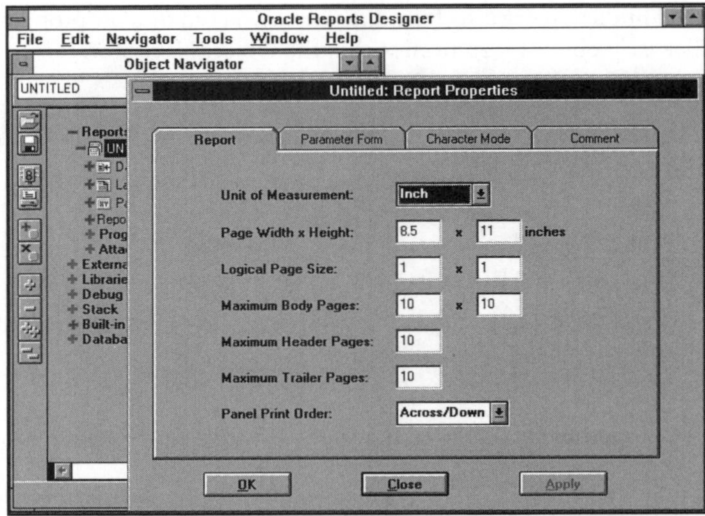

FIGURE 7.8.
Oracle Reports 2.5 Property Sheet.

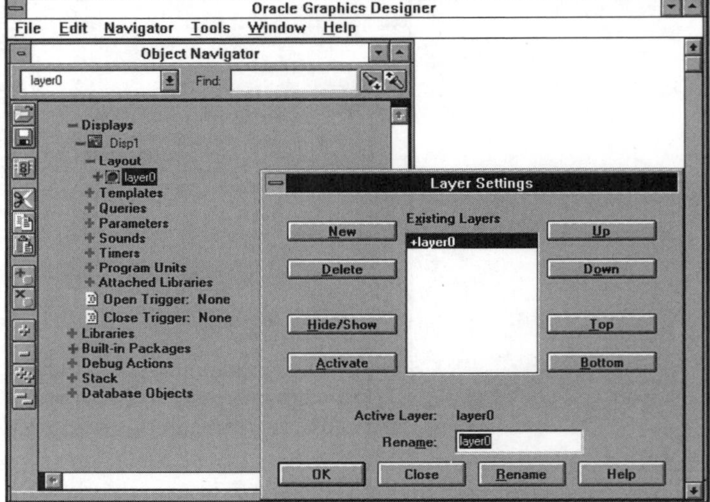

FIGURE 7.9.
Oracle Graphics 2.5 Property Sheet.

Layout Editors

Oracle Forms, Oracle Reports, and Oracle Graphics all use graphical Layout Editors. Layout Editors are used to design the application. From within the Layout Editor you can review and modify the appearance as well as the content of your application. While working in the Layout Editors, you will be able to create new objects, change the properties of any object or group of objects, and even delete objects individually or in groups. Details on working with each Layout Editor will be covered in the following chapters on Forms, Reports, and Graphics.

Each Layout Editor shares some common features with the others. These common features will be reviewed next. An example of the Oracle Graphics Layout Editor is shown in Figure 7.10.

FIGURE 7.10.
Oracle Graphics Layout Editor.

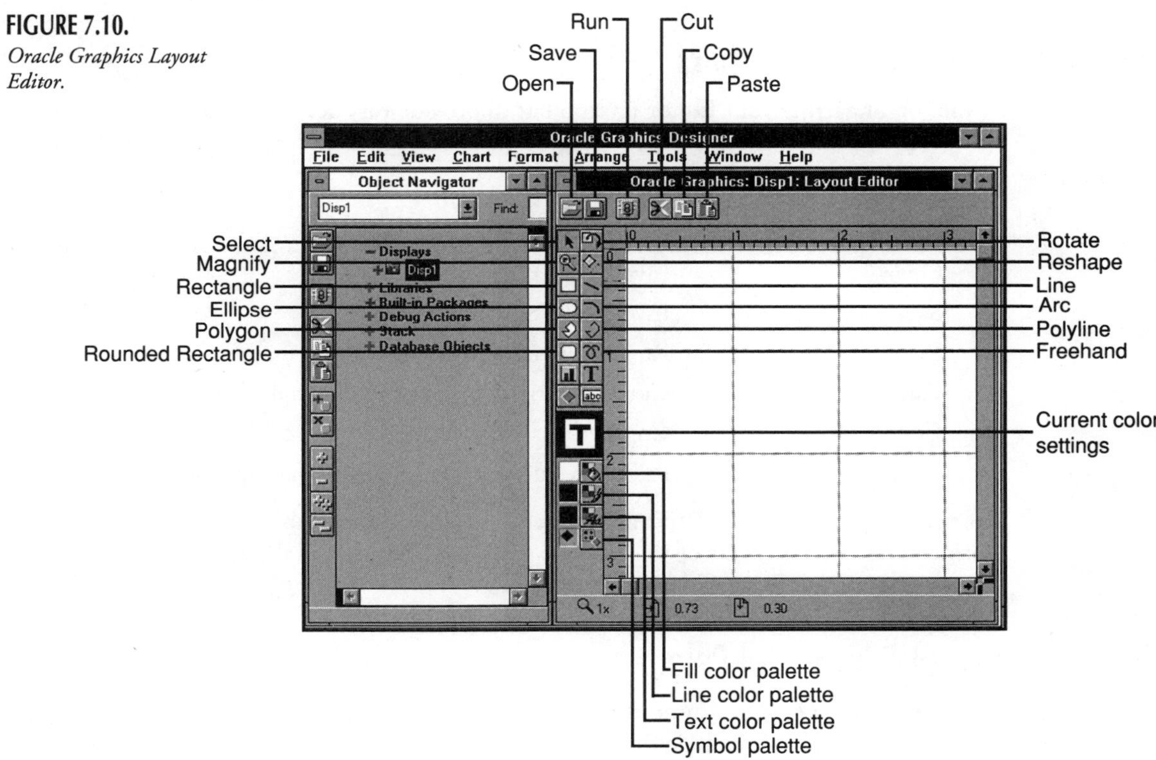

Notice the Layout Editor to the right of the Object Navigator. The Layout Editor can be invoked by double-clicking the Display icon in the Object Navigator from within Oracle Graphics. To invoke the Layout Editor in Oracle Forms, you would double-click the Canvas-View icon, while in Oracle Reports you would double-click the Layout icon.

TIP

Oracle Forms and Oracle Reports also provide access to the Layout Editor from the Tools menu.

TIP

You can also choose the Layout Editor from the pop-up menu from within the Object Navigator in Oracle Forms and Oracle Reports. In Oracle Reports, Layout must first be selected.

Layout Editor Toolbars

At the top of each Layout Editor is a toolbar to provide easy access to frequently performed operations. The toolbar can be seen in Figure 7.10. The common features of the toolbar are as follows:

Button	*Description*
Open	Invokes the Open dialog box.
Save	Invokes the Save dialog box.
Run	Runs the current application.
Cut	Cuts the current contents to the clipboard.
Copy	Copies the current contents to the clipboard.
Paste	Pastes the current contents from the clipboard.

The toolbars in Forms and Reports include some additional capabilities that are application specific. The unique details of the toolbars for Oracle Forms and Oracle Reports will be reviewed in those applications' respective chapters.

Layout Editor Tool Palettes

To the left of each Layout Editor is a Tool palette. The Tool palette can also be seen in Figure 7.10. The Tool palettes include the following four types of tools:

Layout tools

Boilerplate drawing tools

Item drawing tools

File/line color palettes

Each of the Layout Editor Tool palettes includes these layout tools:

Button	*Description*
Select	Provides point-and-click selection of objects.
Rotate	Turns graphics or boilerplate text objects.

Magnify	Magnifies the view in the Layout Editor.
Reshape	Changes the shape of an object.

Each of the Tool palettes also includes these boilerplate drawing tools:

Rectangle
Line
Ellipse
Arc
Polygon
Polyline
Rounded Rectangle
Freehand

The boilerplate drawing tools are used to draw boilerplate objects. Boilerplate means that the objects are not connected to any data. These tools are similar in function to the drawing tools in Paintbrush and are used to enhance the visual presentation of the application.

The item-drawing tools are different for each product and only include Text as a common tool. However, each product's item-drawing tools do support the creation of items for the application being developed. All of the item-drawing tools will be covered for each product in the subsequent chapters.

Lastly, each Tool palette includes File/Line Color palettes. These palettes are used for setting the color of any object within any product. The Current Color setting is shown with a large T followed by the:

Fill Color palette
Line Color palette
Text Color palette

When any of the Color palette buttons are selected, a Color palette appears, allowing the selection of the designated color. The Fill Color is the background color of the object. The Line Color is the color of the surrounding edge, and the Text Color is the color of the font for text fields.

NOTE

Oracle Graphics also includes a Symbol palette within the File/Line Color palette. Detailed discussion of this tool can be found in Chapter 11, "Introducing Oracle Procedure Builder."

Layout Editor Rulers and Gridlines

Each Layout Editor contains controls for rulers and gridlines to aid in the positioning of objects and to help organize the layout during the design of the application. The rulers and gridlines can be seen beneath the toolbar and to the right of the Tool palette. (See Figure 7.10, shown previously.) Rulers and gridlines can be adjusted using the Ruler Setting dialog box. (See Figure 7.11.)

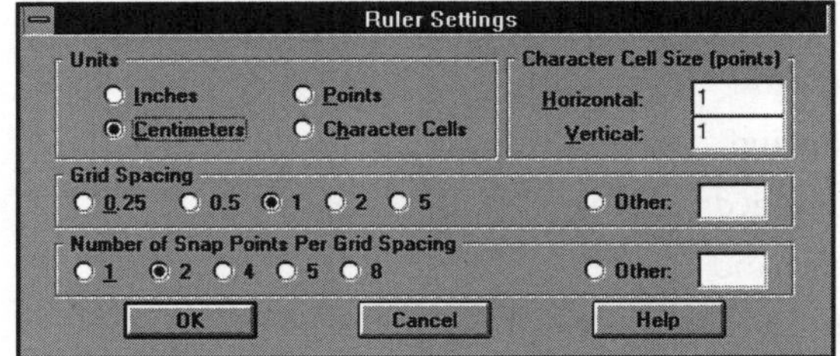

FIGURE 7.11.
The Ruler Settings dialog box.

The Ruler Settings dialog box is invoked by selecting Ruler from the View menu. Ruler is found in the View menu under Settings in Oracle Forms and under View Options in Oracle Reports and Oracle Graphics. A very useful feature is the ability to snap objects into place according to the grid. Snapping to a grid automatically places objects in line with the grid spacing. Grid Snap can be set turned on or off from the View menu.

Layout Settings

The Layout size can be customized using the Layout Settings dialog box as shown in Figure 7.12. The Layout Settings dialog box is invoked by selecting Layout from the View menu. Layout is found in the View menu under Settings in Oracle Forms and under View Options in Oracle Reports and Oracle Graphics.

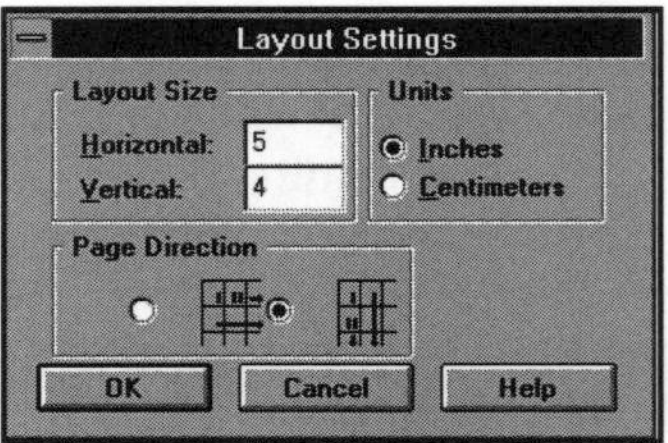

FIGURE 7.12.
The Layout Settings dialog box.

Layout Editor Status Line

The Status Line in the Layout Editor shows the current level of magnification as well as the X and Y coordinates of the current cursor location. The magnification can be increased by selecting the Magnification icon on the Tool palette and clicking the Layout Editor. To reduce the magnification, select the Magnification icon on the Tool palette and hold the shift key while clicking the Layout Editor.

Layout Editor Menus

When the Layout Editor window is active, the Navigator menu item is replaced with View, Format, and Arrange. The View menu contains the following menu items:

Menu Item	*Menu Description*
Zoom In	Increases magnification in Layout Editor.
Zoom Out	Reduces magnification in Layout Editors.
Normal Size	Sets magnification to 1.
Fit to Window	Scales to fit everything in the Layout Editor.
Rulers	Shows or hides the ruler.
Ruler Guides	Shows or hides the ruler guides.
Grid	Shows or hides the grid.
Grid Snap	Turns the Grid Snap on and off.
Page Breaks	Turns the Page Breaks on and off.
Tool Palette	Shows or hides the Tool palette.
Status	Shows or hides the status line.
Settings/View Options	Changes Ruler and/or Layout settings.

The Format menu contains the following menu items:

Menu Item	*Menu Description*
Font	Sets the font for a text item.
Spacing	Sets spacing to single, 1 1/2, double, or custom.
Alignment	Sets justification of text to left, center, or right.
Line	Sets line thickness from 0 to 16 points or custom.
Bevel	Sets bevel to none, inset, outset, raised, or lowered.
Dash	Sets different dash-line styles.
Arrow	Sets arrow location and/or direction on a line.
Drawing Options	General, Arc, Text, Rounded Rectangle, or Image.
Color Palette	Invokes the Color palette.

Many of the Format menu items can be set directly from the menu. However, selecting Font from the Format menu invokes the Font dialog box. (See Figure 7.13.)

FIGURE 7.13.
The Font dialog box.

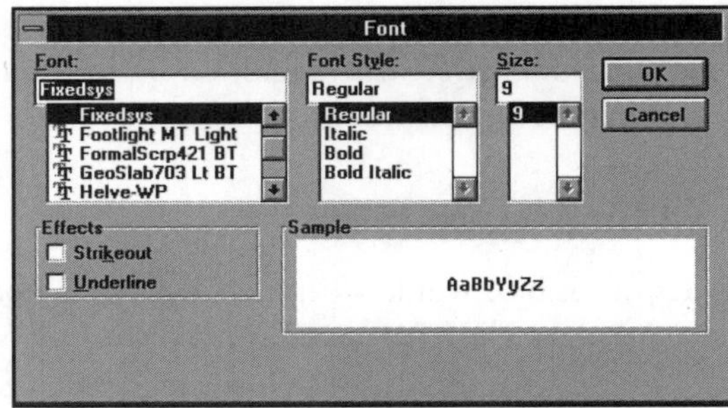

Selecting Drawing Options reveals a submenu with General, Arc, Text, Rounded Rectangle, and Image menu items. Each menu item invokes a separate dialog box to set the drawing options.

The Arrange menu includes the following choices:

Menu Item	*Menu Description*
Bring to Front	Places object on the top layer of layout.
Send to Back	Places object on the bottom layer of layout.
Move Forward	Moves object up one level.
Move Backward	Moves object back one level.
Align Objects	Invokes the Align Objects dialog box.
Repeat Alignment	Applies alignment as previously set.
Size Objects	Invokes the Size Objects dialog box.
Repeat Sizing	Applies sizing as previously set.
Group	Creates a group of all selected objects.
Ungroup	Removes the selected objects from the group.
Group Operations	Select Parent, Select Children, Add to Group, or Remove from Group.

TIP

Oracle Developer/2000 often provides hot-keys to perform frequently used functions. The hot-key appears to the right of the menu items. A handy hot-key on the Arrange menu is Ctrl+L for repeating alignment.

Working with Objects in the Layout Editor

You will work with objects in the Layout Editor and perform a variety of functions. Next we will review creating objects, changing the size of objects, aligning objects, and positioning objects in the Layout Editor.

Creating Objects in the Layout Editor

Objects can be created in the Layout Editor by selecting the object from the Tool palette and placing it in the layout. You can select any of the objects for any of the applications by clicking on the button of the object type that you want from the Tool palette. Once the Tool has been selected, place the object in the layout by pointing, clicking, holding, and dragging to define the area for the object.

Objects can also be created from the Object Navigator as described earlier or by copying and pasting a similar object. Objects can also be created automatically by the Designer when one of the default options is chosen. Defaulting layouts will be discussed in an upcoming section.

Selecting Objects in the Layout Editor

Objects can be selected if they are visible in the Layout Editor by pointing and clicking on them. Objects can also be selected via the Object Navigator.

As discussed in the section on synchronization in the Object Navigator and shown previously in Figure 7.3, the selection of an object in the Layout Editor will also select that object in the Object Navigator.

Multiple objects can be selected in the Layout Editor by clicking the first object and then clicking the remaining items while holding down the shift key. Another method of selecting is to select a group of objects by clicking outside of the objects and dragging a band around the objects you want to select.

CAUTION

When you are selecting a group of objects, all of the objects to be selected must be completely enclosed by the band or they will not be selected.

Sizing Objects in the Layout Editor

To change the size of an existing object in the Layout Editor, do as follows:

1. Select the object.
2. Grab the edge or the corner of the object by pointing, clicking, and holding.

3. Stretch the object to size.
4. Release the mouse button to accept the new size.

Objects can also be sized in the Layout Editor relative to each other. Follow these steps:

1. Select the objects to be sized.
2. Select Arrange from the menu, then Size Objects.

The Size Objects dialog box is shown in Figure 7.14.

FIGURE 7.14.
The Size Objects dialog box.

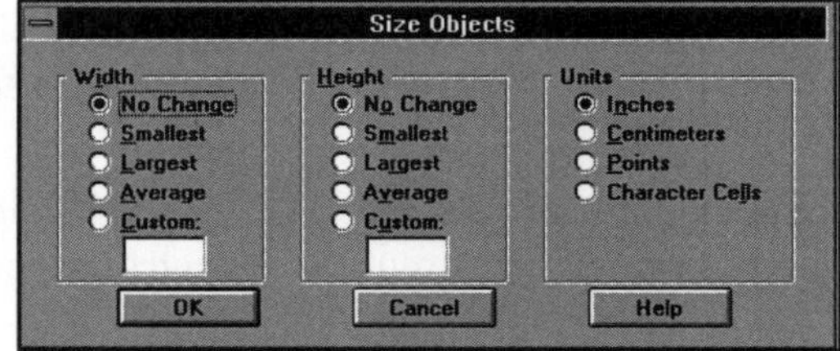

From the Size Objects dialog box, select one of the following for Width and Height:

- No Change
- Smallest
- Largest
- Average
- Custom

NOTE

If Custom is selected from the Size Object dialog box, a numeric value must also be entered.

Then, from the Size Objects dialog box, select one of the following for Units:

- Inches
- Centimeters
- Points
- Character Cells

Finally, to confirm Sizing, click OK.

Aligning Objects in the Layout Editor

Objects can be aligned in the Layout Editor relative to each other or to the grid. To align objects, do as follows:

1. Select the objects to be aligned.
2. Select Arrange from the menu, then Align Objects.

The Alignment Settings dialog box is shown in Figure 7.15.

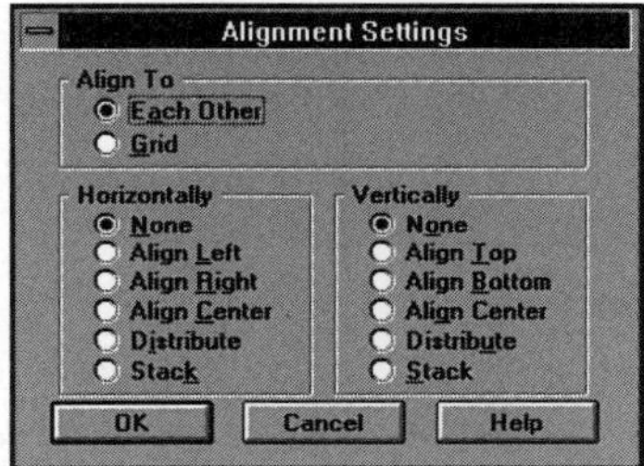

FIGURE 7.15.
The Alignment Settings dialog box.

From the Align Objects dialog box, select one of the following for Align To:

- Each Other
- Grid

Then select one of the following from Horizontally:

- None
- Align Left
- Align Right
- Align Center
- Distribute
- Stack

Then, select one of the following from Vertically:

- None
- Align Top
- Align Bottom
- Align Center
- Distribute
- Stack

Finally, click OK to confirm Alignment.

Positioning Objects in the Layout Editor

Objects can be positioned in the Layout Editor independently or relative to each other. Any object or group of objects can be moved by dragging and dropping or by using the arrow keys. Several objects can be grouped together by selecting them and then selecting Group from the Arrange menu.

Boilerplate items may overlap with other objects. To manage this issue, you can determine which ones are in front of and which ones are behind the others. Select the item and then the Arrange menu item. Objects can be moved forward or backward by selecting Move Forward or Move Backward. Selected items can also be moved directly to the front or to the rear by choosing Bring To Front or Send To Back from the Arrange menu.

PL/SQL Editors

The Oracle Developer/2000 products incorporate the use of PL/SQL Editors. Each of the code segments within an application can be incrementally compiled using the PL/SQL Editor. By using incremental compilation, the current code can immediately be checked for syntax errors. Another advantage of incremental compilation is that the entire application does not need to be recompiled at the end of the development process. The PL/SQL Editors can be invoked using any of the following methods:

- Select PL/SQL Editor from the Tools menu.
- Double-click a PL/SQL object icon in the Object Navigator.
- Right-click in the Object Navigator.
- Right-click a selected object in Layout Editor.

In Figure 7.16, a double-click on the icon of the WHEN-NEW-FORM-INSTANCE trigger launched the PL/SQL Editor.

The PL/SQL Editor contains the following commands on the button bar at the top of the window:

Compile	Compiles the current PL/SQL code.
New	Creates a new PL/SQL object.
Delete	Deletes the current PL/SQL object.
Close	Closes the PL/SQL window.

The current context is displayed in the Type, Object, and Name drop-down lists. The current context is always maintained, meaning that the object selected in the Object Navigator is presented in the PL/SQL Editor.

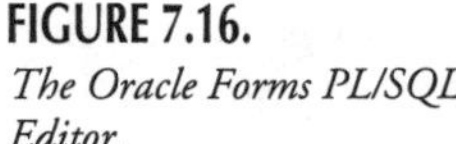

FIGURE 7.16.
The Oracle Forms PL/SQL Editor.

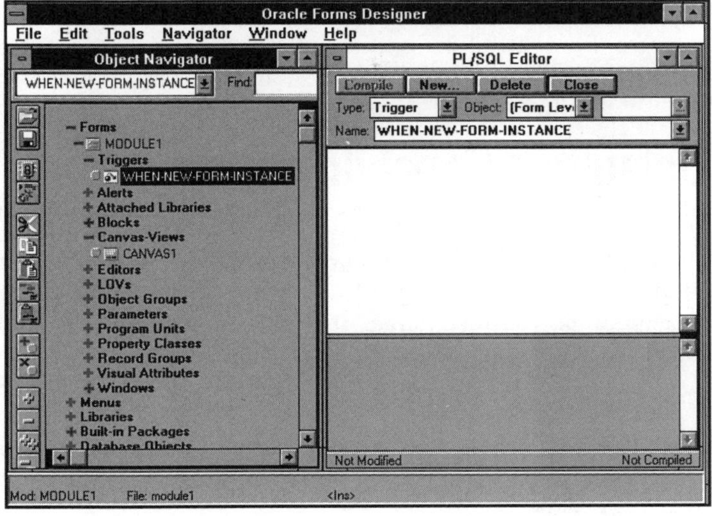

The Type is displayed in the editor window with a drop-down list. The Type can be either Trigger or Program Unit. Program Units are used for Procedures, Functions, Package Specifications, and Package Bodies.

The Object is displayed in the editor window with two drop-down lists. The Object lists show the level in the application that the PL/SQL code is associated with. In the example in Figure 7.16, the WHEN-NEW-FORM-INSTANCE trigger is a form-level trigger. When the context of the object is not at the item level, the Object list to the right is not active. If the context is at the item level, the right drop-down list will contain the item names.

The Name is the last drop-down list in the PL/SQL Editor window, seen just before the Source Code pane.

TIP

The drop-down lists in the PL/SQL Editors show the current context but also allow for navigation to other PL/SQL code by selecting other items from the lists.

The Source Code pane is the large blank space in the PL/SQL Editor, as shown in Figure 7.16. Once the PL/SQL Editor window is open and you have the appropriate context for your source code, you can insert your PL/SQL code into the Source Code pane.

The Message pane is located beneath the Source Code pane in the PL/SQL Editor window and shows compilation errors. If an error occurs during a compilation, simply click on the error message and the PL/SQL Editor will jump via hypertext to the offending line in the source code.

The status bar is located on the bottom of the PL/SQL Editor window and shows information on status. Examples of status messages include information about whether a change has been made to the source code and the success or failure of a compile.

Defaulting Capabilities

Oracle Forms, Reports, and Graphics all have the ability to create applications by default. This capability enables you as a developer to get a quick start on your application. The default application is automatically created simply by selecting a few options about the default style of the application you are creating. Oracle Developer/2000 will do much of the initial work for you. The default applications will work with no additional intervention. The application can then be extended in appearance and function by adding and modifying objects.

Interactive Debuggers

Oracle Forms, Oracle Reports, and Oracle Graphics all allow you to run your applications in Debug mode. Each of the tools leverages the capabilities of Oracle Procedure Builders PL/SQL Interpreter to provide debugging support. Oracle Procedure Builder and the PL/SQL Interpreter will be reviewed in Chapter 11.

To set the Debug mode in Oracle Forms and Oracle Reports, select Tools from the menu, then the Options menu item. The Options dialog box appears. From the Options dialog box, select the tab control for Runtime Options. The check box for Debug mode can be set here to on or off.

NOTE

Oracle Graphics automatically runs in Debug mode from the Designer.

When the application is run, a Debugger window appears. The Debugger window from Oracle Forms has a menu, a toolbar, a source pane, an Object Navigator, and a PL/SQL interpreter. (See Figure 7.17.)

From the Debugger window you can do the following:

- Set break points that will enable you to stop at specific locations within your application
- Create debug triggers that will execute PL/SQL at a given break point
- Use the Object Navigator to locate and select any PL/SQL object to set breaks on

- Edit source code using the Program Unit Editor
- Issue commands from the PL/SQL Interpreter command line

Once you have set break points within the application, you can close the Debugger window. Your application will now run until it encounters a break point. Once a break point is encountered, the Debugger window appears again. (See Figure 7.18.)

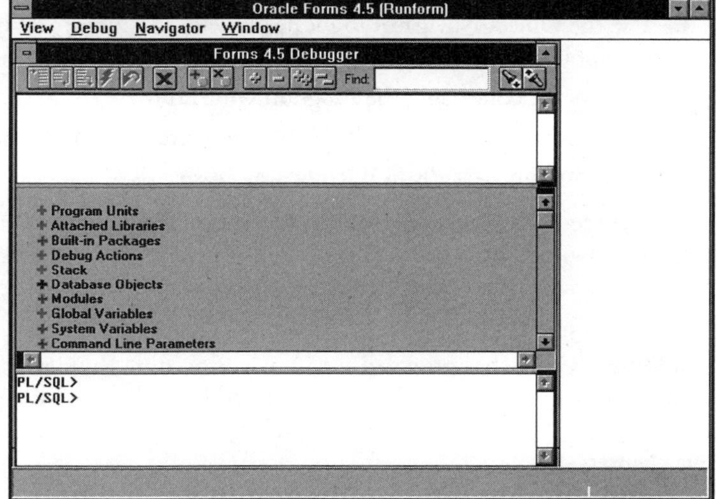

FIGURE 7.17.
The Oracle Forms 4.5 Debugger.

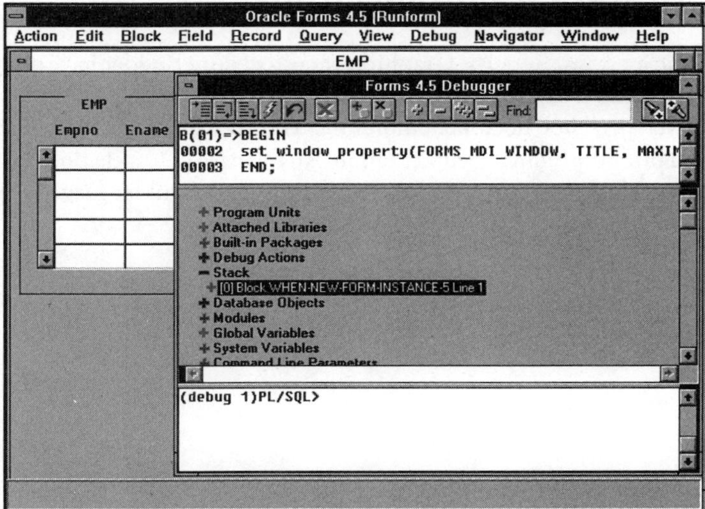

FIGURE 7.18.
The Oracle Forms 4.5 Debugger at a break point.

This time, the available features are somewhat different. The Debugger window will now enable you to do the following:

- Set additional break points
- Remove existing break points
- Create additional debug triggers
- Remove existing debug triggers
- Use the Object Navigator to locate, review, and modify all types of variables within the application
- Edit source code using the Program Unit Editor
- Issue commands from the PL/SQL Interpreter command line
- Step through your PL/SQL code

The source-level debugging capabilities of Oracle Developer/2000 are extremely powerful. The integration with Oracle Procedure Builder provides for a consistent interface and consistent functionality. The use of the Object Navigator within the Debugger further simplifies the locating, setting, and modifying of debugging objects.

In addition, Oracle has provided the Oracle Procedure Builder DEBUG package that can be used from within the PL/SQL Interpreter and by PL/SQL code unit. Using the debuggers in Oracle Forms, Oracle Reports, and Oracle Graphics will be covered in detail in their respective chapters.

Online Documentation

Oracle Forms, Reports, Graphics, and Procedure Builder have online documentation supplied with them. During the installation process, Oracle Book Runtime and each manual in the Oracle Developer/2000 documentation set can be loaded. Oracle Book Runtime is used to view, search, and print the online documentation. An example of Oracle Book is shown in Figure 7.19, which shows the first chapter of the Oracle Procedure Builder Developer's Guide.

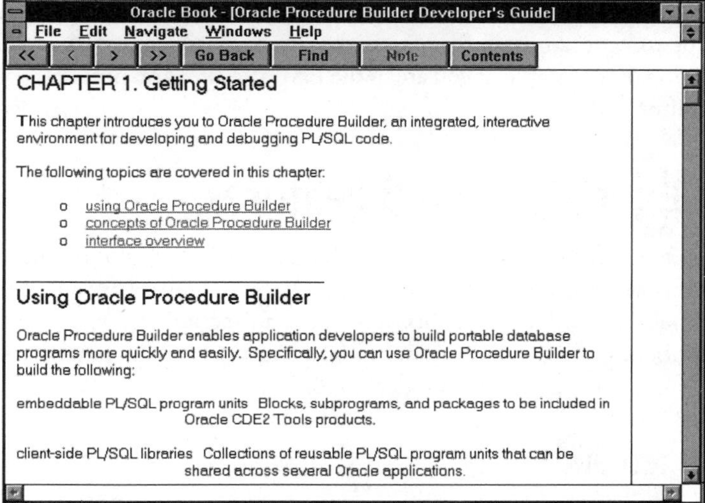

FIGURE 7.19.
Oracle Book online documentation.

Help

Oracle Forms, Reports, Graphics, and Procedure Builder all provide help using the familiar Microsoft Help System. Help can be invoked from the Help menu and includes the ability to review help contents, search on subjects, and navigate using hypertext links. When Help is invoked from the menu, the Help System starts with the Contents window. (See Figure 7.20.)

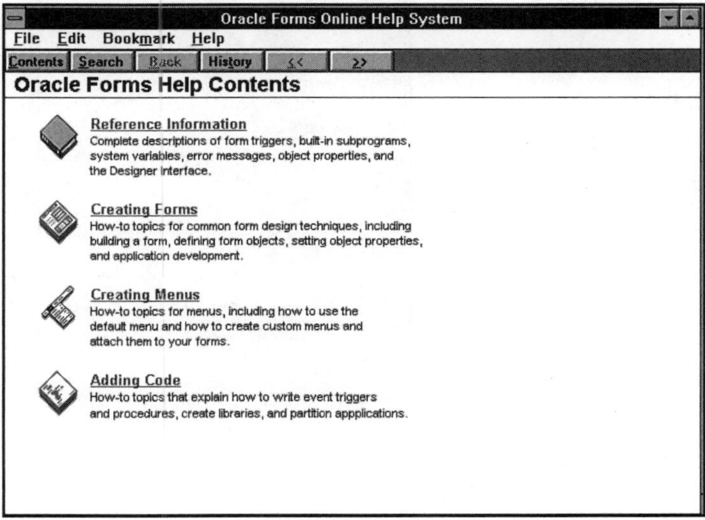

FIGURE 7.20.
The Oracle Forms online help system.

Help can also be invoked using the F1 key. When Help is called using F1, the Help window appears containing information that is context-sensitive to where you are and what you are doing. For example, if you are in the Layout Editor and press F1, you will get help on the Layout Editor.

Object-Oriented Features

Oracle Developer/2000 supports object orientation (OO) in a number of ways utilizing a combination of different features in the Oracle7 database as well as within the Designers. These capabilities will be described here from a practical and functional perspective. I will first describe some OO concepts and then explain the way in which these concepts are supported in Oracle7 and Oracle Developer/2000.

Inheritance

Inheritance is the ability of individual objects to be defined based on another object's definition while also permitting any of its properties to be modified.

Oracle Forms supports inheritance via the use of property classes. As shown in Figure 7.21, the two PUSH_BUTTON items are based on the property class PROPERTY_CLASS_PB.

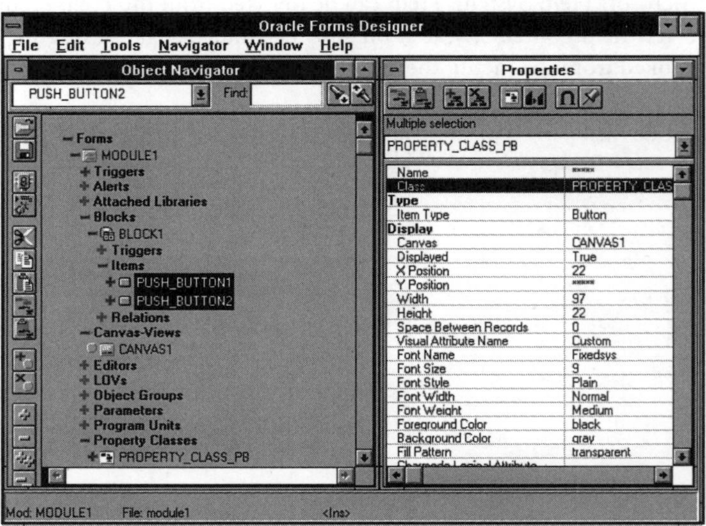

FIGURE 7.21.
Oracle Forms 4.5 property class.

Property classes may include any object, as well as their triggers (methods).

Encapsulation

Encapsulation is the ability to combine and hide data and methods.

Oracle Forms, Reports, and Graphics support encapsulation by utilizing stored functions, procedures, and packages.

These objects may be stored in applications, libraries, or in the Oracle7 database.

Polymorphism

Polymorphism is the ability of individual objects to respond to a given method in their own way.

Oracle Forms supports polymorphism via the use of object class triggers that can fire at the form, block, or item level.

Other OO Features of Oracle7 and Developer/2000

Oracle7 can store application and database objects.

Oracle Developer/2000 applications can reference objects stored in the Oracle7 database.

Oracle Developer/2000 development tools include an Object Navigator with outlining and drag-and-drop code reuse features.

Oracle Developer/2000 development tools provide access to their objects properties for review and editing.

The Properties Window in Oracle Forms 4.5 shows inherited objects and overridden properties.

In Oracle Forms, object groups can be created, further increasing the ease of code reuse.

Product Integration

The Oracle Developer/2000 tools now have the ability to interact with each other in a more tightly integrated fashion. In addition to the OLE2 capabilities that the Oracle Developer/2000 tools support (as shown in Figure 7.22), the tools also support invoking one another from a variety of other methods.

The most traditional method of product integration is the host command. The host command simply invokes the designated product from the operating system command line. The command line can contain parameters to identify the user and the application to run. The Oracle Developer/2000 tools can also be integrated using the `RUN_PRODUCT` built-in function. Each of these integration methods will be explained in further detail in the next few chapters.

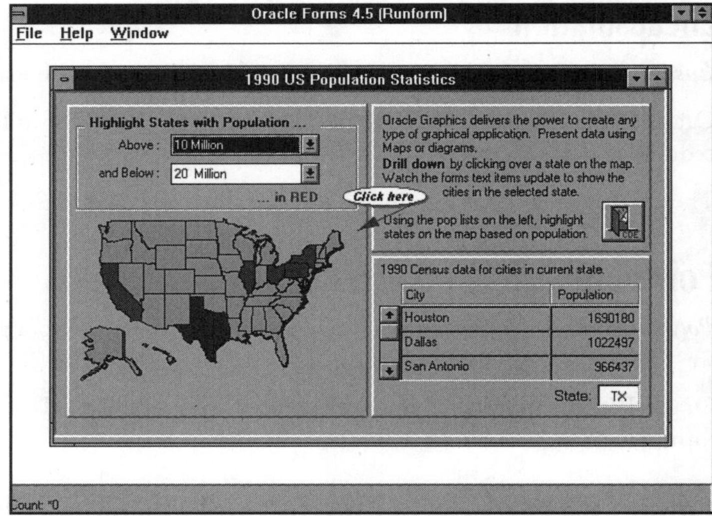

FIGURE 7.22.
An Oracle Forms 4.5 with an Oracle 2.5 graph.

TIP

The Oracle Developer/2000 tools use common Windows dynamic link libraries (DLLs) that can be pre-loaded using CDEINIT.EXE.

OLE2 Support

Oracle Forms, Oracle Reports, and Oracle Graphics all support OLE2. Oracle Forms and Oracle Reports can be OLE2 containers, while Oracle Graphics supports both OLE2 container and OLE2 server objects. Figure 7.23 shows an Oracle Graphics server object (a map of the United States) being used by a Visual Basic application.

Oracle Developer/2000 can contain static or dynamic OLE2 Objects. A static object does not change, while a dynamic object changes based on values in the application.

Both external and in-place activation of OLE objects are supported from within Oracle Developer/2000. This means that any OLE2-compliant application can be integrated with any Oracle Developer/2000 product. For example, an Excel spreadsheet or a Word document can be embedded in an Oracle Forms application.

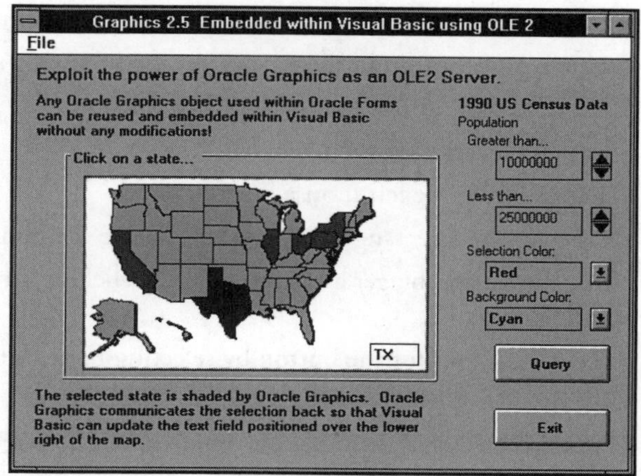

FIGURE 7.23.
An Oracle 2.5 graph embedded within Visual Basic.

Exercise

The purpose of this exercise is to familiarize you with the Oracle Developer/2000 toolset. To simplify the task, this exercise will only use Oracle Forms 4.5. However, each of the exercise items is a review of general functional capabilities. This exercise will also give you some hands-on review of the material just covered in this chapter.

1. Open Oracle Forms 4.5 Designer. Notice the standard Windows interface.
2. Click on the menu. Review each menu item in File, Edit, Tools, Navigator, Window, and Help.
3. Point to a button in the Object Navigator and rest. Notice the bubble help appears, explaining the function of the button.
4. Click an item with a minus symbol in the Object Navigator. Notice the tree collapse.
5. Click an item with a plus symbol in the Object Navigator. Notice the tree expand.
6. Double-click the Module icon. Notice the Properties window appears for the module.
7. Double-click the gray plus sign next to Canvas-Views. Notice a canvas-view is created.
8. Now, double-click the Canvas-View icon. Notice the Layout Editor appears for the canvas. Also notice that the menu has changed from Navigator to View, Format, and Arrange.

9. Click the menu. Review each menu item in View, Format, and Arrange.
10. Create a push-button in the Layout via the following steps:
11. Click the Push Button tool in the Tool palette.
12. Point to a location in the Layout Editor.
13. Click and hold the left mouse button.
14. Drag to create a rectangular shape and release the mouse button.
15. Make the button bigger and/or smaller by clicking an edge or corner of the button and dragging.
16. Select a new font for the button by selecting Font from the Format menu. Notice the button is also selected in the Object Navigator.
17. Change the name of the button via the Object Navigator by clicking on the name and making the change.
18. Invoke the Properties window for the button by double-clicking the button icon in the Object Navigator.
19. Change the name of the button via the Properties window.
20. Search for the button name using Find in the Object Navigator.
21. Delete the button by clicking Delete from the Object Navigator toolbar.
22. Resize the Object Navigator, Layout Editor, and Properties windows.
23. Delete the Canvas by selecting the canvas and clicking Delete from the Object Navigator toolbar. Notice the Canvas window is closed.
24. Right-click to invoke the pop-up menu from the Object Navigator and select Layout Editor. Notice a canvas-view is created automatically.
25. Select Contents from the Help menu. Click Search, type in `Object Navigator`. Click Show Topics and Go To. Exit Help.
26. Right-click to invoke the pop-up menu from the Object Navigator and select Help. Notice Help automatically starts with The Object Navigator.

Summary

This chapter provided an overview of the common components of the Oracle Developer/2000 Designers including:

- Windows interface
- Object navigators
- Toolbars
- Properties

- Layout editors
- PL/SQL editors
- Defaulting capabilities
- Interactive debuggers
- Online documentation
- Help
- Object-oriented features
- Product integration
- OLE2 support

Now that you are familiar with Object Navigators, Layout Editors, and some of the other general features of Oracle Developer/2000, we will take an in-depth look at the features of Oracle Forms 4.5.

8

Introducing Oracle Forms

Introduction

Oracle Forms is the keystone of the Oracle Developer/2000 suite of tools. It is the primary tool that you will be using to develop your database applications. With Oracle Forms you can create applications for queries, data entry, updates, and deletions. In addition, you can create customized menus to attach to your Forms applications. Oracle Forms also provides the capability to define libraries of PL/SQL code that can be referenced from many Forms applications. Within the Oracle Forms Designer you will find support for standard MS Windows objects and functionality.

After reading this chapter you will be familiar with:

- The components of Oracle Forms
- The basics of Oracle Forms, including modules, windows, canvas-views, blocks, items, and triggers
- Object types in the Object Navigator
- The Forms Designer toolbars
- The Properties window
- The Layout Editor and layout objects
- List of values
- The PL/SQL Editor and PL/SQL objects
- Default blocks, items, relations, triggers, and record groups
- The Menu Editor
- Libraries

In the exercise at the end of this chapter, you will develop a Forms application, a menu, and a library.

Oracle Forms is a product that is supported by three primary components: Designer, Generator, and Runform.

The Designer is where your applications will be developed. It is the Designer that will be the primary focus of this chapter, because as a developer most of your time will be spent there. You can find the Oracle Forms Designer executable F45DES.EXE in the \ORACLE\BIN directory.

The Generator converts the 4GL created by the Designer into an executable file. You can find the Oracle Forms Generator executable F45GEN.EXE in the \ORACLE\BIN directory. You will usually generate the executable from within the designer during the development process, just prior to running the application for testing.

The runtime engine is Runform, where the application is run from the executable that was generated. You can find the Oracle Runform F45RUN.EXE executable in the \ORACLE\BIN directory. It is Runform that is deployed for the end users, with the Forms applications that you will develop.

You build applications in Oracle Forms by developing different types of modules. The module types that you can create within Oracle Forms Designer are forms, menus, and libraries. The Oracle Forms Designer incorporates each of the module types into one integrated development environment.

An Oracle Forms application is a screen presentation of related information containing data items from tables in the database. The applications perform functions based on the user's actions and can include components integrated with Oracle Graphics, any OLE2 server, and Visual Basic Custom Controls.

Figure 8.1 shows the Oracle Forms application that will be developed later in this book. Notice that the Runform window contains a menu, toolbar, OLE2 containers, a text item, an image item, list items, a check box, radio groups, a VBX tab control, an Oracle Graphics chart, highlighting, and an imbedded MS Word document.

FIGURE 8.1.
An Oracle Forms application.

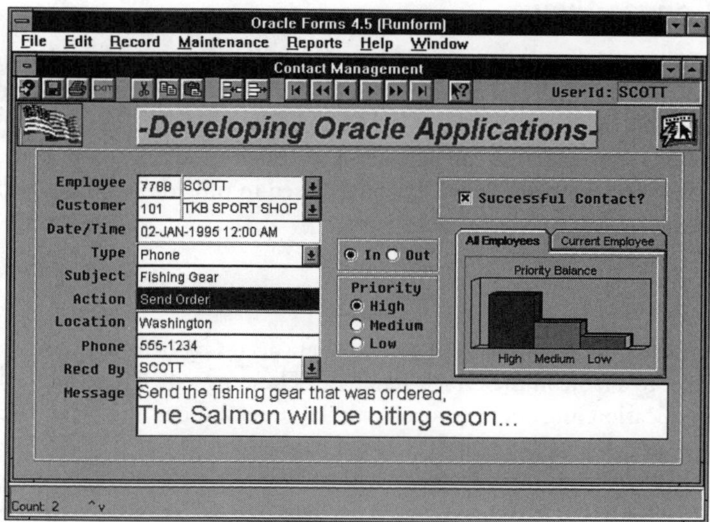

The development of a Forms application is accomplished by defining a forms module and its associated objects. Within the forms module you will create windows, canvases, and blocks that contain items. The form, blocks, and items are capable of executing triggers that use PL/SQL code to carry out functional and database operations.

Forms Modules

An application is made up of one or more forms modules. Forms modules can reference custom menus that you have developed or they can use the default menu. The application can also reference a toolbar to simplify the user's activities and provide a consistent user interface similar to other MS Windows applications. Status information may also be included in the application by referencing the console window. Each of the objects referenced by the forms modules are accessed via the Properties window. A list of each of the module properties can be found in Appendix C, "Oracle Forms Properties."

Windows

Each forms module will contain one or more windows. A window may be a document or dialog-style window and may or may not be modal. Modal dialog windows require the attention of the users and must be dismissed before returning to the application. Document windows that are not modal can coexist with other windows in the application, and focus can change between them without dismissal. Each window may also reference a toolbar. The roperties for each window are accessed via the Properties window. A list of each of the window properties can be found in Appendix C.

Canvas-Views

Canvas-views are the areas within the windows that each of the applications items are placed on. There are several types of canvas-views. The content canvas is the basic type of canvas and usually contains the basic items for the Forms application. The application may also include stacked canvases that can appear on top of an existing content canvas. Additionally, horizontal and vertical toolbar canvases may be used to provide standard toolbars for the Forms application.

Blocks

Oracle Forms applications provide data access by defining blocks and items. Blocks generally refer to a table in the Oracle database. These are called base-table blocks. Each item in a Forms application must belong to a block. Figure 8.2 shows the New Block Options dialog box, with a reference to CUSTOMER as the base table.

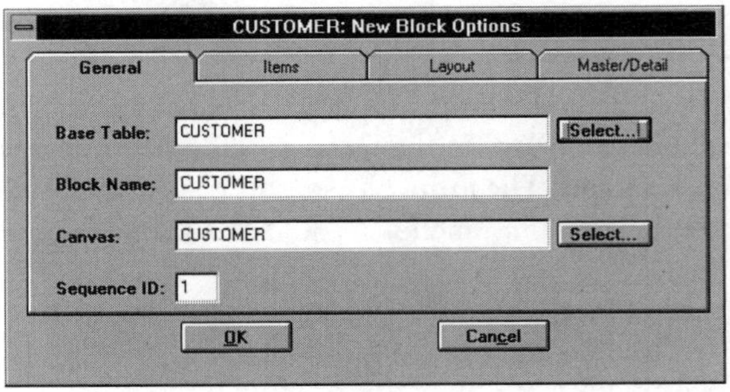

FIGURE 8.2.
The New Block Options dialog box.

Blocks do not have to have an associated table; such blocks are called non-base-table or control blocks. All of the items associated with a non-base-table block are local to the application and do not directly relate to any columns in the database. Blocks may be related to other blocks within the form to create a master detail relationship. Any two tables that can be joined can be used to create blocks that are related.

Use a multirow block when you expect multiple record results from the query and the data is presentable in tabular form. Multiple records may be displayed by defining the block property Number Of Rows. When you create a block with more than one row, you may want to include scroll bars for reviewing the list of records that have been queried but are not visible within the display area.

Blocks may also contain a default `where` clause to filter out some of the records that are queried from the block. The default `where` clause can be modified on the fly by using triggers to dynamically change the functionality of your application. Like the default `where` clause, the block may also contain a default `order by` clause so that the records retrieved will be presented in a logical order to the user.

The block properties may be accessed via the Properties window. A list of each of the block properties can be found in Appendix C.

Items

At the lowest level of your Forms application each object is an item. Each item must belong to a block. If you create an item in the layout without first creating a block, a default block is automatically created. There are many different item types. The following list describes each of the item types as they appear in the Layout Editor.

Item Type	*Description*
Button	Push-button; used for toolbars, and so on.
Check box	Used for selecting from 0 to *n* items.
Radio button	Used for selecting 1 of *n* items.
Text item	Data; usually a column in a table.
Image item	Pictures, bitmaps, and so on.
Chart item	Oracle Graphics chart.
OLE container	An object from any OLE2 server.
VBX control	A control from any VBX Custom Control.
Display item	Boilerplate text; used for labels.
List item	Poplist, tlist, or combo box.

Items may be created manually using the Layout Editor. Also, items can be created automatically by defining a default block. The Items tab in the New Block Options dialog box lists each of the candidate database columns associated with the table the block was based upon. (See Figure 8.3.)

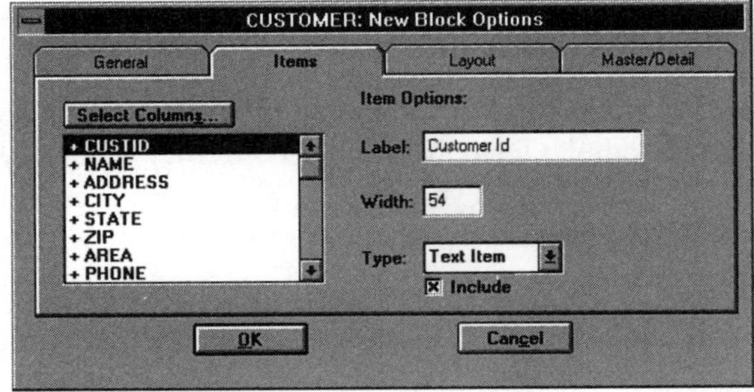

FIGURE 8.3.
The New Block Options dialog box with the Items tab.

Each item type has different properties associated with it. The item properties may be accessed via the Properties window. A list of each of the item properties can be found in Appendix C.

Triggers

Oracle Forms uses triggers to provide the operational functionality of the application. Triggers are written in PL/SQL. PL/SQL is the procedural language Oracle products use to support programming logic and to interact with the database via imbedded SQL commands.

A trigger may be user named or built in. User-named triggers are defined by the developer and are executed via the `execute_trigger` built-in function. Oracle Forms provides many different types of built-in triggers. Each built-in trigger is associated with an event that may occur during the execution of the Forms application. Trigger types include validation, query, transaction, key, and control activities. The following is a brief list of some of the more commonly used triggers:

- ON-LOGON
- ON-CLEAR-DETAILS
- ON-POPULATE-DETAILS
- ON-COMMIT
- WHEN-NEW-FORM-INSTANCE
- WHEN-NEW-ITEM-INSTANCE
- WHEN-BUTTON-PRESSED
- WHEN-VALIDATE-ITEM
- WHEN-CUSTOM-ITEM-EVENT

For a complete list of triggers, see the *Oracle Forms Reference Manual.* In addition to the different types of triggers, there are also different levels with which a trigger can be associated. A trigger may be defined at the form, block, record, or item level. At times, the same trigger may be placed at different levels within the application. This would be done when a specific event would require different action when occurring from within a specific item or block.

Oracle Forms triggers can be defined to fire at only one level or more than one level. This feature provides greater control for the developer than was available in previous versions of Oracle Forms. In the past, the lowest-level trigger would fire and any higher-level triggers of the same type were not processed.

Figure 8.4 shows a form-level trigger that will maximize the window as the application is started.

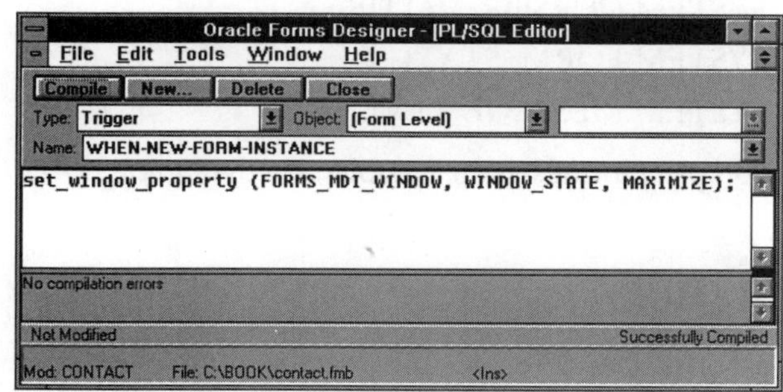

FIGURE 8.4.
The PL/SQL Editor with the NEW-FORM-INSTANCE trigger.

Notice that in Figure 8.4, the PL/SQL code may be incrementally compiled from within the PL/SQL Editor by clicking on the Compile button. Using incremental compilation provides immediate feedback on any compile errors and hastens the generation process.

Triggers may contain conditional logic, SQL, procedure calls, and built-in function calls.

Built-in functions commonly used in triggers:

- CALL-FORM
- DISPLAY-ITEM
- EXECUTE-QUERY
- EXECUTE-TRIGGER
- GET-ITEM-PROPERTY
- GO-BLOCK
- MESSAGE
- RUN-PRODUCT
- SET-ITEM-PROPERTY
- SET-WINDOW-PROPERTY

- SHOW-ALERT
- SHOW-LOV
- SHOW-WINDOW

For a complete list of built-in functions, see the *Oracle Forms Reference Manual*.

Triggers may also contain references to variables. Variables within a trigger may be local, bind, or system variables. A local variable exists only within the scope of the trigger, while a bind variable is associated with an item, and a system variable has its value set by Oracle Forms.

System variables commonly used in triggers include the following:

- SYSTEM.CURSOR_ITEM
- SYSTEM.CURSOR_VALUE
- SYSTEM.FORM_STATUS
- SYSTEM.MESSAGE_LEVEL

For a complete list of system variables, see the *Oracle Forms Reference Manual*.

Designer

Oracle Forms Designer is an integrated development environment used for creating Forms applications, menus, libraries, and database objects. Within the Designer there are several tools and features that are used during the development process. These items include

- The Object Navigator
- Toolbars
- The Properties window
- The Layout Editor
- LOVs
- The PL/SQL Editor
- Defaulting

Figure 8.5 shows the Oracle Forms Designer with the Object Navigator, the Properties window, the Layout Editor, and the PL/SQL Editor.

Notice in the Designer, multiple windows may be open so that several tools can be used together.

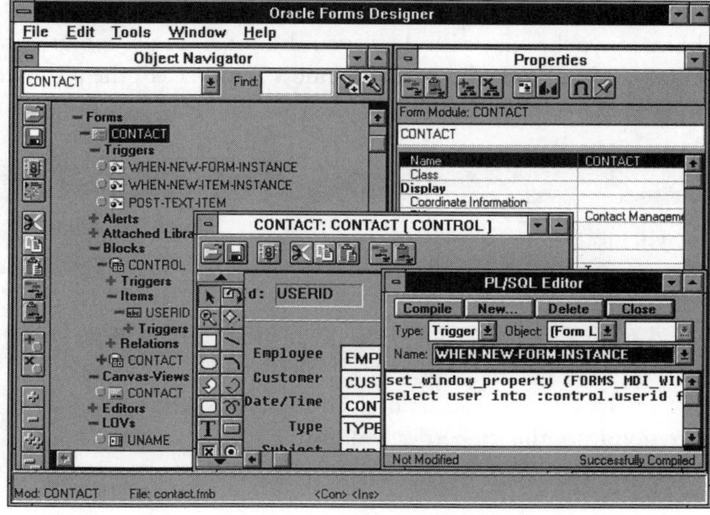

FIGURE 8.5.
The Oracle Forms Designer.

Object Navigator

The Object Navigator was reviewed in Chapter 7, "Introducing Oracle Developer/2000." But Oracle Forms incorporates a few additional features into the Object Navigator that will be examined here. In addition, the specific object types within Oracle Forms will be reviewed. Figure 8.6 shows the Oracle Forms Designer window with the Object Navigator.

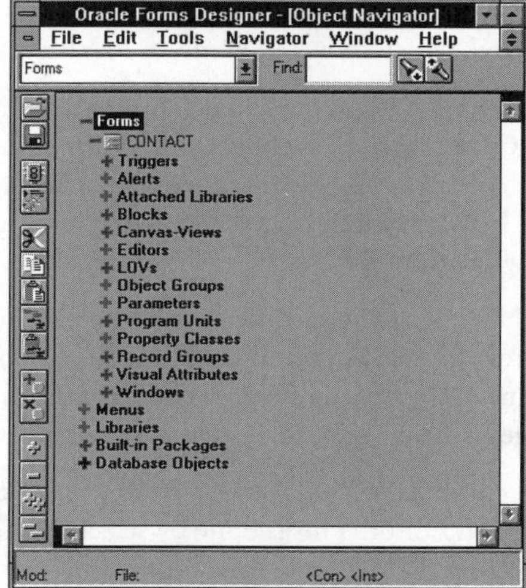

FIGURE 8.6.
The Oracle Forms Designer with the Object Navigator.

An additional navigational feature of the Object Navigator that Oracle Forms provides is the ability to synchronize with the Layout Editor and the Properties window. With synchronization turned on, if the Properties window is displayed, the properties of the object selected in either the Object Navigator or the Layout Editor is shown.

NOTE

Synchronization is selected by default.

CAUTION

Turning off synchronization from the Navigator menu does *not* turn off the synchronization from the Properties window.

TIP

You can turn off the synchronization between the Properties window, the Object Navigator, and the Layout Editor by "pinning" the object in the Properties window. To pin an object, click the icon button of a pin, located in the upper-right corner of the Properties window.

The Object Navigator menu contains radio group menu items for viewing the items either in Ownership View, which shows all items, or in Visual View, which only shows the visual items.

The list of objects shown in the Object Navigator can be restricted to only show objects that contain PL/SQL code, such as triggers, program units, and libraries. This is a convenient feature to use when you are reviewing the code in a Forms application. The Navigator menu provides a check item to switch between showing all of the objects in the Navigator or showing only objects with PL/SQL.

The Object Navigator can also be used as an aid in writing PL/SQL while you are in the PL/SQL Editor. By selecting built-in package objects in the Object Navigator and selecting the Paste Name or Paste Arguments menu items from the Navigator menu, the package name or the package name with its associated parameter list can be inserted into your code.

You can even compile PL/SQL objects from the Object Navigator directly without having to open the PL/SQL Editor. This is done by selecting the PL/SQL object from the Object Navigator and selecting the Compile Selection menu item from the Navigator menu.

The major nodes in the Oracle Forms Object Navigator are:

- Forms
- Menus
- Libraries
- Packages
- Database objects

Form Object Types

While in the Object Navigator, you will notice that the objects are organized by type. There are Forms, Menus, Libraries, and so on. Under the Forms node, you will find all the object types used for designing Oracle Forms applications. Figure 8.7 shows the Object Navigator with the Forms node selected.

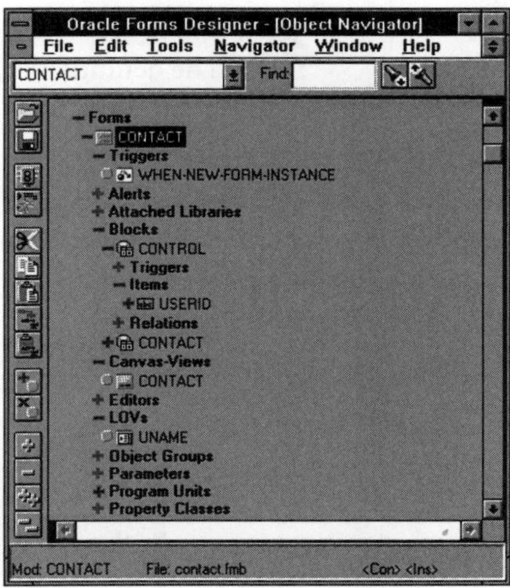

FIGURE 8.7.
The Object Navigator showing forms objects.

Oracle Forms supplies many different object types. Each forms object type, as it is presented in the Object Navigator, is listed here with a description.

Object Type	*Description*
Module	Defines the form.
Triggers	PL/SQL code that fires based on actions.
Alerts	A dialog box that requires a user response.
Attached Libraries	PL/SQL code used by multiple applications.

continues

Object Type	*Description*
Blocks	The basic component of forms; generally based on tables.
Items	All forms widgets; usually connected to columns.
Canvas-Views	The screen that will be presented to the user.
Editors	Used to edit large text strings.
LOVs	List of values; used for lookup and validation.
Object Groups	Related items, grouped for reuse.
Parameters	Items passed in and out of the application.
Program Units	Procedures, functions, and packages.
Property Classes	The definition of a group of properties.
Record Groups	A local array of data, used to support LOVs.
Visual Attributes	The definition of font characteristics.
Windows	The definition of the application windows.

Menu Object Types

Menus are usually created as standard MS Windows-style pull-down menus and are used for the navigation and operation of the application. Under the Menus node, you will find all the object types for menus. Figure 8.8 shows the Object Navigator with the Menus node selected.

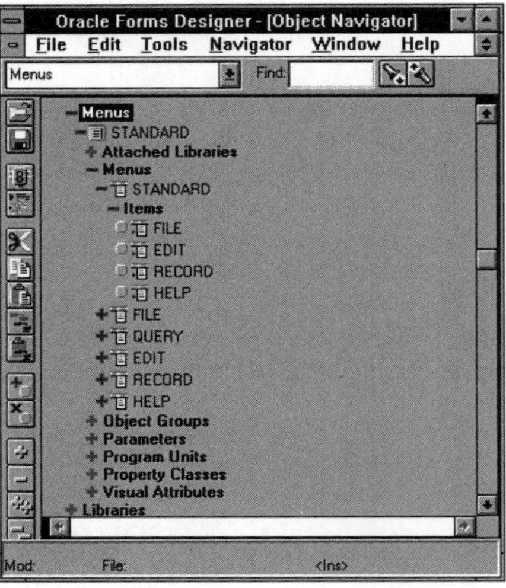

FIGURE 8.8.
The Object Navigator showing menu objects.

Oracle Forms includes several object types to support the creation of menus. Each object type as it is presented in the Object Navigator is listed here with a description.

Object Type	*Description*
Module	Defines the menu.
Attached Libraries	PL/SQL code used by multiple applications.
Menus	Items that appear on a menu.
Object Groups	Related items, grouped for reuse.
Parameters	Items passed in and out of the application.
Program Units	Procedures, functions, and packages.
Property Classes	The definition of a group of properties.
Visual Attributes	The definition of font characteristics.

Library Object Types

Under the Libraries node you will find the object types used for libraries. Libraries are collections of PL/SQL code that can be used by many applications. Figure 8.9 shows the Object Navigator with the Libraries node selected.

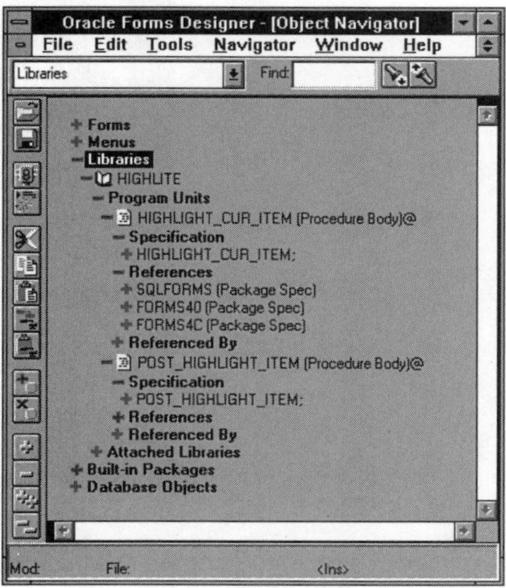

FIGURE 8.9.
The Object Navigator showing library objects.

Each object type used to support the creation and maintenance of libraries as it is presented in the Object Navigator is listed here with a description.

Object Type	*Description*
Module	Defines the library.
Program Units	Procedures, functions, and packages.

continues

Object Type	*Description*
Specification	The program unit name with arguments.
Subprograms	Any subprograms that this program unit includes.
References	Any object that this program unit references.
Referenced By	Any object that is referenced by this program unit.
Attached Libraries	PL/SQL code used by multiple applications.

Built-In Package Object Types

Under the Built-in Packages node you will find all of the built-in programs supplied with Oracle Forms. There are several Built-in Packages, and each one contains a group of supporting functions and procedures. The Object Navigator with the Built-in Packages node selected is shown in Figure 8.10.

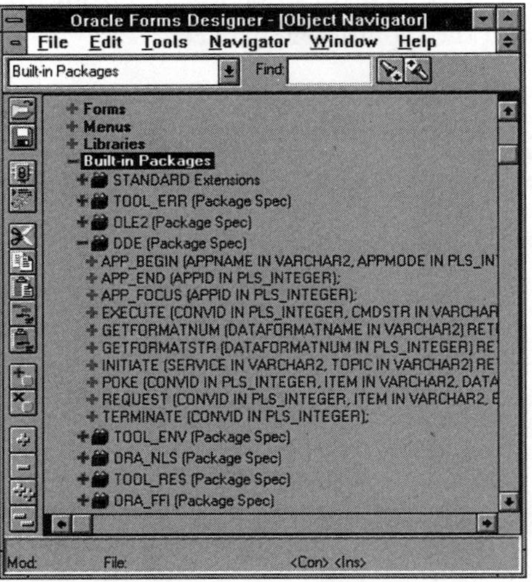

FIGURE 8.10.
The Object Navigator showing built-in package objects.

Oracle Forms provides access to built-in packages via the Object Navigator. By selecting a program unit and Paste Name or Paste Arguments from the Navigator menu, the specification for the program unit is placed into the PL/SQL Editor. The object types are listed here with a description.

Object Type	*Description*
Packages	The name and type of built-in package.
Program Units	The functions and procedures contained in the package.

Database Object Types

All of the database objects for each Oracle user are listed under the Database Objects node. Database objects include programs, libraries, tables, and views. The Object Navigator with the Database Objects node selected is shown in Figure 8.11.

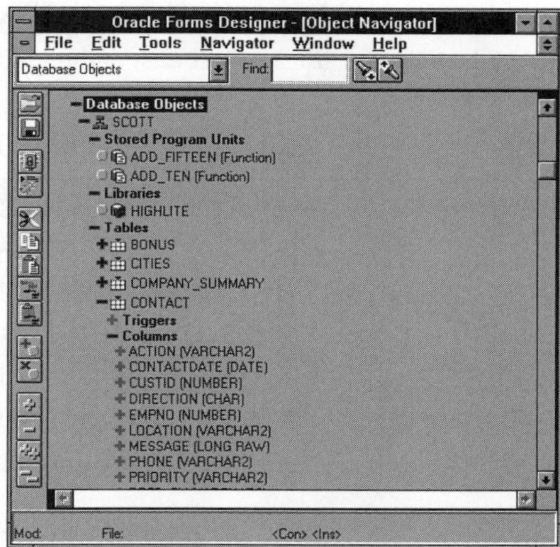

FIGURE 8.11.
The Object Navigator showing database objects.

> **NOTE**
>
> The Database Objects node in the Object Navigator is only enabled when you are connected to the database.

Oracle Forms provides access to each database object type to support the creation and maintenance of objects stored in the database. Each object type as it is presented in the Object Navigator is listed here with a description.

Object Type	*Description*
Owners	The Oracle user ID that owns the database objects.
Stored Program Units	Packages, procedures, and functions.
Libraries	Libraries stored in the database.
Tables	Any tables owned by the user.
Triggers	Any triggers associated with the table.
Columns	The columns that define the table or view.
Views	Any views owned by the user.

Oracle Forms Designer Toolbars

Each of the common toolbars were reviewed in the previous chapter. Here, Oracle Forms' specific items will be reviewed for each of the toolbars that appear in the Designer.

Object Navigator Toolbar

The Oracle Forms Object Navigator has several additional buttons on the toolbar used for forms development. The following list describes each of the additional buttons found on the left side of the Object Navigator.

Button	*Description*
Debug Mode	Enables and disables Debug mode for Runform.
Cut	Cuts the selected object from the Object Navigator.
Copy	Copies the selected object from the Object Navigator.
Paste	Pastes the contents of the clipboard to the Object Navigator.
Copy Properties	Copies the selected objects properties.
Paste Properties	Pastes the copied objects properties.

Figure 8.12 shows the Oracle Forms Object Navigator toolbar.

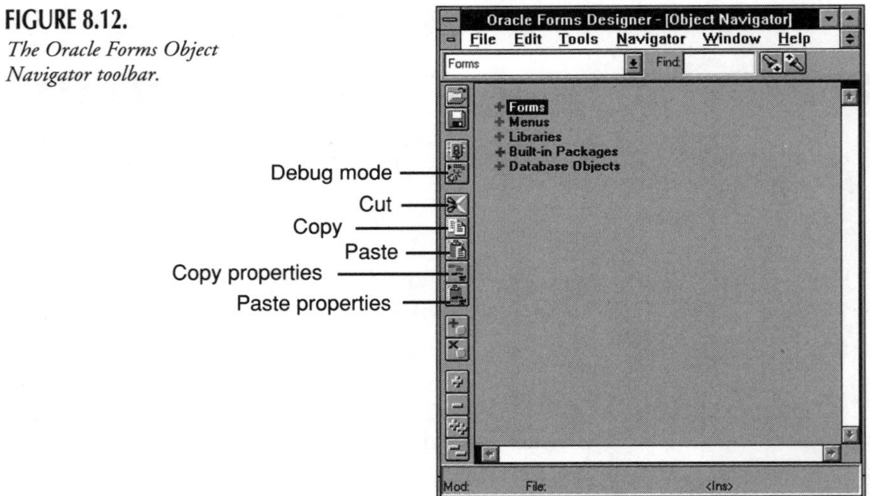

FIGURE 8.12.
The Oracle Forms Object Navigator toolbar.

Layout Editor Toolbar

The Oracle Forms Layout Editor includes the Copy Properties and Paste Properties buttons on the toolbar, just as the Object Navigator toolbar does. Figure 8.13 shows the Oracle Forms Layout Editor toolbar. The toolbar is located at the top of the Layout Editor.

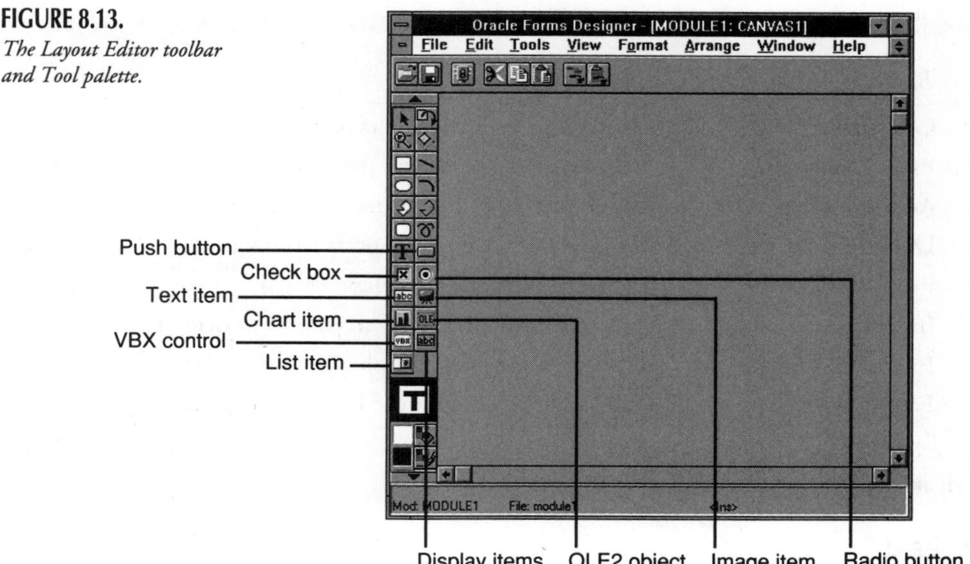

FIGURE 8.13.
The Layout Editor toolbar and Tool palette.

Layout Editor Tool Palette

The Oracle Forms Layout Editor contains the following specific item-drawing tools on the Tool palette, as can be seen in Figure 8.13. The Tool palette appears on the left side of the Layout Editor.

Button	*Description*
Push Button	Creates a push-button item.
Check Box	Creates a check box item.
Radio Button	Creates a radio group with radio-button items.
Text Item	Creates a text item; used for input.
Image Item	Creates an image item.
Chart Item	Creates a chart item for an Oracle Graphics display.
OLE2 Object	Creates a container for any OLE2 server.
VBX Control	Creates a VBX custom control.
Display Items	Creates a display-only item.
List Item	Creates a poplist, tlist, or combo box.

Properties Window Toolbar

Oracle Forms uses a generic Properties window for all object properties. The Properties window has a toolbar used for modifying object properties.

The following list describes each of the buttons found on the Properties window toolbar:

Button	*Description*
Copy Properties	Copies the selected objects properties.
Paste Properties	Pastes the copied objects properties.
Add Property	Provides a list of properties to be added to a class.
Delete Property	Removes the current property from a class.
Property Class	Creates a new property class.
Inherit	Sets the current property to parent, or default value.
Intersection/Union	Display used with multiple properties selected.
Freeze/Unfreeze	Synchronization with the Object Navigator.

Figure 8.14 shows the Properties window. The window is located to the right of the Object Navigator.

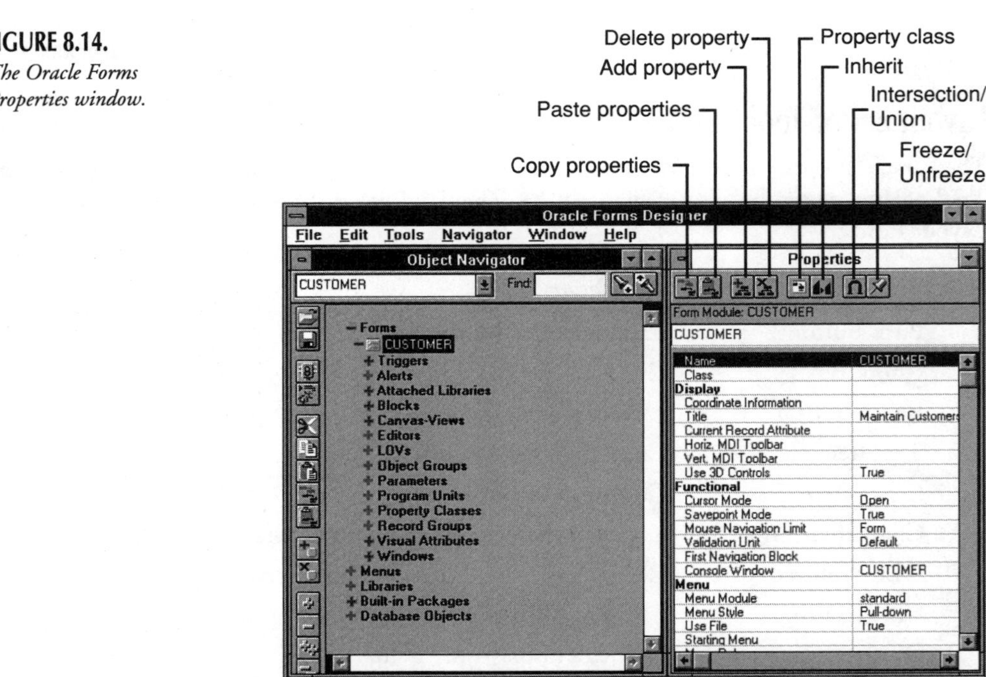

FIGURE 8.14.
The Oracle Forms Properties window.

The Properties Window

As you have seen, the Properties window contains a helpful toolbar as well as a list of the selected objects' properties and their values. The properties for each object are organized by topic.

You will find the name of the property as the first entry in the Properties window. Following the Name property, most objects will have an associated class. The Object Group is the only object that does not have a Class property following the name. In Figure 8.14, the properties of the forms module named "CUSTOMER" are shown.

Most objects will have the following topics:

Topic	*Description*
Display	Size, font, and location information.
Functional	Specific properties of the object.
Miscellaneous	Contains comments and reference information.

Some objects will also include the following:

Topic	*Description*
Menu	Defines the menu to be used for the module.
Data	Data type, range, and defaults for items and parameters.
Records	Record information on blocks and items.
Navigation	Navigation instructions for blocks and items.
Database	Database properties for blocks and items.
Type	The specific type of canvas-view or item.
GUI Hints	Defines GUI properties for windows objects.

NOTE

There are no properties associated with Libraries, Attached Libraries, or Program Units.

All of the properties for each of the Oracle Forms object types are listed in Appendix C. They are organized as they appear in the Object Navigator. You can also locate any specific object property by using the Table Of Contents or the Index.

Properties displayed in the Properties window will often include default values, and some offer drop-down lists for valid choices.

NOTE

You can review and set properties by using the Properties window in Oracle Forms Designer during development, or programatically using the `GET` and `SET` built-in functions.

The Layout Editor

All of the windows objects in your Forms application can be created and detailed in the Layout Editor using the Tool palette, the mouse, and the Properties window. Usually you would begin working with the Layout Editor after creating a default layout. The default layout is created by defining one or more default blocks and setting the properties for the blocks and items. Figure 8.15 shows the Layout Editor with layout objects created from a default block.

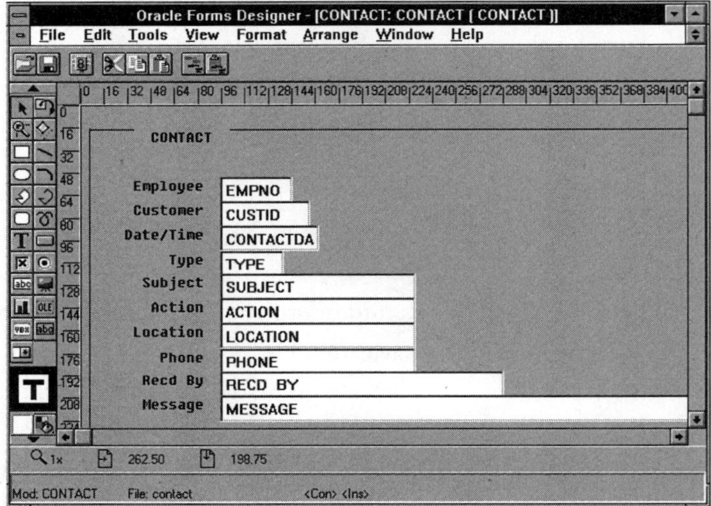

FIGURE 8.15.
The Oracle Forms Layout Editor.

The Oracle Developer/2000 tools use a common Layout Editor, and each contains layout and boilerplate tools as well as color palettes (as was reviewed in the previous chapter).

The specific item-drawing tools of Oracle Forms include:

- Push buttons
- Check boxes
- Radio buttons
- Text items
- Image items
- Chart items
- OLE2 objects
- VBX controls
- Display items
- List items

Push Buttons

Push buttons are used to create list buttons, toolbars, or tool palettes to be used by your Forms applications. But buttons can also be used to provide the user with a convenient method of selecting almost anything. All buttons are created in the Layout Editor. Notice in Figure 8.16 that there is an exit button and a list button for employees.

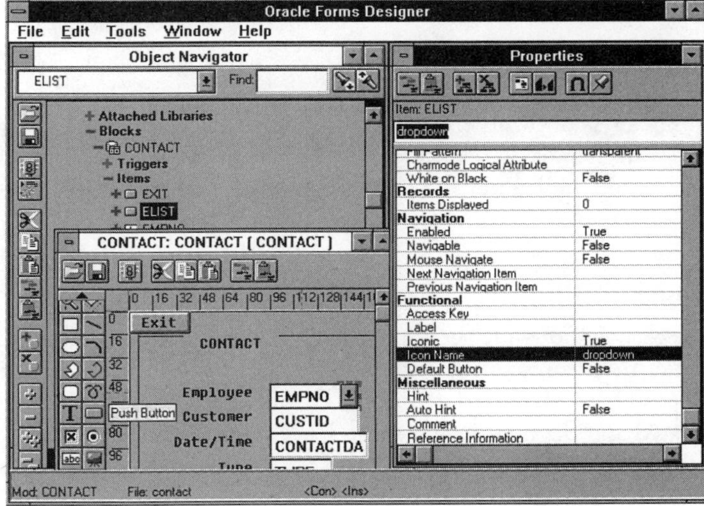

FIGURE 8.16.
Push buttons in the Layout Editor.

As you can see, buttons can display text or icons. You can define the label or the icon to be displayed on the button using the Properties window.

> **NOTE**
>
> You can use the icons supplied with Oracle Forms or with this book, or you can create your own using any icon editor. The Oracle demo icons are in the \ORAWIN\FORMS45\DEMOS\ICONS directory. The book's icons are in the \ICONS directory on the CD-ROM that accompanies this book. The drop-down icon in Figure 8.16 is one of the icons included with this book.

> **CAUTION**
>
> Icons used for buttons do not automatically scale to size as the video resolution is changed on the monitor. Therefore, to support various video resolutions, you will need different icons.

TIP

You can define the directory that Oracle Forms will search for icons in the ORACLE.INI file under the windows directory. The setting is TK21_ICON=*C:\ICONS*, where *C:\ICONS* is the directory where you keep your Forms application icons.

TIP

Create your own standard application toolbar, or use the one provided in the Oracle Forms demos. Reference the toolbar on all of your Forms applications to give them a standard look and feel.

Check Boxes

Check boxes provide the user with a graphical object for making an optional choice. Static values that represent the states of the check box can be directly linked to database columns. Check boxes may be created in the Layout Editor, or as a default item when a default block is created and the item type is set to Check Box. The check box in Figure 8.17 was created by default.

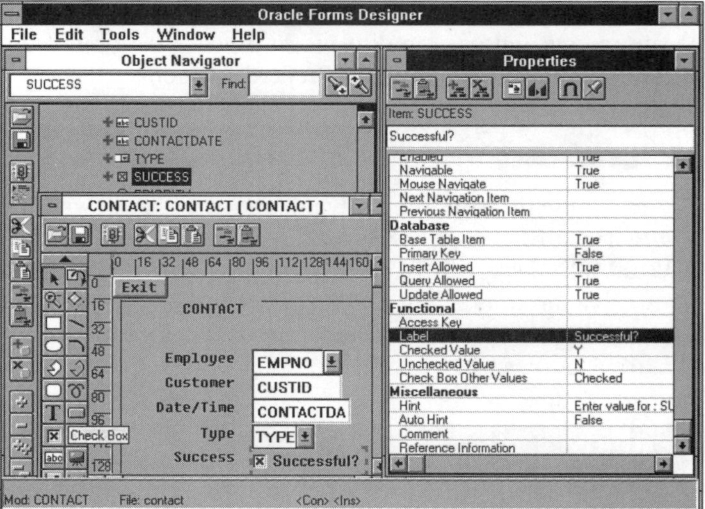

FIGURE 8.17.
A check box in the Layout Editor.

Notice that in Figure 8.17, the label following the check box and the checked and unchecked values are set in the Properties window. When you have several related check boxes, use the rectangle boilerplate drawing tool with a line size of 2 points and a bevel of your choice to create a visual grouping.

Radio Buttons

Radio buttons provide the user with a graphical object for selecting one of many choices. When a radio button is created, a radio group is also created to contain each of the possible selections. Each additional choice is mapped to an additional radio button in the radio group. Static values that represent the various choices in the radio group can be directly linked to database columns. Radio buttons may be created in the Layout Editor, or as a default item when a default block is created and the item type is set to Radio Group. In Figure 8.18, the radio group and radio button were created by default, then the label for the radio button was changed.

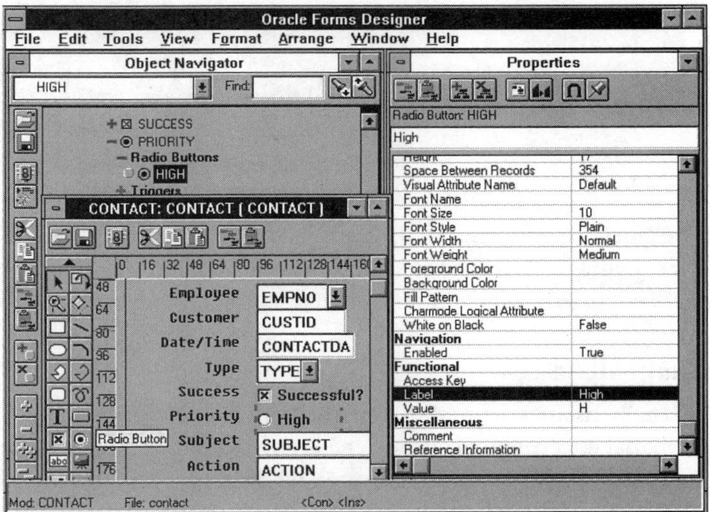

FIGURE 8.18.
A radio button in the Layout Editor.

Notice that in Figure 8.18, the label before the radio button is for the radio group. There is an additional label for the radio button, and a value that has been set in the Properties window. Again, you may want to draw a rectangle around the radio group to provide the user with a visual grouping.

Text Items

Text items are the most common type of layout object and are usually mapped to columns in the database. Text items may be created in the Layout Editor, but they are more often created by default when a default block is created and the item type is set to Text Item. In Figure 8.19, you will notice in the Object Navigator and in the Layout Editor the many text items in the application.

FIGURE 8.19.
Text items in the application.

The labels for text items may be assigned in the Items tab of the New Block dialog box. Once a text item is created, the label must be changed in the Layout Editor using the Text tool from the Tool palette. There is no label property for a text item.

Image Items

Image items are used to display images of various formats in the application. Image items can be mapped to columns in the database or read from the file system. Image items may be created in the Layout Editor or created by default when a default block is created and the item type is set to Image Item. In Figure 8.20, an image item has been added to the upper-left corner of the application.

The image in Figure 8.20 has the sizing style set to Adjust in the Properties window. This scales the image to fit into the area defined in the layout. The image item is populated at runtime with a bitmap via the read_image_file built-in procedure in the WHEN-NEW-FORM-INSTANCE trigger.

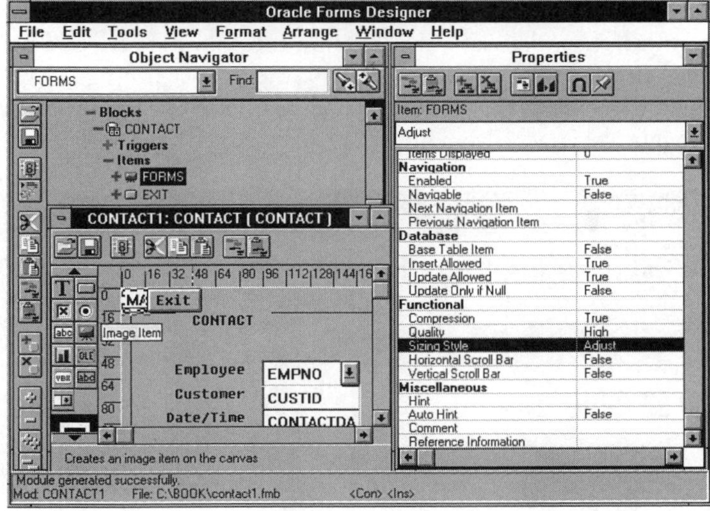

FIGURE 8.20.
An image item in the application.

Chart Items

Chart items are used to display Oracle Graphics displays in the application. The Oracle Graphics display must be created in the Oracle Graphics Designer. Image items must be created in the Layout Editor. There is no item type for chart items in the New Block dialog box. In Figure 8.21, a chart item has been added to the right side of the application.

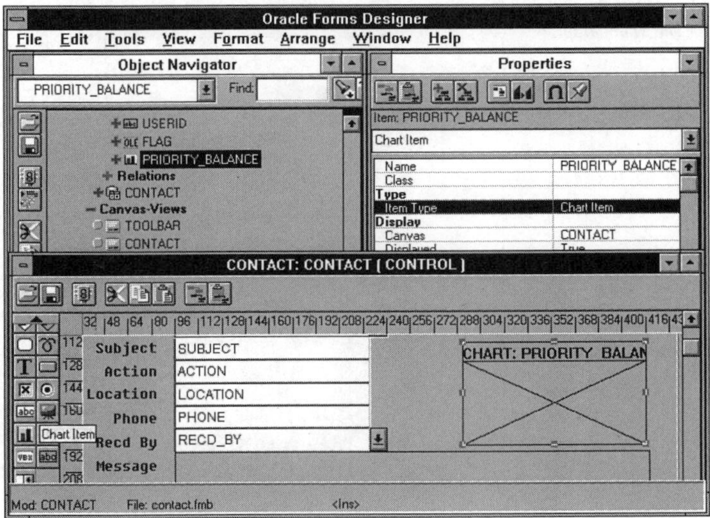

FIGURE 8.21.
A chart item for an Oracle Graphics display.

The Oracle Graphics display in Figure 8.21 will need a trigger to call a procedure to open it at runtime. Also, the sizing style is set in the procedure call and not in the Properties window. The chart item is opened at runtime via the og.open packaged procedure in the WHEN-NEW-FORM-INSTANCE trigger. To use the Oracle Graphics packaged procedures, the OG.PLL file must be attached as a library.

> **NOTE**
>
> The Oracle Graphics packaged procedures are supplied with Oracle Developer/2000. You should find the OG.pll file in the \ORAWIN\FORMS45\PLSQLLIB directory.

OLE2 Objects

OLE2 objects are used to contain any OLE2 server object in the application. The OLE2 object may be an object from an OLE2 server that is registered on your system. OLE2 objects can be mapped to columns in the database, but they can also be static and defined in the designer. OLE2 container objects may be embedded in the Oracle Forms application, or they may be linked to files in the file system. OLE2 objects may be created in the Layout Editor or created by default when a default block is created and the item type is set to Custom Item. A flag from the Microsoft ClipArt Gallery has been added to the upper-right corner of the application in Figure 8.22.

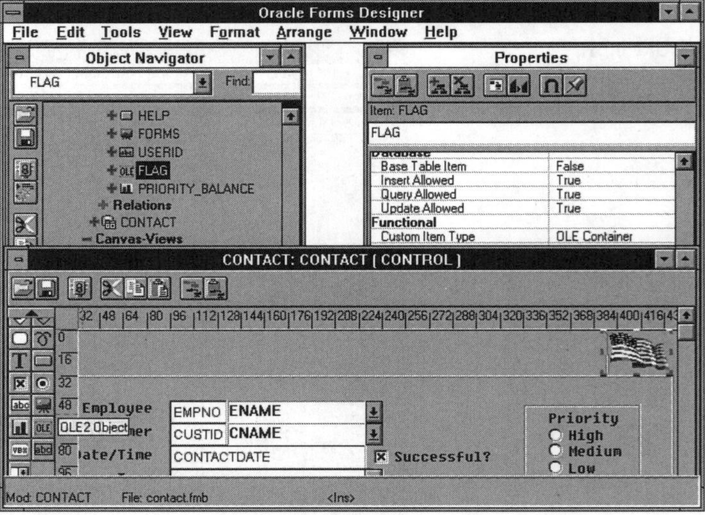

FIGURE 8.22.
An OLE2 object contained in the application.

The flag in Figure 8.22 was embedded as a static object. This was done by selecting the OLE2 Object tool from the Tool palette and defining it in the layout. Then, with a right-mouse click on the OLE2 object, the Insert Object menu item was selected from the pop-up menu as shown in Figure 8.23.

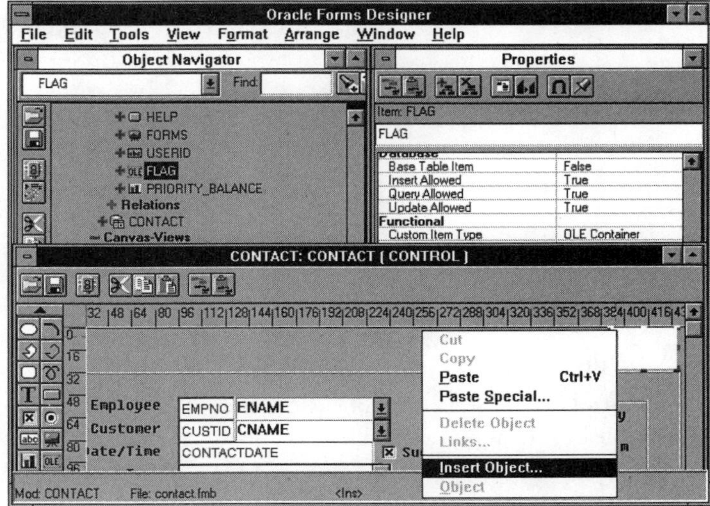

FIGURE 8.23.
The pop-up menu for inserting OLE2 objects.

The Insert Object menu selection invokes the Insert Object dialog box, as shown in Figure 8.24, where the object type of Microsoft ClipArt Gallery was selected.

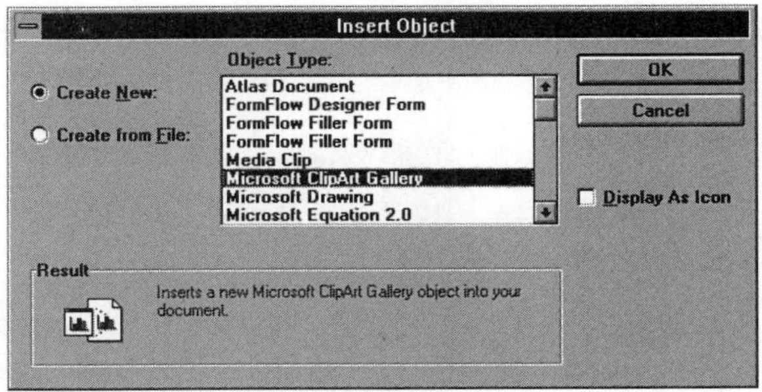

FIGURE 8.24.
The Insert Object dialog box.

Selecting the object type of Microsoft ClipArt Gallery invokes the Microsoft ClipArt Gallery dialog box. (See Figure 8.25.)

Scrolling through the list of available pictures, I selected the United States flag to be embedded in my Forms application.

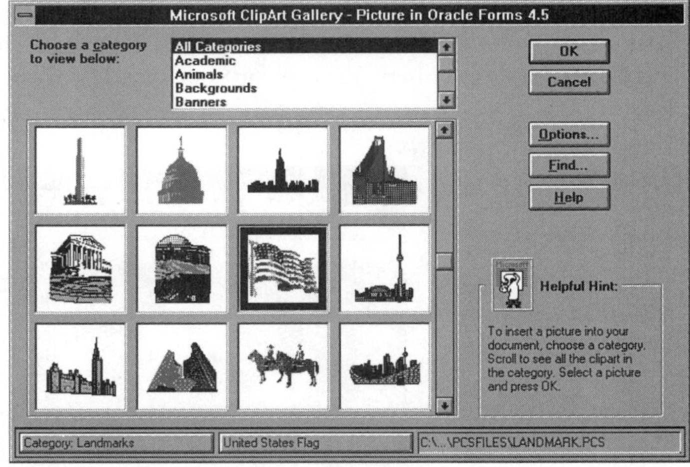

FIGURE 8.25.
The Microsoft ClipArt Gallery dialog box.

VBX Controls

VBX controls are a special type of custom item. You can reference any control from any VBX control file in your application. There are many third-party products on the market that implement a variety of user-interface elements. One of the most commonly seen is the tab control. VBX controls can be mapped to columns in the database, or they can be control items. Custom items, including VBX controls, may be created in the Layout Editor, or they can be created by default when a default block is created and the item type is set to Custom Item. A tab control is being added to the application in Figure 8.26.

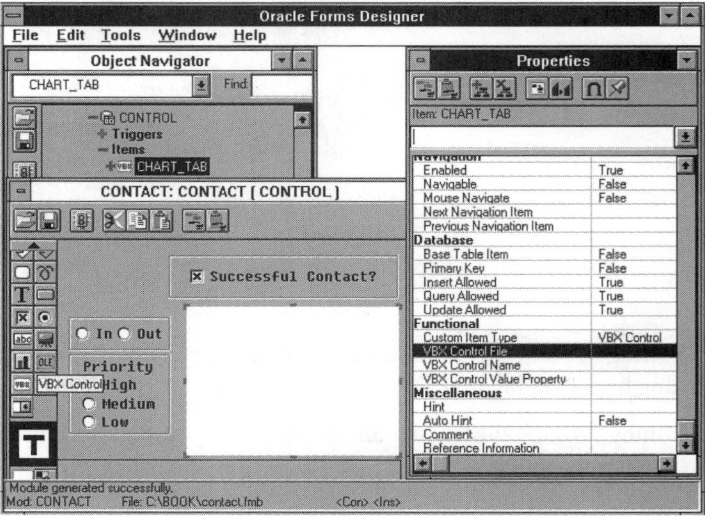

FIGURE 8.26.
Creating a VBX control in the Layout Editor.

Once the VBX control is defined in the layout, the properties for the item must be set in the Properties window. Each control will have its own specific properties to be set, depending on the type of control that it is. In Figure 8.27, the File, Name, Value Property, Caption, Style, and Bevel have all been set, and the tab control is displayed in the layout.

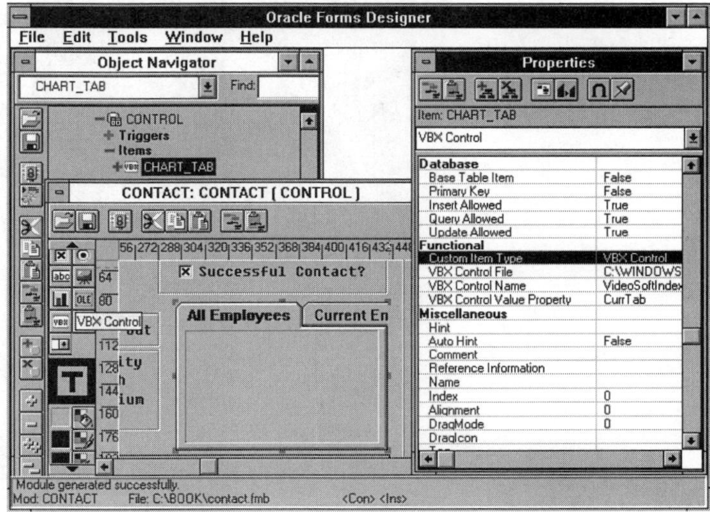

FIGURE 8.27.
A VBX tab control displayed in the layout.

VBX controls will also need a WHEN-CUSTOM-ITEM-EVENT trigger to provide the appropriate actions, based on the user's interaction with the control. VBX files are usually installed in the \WINDOWS\SYSTEM directory. See the vendor documentation for the properties and their settings in the VBX control you are using.

Display Items

Display items are used for labels or control fields, and are not editable, although they may be mapped to columns in the database. Display items may be created in the Layout Editor, or they can be created by defining a default block and setting the item type to Display Item. In Figure 8.28, a display item is created in the layout to show the name of the customer, just to the right of the customer ID.

Display items are often used to describe codes in Forms applications.

List Items

List items may be created in one of three different styles. The default is poplist, which is a drop-down list that must have all the possible values defined. The combo box is like the poplist but allows for a value to be entered that is not in the list. The tlist or text list is not a drop-down style; the tlist items are always displayed, and the list will include a scroll bar if the list is longer than the display area. List items may be mapped to columns in the database, and they may be created in the Layout Editor or by defining a default block and setting the item type to List Item. A poplist was created by the default block in Figure 8.29.

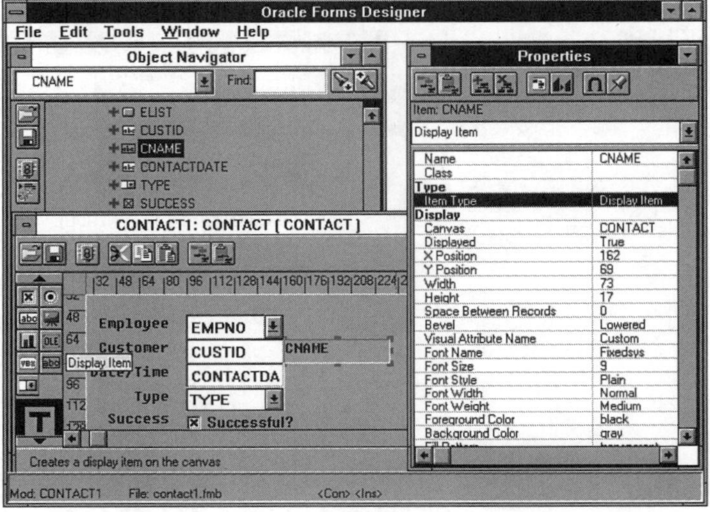

FIGURE 8.28.
Creating a display item in the Layout Editor.

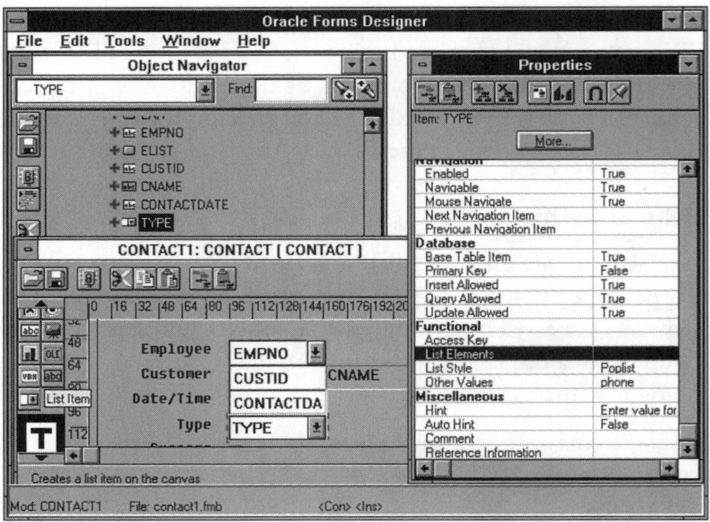

FIGURE 8.29.
A poplist created by a default block.

The values for the poplist are defined in the Properties window using List Elements. When the List Elements property is selected, the More button invokes the List Item Elements dialog box. (See Figure 8.30.)

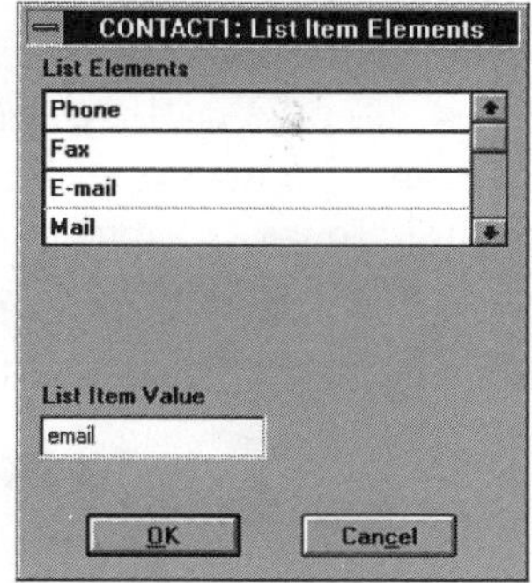

FIGURE 8.30.
The List Item Elements dialog box.

Each of the display labels and valid values for Contact Type are entered using the List Item Elements dialog box.

Color Palettes

There are three color palettes in the Oracle Forms Layout Editors tool palette. They are used to set the fill, line, and text colors of any object in the layout. In Figure 8.31, the three color palettes are shown setting the colors for a text item to display the company name at the top of the Forms application.

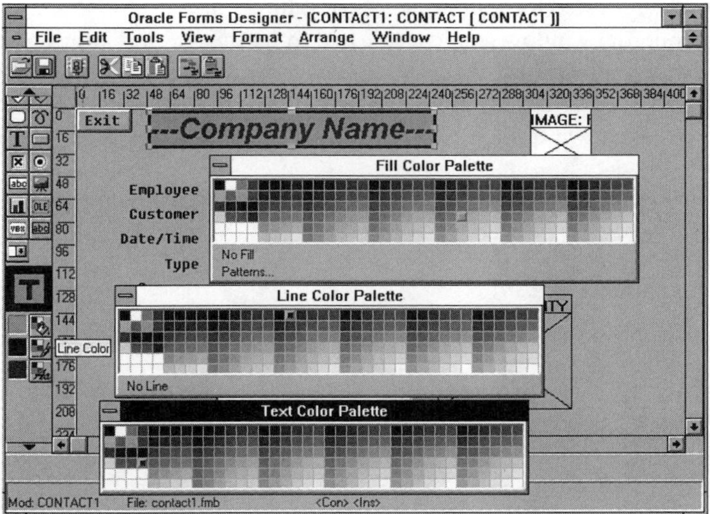

FIGURE 8.31.
Using the color palettes in the Layout Editor.

The color palettes pop up when the tool is selected, but they can be torn away as shown in Figure 8.31. The sample on the Tool palette—just above the color palette tools—shows the current color scheme. Choosing No Fill or No Line makes that portion of the object transparent.

List of Values

Text items can reference a list of values for selection and validation. Lists of values are based on record groups, and a record group can be created automatically when you define the LOV. Oracle Forms uses record groups as the method of storing tables/arrays. In Figure 8.32, the New LOV dialog box is shown containing a SQL statement that selects state and name from the state table.

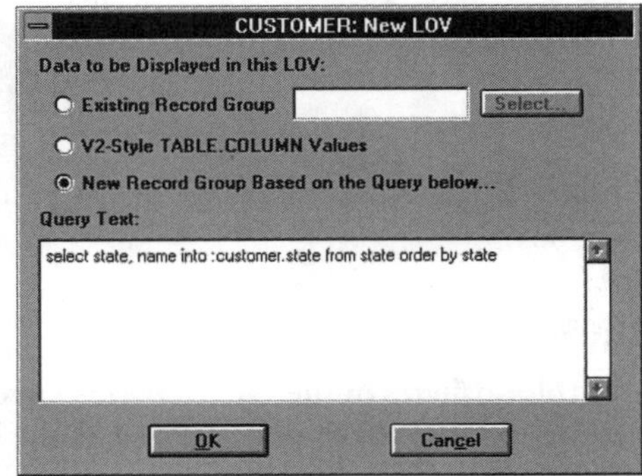

FIGURE 8.32.
The New LOV dialog box shown with a query entered.

Notice that the SQL statement in Figure 8.32 contains an `order by` clause. The `where` clause is also supported for restricting lists of values. Once the LOV is initially defined, you can use the Properties window to add a title and to set the size and location of the display window. In the Properties window, you can also review and modify the column mapping as well as the title and width of the columns displayed for the LOV using the LOV Column Mapping dialog box, as shown in Figure 8.33.

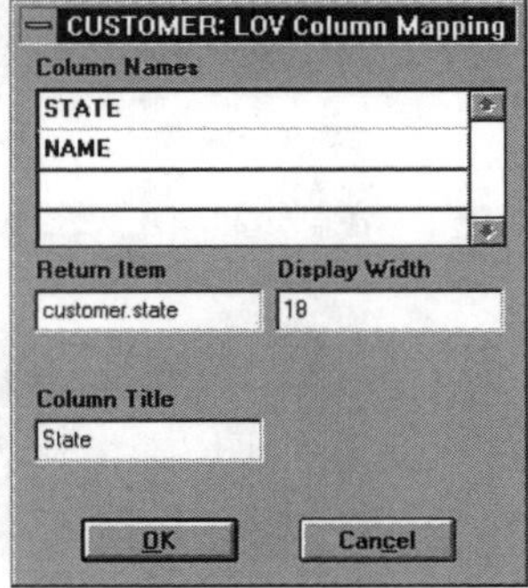

FIGURE 8.33.
The LOV Column Mapping dialog box.

In order for a LOV to be used, it must be referenced by the text item via the LOV property. Also, to provide a drop-down button for the list, the button and the associated WHEN-BUTTON-PRESSED trigger must be created because there is currently no property for including a default list button.

At runtime the list can be invoked from within the application with the F9 key or by selecting the drop-down button, as shown in Figure 8.34.

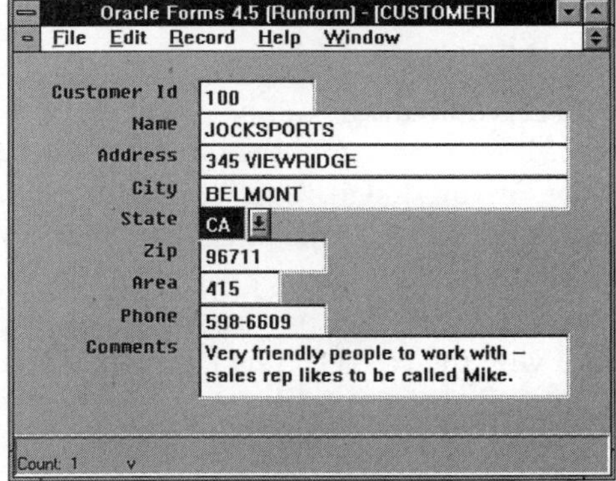

FIGURE 8.34.
A form with a LOV button for states.

When the LOV is selected, a dialog box is presented as shown in Figure 8.35. This dialog box lists values for the current item.

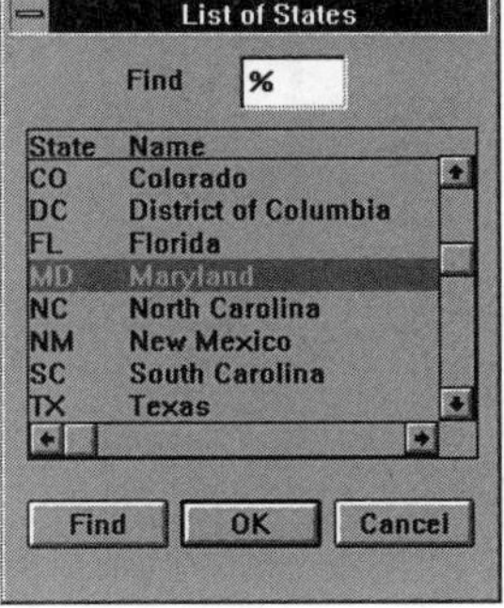

FIGURE 8.35.
The list of states from the LOV selection.

LOV dialogs have a built-in auto-reduce feature that narrows the selections as characters are typed by the user. The Find field may also be used to search for items in the list, and it supports the `%` wildcard as a substitute for the rest of the text string.

The PL/SQL Editor

Oracle Forms Designer is capable of creating robust applications with little or no coding. Your Forms applications can include validation generated by the Designer interrogating constraints in the database. In addition, master-detail block synchronization is automatically managed, and multi-row blocks as well as lists of values can easily be created without writing PL/SQL code.

But, your application's functionality can be extended using the PL/SQL Editor in Oracle Forms Designer. The PL/SQL Editor is automatically invoked whenever you create a trigger or program unit, and it supports incremental compilation of the source code. With incremental compilation, you get immediate feedback on any errors you may have, and the generation of the form's executable is much quicker.

Often, functional requirements can be coded as database constraints and/or procedures that can be referenced from the application. Oracle Forms also supports libraries for PL/SQL objects. Therefore, as you design your application, choose the appropriate place to put your PL/SQL code. Build as much functional definition into the database as possible. Use libraries for code that will be used by many applications. Write code for triggers and program units at the application level when they only support the current application. Figure 8.36 shows the PL/SQL Editor with the HIGHLIGHT_CUR_ITEM procedure successfully compiled.

FIGURE 8.36.
The PL/SQL Editor shown with a procedure.

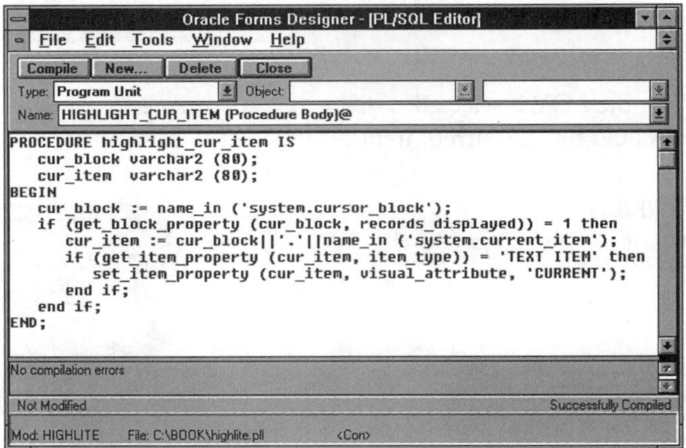

Notice the use of the `NAME_IN` function in the procedure shown in Figure 8.36. The `NAME_IN` function is used so that form objects may be referenced indirectly. Since there is no direct reference to any form-level objects, the PL/SQL code may be stored in libraries outside of the form module.

The PL/SQL Editor supports the creation and maintenance of application triggers and program units. Program units include procedures, functions, and packages. Database program units and triggers can also be created in Oracle Forms Designer. But, the Tools menu does not include menu items to invoke the Stored Program Unit Editor or the Database Trigger dialog box. However, selecting the Stored Program Units or Triggers nodes in the Object Navigator and then selecting Create will invoke the respective interface.

PL/SQL objects can be created and maintained using a variety of products, including any of the Oracle Developer/2000 Designers, Oracle Procedure Builder, SQL*DBA, and SQL*Plus.

Defaulting in Oracle Forms

As mentioned previously, the defaulting capabilities within Oracle Forms are extremely powerful. When Oracle Forms Designer is opened, the form module and window are already defaulted. In addition, just by selecting the canvas-view node, a default canvas-view is created, and when you create an item for the first time via the Layout Editor, a block is created as well. Even the names and properties of new items are set to default values. You only need to change the name and a few properties of the default objects to create a working Forms application.

Here we will review several different forms objects that can be created by default, including blocks, items, relations, triggers, and record groups.

Default Blocks

Default blocks are initiated in Oracle Forms Designer using either the New Block menu item on the Tools menu or by creating an object in the Blocks node of the Object Navigator. In either case, the result is the invocation of the New Block Options dialog box. (See Figure 8.37.)

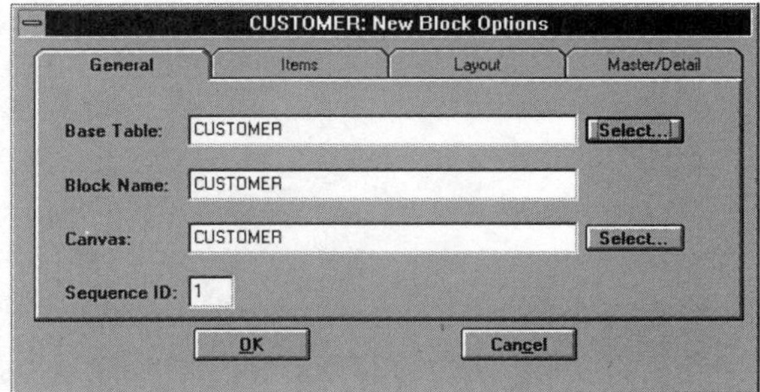

FIGURE 8.37.
The New Block Options dialog box.

The New Block Options dialog box is a tabbed window with tabs for General, Layout, Items, and Master/Detail block information. In the General tab area, a base table may be specified. The block name and canvas will be set by default, but they can be changed if necessary. When creating a base table block, you will also want to select the items to be included.

Default Items

In the Items tab of the New Block Options dialog box is a button to select all the columns from the base table. By default, most columns are included in the layout as text items.

> **NOTE**
>
> The default item type for a long raw column is Image. You should change the item type to Custom Item if you are using this column to store an OLE2 object like an MS Word document.

All items are assigned a label and width based on the column name and definition, respectively. You can change the default label, width, and text type to create a more appropriate layout for your application. (See Figure 8.38.)

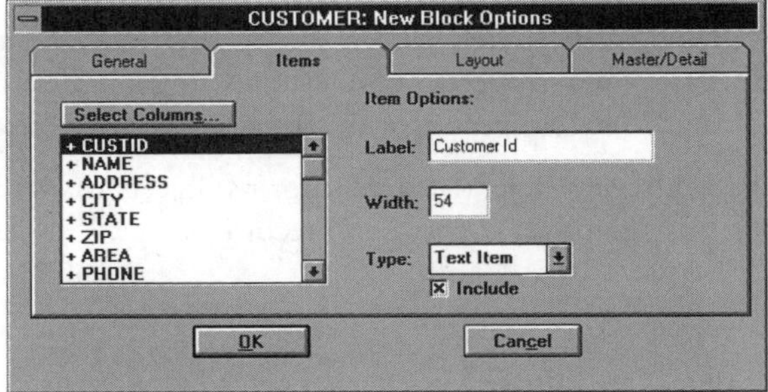

FIGURE 8.38.
The New Block Options dialog box with the Items tab shown.

Once the items have been selected, select the Layout tab of the New Block Options dialog box to determine the way the canvas-view will be populated. (See Figure 8.39.)

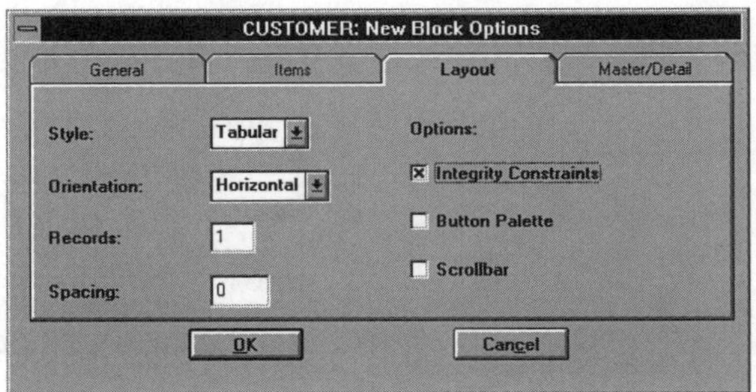

FIGURE 8.39.
The New Block Options dialog box with the Layout tab shown.

By default, the layout style is Tabular, which is good for most Forms applications. The other style is Form, which is a two-column layout. The orientation defaults to Horizontal, which is used for multi-row blocks. For single-row blocks, use the Vertical orientation. The number of records to be displayed and the spacing between records can also be set here. Select the Scrollbar for multi-row blocks, and select Integrity Constraints to have Oracle Forms Designer generate triggers from rules defined in the Oracle database.

TIP

Don't use the Button Palette option for your blocks. Instead, use a toolbar that includes Query, Save, Scroll, and many other features. The toolbar demo or the toolbar from this book are both better choices than the default Button palette.

Default Relations

When you create a master/detail application, Oracle Forms will automatically create a relation joining the two blocks. As a developer, all you do is specify the join condition in the Master/Detail area of the New Block Options dialog box, as shown in Figure 8.40.

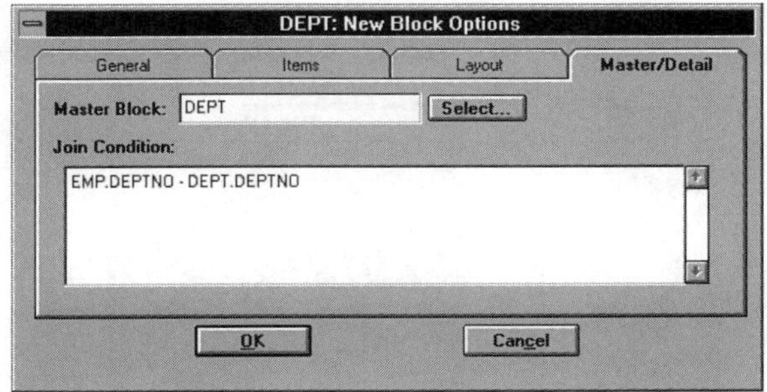

FIGURE 8.40.
The New Block Options dialog box with the Master/Detail tab shown.

The master block contains a reference to the relationship to the detail block, as can be seen in the Object Navigator. (See Figure 8.41.)

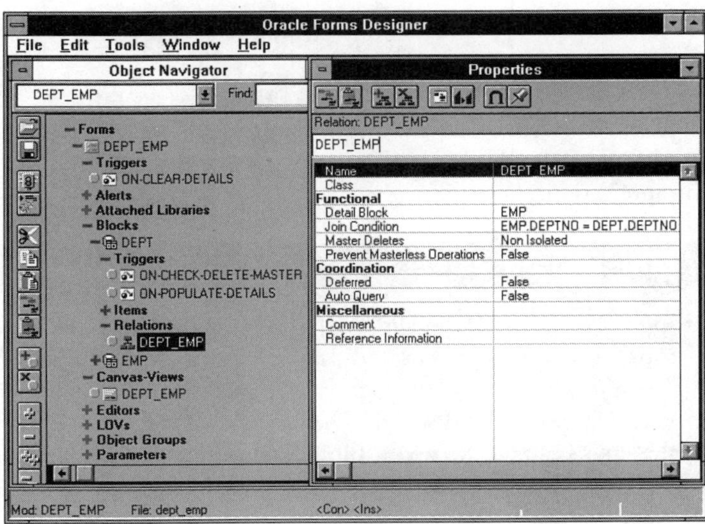

FIGURE 8.41.
A relation shown in Oracle Forms Designer.

The properties of the relation can be reviewed and modified in the Properties window, also shown in Figure 8.41. When a master/detail relationship is defined, program units and triggers are created. In Figure 8.41, notice the triggers in the Object Navigator. The ON-CHECK-DELETE-MASTER, ON-POPULATE-DETAILS, and the form level ON-CLEAR-DETAILS triggers all support the default functionality of master/detail blocks.

Default Triggers

As mentioned previously, Oracle Forms Designer creates triggers automatically for your applications, to provide excellent default capabilities. In Figure 8.42, the ON-CHECK-DELETE-MASTER trigger that was created by default is shown in the Object Navigator and the PL/SQL Editor.

FIGURE 8.42.
The default ON-CHECK-DELETE-MASTER trigger.

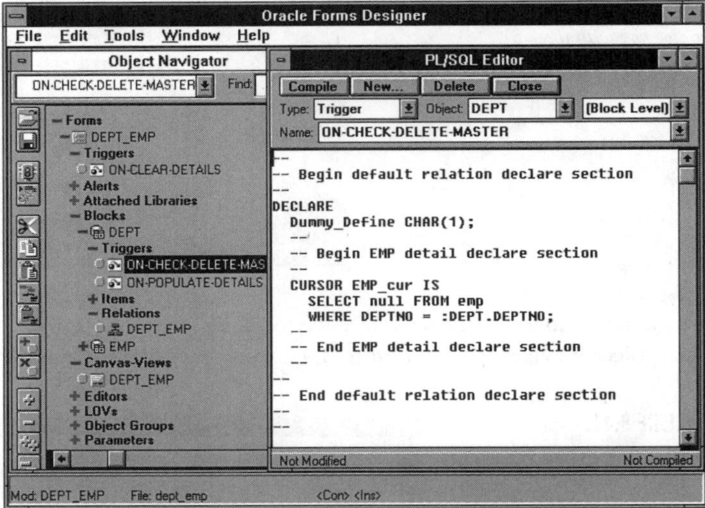

In addition to supporting relations, integrity constraints can also be enforced automatically in the application.

> **NOTE**
>
> A good database design and implementation in Oracle7 is an excellent foundation for supporting the functional and data requirements of your systems. Oracle Forms Designer will leverage the definitions from the Oracle dictionary to create triggers that will enforce constraints in the client-side applications. Client-side validation means that items can be checked without having to attempt to commit to the database.

Oracle Forms will create triggers to enforce the following database constraints:

- Primary key
- Unique key
- Foreign key
- Check
- Not null

This is done by selecting Integrity Constraints in the New Block Options dialog box.

Default Record Groups

Record groups can be created by Oracle Forms by default when a list of values (LOV) is created; they can also be created manually using the Object Navigator.

TIP

I find it easier to just create the LOV and let Oracle Forms default the record group for me. Then I just change the name of the record group to match the LOV name.

Keep in mind that record groups can contain static values or be populated from queries. Either type of record group may be referenced by more than one item and may be defaulted by creating the corresponding LOV first. In Figure 8.43, the record group for STATE is shown in the Object Navigator and the Properties window after being created from the LOV.

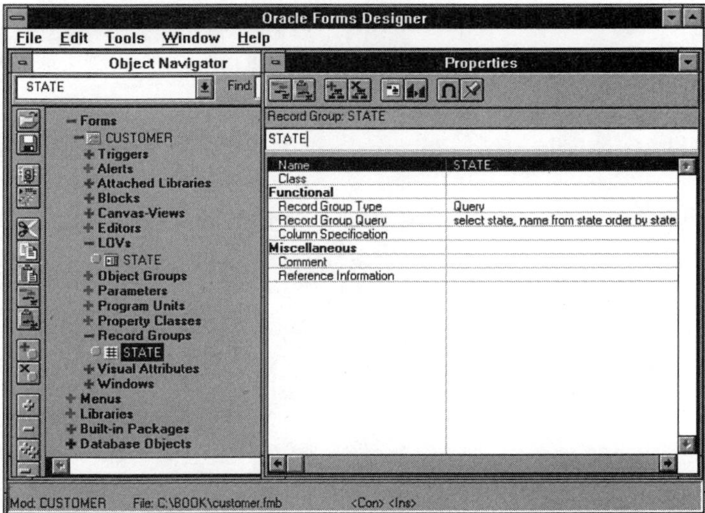

FIGURE 8.43.
A record group shown in Oracle Forms Designer.

The record group can be modified from the Properties window, including changing the query and column specification.

Menu Editor

The Menu Editor is an integrated component of Oracle Forms Designer. This means that you can create the menu for your application at the same time that you are developing the form modules. The Object Navigator, Properties window, and PL/SQL Editor provide the same functionality for developing menus as they do for developing forms. Oracle Forms Designer is shown with each of these windows open in Figure 8.44.

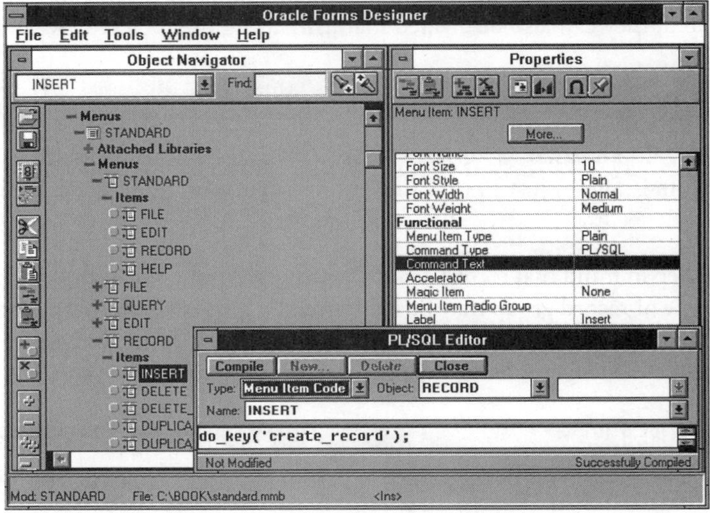

FIGURE 8.44.
The Oracle Forms Designer with menu objects.

The Menu Editor is an additional tool that can be found on the Tools menu. (See Figure 8.45.)

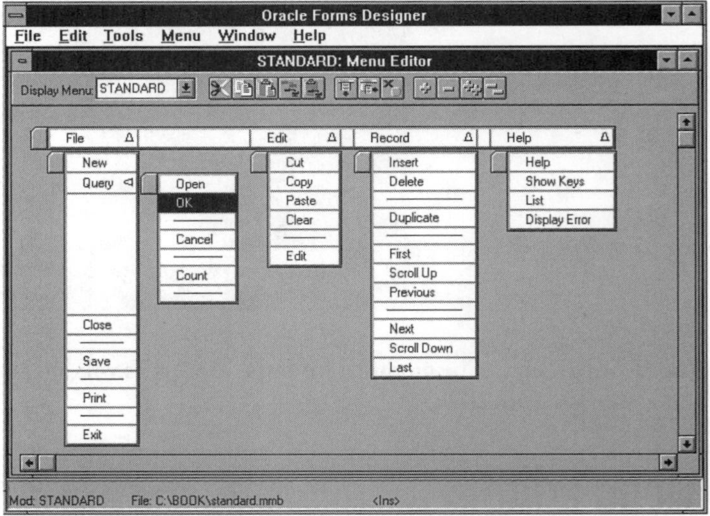

FIGURE 8.45.
The Menu Editor.

The Menu Editor is much more visual and intuitive than the previous versions in Oracle Forms. In Figure 8.45, the layout displays the menu just as it will look during execution of the application. The arrow symbols on parent-menu items expand and collapse the submenus with a click of the mouse. The toolbar at the top of the editor provides a quick and easy interface for developing your menu.

Menu items can be plain, check, radio, separator, or magic items. The Menu Item Type property is set in the Properties window. You may recognize the Check and Radio Style menu items, as they are used in Oracle Forms Designer. The PL/SQL Editor is invoked with a click on the More button when the Command Text property is selected.

Libraries

As mentioned previously, libraries are PL/SQL program units just like the ones in Oracle Forms and in the Oracle database. The only difference is the scope of objects that may be referenced, where the PL/SQL is stored, and how the code is made available to Oracle Forms. Libraries are attached to the form module, but they may start out as program units in the form module or database and later be moved into a library.

When you have procedures, functions, and/or packages that can be used by many Forms applications, it is a good idea to put them in a library. Libraries can also contain their own attached libraries, so you can organize your source code as appropriate.

Oracle provides special functions for indirectly referencing objects in your PL/SQL code. The `NAME_IN` and `COPY` functions enable you to place code into external libraries that reference Forms objects. Oracle also provides the OG.PLL library to support Oracle Graphics, as well as some others that can be found in the \ORAWIN\FORMS45\PLSQLLIB directory.

Exercise

The purpose of this exercise is to familiarize you with the Oracle Forms Designer. In addition to getting a hands-on review of the material just covered in this chapter, you will create a Forms application, a menu, and a library.

Forms

In this exercise you will create a simple application to maintain information on customers.

1. Open Oracle Forms Designer.
2. Click on the menu and review each menu item in the File, Edit, Tools, Navigator, Window, and Help menus.
3. Review the Forms object types in the Object Navigator.

4. Connect to the Oracle database as scott/tiger by selecting Connect from the File menu.
5. Rename the module for your application CUSTOMER.
6. Select Save As from the File menu and save the form as CUSTOMER.FMB.
7. Rename the window CUSTOMER.
8. Double-click the gray plus sign to the left of canvas-views in the Object Navigator. Notice a canvas-view is created.
9. Rename the canvas-view CUSTOMER.
10. Now, double-click the Canvas-View icon. The Layout Editor appears for the canvas. Review the menu as it has changed from Navigator to View, Format, and Arrange.
11. Select New Block from the Tools menu to create a default block.
12. Enter `customer` in the Base Table field and press the tab key.
13. Notice that the block name and canvas are set by default to Customer.
14. Click the Items tab and the Select Columns button.
15. Change the label for CUSTID to Customer ID.
16. Scroll down to the bottom of the list of columns.
17. Double-click REPID and CREDITLIMIT so that they will not be included in the layout.
18. Click the Layout tab, change the Orientation to Horizontal, and click OK to create the default block.
19. Maximize the Layout Editor window.
20. Double-click the Comment item to invoke the Properties window, and change the height from 17 to 34 so that the comment is two lines high.
21. Scroll down to the Multi-Line property and double-click to change the False to True.
22. Return to the layout by selecting Layout Editor from the Tools menu.
23. Shift+click on Name, Address, and City to select these.
24. Select Size Objects from the Arrange menu, set Width to Smallest, and click OK.
25. Select the Save and Run icons from the toolbar.
26. When Runform appears, press F8 to execute a query.
27. Use the down- and up-arrow keys to scroll through the records selected.
28. Select Exit from the Action menu to return to Oracle Forms Designer.

Menus

In this exercise you will create a standard menu that will include some basic menu items, and will be completed later in this book.

1. Select Object Navigator from the Tools menu and collapse the expanded form module.
2. Create a menu in the Object Navigator by double-clicking the gray plus sign of the Menu node.
3. Rename the menu module to STANDARD.
4. Select Save As from the File menu and save the menu as standard.mmb.
5. Double-click the menu icon to invoke the Menu Editor and automatically create a MAIN_MENU with MENU_ITEM1 for your menu.
6. Click the Menu menu, and review each menu item.
7. Review the Menu Editor toolbar using bubble help.
8. Rename the new menu item as File.
9. Create a new menu item by clicking Create Right from the toolbar, and rename it as Edit.
10. Create a new menu item by clicking Create Down from the toolbar, and rename it as Cut.
11. Create menu items under File for New, Save, and Exit.
12. Create menu items under Edit for Edit, Cut, Copy, and Paste.
13. Double-click the Save menu item to invoke the Properties window.
14. Select Command Text and the More button to invoke the PL/SQL Editor.
15. Type `commit;`, click the Compile button and then the Close button.
16. Double-click the Exit menu item to invoke the Properties window.
17. Select Command Text and the More button.
18. Type `exit_form;`, click the Compile button and then the Close button.
19. Save and Generate the menu from the keyboard with Ctrl+S and Ctrl+T, respectively.
20. Double-click the form icon for CUSTOMER to invoke the Properties window for the form module.
21. Set the Menu Module property to STANDARD.
22. Run the application and notice the new menu, then close Runform by selecting Exit from the File menu.

Libraries

In this exercise you will create a library containing several procedures that will be used to highlight fields in a form.

1. Navigate to the Libraries node in the Object Navigator.
2. Create a library in the Object Navigator by double-clicking the gray plus sign of the Libraries node.

3. Double-click the gray plus sign of the Program Units node to invoke the New Program Unit dialog box.
4. Type `highlight_cur_item` as the procedure name, and click OK.
5. Enter the following text in the PL/SQL Editor:

```
PROCEDURE highlight_cur_item IS
   cur_block varchar2 (80);
   cur_item  varchar2 (80);
BEGIN
   cur_block := name_in ('system.cursor_block');
   if (get_block_property (cur_block, records_displayed)) = 1 then
      cur_item := cur_block¦¦'.'¦¦name_in ('system.current_item');
if (get_item_property (cur_item, item_type)) = 'TEXT ITEM' then
         set_item_property (cur_item, visual_attribute, 'CURRENT');
      end if;
   end if;
END;
```

6. Click Compile and then New to create another procedure called `post_highlight_item`.
7. Enter the following text in the PL/SQL Editor:

```
PROCEDURE post_highlight_item IS
   cur_block varchar2 (80);
   cur_item  varchar2 (80);
BEGIN
   cur_block := name_in ('system.cursor_block');
   if (get_block_property (cur_block, records_displayed)) = 1 then
      cur_item := cur_block¦¦'.'¦¦name_in ('system.current_item');
if (get_item_property (cur_item, item_type)) = 'TEXT ITEM' then
         set_item_property (cur_item, visual_attribute, 'DEFAULT');
      end if;
   end if;
END;
```

8. Click Compile and then Close to exit the PL/SQL Editor.
9. Select Save As from the File menu and save the library as HIGHLITE.PLL.
10. Expand the form module to reveal the Attached Libraries node in the Object Navigator.
11. Double-click the gray plus sign of the Attached Libraries node to invoke the Attach Library dialog box, and then click the Find button.
12. Select HIGHLITE.PLL from the Open dialog box.
13. Double-click the gray plus sign of the Visual Attributes node to create a new visual attribute, and change the name to DEFAULT.
14. Click the Create button on the Object Navigator's Tool palette to create another visual attribute. Name this one CURRENT.
15. In the Properties window, change the Foreground Color to White and the Background Color to Blue.

16. Double-click the gray plus sign of the Triggers node, and then type `wni` to create a WHEN-NEW-ITEM-INSTANCE trigger and invoke the PL/SQL Editor.
17. Type `highlight_cur_item;` and click the Compile button. Then click the New button and type `pot`, to create a POST-TEXT-ITEM trigger.
18. Type `post_highlight_item;` and click the Compile button. Then click the Close button.
19. Save, then run the application. Notice the items are highlighted as you navigate from one to the next. Close Runform and then close Oracle Forms Designer to end the exercise.

Summary

This chapter provided you with an overview of Oracle Forms, including:

- The components of Oracle Forms
- The basics of Oracle Forms, including modules, windows, canvas-views, blocks, items, and triggers
- Object types in the Object Navigator
- The Forms Designer toolbars
- The Properties window
- The Layout Editor and layout objects
- List of values
- The PL/SQL Editor and PL/SQL objects
- Default blocks, items, relations, triggers, and record groups
- The Menu Editor
- Libraries

If you worked through the exercise, you should have developed a Forms application, a menu, and a library.

Now that you are familiar with the features of Oracle Forms, Chapter 9, "Introducing Oracle Reports," will take a look at the features of Oracle Reports.

9

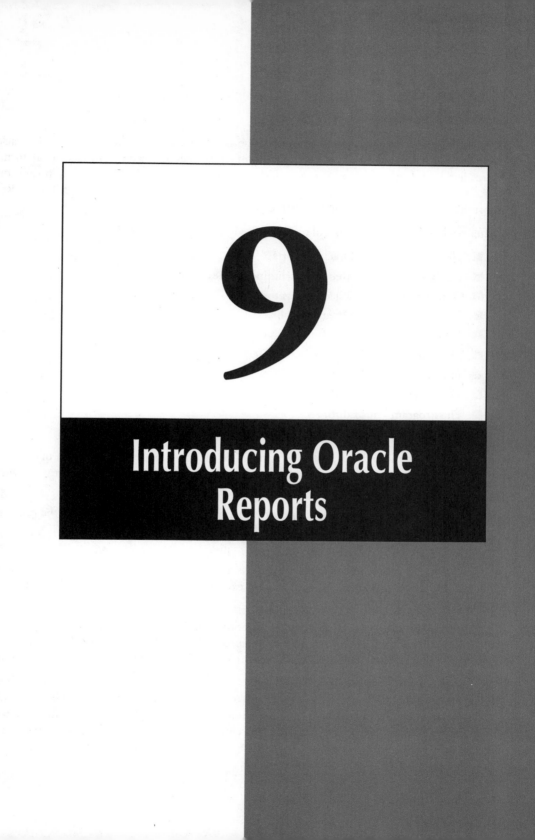

Introducing Oracle Reports

Introduction

Oracle Reports is the report-development environment of Oracle Developer/2000. With Oracle Reports you can create reports in a wide variety of styles, including tabular, master/detail, form, form letter, and matrix. Reports can include OLE2 container objects, providing integration with Oracle Graphics and other MS Windows applications. Like Oracle Forms, Oracle Reports also provides the capability to define libraries of PL/SQL code.

After reading this chapter you will be familiar with:

- The components of Oracle Reports
- The basics of Oracle Reports, including queries, fields, and triggers
- Object types in the Object Navigator
- The Oracle Reports Designer toolbars
- The property sheets
- The Data Model Editor and data objects
- The Layout Editor and layout objects
- The Parameter Form Editor
- The Program Unit Editor
- Defaulting layouts and parameter forms

In the exercise at the end of this chapter you will develop two reports: a tabular list of customers with a page header, and a master/detail report of employees, divided by department, with formula and summary columns.

Oracle Reports is a product that is supported by four components: the Designer, the runtime engine, the converter, and the migration utility.

The Designer is where your report applications will be developed. It is the Designer that will be the primary focus of this chapter, because as a developer, most of your time will be spent there. You can find the Oracle Reports Designer executable R25DES.EXE in the ORACLE\BIN directory.

The runtime engine is where the report application is run from the executable that was generated. You can find the Oracle Reports Runtime executable R25RUN.EXE in the ORACLE\BIN directory. The runtime engine is deployed for the end users, along with the report applications.

The converter can convert the unit of measure or the storage format of an existing report and can generate the 4GL created by the Designer into an executable file, much like Oracle Forms Generator. You can find the Oracle Reports converter executable R25CONV.EXE in the

ORACLE\BIN directory. You will usually generate the executable from within the designer during the development process, just prior to running the report for testing.

The migration utility converts SQL*ReportWriter version 1.1 reports into Oracle Reports format. You can find the Oracle Reports migration utility executable R25MREP.EXE in the ORACLE\BIN directory. You will only need this utility if you are converting existing reports that were created using SQL*ReportWriter.

You build report applications in Oracle Reports by defining queries using the Data Model Editor, laying out the fields using the Layout Editor, and writing triggers using the Program Unit Editor. Oracle Reports Designer incorporates the ability to create reports, libraries, and database objects into one integrated development environment.

An Oracle Reports application is a display or printed presentation of a report containing data items from tables in the database. It can include components integrated with Oracle Graphics or any OLE2 server.

Figure 9.1 shows one of the reports that will be developed later in this book. Notice that the report in the Previewer window contains a title, an OLE2 embedded Excel chart, column labels, database columns, and formula columns.

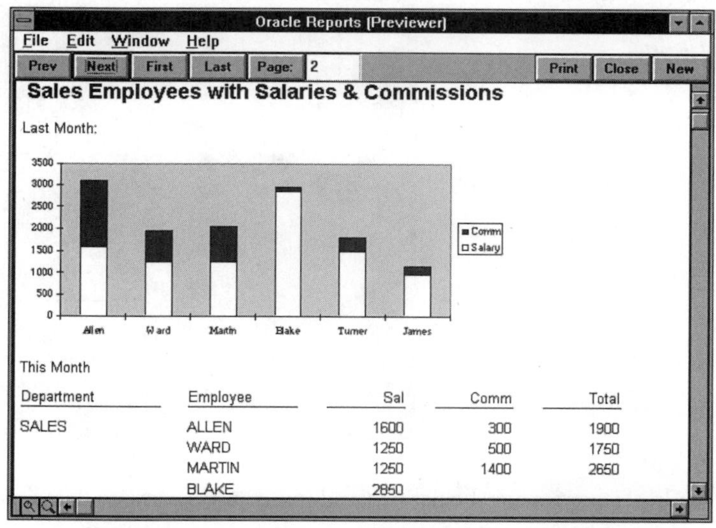

FIGURE 9.1.
An Oracle Reports application.

The development of an Oracle Reports application is accomplished by defining a query and a layout. Within the query you will create groups that contain columns, and within the layout you will create frames that contain fields. A report is capable of executing triggers that use PL/SQL code to carry out special formatting or control operations.

Queries

The development of a report application begins with the definition of a SQL query. The query is defined in the Data Model Editor by clicking the SQL button on the tool palette and drawing it in the layout area. Double-click on the query in the layout, or from the Object Navigator, to invoke the Query dialog box.

TIP

To automatically have the properties dialog boxes invoked when you create an object, just uncheck the Suppress Define Property Sheets option in the Preferences tab of the Tools Options dialog box.

Figure 9.2 shows the Data Model Editor with the Query dialog box containing a SQL select statement.

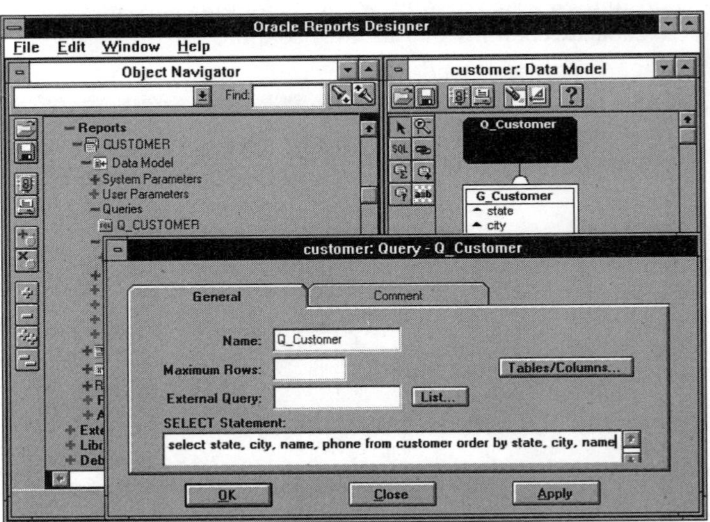

FIGURE 9.2. *The Data Model Editor and the Query dialog box with a SQL select statement.*

Multiple queries may be defined and joined together with data links. When a query is defined, a group containing the query columns is created, as shown in Figure 9.2.

Fields

Once the data model is complete, the selected columns are mapped in the layout. Each column may be referenced by a field in the layout, and each group is referenced by a frame containing the fields. Usually the fields and frames are created by using the Default Layout tool as shown in Figure 9.3.

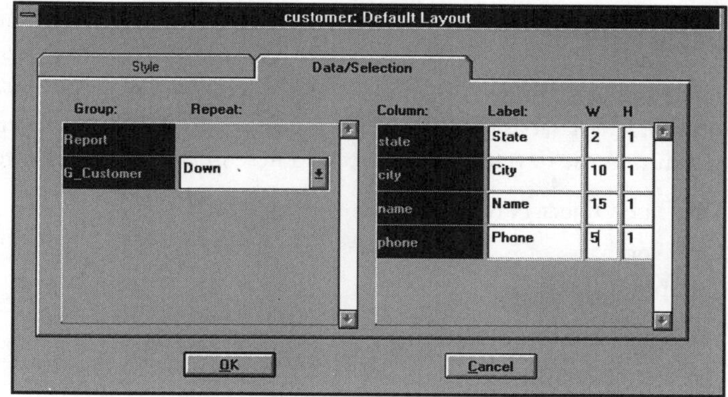

FIGURE 9.3.
The Default Layout showing groups and columns.

Each of the selected groups and columns will be placed in the layout according to the layout style for the report, the repeat direction for the group, and the label and size of the columns.

Triggers

Oracle Reports supports the definition of format and report triggers utilizing PL/SQL and the Program Unit Editor. Format triggers can be defined for each object in the report. Figure 9.4 shows a format trigger for a field.

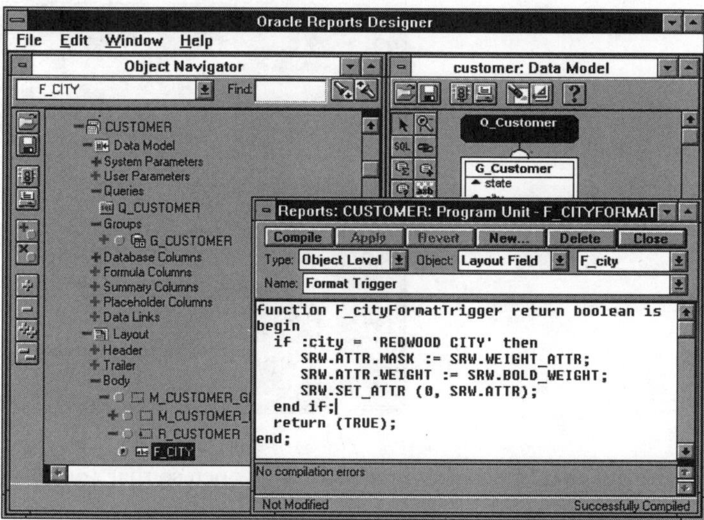

FIGURE 9.4.
The Program Unit Editor showing a format trigger.

You will notice in Figure 9.4 that the Object Navigator shows a letter *P* on the bullet of the city field that contains a PL/SQL format trigger.

Designer

Oracle Reports Designer is an integrated development environment used for creating reports, libraries, and database objects. Within the Designer there are several tools and features that are used during the development process. These items will be reviewed next, and include:

- The Object Navigator
- Toolbars
- Property sheets
- The Data Model Editor
- The Layout Editor
- The Parameter Form
- The Program Unit Editor
- Defaulting

Figure 9.5 shows the Oracle Reports Designer, along with the Object Navigator, the Data Model Editor, the Layout Editor, and the Program Unit Editor.

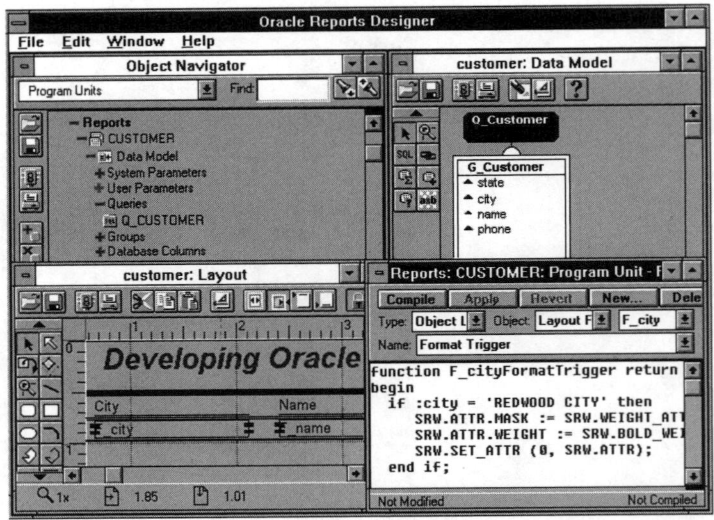

FIGURE 9.5.
The Oracle Reports Designer with tools windows open.

In the designer, multiple windows may be open so that several tools can be used together.

Object Navigators

The Object Navigator was reviewed in Chapter 7, "Introducing Oracle Developer/2000." But Oracle Reports incorporates a few additional features into the Object Navigator that will be reviewed here. In addition, the specific object types within Oracle Reports will be reviewed. Figure 9.6 shows the Oracle Reports Designer window with the Object Navigator displaying the major nodes.

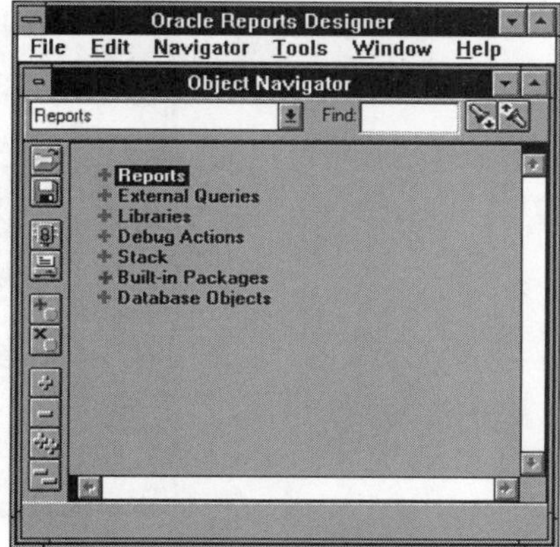

FIGURE 9.6.
The Oracle Reports Designer with the Object Navigator.

The Object Navigator toolbar contains an additional Print button for printing the current report. In addition, the Object Navigator menu contains a check menu item for turning the toolbar in the Object Navigator on and off, and a Navigator Options menu item that invokes the Object Navigator Options dialog box.

You can compile PL/SQL objects from the Object Navigator directly without having to open the Program Unit Editor. This is done by selecting the PL/SQL object from the Object Navigator and selecting the Compile Selection menu item from the Navigator menu.

The major nodes in the Oracle Reports Object Navigator are:

- Reports
- External Queries
- Libraries
- Debug Actions
- Stack
- Built-in Packages
- Database Objects

Report Object Types

While you are in the Object Navigator, you will notice that the objects are organized by type. Under the Reports node, you will find all the object types used for designing report applications. Figure 9.7 shows the Object Navigator with the Reports node expanded.

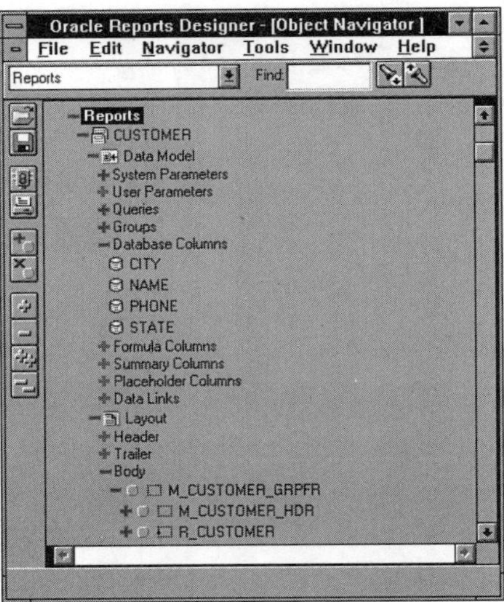

FIGURE 9.7.
The Object Navigator showing report objects.

Oracle Reports supplies many different object types. Each report object type, as it is presented in the Object Navigator, is listed here with a description.

Object Type	*Description*
Module	Defines the report.
Data Model	Invokes the Data Model Editor and contains data objects.
System Parameters	Parameters that are predefined by the system.
User Parameters	Parameters that can be defined by the developer.
Queries	SQL select statements.
Groups	Contains columns for the report.
Database Columns	Columns mapped to columns in the database.
Formula Columns	Columns defined by functions.
Summary Columns	Columns for break and report summaries.
Placeholder Columns	Local variables set via PL/SQL.
Data Links	Join two queries.
Layout	Invokes the Layout Editor and contains layout objects.
Header	The header page(s) preceding the report.
Trailer	The trailer page(s) following the report.
Body	The layout area for the report detail.
Margin	The margin surrounds the body of the report.

Frames	Contain non-database fields.
Repeating Frames	Contain database fields.
Fields	Data items in the layout.
Boilerplate	Static text or graphical items in the layout.
Anchors	Orients layout objects to each other.
Buttons	Used to execute PL/SQL and to activate sounds or images.
OLE2 Objects	OLE2 containers.
Parameter Form	Provides input parameter values at runtime.
Report Triggers	PL/SQL code that fires based on events.
Program Units	Procedures, functions, and packages.
Attached Libraries	PL/SQL code used by multiple applications.

Fields and boilerplate may be found in the layout header, margin, body, or trailer, as well as in the parameter form.

External Query Object Types

Oracle Reports provides the capability to create, save, and reference queries as ASCII files containing SQL select statements. When you create an external query, the External Query Definition window is invoked. (See Figure 9.8.)

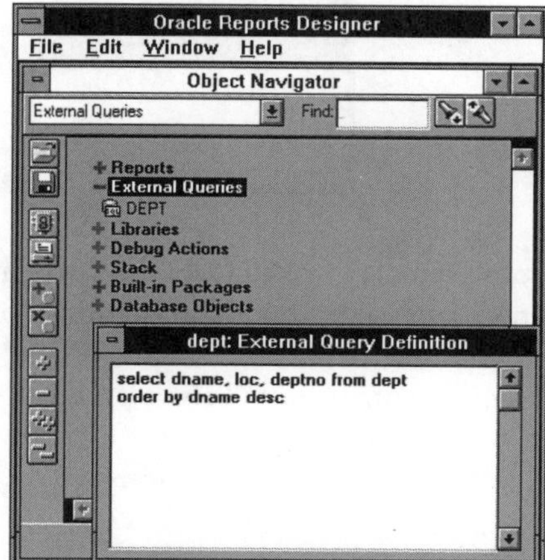

FIGURE 9.8.
The Object Navigator showing an external query.

Queries in the Data Model may reference external queries that have been saved to the file system, or they may contain a local SQL select statement.

Library Object Types

Oracle Reports supports the creation and maintenance of libraries, just as was reviewed in the previous chapter introducing Oracle Forms. Libraries are external to the report and may be saved to the database or the file system. Libraries are then attached to the report, so that the PL/SQL program units may be referenced.

Debug Action Object Types

When debugging your Oracle Reports applications, you will create breakpoints and triggers using the PL/SQL Interpreter. Each of the breakpoints and triggers are associated with a program unit in the report and appear as debug actions in the Object Navigator. (See Figure 9.9.)

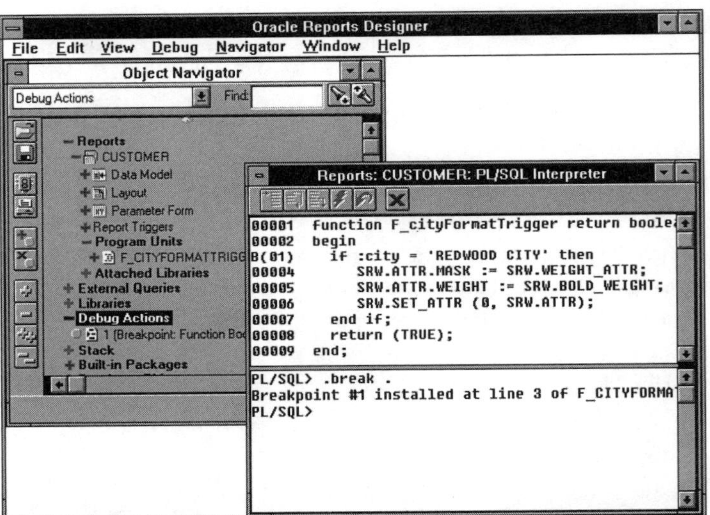

FIGURE 9.9.
The Object Navigator showing debug actions.

The PL/SQL Interpreter is invoked from the Tools menu. The selected program unit will appear in the source frame at the top of the window. Position your cursor at the desired location in the source code, and choose either Break or Trigger from the Debug menu. Double-clicking on a source line will also set a break on that line, while double-clicking again will remove the break. A break will stop the execution of the program unit, and a trigger will execute the PL/SQL code associated with it.

Stack Object Types

When debug actions have been set and the report is run, the PL/SQL Interpreter appears containing the Navigator pane. The Stack node in the Object Navigator will contain a list of each of the program units called and a list of variables with their current values.

Built-in Package Object Types

Under the Built-in Packages node, you will find all of the built-in programs supplied with Oracle Reports. There are several built-in packages, and each one contains a group of supporting functions and procedures. Many of the built-in packages are the same ones found in Oracle Forms. However, Oracle Reports also includes the SRW, LIST, and DEBUG packages. You can find more information on available packages in the Oracle Reports Reference Manual.

Database Object Types

All database objects for each Oracle user are listed under the Database Objects node in the Object Navigator. Database objects include programs, libraries, tables, and views. Having the database objects available from the Oracle Reports Designer provides the developer with an integrated development environment. This means that you don't have to leave the Designer to locate, review, create, or modify database objects that will be used by your report application.

Oracle Reports Designer Toolbars

Each of the common toolbars were reviewed in Chapter 7. Here the Oracle Reports-specific items will be reviewed for each of the toolbars that appear in the Designer.

Data Model Toolbar

The Oracle Reports Data Model Editor includes the Open, Save, Run, and Print buttons on the toolbar, just as on the Object Navigator. In addition, the following buttons also appear:

Button	*Description*
Clear	Deletes the current selection.
Default Layout	Invokes the Default Layout dialog box.
Help	Invokes the Oracle Reports Help System.

The Oracle Reports Data Model Editor is shown in Figure 9.10.

Data Model Tool Palette

The Oracle Reports Data Model Editor also contains a tool palette for creating objects in the data model. The tool palette appears on the left side of the Data Model Editor. The following tools appear on the tool palette, as shown in Figure 9.10:

Button	*Description*
Select	Selects the object in the data model.
Magnify	Doubles the magnification.

continues

Button	Description
Query	Creates a query.
Data Link	Creates a link between two queries.
Summary Column	Creates a column to calculate summary information.
Formula Column	Creates a column containing a formula.
Placeholder Column	Creates a local variable.
Cross Product	Used to create a matrix.

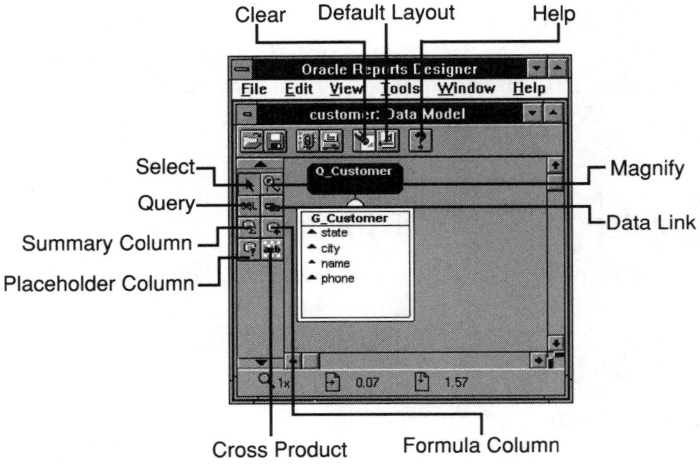

FIGURE 9.10.
The Data Model Editor.

Layout Editor Toolbar

The Oracle Reports Layout Editor contains the standard tools for Open, Save, Run, Print, Cut, Copy, Paste, and Help on the toolbar. In addition, the toolbar contains the following tools, as shown in Figure 9.11:

Button	Description
Default Layout	Invokes the Default Layout dialog box.
Body	Shows the body of the report in the layout.
Margin	Shows the page margin in the layout.
Header	Shows the report header in the layout.
Trailer	Shows the report trailer in the layout.
Confine	Toggles the Confine mode on and off.
Flex	Toggles the Flex mode on and off.

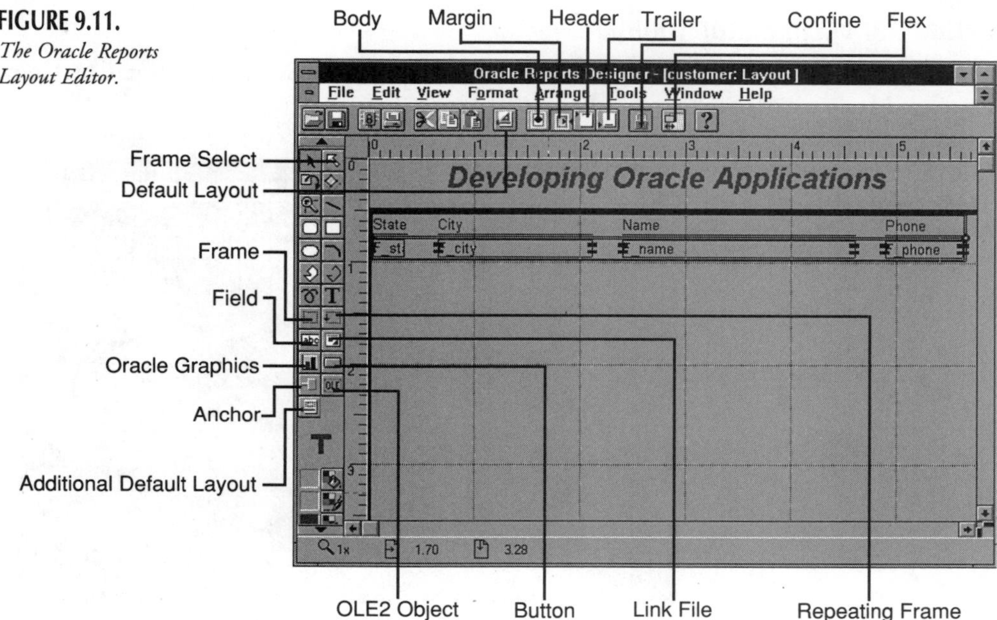

FIGURE 9.11.
The Oracle Reports Layout Editor.

Using Confine mode in the layout will prevent an object from being moved outside of its enclosing frame. The Flex mode will stretch the enclosing frame(s) to allow the movement of objects without having to manually adjust the enclosing frame(s).

Layout Editor Tool Palette

The Oracle Reports Layout Editor contains the following item-drawing tools on the tool palette, as can be seen in Figure 9.11. The tool palette appears on the left side of the Layout Editor.

Button	*Description*
Frame Select	Selects all objects in the frame.
Frame	Creates a frame.
Repeating Frame	Creates a repeating frame.
Field	Creates a display field.
Link File	Inserts a link to a file on the file system.
Oracle Graphics	Creates a chart item for an Oracle Graphics display.
Button	Creates a push-button item.
Anchor	Creates an anchor for two objects.
OLE2 Object	Creates a container for any OLE2 server.
Additional Default Layout	Creates an addition to the layout.

Parameter Form Editor Toolbar

The Parameter Form Editor contains the standard tools for Open, Save, Run, Print, Cut, Copy, Paste, and Help on the toolbar. (See Figure 9.12.)

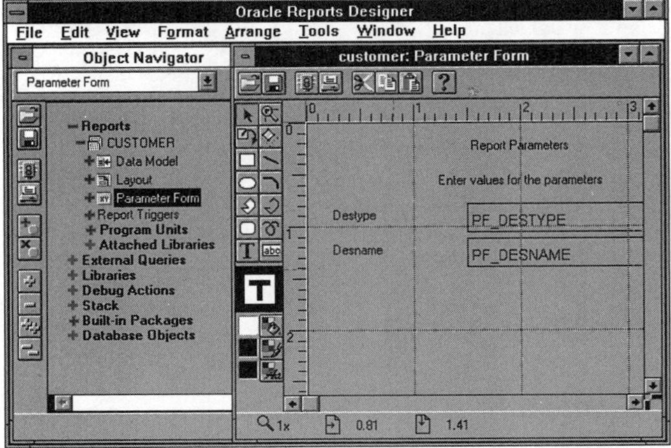

FIGURE 9.12.
The Parameter Form Editor.

Parameter Form Editor Tool Palette

The Oracle Reports Parameter Form Editor contains tools for Select, Magnify, Rotate, Reshape, Rectangle, Line, Ellipse, Arc, Polygon, Polyline, Rounded Rectangle, Freehand, Text, and Field on the tool palette.

Property Sheets

Oracle Reports uses property sheets that appear as tab-controlled dialog boxes for managing object properties. Unlike Oracle Forms, which uses a common Properties window, Oracle Reports uses different property sheets for each object type. An example of a property sheet is shown in Figure 9.13.

All of the properties for each of the Oracle Reports object types are listed in Appendix E, "Oracle Reports Properties." You will notice that almost all property sheets contain a Comment tab. This is used for documenting the application.

NOTE

The property sheets can remain open while you are working in other windows in the Designer. However, they are fixed in size and are therefore often difficult to organize on the desktop without obstructing your work area.

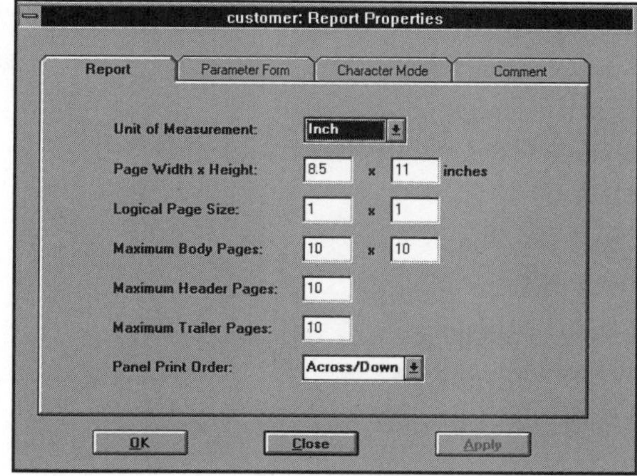

FIGURE 9.13.
The Reports Properties tab-controlled dialog box.

Like the Oracle Forms properties, the Oracle Reports properties are often initialized with default values, and some offer drop-down lists of valid choices.

The Data Model Editor

The definition of each report begins with the creation of a data model, using the Data Model Editor. The data model will contain queries, groups, columns, links, and parameters. The Data Model Editor, containing each of these objects, is shown in Figure 9.14.

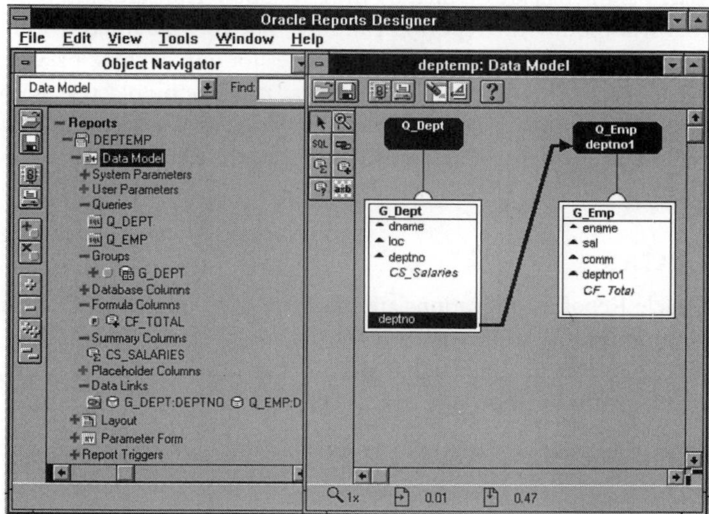

FIGURE 9.14.
The Oracle Reports Data Model Editor.

The data model objects include:

- System parameters
- User parameters
- Queries
- Groups
- Database columns
- Formula columns
- Summary columns
- Placeholder columns
- Data Links

System Parameters

The list of system parameters is predefined by Oracle Reports. They are used to manage the general types of options that might be modified at runtime, such as the number of copies to be printed or the output destination. The commonly used system parameters contain initial values. For example, the default number of copies is one, and the default destination is the screen. The values for any of these parameters may be changed in the Designer via their property sheets or at runtime by placing the parameter on the Parameter form.

User Parameters

User parameters are defined by the developer. They are used to provide the user with options that will modify the report at runtime. The user parameters also can contain initial values as defined during development. The values for any of these parameters may be changed in the Designer via their property sheets or at runtime by placing the parameter on the Parameter form. In addition, a user parameter may be based on a list of static values or on a SQL select statement. The list of values is defined in the Data/Selection tab of the Parameter property sheet.

Queries

Oracle Reports applications are based on SQL queries that return data from the database to your report. Creating a query is the starting point for defining the report. All queries are based on SQL select statements that are either external or local to the report. Figure 9.15 shows the query for the exercise later in this chapter.

Once the query is accepted, a group containing its columns is created in the data model.

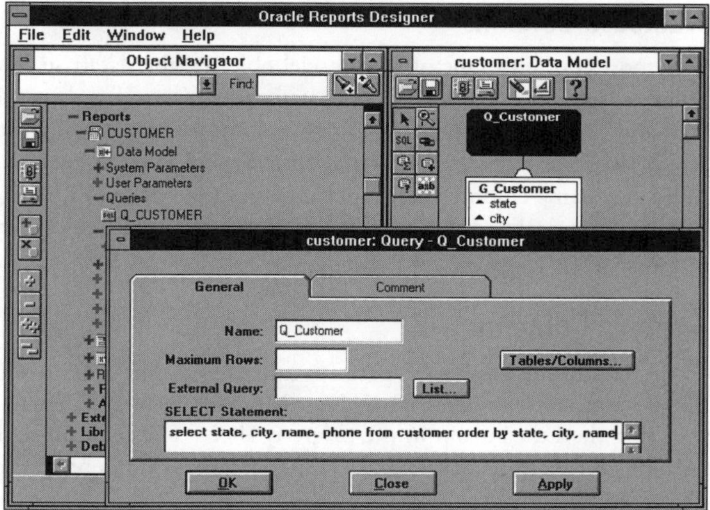

FIGURE 9.15.
The SQL query for the customer report.

Groups

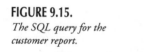

As already mentioned, groups are initially created from queries and are used to organize the data in the report. (See Figure 9.15.) Groups can also be created manually to further organize the data for breaks or subtotals. By clicking and dragging a column outside of an existing group, a new group is created. The creation of addition groups will result in additional frames in the default layout, and additional breaks in the data that is output. Groups may also contain additional columns created in the Data Model Editor. In Figure 9.16, groups are shown containing summary and formula columns.

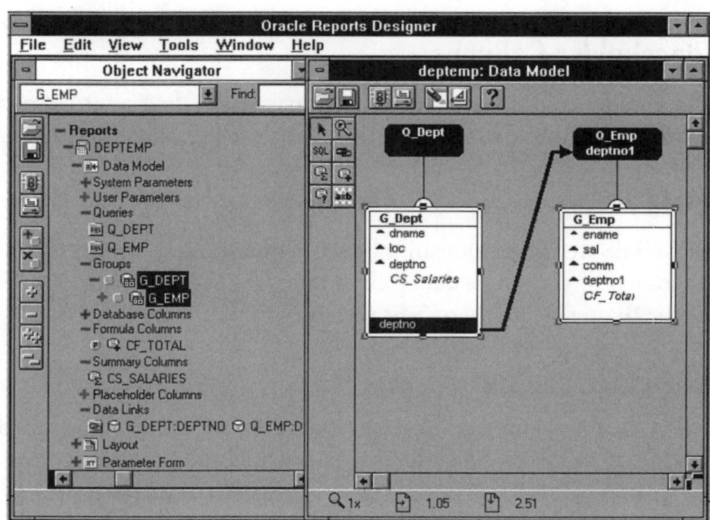

FIGURE 9.16.
The Data Model Editor showing groups.

Database Columns

The most common type of data model object is the database column. It is created from the columns specified in the SQL select statement. You will only get database columns from queries, and you will notice there is no tool on the tool palette to create them independently. The database columns derive their names from the column names, or aliases in the select statement. When the same column name appears more than once in Oracle Reports, it is automatically given a numerical addition to make it unique. Notice the column name is deptno in G_DEPT and deptno1 in G_EMP in Figure 9.16.

Formula Columns

Formula columns are used to perform calculations that contain one or more database columns. They are created manually in the Data Model Editor. Once created, the formula is defined by selecting the Edit button in the property sheet. The Program Unit Editor is invoked, and it contains a function shell. The PL/SQL statements are entered in the begin block and then compiled to complete the process.

NOTE

Many formulas can be defined directly in the SQL statement.

Summary Columns

Summary columns provide support for the aggregation of data values. The Summary Columns property sheet contains a list of available functions, including sum, count, average, first, last, maximum, minimum, percent of total, standard deviation, and variance.

Placeholder Columns

Placeholder columns are not directly mapped to data returned from the query. The values for placeholder columns must be set by the developer in a program unit.

Data Links

Data links define relationships between queries. Any two queries with a common column may be joined by creating a data link in the Data Model Editor. You will create a data link as part of the master/detail exercise at the end of this chapter.

The Layout Editor

All of the display objects in your report applications can be created and detailed in the Layout Editor using the tool palette, the mouse, and the properties sheets. Usually, you would begin working with the Layout Editor after creating a default layout. The default layout is created by defining one or more queries, selecting the layout style, and selecting the columns for the display. Figure 9.17 shows the Layout Editor containing layout objects that were created from a default layout.

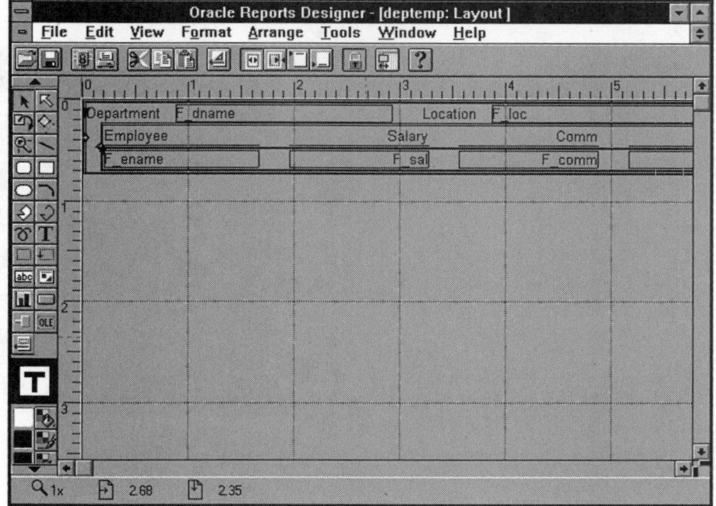

FIGURE 9.17.
The Oracle Reports Layout Editor.

The Oracle Developer/2000 tools use a common layout editor, and each contains layout and boilerplate tools as well as color palettes, as was reviewed in Chapter 7.

The specific item-drawing tools of Oracle Reports include:

- The report header
- The report trailer
- The report body
- The margin
- Frames
- Repeating frames
- Layout fields
- Boilerplate
- Anchors
- Buttons
- Oracle Graphics displays
- OLE2 containers

The Report Header

Report headers are sometimes useful additions to reports. When many different users are sharing a printer in an office, a report header can identify the report and create a separation page between printouts. A report header can be created for your report via the Layout Editor. (See Figure 9.18.)

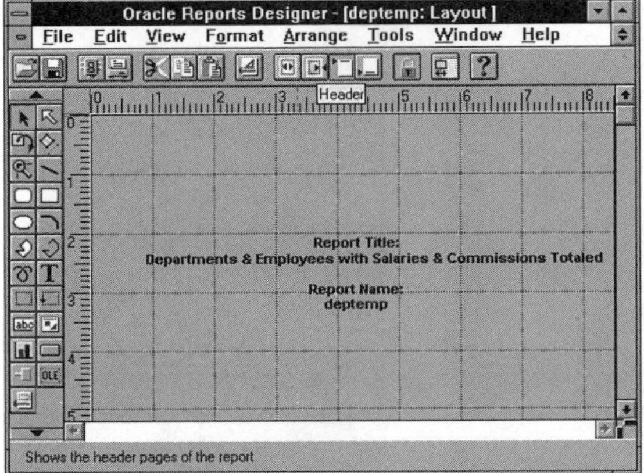

FIGURE 9.18.
The Layout Editor showing the report header.

In Figure 9.18, the report title and name are included as boilerplate text items in the header. Other items can be included as well, such as the date, time, and user ID of the originator.

The Report Trailer

Like report headers, trailers are sometimes useful additions to reports. A report trailer can identify the end of the report and create a separation page between printouts. A report trailer can be created for your report via the Layout Editor. (See Figure 9.19.)

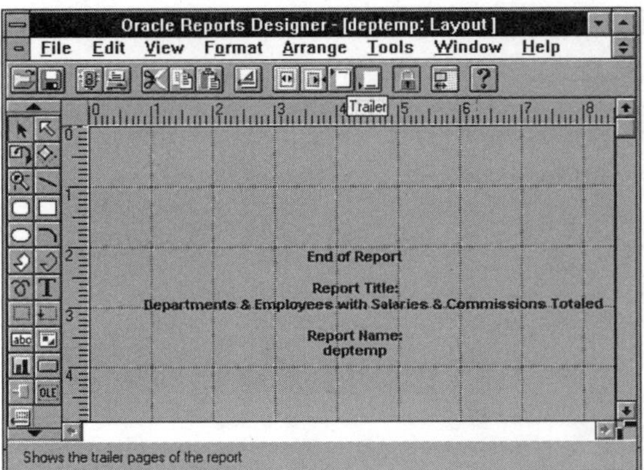

FIGURE 9.19.
The Layout Editor showing the report trailer.

Use the tools on the Layout Editor toolbar to switch between the report header, body, margin, and trailer.

The Report Body

The body of the report is where the data is laid out. Whether the layout objects are created by the default layout or manually in the Layout Editor, the body will contain the bulk of the information provided in your report. Figure 9.20 shows the Layout Editor containing frames, repeating frames, boilerplate text, and fields.

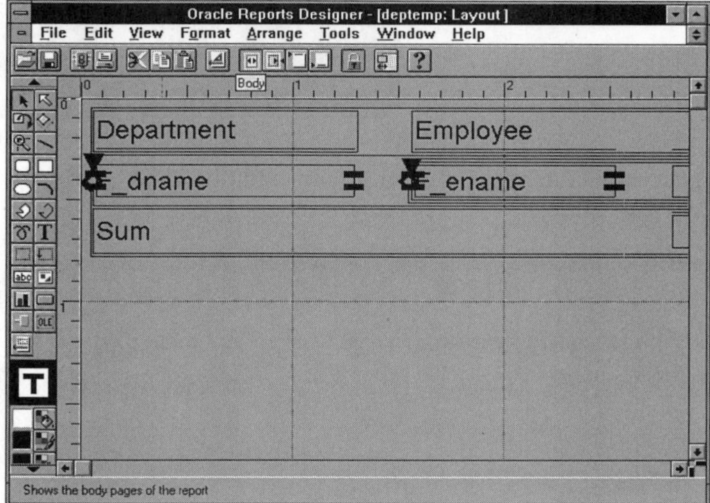

FIGURE 9.20.
The Layout Editor showing the report body.

Notice also in Figure 9.20, that the layout objects appear large. This is the result of increasing the magnification in the layout.

TIP

Enlarging the appearance of objects can be useful when editing, as otherwise the individual objects may be difficult to select.

The Margin

The margin is where page headers and footers can be defined. It also creates space around the report layout. The size of the margin may be adjusted by dragging the handles of the body. The margin is shown containing a boilerplate text item for the page header in Figure 9.21.

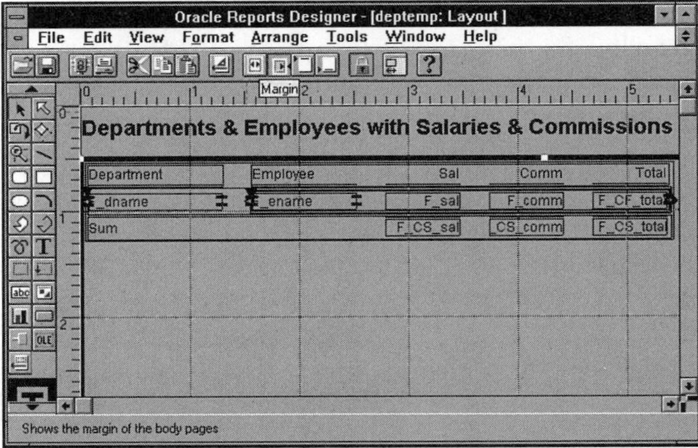

FIGURE 9.21.
The Layout Editor showing the margin.

The margin can contain layout fields in addition to boilerplate. For example, you may want to add page numbers to the bottom of the page.

> **TIP**
>
> While working with the margin, reduce the magnification in the layout to display the entire page.

Frames

A frame is a container for grouping related layout objects in the report. Frames may contain other frames, repeating frames, boilerplate, and fields. In the Layout Editor, frames appear as rectangular lines with diamond symbols on the edges to indicate that the frame can expand.

Repeating Frames

Like a frame, a repeating frame is also a container for grouping related layout objects in the report. And like a frame, repeating frames may contain other frames, repeating frames, boilerplate, and fields. The difference is that repeating frames are used to contain rows of data. In the Layout Editor, frames appear as rectangular lines with down arrows on the edges to indicate repeat direction. Most often you will see data repeated in a downward direction.

Layout Fields

The data returned from the query appears in the layout as fields. But layout fields can also be mapped to parameters, formula columns, summary columns, or placeholder columns. The default layout will create a field in the layout for each column in the data model. You can also create fields in the Layout Editor and map them to any source object. Oracle Reports also provides source objects for the date and page count that can be mapped to layout fields. While most layout fields are found in the body of the report, the header, trailer, and margin can also contain layout fields.

Boilerplate

Oracle Reports provides many types of boilerplate for the layout. Boilerplate text items are used for column headers and labels. Several types of graphics boilerplate are available from the tool palette, including lines, rectangles, and many others. Boilerplate text items and lines are created by the default layout. The label assigned in the Data/Selection tab of the Default Layout dialog box appears as boilerplate text. Files that are linked are also considered to be boilerplate, although the contents of the file could change between runs of the report. Imported text, drawings, or images become static boilerplate objects.

Anchors

Anchors are used to keep objects aligned to one another. Oracle Reports creates implicit anchors automatically at runtime. But you can create explicit anchors to ensure that the two objects are organized in the layout according to your requirements. Each of the objects is attached to the anchor from one of its edges and can be offset by a designated percentage. It is often good to use the property sheet to specify the anchors as collapsible, in order to reduce the space between objects.

Buttons

Buttons can be used to execute PL/SQL or to activate a multimedia object. At runtime the button appears in the Previewer but does not get printed. Buttons may be given a text or iconic label via the Button Face options in the property sheet.

Oracle Graphics Displays

Oracle Graphics displays can be included in your report applications. The display must first be created using Oracle Graphics Designer. By passing a report column as a display parameter to Oracle Graphics, the display can dynamically represent the data in the report. The Oracle Graphics Display property sheet contains the name of the display file as well as a list of all report columns that are available to be passed to Oracle Graphics as parameters.

OLE2 Objects

OLE2 objects are used to contain any OLE2 server object in the application. The OLE2 object may be any object from an OLE2 server that is registered on your system. OLE2 container objects may be embedded in the report or linked to files in the file system.

The Parameter Form Editor

The Parameter Form Editor is used to create and modify parameter forms. A parameter form is used to provide an interface to the user prior to execution of the report. Parameter forms contain parameter fields that are usually set to a default value, but may be changed by the user at runtime. Parameter fields may be used to filter the results of the query, or to modify settings like output destination. The Parameter Form Editor is similar to the Layout Editor in Oracle Reports and Oracle Forms, although parameter forms are very limited in the types of objects they contain. Only parameter fields and boilerplate objects are included in a parameter form, although all of the various types of boilerplate objects are supported. Parameter fields are mapped to system or user parameters. The parameter form may be created by default and/or may be edited in the Parameter Form Editor. Figure 9.22 shows an example of a parameter form created by default.

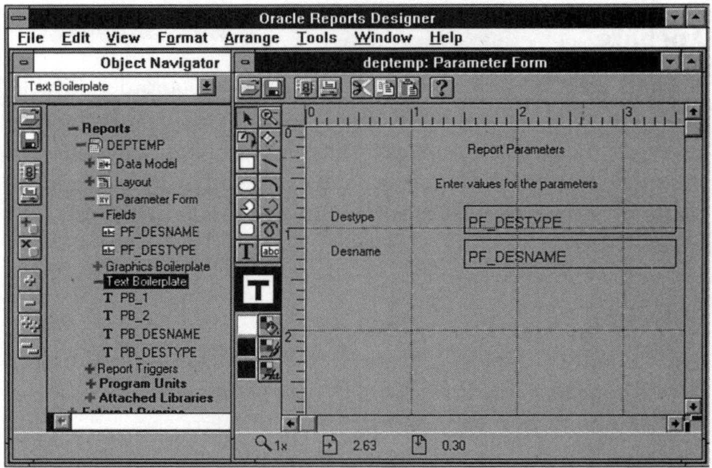

FIGURE 9.22.
The Parameter Form Editor with a default form.

Notice the parameter form contains text boilerplate field labels and parameter fields for the destination type and destination name.

Program Unit Editor

The Program Unit Editor in Oracle Reports is almost identical in appearance and function to the PL/SQL Editor in Oracle Forms that was reviewed in the preceding chapter. One difference is that in Oracle Reports, all PL/SQL objects become program units. Even report triggers are created as functions in the Program Unit Editor. But you will recognize the button bar, the identification fields, the source pane, and the status line as shown in Figure 9.23.

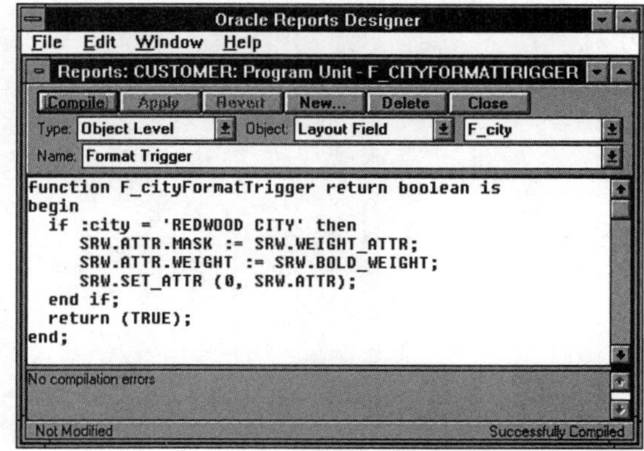

FIGURE 9.23.
The Program Unit Editor.

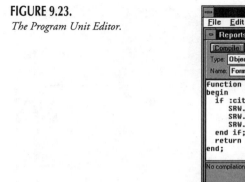

Whether you are creating report triggers, format triggers, procedures, functions, or packages in Oracle Reports, the Program Unit Editor will be where this work is done.

Report Triggers

There are five standard report triggers provided with Oracle Reports. They are *before report*, *after report*, *between pages*, *before parameter form*, and *after parameter form*. As mentioned previously, each of these report triggers are really program units of the type Function Body. But, they are different from other functions in that Oracle Reports manages when they are executed.

Format Triggers

Almost every object in Oracle Reports can contain a format trigger, from frames to fields. Like report triggers, format triggers are functions and are created via the Program Unit Editor. The execution of format triggers is also managed by Oracle Reports. Each time an object is being formatted for output, the associated trigger is executed.

Default Layout

Oracle Reports provides six different report-style formats by default. They include tabular, master/detail, form, form letter, mailing label, and matrix. The default report style is tabular. When the Default Layout dialog box is invoked, select one of the radio buttons to indicate the style of report to create. (See Figure 9.24.)

Notice that each style in the radio group is shown with an iconic example of that style.

Next, select the Data/Selection tab to choose which columns are to be included in the layout. (See Figure 9.25.)

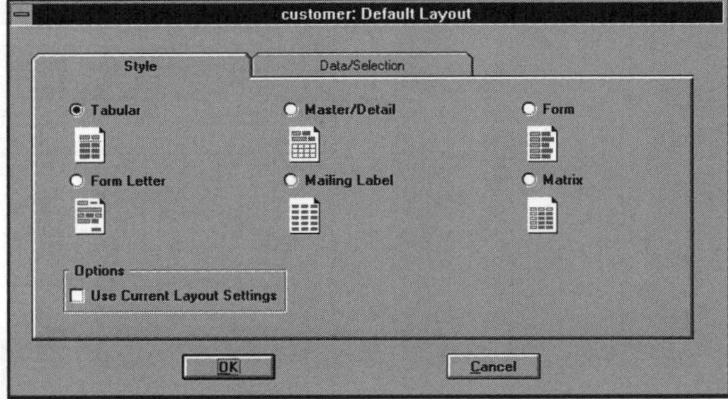

FIGURE 9.24.
The Default Layout dialog box showing the Style tab.

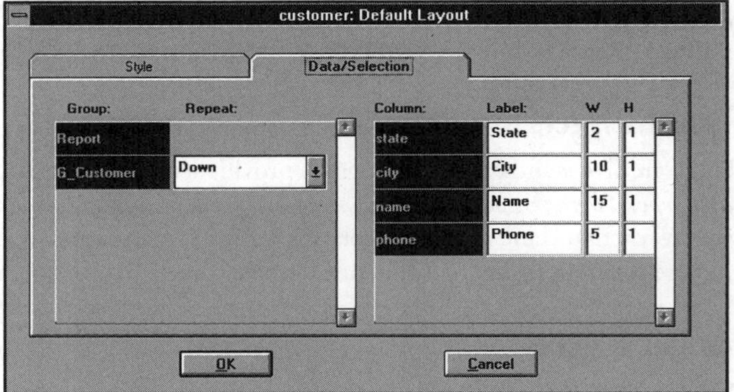

FIGURE 9.25.
The Oracle Reports Default Layout Data/Selection.

By default, all groups containing all columns are selected. The labels for the columns are also defaulted. When a group is deselected, all of the columns that it contains are also deselected. Review, and modify if necessary, which groups and columns to include, the repeat direction of the groups, and the labels, width, and height of the columns.

TIP

Choose the font size and style for your report before you create the default layout. If, after reviewing the results in the Layout Editor, you are not satisfied with the results, re-default the layout, making adjustments to the width of your columns.

Next we will review each of the default layout styles available from the Default Layout dialog box.

Tabular

Tabular reports are the most common style reports. They provide simple columnar lists of data. The Layout Editor is shown in Figure 9.26 with a layout that was defaulted using a tabular style.

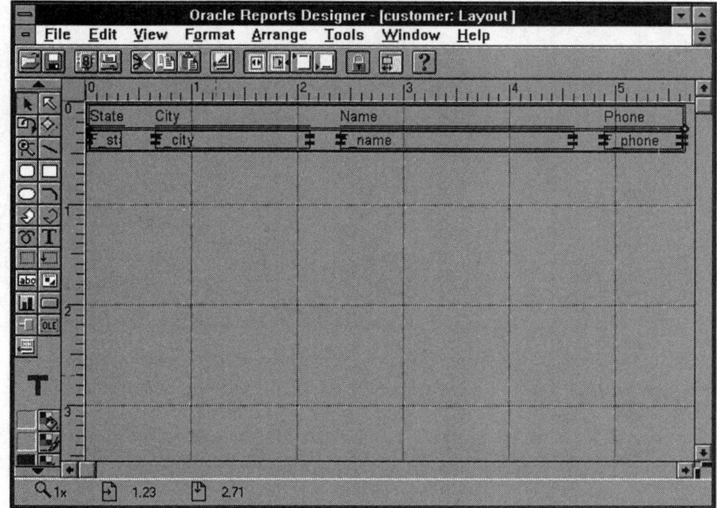

FIGURE 9.26.
A tabular style default layout.

The first part of the exercise at the end of this chapter is to create a tabular report just as in Figure 9.26. Notice in the layout that each field has a column header that was created from the label, and the repeat direction for the group of records displayed is Down.

Master/Detail

Master/detail reports are created from two or more groups of data where one group is dependent on the other. The layout fields of the master group precede the layout fields of the detail group. The second part of this chapter's exercise is to create a master/detail report. The default layout from the master/detail exercise is shown in Figure 9.27.

You will notice in Figure 9.27 that each Designer contains an Object Navigator window, complete with an item.

Form

The form-style default layout organizes each record on a separate page and places the labels on the left side of the fields. The labels and fields are placed on the page from left to right, and then down.

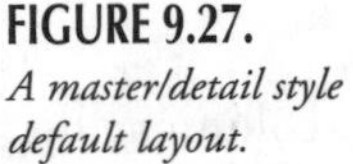

FIGURE 9.27.
A master/detail style default layout.

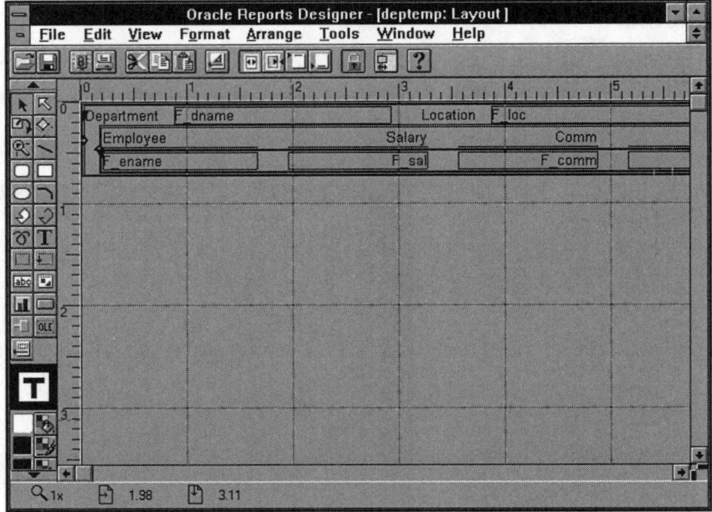

Form Letter

The form-letter style default layout organizes each record on a separate page, but no labels are assigned to the fields. The fields are placed on the page along the right margin and down, but they are not displayed. Instead, a boilerplate text field is created containing a list of reference fields to each of the layout fields. From this default layout, the boilerplate text field may be edited to create the form letter.

Mailing Label

The mailing-label style default layout organizes each record immediately following the preceding record. It does not include field labels. The fields are placed on the page along the left side, and then down. This default will produce a single-column list. Change the repeat direction for the group to produce a multicolumn list.

Matrix

A matrix style default layout creates a report much like a grid or spreadsheet. It includes layout fields as labels across the top and down the left side. Additional layout fields are created where the columns intersect. To create a matrix report, you must first have one or more queries that result in at least three columns and three groups: one for the top label, one for the left side label, and one for the intersection of the other two. In addition, a fourth group must be created in the Data Model Editor that encloses the two label groups.

Default Parameter Form

Just as default layouts are created in Oracle Forms and Oracle Reports, default parameters forms can also be created for your report applications. From the Default Parameter Form dialog box, select the system and/or user parameters that you would like to include. (See Figure 9.28.)

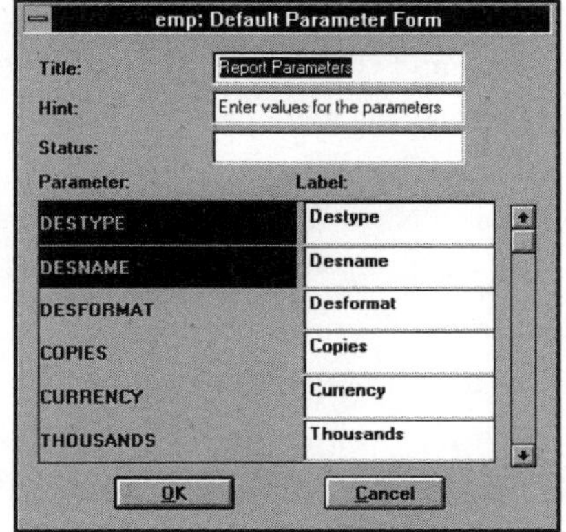

FIGURE 9.28.
The Default Parameter Form dialog box.

Change the default title and labels for your parameter form, then from the Parameter Form Editor make any other cosmetic changes that are necessary.

Exercise

The purpose of this exercise is to familiarize you with Oracle Reports Designer. In addition it will give you some hands-on review of the material that has been covered in this chapter. You will create a tabular report and a master/detail report, make changes in the Designer, and review the reports using the Previewer.

A Tabular Customer Report

In this exercise you will create a tabular report to list information about customers.

1. Open Oracle Reports Designer.
2. Notice the default report is named UNTITLED.
3. Connect to the Oracle database as scott/tiger by selecting Connect from the File menu.
4. Select Save As from the File menu and save the report as CUSTOMER.RDF.
5. Double-click on the Data Model icon in the Object Navigator to invoke the Data Model Editor.

6. Click the SQL Query button on the tool palette, then point, click, and drag in the layout to create a SQL query.
7. Double-click on the query to invoke the Query properties sheet.
8. Change the query name from Q_1 to Q_Customer.
9. Enter the following text in the SELECT Statement field: `select state, city, name, phone from customer order by state, city, name`, and press OK.
10. Notice a group and columns are created in the layout of the data model.
11. Close the Data Model window.
12. Review the query, group, and database column objects created in the data model, using the Object Navigator and the property sheets.
13. Double-click the Layout icon in the Object Navigator to invoke the Layout Editor.
14. Select Font from the Format menu.
15. Set the font to Arial, Regular, 10.
16. Select Default Layout from the Tools menu or the Layout Editor toolbar.
17. Leave the default Style as Tabular, and click the Data/Selection tab.
18. Change the width of City to 10, Name to 15, and Phone to 5, then press OK.
19. Notice the default layout created in the Layout Editor.
20. Review the group frame, header frame, boilerplate, repeating frame, and layout field objects created in the layout, using the Object Navigator and the property sheets.
21. Select Save and then Run from the File menu or from one of the toolbars.
22. Select Run Report from the Runtime Parameter Form.
23. Review the report in the Previewer, and press Close to return to Oracle Reports Designer.
24. Select Tools Options from the Tools menu.
25. Select the Runtime Settings tab, uncheck Parameter Form, and click OK.
26. Select and maximize the Layout Editor.
27. Select Margin from the toolbar.
28. Notice the margin area appears above the layout.
29. Click the Text tool on the tool palette, and create a text item in the upper-left corner of the margin.
30. Type `Developing Oracle Applications` as the text string.
31. Using the Color palettes, set the fill color to No Fill, the line color to No Line, and the text color to Red.
32. Select Font from the Format menu.
33. Set the font to Arial, Bold Italic, 20.

34. Select Alignment, Center from the Format menu.
35. Grab the upper-left corner of the text item and stretch it to the upper-left corner of the margin.
36. Grab the lower-right corner of the text item and stretch it to the right, just above the end of the last layout field.
37. Save, Run, Review, and return to Oracle Reports Designer.

A Master/Detail Department/Employee Report

In this exercise you will create a master/detail report to list employees by department that includes formula and summary columns.

1. Close the current report and create a new one.
2. Select Save As from the File menus and save the report as DEPTEMP.RDF.
3. Invoke the Data Model Editor, create a query, and change the name to Q_Dept.
4. Enter the following text in the SELECT Statement field: `select dname, loc, deptno from dept order by dname desc`, then press OK.
5. Create a query named Q_Emp just to the right of Q_Dept.
6. Enter the following text in the SELECT Statement field: `select ename, sal, comm, deptno from emp`, then press OK.
7. Click the Data Link button on the tool palette, then click on the deptno column in the G_Dept group and drag to the deptno1 column in the G_Emp group.
8. Select Default Layout from the Layout Editor toolbar.
9. Change the default Style to Master/Detail, and click on the Data/Selection tab.
10. Change the label of dname to Department, loc to Location, ename to Employee, and sal to Salary.
11. Click deptno and deptno1 to deselect them, then press OK.
12. Save, run, review, and return to Oracle Reports Designer.
13. Go to the Data Model and click the Formula Column button on the tool palette.
14. Then click in the white space under the deptno1 column in the G_Emp group.
15. Double-click CF_1 to invoke the property sheet, change the name to CF_Total, and click the Edit button to define the formula. You may need to move or close the property sheet to see the Program Unit Editor.
16. In the function shell, just under the begin statement, type `return (:sal + :comm);`. Click the Compile and Close buttons.
17. Select Default Layout from the Layout Editor toolbar.
18. Change the label for CF_Total to Total, then press OK, and select Yes to replace the existing layout.

19. Save, run, review, and return to Oracle Reports Designer.
20. Go to the Data Model, and click the Summary Column button on the tool palette.
21. Then click just under the deptno column in the G_Dept group to create a summary column.
22. Double-click CS_1 to invoke the property sheet, change the name to CS_Salaries, Source to sal, Reset At to G_Dept, and click OK.
23. Select Default Layout from the Layout Editor toolbar.
24. Change the label for CS_Salaries to Salaries, then press OK, and select Yes to replace the existing layout.
25. Save, run, review, and return to Oracle Reports Designer.
26. Go to the Data Model, and click the Summary Column button on the tool palette.
27. Click just under the G_Dept group in the layout and drag to create a report summary column.
28. Double-click CS_1 to invoke the property sheet, change the name to CS_Total_Salaries, Source to sal, and click OK.
29. Select Default Layout from the Layout Editor toolbar.
30. Change the label for CS_Total_Salaries to Total Salaries, then press OK, and select Yes to replace the existing layout.
31. Select the total salaries field in the layout.
32. Select Alignment, Right from the Format menu.
33. Save, run, review, return, and close Oracle Reports Designer to end the exercise.

Summary

This chapter provided you with an overview of Oracle Reports, including:

- The components of Oracle Reports
- The basics of Oracle Reports including: queries, fields, and triggers
- Object types in the Object Navigator
- The Oracle Reports Designer toolbars
- The property sheets
- The Data Model Editor and data objects
- The Layout Editor and layout objects
- The Parameter Form Editor
- The Program Unit Editor
- Defaulting layouts and parameter forms

If you worked through the exercise, you have developed a tabular report and a master/detail report. You should also now know how to add a page header in the margin, as well as how to create formula and summary columns.

Now that you are familiar with the features of Oracle Reports, next we will take a look at the features of Oracle Graphics.

10

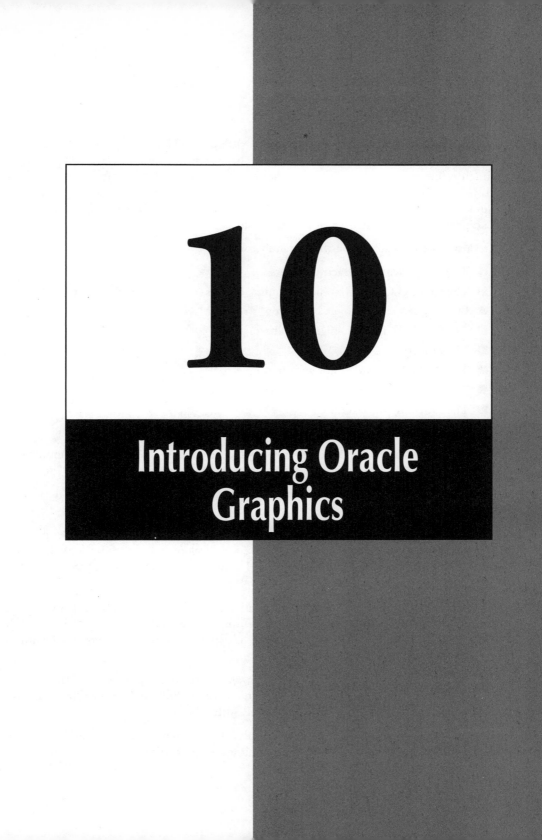

Introducing Oracle Graphics

Introduction

Oracle Graphics is the component of Oracle Developer/2000 that is used to create graphical displays. With Oracle Graphics you can create charts in a wide variety of styles, including column, bar, line, mixed, and pie. Oracle Graphics can include OLE2 container objects and is an OLE2 server, thus providing integration with Oracle Forms, Oracle Reports, and other MS Windows applications. Like Oracle Forms and Oracle Reports, Oracle Graphics also provides the capability to define libraries of PL/SQL code.

After reading this chapter, you will be familiar with:

- The components of Oracle Graphics
- The basics of Oracle Graphics, including queries, charts, templates, and triggers
- Object types in the Object Navigator
- The Oracle Graphics Designer toolbars
- The property sheets
- The Chart Template Editor and chart objects
- The Layout Editor and layout objects
- The Program Unit Editor
- Defaulting charts

In the exercise at the end of this chapter you will develop a pie chart and two column charts. You will also modify chart objects using property sheets and the Layout Editor.

Oracle Graphics is a product that is supported by three components; the Designer, the runtime engine, and the batch engine.

The Designer is where your Graphics applications will be developed. It is the Designer that will be the primary focus of this chapter, because as a developer most of your time will be spent there. You can find the Oracle Graphics Designer executable G25DES.EXE in the ORACLE\BIN directory.

The runtime engine is where the report application is run from the executable that was generated. You can find the Oracle Graphics runtime executable G25RUN.EXE in the ORACLE\BIN directory. The runtime engine is deployed for the end users, along with the graphics applications.

The batch engine enables you to run graphics displays in the background so they can be sent to a printer, file, or database without appearing on the screen. You can find the Oracle Graphics batch executable G25BAT.EXE in the ORACLE\BIN directory.

You build graphics applications in Oracle Graphics by defining queries, selecting a chart type, editing the chart objects using the Layout Editor and property sheets, and writing triggers using the Program Unit Editor. Oracle Graphics Designer incorporates the ability to create displays, libraries, and database objects into one integrated development environment.

An Oracle Graphics application is a display or printed presentation of data items from tables in the database, and it can be integrated with Oracle Forms or Oracle Reports. Oracle Graphics is an OLE2 server, so any OLE2 container can include a display created in Oracle Graphics Designer.

A display that will be developed in the third exercise at the end of this chapter is shown in Figure 10.1. Notice that the display contains a chart title, a plot frame, three-dimensional columns, and an axis label. Also notice that this display is in the Oracle Graphics Runtime window and that this is the same display that was integrated into the sample application in Chapter 8, "Introducing Oracle Forms."

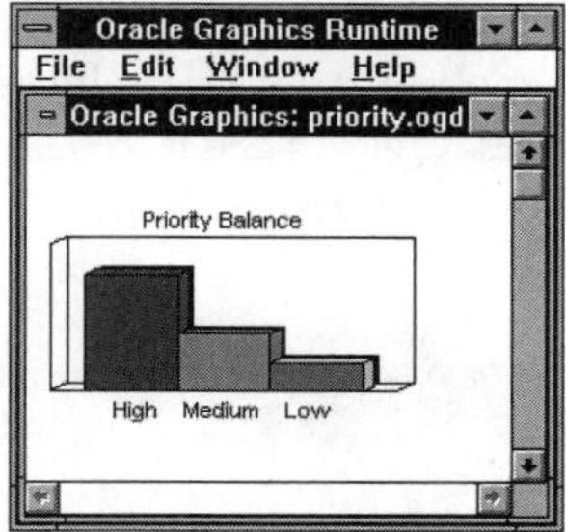

FIGURE 10.1.
An Oracle Graphics display.

The development of a graphics display is accomplished by defining a query and a layout. To create the initial layout, you will use the Chart Properties dialog box, which contains tabs for selecting the chart type, the query for the data, the categories for the X axis, and the values for the Y axis. The layout is further modified via the Layout Editor and property sheets. A display is also capable of executing triggers that use PL/SQL code to carry out special formatting or control operations.

Queries

The development of a chart begins with the definition of a SQL query. A query may be defined in the Query Properties dialog box, which can be invoked from the Object Navigator or the Tools menu. But, Oracle Graphics provides a Chart Genie that will enable you to define the query while you are creating the chart. The Chart Genie appears when the Create Chart menu item is selected from the Chart menu.

In Figure 10.2, the Chart Genie is shown with the Query tab containing a SQL statement from the first exercise at the end of this chapter.

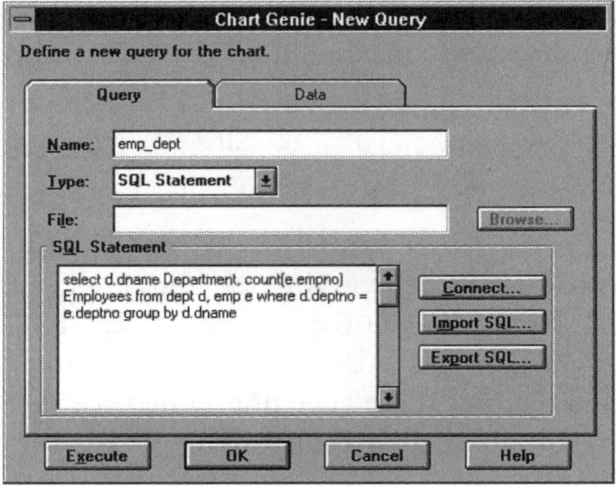

FIGURE 10.2.
The Chart Genie dialog box with the Query tab containing a SQL statement.

You can use the Query Properties dialog box to create queries without creating a chart, or to modify existing queries. Queries can also be developed outside of Oracle Graphics and saved to a file; then they can be referenced from the Query Properties dialog box by the filename or by importing the SQL.

TIP

For complex queries, you may find it easier to develop the query outside of Oracle Graphics. For example, Oracle Procedure Builder or SQL*Plus will give you more information on syntax errors than Oracle Graphics will.

Whichever method you choose to develop your query, the result will be data that is returned to be displayed on an Oracle Graphics chart. The Data tab on the Query Properties dialog box and the Chart Genie dialog box allow you to review the results of the query. The data returned from the query shown in Figure 10.2 is shown in Figure 10.3 in the Data tab of the Chart Genie dialog box.

Charts

As mentioned previously, Oracle Graphics provides the Chart Genie to assist in the development of your displays. Select Create Chart from the Chart menu and the Chart Genie will check to see if there are any existing queries. If so, you will have the option to base the chart on one of the existing queries or to define a new one. When no queries exist in the display, the Chart Genie automatically begins with the New Query dialog box.

Once you have selected a query, the Chart Genie invokes the Chart Properties dialog box to define the default chart type for the layout. The pie chart with depth has been selected for the Employees by Department display in Figure 10.4.

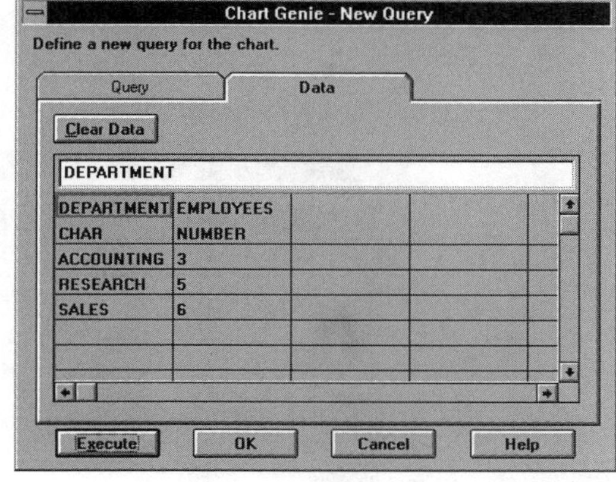

FIGURE 10.3.
The Chart Genie dialog box with the Data tab displaying the results of a SQL statement.

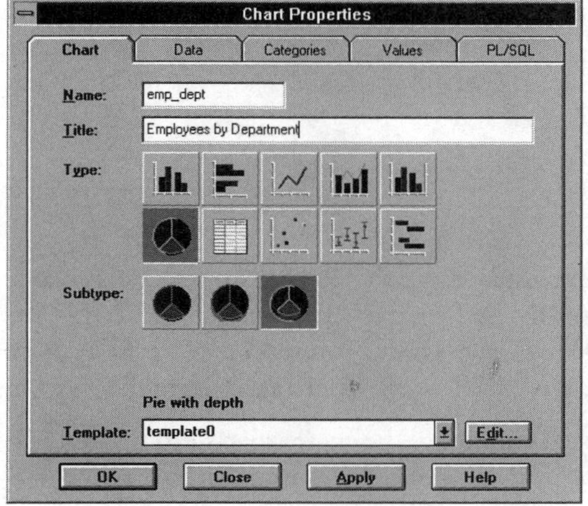

FIGURE 10.4.
The Chart Properties dialog box with a pie chart.

There are 10 different types of charts that can be selected from the Chart Properties' Chart tab. Each chart type has several subtypes. The column, pie, table, and Gantt charts include subtypes for chart frames with shadows and depth. The categories and values for the chart are set by default, but these can be modified via the tabs in the Chart Properties dialog box.

Templates

Oracle Graphics uses templates to define the visual characteristics of the frame and fields in the chart. Each chart type has a default template defined for it. This template will be used unless a new template is created and referenced in the Chart Properties dialog box.

When a change is made to the chart in the layout, the layout changes are recorded automatically in the current template, and these take precedence over the previous values in the template. You can create your own templates using the Object Navigator or the Chart Template Editor. The default column-chart frame template is displayed in the Chart Template Editor in Figure 10.5.

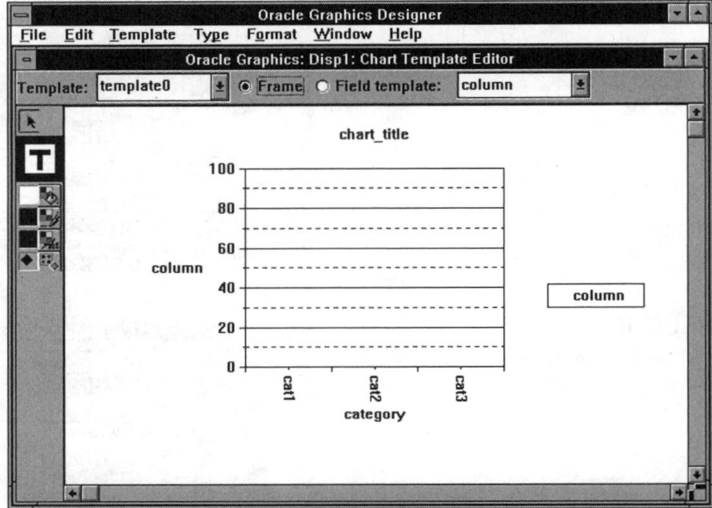

FIGURE 10.5.
The frame in the Chart Template Editor.

All of the templates for the current display are available to be switched to via the Template drop-down list in the upper-left corner of the Chart Template Editor. The frame template can be modified using the frame and axes property sheets that are available from the Template menu. Also, the type of chart can be changed using the Type menu and its iconic submenu items.

The visual attributes of the chart objects can be set using the color palettes in the Chart Template Editor or the Format menu items. The frame and field views are toggled in the editor using the radio buttons at the top of the window. The default column-chart field template is displayed in the Chart Template Editor in Figure 10.6.

The default field template name is the chart type. This name can be changed, and new field templates can be created using the Field Template Properties dialog box by selecting Field Templates from the Template menu.

Triggers

Oracle Graphics supports the definition of format and event triggers utilizing PL/SQL and the Program Unit Editor. Format triggers can be defined for each chart object in the display. Event triggers can be defined for the display, the query, buttons, or timers. Using the Object Navigator, double-click on the trigger icon of any object. The Program Unit Editor is thus invoked, creating a new program unit or providing access to the existing PL/SQL code.

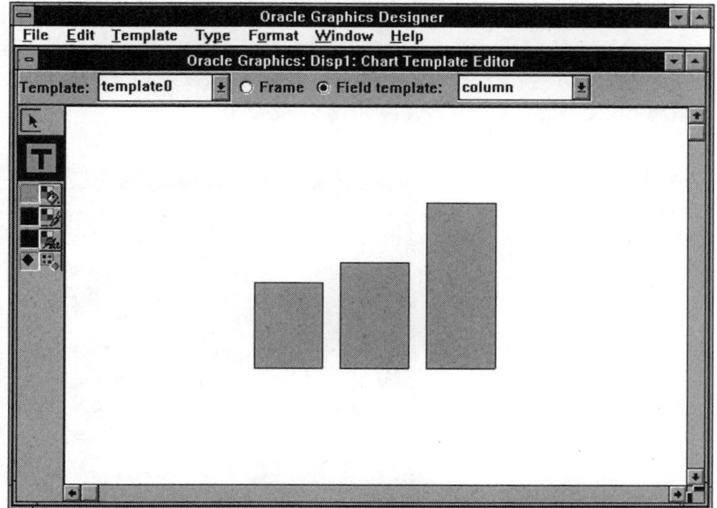

FIGURE 10.6.
The fields in the Chart Template Editor.

Designer

Oracle Graphics Designer is an integrated development environment used for creating displays, libraries, and database objects. Within the Designer there are several tools and features that are used during the development process. These items will be reviewed next, and include:

- The Object Navigator
- Toolbars
- Property sheets
- The Chart Template Editor
- The Layout Editor
- The Program Unit Editor
- Defaulting

Oracle Graphics Designer is shown in Figure 10.7 with the Object Navigator, the Layout Editor, and the Chart Template Editor displayed.

In the Designer, multiple windows may be open at the same time, so that several tools can be used in combination with one another. The tools are synchronized with each other and automatically reflect the changes as they are made.

Object Navigator

The Object Navigator was reviewed in Chapter 7, "Introducing Oracle Developer/2000." However, Oracle Graphics incorporates an additional feature into the Object Navigator that will enable you to optionally view reference information. The Object Navigator menu contains a Navigator Options menu item, which invokes the Object Navigator Options dialog box. The dialog box contains checkboxes for showing which objects each object references and which objects are referenced by which objects.

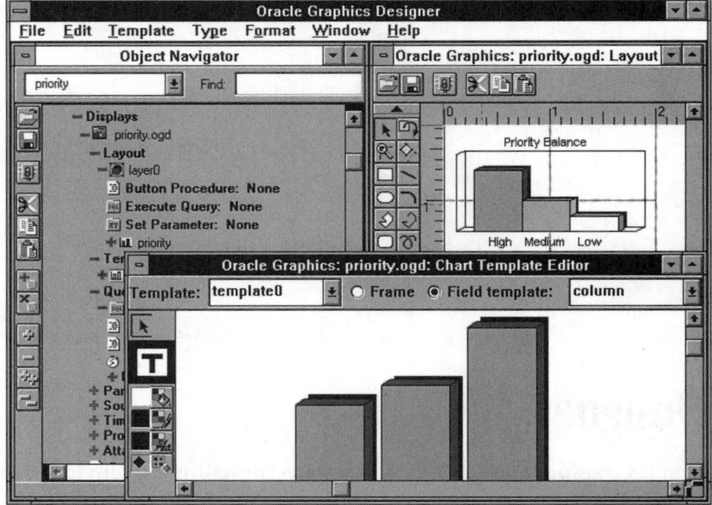

FIGURE 10.7.
Oracle Graphics Designer with tools windows open.

Next, the specific object types within Oracle Graphics will be reviewed. In Figure 10.8, the Oracle Graphics Designer window is shown with the Object Navigator displaying the major nodes.

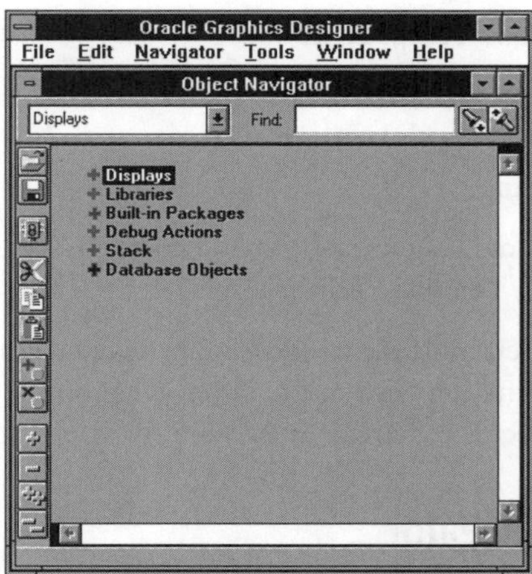

FIGURE 10.8.
Oracle Graphics Designer with the Object Navigator.

The major nodes in the Oracle Graphics Object Navigator are

- Displays
- Libraries
- Built-in Packages
- Debug Actions
- Stack
- Database Objects

Display Object Types

Notice that the objects in the Object Navigator are organized by type. Under the Displays node, you will find all the object types used for designing Graphics applications. The Object Navigator is shown in Figure 10.9, with the Displays node expanded.

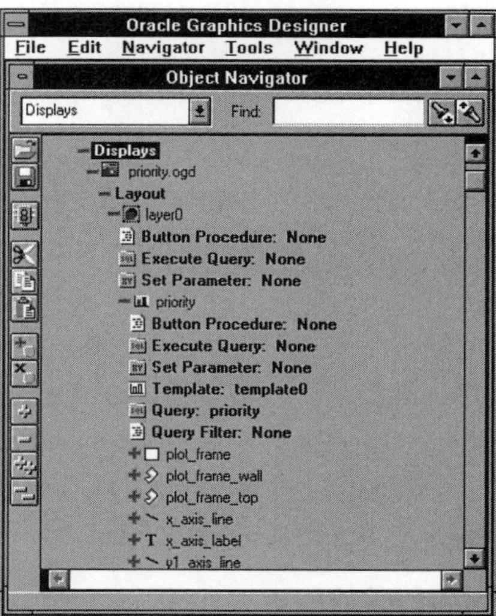

FIGURE 10.9.
The Object Navigator showing display objects.

Oracle Graphics supplies many different display object types. Each display object type, as it is presented in the Object Navigator, is listed here with a description.

Object Type	*Description*
Module	The name of the display; invokes the Display Properties.
Layout	Owns the layout objects for the display.
Layer	Owns the chart objects; invokes the Layer Settings.

continues

Object Type	*Description*
Button Procedure	PL/SQL that is executed when the object is clicked on.
Execute Query	A reference to a query to be executed.
Set Parameter	A reference to a parameter value.
Chart	The basic component of Graphics; based on a template.
Templates	Templates for the chart.
Queries	SQL select statements.
Custom Exec Trigger	A function to populate a custom query.
Post Exec Trigger	PL/SQL that is executed after the query is executed.
Timer	A reference to a timer.
Referenced By	Objects that are referenced by the current object.
Query Filter	A function to filter out rows from the query.
Boilerplate	Any static graphics or text.
Symbols	Static graphical symbols from the symbol palette.
Chart Objects	All objects in the chart, based on chart type.
Format Trigger	PL/SQL that is executed during formatting.
Parameters	Items passed into the application.
Sounds	Recorded sound files.
Timers	A clock that fires event triggers.
Timer Procedure	Procedures that are referenced by the timer.
Program Units	Procedures, functions, and packages.
Attached Libraries	PL/SQL code used by multiple applications.
Open Trigger	PL/SQL that is executed when the display is opened.
Close Trigger	PL/SQL that is executed when the display is closed.

Most layout objects can contain a reference to a button procedure, a query that can be executed, and a parameter that can be set. In addition, chart objects can contain a reference to a format trigger.

Library Object Types

Like Oracle Reports and Oracle Forms, Oracle Graphics supports the creation and maintenance of libraries. Libraries are external to the display and may be saved to the database or the file system. Libraries are then attached to the display, so that the PL/SQL program units may be referenced.

Built-In Package Object Types

Under the Built-in Packages node, you will find all of the built-in programs supplied with Oracle Graphics. There are several built-in packages, and each one contains a group of supporting functions and procedures. Many of the built-in packages are the same ones found in Oracle Forms and Oracle Reports. Oracle Graphics includes the same LIST and DEBUG packages found in Oracle Reports. You can find more information on available packages in the Oracle Graphics Reference Manual.

Debug Action Object Types

When debugging your Oracle Graphics applications, you will create breakpoints and triggers using the PL/SQL Interpreter. Each of the breakpoints and triggers are associated with a program unit in the display, and they appear as debug actions in the Object Navigator.

The PL/SQL Interpreter is invoked from the Tools menu. The selected program unit will appear in the source frame at the top of the window. Position your cursor at the desired location in the source code, and choose either Break or Trigger from the Debug menu. Double-clicking on a source line will also set a break on that line, while double-clicking again will remove the break. A break will stop the execution of the program unit, and a trigger will execute the PL/SQL code associated with it.

Stack Object Types

When debug actions have been set and the display is run, the PL/SQL Interpreter appears containing the Navigator pane. The Stack node in the Object Navigator will contain a list of each of the program units called and a list of variables with their current values.

Database Object Types

All of the database objects for each of Oracle users are listed under the Database Objects node in the Object Navigator. Database objects include programs, libraries, tables, and views. Having the database objects available from the Oracle Graphics Designer provides you as a developer with an integrated development environment. This means that you don't have to leave the Designer to locate, review, create, or modify database objects that will be used by your Graphics application.

Oracle Graphics Designer Toolbars

Each of the common toolbars were reviewed in Chapter 7. In the following sections, the Oracle Graphics-specific items will be reviewed for each of the toolbars that appear in the Designer.

Layout Editor Toolbar

The Oracle Graphics Layout Editor contains the standard tools for Open, Save, Run, Cut, Copy, and Paste on the toolbar. The additional tools are found on the pop-up menu in the Layout Editor, but not on the toolbar. The Layout Editor is shown in Figure 10.10 containing the pie chart that will be developed in the first exercise at the end of this chapter.

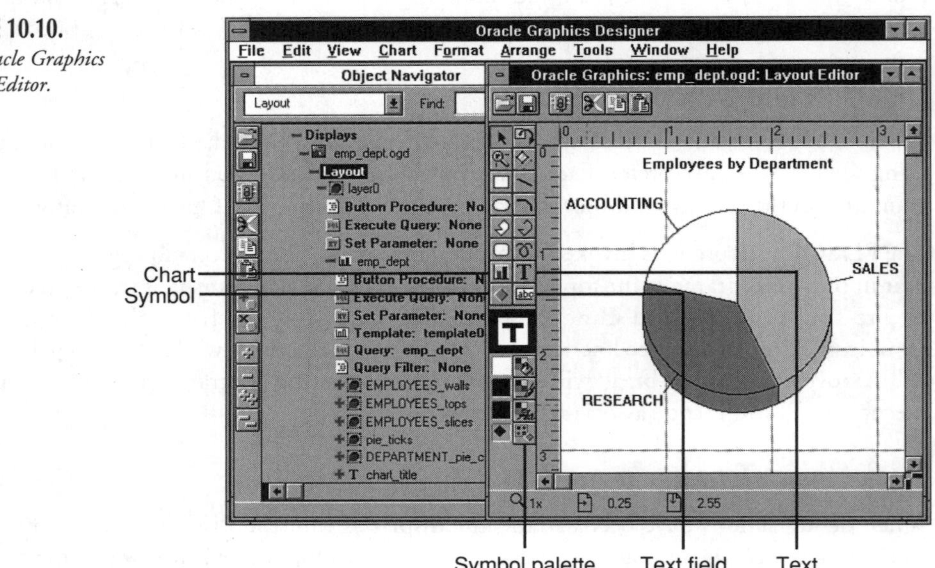

FIGURE 10.10.
The Oracle Graphics Layout Editor.

Layout Editor Tool Palette

The Oracle Graphics Layout Editor contains the following specific item-drawing tools on the tool palette, as can be seen in Figure 10.10. The tool palette appears on the left side of the Layout Editor.

Button	*Description*
Chart	Creates a chart item for an Oracle Graphics display.
Text	Creates a text item.
Symbol	Creates a symbol in the layout.
Text Field	Creates a text field.
Symbols	Invokes the Symbol palette.

Notice, on the lower-left side of the Layout Editor, that Oracle Graphics contains an additional palette for selecting symbols that is not found in Oracle Forms or Oracle Reports. The symbol palette is also found in the tool palette of the Chart Template Editor in Oracle Graphics.

Property Sheets

Oracle Graphics uses property sheets that appear as tab-controlled dialogs for managing object properties. Unlike Oracle Forms, which uses a common Properties window, Oracle Graphics is like Oracle Reports in that it uses different property sheets for each object type. An example of a property sheet is shown in Figure 10.11.

FIGURE 10.11.
The Chart Properties tab-controlled dialog box.

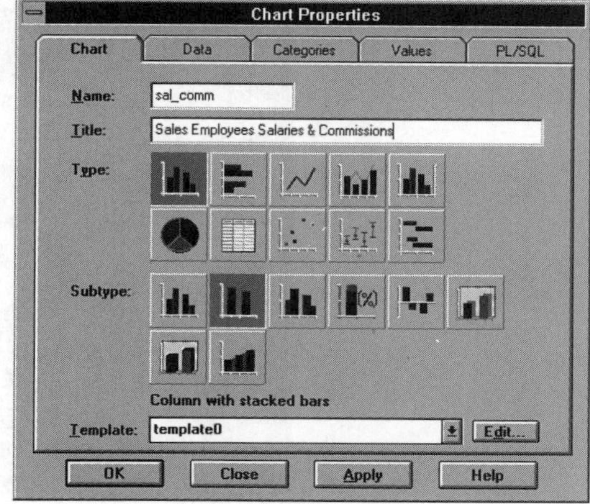

Figure 10.11 shows the chart properties for the second exercise at the end of this chapter, which uses a column chart with stacked bars. All of the properties for each of the Oracle Graphics object types are listed in Appendix G, "Oracle Graphics Properties."

> **NOTE**
>
> The property sheets can remain open while you are working in other windows in the Designer. However, they are fixed in size and are therefore often difficult to organize on the desktop without obstructing your work area.

Like the Oracle Forms and Oracle Reports properties, the Oracle Graphics properties are often initialized with default values, and many offer drop-down lists of valid choices.

The Layout Editor

The Layout Editor displays the chart as it will be at runtime. You can modify the visual attributes of the chart objects using the editor. Usually you would begin working with the Layout Editor after creating a default layout. The default layout is created by defining a query, selecting the chart type, and setting the properties for the various display objects. Changes made to the chart template, the object properties, and the layout are all reflected in the Layout Editor. Boilerplate objects can also be added to the chart using the editor and the tool palette. In Figure 10.12, the Layout Editor is shown containing the column chart with stacked bars from the second exercise at the end of this chapter.

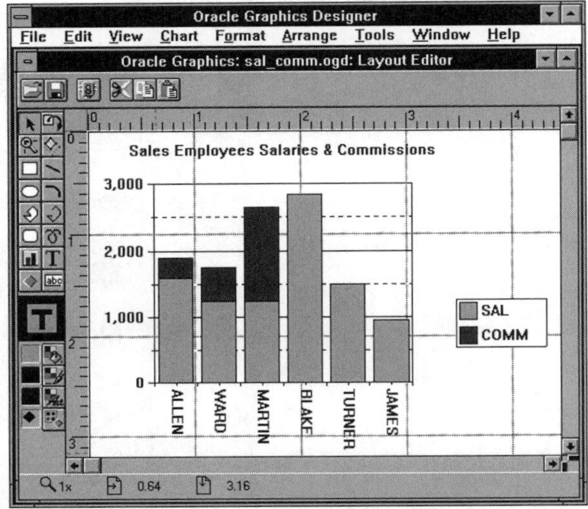

FIGURE 10.12.
The Layout Editor with a stacked bar chart.

You will notice in Figure 10.12 that the chart in the Layout Editor contains the actual data that was returned from the query.

Layers

An Oracle Graphics display contains one or more charts that are placed on one or more layers. When only a single chart is needed, it will automatically be placed on the default layer. Additional charts may be placed on the existing layer. However, each chart on the layer is displayed with that layer. So, to manage the display of multiple charts in the same application, you may want to place each chart on a separate layer. The charts may be based on the same query, but they can be displayed independently of one another. In Figure 10.13, the Layer Settings dialog box is shown with the active layer containing a table and the other layer containing a pie chart.

You will notice in Figure 10.13 that each layer is preceded by a plus or minus symbol indicating whether or not it is displayed. More than one layer may be displayed at the same time. However, at least one layer must be active, and the active layer must be displayed.

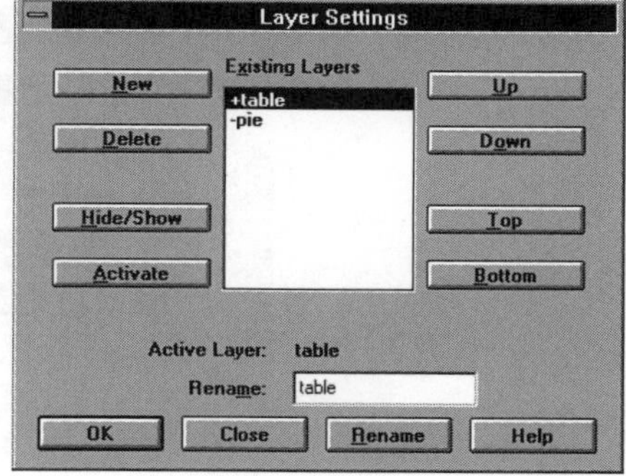

FIGURE 10.13.
The Layer Settings dialog box.

TIP

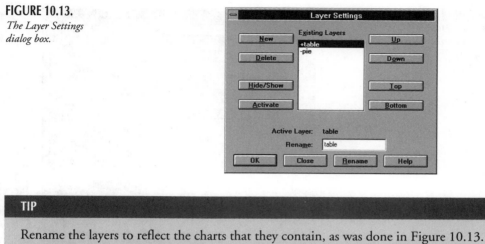

Rename the layers to reflect the charts that they contain, as was done in Figure 10.13. Doing this will give you a more intuitive reference to the layers than using the default names.

Queries

Oracle Graphics supports many different types of queries to provide the data to the chart application. The most common types of queries are the SQL statement and the external SQL file. Each of these types result in data being returned from an Oracle database. Figure 10.14 shows the Query Properties dialog box containing a reference to an ASCII file that contains the SQL statement for the third exercise at the end of this chapter.

Oracle Graphics also supports query types based on files from non-Oracle sources, including Microsoft Excel SYLK files, Lotus WKS files, and ASCII PRN files. Lastly, the data for the query may be created via PL/SQL using the query type of Custom. The Custom query type requires the schema to be defined. The schema contains the column name, data type, and maximum length for each column in the query.

The Options tab of the Query Properties dialog box defines when the query is to be executed, how the data is managed, which procedure is to be executed for a custom query, and which trigger to fire after query execution. The default settings for query options are shown in Figure 10.15.

You will notice in Figure 10.15 that the query will be executed when the display is opened by default, but it can be executed based on a timer trigger.

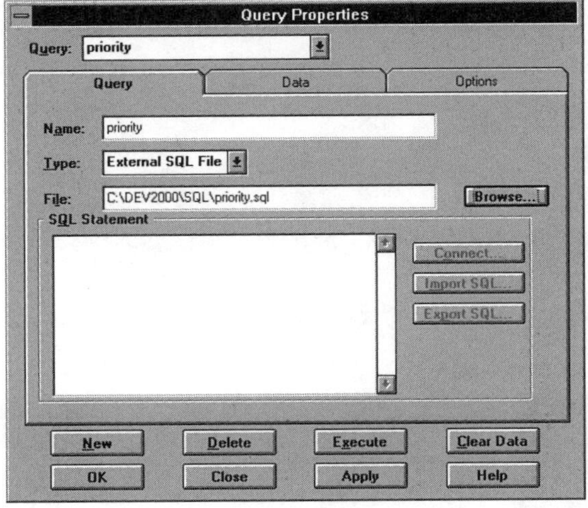

FIGURE 10.14.
The Query Properties dialog box referencing an external SQL file.

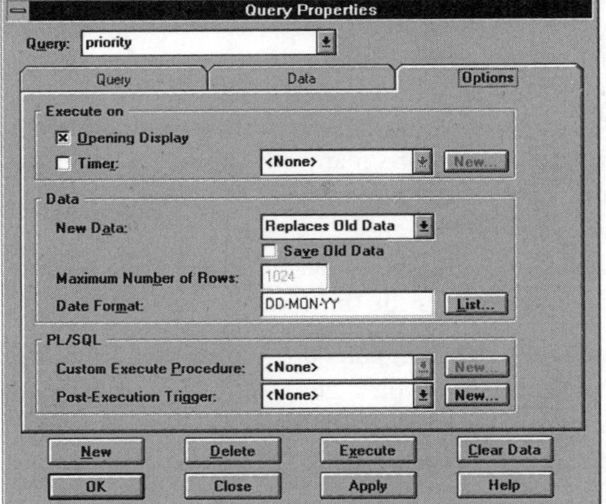

FIGURE 10.15.
The Query Properties dialog box showing the Options tab.

NOTE

Using a timer to execute the query will enable you to monitor activity in the database with the Graphics application without additional user intervention.

Each chart may contain a query filter function that will be executed for each row. The query filter is written in PL/SQL and returns True to keep the row or False to remove the row.

Parameters

Parameters are used to pass information to or from Oracle Graphics. The name and data type of the parameter is set in the Designer. The initial value may be set in the Designer and then overridden either programatically or by passing the name and value on the command line. If a SQL statement contains a reference to a parameter, then the parameter is created automatically. Parameters are commonly used to change the results of a query by modifying the Where clause. The Parameters dialog box is shown with the initial value set to the percent symbol in Figure 10.16.

FIGURE 10.16.
The Parameters dialog box.

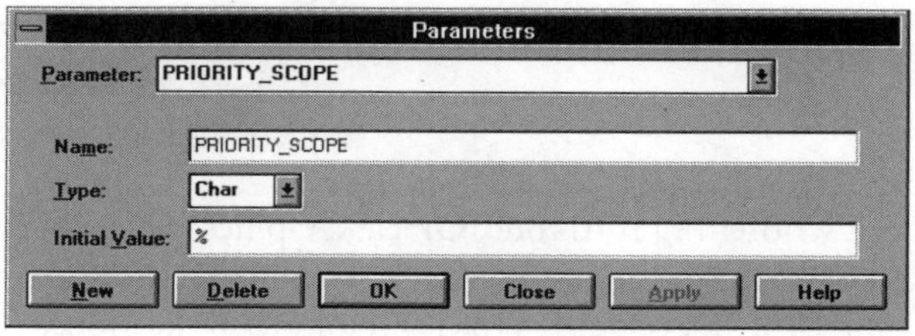

Setting the initial value for the parameter to the percent symbol and using the parameter in the Where clause will result in the selection of all rows for the priority query unless the parameter value is overridden. Using the parameter in this way will enable us to use one chart to display all priorities as well as priorities by employee.

Boilerplate

Oracle Graphics creates boilerplate objects to represent labels, axes, lines, frames, and other static information for the display from the chart template. Additional boilerplate objects may be added to the layout using the Layout Editor's tool palette. Boilerplate objects do not have format triggers like other chart objects do.

Symbols are boilerplate objects unique to Oracle Graphics and are found at the bottom of the tool palette in the Layout Editor. There is a symbol palette for selecting the type of symbol to be used. The symbol palette works much like the color palettes. From the Format menu, the symbol size may be set to small, medium, or large.

Chart Objects

Objects contained in the display that are not static are called chart objects. Chart objects have an associated value that is set at runtime, based on the data retrieved from the query. The types of chart objects in the display are dependent on the chart type, the current template, and the property settings of the frame and axes. Chart objects may contain mouse-activated procedures as well as format triggers. Format triggers and mouse procedures are written in PL/SQL and fire for each object as it is processed in the display. In addition, each chart object may be automatically connected to another chart by defining the Drill-down parameter, value, and query in the Object Properties dialog box as shown in Figure 10.17.

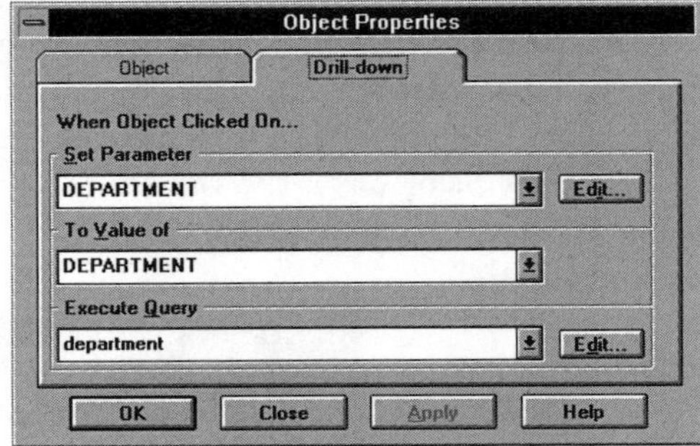

FIGURE 10.17.
The Object Properties dialog box with the Drill-down tab.

Without writing PL/SQL code, Oracle Graphics will enable you to create master/detail charts that populate the detail information by clicking on the chart object in the master. For example, in Chapter 14, "Developing Oracle Graphics Applications," we will modify the pie chart from the first exercise at the end of this chapter to include a tabular chart listing the employees for each of the departments.

Sounds

Sounds can be incorporated into your Oracle Graphics applications to further enhance the user interface. If you have a microphone attached to your computer, you can record your own sounds. In addition, you can import existing sound files from the file system. Oracle Graphics supports a wide variety of sound file formats, including the popular WAV files of Microsoft Windows. Figure 10.18 shows the Sound Player dialog box after having recorded a sound.

FIGURE 10.18.
The Sound Player dialog box.

The Sound Player dialog box is used to record your own sounds and to play existing sounds. Once a sound is recorded or imported into the display, it is played at runtime using a PL/SQL program unit. The program unit is usually a button procedure or timer trigger. Oracle Graphics provides the built-in procedures OG_SET_SOUND and OG_PLAY_SOUND to simplify the development process and reduce the amount of PL/SQL code to a minimum.

Timers

Timers can be created in your display to automatically cause the execution of a procedure or the re-querying of the data for the chart. By assigning a timer to a query, the database can be continually monitored by your application, and the chart will be updated to reflect any change that has occurred since the previous query. When a timer is created, the Timer Triggers dialog box is invoked, as shown in Figure 10.19.

FIGURE 10.19.
The Timer Triggers dialog box.

You will notice in Figure 10.19 that the timer will execute the procedure at each five-second interval and is set to Active by default. To associate a timer with a query, use the Options tab in the Query Properties dialog box.

Chart Template Editor

The Chart Template Editor is used to manage the templates for the display. The default templates may be edited, and additional templates may be created. Templates provide a consistent style for the chart type and may be referenced by many different charts to give them all the same presentation style. The Chart Template Editor enables you to manage the frame and field templates. In addition, the current setting of the axis properties are reflected in the editor.

Frames

Each chart has a chart frame that surrounds the chart. The frame defines the three-dimensional appearance of the chart, as well as the information displayed with the chart. The properties of the chart frame are dependent on the chart type. The depth and shadow of the frame can be automatically set using the chart subtypes in the Chart Properties dialog box. In Figure 10.20, the Frame Properties dialog box is shown with the depth size automatically set, because the pie with depth chart subtype was chosen in the Chart Properties dialog box.

Notice the Pie Frame tab to the right of the Frame tab in Figure 10.20. The additional frame properties are found on the second tab of the Frame Properties dialog box and are dependent on the chart type. The pie and table charts have their own properties tabs, while each of the other chart types share the Axis Frame properties tab.

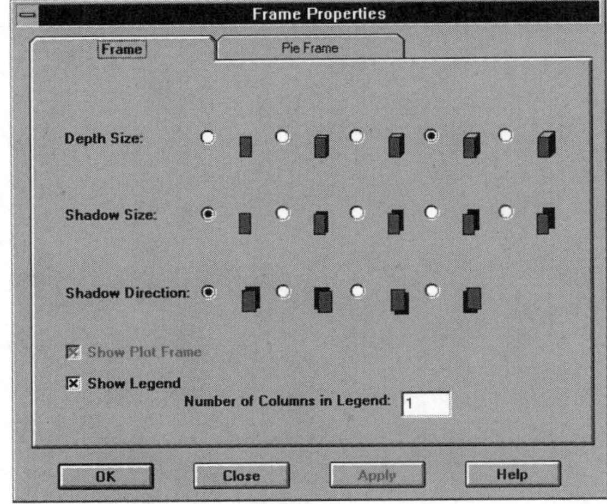

FIGURE 10.20.
The Frame Properties dialog box.

Axes

The location and direction of the axis information, as well as the display of tick marks, grid lines, and labels, are set using the Axis Properties dialog box as shown in Figure 10.21.

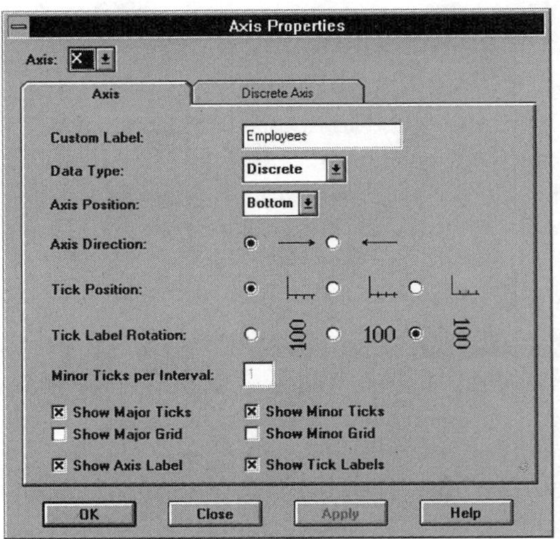

FIGURE 10.21.
The Axis Properties dialog box.

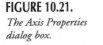

Notice that in Figure 10.21, the custom label is set and therefore replaces the default from the column name in the select statement.

Each chart contains an X and Y axis. Some charts may contain more than one Y axis. The drop-down list at the top of the dialog box enables you to switch between the different axes in the chart. The Axis Properties dialog box contains an additional tab to the right of the Axis tab that is dependent on the data type. There are a number of additional properties for formatting the axis when the data is in the form of a date. Each of the axis properties is reviewed in Appendix G.

TIP

The column labels from the SQL statement are used for the default axis labels. Therefore, by assigning aliases to the database columns in your queries you can create a more presentable chart without modifying the axes' properties.

Fields

Each value column from the query is plotted in the chart as a field. The plot type for the field is dependent on the chart type. The plot types include bar, line, fill, symbol, spike, and label. Field templates define the characteristics of each field in the display and can be modified via the Field Template Properties dialog box. The color pattern for the plotted fields can be set automatically by default in the field template or in the Layout Editor. Changes made to the field properties in the layout are automatically reflected in the field template. Like frame templates, field templates are a useful tool for standardizing the appearance of your display applications.

Reference Lines

You can add reference lines to the chart to mark a given point on the graph and show a static value that can be used to compare the values returned from the query. The Reference Line Properties dialog box enables you to define a label and value for the reference line as well as a selection for which axis the reference line should be mapped to.

Program Unit Editor

The Program Unit Editor in Oracle Graphics is identical in appearance and function to the Program Unit Editor in Oracle Reports that was reviewed in the preceding chapter. As in Oracle Reports, all PL/SQL objects become program units. Even timer triggers are created as functions in the Program Unit Editor. You will recognize the button bar, the identification fields, the source pane, and the status line as shown in the Program Unit Editor in Figure 10.22.

In Figure 10.22, a button procedure is referencing Oracle Graphics built-in procedures to play a sound when the user clicks on a chart object. The Program Unit Editor is used for creating button procedures, format triggers, timer procedures, open triggers, close triggers, procedures, functions, and packages in Oracle Graphics.

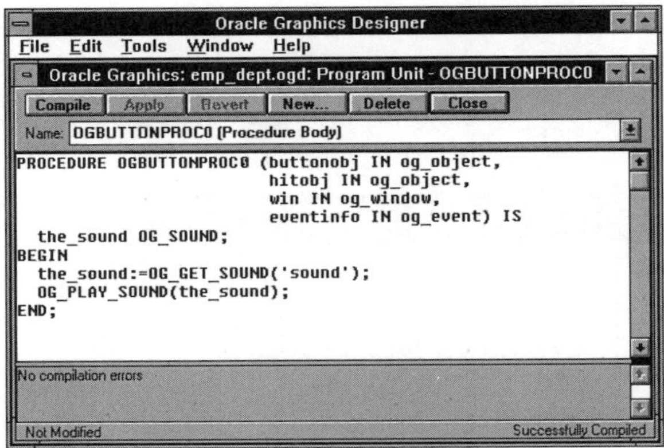

FIGURE 10.22.
The Program Unit Editor.

Whenever a new function or procedure is created, the Program Unit Editor is automatically initialized with a default template of PL/SQL that includes the required parameters.

Button Procedures

Unlike Oracle Forms and Oracle Reports, Oracle Graphics does not include button items. Instead, any and all chart objects may contain button procedures and therefore be like buttons in function (though not in appearance). Button procedures are executed when the object to which they are attached is clicked on by the user at runtime. A button procedure can be executed during a drill-down from higher to lower level detail in the display, or it can support any other functionality you may wish to assign to the object that is clicked on.

Format Triggers

All chart elements may contain format triggers to modify or conditionally modify the appearance of the object prior to presentation. The format trigger is created as a procedure in the Program Unit Editor and is associated with the object via the Object Navigator or the Object Properties dialog box. A single program unit may be referenced by several different chart elements.

Timer Procedures

A timer can reference a procedure to be executed each time the timer interval expires. The timer procedure does not contain any parameters, but it can reference objects in the display by using the Oracle Graphics built-in procedures. Any existing procedure may be referenced from a timer.

Open Trigger

Each display may reference an open trigger that will execute the associated procedure when the application is started at runtime. As with the timer procedure, any existing procedure may be referenced for the open trigger. Open triggers are generally used to initialize objects, execute queries, hide layers, or activate layers in the display.

Close Trigger

Each display may also reference a close trigger that will execute the associated procedure when the application is closed at runtime. Again, any existing procedure may be referenced for the close trigger.

Defaulting in Oracle Graphics

Oracle Graphics provides 10 different chart types by default. Each chart type contains subtypes, which can result in 56 different styles of charts automatically. The chart types include column, bar, line, mixed column and line, double-Y, pie, table, scatter, high-low, and Gantt. The default chart type is a column chart with no 3-D properties set, but the chart type and subtype are easily changed when the Chart Properties dialog box is invoked by selecting one of the iconic radio buttons.

Each chart must be based on a query. When a new chart is created and queries exist in the display, the Chart Genie invokes a query selection dialog box. (See Figure 10.23.)

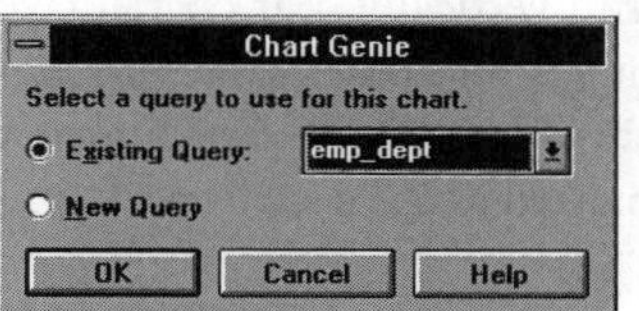

FIGURE 10.23.
The Chart Genie listing existing queries.

The drop-down list provides access to the existing queries in the display, and the radio buttons allow a new or existing query to be selected. Following the selection of an existing query or the entry of a new query, the Chart Properties dialog box is invoked to select the chart type and to set other properties that will create the default chart in the layout.

Column Chart

The default chart type is column, and this is the type of chart that will be created in the second and third exercises at the end of this chapter. Column charts have the following subtypes: stacked bars, overlapping bars, percent scaling, baseline at zero, with shadows, with depth, and with connecting lines. Figure 10.24 shows the Layout Editor with the Sales Employees Salaries & Commissions display from the second exercise at the end of this chapter.

Notice in the layout that the axis label is defaulted from the column name in the query. This will be modified during the exercise.

FIGURE 10.24.
A column chart containing stacked bars.

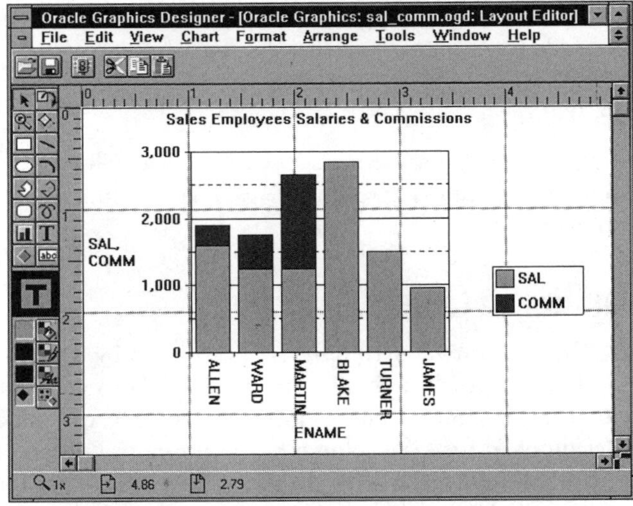

Bar Chart

The bar chart is like the column chart, except that the bars run horizontally, as opposed to columns, which run vertically. Bar charts have the following subtypes: stacked bars, overlapping bars, percent scaling, baseline at zero, with shadows, with depth, and with connecting lines. Figure 10.25 shows the Layout Editor with the Sales Employees Salaries & Commissions display formatted as a bar chart with stacked bars.

FIGURE 10.25.
A bar chart containing stacked bars.

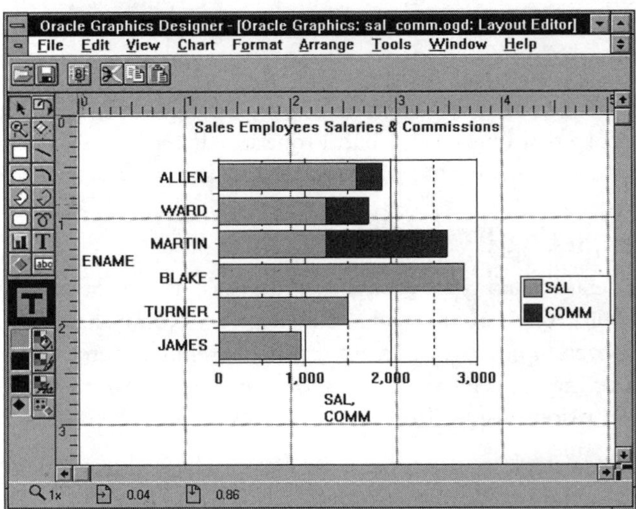

Line Chart

The line chart plots the values vertically from left to right and connects the points with a solid line. Line charts have the following subtypes: with symbols, stacked lines, stacked lines with fill, step, step with symbols, stacked step, stacked step with fill, curved line, curved line with symbols, stacked curved lines, and stacked curved lines with fill. Figure 10.26 shows the Layout Editor with the Sales Employees Salaries & Commissions display formatted as a line chart with stacked lines.

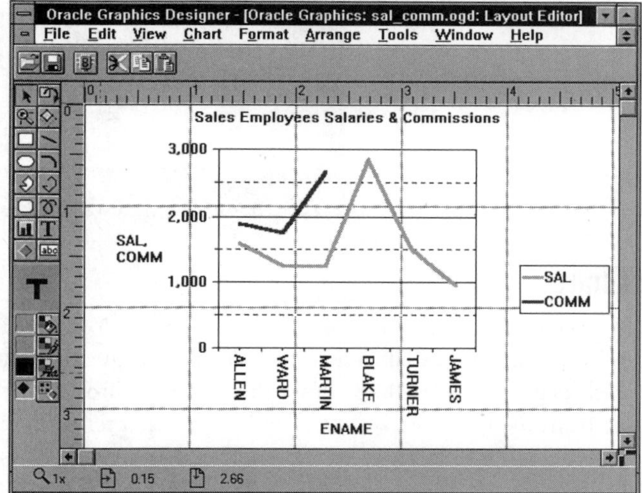

FIGURE 10.26.
A default line chart with stacked lines.

Mixed Chart

Mixed charts combine the column and line chart types; they represent one set of values as a column and the next as a line. Mixed charts have the following subtypes: column and fill, column and curved line, and column and curved lines with fill. Figure 10.27 shows the Layout Editor with the Sales Employees Salaries & Commissions display formatted as a mixed chart with columns and lines.

Double-Y Chart

Double-Y charts have two vertical axes. One axis is on the left side, and the other is on the right side. Each vertical axis contains tick labels for the plotted values. Double-Y charts are columnar by default and have the following subtypes: column with overlapping bars, line, and line with symbols.

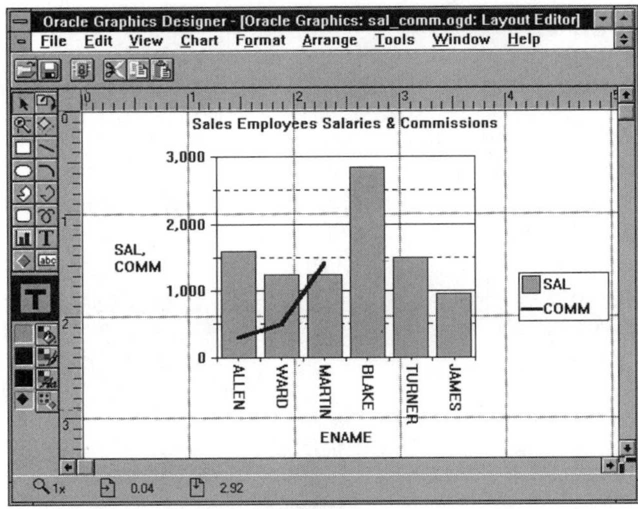

FIGURE 10.27.
A mixed chart with columns and lines.

Pie Chart

Pie charts represent each value as a slice of the total. You can optionally combine the smaller values into a single slice labeled Other. Pie charts have the following subtypes: with shadow, and with depth. Figure 10.28 shows the Layout Editor with the Employees by Department display from the first exercise at the end of this chapter formatted as a pie chart with depth.

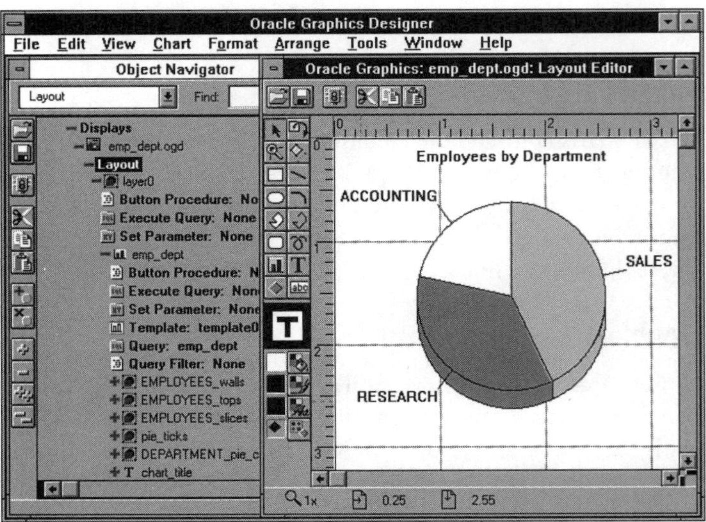

FIGURE 10.28.
A default pie chart.

Pie charts are a good choice for the master chart in master/detail displays. The user can drill-down on any one slice of the pie by clicking on that slice.

Table Chart

Table charts are very basic and are the equivalent of a simple columnar report. Use a table chart when you have a list of data to be displayed that is not as well suited for a graphical display. Table charts have the following subtypes: with shadow, and with depth. Figure 10.29 shows the Layout Editor with the Employees by Department display formatted as a table.

FIGURE 10.29.
A table chart listing the number of employees in each department.

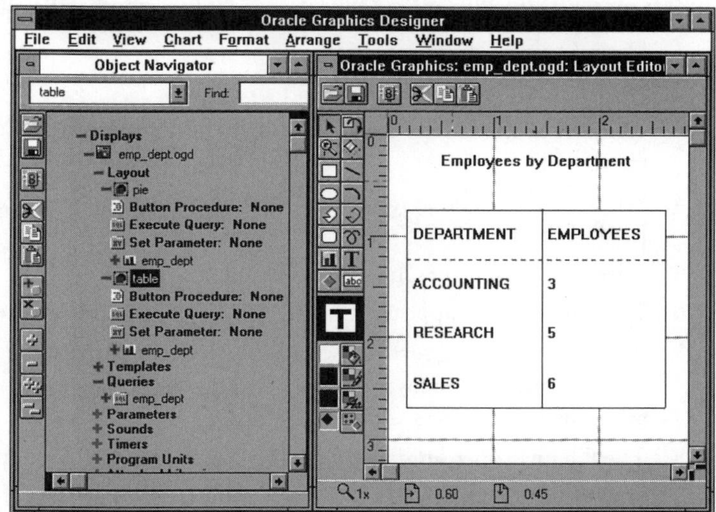

Scatter Chart

Scatter charts plot each value as a symbol on a grid and have the following subtypes: with regression line, with grid, logarithmic scatter, log-log scatter, and with connecting lines.

High-Low Chart

High-low charts plot two sets of data values as symbols on a grid and have the following subtypes: spikes with close symbols, close symbols with spikes, close with connecting lines, and close with fill. High-low charts are useful when displaying a comparison between two sets of numbers.

Gantt Chart

Gantt charts plot sets of date values as horizontal bars with the first value as the start and the second value as the end. Gantt charts have the following subtypes: with shadow, and with depth. Gantt charts are most often used to display scheduling information.

Exercises

The purpose of these exercises is to familiarize you with Oracle Graphics Designer. In addition they will give you some hands-on review of the material that has been covered in this chapter. You will create a pie chart and two column charts, make changes in the Designer, and review the displays.

Creating a Pie Chart of Employees by Department

In this exercise you will create a pie chart of employees by department.

1. Open Oracle Graphics Designer.
2. Notice that the default display is named 'Disp1'.
3. Connect to the Oracle database as scott/tiger by selecting Connect from the File menu.
4. Select Save As, File System from the File menu, and save the display as EMP_DEPT.OGD.
5. Select Chart, Create Chart from the menu.
6. The Chart Genie appears. Change the query name from query0 to emp_dept.
7. Enter the following text in the SQL statement field: `select d.dname Department, count(e.empno) Employees from dept d, emp e where d.deptno = e.deptno group by d.dname`, and press OK.
8. The Chart Properties dialog box appears. Name the chart emp_dept, and set the title to Employees by Department.
9. Set the chart type to Pie and the subtype to Pie With Depth, and press OK.
10. Notice the chart is created in the layout.
11. Select Save, and Run from the File menu or one of the toolbars.
12. Review the chart in the Graphics Debugger window, and select Close from the File menu to return to Oracle Graphics Designer.

Creating a Stacked Bar Chart of Sales Employees Salaries and Commissions

In this exercise you will create a stacked bar chart of sales employees displaying salaries and commissions.

1. Close the current display and create a new one.
2. Select Save As, File System from the File menu, and save the display as SAL_COMM.OGD.

3. Select Chart, Create Chart from the menu.
4. The Chart Genie appears. Change the query name from query0 to sal_comm.
5. Enter the following text in the SQL statement field: `select ename, sal, comm from emp where deptno = 30`, and press OK.
6. The Chart Properties dialog box appears. Name the chart sal_comm, and set the title to Sales Employees Salaries & Commissions.
7. Set the subtype to Column With Stacked Bars, and press OK.
8. Notice the chart is created in the layout.
9. Select Save and Run from the File menu or one of the toolbars.
10. Review the chart in the Graphics Debugger window, and select Close from the File menu to return to Oracle Graphics Designer.
11. Select Axes from the Chart menu.
12. Uncheck Show Axis Label for Axis Y1 in the Axis Properties dialog box.
13. Select Axis X from the drop-down list.
14. Enter Employees as the custom label, and press OK.
15. Save, run, review, and return to Oracle Graphics Designer.

Creating a Column Chart for Priority Balance

In this exercise you will create a column chart displaying the balance of contact priorities between high, medium, and low.

1. Close the current display, and create a new one.
2. Select Save As, File System from the File menu and save the display as PRIORITY.OGD.
3. Select Chart, Create Chart from the menu.
4. The Chart Genie appears. Change the query name from query0 to priority.
5. Set the type to External SQL File from the drop-down list.
6. Click the Browse button to locate and select the \DEV2000\SQL\PRIORITY.SQL file, and press OK.
7. Answer Yes to create the PRIORITY_SCOPE bind variable.
8. Set the parameter type to Char and the initial value to %, and press OK.
9. In the Chart Properties dialog box, name the chart priority, and set the title to Priority Balance.
10. Select the Values tab, and add HIGH from the Query Columns to the Chart Values by selecting it and pressing the Insert button.
11. Select HIGH in the Chart Values list, press the Top button, and press OK.

12. Notice the chart frame is created in the layout without any chart data.
13. Select Axes from the Chart menu, the Axis Properties dialog box appears.
14. Select Axis Y1 from the drop-down list, and uncheck each Show check box.
15. Select Axis X from the drop-down list.
16. Enter High Medium Low as the custom label.
17. Check only Show Axis Label, and press OK.
18. Select Frame from the Chart menu.
19. Select the middle radio button for Depth Size in the Frame Properties dialog box.
20. Uncheck Show Legend, and press OK.
21. Select Query from the Tools menu.
22. Press the Execute button and then OK.
23. Notice the chart appears in the layout with data.
24. In the Layout Editor, select the bar, top, and wall for each column, and set the fill colors to red, blue, and green respectively.
25. Save, run, review, return, and close Oracle Graphics Designer to end the exercise.

Summary

This chapter provided you with an overview of Oracle Graphics, including:

- The components of Oracle Graphics
- The basics of Oracle Graphics, including queries, charts, templates, and triggers
- Object types in the Object Navigator
- The Oracle Graphics Designer toolbars
- The property sheets
- The Chart Template Editor and chart objects
- The Layout Editor and layout objects
- The Program Unit Editor
- Defaulting charts

If you worked through the exercises, you have developed a pie chart and two column charts. You also now know how to modify chart objects using property sheets and the Layout Editor.

Now that you are familiar with the features of Oracle Graphics, next we will take a look at the features of Oracle Procedure Builder.

11

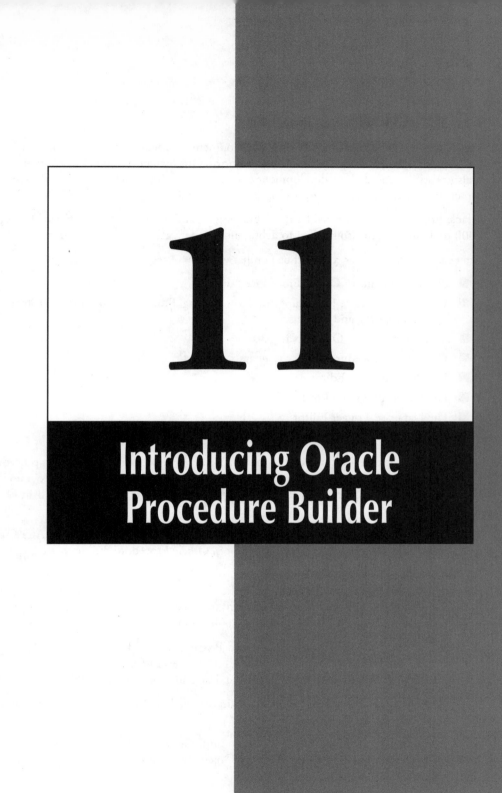

Introducing Oracle Procedure Builder

Introduction

Oracle Procedure Builder is the PL/SQL development and debugging environment of Oracle Developer/2000. It is integrated with Oracle Forms, Oracle Reports, and Oracle Graphics, but it also exists as a stand-alone development environment. With Oracle Procedure Builder, you can create functions, procedures, packages, libraries, and database triggers.

Oracle Procedure Builder provides the debugging capability to each of the Oracle Developer/2000 tools, and it can also be used to debug independent PL/SQL program units.

After reading this chapter, you will be familiar with:

- The components of Oracle Procedure Builder
- The basics of Oracle Procedure Builder including, functions, procedures, packages, libraries, triggers, and debugging
- Object types in the Object Navigator
- The Oracle Procedure Builder toolbars
- The Program Unit Editor
- The Stored Program Unit Editor
- The Database Trigger Editor
- Debugging with the PL/SQL Interpreter

In addition, in the exercise at the end of this chapter, you will develop a function, a procedure, a package, and a database trigger. You will create these PL/SQL objects using the Program Unit Editor, the Stored Program Unit Editor, and the Database Trigger Editor found in Oracle Procedure Builder.

The Oracle Procedure Builder executable PB15DES.EXE is located in the ORACLE\BIN directory. Unlike the other Developer/2000 tools, Oracle Procedure Builder has only one independent component.

You build PL/SQL components for your applications in Oracle Procedure Builder by using the various editors. Using the Program Unit Editor, you can write PL/SQL program units that may be placed in a library or directly into an application.

PL/SQL code may be written using the Stored Program Unit Editor to create PL/SQL program units in the database. Stored Program Units may also be created in the Program Unit Editor and copied or moved to the database via drag and drop from the Object Navigator.

Database triggers may be created for each table in the database and are created and maintained via the Database Trigger Editor.

All of the debugging of your PL/SQL program units and applications will be done using the PL/SQL Interpreter in combination with the Object Navigator.

Oracle Procedure Builder incorporates the ability to create program units, libraries, and database objects into one integrated development environment. A PL/SQL object is a function, procedure, package, or trigger that may reference other PL/SQL objects, tables, and views, as well as any other objects in the database. PL/SQL objects may also reference built-in functions and procedures that are provided as packages with Procedure Builder.

Figure 11.1 shows a function to calculate salary increases that will be developed in the exercise at the end of this chapter.

FIGURE 11.1.
A function that calculates salary increases.

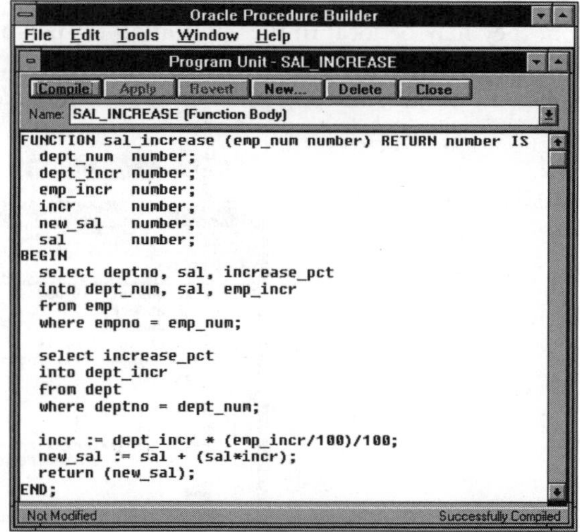

The development of each type of PL/SQL program unit is accomplished by utilizing the various editors within Oracle Procedure Builder. Functions, procedures, packages, and libraries may be moved between the local application and the database by dragging and dropping them in the Object Navigator.

NOTE

You must be using version 7 or higher of the Oracle database to be able to store PL/SQL objects in the database.

Functions

A function is a PL/SQL program unit that returns a single value. Functions can accept arguments. They may be local to the application or stored in the database. A function that is stored in the database may be referenced in a SQL statement, as will be demonstrated in the first exercise at the end of this chapter.

> **NOTE**
>
> You must be using version 7.1 or higher of the Oracle database to be able to reference a function that is stored in the database in a SQL statement.

Procedures

Procedures are PL/SQL program units that can pass one or more arguments in and out. Like a function, they may be local to the application or may be stored in the database. Unlike a function, a procedure is not required to return a value, but may accept and return multiple values. Figure 11.2 shows the procedure to update employee salaries.

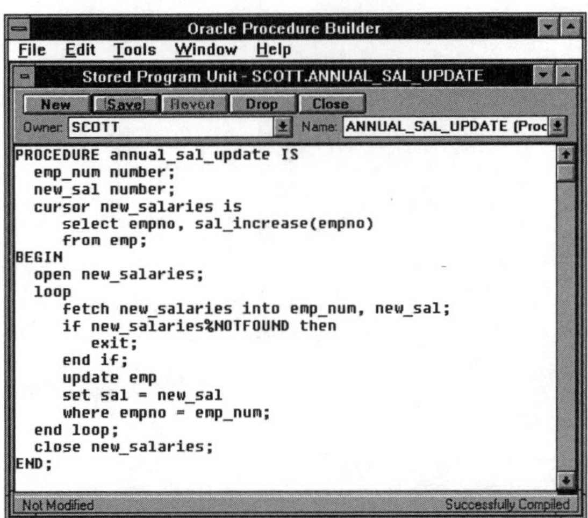

FIGURE 11.2.
A procedure that updates employee salaries.

The `annual_sal_update` procedure will be created in the second exercise at the end of this chapter. You will notice that in Figure 11.1 the `sal_increase` function returns a number, while in Figure 11.2 the `annual_sal_update` procedure does not accept or return any values.

Packages

Functions and procedures may exist independently or may be placed in a package. A package includes a specification and a body. The package specification includes the name and parameters for each of the functions and/or procedures in the package, as well as any common variables. The package body includes the PL/SQL source code for the functions and/or procedures. Functions and procedures may be placed in the package body and not included in the package specification in order to hide them from external references. Like functions and procedures, packages may exist in the local application or may be stored in the Oracle database.

CAUTION

Any program units that reference built-in packages that are specific to a product will only compile from within that product. For example, a procedure that uses SET_ITEM_PROPERTY from Oracle Forms will not compile in Oracle Procedure Builder.

Libraries

Libraries are collections of program units and attached libraries. They are external to the application and may be saved to the file system or the database. Libraries that have been saved to the database may be used by other Oracle users. Library access is granted or revoked by selecting Library Access from the File menu, and using the Grant Access List dialog box.

Libraries may be attached to Oracle Procedure Builder so that the program units they contain may be referenced. But, to edit a library it must be opened in Oracle Procedure Builder, and not just attached. Libraries may be opened from ASCII files on the file system, or from the database by selecting Open from the File menu.

Triggers

Oracle Procedure Builder supports the definition of database triggers utilizing PL/SQL and the Database Trigger Editor. One or more database triggers may be defined for each table in the database. Figure 11.3 shows a database trigger for the EMP table.

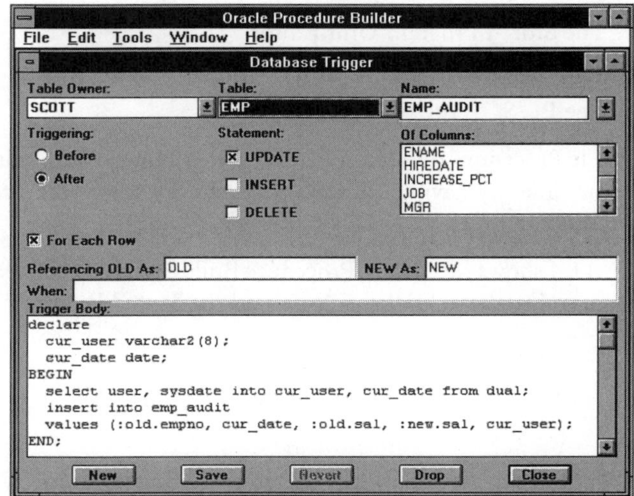

FIGURE 11.3.
A database trigger for the EMP table.

The Database Trigger Editor is a GUI front end for the create trigger command and makes the selection of database objects and trigger options very easy. The same database triggers can be created at the SQL command line in the PL/SQL Interpreter, SQL*Plus, SQL*DBA, or any product that provides a SQL command-line interface to an Oracle database.

Debugging

Oracle Procedure Builder includes the PL/SQL Interpreter for debugging program units that are being developed and tested as independent PL/SQL objects. For debugging PL/SQL objects that are dependent on a specific tool, use the PL/SQL Interpreter that is integrated within the tool, as opposed to using Oracle Procedure Builder.

Oracle Procedure Builder

Oracle Procedure Builder is an integrated development environment used for creating program units, libraries, and database objects. Since there is only one independent component of Oracle Procedure Builder, Oracle Procedure Builder is the equivalent of the Designer tools for Oracle Forms, Oracle Reports, and Oracle Graphics. For example, Oracle Procedure Builder does not include a runtime, batch, or conversion component.

Within Oracle Procedure Builder there are several tools and features that are used during the development process. These items will be reviewed next. They include:

- The Object Navigator
- Toolbars
- The Program Unit Editor
- The Stored Program Unit Editor
- The Database Trigger Editor
- The PL/SQL Interpreter

In Oracle Procedure Builder, like the other Designer tools, multiple windows may be open at the same time. By having multiple windows open, you can use the tools together or you can return to them quickly.

Figure 11.4 shows the Oracle Procedure Builder with the Object Navigator, the Program Unit Editor, the Database Trigger Editor, and the Stored Program Unit Editor windows open.

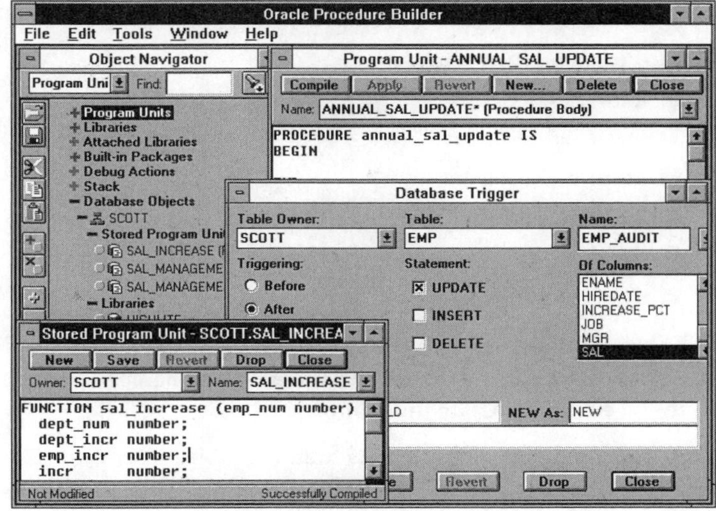

FIGURE 11.4.
Oracle Procedure Builder with multiple tools and windows open.

Object Navigator

The Object Navigator was reviewed in Chapter 7, "Introducing Oracle Developer/2000." But Oracle Procedure Builder incorporates a few additional features into the Object Navigator that will be reviewed here. In addition, the specific object types within Oracle Procedure Builder will be reviewed. Figure 11.5 shows the Oracle Procedure Builder window, with the Object Navigator displaying the major nodes.

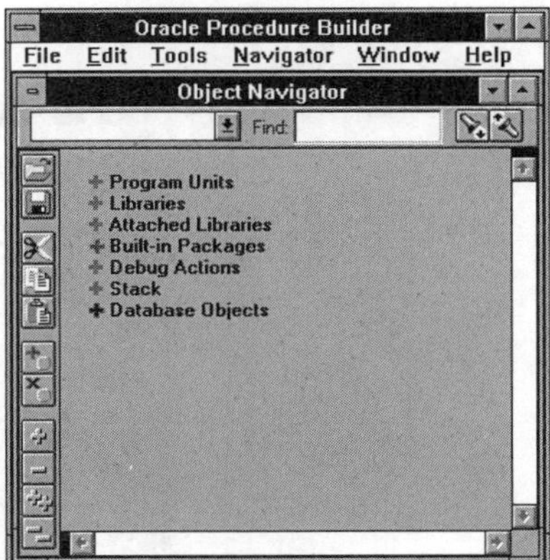

FIGURE 11.5.
Oracle Procedure Builder with the Object Navigator.

The major nodes in the Oracle Procedure Builder Object Navigator are:

- Program Units
- Libraries
- Attached Libraries
- Built-in Packages
- Debug Actions
- Stack
- Database Objects

The Navigator menu contains menu items for enabling and disabling debug actions, as well as menu items for pasting the selected program unit name or program unit name with arguments into the current program unit editor.

You can compile PL/SQL objects from the Object Navigator directly without having to open the Program Unit Editor. This is done by selecting the PL/SQL object from the Object Navigator and selecting the Compile menu item from the Navigator menu.

While in the Object Navigator, you will notice that the objects are organized by type. There are Program Units, Libraries, Attached Libraries, and so on.

Program Unit Object Types

Under the Program Units node you will find all the object types used for designing program units for your applications. Figure 11.6 shows the Object Navigator with the Program Units node expanded and containing the `SAL_INCREASE` function, its specification, and references from the first exercise at the end of this chapter.

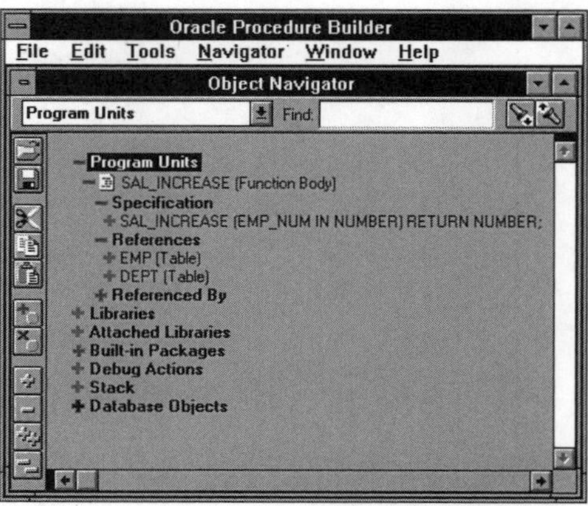

FIGURE 11.6.
The Object Navigator showing program units.

Oracle Procedure Builder supplies four object types under the Program Units node. Each object type, as it is presented in the Object Navigator, is listed here with a description.

Object Type	*Description*
Program Unit	The name and type of program unit.
Specification	The name and parameters of the program unit.
References	A list of objects referenced in the program unit.
Referenced By	A list of objects that reference the program unit.

Program units may be loaded from ASCII files on the file system by selecting Load from the File menu. ASCII text may also be imported or exported to and from the program unit editors using Import or Export from the File menu.

Library Object Types

Oracle Procedure Builder supports the creation and maintenance of libraries via the Libraries node in the Object Navigator. Under the Libraries node, you will find any open libraries with their associated program units, and attached libraries.

Attached Library Object Types

Oracle Procedure Builder is the only tool that includes Attached Libraries as a major node in the Object Navigator. This is because in each of the other tools, attached libraries support a specific module, while within Oracle Procedure Builder, independent PL/SQL objects may be created that are not necessarily part of an application module.

Built-in Package Object Types

Under the Built-in Packages node, you will find all of the built-in programs supplied with Oracle Procedure Builder. There are several built-in packages, and each one contains a group of supporting functions and procedures. Many of the built-in packages are the same ones found in Oracle Forms, Oracle Reports, and Oracle Graphics. You can find more information on the available packages, and the program units they contain in the Oracle Procedure Builder Reference Manual.

Debug Action Object Types

When debugging your PL/SQL program units, you will create breakpoints and triggers using the PL/SQL Interpreter. Each of the breakpoints and triggers are associated with a program unit and appear as debug actions in the Object Navigator.

Stack Object Types

When debug actions have been set and the application is run, the PL/SQL Interpreter appears containing the Navigator pane. The Stack node in the Object Navigator will contain a list of each of the program units called, as well as a list of all of the variables within the application, along with their current values. During the break in execution, the variables within the applications may be reviewed and modified prior to resuming the process.

Database Object Types

Once you are connected to an Oracle database, all of the database objects for each of the Oracle users are listed under the Database Objects node in the Object Navigator. Database objects include stored program units, libraries, tables, and views. Under the tables and views nodes, you will find their respective columns. Database triggers are also listed under the tables node.

Having the database objects available from Oracle Procedure Builder provides you as a developer with an integrated development environment. This means that you don't have to leave Oracle Procedure Builder to locate, review, create, or modify many of the database objects that will be used by your applications.

Figure 11.7 shows the Object Navigator, with the Database node expanded, revealing each of the database objects owned by SCOTT, including the database trigger from the final exercise at the end of this chapter.

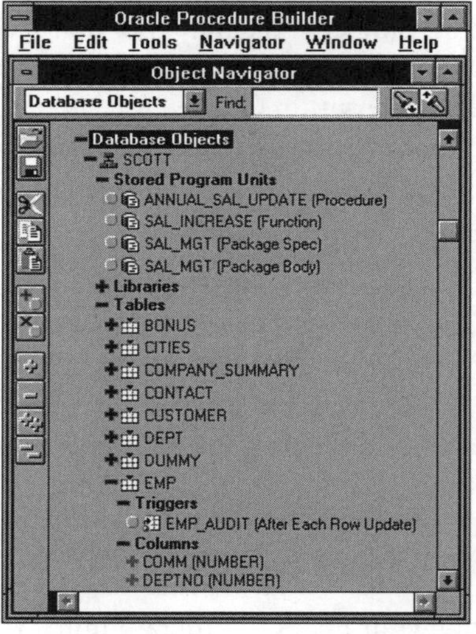

FIGURE 11.7.
The Object Navigator showing the database objects owned by SCOTT.

Oracle Procedure Builder Toolbars

The Oracle Procedure Builder only includes two toolbars: the standard toolbar on the Object Navigator and a toolbar for the PL/SQL Interpreter.

The Object Navigator Toolbar

The Object Navigator toolbar contains additional buttons for Cut, Copy, and Paste. Interestingly, the toolbar does not contain buttons for Copy Properties and Paste Properties as found in Oracle Forms and on the Oracle Procedure Builder Navigator menu.

PL/SQL Interpreter Toolbar

The PL/SQL Interpreter has several buttons on the toolbar used for debugging. The Create, Delete, Expand, Collapse, and Search buttons are only present when a break has been encountered and the navigator pane is displayed. The following list describes the buttons that are found on the toolbar.

Button	*Description*
Step Into	Steps into called program units.
Step Over	Steps over a called program unit.
Step Out	Stops after the called program unit is executed.
Go	Resumes execution of the current program unit.
Reset	Terminates execution of the current program unit.
Close	Closes the PL/SQL Interpreter window.
Create	Creates an object of the type selected.
Delete	Deletes the selected object(s).
Expand	Expands the current branch one level.
Collapse	Collapses the current branch one level.
Expand All	Expands all branches under the current node.
Collapse All	Collapses all branches under the current node.
Search Forward	Searches forward for the find string.
Search Back	Searches backward for the find string.

Figure 11.8 shows the PL/SQL Interpreter toolbar as it initially appears.

Figure 11.9 shows the PL/SQL Interpreter toolbar as it appears during a break in a debugging session.

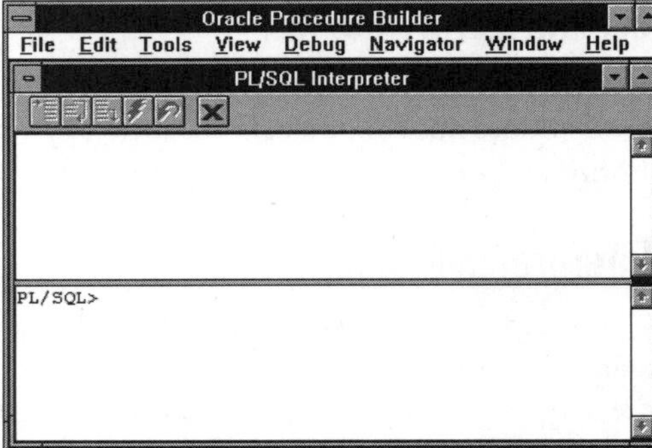

FIGURE 11.8.
The initial PL/SQL Interpreter toolbar.

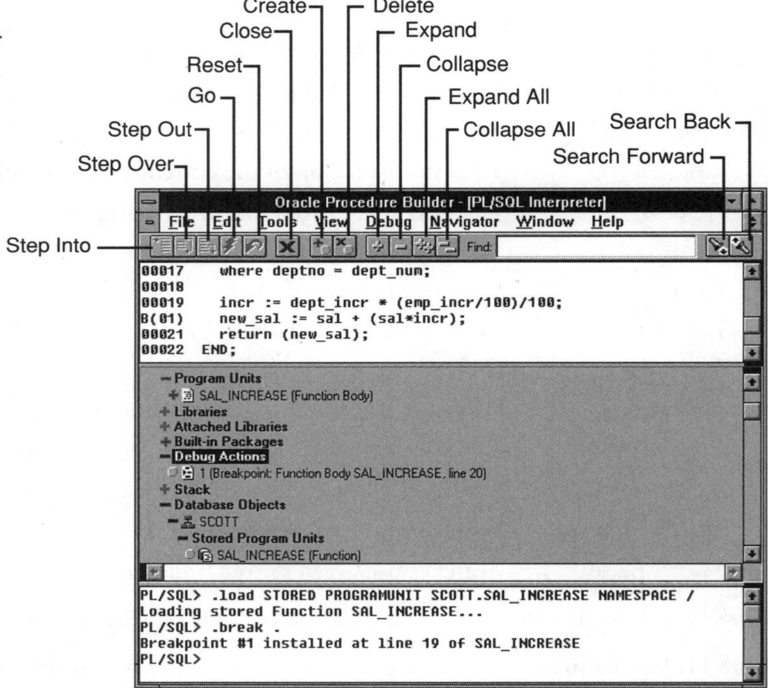

FIGURE 11.9.
The PL/SQL Interpreter toolbar during a break.

Program Unit Editor

The Program Unit Editor in Oracle Procedure Builder is used to create and maintain local program units. It is identical in appearance and function to the PL/SQL Editor in Oracle Forms as well as the Program Unit Editor in Oracle Reports and Oracle Graphics. Functions, procedures, package bodies, and package specifications are all PL/SQL program units that can be edited using the Program Unit Editor. You will recognize the button bar, the identification fields, the source pane, and the status line as shown in the Program Unit Editor in Figure 11.10.

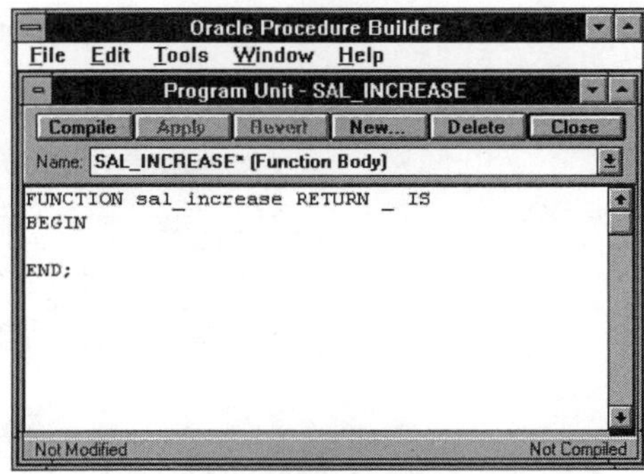

FIGURE 11.10.
The Program Unit Editor.

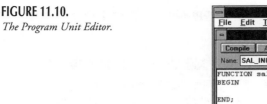

Whenever a new function, procedure, or package is created, the Program Unit Editor is automatically initialized with a default template of PL/SQL that includes a shell for the program unit.

Functions

A local function is created in the Object Navigator by selecting the Program Units node and clicking the Create button on the tool palette, then selecting the program unit type and giving it a name. Figure 11.11 shows the New Program Unit dialog box that is displayed while the user creates the `sal_increase` function.

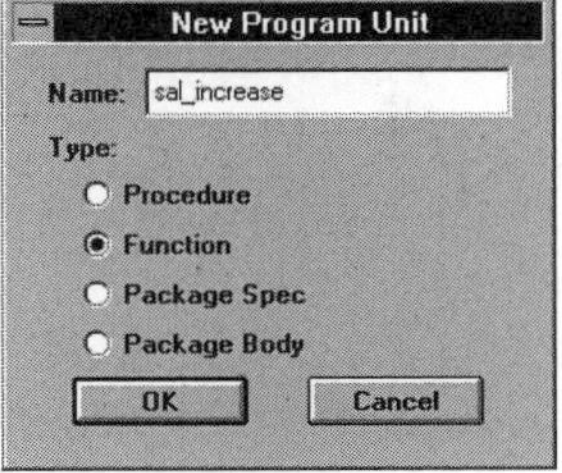

FIGURE 11.11.
The New Program Unit dialog box creating a function.

Once the program unit type and name are entered, the Program Unit Editor is invoked. The function is initialized as a shell of PL/SQL code containing the function name, a return, a begin statement, and an end statement. You identify the return type as number, char, or date. Then enter any declarations before the begin statement. Enter the PL/SQL in the begin block, and compile.

Procedures

Local procedures are created in the same manner as functions, except that Procedure is selected from the New Program Unit dialog box. The Program Unit Editor is shown in Figure 11.12 with the source pane containing the `annual_sal_update` procedure, the status line indicating that the procedure compiled with errors, and the compilation messages pane containing the compile errors.

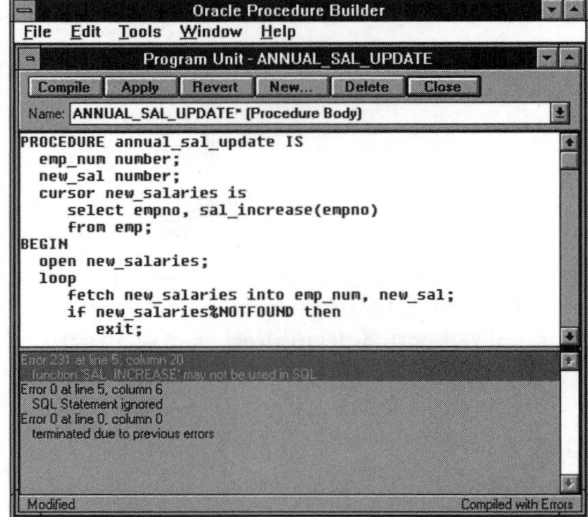

FIGURE 11.12.
The Program Unit Editor with a compile error.

> **NOTE**
>
> The compile error was caused by the procedure trying to reference a local function in a SQL select statement. When we move the function to the database, it becomes a database function and then may be referenced in the select statement without any compiled errors.

Packages

Local packages are created by creating a program unit of type Package Spec and entering the package-specification information. Then you create a program unit of type Package Body and enter the PL/SQL source code.

Package Specifications

Package specifications define the package by naming each of the functions and/or procedures in the package with their associated parameter lists. Also found in the package specification are any common declarations of variables or cursors.

Package Bodies

Package bodies include all of the PL/SQL source code to support the specified functions and/or procedures. The package body may also include additional functions and/or procedures internally that are not available to be referenced directly.

Stored Program Unit Editor

The Stored Program Unit Editor in Oracle Procedure Builder provides you with a graphical user interface to the create function, create procedure, create package, and create package body SQL commands. Stored program units reside within the Oracle database. Each type of stored program unit could be created using any SQL command-line interface to the Oracle database. Notice in Figure 11.13, the `annual_sal_update` procedure is created using the SQL command line from SQL*Plus.

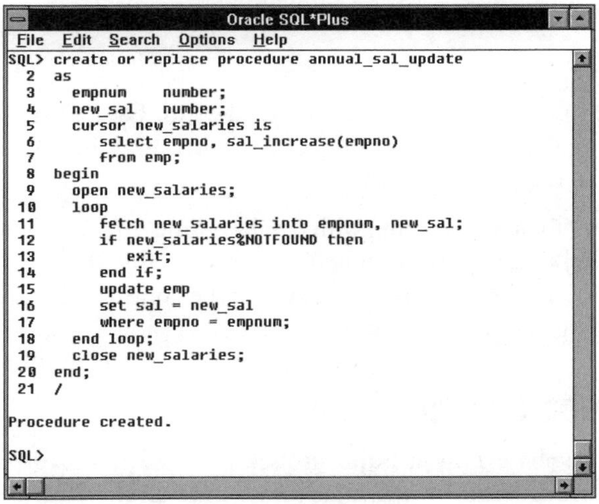

FIGURE 11.13.
*Oracle SQL*Plus creating a procedure.*

Oracle SQL*Plus

File Edit Search Options Help

```
SQL> create or replace procedure annual_sal_update
as
  empnum    number;
  new_sal   number;
  cursor new_salaries is
     select empno, sal_increase(empno)
     from emp;
begin
  open new_salaries;
  loop
     fetch new_salaries into empnum, new_sal;
     if new_salaries%NOTFOUND then
        exit;
     end if;
     update emp
     set sal = new_sal
     where empno = empnum;
  end loop;
  close new_salaries;
end;
/

Procedure created.

SQL>
```

The Stored Program Unit Editor in Oracle Procedure Builder is similar in appearance and function to the Program Unit Editor. As with the Program Unit Editor, all PL/SQL objects created in the Stored Program Unit Editor become program units. Notice, however, that the button bar and the identification fields are somewhat different, as shown in Figure 11.14.

The Stored Program Unit Editor button bar contains New, Save, Revert, Drop, and Close buttons, while the Program Unit Editor button bar has Compile, Apply, Revert, New, Delete, and Close. In the Stored Program Unit Editor, the program unit is compiled automatically when it is saved.

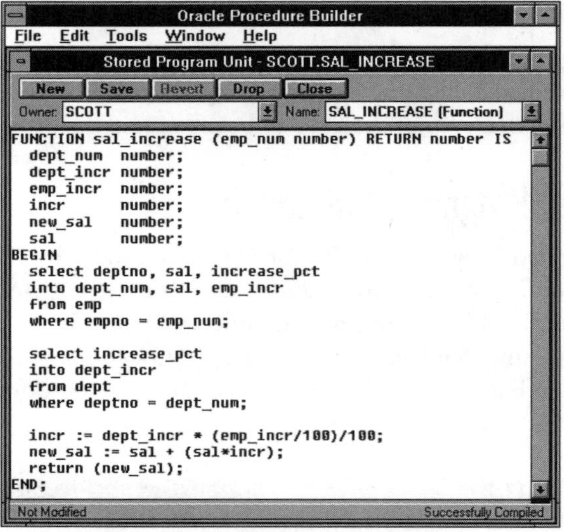

FIGURE 11.14.
The Stored Program Unit Editor.

Stored program units must be owned by an Oracle user, and just under the button bar is a drop-down list that shows the current user as well as all of the other Oracle users that could own stored program units.

Whether you are working with database functions, database procedures, or database packages, you will find the process much the same as using the Program Unit Editor that was discussed earlier. Local program units may even be copied to become stored program units simply by dragging and dropping in the Object Navigator.

Database Trigger Editor

The Database Trigger Editor is used to create and maintain database triggers. Each database trigger is associated with a table owner and a table. The Database Trigger Editor provides drop-down lists to select the table owner, table name, and trigger name as well as radio groups, check boxes, text lists, and text items to enable you to quickly and easily build triggers in the Oracle database.

Database Triggers

A database trigger is created by selecting an owner, a table, and the other options in the editor, and then adding PL/SQL to the trigger body. Figure 11.15 shows the Database Trigger Editor as it appears while the user creates the audit trigger for the EMP table.

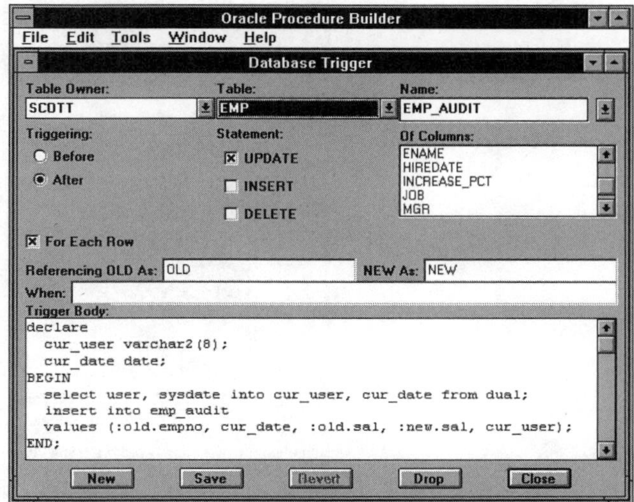

FIGURE 11.15.
The Database Trigger Editor.

The `create trigger`, `alter trigger`, or `drop trigger` SQL commands are built in the background and processed by Oracle Procedure Builder, and the Oracle database as you work in the Database Trigger Editor.

Debugging

When debugging your PL/SQL program units, you will create breakpoints and break triggers using the PL/SQL Interpreter. During any break, you can review and modify the contents of any of the items in your application by using the navigator. You may also use a debug script that was created and saved earlier, or save the contents of the debugging session to a log file.

The PL/SQL Interpreter

You can debug your PL/SQL program units by selecting them in the Object Navigator, then invoking the PL/SQL Interpreter from the Tools menu. The selected program unit will appear in the source frame at the top of the window. From the source frame you can set your breaks for debugging. During a break in execution, the navigator frame will appear in the middle of the PL/SQL Interpreter. The navigator frame functions just as the Object Navigator does, but it also enables you to review and modify item values.

The PL/SQL Interpreter is shown in Figure 11.16 with the `sal_increase` function containing a breakpoint on line 20.

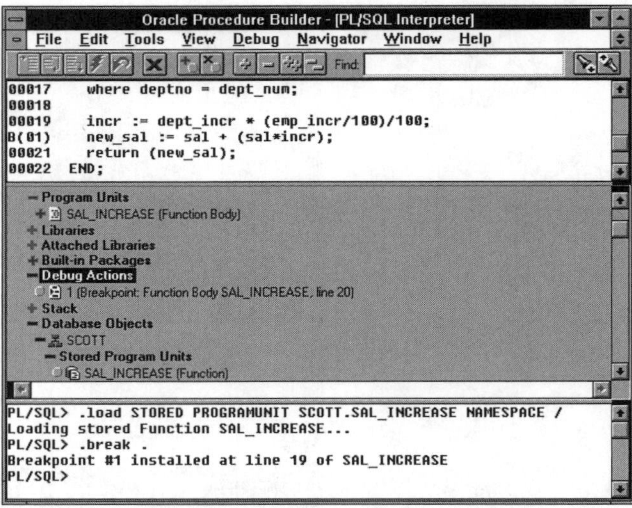

FIGURE 11.16.
The PL/SQL Interpreter.

At the bottom of the PL/SQL Interpreter window is a PL/SQL command line. The PL/SQL command line supports any PL/SQL statement or anonymous block, as well as standard SQL statements like those used in SQL*Plus, or SQL*DBA.

Figure 11.17 shows the PL/SQL Interpreter with the PL/SQL command line containing the create statement for the EMP_AUDIT table.

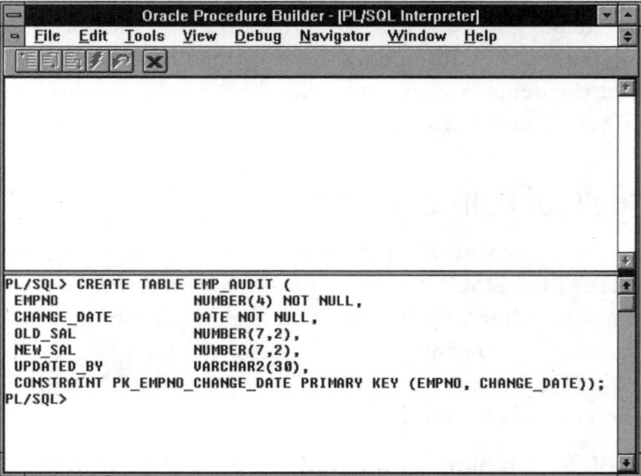

FIGURE 11.17.
The PL/SQL Interpreter creates a table.

Breakpoints

A breakpoint will stop the execution of a program unit at that location. To create a breakpoint, position your cursor at the desired location in the source code and choose Break from the Debug menu. Double-clicking on a source line will also set a breakpoint on that line, while double-clicking again will remove the break.

Figure 11.16 shows the PL/SQL Interpreter Navigator pane with a breakpoint under the Debug Actions node.

Break Triggers

Break triggers execute PL/SQL at a specified point of program execution. To create a break trigger, position your cursor at the desired location in the source code and select Trigger from the Debug menu. The PL/SQL Breakpoint dialog box will appear with the program unit and line number specified, as well as a text item where you can enter the PL/SQL for the trigger body.

PL/SQL Interpreter Script Files

Oracle Procedure Builder supports the use of script files for the PL/SQL Interpreter. Script files contain PL/SQL Interpreter commands and may be created using any ASCII text editor, such as Notepad, or they may be created by logging the PL/SQL Interpreter commands. Once a script file is loaded, each of the PL/SQL or Oracle Procedure Builder commands in that script file are executed. To load a script file, select Interpret from the File menu, then select the script file and options from the Interpret Debug Script dialog box. (See Figure 11.18.)

FIGURE 11.18.
The Interpret Debug Script dialog box.

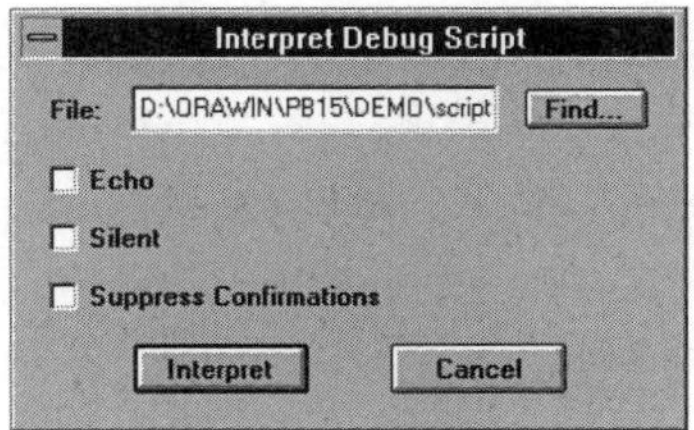

PL/SQL Interpreter Logs

You can save the results of the current debugging session to a log file by selecting Log from the File menu and then selecting a log filename and log options from the Log Interpreter dialog box. (See Figure 11.19.)

When Show Log is selected, the PL/SQL Interpreter Log window is displayed. The PL/SQL Interpreter Log is used to review the current log file during debugging.

FIGURE 11.19.
The Log Interpreter dialog box.

Exercises

The purpose of these exercises is to familiarize you with Oracle Procedure Builder. In addition, it will give you some hands-on review of the material that has been covered in this chapter. You will create a function, a procedure, a package, and a database trigger.

A Function To Calculate Salary Increases

In this exercise a function is created to calculate a salary increase for an employee. The function receives the value of EMP_NUM and returns a new value for salary.

1. Open Oracle Procedure Builder.
2. Close the PL/SQL Interpreter window.
3. Connect to the Oracle database as scott/tiger by selecting Connect from the File menu.
4. Invoke the New Program Unit dialog box by double-clicking the Program Units node in the Object Navigator.
5. Select the Function radio button for the Type.
6. Enter the function name as `sal_increase`, and press OK.
7. The Program Unit Editor appears. Notice the function shell is initialized in the editor.
8. Add the following text before the `RETURN` statement `(emp_num number)`. This is the input parameter.
9. For the return type, change the _ to `number`.
10. Enter the following declarations before the `BEGIN` statement:

```
dept_num  number;
dept_incr number;
emp_incr  number;
incr      number;
new_sal   number;
sal       number;
```

11. Enter the following PL/SQL after the `BEGIN` statement:

```
select deptno, sal, increase_pct
into deptnum, sal, emp_incr
```

```
from emp
where empno = emp_num;

select increase_pct
into dept_incr
from dept
where deptno = dept_num;

incr := dept_incr * (emp_incr/100)/100;
new_sal := sal + (sal*incr);
return (new_sal);
```

12. Compile the function by clicking the Compile button, and then press Close.
13. Notice the function appears in the Object Navigator.
14. Click on the Database Objects node in the Object Navigator, then click on SCOTT, then click on Stored Program Units. This will reveal the stored program units that the user SCOTT owns.
15. Click and drag the SAL_INCREASE program unit down to the Stored Program Units node in the Object Navigator. This will copy the function from the local application to the Oracle database.
16. Delete SAL_INCREASE under the local Program Units node.
17. Note that the function could have been created initially under the Stored Program Units node in the Object Navigator.

A Procedure To Update Salaries Annually

In this exercise a procedure is created to update the salaries of all employees. This procedure includes the use of the `sal_increase` function in the SQL select statement.

1. Invoke the New Program Unit dialog box by selecting the Stored Program Units node in the Object Navigator and clicking the Create button on the tool palette.
2. Select the Procedure radio button for the Type.
3. Enter the procedure name as `annual_sal_update`, and press OK.
4. The Stored Program Unit Editor appears. Notice the procedure shell is initialized in the editor.
5. Enter the following declarations before the `BEGIN` statement:

```
empnum    number;
new_sal   number;
cursor new_salaries is
   select empno, sal_increase(empno)
   from emp;
```

6. Enter the following PL/SQL after the `BEGIN` statement:

```
open new_salaries;
loop
   fetch new_salaries into empnum, new_sal;
   if new_salaries%NOTFOUND then
```

```
      exit;
   end if;
   update emp
   set sal = new_sal
   where empno = empnum;
end loop;
close new_salaries;
```

7. Compile and save the procedure by clicking the Save button, and then press Close.
8. Notice the procedure appears in the Object Navigator.

A PackageTo Contain the Function and Procedure

In this exercise a package is created that contains a procedure, and a function. This package also supports the calculation, and update of salary increases for employees.

1. Invoke the New Program Unit dialog box by selecting the Stored Program Units node in the Object Navigator and clicking the Create button on the tool palette.
2. For the Type, select the Package Spec radio button.
3. Enter the package name as `sal_mgt`, and press OK.
4. The Stored Program Unit Editor appears. Notice the package specification shell is initialized in the editor.
5. Enter the following package specifications before the `END` statement:

```
procedure sal_update;
function sal_incr (emp_num number) return number;
```

6. Compile and save the package specification by clicking the Save button, and then press Close.
7. Notice the package specification appears in the Object Navigator.
8. Invoke the New Program Unit dialog box by selecting the Stored Program Units node in the Object Navigator and clicking the Create button on the tool palette.
9. Select the Package Body radio button for the Type.
10. Enter the package name as `sal_mgt`, and press OK.
11. The Stored Program Unit Editor appears. Notice the package body shell is initialized in the editor.
12. Enter the following package body before the `END` statement:

```
procedure sal_update is
  empnum    number;
  new_sal   number;
  cursor new_salaries is
     select empno
     from emp;
begin
  open new_salaries;
  loop
     fetch new_salaries into empnum;
```

```
      if new_salaries%NOTFOUND then
         exit;
      end if;
      new_sal := sal_incr(empnum);
      update emp
      set sal = new_sal
      where empno = empnum;
   end loop;
   close new_salaries;
end;
function sal_incr (emp_num number) return number is
   dept_num  number;
   dept_incr number;
   emp_incr  number;
   incr      number;
   new_sal   number;
   sal       number;
begin
   select deptno, sal, increase_pct
   into dept_num, sal, emp_incr
   from emp
   where empno = emp_num;

   select increase_pct into dept_incr
   from dept
   where deptno = dept_num;

   incr := dept_incr * (emp_incr/100)/100;
   new_sal := sal + (sal*incr);
   return (new_sal);
end;
```

13. Compile and save the package body by clicking the Save button, and then press Close.
14. Notice the package body appears in the Object Navigator.

A Database Trigger To Audit Employee Salary Increases

In this exercise a database trigger is created that captures audit information on employee salary increases. This trigger inserts a record into the EMP_AUDIT table whenever the salary of an employee is updated.

1. Click on the Tables node in the Object Navigator, then click on EMP. This will reveal the Triggers and Columns nodes for the EMP table.
2. Invoke the Database Trigger Editor by double-clicking on the Triggers node in the Object Navigator.
3. Press the New button to create a new database trigger.
4. Change the trigger name to EMP_AUDIT.
5. Select the After radio button for Triggering.
6. Select the Statement UPDATE check box. Notice the list of columns appears.
7. Scroll down and select the SAL column.

8. Select the For Each Row check box. Notice that the Referencing and When fields are enabled.
9. Enter the following declarations before the BEGIN statement in the Trigger Body:

```
declare
  cur_user varchar2(8);
  cur_date date;
```

10. Enter the following PL/SQL after the BEGIN statement:

```
select user, sysdate
into cur_user, cur_date from dual;
insert into emp_audit
values (:old.empno, cur_date, :old.sal, :new.sal, cur_user);
```

11. Compile and save the procedure by clicking the Save button, and then press Close.
12. Notice the trigger appears in the Object Navigator.

Summary

This chapter provided you with an overview of Oracle Procedure Builder including:

- The components of Oracle Procedure Builder
- The basics of Oracle Procedure Builder, including functions, procedures, packages, libraries, triggers, and debugging
- Object types in the Object Navigator
- The Oracle Procedure Builder toolbars
- The Program Unit Editor
- The Stored Program Unit Editor
- The Database Trigger Editor
- Debugging with the PL/SQL Interpreter

If you worked through the exercise, you have created a function, a procedure, a package, and a database trigger. You also now know how to copy PL/SQL objects from the local application to the database by dragging and dropping via the Object Navigator.

Now that you are familiar with the features of Oracle Procedure Builder, we will continue with the development of Oracle Forms applications.

IV

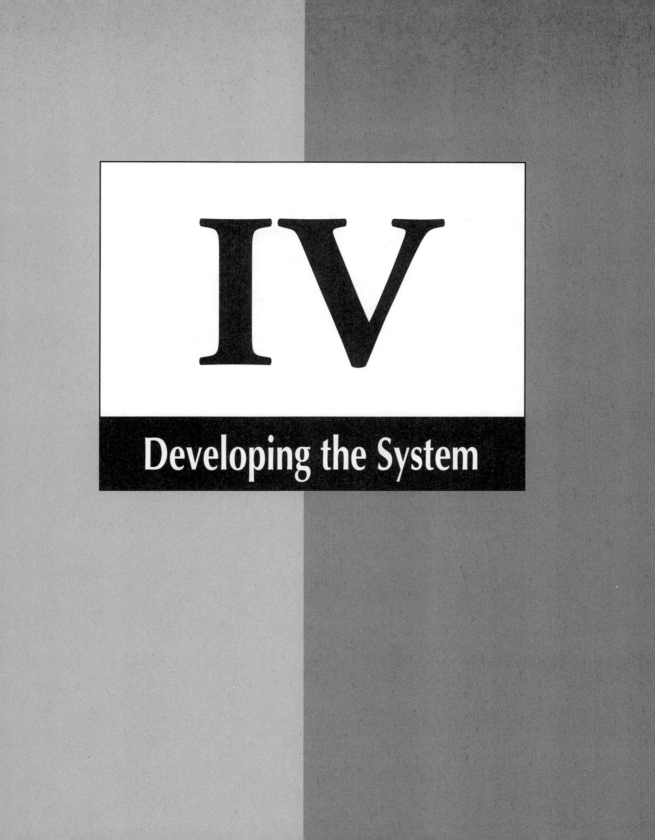

Developing the System

12

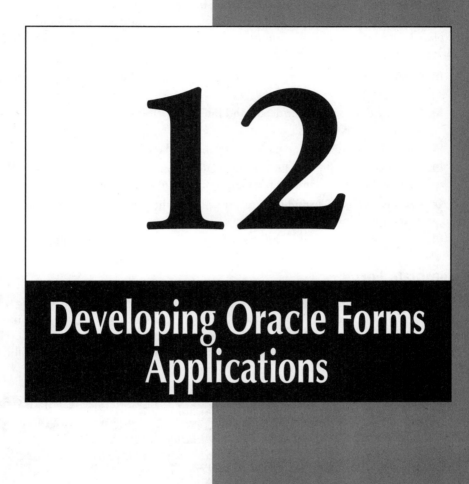

Developing Oracle Forms Applications

Introduction

Now that we've had a look at each of the tools in Oracle Developer/2000 and have completed a few exercises that introduced us to the components and features of the products, we will now explore in greater depth the development of applications. In reading and working through this chapter, you will do the following:

- Create Oracle Forms templates containing visual attributes, property classes, a toolbar, and triggers
- Create multi-row, master/detail, and integrated Oracle Forms applications using the template forms
- Create lists of values for data selection and validation
- Use Object Linking and Embedding (OLE) from sources such as the MS ClipArt Gallery, MS Word, and Oracle Graphics in your application
- Use Visual Basic Custom Controls to enhance the user interface and functionality of your application
- Complete the standard Windows-style pull-down menus for your applications

Template Forms

In this chapter we will develop several Oracle Forms applications, but we will begin by creating two template forms. Template forms contain objects that will be common to all of our Forms applications. By creating the templates once and using them in all of our development, we achieve consistent and standardized applications. Each of the applications will use a template to get started, including the one shown in Figure 12.1.

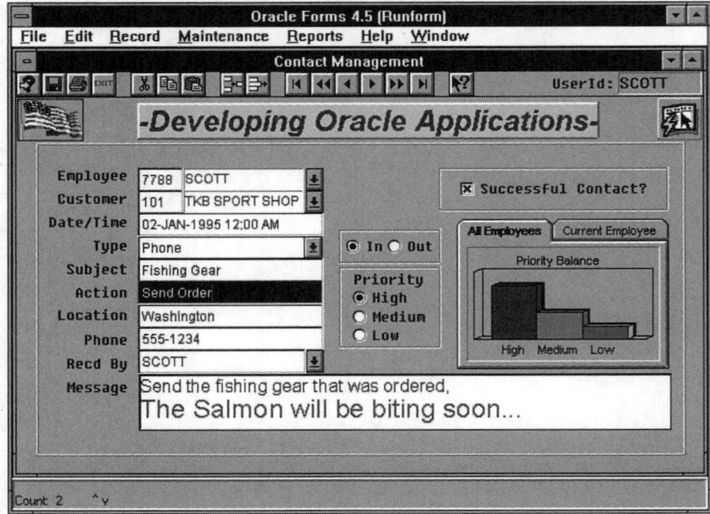

FIGURE 12.1.
The Contact Management forms application.

The template forms will be created by setting the module properties and creating visual attributes, a canvas, a control block, some items, some property classes, a toolbar, and attaching a library. To create the template forms, follow these steps:

1. Open Oracle Forms Designer.
2. Connect to the Oracle database as scott/tiger.
3. Rename the module to TEMPLIST.
4. Select Save As from the File menu and save the form as TEMPLIST.FMB.

Module Properties

Use the module properties of Oracle Forms to name the application and associate our standard menu with it. (See Figure 12.2.) The standard menu was created in Chapter 8, "Introducing Oracle Forms," and will be completed later in this chapter. To name the application follow these steps:

1. Double-click on the form module icon under Forms in the Object Navigator to invoke the Properties window.
2. Change the menu module from DEFAULT to standard.

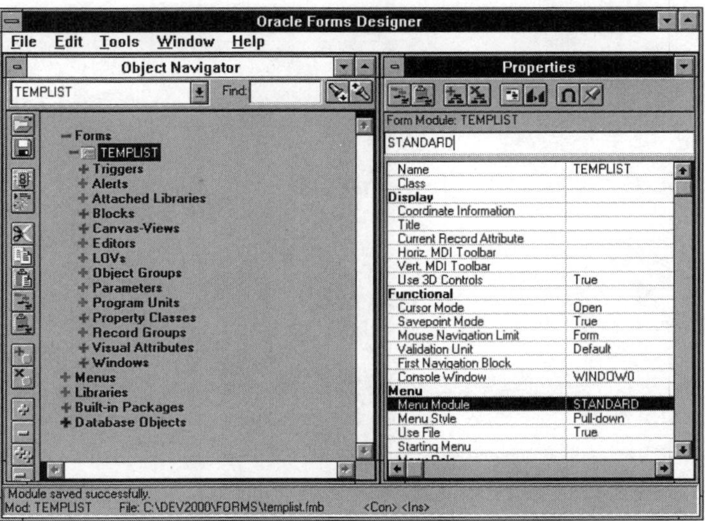

FIGURE 12.2.
Form module properties referencing our standard menu.

Visual Attributes

We will create two standard visual attributes to use in our applications. The first is used to highlight the current row in a multi-row block or the current item in a single row block. The second visual attribute returns the item(s) to their original appearance. To create two standard visual attributes, follow these steps:

1. Double-click on the gray plus sign to the left of Visual Attributes in the Object Navigator to create a new visual attribute.
2. Change the visual attribute name to CURRENT.
3. Set the Font Name to Arial.
4. Set the Font Size to 9.
5. Set the Foreground Color to white.
6. Set the Background Color to blue.
7. Click on the Visual Attributes node in the Object Navigator, and then click the create button to create another visual attribute.
8. Change the visual attribute name to DEFAULT.
9. Set the Font Name to Arial.
10. Set the Font Size to 9.

The visual attributes we just created are shown in Figure 12.3, and will be used in all the Forms applications we develop.

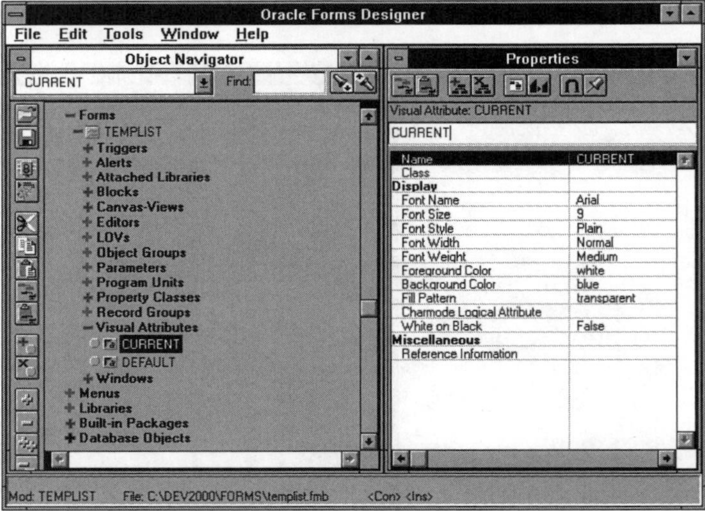

FIGURE 12.3.
Visual attributes for highlighting items.

Canvases

Oracle Forms supports several canvas types including content, stacked, horizontal toolbar, and vertical toolbar. All Oracle Forms applications contain canvases, blocks, and items. Our templates will contain a canvas for a horizontal toolbar as well as a control block and items that will be standard throughout our development. First we will create the canvas, then we will add the control block and the other items.

1. Select Layout Editor from the Tools menu.
2. Notice a default canvas-view has been created.
3. Change the canvas-view name to TOOLBAR.
4. In the Properties window, change the canvas-view type to Horizontal Toolbar.
5. Change the height to 17.
6. Select WINDOW0 from the Object Navigator.
7. Set Horizontal Toolbar to TOOLBAR.

Later in this chapter we will create Forms applications that also contain content canvases and a stacked canvas.

Blocks and Items

Here we will create a non-base table control block, a button, and a display item for the template forms.

1. Return to the Layout Editor, and select the Push Button icon from the tool palette.
2. Create a button in the layout; notice that a non-base table default block has been created.
3. Change the block name to CONTROL.
4. Return to the Layout Editor, and double-click on the button item to activate the Properties window.
5. Change the item name to TOOL_BUTTON.
6. Set the X and Y positions to 0.
7. Change the width and height to 17.
8. Set Navigable to False.
9. Set Mouse Navigate to False.
10. Delete the label.
11. Set Iconic to True.
12. Create a WHEN-BUTTON-PRESSED trigger for the button item.
13. Close the PL/SQL Editor.

Now we will create a display item to show the current user on the toolbar.

1. Create a new item via the Object Navigator.
2. Change the item name to USERID.
3. Change the item type to Display Item.
4. Select TOOLBAR from the drop-down list for the Canvas.
5. Set the X position to 410 and the Y position to 0.

6. Set the width to 57 and the height to 17.
7. Set Base Table Item to False.
8. Return to the Layout Editor, click the text tool button, and add `Userid:` as the label to the left side of the USERID display item.

Now we have a canvas, a control block, a button, and a display item for the current user. Later we will add the rest of the buttons to the toolbar, but first we will create the tool button property class.

Property Classes

Property classes are one of the object-oriented features of Oracle Forms. In this chapter we will create two property classes for the template forms. One property class will be used for the buttons on the toolbar, and the other will be used for the list of value buttons. We will create the property class now for the tool buttons as shown in Figure 12.4, and we will create the property class for the list of values later in this chapter. To create the property class for the tool buttons:

1. Select TOOL_BUTTON, then click the Property Class button on the toolbar in the Properties window to create a new property class.
2. Click OK to acknowledge that the new property class has been created.
3. Select the new property class from the Object Navigator.
4. Change the property class name to TOOL_BUTTON.
5. Select X position from the Properties window, then click the Delete Property button on the toolbar.
6. Select Icon Name from the Properties window, then click the Delete Property button on the toolbar.
7. Save the form.

We deleted the X position and the icon-name properties for the tool button because they will be unique to each button.

Toolbar

Each Forms application we develop will contain a standard toolbar. The toolbar will contain button items, triggers, and a display item for the current user. Now that we have a toolbar property class, we can create each of the tool buttons and their associated triggers. There are a total of 16 buttons on the toolbar, and each one will have a WHEN-BUTTON-PRESSED trigger. To create a tool button, do the following:

1. Select the TOOL_BUTTON item in the Object Navigator, then change the property class to TOOL_BUTTON.

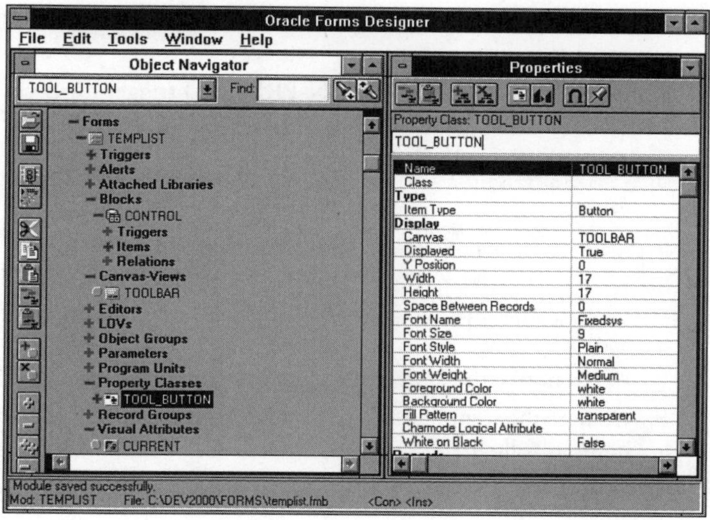

FIGURE 12.4.
The TOOL_BUTTON property class for the toolbar.

2. Click on the Copy button on the tool palette in the Object Navigator, then click on the Paste button 15 times to create all the buttons on the toolbar.
3. Change the name of TOOL_BUTTON to ENTERQRY, then set the icon name to entquery.
4. Open the WHEN-BUTTON-PRESSED trigger for ENTERQRY and enter the following PL/SQL code:

```
declare
item_id item;
begin
  item_id := find_item ('CONTROL.ENTERQRY');
  if :System.Mode = 'ENTER-QUERY' then
     set_item_property (item_id, ICON_NAME, 'entquery');
     do_key ('execute_query');
  else
     set_item_property (item_id, ICON_NAME, 'exequery');
     do_key ('enter_query');
  end if;
end;
```

   Notice we are using two different icons for the query tool button, depending on the system mode.

5. Change the item names, icon names, and triggers of the next two button items to the following:

ITEM NAME	*ICON NAME*	*TRIGGER TEXT*
SAVE	saveb	`do_key('commit_form');`
PRINTER	printer	`execute_trigger('print_doc');`

6. Select the next button item, change the name of the button to EXIT, then set the icon name to exitb.
7. Open the WHEN-BUTTON-PRESSED trigger for EXIT and enter the following PL/SQL code:

```
declare
item_id item;
begin
   if :System.Mode = 'ENTER-QUERY' then
      item_id := find_item ('CONTROL.ENTERQRY');
      set_item_property (item_id, ICON_NAME, 'entquery');
   end if;
   do_key('exit_form');
end;
```

   Again notice the icon name is set based on the system mode.
8. Change the item names, icon names, and triggers of each of the remaining new button items as follows:

ITEM NAME	*ICON NAME*	*TRIGGER TEXT*
CUT	cut	`cut_region;`
COPY	copy	`copy_region;`
PASTE	paste	`paste_region;`
INSERT	insert	`do_key('create_record');`
DELETE	delete	`do_key('delete_record');`
FIRSTREC	firstrec	`first_record;`
PREVSET	prevset	`do_key('scroll_up');`
PREVREC	prevrec	`do_key('previous_record');`
NEXTREC	nextrec	`do_key('next_record');`
NEXTSET	nextset	`do_key('scroll_down);`
LASTREC	lastrec	`last_record;`
HELP	helpb	`help;`

   Notice the icon names are generally the same as the item name, with the exceptions of help, exit, save, and enterqry. All of the icons are included on the CD-ROM; however, Oracle has provided icons with the Oracle demos as well. The icons were named to avoid a confict between the two sets.
9. Select all of the toolbar buttons in the Object Navigator by selecting the ENTERQRY button item, then shift-clicking on the HELP button item.
10. Select Layout Editor from the Tools menu, then select Align Objects from the Arrange menu to invoke the Alignment Settings dialog box.
11. Select Stack Horizontally, then click OK.
12. Notice that the entire toolbar is now visible.
13. Select the HELP button in the layout, then press the right arrow key five times.

14. Select the buttons from HELP to FIRST RECORD, then press the right arrow key five times.
15. Select the buttons from HELP to CUT, then press the right arrow key five times.
16. Save the form.

Notice how we used the copy, paste, and alignment features to facilitate the creation of the toolbar. The separation of tool buttons with some space organizes them into functional groups.

Triggers

The template forms will also contain some form-level triggers. We will start with a WHEN-NEW-FORM-INSTANCE trigger and a user-named trigger. Later we will add a WHEN-NEW-ITEM-INSTANCE and a POST-TEXT-ITEM trigger. To add a form-level trigger, follow these steps:

1. Double-click the Triggers node in the Object Navigator to invoke the Triggers list of values.
2. Type the letters W, N, and F to select the WHEN-NEW-FORM-INSTANCE trigger, then press enter to invoke the PL/SQL Editor.
3. Type the following text:

```
set_window_property (FORMS_MDI_WINDOW, TITLE, 'Set in WHEN-NEW-FORM-INSTANCE
➥trigger');
select user into :control.userid from dual;
execute_query;
```

As we work through this chapter, we will return to the WHEN-NEW-FORM-INSTANCE trigger as shown in Figure 12.5 and add more PL/SQL. The additional code will be added as the feature is explained.

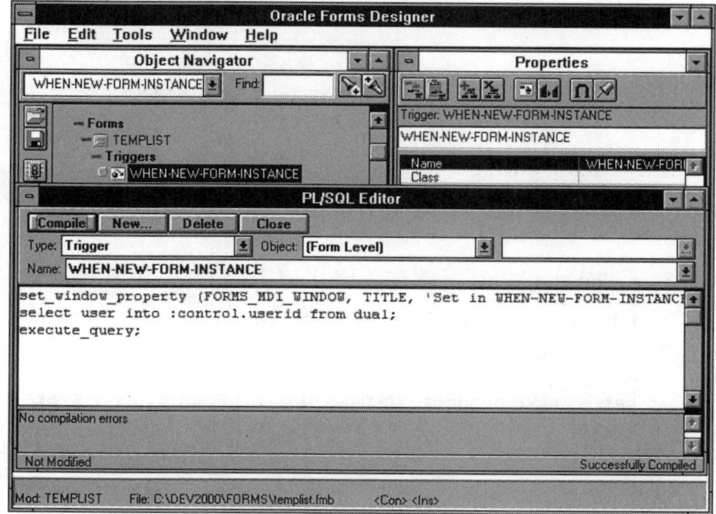

FIGURE 12.5.
The PL/SQL Editor with the WHEN-NEW-FORM-INSTANCE trigger shown.

Now we will add the user-named trigger to the template form, as follows:

1. Press the Compile button, then the New… button.
2. Press enter to select a user-named trigger.
3. Change the name to PRINT_DOC using the Object Navigator.
4. Return to the PL/SQL Editor and enter print;
5. Compile the trigger, and close the PL/SQL Editor.
6. Save the form.

The PL/SQL for the PRINT_DOC trigger as shown in Figure 12.6 will be changed in Chapter 15, "Integration and Deployment in the Windows Environment." For now, using print in the trigger allows us to create a placeholder in the template form, and the default behavior is to print the screen.

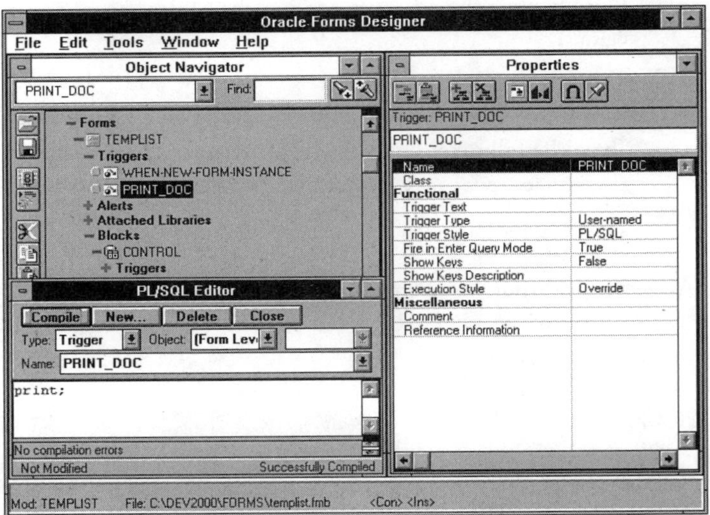

FIGURE 12.6.
The PL/SQL Editor with a user-named trigger shown.

The user-named trigger will be executed from our standard menu as well as our toolbar. Next we will create the second form template with the window maximized, as well as a property class for the list of values button.

1. Open the WHEN-NEW-FORM-INSTANCE trigger.
2. Change the trigger text to the following:

```
set_window_property (FORMS_MDI_WINDOW, TITLE, 'Set in WHEN-NEW-FORM-INSTANCE
➥trigger');
set_window_property (FORMS_MDI_WINDOW, WINDOW_STATE, MAXIMIZE);
select user into :control.userid from dual;
```

Notice we set the window size to Maximize and removed the execute query statement.

3. Change the module name to TEMPLATE.
4. Select the TOOL_BUTTON property class in the Object Navigator, then click on the Copy and Paste buttons on the tool palette.
5. Change the property class name to LOV_BUTTON.
6. Change the Canvas to <Null> from the Properties window.
7. Select Y Position, then click the Delete Property button on the toolbar.
8. Change the width to 13.
9. Click the Add Property button on the toolbar, then type the letter I, and press enter to automatically reduce the list and select Icon Name.
10. Set the Icon Name to Dropdown.
11. Create a WHEN-BUTTON-PRESSED trigger for LOV_BUTTON with the following code.

```
do_key('list_values');
```

12. Save the form as TEMPLATE.FMB.

The LOV_BUTTON property class is shown in Figure 12.7.

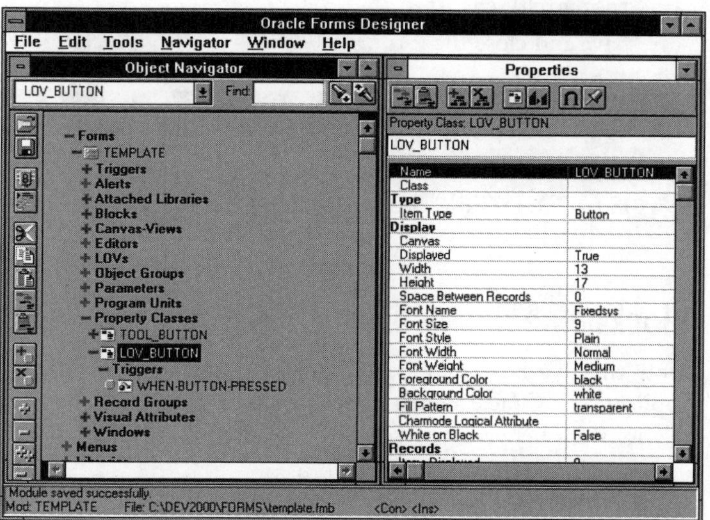

FIGURE 12.7.
The LOV_BUTTON property class for the template.

Attach Library

Now we will attach the HIGHLITE.PLL library file, which contains program units for highlighting the current form field. This highlite library was created in Chapter 8 and will be used in our single-row template. For multi-row blocks, Oracle Forms provides the current row highlighting.

To attach the library, do as follows:

1. Double-click on the gray plus sign to the left of Attached Libraries in the Object Navigator to invoke the Attach Library dialog box.
2. Click the Find button to invoke the Open dialog box.
3. Locate and select the HIGHLITE.PLL file.

You should find the HIGHLITE.PLL file in the \DEV2000\LIBS directory.

4. Click the Attach button.
5. Click Yes to remove the directory path.

Removing the path will cause Oracle Forms to search for the library file, whereas leaving the path hard-codes the location into the Forms application.

Now we will create the triggers that will call the procedures from the attached library to do the field highlighting.

1. Create a form-level WHEN-NEW-ITEM-INSTANCE trigger with the following PL/SQL code:
   ```
   highlight_cur_item;
   ```
2. Create a form-level POST-TEXT-ITEM trigger with the following PL/SQL code:
   ```
   post_highlight_item;
   ```
3. Save and close the form.

CAUTION

If you create any block or item-level triggers for WHEN-NEW-ITEM-INSTANCE or POST-TEXT-ITEM, be sure to include the call to the appropriate procedure.

Blocks

Now that we have created our form templates, we will use them to create our Forms applications. Oracle Forms supports single- and multi-row blocks, as well as master/detail relationships between blocks.

Multi-Row Blocks

We will develop a simple Forms application to maintain the list of states. This form will contain a multi-row block with a scroll bar so we can review many records on the screen at once.

1. Open the form module TEMPLIST.
2. Change the form module name from TEMPLIST to STATE.
3. Save the form module as STATE.FMB.

4. Change the MDI window title to Maintain Table in the WHEN-NEW-FORM-INSTANCE trigger.
5. Select WINDOW0 in the Object Navigator, then set the title to States using the Property window.
6. Create a new block for STATE; set the base table and canvas name to STATE.
7. Select the Items tab, click the Select Columns button, and change the label of Code to STATE and the width from 18 to 30.
8. Select the Layout tab, change Records from 1 to 7, click on Integrity Constraints and Scrollbar, then press OK.

The New Block Options dialog box contains the Layout tab with the number of records to be displayed, as well as the selection to include constraints, and the scrollbar. (See Figure 12.8.)

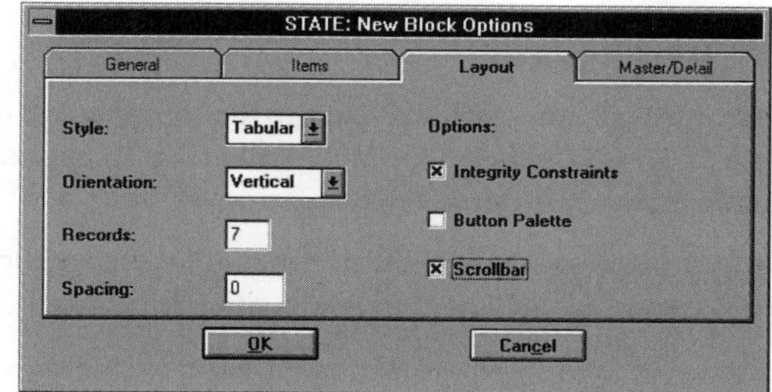

FIGURE 12.8.
The New Block Options dialog box with the Layout tab shown.

Next we will make some layout adjustments then set the current row highlighting.

1. Notice the new STATE block and canvas.
2. Double-click the canvas icon for STATE in the Object Navigator to invoke the Layout Editor.
3. Select and delete the border line and label.
4. Move the scrollbar to the right side.
5. Set the Current Record Attribute to CURRENT in the Properties windows for the block.
6. Save, run, then close the form.

Notice in Figure 12.9 that the Forms application displays many records, and the current record is highlighted.

You can use this type of form to create each of the maintenance forms for the lookup or reference tables in the database.

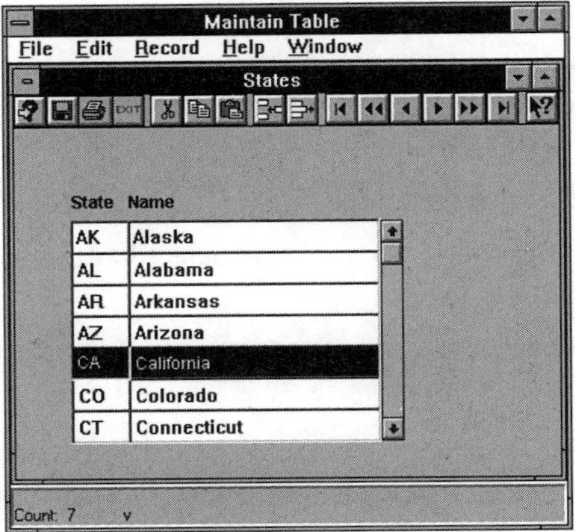

FIGURE 12.9.
Runform with a multi-row block listing states.

Master/Detail Blocks

Oracle Forms will automatically manage the coordination of data in different blocks that are related with a join condition. Next we will create an application to maintain the department and employee salary increase percentages.

1. Open the form module TEMPLIST, then change the module name to DEPT_EMP.
2. Save the form as DEPT_EMP.FMB.
3. Change the MDI window title to Maintain Increases in the WHEN-NEW-FORM-INSTANCE trigger.
4. Set the title to Departments and Employees.
5. Create a new block for DEPT, set the base table to DEPT, and set the canvas name to DEPT_EMP.
6. Select the Items tab, select the following items, and change the labels and widths as listed here:

Deptno	Num	30
Dname	Department	80
Loc	Location	70
Increase Pct	Incr	20

7. Select the Layout tab, change Records from 1 to 3, click on Integrity Constraints and Scrollbar, then press OK.
8. Notice the new DEPT block and the DEPT_EMP canvas.
9. Double-click the canvas icon for DEPT_EMP to invoke the Layout Editor.
10. Select and delete the border line and label.
11. Move the scrollbar to the right side.

12. Set the Current Record Attribute to CURRENT in the Properties windows for the DEPT block.
13. Create a new block for EMP, set the base table to EMP, and set the canvas name to DEPT_EMP.
14. Select the Items tab, select only the following items, and change the labels and widths as listed here:

Empno	Num	30
Ename	Employee	80
Job	Job	70
Deptno	Num	30
Increase Pct	Incr	20

    Remove the other columns from selection by double-clicking on them, or by removing the check in the Include checkbox for each one.
15. Select the Layout tab, change Records from 1 to 3, and click on Integrity Constraints and Scrollbar.
16. Select the Master/Detail tab, click the Select button and choose DEPT as the master block. Notice the join condition is automatically created. (See Figure 12.10.) Press OK.

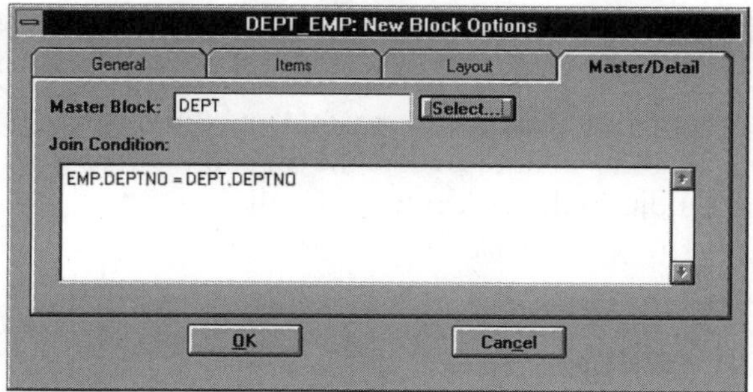

FIGURE 12.10.
The New Block Options dialog box with the Master/Detail tab shown.

Now we will make the final adjustments in the layout and test the form.

1. Double-click the canvas icon for DEPT_EMP to invoke the Layout Editor.
2. Select and delete the border line and label.
3. Move the scrollbar to the right side.
4. Select all of the department objects in the layout and move them up.
5. Select all of the employee objects in the layout and move them up as well.

6. Set the Current Record Attribute to CURRENT in the Properties windows for the EMP block.
7. Save and run the form, then exit, and close the DEPT_EMP form module.

In Figure 12.11 the standardized form is shown, revealing the coordination between the department and employee blocks. The highlighting is provided by Oracle Forms by setting the current record attribute property.

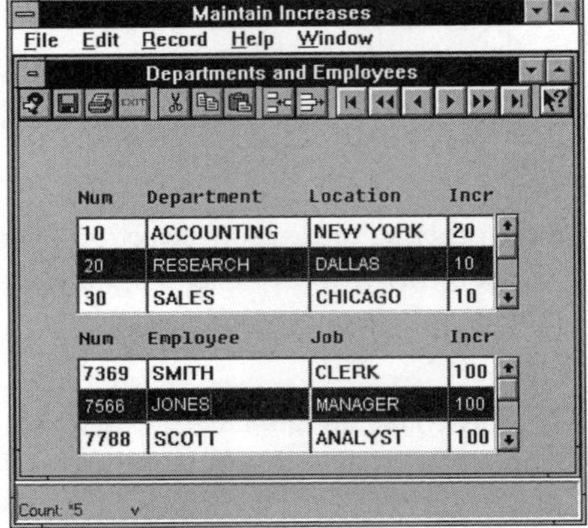

FIGURE 12.11.
Runform with master and detail rows highlighted for Department and Employees.

> **NOTE**
>
> Notice that we used the same template form for this application. The presentation and functional capabilities are like the state form. This makes learning and using the applications in the system easier for the user.

List of Values

List of values provide value selection, and validation for text items in your Forms applications. Now we will modify the customer form that was created in Chapter 8 to include a list of values.

1. Open the form module CUSTOMER.
2. Double-click the LOVs node in the Object Navigator to invoke the New LOV dialog box.
3. Enter the following query text:

```
select code state, name into :customer.state from state order by code
```

4. Press the OK button.

In Figure 12.12, the New LOV dialog box is shown containing the SQL statement selecting state and selecting name from the state table.

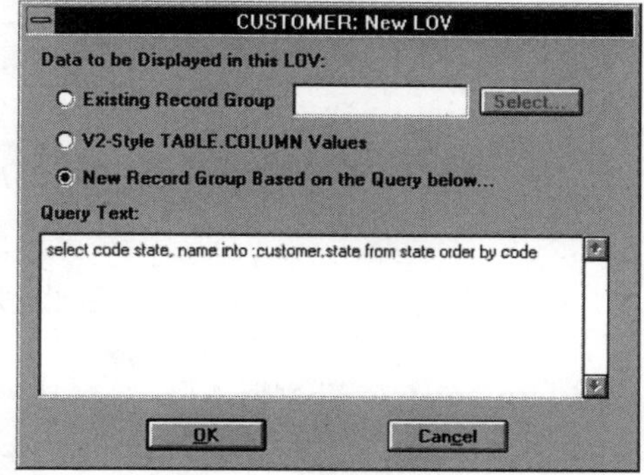

FIGURE 12.12.
The New LOV dialog box shown with a query entered.

Notice the preceding SQL statement contains an `order by` clause. The `where` clause is also supported for restricting the list of values.

Once the LOV is defined, a record group is automatically created. You can use the Properties window to add a Title and set the size and location of the display window.

1. Using the Object Navigator, change the LOV name and the record group name to STATE.
2. Select the STATE LOV, then set the title in the Properties window to List of States.
3. Select Column Mapping in the Properties window, then click the More button to invoke the LOV Column Mapping dialog box.
4. Change the display width of state from 18 to 30.
5. Press the OK button.

In the Properties window, you can review and modify the column mapping, as well as the title and width of the columns displayed for the LOV, using the LOV Column Mapping dialog box, as shown in Figure 12.13.

In order for an LOV to be used, it must be referenced by a text item via the LOV property. Also, to provide a drop-down button for the list, the button and the associated WHEN-BUTTON-PRESSED trigger must be created. We will use the LOV_BUTTON property class from the template form to define the list-of-values button properties and the trigger.

1. Select the STATE item, then set LOV in the Properties window to STATE.
2. Create a button in the layout to the right of the STATE item.
3. Change the button name to STATE_LOV.

Because the CUSTOMER form was originally created without using the template form, we will copy the LOV_BUTTON property class from the TEMPLATE form.

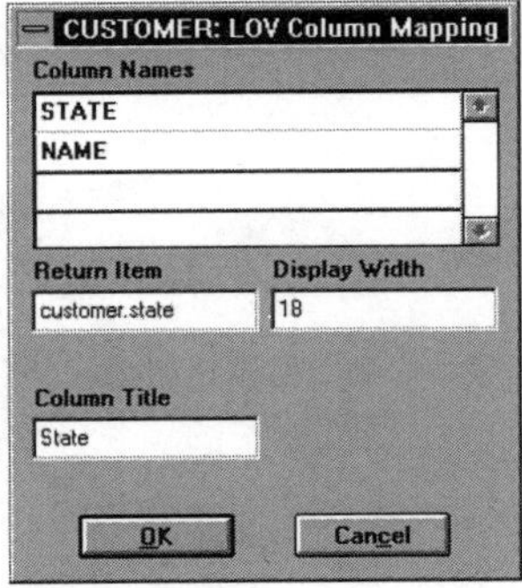

FIGURE 12.13.
The LOV Column Mapping dialog box.

4. Open the form module TEMPLATE.
5. Drag and drop the LOV_BUTTON property class from TEMPLATE to CUSTOMER.
6. Click the Copy and OK buttons.
7. Close the form module TEMPLATE.
8. Select STATE_LOV in the Object Navigator.
8. Set Canvas to CUSTOMER using the Properties window.
9. Set the property class to LOV_BUTTON.
10. Save and run the form to test the list-of-values button.

At runtime, the list of values for the state can be invoked from within the application by selecting the state item, then pressing the F9 key or selecting the drop-down button, as shown in Figure 12.14.

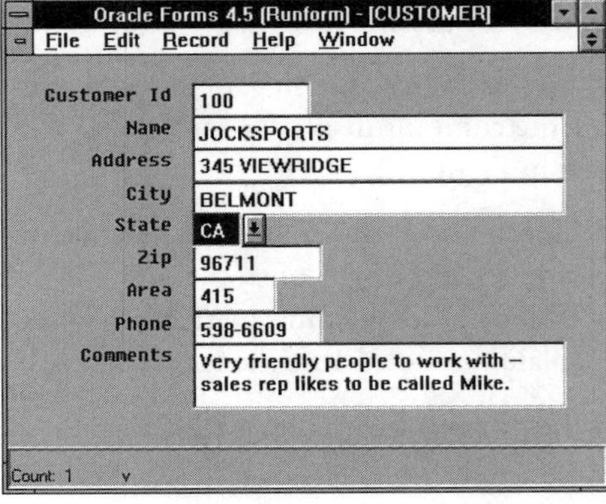

FIGURE 12.14.
A form with an LOV button for states.

NOTE

Notice that there is no WHEN-BUTTON-PRESSED trigger for the STATE_LOV button. The trigger fires from the LOV_BUTTON property class.

LOV dialog boxes have a built-in auto-reduce feature that narrows the selections as characters are typed by the user. The Find field may also be used to search for items in the list, and it supports the % wild-card character as a substitute for the rest of the text string.

When the LOV is selected, a dialog box is presented, as shown in Figure 12.15, listing values for the current item.

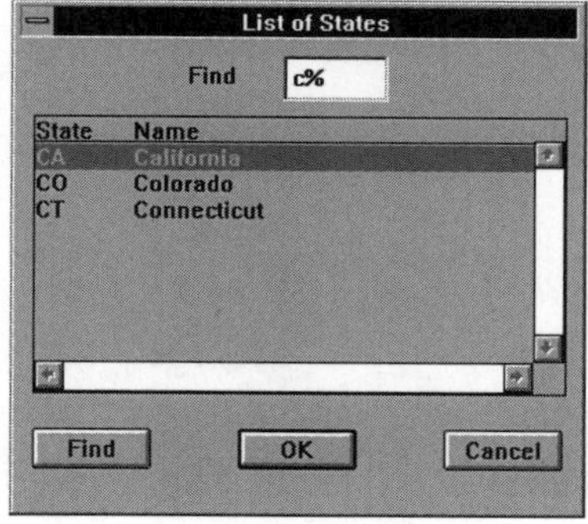

FIGURE 12.15.
The list of states from the LOV selection.

In Figure 12.15, the LOV dialog box is shown with the list of states automatically reduced to include only those states whose names begin with the letter C.

Layout

Now that we have created two multi-row block forms that used the TEMPLIST template form, next we will create the contact-management application using the TEMPLATE template form. In this section we will be using many different types of layout items, and we will create some of them during the creation of the default block.

Default Layout

The default layout created by the Oracle Forms default block facility can include text, list, custom, checkbox, and radio items. Using the default layout is a good starting point for developing your applications. Once the default layout is complete, we will add the other items and modify the layout using the Layout Editor.

1. Open the form module TEMPLATE, then change the module name to CONTACT.
2. Save the form as CONTACT.FMB.

3. Change the MDI window title to Developing Oracle Applications in the WHEN-NEW-FORM-INSTANCE trigger.
4. Change the window title to Contact Management.
5. Create a new block for CONTACT, set the base table to CONTACT and set the canvas name to CONTACT.
6. Select the Items tab, select the following items, and set the labels, widths, and item types as shown here:

EMPNO	Employee	36	Text Item
CUSTID	Customer	36	Text Item
CONTACT_DATE	Date/Time	126	Text Item
TYPE	Type	126	List Item
SUBJECT	Subject	126	Text Item
ACTION	Action	126	Text Item
LOC	Location	126	Text Item
PHONE	Phone	126	Text Item
RECD_BY	Recd By	114	Text Item
MESSAGE	Message	306	Custom Item
SUCCESS	Success	138	Check Box
DIRECTION	In	25	Radio Group
PRIORITY	Priority	25	Radio Group

7. Select the Layout tab, change the Orientation from Vertical to Horizontal, click on Integrity Constraints, then press OK.
8. Notice the new CONTACT block and CONTACT canvas.
9. Double-click the canvas icon for CONTACT to invoke the Layout Editor, then maximize the window.
10. Select and delete the border line and label.
11. Save the form.

CAUTION

Do not run the form yet, because the default objects for the check box and the radio groups are not complete.

The results of the layout specifications made during the creation of the default block should appear in the Layout Editor as shown in Figure 12.16.

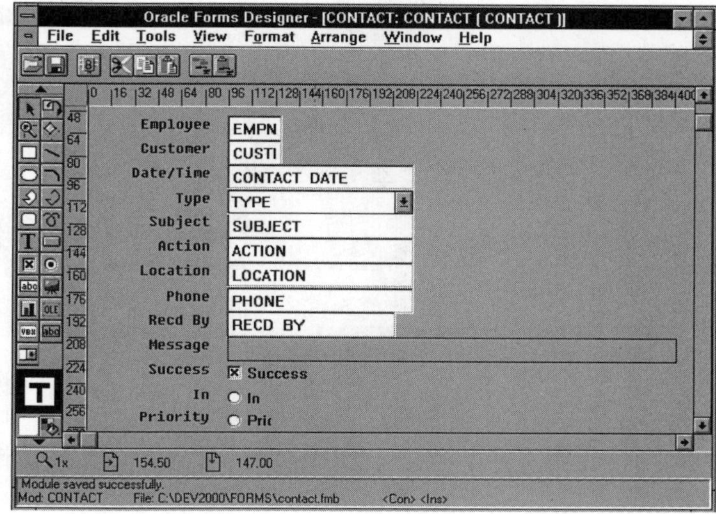

FIGURE 12.16.
Default layout for contact management.

The default layout will be modified over the next several sections.

Display Items

Next we will create display items for the fields EMPNO and CUSTID. These items are the keys to their respective tables, and we want to display the associated names as well.

1. Click on the Display Item tool on the tool palette and create a display item to the right of the EMPNO item.
2. Change the item name to EMP_NAME using the Properties window.
3. Set the height to 17 and the width to 77.
4. Set Base Table Item to False.
5. Press Ctrl+C and then Ctrl+V to copy and paste the display item.
6. Move the new item down to align with CUSTID.
7. Change the item name to CUST_NAME.
8. Change the maximum length from 30 to 45.
9. Select the display, text, and list items in the CONTACT block.
10. Set Visual Attribute Name to DEFAULT.

The form should now look like Figure 12.17.

Now we will create the trigger to populate the display items with their names from their respective tables.

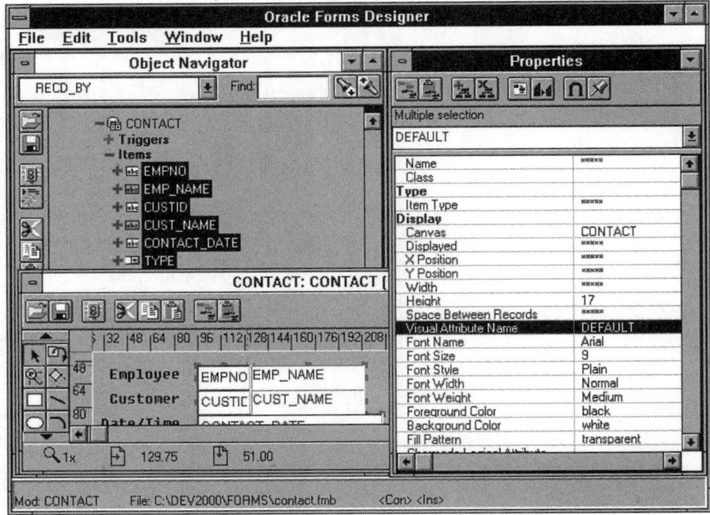

FIGURE 12.17.
Display items for employees and customers.

1. Create a POST-CHANGE trigger for EMPNO with the following select statement:

```
select ename into :contact.emp_name
from emp
where empno = :contact.empno;
```

2. Create a POST-CHANGE trigger for CUSTID with the following select statement:

```
select name into :contact.cust_name
from customer
where custid = :contact.custid;
```

3. Save the form.

More LOVs

Next we will create LOVs and LOV buttons for the fields EMPNO, CUSTID, and RECD_BY.

1. Double-click the LOVs node in the Object Navigator to invoke the New LOV dialog box.
2. Enter the following query text, and press OK.

```
select ename, empno into :contact.emp_name, :contact.empno from emp order by
➥ename
```

3. Using the Object Navigator, change the LOV name and the record group name to EMP.
4. Select EMPNO, then set LOV in the Properties window to EMP, and set LOV for Validation to True.
5. Create another LOV, using the following text:

```
select name, custid into :contact.cust_name, :contact.custid from customer
➥order by name
```

6. Using the Object Navigator, change the LOV name and the record group name to CUST.
7. Select CUSTID, then set LOV in the Properties window to CUST and set LOV for Validation to True.
8. Create another LOV, using the following text:

```
select username into :contact.recd_by from all_users
where username ^= 'SYS' and username ^= 'SYSTEM'
order by username
```

9. Using the Object Navigator, change the LOV name and the record group name to USER.
10. Select RECD_BY, then set LOV in the Properties window to USER and set LOV for Validation to True.

Now that we have the LOVs, we will create drop-down buttons for them using the LOV_BUTTON property class.

1. Create a button in the layout to the right of the EMP_NAME item.
2. Change the button name to EMP_LOV.
3. Select EMP_LOV in the Object Navigator.
4. Set Canvas to CONTACT using the Properties window.
5. Set the property class to LOV_BUTTON.
6. Copy and paste EMP_LOV to create CUST_LOV and RECD_BY_LOV buttons.
7. Move CUST_LOV and RECD_BY_LOV to the right of CUST_NAME and RECD_BY, respectively.
8. Save and run the form to test the list-of-values buttons.

Format Masks

Format masks are useful in presenting date and numeric items. Next we will create a format mask for the date and time that the contact was made.

1. Select the CONTACT_DATE item, then invoke the Properties window.
2. Set Format Mask to DD-MON-YYYY HH:MI AM.
3. Set Default Value to $$DATETIME$$.
4. Change Maximum Length and Query Length from 9 to 20, then save the form.

In Figure 12.18, the Properties windows is shown with the format mask being defined.

Notice that we used the system variable for the date and time to initialize the value to the current date and time.

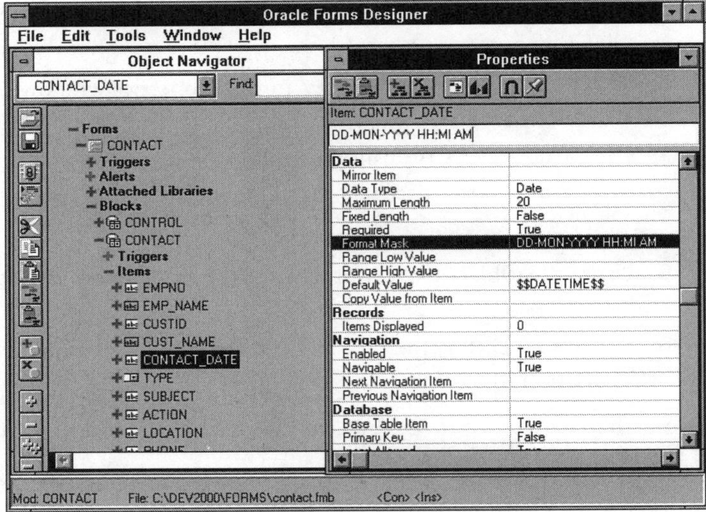

FIGURE 12.18.
A format mask for the Date/Time field.

List Items

There are three different list styles that are supported by Oracle Forms. We are using the default style of Poplist. This style is often refered to as a drop-down list. The Tlist and the Combo Box are the other styles that may be used.

An example of each of the list styles is shown in Figure 12.19.

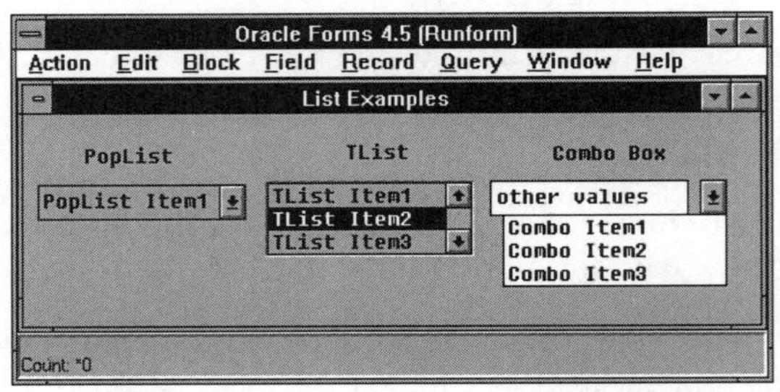

FIGURE 12.19.
A form with examples of the list styles.

Notice the different list styles shown in Figure 12.19. The poplist has a drop-down button and can only contain values from the list. The tlist has no drop-down button but instead lists all of the items all of the time and automatically adds a scrollbar if the list is larger than the display area. Lastly, the combo box has a drop-down button just to the right of the list and may contain other values that are not provided in the list.

We defined TYPE to be a list item during the creation of the default block; now we will complete the list item details for TYPE. While the default block initially created a single default list item, each of the list items with their associated valid values must be entered.

1. Select the TYPE list item in the Object Navigator, then activate the Properties window.
2. Set Default Value to Phone.
3. Select List Elements, and press the More button to invoke the List Item Elements dialog box.
4. Enter the following items and values for the list:

Phone	phone
Fax	fax
E-Mail	email
Mail	mail
Visit	visit

5. Press the OK button.
6. Save the form.

The List Item Elements dialog box is shown Figure 12.20.

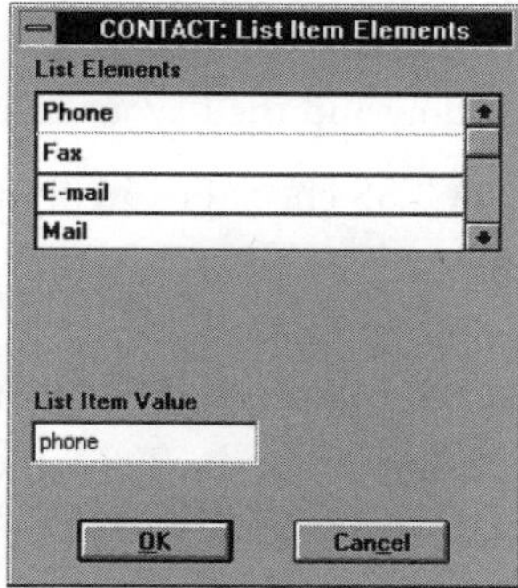

FIGURE 12.20.
The List Item Elements dialog box.

Notice that the list elements are presented with a tlist and that the scrollbar appears as the fifth item is added. In Figure 12.21, the list for contact type is exposed for selection during runtime.

Notice in Figure 12.21 that the presentation and function of the poplist is different from the lists of values we created earlier in this chapter.

TIP

Consider using list items when the number of choices in the list is small and the values are stable.

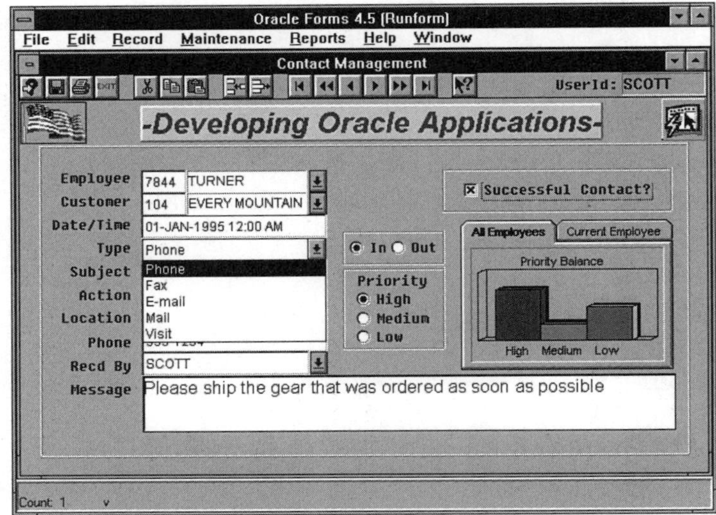

FIGURE 12.21.
Runform with the poplist shown for contact type.

A Check Box

The check box item for SUCCESS was created by the default block, but it requires a few changes in the Properties window and the Layout Editor.

1. Select the SUCCESS check box item in the Object Navigator, then activate the Properties window.
2. Set Default Value to Y.
3. Change the Label to Successful Contact?.
4. Select Layout Editor from the Tools menu, then maximize the Layout Editor.
5. Select and delete the label to the left of the check box.
6. Click and drag the check box to the upper right corner of the layout, to the right of EMP_NAME, then save the form.

The check box item SUCCESS should now appear as in Figure 12.22.

Radio Groups

We created two radio groups during the default block specification. Now we will add additional radio buttons to these groups, set the default values, and make a few changes in the layout.

First we will complete the DIRECTION radio group, then we will complete the PRIORITY radio group.

1. Select and delete the In label to the left of the DIRECTION radio button.

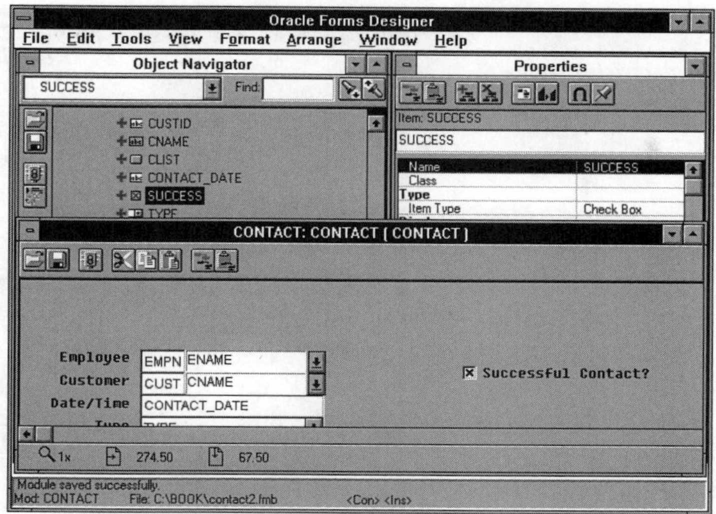

FIGURE 12.22.
The check box displayed in the Layout Editor.

2. Select and move the radio button, just to the right of the TYPE list item.
3. Press Ctrl+C and then Ctrl+V to copy and paste the radio-button item.
4. Move the new item to the right.
5. Change the original radio-button item name to IN.
6. In the Properties window, set the Value for IN to I.
7. Change the new radio-button item name to OUT.
8. In the Properties window, set the Label for OUT to Out.
9. Set the Value for OUT to O.
10. Select the radio group DIRECTION in the Object Navigator, then in the Properties window set the Default Value and Other Values to I.

The radio group DIRECTIONS should now appear in the layout as in Figure 12.23.

Now we will complete the PRIORITY radio group.

1. In the Layout Editor, select the Priority label to the left of the radio button, and move it to the right of the SUBJECT text item.
2. Select and move the radio button, just under the Priority label.
3. In the Properties window, change the name from PRIORITY to HIGH.
4. Set the Label for HIGH to High.
5. Set the Value for HIGH to H.
6. Select the radio group PRIORITY in the Object Navigator, then in the Properties window set the Default Value and Other Values to L.

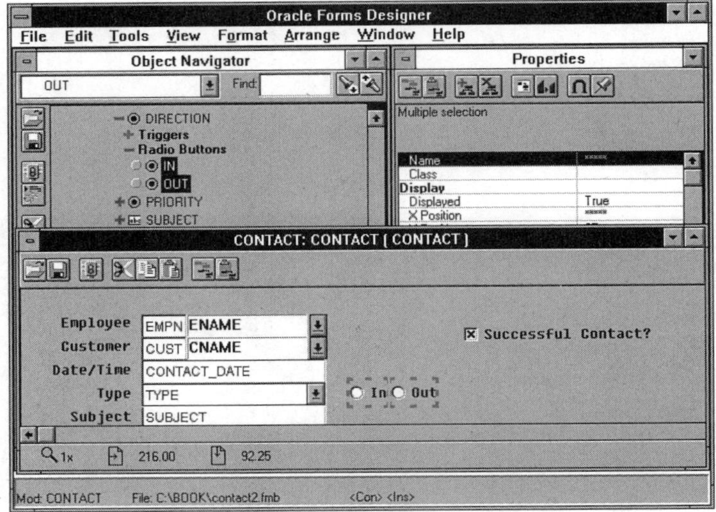

FIGURE 12.23.
The radio buttons in the DIRECTIONS group.

7. Select the HIGH radio button, then press Ctrl+C and Ctrl+V twice to create two more radio buttons.
8. Click and drag the right edge of the selected radio buttons to the right to increase the space for the labels.
9. Select all three buttons, then in the Layout Editor select Align Objects from the Arrange menu.
10. Select Horizontally Align Left and Vertically Stack, then press OK.
11. Change the new radio-button item names to MEDIUM and LOW.
12. In the Properties window, set the Label for MEDIUM to Medium and the Value for MEDIUM to M.
13. Set the Default Value for LOW to L and the Value for LOW to L.
14. Save and run the form.

Notice in Figure 12.24 that the DIRECTION radio group is horizontally aligned, whereas the PRIORITY radio group is vertically aligned.

Product Integration

Oracle Forms can display images from a variety of formats, can be integrated with Oracle Graphics or any OLE2 server, and can also use Microsoft Visual Basic Custom Controls.

In the upcoming sections, we will modify the Contact Management application to include a bitmap image file, OLE2 containers, a VBX tab control, and an Oracle Graphics display.

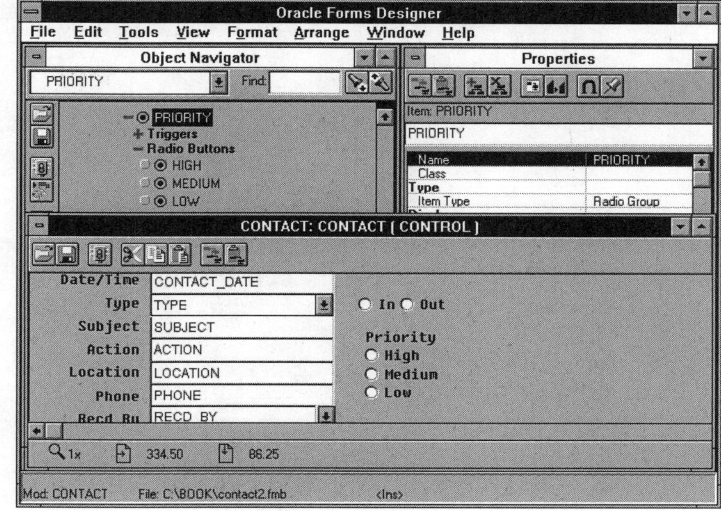

FIGURE 12.24.
Both radio groups completed in the layout.

Image Items

An image item may be static, or it may be associated with a database column. Here we will create a static image item in the form, then read the image of the bitmap using a form-level trigger. The bitmap was created using MS Paintbrush and saved to the local file system.

1. Select and maximize the Layout Editor.
2. Click on the Image Item tool on the tool palette and create an image item in the upper right corner of the layout.
3. From the Properties windows, change the item name to FORMS_BMP.
4. Set the X position to 437 and the Y position to 1.
5. Set the width and the height to 30.
6. Set Bevel to Raised.
7. Set Background Color to gray.
8. Set Navigable to False.
9. Set Base Table Item to False.
10. Set Sizing Style to Adjust.
11. Move FORMS_BMP from the CONTACT block to the CONTROL block using drag and drop in the Object Navigator.

The image item should appear in the layout as in Figure 12.25.

The image item will be populated using a procedure call in the WHEN-NEW-FORM-INSTANCE trigger.

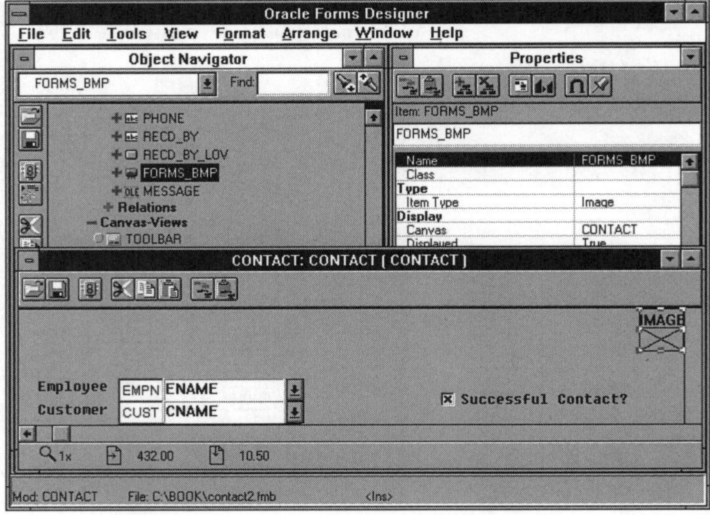

FIGURE 12.25.
An image item that will display a bitmap.

1. From the Object Navigator, select the WHEN-NEW-FORM-INSTANCE trigger, then add the following:

```
read_image_file('\dev2000\bitmaps\f45run.bmp','BMP','control.forms_bmp');
```

2. Save and run the form.

Notice the use of the built-in procedure to read the bitmap image from the file system.

OLE2 Objects

Oracle Forms provides support for including OLE2 container objects in your Forms applications. Next we are going to add an OLE2 object from the Microsoft ClipArt Gallery and one from Microsoft Word to our application. The picture from the ClipArt Gallery will be a static object, while the MS Word document will be part of the contact data stored in the Oracle database.

The ClipArt item will be placed in the control block and not in the base table block, because it is not based on data contained in a given column in the database. Although the ClipArt item is a static OLE2 container, the contents may be changed at runtime.

1. Select and maximize the Layout Editor.
2. Click on the OLE2 Object tool on the tool palette and create a custom item in the upper-left corner of the layout.
3. From the Properties windows, change the item name to OLE_FLAG.
4. Set the X position and the Y position to 1.
5. Set the width to 45 and the height to 30.

6. Set Bevel to None.
7. Set Mouse Navigate to False.
8. Set Base Table Item to False.
9. Set OLE In-place Activation to True.
10. Set OLE Resize Style to Scale.
11. Move OLE_FLAG from the CONTACT block to the CONTROL block using drag and drop in the Object Navigator.
12. From the Layout Editor, select the OLE2 item, then right-mouse click to invoke the pop-up menu. The OLE pop-up menu should appear in the layout as shown in Figure 12.26

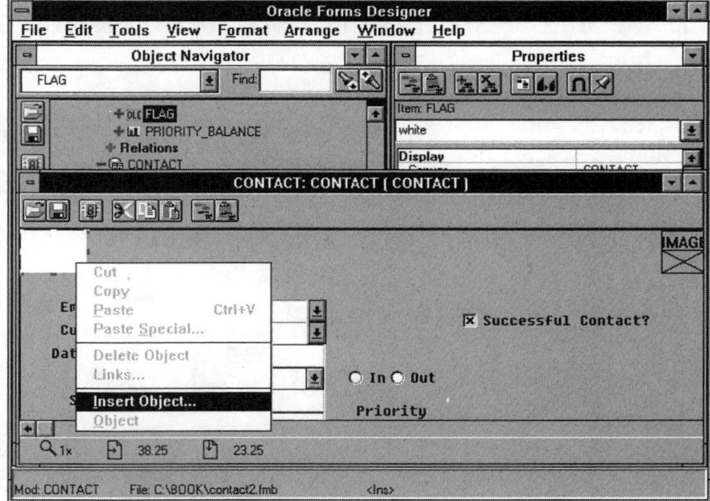

FIGURE 12.26.
OLE pop-up menu from the OLE2 object.

13. Select Insert Object from the pop-up menu to invoke the Insert Object dialog box.
14. Select Microsoft ClipArt Gallery from the Insert Object dialog box, then select the picture of Old Glory from the Landmarks category.

In Figure 12.27, the Insert Object dialog box is shown with the Microsoft ClipArt Gallery selected.

Since the OLE2 object is in the control block and is navigable, we will go to the CONTACT block in the WHEN-NEW-FORM-INSTANCE trigger.

1. From the Object Navigator, select the WHEN-NEW-FORM-INSTANCE trigger, then add the following:

```
go_block('CONTACT');
```

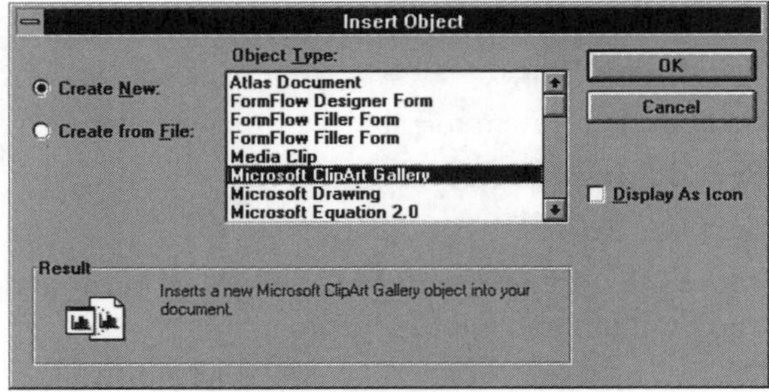

FIGURE 12.27.
The Insert Object dialog box.

2. Save and run the form, then double-click on the flag to invoke the Microsoft ClipArt Gallery and select a different picture.

The new OLE2 object is selected from the Microsoft ClipArt Gallery during runtime, as shown in Figure 12.28.

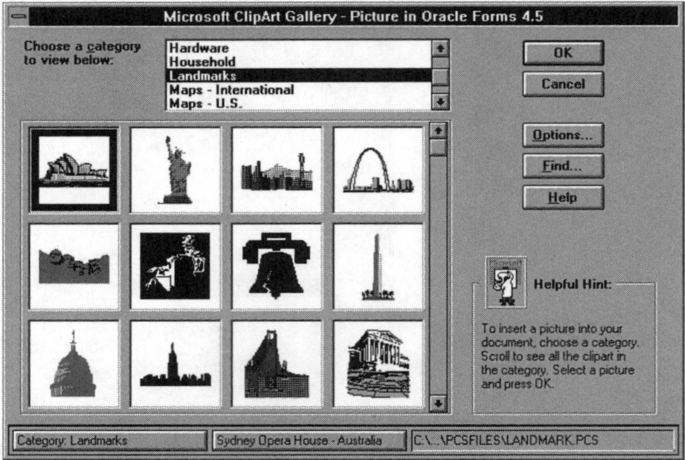

FIGURE 12.28.
The Microsoft ClipArt Gallery dialog box.

Now we will complete the specification for the message item. The message item is an OLE2 custom item that was defined earlier during the creation of the default block. This container will allow each row in the database to contain an MS Word document (or any other OLE2 compliant object). We will use in-place activation to enter text during runtime.

1. Select the MESSAGE item.
2. Set the width to 363 and the height to 40.
3. Set OLE In-place Activation to True.
4. Save and run the form to test the OLE2 container.

Now that we have an OLE2 container in our Forms applications, let's test the in-place activation.

1. Right-click on the message item to invoke the pop-up menu.
2. Select Insert Object from the pop-up menu.
3. Select Microsoft Word 6.0 Document from the Insert Object dialog box, then press OK.

Notice in Figure 12.29 that the message item has become an MS Word document and that the menu and toolbars have been replaced.

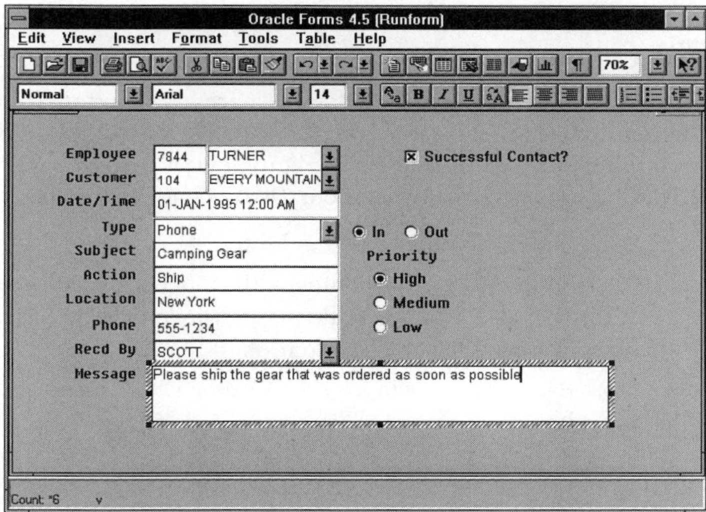

FIGURE 12.29.
The message item as an MS Word OLE2 object.

Once MS Word is activated in our Forms application, let's enter some text and try a few features from MS Word.

1. Type in some text, then change the font style and size.
2. Click outside of the document area to return the focus to Oracle Forms.
3. Exit to return to Oracle Forms Designer.

TIP

Use in-place activation when you want the focus to remain in the form and have the OLE2 application appear within the form.

In-place activation will replace the current Forms toolbar and menus with the OLE2 application's toolbar and menus, while external activation will change the focus from Oracle Forms to the OLE2 application being invoked.

> **NOTE**
>
> In-place activation is only available for embedded objects.

We will come back to this application and review additional capabilities of OLE2 objects in Oracle Forms in Chapter 15.

VBX Custom Controls

Oracle Forms can include items that reference VBX Custom Controls. There are many standard Custom Controls that are shipped with Microsoft Visual Basic and many more available from third-party vendors. In our application we will create a VBX custom item in the layout that will contain a tab control for our Oracle Graphics displays.

1. Select and maximize the Layout Editor.
2. Click on the VBX Control tool on the tool palette and create a item on the right side of the layout. Notice in the Properties window that a Custom Item is created with the Custom Item Type of VBX Control.
3. From the Properties windows, change the item name to PRIORITY_TAB.
4. Set the X position to 300 and the Y position to 86.
5. Set the width to 145 and the height to 105.
6. Set Bevel to None.
7. Set Font Name to Arial.
8. Set Font Size to 8.
9. Set Navigable to False.
10. Set Mouse Navigate to False.
11. Set Base Table Item to False.
12. Set VBX Control File to C:\WINDOWS\SYSTEM\VSVBX.VBX.

> **NOTE**
>
> We are using the VideoSoft Custom Control Library shipped with the Oracle demos. Usually VBX files are installed to the \WINDOWS\SYSTEM directory.

13. Select VideoSoftIndexTab from the drop-down list for VBX Control Name.

NOTE

Some VBX files contain more than one control name. Use the list button on the top of the properties palette to provide a list of available controls from the VBX file.

14. Set Caption to All Employees|Current Employee.
15. Copy the Back TabColor to the Front TabColor.
16. Set Style to 5.
17. Set Position to 0.
18. Set BackSheets to 1.
19. Move PRIORITY_TAB from the CONTACT block to the CONTROL block.

The VBX control should appear in the layout as shown in Figure 12.30.

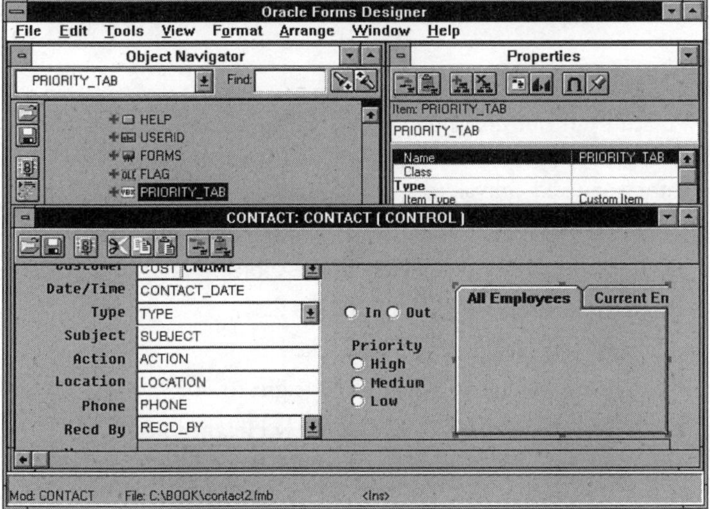

FIGURE 12.30.
Creating a VBX control in the Layout Editor.

20. Save and run the form.

Your application should now look like Figure 12.31.

The tab control is in place and ready to provide an interface to view the charts that we will add. After we create a canvas and the chart item, we will add a custom trigger to display the appropriate chart based on the selection of one of the tabs.

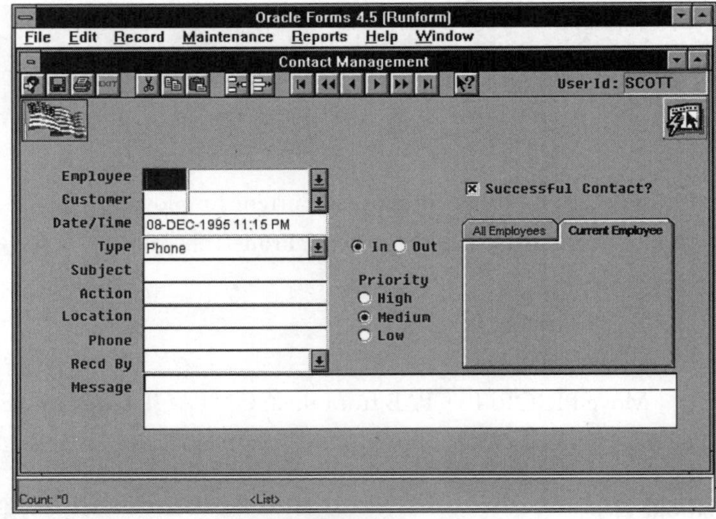

FIGURE 12.31.
The VBX tab control in the application.

A Stacked Canvas

We can't put objects directly onto VBX custom controls. However, we can display a stacked canvas over a portion of the control and place our objects on that stacked canvas. Next, we will create a stacked canvas that will contain the Oracle Graphics display and appear on the tab control.

1. Create a new canvas-view in the Object Navigator.
2. Set the name to ALL_EMPLOYEES.
3. Set Canvas-view Type to Stacked.
4. Set the width to 132 and the height to 80.
5. Set View Width to 132 and View Height to 80.
6. Set Display X Position to 307 and Display Y position to 106.
7. Save the form.

If you select Stacked Views from the View menu and then select ALL_EMPLOYEES, the layout will reveal the placement of the stacked canvas on the tab control as shown in Figure 12.32.

Oracle Graphics

Oracle Graphics is an OLE2 server, and Oracle Forms supports OLE2 containers. But, Oracle Forms applications include Oracle Graphics displays as chart items. Chart items are a specific type of item, used just for Oracle Graphics displays.

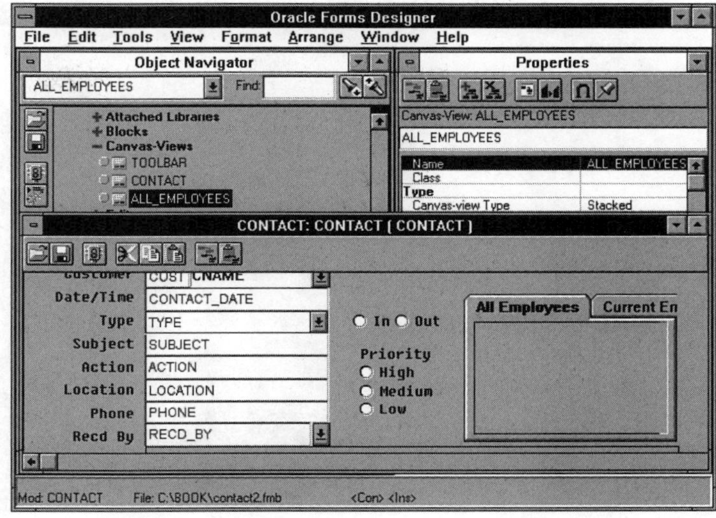

FIGURE 12.32.
A stacked canvas shown in the Layout Editor.

Now we will create an Oracle Graphics display item that will display the chart that was created in Chapter 10, "Introducing Oracle Graphics." Like the bitmap and the clip art, the Oracle Graphics display will be placed in the control block.

1. Double-click on the ALL_EMPLOYEES canvas-view in the Object Navigator to invoke the Layout Editor.
2. Select Show View from the View menu.
3. Click on the Chart Item tool on the tool palette and create a chart item in the layout.
4. From the Properties windows, change the item name to PRIORITY_BALANCE.
5. Set the X position to 3 and the Y position to 4.
6. Set the width to 124 and the height to 72.
7. Set the Bevel to None.
8. Move PRIORITY_BALANCE from the CONTACT block to the CONTROL block.

The chart item should appear in the layout as shown in Figure 12.33.

Next we attach the Oracle Graphics library, so that the display can be opened with a procedure call from within a trigger.

1. Create an attached library in the Object Navigator.
2. Locate the OG.PLL library in the file system. You should find it in the \ORAWIN\GRAPH25\DEMOS\FORMS or \DEV2000\LIBS directories.

Now we will open the display using one of the packaged procedures in the Oracle Graphics library. Then we will create a custom trigger.

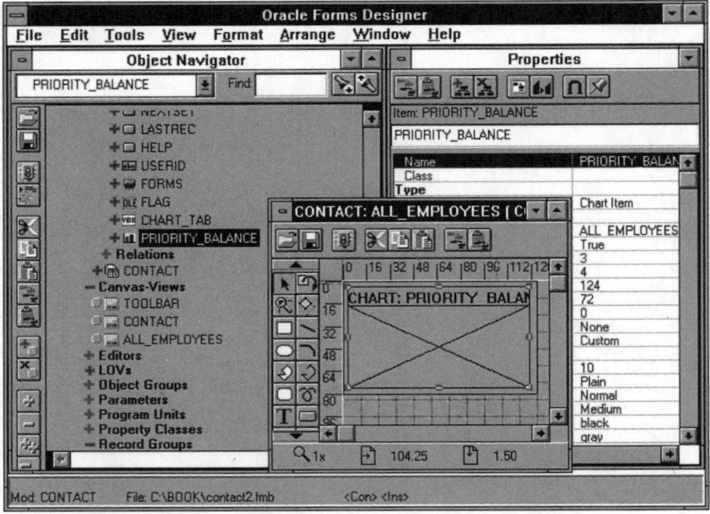

FIGURE 12.33.
A chart item in the Layout Editor.

1. From the Object Navigator, select the WHEN-NEW-FORM-INSTANCE trigger, then add the following:

```
og.open('priority.ogr', 'control.priority_balance', FALSE);
```

2. Create a new WHEN-CUSTOM-ITEM-EVENT trigger for the PRIORITY_TAB item with the following text:

```
DECLARE
   TabEvent  VARCHAR2(80);
   TabNumber NUMBER;
BEGIN
   TabEvent := :system.custom_item_event;
   IF (UPPER(TabEvent) = 'CLICK') then
      TabNumber := VBX.Get_Property('PRIORITY_TAB', 'CurrTab');
      IF TabNumber = 0 then
         show_view('ALL_EMPLOYEES');
      ELSIF TabNumber = 1 then
         show_view('CONTACT');
      END IF;
   END IF;
END;
```

3. Save and run the form.

Boilerplate

The Contact Management application will contain two different types of boilerplate. We will use a text item for the application title and beveled lines for functional grouping.

Text Items

First we will add an application title to the form using a text item with some three-dimensional attributes.

1. Select and maximize the Layout Editor.
2. Click on the Text Item tool on the tool palette and create a text item at the top of the layout.
3. Enter `-Developing Oracle Applications-` as the text.
4. Select Font from the Format menu, then set the Font to Arial, the Font Style to Bold Italic, and the Size to 20.
5. Select Line from the Format menu, then set the line size to 2 point.
6. Select Bevel from the Format menu, then set the bevel to Raised.
7. Using the Color Palette, set the Fill Color to gray12, the Line Color to black, and the Text Color to red.

The application title should appear. (See Figure 12.34.)

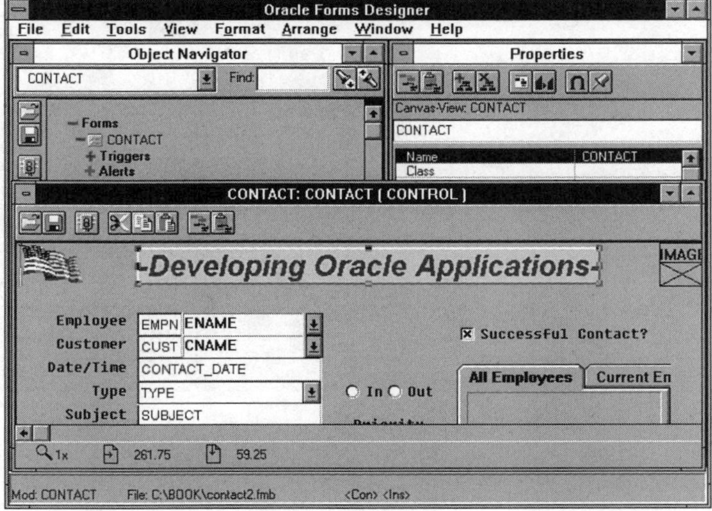

FIGURE 12.34.
A 3-D text item for the application title.

Beveled Lines

Next we will add beveled lines to group and/or separate items in the layout.

1. Click on the Rectangle tool on the tool palette and draw a box around the SUCCESS checkbox item.
2. Select Bevel from the Format menu, then set the bevel to Inset.

3. Using the Color Palette, set the Fill Color to No Fill and the Line Color to black.
4. Select Line from the Format menu, then set the line size to 2 point.
5. Draw another box around the DIRECTION radio group.
6. Add another box around the PRIORITY radio group.
7. Add another box around all the items in the CONTACT block.

Arrange the Layout

The final step in the development of the application is to arrange the items so that they are presentable. We will accomplish this by aligning and sizing the items.

Use the example of the Contact Management application in Figure 12.35 to do the final adjustments to your Forms application.

FIGURE 12.35.
The Contact Management application.

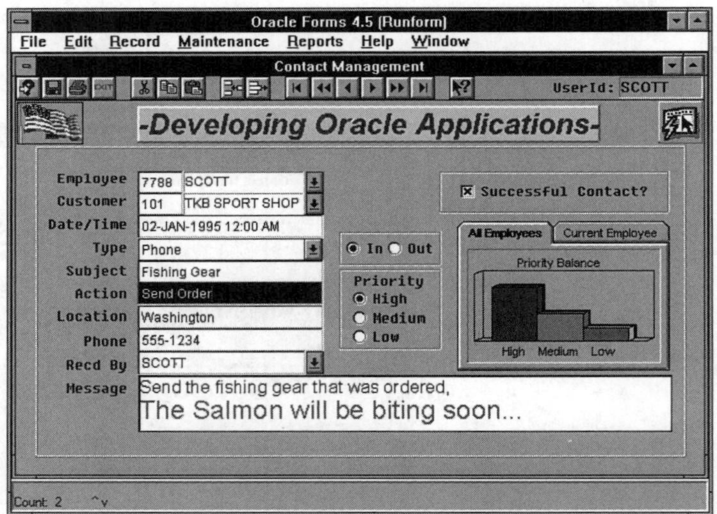

You can take advantage of the rulers, ruler guides, ruler grids, and the arrange menu items to complete the layout.

TIP

Create sight lines by aligning objects on the right, left, top, and bottom edges.

DDE Support

Oracle Forms supports the DDE (Dynamic Data Exchange) messaging protocol, although the use of OLE2, which is a higher-level protocol, may be sufficient for most of your requirements. DDE messages are supported through the DDE built-in package procedures. For more information on DDE, refer to the Oracle Forms Advanced Techniques Manual.

ODBC Support

Oracle Forms supports the ODBC (Open Database Connectivity) protocol to enable access to data sources other than an Oracle database. For more information on ODBC, refer to the *Oracle Forms Advanced Techniques Manual.*

Menus

In Chapter 8, we created a standard menu to be used by our Forms applications. Now we will complete that menu by adding the remaining menu items. Following that, we will also create an application menu for Contact Management that will include additional menus for maintenance and reports.

1. Open the menu module STANDARD.MMB.
2. Invoke the Menu Editor and maximize the window.
3. Click on File to expand the menu.
4. Modify the File menu to include the following items:
   - New
   - Query
   - Close
   - Close Sep
   - Save
   - Save Sep
   - Print
   - Sep
   - Exit
5. Click on Edit to expand the menu.
6. Modify the Edit menu to include the following items:
   - Cut
   - Copy
   - Paste

- Clear
- Clear Sep
- Edit

7. Create an Open menu item to the right of Query.
8. Add the following menu items under Open:
   - OK
   - OK Sep
   - Cancel
   - Cancel Sep
   - Count
9. Create a Record menu item to the right of Edit.
10. Add the following menu items under Record:
    - Insert
    - Delete
    - Delete Sep
    - Duplicate
    - Duplicate Sep
    - First
    - Scroll Up
    - Previous
    - Previous Sep
    - Next
    - Scroll Down
    - Last
11. Create a Help menu item to the right of Record.
12. Add the following menu items under Help:
    - Help
    - Show Keys
    - List
    - Display Error
13. Select each of the Sep menu items, and set the Menu Item Type to Separator in the Properties window. The menu in the Menu Editor should now look like Figure 12.36.

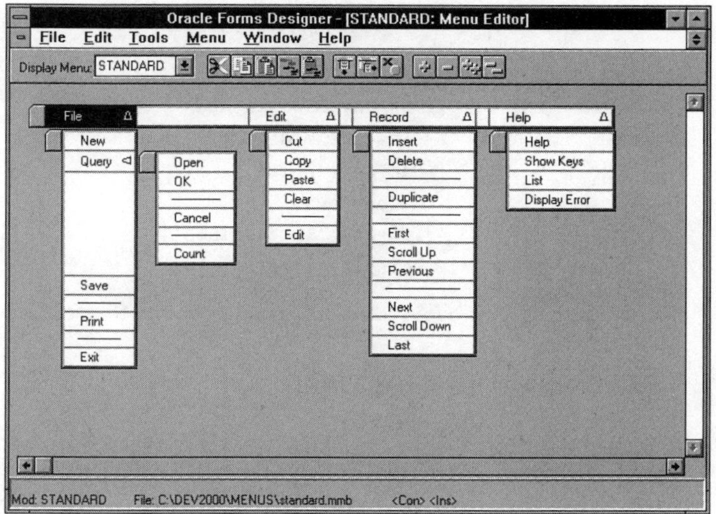

FIGURE 12.36.
The STANDARD menu in the Menu Editor.

14. Select Command Text and the More button to invoke the PL/SQL Editor, and enter the following text for each of the menu items:

MENU ITEM	*COMMAND TEXT*
New	`do_key('create_record');`
Save	`do_key('commit_form');`
Print	`execute_trigger('print_doc');`
Exit	`do_key('exit_form');`
Open	`do_key('enter_query');`
OK	`do_key('execute_query');`
Cancel	`do_key('exit_form');`
Count	`do_key('count_query');`
Cut	`cut_region;`
Copy	`copy_region;`
Paste	`paste_region;`
Clear	`clear_field;`
Edit	`edit_field;`
Insert	`do_key('create_record');`
Delete	`do_key('delete_record');`
Duplicate	`do_key('create_record');`
	`do_key('duplicate_record);`
First	`first_record;`
Scroll Up	`do_key('scroll_up');`
Previous	`do_key('previous_record');`

continues

MENU ITEM	*COMMAND TEXT*
Next	`do_key('next_record');`
Scroll Down	`do_key('scroll_down');`
Last	`last_record;`
Help	`do_key('help');`
Show Keys	`show_keys;`
List	`do_key('list_values');`
Display Error	`display_error;`

15. Select the menu STANDARD, and invoke the Properties window for the menu module.
16. Set Main Menu to STANDARD.
17. Set File to STANDARD.
18. Save and generate the menu from the keyboard with Ctrl+S and Ctrl+T respectively.

Next we will create an application menu by modifying the standard menu to include menu items that will call other forms and reports.

1. Change the menu module name and file from STANDARD to CONTACT, then save the menu module as CONTACT.MMB.
2. Invoke the Menu Editor and maximize the window.
3. Select the Record menu item.
4. Create a Maintenance menu item to the right of Record.
5. Create a Reports menu item to the right of Maintenance.
6. Add the following items under the Maintenance menu:
   - Customers
   - States
7. Double-click on the menu icon for CUSTOMERS under the Maintenance menu in the Object Navigator to invoke the PL/SQL Editor, and enter the following text:
   ```
   call_form('customer', no_hide, do_replace);
   ```
8. Double-click on the menu icon for CUSTOMERS under the Maintenance menu in the Object Navigator to invoke the PL/SQL Editor, and enter the following text:
   ```
   new_form('state');
   ```
9. Add a Customers menu item under the Reports menu.
10. Double-click on the menu icon for CUSTOMERS under the Reports menu in the Object Navigator to invoke the PL/SQL Editor, and enter the following text:
    ```
    run_product (REPORTS, 'customer', ASYNCHRONOUS, RUNTIME, FILESYSTEM, NULL,
    ➥NULL);
    ```
11. Save and generate the menu from the keyboard with Ctrl+S and Ctrl+T, respectively.

12. Close the menu module, and open the CONTACT form.
13. Change the menu from STANDARD to CONTACT.
14. Save and run the form to test the completed application. (See Figure 12.37.)

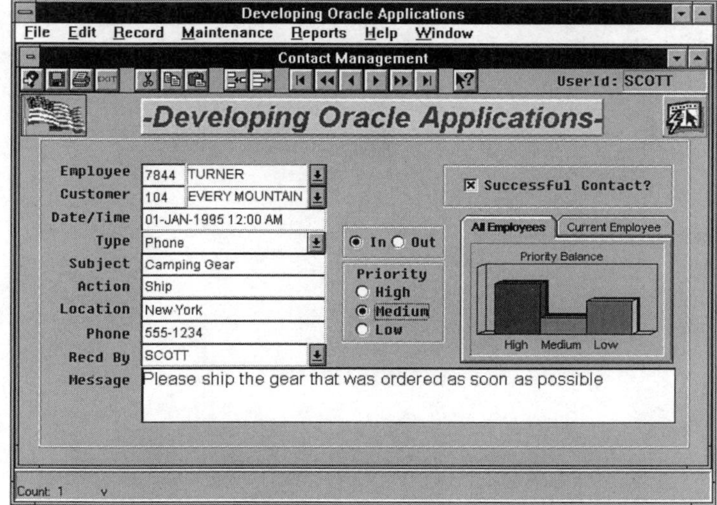

FIGURE 12.37.
The completed Contact Management application.

Summary

This chapter provided you with a variety of examples of Forms application development, including:

- Creating Oracle Forms templates with toolbars
- Creating multi-row, master/detail, and integrated applications using templates
- Adding List of Values
- Using OLE2
- Adding VBX Custom Controls
- Creating standard and custom application menus

If you worked through each section in the chapter, you will have completed the development of several different types of Forms applications and menus.

Now that you have developed applications with Oracle Forms, next we will create applications using Oracle Reports.

13

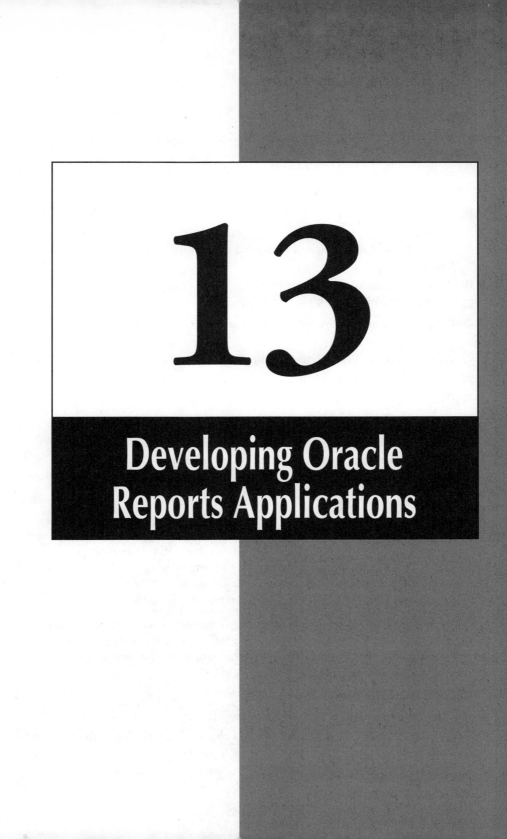

Developing Oracle Reports Applications

Introduction

Now that we've done some development using Oracle Forms and have completed an application that calls a report, we will explore in greater depth the development of report applications, building on the knowledge you've already gained. In reading and working through this chapter, you will learn how to do the following:

- Create Oracle Reports templates containing standard headers, trailers, and margin items
- Create break, drill-down, and integrated application reports using templates and OLE2
- Create format masks for report fields
- Use OLE2 to link an MS Excel file in a report
- Create a parameter form with a list of values from a SQL select statement to filter a query
- Add buttons and PL/SQL to drill-down into a detail report
- Add a link to an image file to a report
- Create a report with a Long Raw column for MS Word
- Embed an Oracle Graphics display in a report
- Create a report trigger for auditing
- Add reports to the application menu in Oracle Forms

Report Templates

In this chapter we will develop several report applications, but we will begin by creating two template reports. Template reports contain objects that will be common to all of our report applications. By creating the templates once and using them in all of our developments, the result will be consistent and standardized applications. Each of the applications will use a template to get started, including the application shown in Figure 13.1.

The template reports will be created by setting two system parameters, creating formula and placeholder columns, creating a header page, a trailer page, and a standard margin. The first template will have a portrait orientation, and the second template will be a landscape. To create the portrait report template, follow these steps:

1. Open Oracle Reports Designer.
2. Connect to the Oracle database as scott/tiger.
3. Select the System Parameter `DESTYPE` and change the Initial Value from Screen to Preview.

4. Select the System Parameter `ORIENTATION` and change the Initial Value from Default to Portrait.
5. Invoke the Data Model Editor, and create a Formula Column. Change the name to CF_USER, the Datatype to Char, Width to 30, and click the Edit button to invoke the Program Unit Editor.
6. Enter the following text before the begin statement:

```
declare userid varchar2(30);
```

7. Enter the following text after the begin statement:

```
select user into userid from dual;
```

8. Compile, then close the Program Unit Editor.
9. Create a Placeholder Column. Change the name to CP_PAGE_TITLE, change the Datatype to Char, change the Width to 50, and change Value If Null to Enter The Page Title Here.
10. Create another Placeholder Column. Change the name to CP_REPORT_NAME, change the Datatype to Char, change the Width to 8, and change Value If Null to rpt_name.
11. Create one more Placeholder Column. Change the name to CP_REPORT_TITLE, change the Datatype to Char, change the Width to 50, and change Value If Null to Enter the Report Title Here.
12. Select Save As from the File menu and save the report template as TEMPPORT.RDF.

FIGURE 13.1.
An Oracle Reports application.

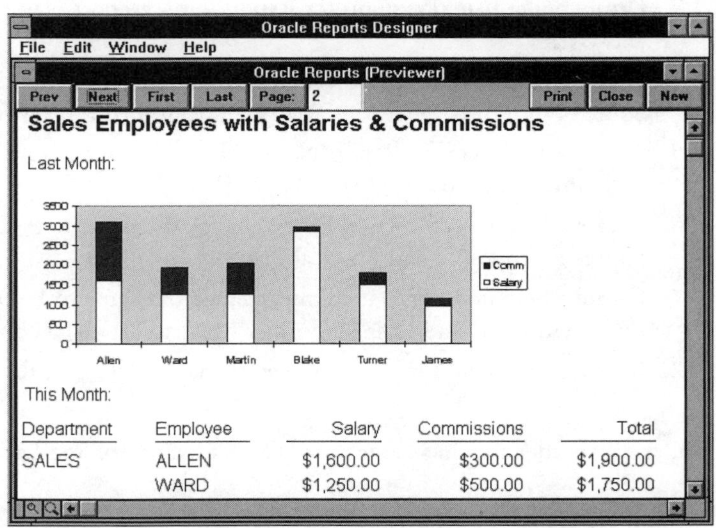

TIP

Group the formula, summary, and placeholder columns together at the top of the Data Model Editor so they are organized, but leave plenty of space for the data model.

Now we will create a report header that will use some of the columns we've just created.

The Report Header

Report headers are useful additions to reports. When many different users are sharing a printer in an office, a report header can identify the report and create a separation page between printouts. We are going to create a report header that contains the report title, name, page count, date, and userid. To create a report header, follow these steps:

1. Select and maximize the Layout Editor.
2. Reduce the magnification to 1/2x.
3. Select Header from the Layout Editor toolbar.
4. Select Font from the Format menu, then set the Font to Arial, the Font Style to Bold, and the Size to 14.
5. Select Alignment from the Format menu, then select Center.
6. Using the Color Palettes, set the Fill Color to No Fill and the Line Color to No Line.
7. Create boilerplate text items for Report Title, Report Name, Total Pages, Date/Time, and User.
8. Create a field item for Report Title, change the name to F_REPORT_TITLE, and set Source From to CP_REPORT_TITLE from the drop-down list.
9. Create a field item for Report Name, change the name to F_REPORT_NAME, and set Source From to CP_REPORT_NAME.
10. Create a field item for Total Pages, change the name to F_TOTAL_PAGES, and set Source From to &Total Physical Pages.
11. Create a field item for Date/Time, change the name to F_DATE, set Source From to &Current Date, and Display Format Mask to DD-MON-YY HH:MI AM.
12. Create a field item for User, change the name to F_USER, and set Source From to CF_USER.

The report header should appear in the Object Navigator and Layout Editor as shown in Figure 13.2.

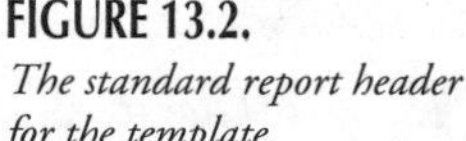

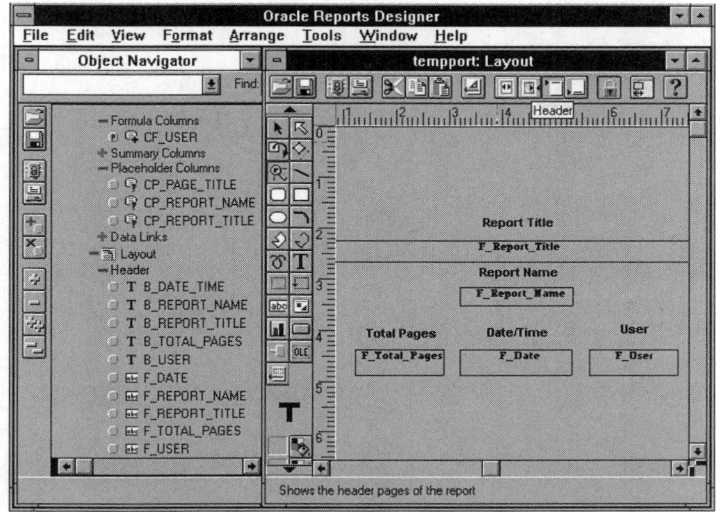

FIGURE 13.2.
The standard report header for the template.

In Figure 13.2, the labels are boilerplate text items, but the values for report title, report name, total pages, date/time, and user fields will be assigned from columns.

The Report Trailer

Like report headers, trailers are useful additions to reports. The report trailer is used to identify the end of the report and create a separation page between printouts. We are going to create a report trailer that contains an end of report, the report title, and a report name. To create a report trailer, follow these steps:

1. Select the boilerplate text and fields for the report title and report name.
2. Copy the selected objects.
3. Select Trailer from the Layout Editor toolbar.
4. Paste the objects into the layout.
5. Create a boilerplate text item for End of Report just above the report title.
6. Save the report template.

The report trailer should appear in the Object Navigator and Layout Editor as shown in Figure 13.3.

The report trailer was created very quickly using the copy-and-paste technique, but it will still reference the appropriate columns to populate the field items.

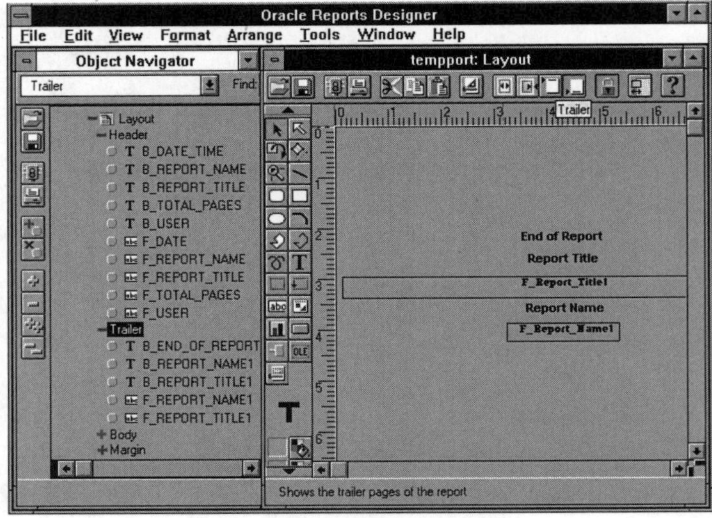

FIGURE 13.3.
The Layout Editor showing the report trailer.

The Margin

The margin is where page header and footers can be defined. It also creates space around the report layout. The size of the margin may be adjusted by dragging the handles of the margin in the Layout Editor. We are going to create a margin that contains the page title at the top and the page-count information at the bottom.

1. Select Margin from the Layout Editor toolbar.
2. Notice the margin area is above and below the dark line that defines the body area of the layout.
3. Create a field item for Page Title in the margin area at the top of the page, change the name to F_PAGE_TITLE, set Source From to CP_PAGE_TITLE, and set the alignment to left.
4. Create boilerplate text items in the margin area at the bottom of the page for Page and of.
5. Create a field item for Current Page, change the name to F_CURRENT_PAGE, and set Source From to &Physical Page Number.
6. Create a field item for Page Total, change the name to F_PAGE_TOTAL, and set Source From to &Total Physical Pages.
7. Arrange the page information items as they appear in Figure 13.4, aligned at the bottom and stacked.
8. Save the report template.

Figure 13.4 shows the margin containing boilerplate text and field items for the page-count information.

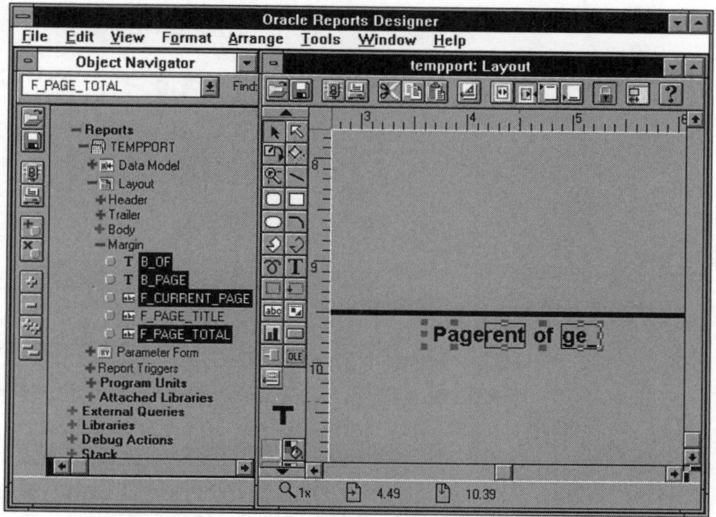

FIGURE 13.4.
The Layout Editor showing the margin.

The margin could contain other layout fields and boilerplate. For example, you may want to add the report name and/or the date/time to each page.

A Parameter Form

Just as default layouts are created in Oracle Forms and Oracle Reports, default parameters forms can also be created for your Oracle Reports applications. Next we will create a default parameter form for our report template that contains the system parameters that we modified earlier in this chapter.

1. Select Default Parameter Form from the Tools menu.
2. Select `DESTYPE` and `ORIENTATION` from the list of parameters.
3. Change the label from Destype to Output Type, then press OK.
4. Save the report template.

The system parameters are selected from the Default Parameter Form dialog box, as shown in Figure 13.5.

Notice that the titles and labels for the parameter form appear in the Default Parameter Form dialog box and then in the Parameter Form Editor. We modified the label for `DESTYPE` in the Default Parameter Form dialog box to give it a more intuitive name. Figure 13.6 shows the Parameter Form Editor containing the `DESTYPE` and `ORIENTATION` system parameters.

FIGURE 13.5.
The Default Parameter Form dialog box.

tempport: Default Parameter Form
Title: Report Parameters
Hint: Enter values for the parameters
Status:

Parameter:	Label:
DESTYPE	Output Type
DESNAME	Desname
DESFORMAT	Desformat
COPIES	Copies
CURRENCY	Currency
THOUSANDS	Thousands

OK Cancel

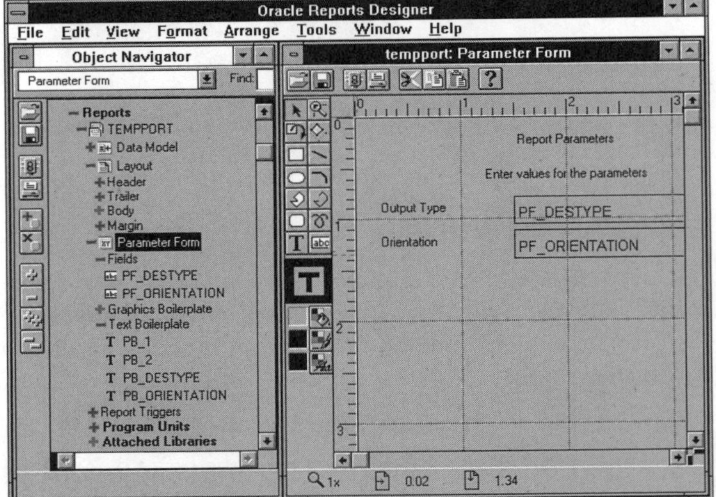

FIGURE 13.6.
The Parameter Form Editor with the default parameter form.

The Landscape Template

Now that we have completed the report template for the portrait orientation, we will make a few changes to the template to use for landscape reports.

1. Select the System Parameter `ORIENTATION` and change the Initial Value from Portrait to Landscape.
2. Select Save As from the File menu and save the report template as TEMPLAND.RDF.

Next we will temporarily adjust the margin, then change the report properties for page width and height.

1. Select and maximize the Layout Editor.
2. Select Margin from the Layout Editor toolbar.
3. Drag the bottom of the margin up a few inches.
4. Select the page-count items and drag them up just below the bottom margin.

Now we can change the report properties for page width and height without the margin objects being off the page. We will also adjust the header, trailer, and margins so that the objects will be centered.

1. Select TEMPLAND in the Object Navigator, click the right mouse button to invoke the pop-up menu, and select Properties to invoke the Report Properties dialog box.
2. Change the Page Width from 8.5 to 11 and the Page Height from 11 to 8.5.
3. Return to the Layout Editor and select Header from the Layout Editor toolbar.
4. Select all of the header items and drag them to the right about an inch, to center them. Then select Trailer from the Layout Editor toolbar.
5. Select all of the trailer items and drag them to the right about an inch to center them. Then select Margin from the Layout Editor toolbar.
6. Select the page title, and stretch it to the right, just short of the right margin.
7. Drag the bottom of the margin down to 7 1/2 inches.
8. Select the page-count items, drag them to just below and in the center of the bottom margin.
9. Save and close the report template.

We now have two templates to use in developing our report applications. In the remainder of this chapter, we will use the templates as a starting point for developing several different reports. The first report will be a list of sales employees that contains an Excel chart and calculates their total salaries and commissions.

The Sales Employees Report

We will start the development of our report by opening one of the templates and setting the values for our placeholder columns.

1. Open TEMPORT.RDF and save the report as SAL_COMM.RDF.
2. Select CP_PAGE_TITLE from the Placeholder Columns in the Object Navigator, invoke the Properties dialog box, and set Value If Null to Sales Employees with Salaries and Commissions.
3. Select CP_REPORT_NAME, and set Value if Null to sal_comm.
4. Select CP_REPORT_TITLE, and set Value If Null to Sales Employees with Salaries and Commissions.

A Data Model with Data Links and a Formula Column

Now we will create the data model for the report. The data model will contain two queries, a data link, and a formula column.

1. Invoke the Data Model Editor and create a query. Then change the name to Q_DEPT and enter the following select statement:

   ```
   select dname, deptno from dept where dname = 'SALES'
   ```

2. Create another query. Then change the name to Q_EMP and enter the following select statement:

   ```
   select ename, sal, comm, deptno from emp
   ```

3. Click the Data Link button on the tool palette, then click on Q_DEPT and drag to Q_EMP to create the data link joining the two queries.

TIP

If your foreign-key reference constraints are defined in the Oracle database, then Oracle Reports will be able to automatically create the data links from the queries without you having to identify the appropriate columns.

4. Click the Formula Column button on the tool palette.
5. Click just under the deptno1 column in the G_EMP group.
6. Double-click CF_1 to invoke the property sheet, change the name to CF_Total, and click the Edit button to define the formula. You may need to move or close the property sheet to see the Program Unit Editor.
7. In the function shell, just under the begin, type `return (:sal + :comm);`. Then click the Compile and Close buttons.

The objects in the data model should appear in the Object Navigator and Data Model Editor as shown in Figure 13.7.

NOTE

The formula column could have been created as a database column by including the calculation in the SQL select statement.

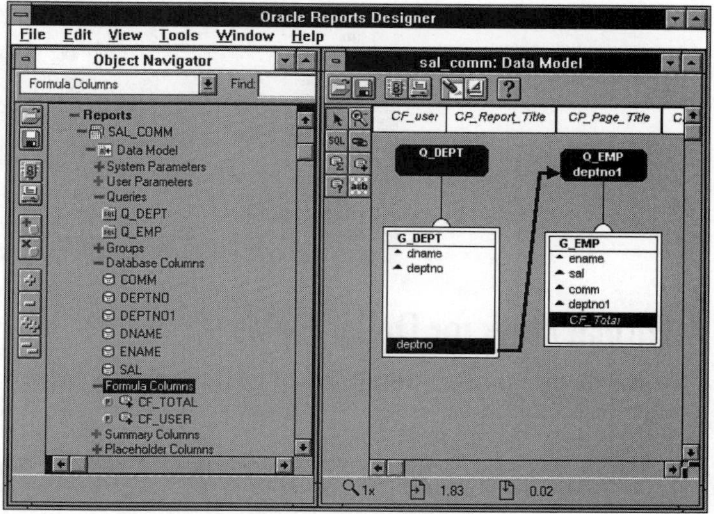

FIGURE 13.7.
The data model for the sal_comm report.

A Default Tabular Layout

Now we will create the layout for the report. The layout will contain the department name, employee name, salary, commissions, and the total columns.

1. Select Layout Editor from the Tools menu, then select Font from the Format menu and set the font to Arial, regular, 12 point.
2. Select Default Layout from the Layout Editor toolbar.
3. Click the Data/Selection tab.
4. Change the label of dname to Department, ename to Employee, sal to Salary, comm to Commissions, and CF_Total to Total.
5. Change the width of dname, ename, sal, comm, and CF_Total to 5.
6. Click deptno and deptno1 to deselect them, then press OK.
7. Save, run, preview, and return to Oracle Reports Designer.

The fields created during the default layout should appear in the Layout Editor as shown in Figure 13.8.

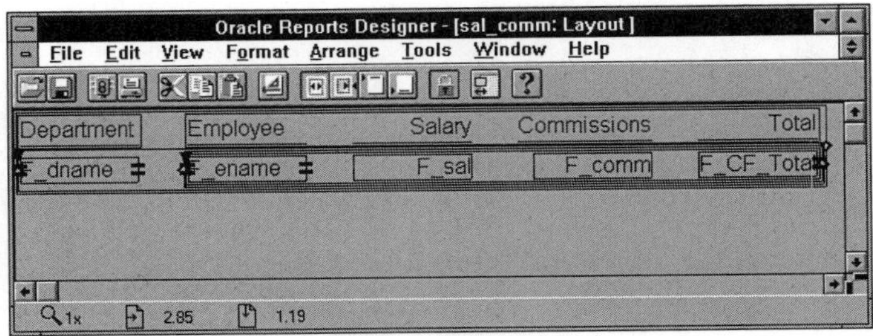

FIGURE 13.8.
The Layout Editor after default layout.

A Format Mask for Dollar Fields

The sal, comm, and total fields will need a format mask to display the numeric data as dollars. Format masks are added using the property sheets of the layout fields.

> **TIP**
>
> The layout fields may be found under the group frames and repeating frames in the body under the Layout node in the Object Navigator. But, the easiest way to access the property sheets of the layout fields is to select them in the Layout Editor.

1. Select and maximize the Layout Editor. Then select Body from the Layout Editor toolbar.
2. Select F_sal, F_comm, and F_CF_Total in the layout.
3. Right mouse click and select Properties from the pop-up menu.
4. The three Layout Field property sheets all appear stacked on each other.
5. Enter `-$NNN,NN0.00` as the Display Format Mask for F_CF_Total, then press OK. Notice the property sheet for F_comm is now available.
6. Select -$NNN,NN0.00 from the drop-down list of Format Masks for F_comm, and press OK. The property sheet for F_sal is now available.
7. Select -$NNN,NN0.00 from the drop-down list of Format Masks for F_sal, and press OK.

The drop-down list for the display format mask appears in the Object tab of the Layout Field property sheet as shown in Figure 13.9.

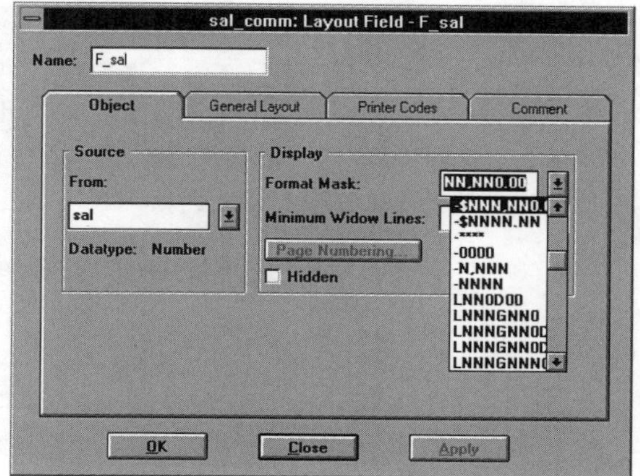

FIGURE 13.9.
The list of format masks from the property sheet.

An OLE2 Object Linked to an Excel File

Next we will add an Excel spreadsheet that contains a chart from the file system to the top of the report. To do this, we will increase the upper margin area and then add an OLE2 container in the margin area. The OLE2 container will be linked to a file on the file system.

1. Select and maximize the Layout Editor. Then select Margin from the Layout Editor toolbar.
2. Reduce the magnification in the layout so that the entire page width is displayed.
3. Click and drag the margin area down three inches from the top of the page to make room for the chart.
4. Select OLE2 Object from the toolbar.
5. Create the OLE2 item in the margin area. The Insert Object dialog box is invoked.
6. Select Create from File in the Insert Object dialog box, then select the Link checkbox and enter the absolute path name of the Excel chart (as shown in Figure 13.10), and press OK.

NOTE

You should find the Excel file in the \DEV2000\REPORTS directory. The Browse button in the Insert Object dialog box will invoke the Browse dialog box to enable you to locate the file on the file system.

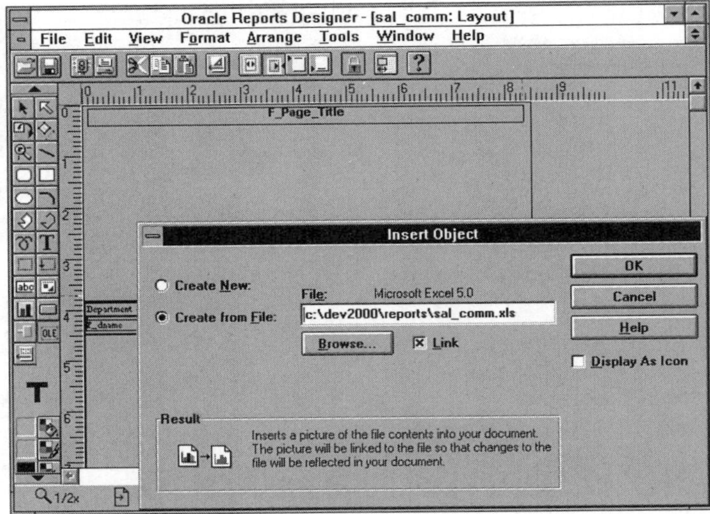

FIGURE 13.10.
The Insert Object dialog box for an Excel chart.

> **TIP**
>
> When you select the Link option in the Insert Object dialog box, the report will contain the latest version of the object at runtime.

The OLE2 container should now appear in the layout as shown in Figure 13.11.

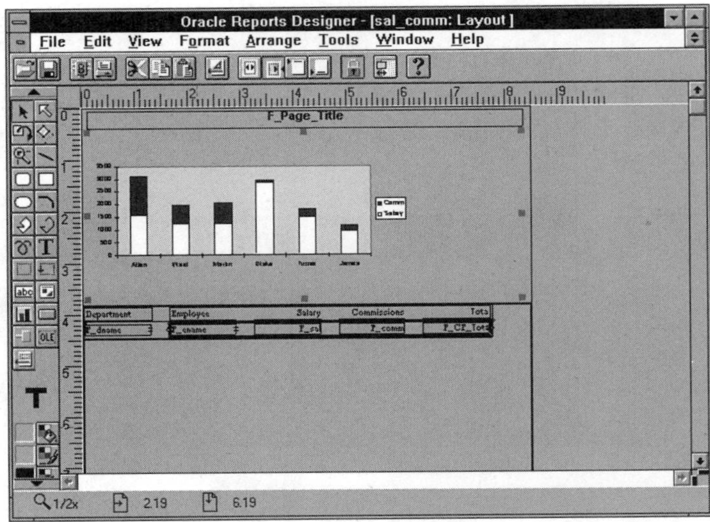

FIGURE 13.11.
The Layout Editor showing the OLE2 linked object from MS Excel.

Adding Boilerplate Text to the Margin

The final steps to complete the sal_comm report are to add some boilerplate text to the margin area to identify the chart information and the report data that follows.

1. Create boilerplate text items for Last Month: and This Month:, before and after the OLE2 container respectively.
2. Save, run, preview, return to Oracle Reports Designer, and close the report.

The completed sal_comm report should appear in the Previewer as shown in Figure 13.12.

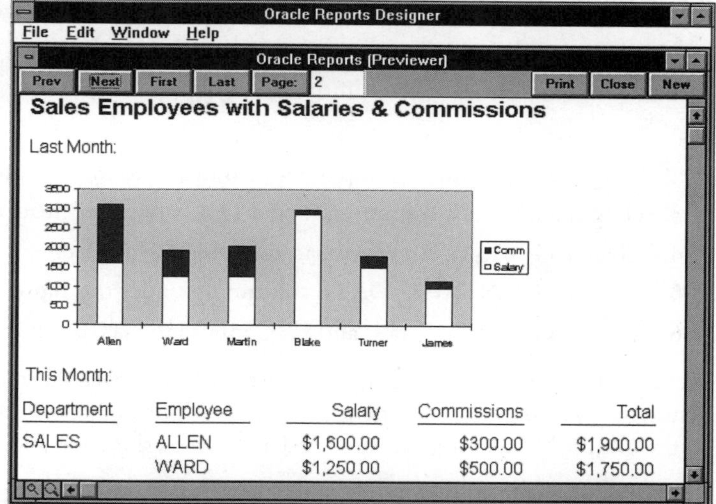

FIGURE 13.12.
The completed sal_comm report shown in the Previewer.

The Employee Contact Details Report

The next report we will create will list all of the contacts made by a given employee. We will start the development of our report by opening one of the templates and setting the values for our placeholder columns. Then we will define the data model, define the layout, and modify the parameter form. This report can be run independently and can also serve as the detail report to be called from the drill-down report we will develop next in this chapter.

1. Open TEMPPORT.RDF and save the report as CONTACTS.RDF.
2. Select CP_PAGE_TITLE from the Placeholder Columns in the Object Navigator, invoke the Properties dialog box, and set Value if Null to Contacts by Employee.
3. Select CP_REPORT_NAME, and set Value If Null to Contacts.
4. Select CP_REPORT_TITLE, and set Value If Null to Employee Contacts.

A Data Model with Break Groups and a User Parameter

Now we will create the data model for the report. The data model will contain a query, two break groups, and a user parameter.

1. Invoke the Data Model Editor and create a query. Then change the name to Q_Contacts and enter the following select statement:

```
select * from contact_list
where ename = :emp_name
order by contact_date
```

> **NOTE**
>
> Notice that this query is based on a view, it selects all columns, and it includes a reference to a user parameter in the where clause.

2. Drag the G_Contacts group down two inches to make room for two break groups.
3. Drag the ENAME column up under Q_Contacts to create a new break group.
4. Change G_1 to G_Employees in the Object Navigator.
5. Drag the CONTACT_DATE column up under the Employees group.
6. Change G_1 to G_Dates, and G_Contacts to G_Customers in the Object Navigator.

Notice in the Object Navigator that the User Parameter was automatically created via the where clause in the SQL select statement of the query. The objects in the data model should appear in the Object Navigator and Data Model Editor as shown in Figure 13.13.

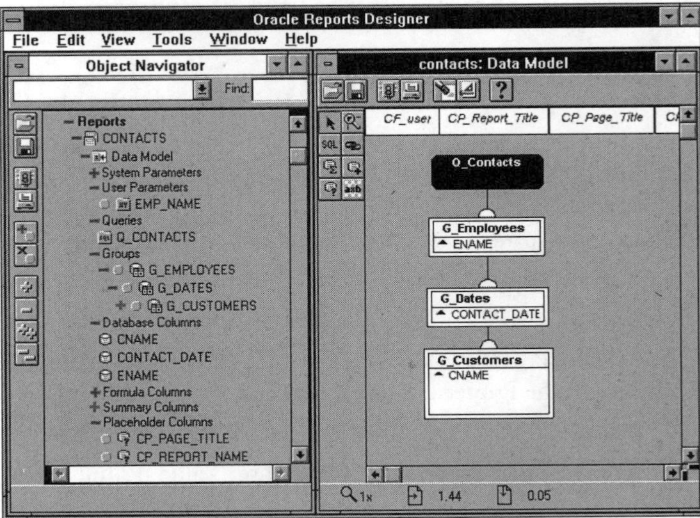

FIGURE 13.13.
The data model for the contacts report.

Adding a List of Values for the User Parameter

This report will filter the query based on the value of employee name in the user parameter. We will provide a list of valid employee names for the user parameter by defining a list of values based on a SQL select statement.

1. Select EMP_NAME from User Parameters in the Object Navigator and invoke the property sheet.
2. Click the Data/Selection tab from the Parameter dialog box, then change List of Values from Static Values to SELECT Statement.
3. Enter the following query, then press OK.

```
select ename from emp
```

A Default Tabular Layout with Break Groups

Now we will create the layout for the report. The layout will contain the employee name, date of contact, and the customer name.

1. Select Layout Editor from the Tools menu, then select Font from the Format menu, and set the font to Arial, regular, 10 point.
2. Select Default Layout from the Layout Editor toolbar.
3. Click the Data/Selection tab.
4. Change the label of ename to Employee, contact_date to Date, and cname to Customer.
5. Change the width of cname to 30, then press OK.
6. Save the report.

Frames

A frame is a container for grouping related objects in the report. Frames may contain other frames, boilerplate, and fields. Each group in the data model will have an associated group frame, header frame, and repeating frame in the layout body. The frames are created automatically by the default layout. In the Object Navigator frames appear as rectangular icons in the Body under the Layout node.

Figure 13.14 shows the Object Navigator with the Body node expanded and containing the group frames, header frames, and repeating frames from the Contacts report.

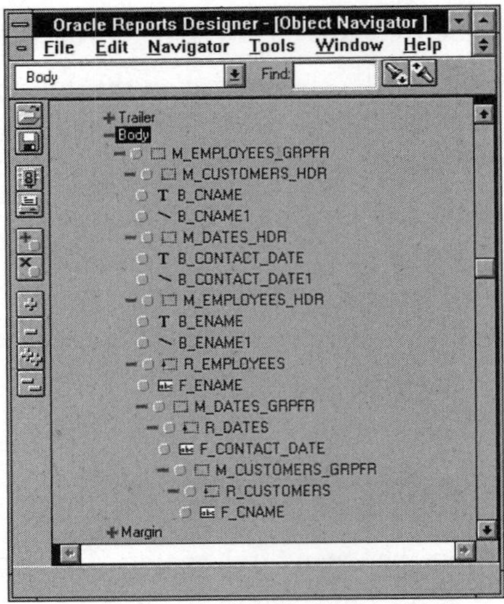

FIGURE 13.14.
The Object Navigator showing the frames from the Contacts report.

Group Frames

Group frames contain repeating frames and sometimes header frames. The group frames are nested under each other just as the groups are in the data model.

Header Frames

Header frames contain the boilerplate text and graphics for labeling the report columns. Generally, the highest group frame in the data model contains the header frames for the report.

Repeating Frames

A repeating frame is similar to a group frame except that the repeating frame contains report fields. In the Object Navigator, repeating frames appear as rectangles with an arrow. The repeating frames are under their group frames.

Figure 13.15 shows the Layout Editor displaying some of the group frames, header frames, and repeating frames from the contacts report.

Notice in the layout that the outside frame is an expandable group frame, the header frame contains boilerplate text, and the repeating frame contains a field as well as additional frames.

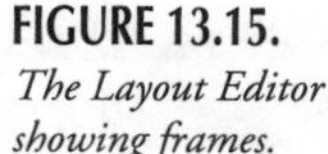

FIGURE 13.15.
The Layout Editor showing frames.

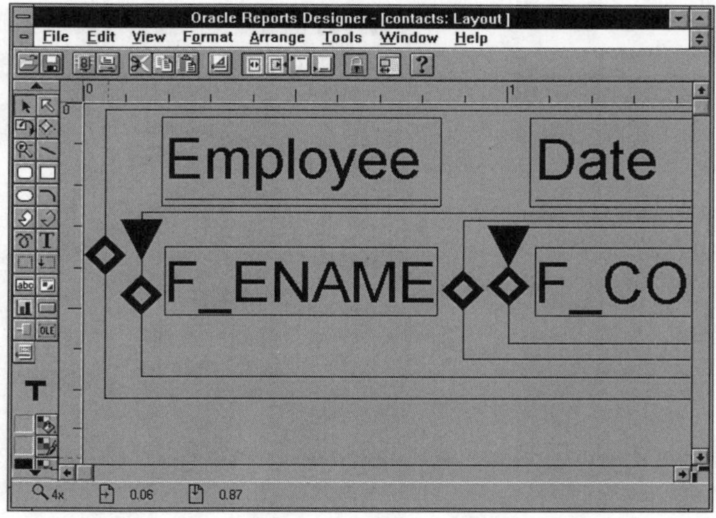

Adding a User Parameter to the Parameter Form

Next we will add the new parameter to the parameter form. To do that, we will just re-create the default parameter form and include the selection of EMP_NAME.

1. Select Default Parameter Form from the Tools menu.
2. Notice `DESTYPE` and `ORIENTATION` are already selected, based on the existing parameter form.
3. Scroll down and select EMP_NAME, change the label from Emp_Name to Employee, then press OK.
4. Save the report.

Figure 13.16 shows the Parameter Form Editor containing the `DESTYPE`, `ORIENTATION`, and `EMP_NAME` parameters.

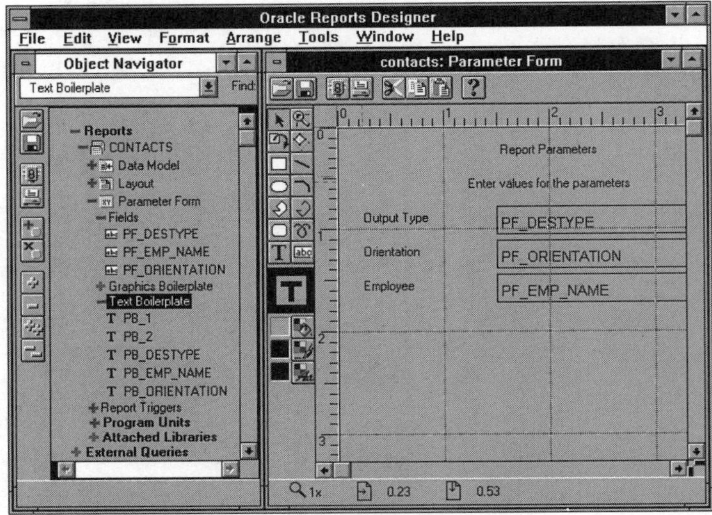

FIGURE 13.16.
The Parameter Form Editor with the user parameter added.

The Employee Contact Totals Report

The next report we will create lists the employees and the number of contacts they have made to their customers. This report will be able to drill-down from any given employee and display the details of their contacts.

But first we will make a few changes to the contacts report, so when we call it from the drill-down report, it will not contain the header, trailer, or parameter form.

1. Save the report as ECONTACT.RDF.
2. Select Tools Options from the Tools menu to invoke the Tools Options dialog box.
3. Select the Runtime Settings tab, and uncheck the Parameter Form check box, then press OK.
4. Expand the Header node in the Object Navigator, select all of the header items, then click the Delete button from the tool palette.
5. Expand the Trailer node in the Object Navigator, select all of the trailer items, then press the Delete key.
6. Save the report.

Now we will create the contact-totals report that will contain a button item to invoke the contact detail report.

1. Open TEMPPORT.RDF and save the report as ECONTOTS.RDF.
2. Select CP_PAGE_TITLE from the Placeholder Columns in the Object Navigator, invoke the Properties dialog box, and set Value If Null to Contact Totals By Employee w/Drilldown to Details.
3. Select CP_REPORT_NAME and set Value If Null to econtots.
4. Select CP_REPORT_TITLE and set Value If Null to Employee Contact Totals.
5. Invoke the Data Model Editor and create a query. Then change the name to Q_Contact_Totals and enter the following select statement:
```
select e.ename Employee, count(e.empno) Contacts
from contact c, emp e
where e.empno = c.empno
group by e.ename
```
6. Select Layout Editor from the Tools menu, then select Font from the Format menu, and set the font to Arial, Bold, 16 point.
7. Select Default Layout from the Layout Editor toolbar.
8. Click the Data/Selection tab, and change the width of Contacts to 10, then press OK.
9. Save the report.

The layout appears in the Layout Editor with the two fields to list the employees and contact totals. The next steps are to create some room on the left side of the layout and then add a button item to create the drill-down function.

Flex Mode in the Layout Editor

We will create the space in the layout by using the flex mode feature in the Layout Editor. Flex mode enables you to easily move one or more objects in the layout without inadvertently moving any object outside of its group boundary.

1. Select and maximize the Layout Editor.
2. Toggle the flex mode on by selecting the Flex button on the toolbar.
3. Select all of the items in the layout, then deselect the group frame by shift-clicking on it.
4. Drag the selected items to the right of the layout about 2 inches.
5. Select the repeating group, then stretch it back to the left to create space for the button between the left margin and the employee field.

Now we can add the button and the PL/SQL code associated with it to drill-down to the contact details report.

A Drill-Down Button

Buttons can be used to execute PL/SQL or to activate a multimedia object. We are using the button and PL/SQL to drill-down to a detail report. Button labels may be text or iconic. Our button will contain a text string to indicate the function of the button to the user. At runtime the button appears in the Previewer but does not get printed.

1. Select Font from the Format menu and set the font to Arial, Regular, 8 point.
2. Select Button from the tool palette and create a button in the repeating group.
3. Select Properties from the pop-up menu in the Layout Editor to invoke the Button property sheet.
4. Change the name to U_Drill_Down.
5. Set the Text String to Show Contact Details.
6. Set the Action to Execute PL/SQL, then click the Edit button to invoke the PL/SQL Editor.
7. Enter the following text after the begin statement:

```
srw.run_report('econtact.rdf paramform=no EMP_NAME="'¦¦:employee¦¦'"');
```

Notice that we are using one of the Oracle Reports packaged procedures to run the report. The completed button should appear in the Object Navigator and Layout Editor as shown in Figure 13.17.

Notice also that the button-object bullet in the Object Navigator contains the letter P, indicating that the button contains a PL/SQL program unit.

8. Save and run the report.

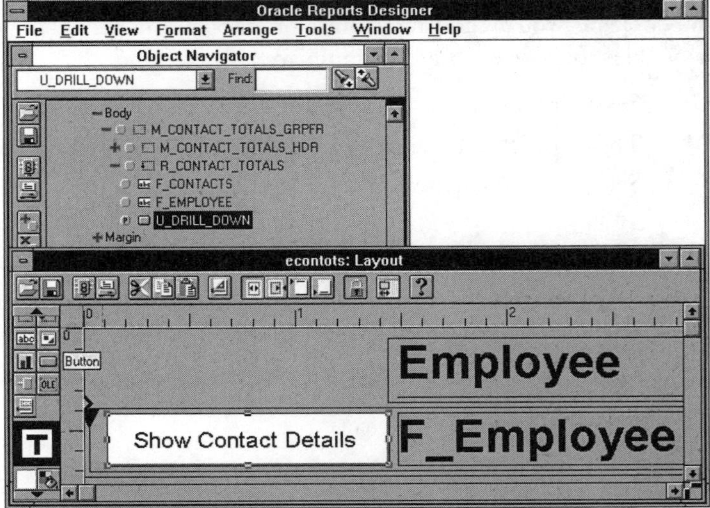

FIGURE 13.17.
The button to show contact details.

Since the button was placed in the repeating frame, when the Employee Contact Totals report is run, the button appears alongside each of the employees as shown in Figure 13.18.

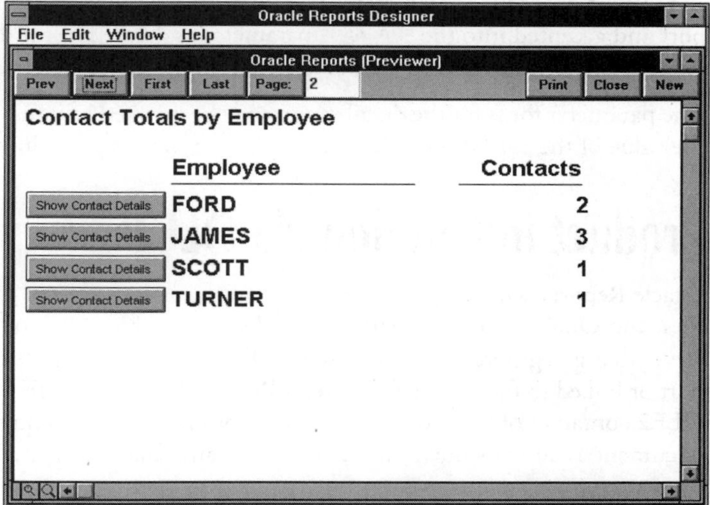

FIGURE 13.18.
The Employee Contact Totals report.

When the user wishes to see the contact details for one of the employees, they press the Show Contact Details button. The name of the associated employee is passed down to the Employee Contacts report, and a second Previewer is displayed containing that employee's contact details, as shown in Figure 13.19.

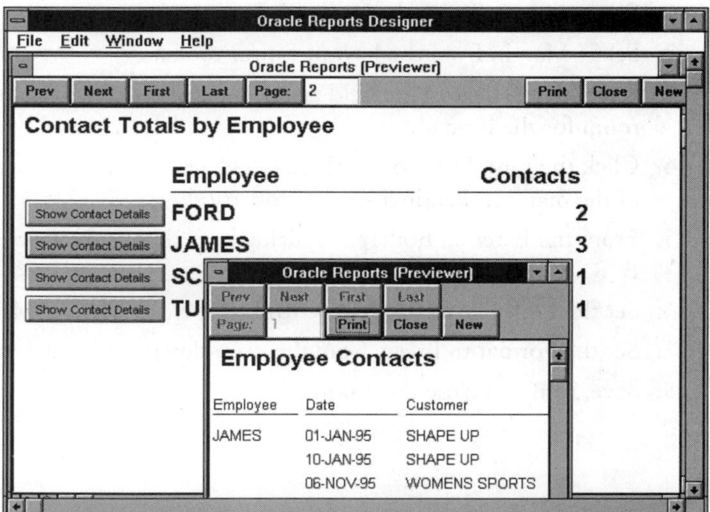

FIGURE 13.19.
The Employee Contacts report.

Passing Parameters

The parameter field for employee name is passed to the detail report as a text string in the run_report procedure parameters. The bind variable `:employee` is assigned by the calling report and accepted into the `EMP_NAME` parameter as defined in the detail report. More than one parameter may be passed to detail reports as required.

The parameter form for the detail report may be invoked or it may be excluded, depending on the value of the `paramform` parameter in the run_report procedure.

Product Integration via OLE2

Oracle Reports achieves product integration through the use of OLE2 container objects, link files, and Oracle Graphics chart items. The OLE2 object may be any object from any OLE2 server that is registered on your system. OLE2 container objects may be embedded in the report or linked to files in the file system. Previously we linked an Excel file to a report using an OLE2 container object. Now we will add a bitmap image as a link file, then add an MS Word document as an embedded OLE2 container, and finally add an Oracle Graphics chart.

Link File to an Image Item

Oracle Reports can display images from a variety of formats, including BMP, PCX, TIFF, and others. An image item may be associated with a file or a database column. Here we will link an image file in the margin of the report. The bitmap was created using MS Paintbrush and saved to the local file system.

1. Select and maximize the Layout Editor.
2. Select Margin from the Layout Editor toolbar.
3. Select the F_Page_Title field and move the left side over about a half inch to make room for the bitmap.
4. Click the Link File tool on the tool palette and create an item in the upper-left corner of the margin, then invoke the property sheet.
5. From the External Boilerplate dialog box, change the name of the item to B_REPORT_BITMAP.
6. Set the Link File to \DEV2000\BITMAPS\R25RUN.BMP.
7. Set the Format to Image from the drop-down list, then press OK.
8. Save, run, and close the report.

The boilerplate image item should now appear in the Layout Editor and Object Navigator. (See Figure 13.20.)

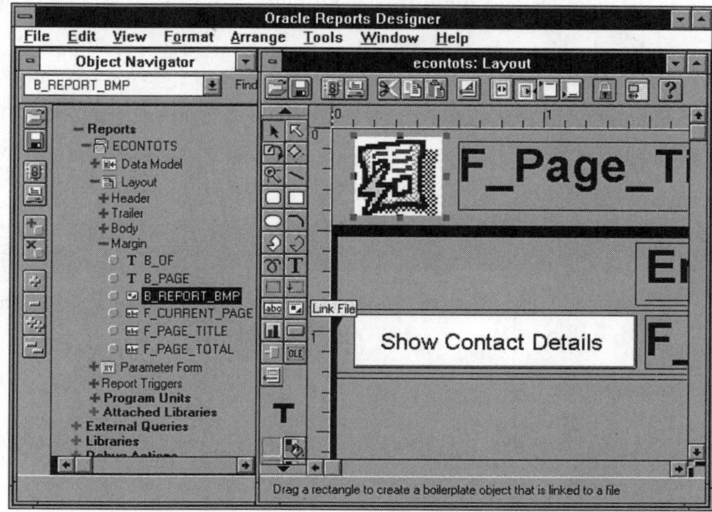

FIGURE 13.20.
An image item that will display a bitmap.

TIP

You may want to add your company logo to the page header of your report templates using a link file to an image.

An Embedded OLE2 Object from MS Word

We will now create a report that will contain an embedded OLE2 object from MS Word that is connected to a database column.

1. Open TEMPLAND.RDF and save the report as CONT_MSG.RDF.
2. Select CP_PAGE_TITLE from the Placeholder Columns in the Object Navigator, invoke the Properties dialog box, and set Value If Null to Contact Messages via MS Word.
3. Select CP_REPORT_NAME and set Value If Null to cont_msg.
4. Select CP_REPORT_TITLE and set Value If Null to Contact Messages.

A Data Model with Multiple Joins and a Long Raw Column

Now we will create the data model for the report. The data model will contain a query that joins three tables and includes a long raw column for the MS Word message.

1. Invoke the Data Model Editor and create a query. Then change the name to Q_Contact_Msgs and enter the following select statement:

```
select e.ename Employee, cus.name Customer, c.contact_date When, c.message
➥Message
from emp e, customer cus, contact c
where e.empno = c.empno and cus.custid = c.custid
```

> **NOTE**
>
> Notice that this query contains the long raw message column from the contact table, which will be the source for our OLE2 container.

2. Select the Message column and invoke the property sheet.
3. Change the Format from Text to OLE2 in the Database Column dialog box, then press OK.
4. Select Layout Editor from the Tools menu, then select Font from the Format menu, and set the font to Arial, Regular, 10 point.
5. Select Default Layout from the Layout Editor toolbar, then select Form as the layout style.
6. Click the Data/Selection tab, change the width of Employee to 5, Customers to 10, the height of Message to 3, and add a colon to each label. Then press OK.

> **NOTE**
>
> Notice that this report is a Form-style layout and that we added colons to the labels because the data prints to the right of the labels, as opposed to under them.

7. Save and run the report.

The completed cont_msg report should appear in the Oracle Reports Designer and Previewer. (See Figure 13.21.)

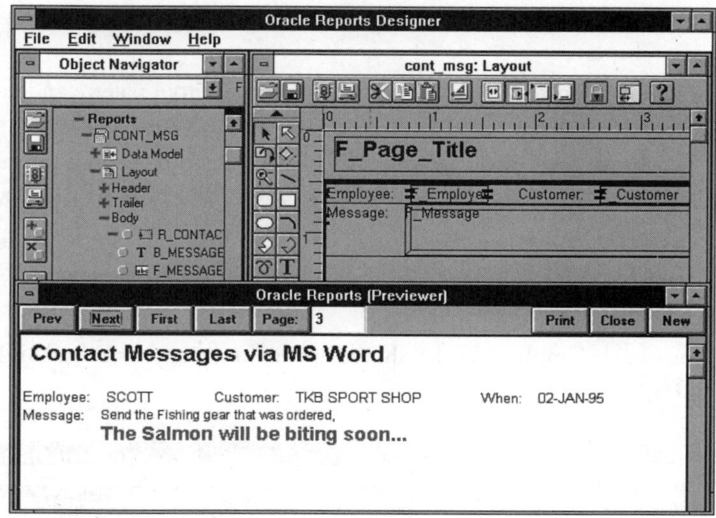

FIGURE 13.21.
The cont_msg report shown with an embedded MS Word document.

An Oracle Graphics Display

Next we will create a report that will contain a summary of contact priorities and a display from Oracle Graphics. We will use the display created in Chapter 10, "Introducing Oracle Graphics." Later we will add a second query to this report for employee details.

1. Open TEMPPORT.RDF and save the report as PRIORITY.RDF.
2. Set Value if Null for CP_PAGE_TITLE to Contact Priorities.
3. Set Value if Null for CP_REPORT_NAME to priority.
4. Set Value if Null for CP_REPORT_TITLE to Contact Priorities.
5. Invoke the Data Model Editor and create a query. Then change the name to Q_Priorities and enter the following select statement:

```
select count (decode (priority, 'H', 'High')) High,
count (decode (priority, 'M', 'Medium')) Medium,
count (decode (priority, 'L', 'Low')) Low
from contact
```

6. Select Layout Editor from the Tools menu, then select Font from the Format menu, and set the font to Arial, Bold, 16 point.
7. Select Default Layout from the Layout Editor toolbar.
8. Click the Data/Selection tab, and change the width of High, Medium, and Low to 5. Then press OK.
9. Select and maximize the Layout Editor, then select Margin.

10. Move the top of the margin down three inches to make room for the Oracle Graphics display.
11. Click on the Oracle Graphics tool on the tool palette and create an item in the upper-left corner of the margin, then invoke the property sheet.
12. From the Oracle Graphics Display dialog box, change Name to D_Priorities and change Display Name to \DEV2000\GRAPHICS\PRIORITY.OGD. Then press OK.
13. Set Line Color to No Line from the Color Palette.
14. Save and run the report.

The Oracle Graphics display should appear in the Layout Editor and Object Navigator as shown in Figure 13.22.

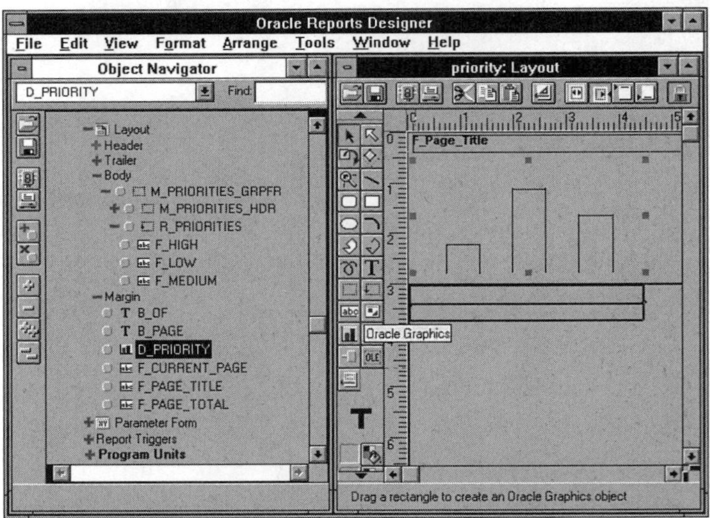

FIGURE 13.22.
An Oracle Graphics display in the layout.

Adding a Second Query and Default Layout

Now that we have developed a summary report with a graph, we will add another query to show the priority details by employee.

1. Invoke the Data Model Editor and create a query. Then change the name to Q_Emp_Priorities and enter the following select statement:

```
select e.empno,
e.ename Employee,
count (decode (c.priority, 'H', 'High')) High,
count (decode (c.priority, 'M', 'Medium')) Medium,
count (decode (c.priority, 'L', 'Low')) Low
from contact c, emp e
```

```
where e.empno = c.empno
group by e.empno, e.ename
```

2. Select and maximize the Layout Editor, then select Body and reduce the magnification so the entire body is visible.
3. Select Additional Default Layout from the Layout Editor toolbar, then define the layout area by drawing a rectangle just under the existing layout items using the remaining space in the body.
4. Click the Data/Selection tab, deselect ename, and change the width of Employee, High, Medium, and Low to 5. Then press OK.
5. Return to the Layout Editor, select all of the previous layout items, and move them to the right to align with the new columns.

TIP

Use the ruler guides to align the first group of layout items with the group of items beneath them.

6. Select Margin, then move the center of the Oracle Graphics display over the summary items. (See Figure 13.23.)
7. Save and run the report.

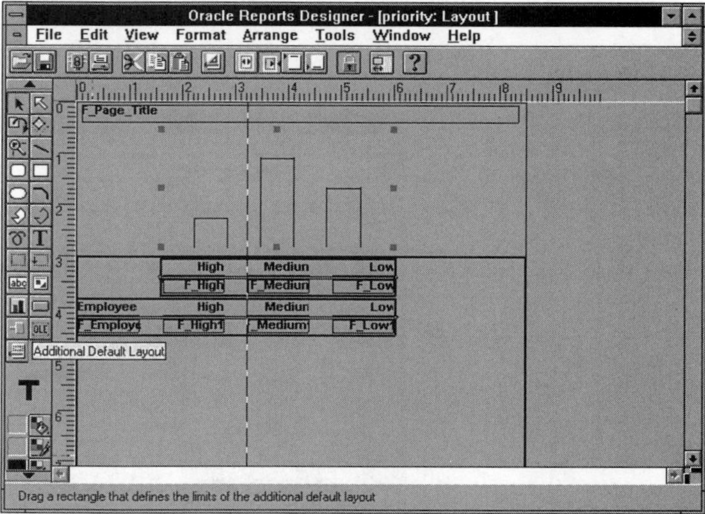

FIGURE 13.23.
Additional Default Layout items aligned in the Layout Editor.

> **NOTE**
>
> In Chapter 14, "Developing Oracle Graphics Applications," we will create an additional display and then return to this report to add a detail graph for each employee.

Report Triggers

There are five standard report triggers provided with Oracle Reports. They are Before Report, After Report, Between Pages, Before Parameter Form, and After Parameter Form. We will create a Before Report trigger to insert audit records into the rpt_audit table.

1. Invoke the Program Unit Editor for the Before Report trigger by double-clicking it in the Object Navigator, then enter the following text before the begin statement:

```
cur_user varchar2(8);
cur_date date;
```

2. Then enter the following text after the begin statement:

```
select user, sysdate into cur_user, cur_date
from dual;
insert into rpt_audit
values ('priority', cur_user, cur_date);
```

3. Compile the trigger, then close the Program Unit Editor.
4. Save and run the report.

The Before Report trigger appears in the Program Unit Editor as shown in Figure 13.24.

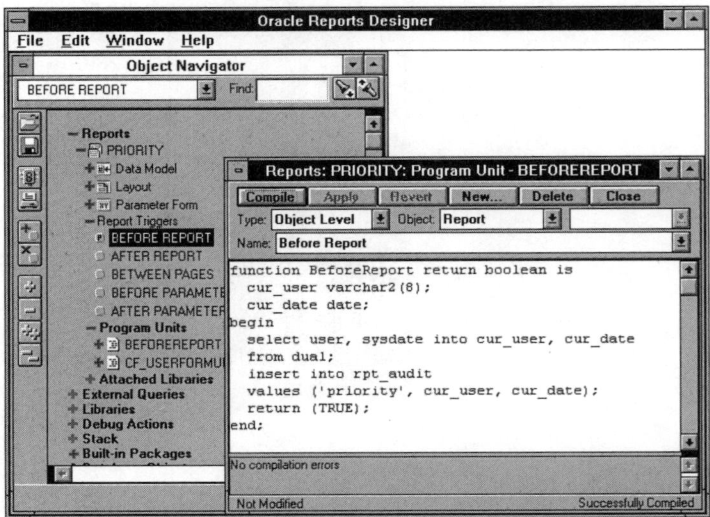

FIGURE 13.24.
The Program Unit Editor showing a Report Trigger.

NOTE

By creating an audit table and using the Before Report trigger, we can monitor which reports have been run by which users, and when.

Format Triggers

In addition to report-level triggers, Oracle Reports also supports format triggers. Like report triggers, format triggers are functions and are created via the Program Unit Editor. If an object contains a format trigger, then it is executed each time that object is being formatted for output. Format triggers extend the formatting capabilities of field items beyond the simple format masks. An example of a format trigger is shown in Figure 13.25.

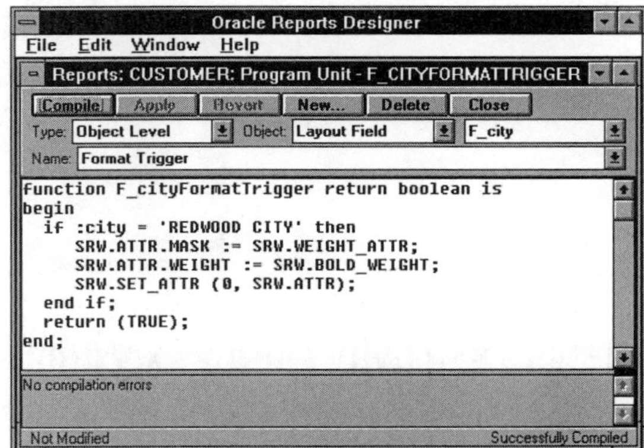

FIGURE 13.25.
The Program Unit Editor showing a Format Trigger.

Runtime

The Oracle Reports runtime environment includes many features to increase your productivity, including the following:

- List of values in the Parameter Form
- Client/Server activity monitoring
- Oracle Reports Server for background processing

Now we will look at each of these features.

The Parameter Form with Lists of Values

During the presentation of the Parameter Form at runtime, the parameter fields may contain lists of values to facilitate the selection of valid responses. The lists of values may be static or dynamic, and they may or may not restrict the available entries.

You will notice in Figure 13.26, that the Parameter Form contains a static list of values for the system parameters and a dynamic list of values for the user parameters.

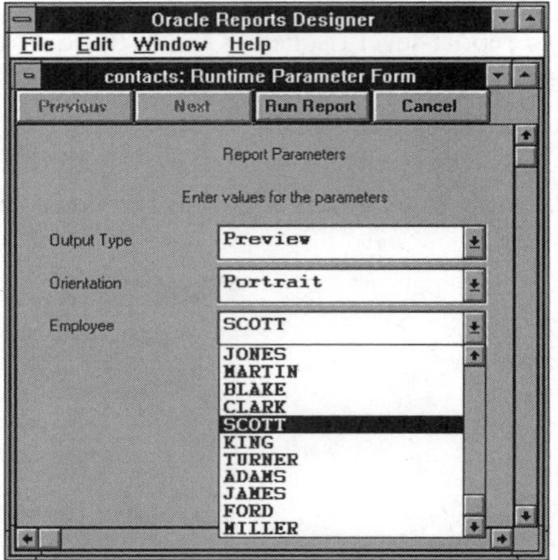

FIGURE 13.26.
The Parameter Form at runtime.

Monitoring C/S Activity During Execution

Oracle Reports enables you to monitor the activity of your report applications at runtime. The client and server activity is indicated visually by the use of simple automation in the Report Progress dialog box. The Report Progress dialog box is shown in Figure 13.27.

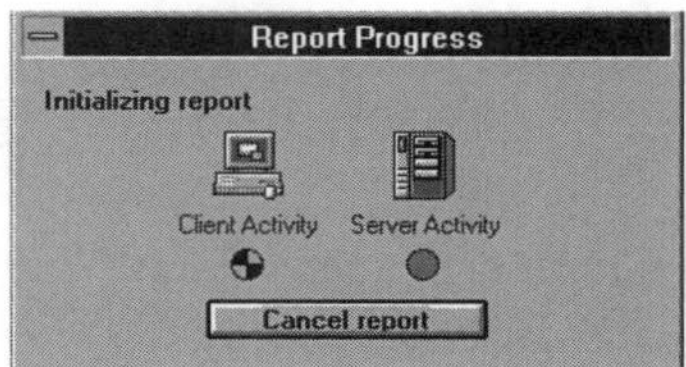

FIGURE 13.27.
The Progress dialog box showing Client/Server activity.

The initialization of the report, the execution of report triggers, and the formatting of the report pages are indicated by the message area at the top of the dialog box. To demonstrate the ability to interrupt the execution of a report while it is in process, we will now cancel a report during execution.

1. Run the current report.
2. When the Report Progress dialog box appears, click on the Cancel report button.
3. Click OK when you receive the warning from Oracle Reports that the report has been aborted upon user request.
4. Notice that the report has been interrupted and that you are returned to the Designer.

> **NOTE**
>
> This feature was not available in versions of Oracle Reports prior to 2.5. It is useful when a job is running too long or was started inadvertently.

Oracle Reports Server

Oracle Reports supports the ability to run reports in the background via Oracle Reports Server. If the `BACKGROUND` system parameter is set to YES, Oracle Reports will place the report in the server queue. Running a report in the background frees the client workstation to be used for other applications. In addition to the `BACKGROUND` system parameter, the `BATCH` system parameter may be set to YES to eliminate any screen output and user interaction.

> **NOTE**
>
> Run reports in the background in batch mode when they are to be printed and no preview is needed.

In Figure 13.28, a report is displayed in the Previewer that was run from the contact-management application menu. At the bottom of the screen, the other applications that are running are shown minimized.

Notice in Figure 13.28 that Oracle7, Microsoft Excel, Program Manager, Oracle Graphics Batch, Oracle Reports Server, and Oracle Forms are all running.

> **NOTE**
>
> Reports that are run from Oracle Forms or Oracle Graphics will automatically start Oracle Reports Server.

FIGURE 13.28.
Oracle Reports with minimized applications in the background at runtime.

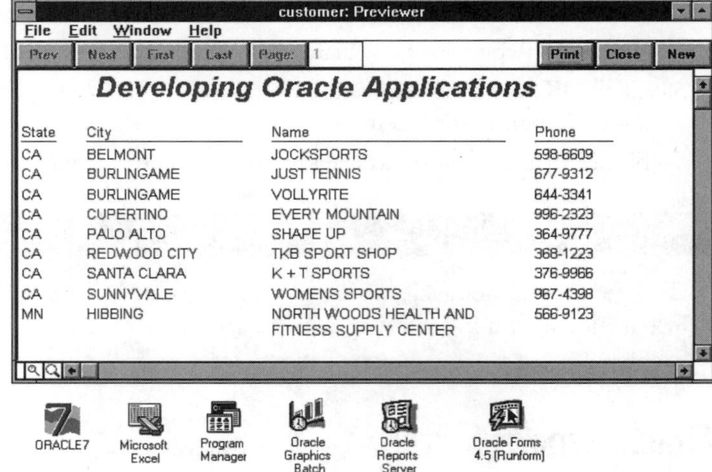

Debugging Oracle Reports

Oracle Reports supports the debugging of PL/SQL program units via the PL/SQL Interpreter and via the Debug Actions and Stack nodes in the Object Navigator, as shown in Figure 13.29.

FIGURE 13.29.
The PL/SQL Interpreter with a breakpoint set.

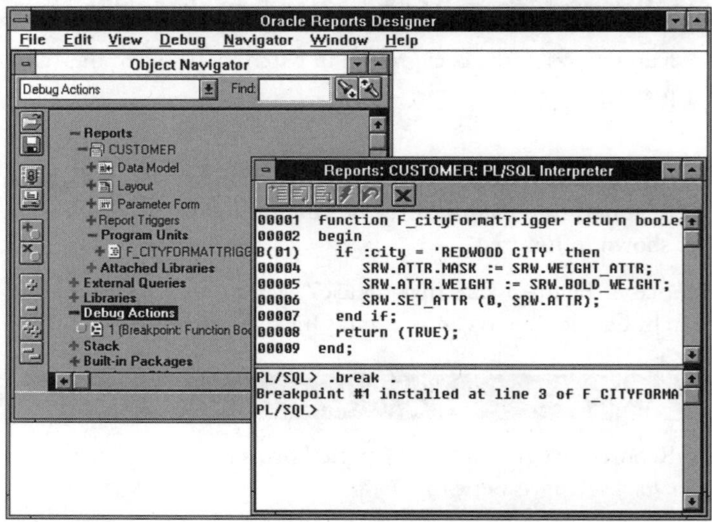

The PL/SQL Interpreter enables you to set breakpoints and break triggers to debug PL/SQL program units using the same methods as in Oracle Forms and Oracle Procedure Builder.

DDE Support

Oracle Reports supports the DDE (dynamic data exchange) messaging protocol, although the use of OLE2, which is a higher-level protocol, may be sufficient for most of your requirements. DDE messages are supported through the DDE built-in package procedures. For more information on DDE, refer to the *Oracle Procedure Builder Reference Manual.*

ODBC Support

Oracle Reports supports the ODBC (open database connectivity) protocol to enable access to data sources other than an Oracle database. For more information on ODBC, refer to the CDE2 Installation Guide.

Adding Reports to the Forms Menu

In Chapter 12, "Developing Oracle Forms Applications," we created an application menu to be used by the contact-management application. Now we will add the menu items for each of our reports.

1. Open Oracle Forms Designer and the CONTACT menu module menu.
2. Invoke the Menu Editor and maximize the window.
3. Select the Reports menu item, then select Customers.
4. Add the following items under the Customers menu:

   ```
   Contact Messages
   Contact Priorities
   Contact Totals
   Contacts by Employee
   Employees by Department
   Sales Salaries + Commissions
   ```

   The Menu Editor with the Reports menu displayed should now appear as shown in Figure 13.30.
5. Double-click the menu icon for CUSTOMERS under the Reports menu in the Object Navigator to invoke the PL/SQL Editor, then copy the following text:

   ```
   run_product (REPORTS, 'customer',
                ASYNCHRONOUS, RUNTIME,
                FILESYSTEM, NULL, NULL);
   ```

   The Object Navigator with the CUSTOMERS menu item selected and the PL/SQL Editor displayed are shown in Figure 13.31.

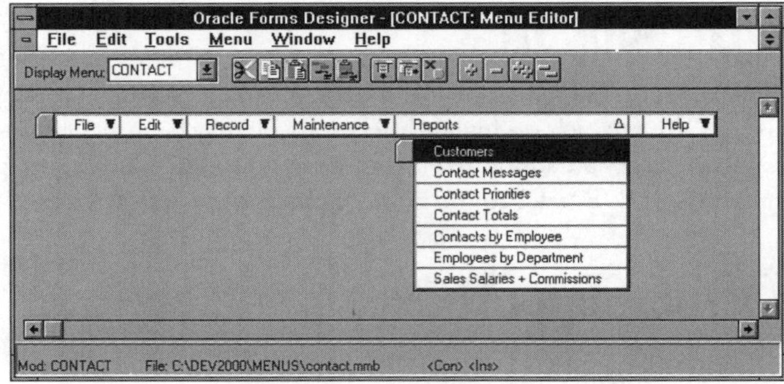

FIGURE 13.30.
The Menu Editor with the Reports menu.

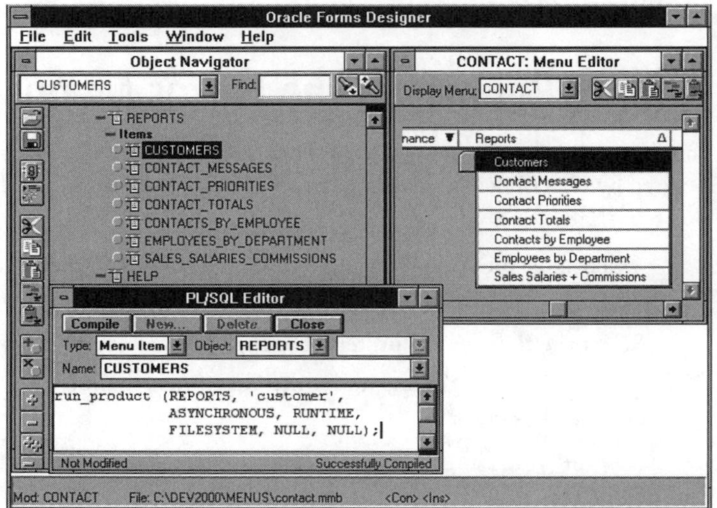

FIGURE 13.31.
The PL/SQL Editor with the CUSTOMERS PL/SQL.

6. Now double-click the new menu items icon under the Reports menu, paste the text that was copied, and change the report name as follows:

```
Menu Description                  Report Name
Contact Messages                  cont_msg
Contact Priorities                priority
Contact Totals                    econtots
Contacts by Employee              contacts
Employees by Department           deptemp
Sales Salaries + Commissions      sal_comm
```

7. Save and Generate the menu from the keyboard with Ctrl+S and Ctrl+T, respectively.
8. Close the menu module and open the CONTACT form.
9. Save and run the form to test the additional application menu items.

Summary

This chapter provided you with a variety of examples of report applications development including:

- Creating Oracle Reports templates
- Creating break, drill-down, and integrated application reports using templates and OLE2
- Creating format masks
- Using OLE2 to link to a MS Excel file
- Creating a parameter form to filter a query
- Adding buttons with PL/SQL to drill-down
- Adding a link to an image file
- Using a Long Raw database column for MS Word
- Embedding Oracle Graphics displays
- Creating a report trigger
- Updating the Oracle Forms application menu

If you worked through each section in the chapter, you should have completed the development of several different types of reports applications.

Now that you have developed report applications with Oracle Reports, we will create more displays and enhance our existing applications using Oracle Graphics.

14

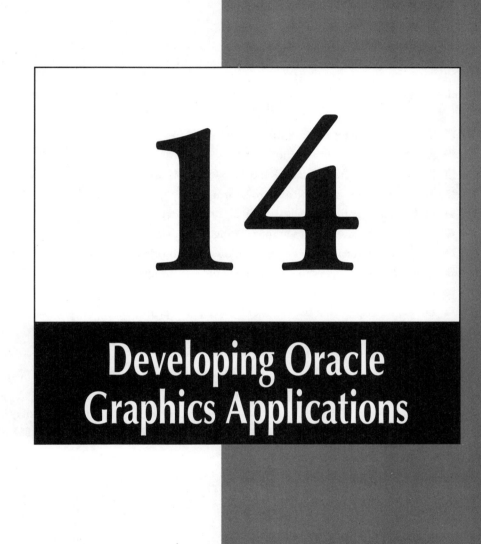

Developing Oracle Graphics Applications

Introduction

Now that we've developed several applications using Oracle Forms and Oracle Reports, we will extend the functionality of some of those applications even further by developing and incorporating Oracle Graphics displays. In addition, we will develop some stand-alone Oracle Graphics applications and add them to the Contact Management application menu. In reading and working through this chapter, you will do the following:

- Create a parameter-driven display
- Add graphical detail to a report
- Pass parameters from Oracle Reports to Oracle Graphics
- Add a parameter-driven display to a form
- Pass parameters from Oracle Forms to Oracle Graphics
- Create a drill-down chart without coding
- Create an open trigger to set the window size and title
- Create a format trigger to conditionally modify the chart
- Create a format mask for a chart item
- Develop a display that uses a timer to update the chart
- Import an image file
- Add a button trigger using PL/SQL
- Add Oracle Graphics displays to the application menu in Oracle Forms

Oracle Graphics enables you to develop your own graphical displays. These displays may be used in Oracle Forms, Oracle Reports, or any OLE2 container. The same display may be used in many different applications and can also be run as an independent application as shown in Figure 14.1.

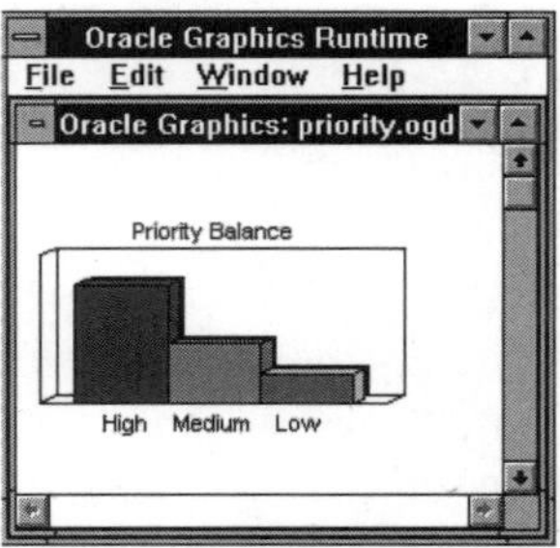

FIGURE 14.1.
An Oracle Graphics application.

You will recognize the display in Figure 14.1 as the one we created in Chapter 10, "Introducing Oracle Graphics." It was used in our Oracle Forms and Oracle Reports applications.

Graphics Templates

Oracle Graphics includes 56 templates for display frames and fields. Rather than beginning this chapter by creating our own standard templates as we did in Oracle Forms and Oracle Reports, we will simply use the templates provided to us.

> **NOTE**
>
> Oracle Graphics does support the creation of additional templates, as well as the editing of the existing templates.

Later in this chapter, we will change the default color scheme for a field template using the Chart Template Editor.

The Contact Priorities by Employee Display

We developed a report in the previous chapter that contained an Oracle Graphics display for reviewing the contact priorities. This was the same display developed in Chapter 10 and used in Chapter 12, "Developing Oracle Forms Applications."

Now we will create a display for the contact priorities detail by employee. This display will accept a parameter containing the employee number. We will then return to Oracle Reports Designer and Oracle Forms Designer to add this display to the priority report and the contact form, respectively. To create a display for the contact priorities by employee, follow these steps:

1. Open Oracle Graphics Designer.
2. Connect to the Oracle database as scott/tiger.
3. Open PRIORITY.OGD and save the display as PRIORITE.OGD.

Reference a Parameter in the SQL Statement

We will begin by modify the existing display by adding a `where` clause, and creating a parameter.

1. Double-click the PRIORITY query to invoke the Query Property dialog box. Append the following where clause to the SQL statement, then press Execute.

   ```
   where empno = :employee
   ```

Figure 14.2 shows the Query Property dialog box with the modification to the existing query.

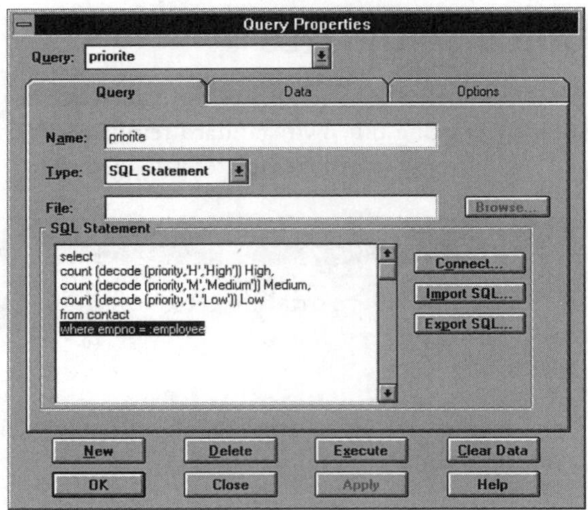

FIGURE 14.2.
The Query Property dialog box for Priorite.

Oracle Graphics responds with a warning dialog box that says the bind variable EMPLOYEE does not exist. Create it Now?

2. Click Yes, and the Parameters dialog box is invoked, initialized with the appropriate values. (See Figure 14.3.)

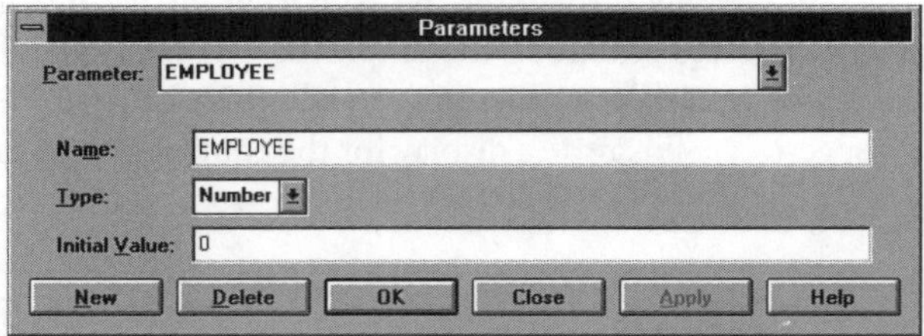

FIGURE 14.3.
The Parameters dialog box for EMPLOYEE.

3. Change the Initial Value from 0 to 7788, then click OK to close the Parameters dialog box. The value 7788 is the empno assigned to SCOTT in the DEMOBLD.SQL and DEMOBLD7.SQL scripts.
4. Press the Execute button in the Query Property dialog box to refresh the query data and the display in the layout with the priority details for SCOTT, then click OK to close the Query Property dialog box.
5. Save the display.

6. Generate the display by selecting Administration from the File menu, then Generate, then File System.
7. Save the generated display as PRIORITE.OGR, and close the display.

The generated display will be used by Oracle Reports and Oracle Forms at runtime.

Add the Detail Display to the Priority Report

Now we have a display that will accept a parameter. Next, we will return to Oracle Reports Designer to add the display to the repeating group of employees by following these steps:

1. Open Oracle Reports Designer.
2. Connect to the Oracle database as scott/tiger.
3. Open PRIORITY.RDF.
4. Select and maximize the Layout Editor, then select Body.
5. Select the group frame and repeating frame, then stretch them to the right near the margin.
6. Select the group frame and stretch it down another half inch.
7. Select the repeating frame and stretch it down another half inch as well.
8. Click on the Oracle Graphics tool on the tool palette and create an item on the right side of the repeating frame, then invoke the property sheet.
9. From the Oracle Graphics Display dialog box, change Name to D_Emp_Priorities, and change Display Name to \DEV2000\GRAPHICS\PRIORITE.OGD.

Passing Parameters from Oracle Reports

By passing a report column as a display parameter to Oracle Graphics, the display can dynamically represent the data in the report. To pass a report column as a display parameter to Oracle Graphics do the following:

1. From the Oracle Graphics Display dialog box, scroll down and select empno from the Report Column list, enter EMPLOYEE in the Display Parameter field, then press OK.

The Oracle Graphics Display property sheet contains the name of the display file as well as a list of all report columns that are available to be passed to Oracle Graphics as display parameters. (See Figure 14.4.)

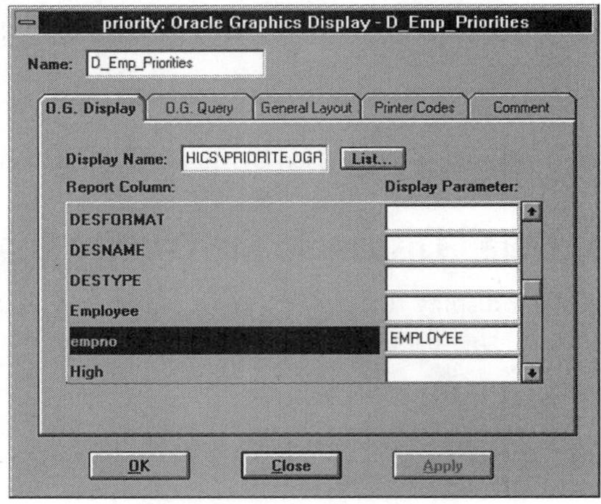

FIGURE 14.4.
The Oracle Graphics Display property sheet.

2. Set Line Color to No Line from the Color Palette.

The Oracle Graphics display should appear in the Layout Editor and Object Navigator. (See Figure 14.5.)

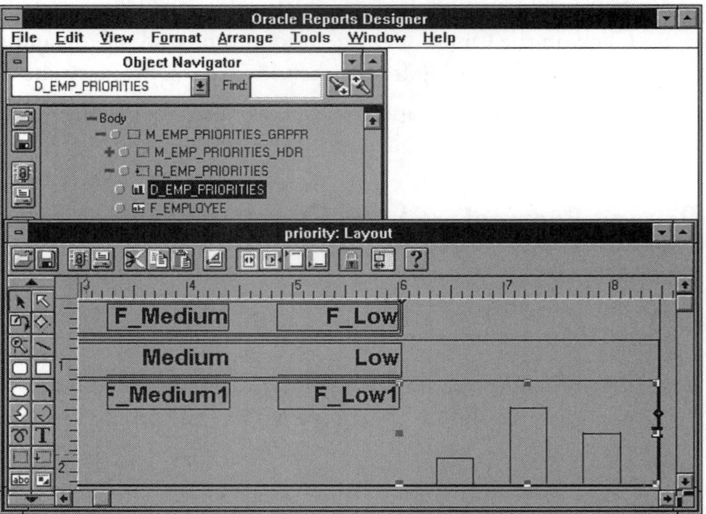

FIGURE 14.5.
An Oracle Graphics display in the layout.

3. Save and run, then close the report.

Add the Detail Display to the Contact Form

Now that we have added the display to our report, we will now return to Oracle Forms Designer to add the display to the tab control of the Contact Management application. To do this, we will copy the existing stacked canvas and chart item, then modify the WHEN-CUSTOM-ITEM-EVENT trigger.

1. Open Oracle Forms Designer.
2. Connect to the Oracle database as scott/tiger.
3. Open CONTACT.FMB.
4. Select the canvas-view ALL_EMPLOYEES in the Object Navigator, then copy and paste.
5. Change the name of the canvas-view to CUR_EMPLOYEE.
6. Select the PRIORITY_BALANCE chart item from the CONTROL block in the Object Navigator, then copy and paste.
7. Change the name of the chart item to PRIORITE_BALANCE.
8. Change the display canvas for PRIORITE_BALANCE to CUR_EMPLOYEE from the drop-down list in the Properties window.

The chart item should appear in the Properties window and Object Navigator. (See Figure 14.6.)

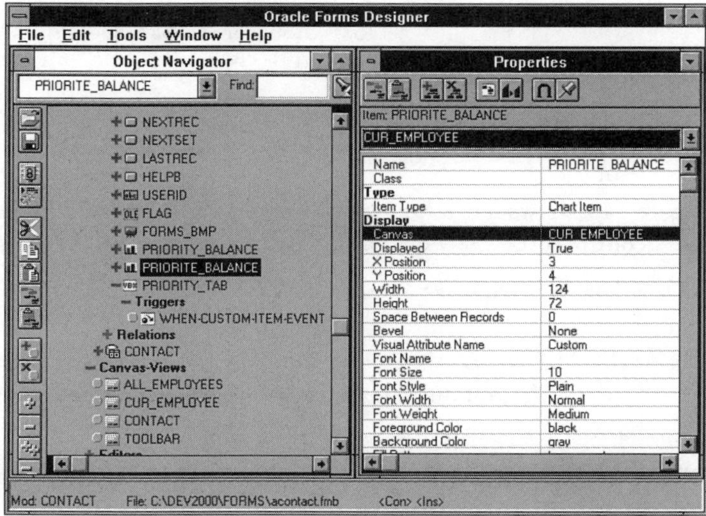

FIGURE 14.6.
The PRIORITE_BALANCE chart item.

9. Change the WHEN-CUSTOM-ITEM-EVENT trigger of the VBX control PRIORITY_TAB to the following.

```
DECLARE
   TabEvent  VARCHAR2(80);
   TabNumber NUMBER;
   Parm_Id   ParamList;
   cur_emp   varchar2(8) := to_char(:contact.empno);
```

```
BEGIN
   TabEvent := :system.custom_item_event;
   IF (UPPER(TabEvent) = 'CLICK') then
      TabNumber := VBX.Get_Property('PRIORITY_TAB',
                                    'CurrTab');
      IF TabNumber = 0 then
         show_view('ALL_EMPLOYEES');
         Run_Product(GRAPHICS,
                     'priority.ogr',
                     SYNCHRONOUS,
                     BATCH,
                     FILESYSTEM,
                     NULL,
                     'control.priority_balance');
      ELSIF TabNumber = 1 then
         show_view('CUR_EMPLOYEE');
         Parm_Id := Create_Parameter_List('emp');
         Add_Parameter(Parm_Id,
                       'EMPLOYEE',
                       TEXT_PARAMETER,
                       cur_emp);
         Run_Product(GRAPHICS,
                     'priorite.ogr',
                     SYNCHRONOUS,
                     BATCH,
                     FILESYSTEM,
                     Parm_Id,
                     'control.priorite_balance');
         Destroy_Parameter_List(Parm_Id);
      ELSE
         show_view('CONTACT');
      END IF;
   END IF;
END;
```

Figure 14.7 shows the WHEN-CUSTOM-ITEM-EVENT trigger for the PRIORITY_TAB VBX control successfully compiled.

10. Compile, then select (Form Level) from the object drop-down list in the PL/SQL Editor.
11. Select the WHEN-NEW-FORM-INSTANCE trigger from the name drop-down list in the PL/SQL Editor, then remove the following statement:

```
og.open('priority.ogr', 'control.priority_balance', FALSE);
```

NOTE

Notice that we originally used OG.OPEN in the WHEN-NEW-FORM-INSTANCE trigger to populate the chart item, and now we are using Run_Product in the WHEN-CUSTOM-ITEM-EVENT trigger. This change was made so that each time the tab control is selected, the chart item is updated with the current information.

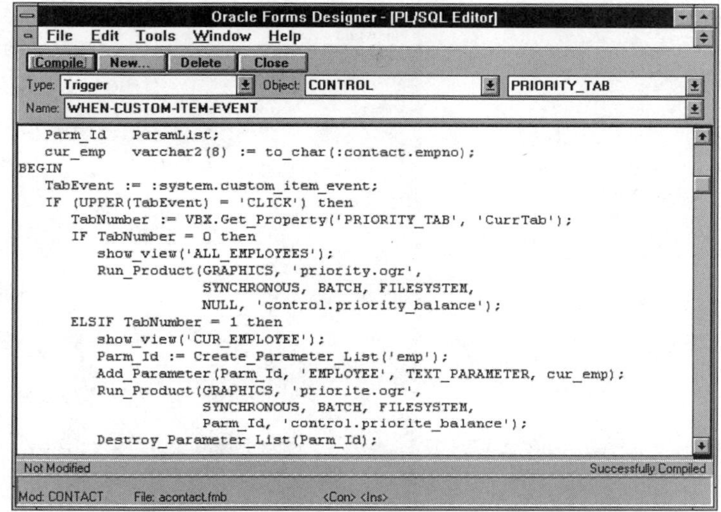
Oracle Forms Designer - [PL/SQL Editor]
File Edit Tools Window Help
Compile New... Delete Close
Type: Trigger
Object: CONTROL
PRIORITY_TAB
Name: WHEN-CUSTOM-ITEM-EVENT
Parm_Id ParamList;
cur_emp varchar2(8) := to_char(:contact.empno);
BEGIN
TabEvent := :system.custom_item_event;
IF (UPPER(TabEvent) = 'CLICK') then
TabNumber := VBX.Get_Property('PRIORITY_TAB', 'CurrTab');
IF TabNumber = 0 then
show_view('ALL_EMPLOYEES');
Run_Product(GRAPHICS, 'priority.ogr',
SYNCHRONOUS, BATCH, FILESYSTEM,
NULL, 'control.priority_balance');
ELSIF TabNumber = 1 then
show_view('CUR_EMPLOYEE');
Parm_Id := Create_Parameter_List('emp');
Add_Parameter(Parm_Id, 'EMPLOYEE', TEXT_PARAMETER, cur_emp);
Run_Product(GRAPHICS, 'priorite.ogr',
SYNCHRONOUS, BATCH, FILESYSTEM,
Parm_Id, 'control.priorite_balance');
Destroy_Parameter_List(Parm_Id);
Not Modified
Successfully Compiled
Mod: CONTACT
File: acontact.fmb
<Con> <Ins>

FIGURE 14.7.
The PL/SQL Editor for the VBX trigger.

12. Compile, and close the PL/SQL Editor.
13. Delete the Oracle Graphics attached library.

Passing Parameters from Oracle Forms

By passing a bind variable as a display parameter to Oracle Graphics, the display can dynamically represent the data in the form. The display parameter is passed by creating a parameter list and adding a parameter to that list. The parameter value is set in the declare section of the program unit.

> **NOTE**
>
> The parameter must be passed as a character string, or a record group. We declared a local variable as VARCHAR2 and used the `to_char` function to convert the numeric EMPNO in the assignment statement.

1. Save and run the form.
2. Execute a query, select the Current Employee tab, modify the priority, commit the change, select the Current Employee tab again, then close the form.

When the form is run and the Current Employee tab is selected, the stacked canvas appears and the chart item is populated with the current employee information. (See Figure 14.8.)

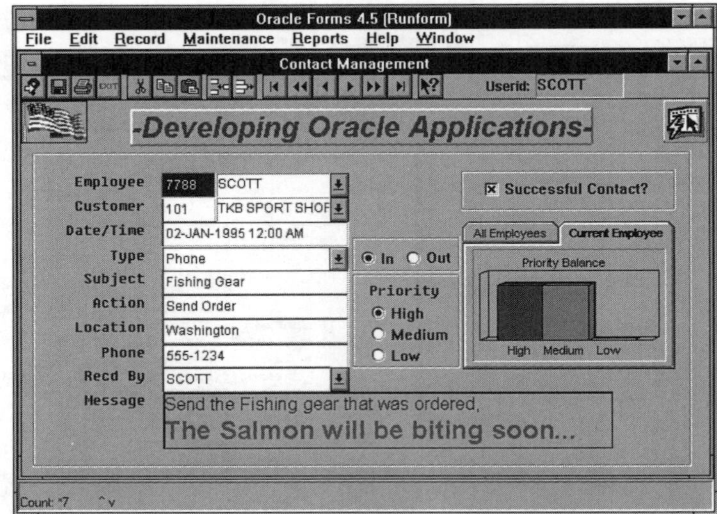

FIGURE 14.8.
The Current Employee display in Runform.

A Drill-Down Chart

Oracle Graphics enables you to create drill-down charts without any PL/SQL code. A drill-down chart represents a master/detail relationship. The first chart is the master, and a click on one of the chart objects populates the details of a second chart. Now we will create a drill-down chart by adding a second query, a parameter, and a table chart to the Employees By Department applications we created in Chapter 10. To create a drill-down chart, follow these steps:

1. Return to Oracle Graphics Designer.
2. Open EMP_DEPT.OGD.
3. Invoke the Query Properties dialog box for emp_dept.
4. Change the SQL statement to the following:
```
select d.deptno, d.dname Department, count(e.empno) Employees from dept d,
➥emp e where d.deptno = e.deptno group by d.deptno, d.dname
```
5. Press Execute and OK.
6. Select Create Chart from the Chart menu.
7. Create a new query named Employees with the following SQL statement:
```
select d.dname Department, e.ename Employee
from dept d, emp e
where d.deptno = :deptno
and d.deptno = e.deptno
```
8. Accept the `DEPTNO` parameter that was automatically created.
9. Set the chart name and title to Employees in the Chart tab of the Chart Properties dialog box.

10. Set the chart type to table, then select the Values tab.
11. Select Department and Employee from the Query Columns list, then press OK.
12. Select the Frame Properties dialog box for Employees, then select the Table Frame tab, uncheck the Show Horizontal Gridlines option, and press OK.

Next we will change the default color scheme for the field template of the pie chart. Then we will adjust the layout of the table in the Layout Editor, add some boilerplate, and create the drill-down specification from the pie chart.

1. Select Templates from the Tools menu to invoke the Chart Template Editor, then maximize the window.
2. Select template0 from the Template drop-down list, then click on the Field template radio button.
3. Click on the pie chart to select it, then select light gray from the Fill Color Palette. (See Figure 14.9.)

The default field template for the pie chart appears in the Chart Template Editor as shown in Figure 14.9.

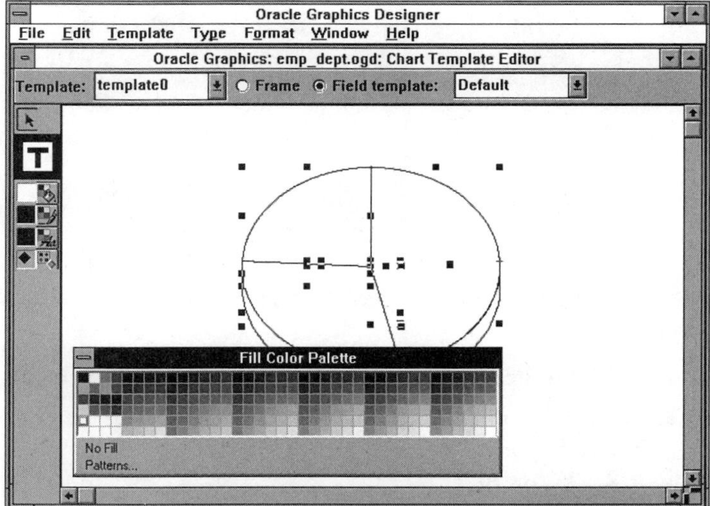

FIGURE 14.9.
The Chart Template Editor with a default field template and the Fill Color Palette.

The default layout of the table placed it under the pie chart, but we want it on the right side. We will also add some boilerplate text inside of an ellipse for a comment to the user.

1. Select and maximize the Layout Editor.
2. Select the Employee chart and move it from under the pie to the right of the pie.
3. Click on the Ellipse button on the toolbar and create a boilerplate graphics object between the two charts, near the top.

4. Set the Fill Color to light gray and the Line Color to blue.
5. Select 2pt. from the Format, Line menu.
6. Create a text item inside of the ellipse with the following text:

```
Click on a pie slice
to list the employees
```

7. Set the Fill Color to No Fill, the Line Color to No Line, and the Font to Arial, Regular, 8 pt.

The two charts should now appear in the Layout Editor. (See Figure 14.10.)

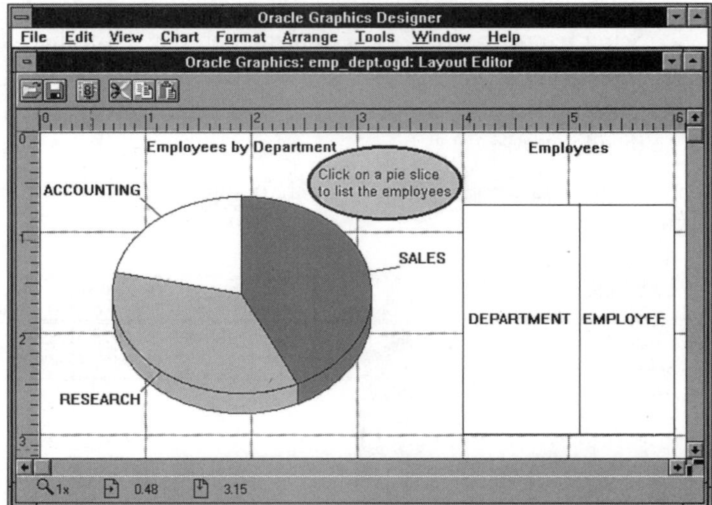

FIGURE 14.10.
The Layout Editor with two charts.

Now we can define the drill-down properties of the pie chart, including the parameter and query information.

1. Click on the pie chart in the Layout Editor, then click on a slice of the pie.
2. Right-click and select Properties from the pop-up menu to invoke the Object Properties dialog box.
3. Select the Drill-down tab, then select `DEPTNO` from Set Parameter and To Value Of. Set Execute Query to Employees, then press OK.
4. Save and run the display.

Oracle Graphics will simulate the runtime environment in the Designer by displaying the Oracle Graphics Debugger window. (See Figure 14.11.)

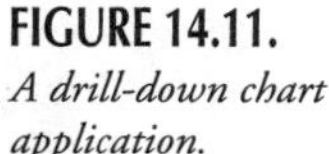

FIGURE 14.11.
A drill-down chart application.

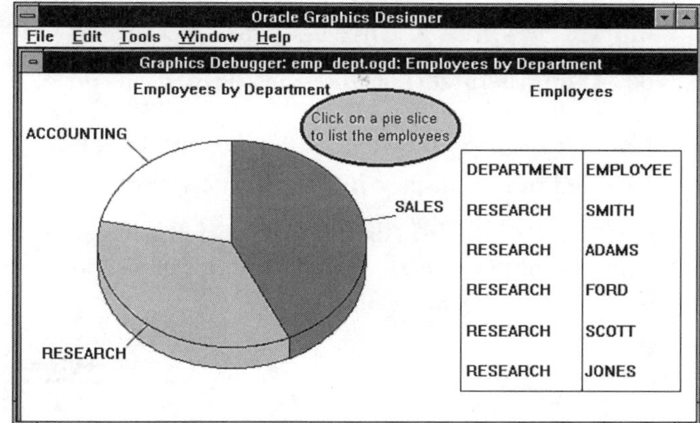

5. Click on one of the pie slices, and notice that the table to the right lists the names of the associated employees.

That's all you have to do to create a drill-down Oracle Graphics application. Next we will create a trigger to set the window size and title.

Triggers

Oracle Graphics provides five types of triggers that may be used in your chart applications. They are Open Display, Query, Format, Timer, and Close Display. In addition there are button procedures that are functionally similar to triggers. We will create an Open Display trigger to set the window size and title.

An Open Trigger

In the following trigger, we will be using two built-in data types, several built-in subprograms, and two built-in global variables provided by Oracle Graphics. To create the Open trigger follow these steps:

1. Invoke the Program Unit Editor for the Open trigger by double clicking on it in the Object Navigator, then entering the following text before the begin statement:

```
the_win OG_WINDOW;
win_pos OG_POINT;
win_wid NUMBER;
win_ht  NUMBER;
```

2. Enter the following text after the begin statement:

```
the_win := OG_GET_WINDOW('Main Layout');
win_pos.x := 0;
win_pos.y := 0;
```

```
OG_SET_POSITION(the_win, win_pos);
win_wid := 6.5*OG_APP.HSCREEN_RES;
win_ht := 3*OG_APP.VSCREEN_RES;
OG_SET_WINDOW_SIZE(the_win, win_wid, win_ht);
OG_SET_NAME(the_win, 'Employees by Department');
```

3. Compile the trigger, then close the Program Unit Editor.
4. Save and run the display. Then generate a runtime version of the display and close.

Notice the use of the built-in data types, global variables, and subprograms. By setting the size of the window, both charts are visible when the application is run. Figure 14.12 shows an example of an Open trigger.

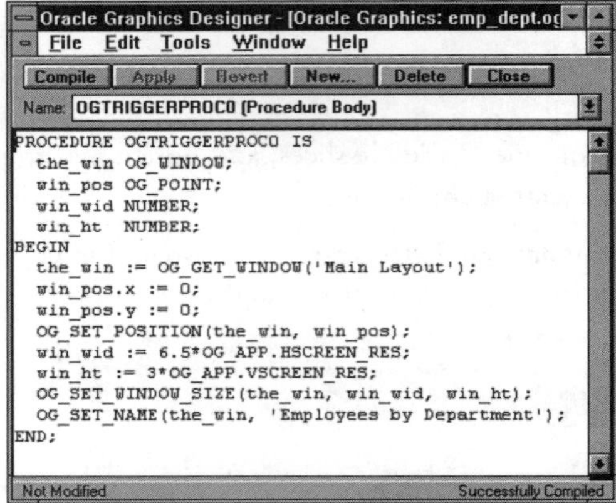

FIGURE 14.12.
The Program Unit Editor showing an Open Trigger.

A Format Trigger

Oracle Graphics also supports format triggers. Format triggers, like some of the other triggers are actually program units of type procedure body, and are created via the Program Unit Editor. If an object contains a format trigger, then it is executed each time that object is being formatted for output. Format triggers extend the formatting capabilities of chart items to include conditional logic.

1. Open SAL_COMM.OGD.
2. Select and maximize the Layout Editor.
3. Select COMM_BARS in the chart and invoke the Object Properties sheet.
4. Click on New to the right of the Format Trigger drop-down list to create a new format trigger.
5. Enter the following text before the begin statement:

```
commission number;
```

6. Enter the following text after the begin statement:

```
commission := OG_GET_NUMCELL(query,
                             OG_NEWDATA,
                             'comm');
if commission > 1000 then
   OG_SET_BFCOLOR (elem, 'green');
end if;
```

7. Compile and close the PL/SQL Editor. Then click OK to dismiss the Object Properties dialog box.
8. Save and run the display. Then generate a runtime version of the display and close.

The result of the format trigger is shown at runtime in Figure 14.13, where the commission bar is green (dark gray in the figure) for the one that is over $1,000.

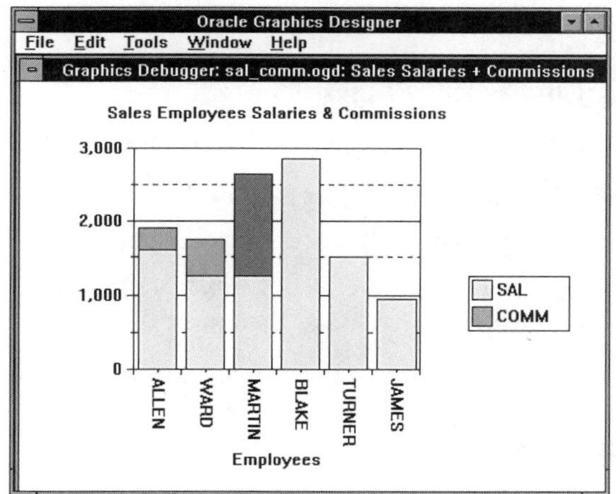

FIGURE 14.13.
The commission highlighted via a format trigger.

A Timer Trigger

Timer triggers can be associated with a query so that the query is re-executed each time the timer expires. Optionally, a timer trigger may execute any PL/SQL procedure. In the previous chapter, we captured the report name, user, and run date in the report audit table. Now we will create a display to monitor the report auditing information using a timer trigger.

1. Create a new display and save it as RPTAUDIT.OGD.
2. Select Create Chart from the Chart menu.
3. Create a new query named Date_Time with the following SQL statement:

```
select sysdate
from dual
```

4. Set the chart name to Date_Time, and set the title to Date Time in the Chart tab of the Chart Properties dialog box.

5. Set the chart type to table, then select the Values tab.
6. Select SYSDATE from the Query Columns list, then press OK.
7. Select the chart in the Layout Editor, move it to the upper-left corner, and make it about 2-1/2-inches wide and 1/2-inch high.
8. Invoke the Frame Properties dialog box from the pop-up menu, uncheck the Show Plot Frame check box, then select the Table Frame tab.
9. Remove the checks from the three Show check boxes.
10. Invoke the Query Properties dialog box and select the Options tab.
11. Check the Execute on Timer check box, then click on the New button to the right of the drop-down list to invoke the Timer Triggers dialog box.
12. Change the Name to 15seconds and the Interval to 0 min. and 15 sec., then press OK.

A Date Time Format Mask

Now we will format the current date and time in the display using a format mask.

1. Select the SYSDATE chart item in the Layout Editor.
2. Select Alignment and Center from the Format menu.
3. Invoke the Date Format dialog box from the pop-up menu, select the DD-MON-YY HH24:MI:SS format mask, then press OK.

Figure 14.14 shows the Date Format dialog box with the format mask selected from the list. The list provides easy access to all of the format masks that have been defined. Additional format masks may be added here as well.

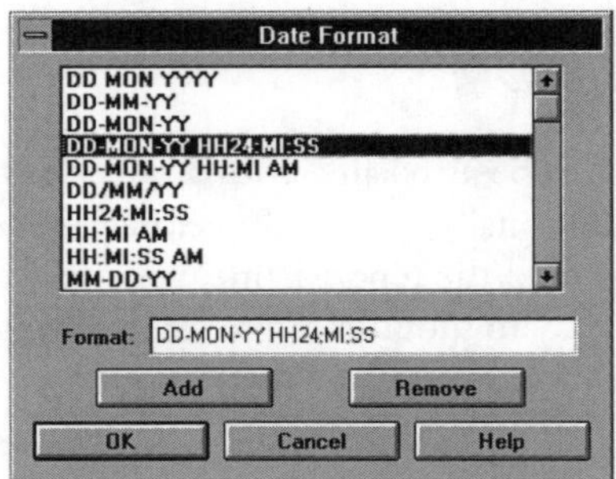

FIGURE 14.14.
The Date Format dialog box.

Next we will add another table chart to the display. This one will list the details of the report auditing table.

A Table Chart for Report Auditing

This table chart will be based on the same timer trigger that we just created. Therefore, the query will re-execute at each interval defined by the timer.

1. Select Create Chart from the Chart menu.
2. Create a new query named Report_Auditing with the following SQL statement:
```
select *
from rpt_audit
```
3. Set the chart name to Report_Auditing and set the title to Report Auditing in the Chart tab of the Chart Properties dialog box.
4. Set the chart type to table, then select the Values tab.
5. Select all three of the items in the Query Column list, then press OK.
6. Select the Report Auditing chart in the Layout Editor and move it down under the Date Time chart.
7. Invoke the Query Properties dialog box and select the Options tab.
8. Check the Execute On Timer check box, select 15seconds from the drop-down list, then press OK.
9. Save and run the display.

Figure 14.15 shows the Report Auditing display with both charts updated via the timer trigger.

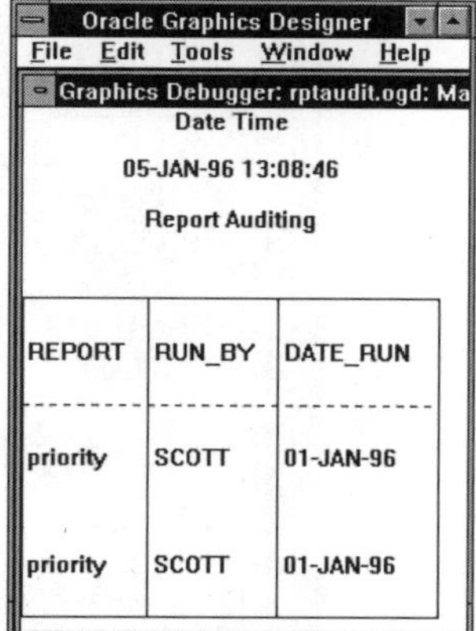

FIGURE 14.15.
The Report Auditing display.

Importing an Image

Oracle Graphics can display images from a variety of formats including BMP, PCX, TIFF, and others. An image item may be imported from a file or from the database. Here we will import a bitmap image file of a button into the display. The bitmap was created using MS Paintbrush and saved to the local file system.

1. Select the Layout Editor.
2. Select Import Image from the Edit menu.
3. Set the name to \DEV2000\BITMAPS\CLOSE.BMP, set the type to BMP, and press OK.

Figure 14.16 shows the Import Image dialog box referencing a bitmap image of a close button from the file system.

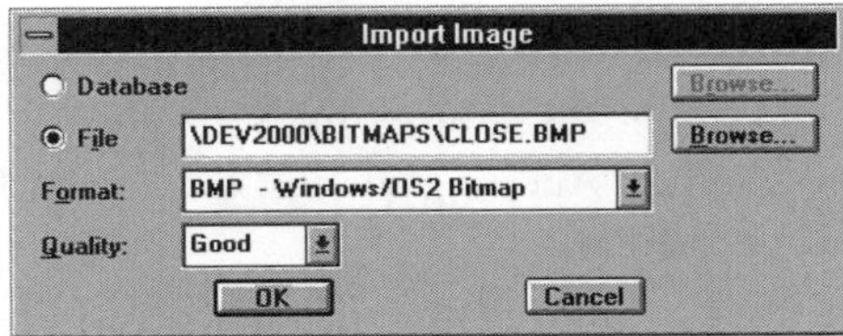

FIGURE 14.16.
The Import Image dialog box referencing a bitmap.

4. Center the bitmap between the charts.
5. Select Send To Back from the Arrange menu.

The imported image item should appear in the Layout Editor and Object Navigator as shown in Figure 14.17.

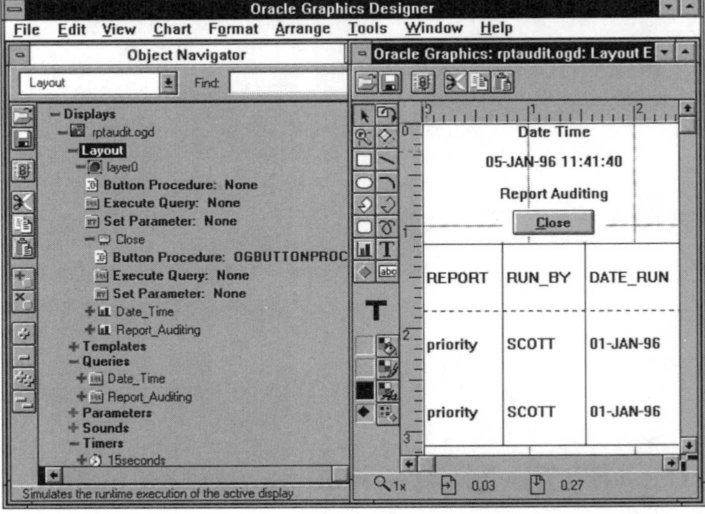

FIGURE 14.17.
An image item that will display a bitmap.

TIP

Oracle Graphics does not include a button layout object as in Oracle Forms and Oracle Reports. But it does support button procedures and image items. Therefore I've included some bitmap images of buttons with this book. We've just used one here, and now we'll add the button procedure to it.

A Button Procedure

Buttons can be used to execute PL/SQL or to activate a multimedia object. We are using the button and PL/SQL to drill-down to a detail report. Button labels may be text or iconic. Our button will contain a text string to indicate the function of the button to the user. At runtime the button appears in the Previewer but does not get printed. Create a procedure for the button image item as follows:

1. Select the image item in the Object Navigator and expand the objects under it.
2. Invoke the Program Unit Editor for the button procedure by double-clicking in it, then enter the following text before the begin statement:
   ```
   cur_display og_display;
   ```
3. Enter the following text after the begin statement:
   ```
   cur_display := og_get_display ('rptaudit.ogd',
                                  OG_FILESYSTEM);
   og_close_display(cur_display);
   ```
4. Compile, then close the PL/SQL Editor.
5. Save and run the display. Close the display using the button.

   Notice the Button Procedure in the Object Navigator as it appears in Figure 14.17 (shown previously). At runtime, the Report Auditing display appears as in Figure 14.18 with the button added.
6. Generate a runtime version of the display, then close.

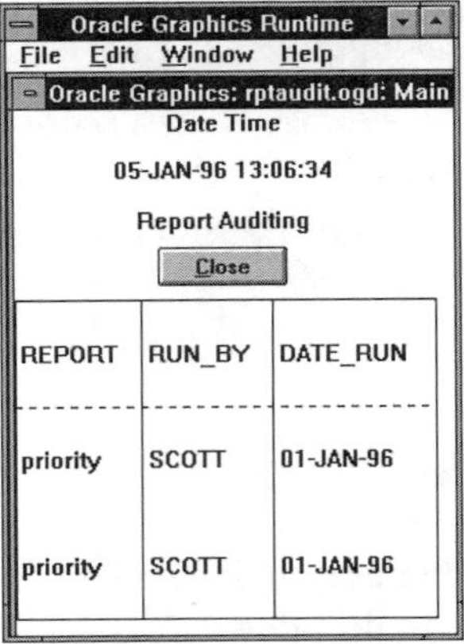

FIGURE 14.18.
A display with an image of a button.

Runtime

The Oracle Graphics runtime environment enables us to develop and execute stand-alone Graphics applications. In this chapter the Contact Priorities, Employees by Department, Report Auditing, and Sales Salaries + Commissions applications can all be run as stand-alone applications. Later we will add each of these applications to our Contact Management application menu.

Oracle Graphics Batch

Oracle Graphics enables you to run reports in the background via Oracle Graphics Batch. Running a display in the background frees the client workstation to be used for other applications.

> **NOTE**
>
> You should run displays in the background in batch mode when they are to be printed or saved to a file and no review is needed.

> **NOTE**
>
> Displays that are run from Oracle Forms or Oracle Reports will automatically start Oracle Graphics Batch.

DDE Support

Oracle Graphics supports the DDE (dynamic data exchange) messaging protocol, although the use of OLE2, which is a higher-level protocol, may be sufficient for most of your requirements. DDE messages are supported through the DDE built-in package procedures. For more information on DDE, refer to the Oracle Procedure Builder Reference Manual.

ODBC Support

Oracle Graphics supports the ODBC (open database connectivity) protocol to enable access to data sources other than an Oracle database. For more information on ODBC, refer to the CDE2 Installation Guide.

Adding Displays to the Forms Menu

In Chapter 13, "Developing Oracle Reports Applications," we added reports to the application menu. Now we will add the menu items for each of our displays.

1. Open Oracle Forms Designer and the CONTACT menu module.
2. Invoke the Menu Editor and maximize the window.
3. Select the Reports menu item.
4. Create a Graphics menu item to the right.
5. Add the following items under the Graphics menu:
```
Contact Priorities
Employees by Department
Report Auditing
Sales Salaries + Commissions
```
6. Double-click the menu icon for CUSTOMERS under the Reports menu in the Object Navigator to invoke the PL/SQL Editor, then copy the following text:
```
run_product (REPORTS, 'customer',
             ASYNCHRONOUS, RUNTIME,
             FILESYSTEM, NULL, NULL);
```
7. Double-click the new menu items icon under the Graphics menu, paste the text that was copied, change REPORTS to GRAPHICS, and change the display name as follows:

Menu Description	*Display Name*
Contact Priorities	PRIORITY.OGR
Employees by Department	EMP_DEPT.OGR
Report Auditing	RPTAUDIT.OGR
Sales Salaries + Commissions	SAL_COMM.OGR

Figure 14.19 shows the Object Navigator, Menu Editor, and PL/SQL Editor with the Graphics menu displayed and the PL/SQL to run an Oracle Graphics display compiled.

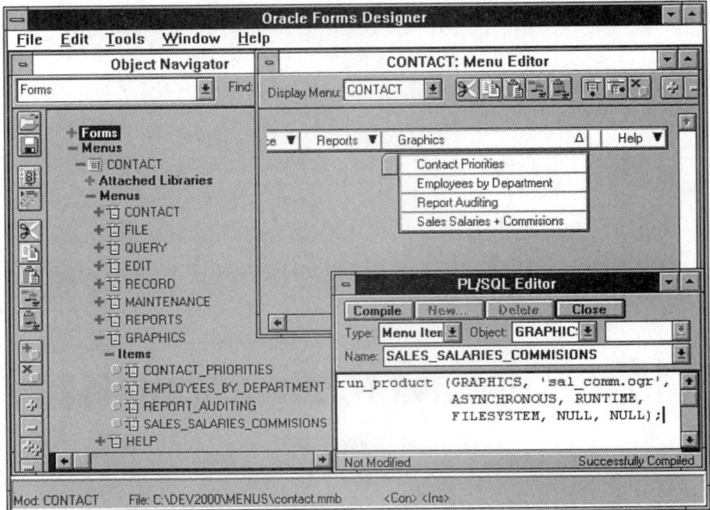

FIGURE 14.19.
The Menu Editor with the Graphics menu.

8. Save and Generate the menu from the keyboard with Ctrl+S and Ctrl+T, respectively.
9. Close the menu module and open the CONTACT form.
10. Save and run the form to test the Graphics application menu items. Then close the form and Oracle Forms Designer.

The Contact Management form appears with the Graphics menu displayed. (See Figure 14.20.)

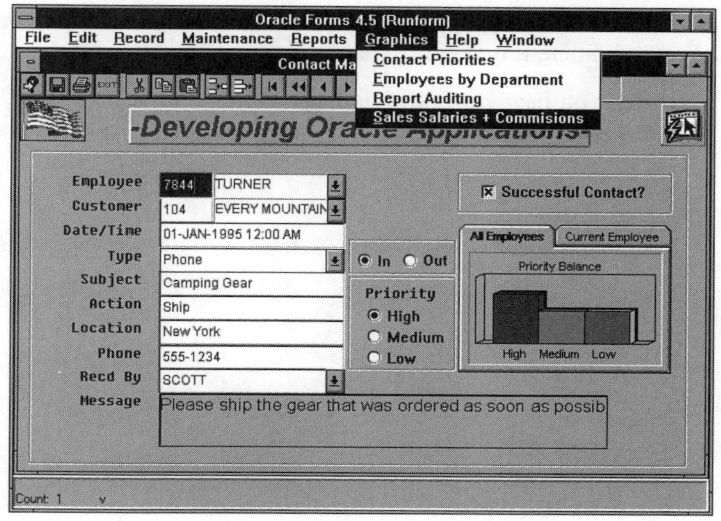

FIGURE 14.20.
The Contact Management form with the Graphics menu displayed.

Summary

This chapter provided you with a variety of examples of Oracle Graphics applications development, including:

- Creating a parameter-driven display
- Adding Oracle Graphics displays in reports
- Passing parameters from a report to a display
- Adding Oracle Graphics displays in forms
- Passing parameters from a form to a display
- Creating a drill-down chart
- Creating an open trigger
- Creating a format trigger
- Creating a format mask
- Creating a timer trigger
- Importing an image file
- Adding buttons with PL/SQL
- Updating the Oracle Forms application menu

If you worked through each section in the chapter, you will have completed the development of several different types of chart applications.

Now that you have developed applications with Oracle Forms, Oracle Reports, and Oracle Graphics, next we will learn how to integrate and deploy them in a Windows environment.

15

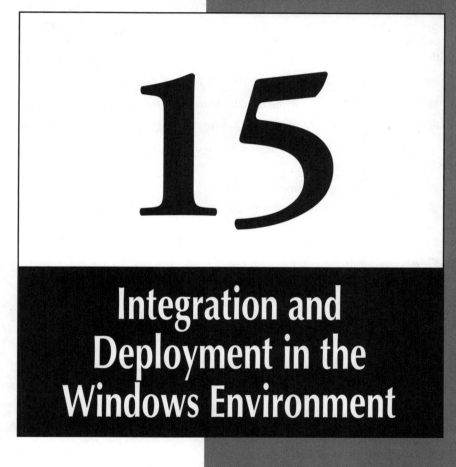

Integration and Deployment in the Windows Environment

Introduction

Now that you have developed applications with Oracle Forms, Oracle Reports, Oracle Graphics, Oracle Procedure Builder, and the Oracle7 database, we will integrate all of these applications through a single point of entry for the user. Then we will review the issues associated with deploying our application system in a Windows environment. Then we will finish this book with a series of exercises that leverage the power of OLE2 in your applications.

In reading and working through this chapter, you will do the following:

- Create the Contact Management Information System menu
- Create the Contact Management Information System entry point using Oracle Forms

Then we will review deployment and configuration issues in the Windows environment, including:

- Setting up the application environment
- Creating multiple environments for development, testing, demonstration, training, and production
- Referencing a database for each environment
- Application installation
- GUI styles and standards
- Memory, disk space, and performance
- OLE2 options
- Advanced topic for application enhancements

And we will conclude by exploring the power of OLE2, including:

- Editing OLE2 objects
- Inserting OLE2 objects into the Oracle database
- Linking to sound files
- Running video clips

The Contact Management Information System

Now that we have developed many applications using Oracle Developer/2000, we will create an easy way for our users to access all of these applications. We will use Oracle Forms to create a single entry point containing a welcome screen and an application system menu.

The completed welcome screen appears in Figure 15.1, with the menu, tool buttons, a welcome for the current user, a picture from the ClipArt Gallery, and iconic launch buttons to some of the forms applications.

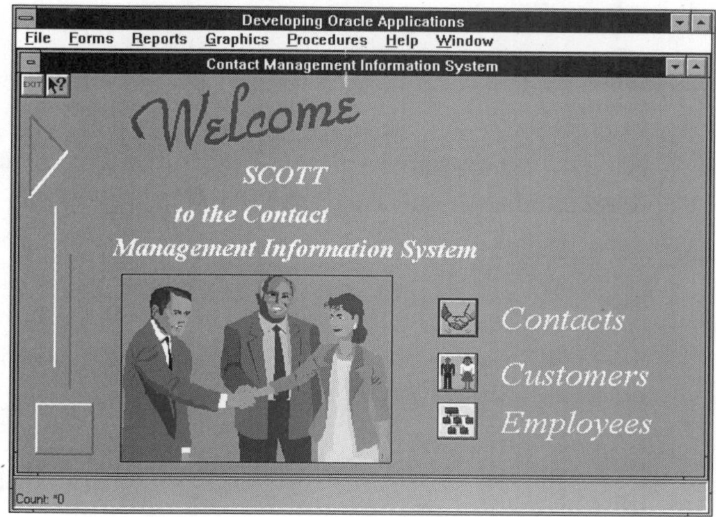

FIGURE 15.1.
The Oracle Forms welcome screen.

The Contact Management Information System Menu

We will begin by creating the Contact Management Information System menu. This menu will enable us to access each of the applications that we have developed in this book.

In Chapter 14, "Developing Oracle Graphics Applications," we updated the CONTACT menu that is used by the contact-management application. Because this menu contains many of the applications already, we will use this menu as the starting point for developing the CMIS menu. To create the Contact Management Information System menu, follow these steps:

1. Open Oracle Forms Designer and connect to the Oracle database as scott/tiger.
2. Open the CONTACT menu module. Change the menu module name to CMIS, and save the menu as CMIS.MMB.
3. Invoke the Menu Editor and maximize the window.
4. Select and expand the File menu. Select and delete the New, Query, Save, and the save separator menu items—leaving only Print, a print separator, and the Exit menu items.
5. Select the Edit, Record, and Maintenance menu items, then delete.
6. Select the Object Navigator. Then select the old Query, Edit, Record, and Maintenance menus, then delete.
7. Select the File menu item in the Menu Editor, and add a Forms menu item to the right.

8. Select the Forms menu item and add the following menu items under it:

```
Contacts
Customers
Employees
Maintenance
```

9. Select the Maintenance menu item and add a States menu item to the right.
10. Select the Graphics menu item and add a Procedures menu item to the right.
11. Select the Procedures menu item and add the following items under it:

```
Salary Update
Save Salary Changes
Undo Salary Changes
```

12. Select the Salary Update menu item and add the following Hint:

```
Execute the Annual Salary Update Procedure...
```

13. Select the Save Salary Changes menu item, and add the following Hint:

```
Commit changes to the database...
```

14. Select the Undo Salary Changes menu item, and add the following Hint:

```
Rollback changes...
```

The Menu Editor with the CMIS menu displayed should now appear as shown in Figure 15.2.

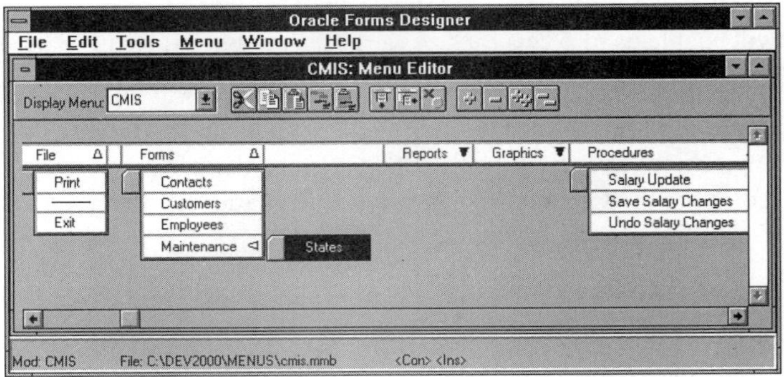

FIGURE 15.2.
The Menu Editor with the CMIS menu.

Now that we have the structure of the CMIS menu defined, we will add the PL/SQL for each new menu item.

1. Select the Contacts menu item from the Forms menu in the Object Navigator, and invoke the PL/SQL Editor. Then enter the following:

```
call_form('contact', no_hide, do_replace);
```

2. Select the Customers menu item, invoke the PL/SQL Editor, and enter the following:

```
call_form('customer', no_hide, do_replace);
```

3. Select the Employees menu item, invoke the PL/SQL Editor, and enter the following:

```
call_form('dept_emp', no_hide, do_replace);
set_window_property (FORMS_MDI_WINDOW, TITLE, 'Developing Oracle
➥Applications');
```

4. Select the States menu item, invoke the PL/SQL Editor, and enter the following:

```
call_form('state', no_hide, do_replace);
set_window_property (FORMS_MDI_WINDOW, TITLE, 'Developing Oracle
➥Applications');
```

CAUTION

We must reset the FORMS_MDI_WINDOW title after the call_form for Employees and for States. This is because the DEPT_EMP form sets the title to Maintain Increases, and the STATE form sets the title to Maintain Tables in the WHEN-NEW-FORM-INSTANCE triggers respectively. When we return from those forms, we want the title to be Developing Oracle Applications.

5. Select the Salary Update menu item, invoke the PL/SQL Editor, and enter the following code, which executes the procedure, disables itself, enables the other two procedure menu items, and sends an acknowledgment message:

```
annual_sal_update;
set_menu_item_property ('procedures_menu.salary_update',
ENABLED, PROPERTY_OFF);
set_menu_item_property ('procedures_menu.save_salary_changes',
ENABLED, PROPERTY_ON);
set_menu_item_property ('procedures_menu.undo_salary_changes',
ENABLED, PROPERTY_ON);
message('Salary Updates have been Processed.');
```

6. Select the Save Salary Changes menu item, invoke the PL/SQL Editor, and enter the following code, which commit the changes to the database, enables Salary Update, disables itself and Undo Salary Changes, then sends an acknowledgment message:

```
commit;
set_menu_item_property ('procedures_menu.salary_update',
ENABLED, PROPERTY_ON);
set_menu_item_property ('procedures_menu.save_salary_changes',
ENABLED, PROPERTY_OFF);
set_menu_item_property ('procedures_menu.undo_salary_changes',
ENABLED, PROPERTY_OFF);
message('Salary Updates have been Saved.');
```

7. Select the Undo Salary Changes menu item, invoke the PL/SQL Editor, and enter the following code, which rolls back the changes to the database, enables Salary Update, disables itself and Save Salary Changes, then sends an acknowledgment message:

```
rollback;
set_menu_item_property ('procedures.salary_update',
ENABLED, PROPERTY_ON);
set_menu_item_property ('procedures.save_salary_changes',
ENABLED, PROPERTY_OFF);
set_menu_item_property ('procedures.undo_salary_changes',
ENABLED, PROPERTY_OFF);
message('Salary Updates have been Undone.');
```

To finish the CMIS menu, we will add startup code to the CMIS menu module that will initially disable the Save Salary Changes and Undo Salary Changes menu items.

1. Invoke the PL/SQL Editor for the startup code in the menu module Properties window, and enter the following:

```
set_menu_item_property ('procedures_menu.save_salary_changes', ENABLED,
➥PROPERTY_OFF);
set_menu_item_property ('procedures_menu.undo_salary_changes', ENABLED,
➥PROPERTY_OFF);
```

2. Save, generate, and close the menu module.

The CMIS menu module and the PL/SQL Editor with the menu startup code displayed should appear as shown in Figure 15.3.

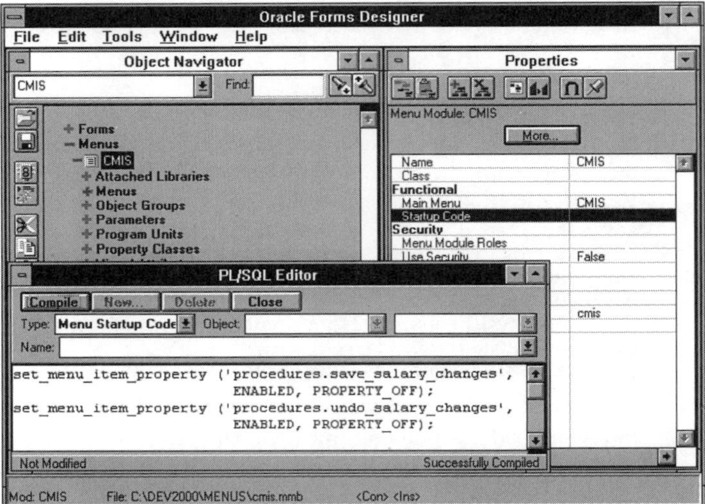

FIGURE 15.3.
The PL/SQL Editor with the menu startup code.

The Oracle Forms Welcome Screen

By creating a single point of entry for the application system, we give the user a simple launching pad for any work that needs to be done. So now we will create that launch point as a welcome screen using Oracle Forms.

The welcome screen will be created by setting a few properties and copying objects from our contact application. Then we will add a drawing, text, graphics boilerplate, launch buttons, an OLE2 container, and some color.

1. Select the default form module. Change the name to CMIS, and save as CMIS.FMB.
2. Invoke the Properties window for the form module.
3. Change the menu module from DEFAULT to CMIS.
4. Change the window title to Contact Management Information System.

Copy Objects

Now we will open another form that contains objects that we will copy into this form.

1. Open the form module CONTACT.
2. Drag and drop in the Object Navigator to copy the WHEN-NEW-FORM-INSTANCE trigger. Select Copy when prompted for either Copy or Reference, and select OK in the Copy Object Options dialog box.
3. Invoke the Program Unit Editor and remove the read_image_file and go_block statements.
4. Create a canvas, and set the name to CMIS.
5. Create a new non-base table block. Set the name and canvas to CMIS.
6. Drag and drop in the Object Navigator to copy the Exit button. Then, in the Copy Object Options dialog box, select the Items tab and change Copy canvas-view to Replace with <NULL>.

The Items tab of the Copy Object Options dialog box appears as shown in Figure 15.4.

FIGURE 15.4.
The Items tab of the Copy Object Options dialog box.

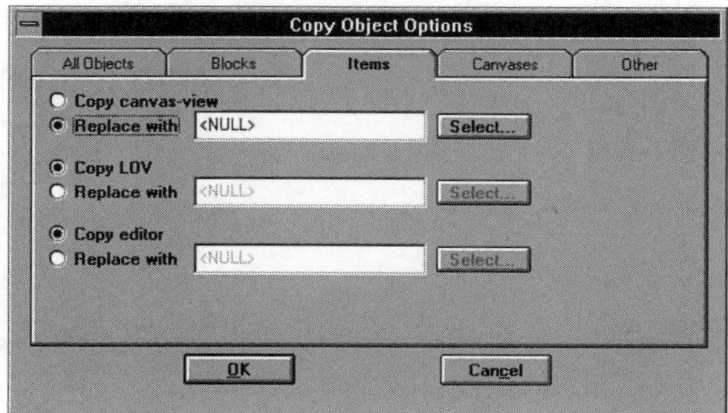

7. Set X Position to 0.
8. Remove all of the PL/SQL from the WHEN-BUTTON-PRESSED trigger except the do_key('exit_form') statement.
9. Copy the Help button. Select Copy. In the Copy Object Options dialog box, select the Items tab, and change Copy canvas-view to Replace with <NULL>.
10. Set the X position to 18.
11. Copy the USERID display item. Select Copy. In the Copy Object Options dialog box, select the Items tab, and change Copy canvas-view to Replace with <NULL>.
12. Set the x position to 142 and the y Position to 59.
13. Set the width to 69 and the height to 24.

14. Set Bevel to None.
15. Set Foreground Color to White and Background Color to r50g75b75.
16. Set the font to Times New Roman, Bold Italic, 18.
17. Set Alignment to Right.
18. Select the two buttons and the display item. Then set the canvas to CMIS.
19. Close the form module CONTACT.

Import a Drawing in Oracle Format

Next we will import a welcome drawing that is in Oracle format on the file system. Then we will add the rest of the text and graphics boilerplate.

1. Select and maximize the Layout Editor.
2. Select Drawing and Import from the Edit menu.
3. Enter \DEV2000\FORMS\WELCOME.ODF as the filename in the Import dialog box, and press OK.

Figure 15.5 shows the Import dialog box with the welcome drawing identified.

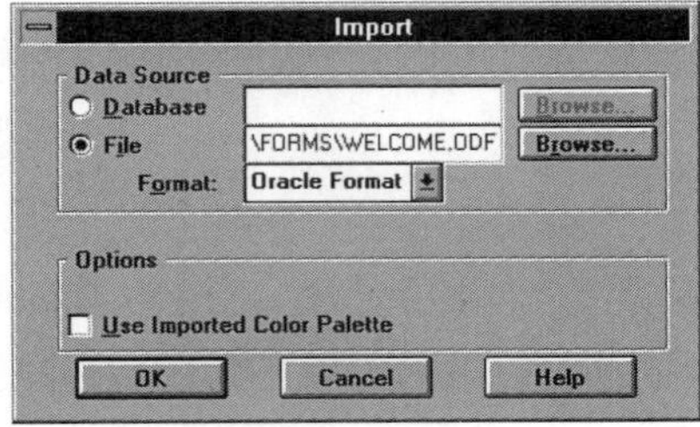

FIGURE 15.5.
The Import dialog box with the welcome drawing.

Text and Graphics Boilerplate

Now we will add the boilerplate text and graphics.

1. Create two text items under the USERID display item with the following text:
```
to the Contact
Management Information System
```
2. Set the font for these text items to Times New Roman, Bold Italic, 18.
3. Create three text items on the lower-right side with the following text:
```
Contacts
Customers
Employees
```
4. Set the font for these text items to Times New Roman, Italic, 24.

5. Create the three gray lines on the left side of the layout that make up two sides of the triangle and one of the bars. (See Figure 15.1, shown previously.)
6. Set the line color to gray.
7. Set the line size to 2 pt.
8. Create the two white lines on the left side of the layout that make up one side of the triangle and one of the bars as shown in Figure 15.1.
9. Set the line color to white.
10. Draw a rectangle on the left side of the layout as shown in Figure 15.1.
11. Set the line color to black.
12. Set the bevel to Raised.

Launch Buttons

Next we will create the buttons to launch some of the Oracle Forms applications.

1. Select the EXIT button. Then copy and paste.
2. Change the name to CONTACTS.
3. Change the X position to 286 and the Y position to 156.
4. Change the width and height to 28.
5. Change the icon name to contact.
6. Change the WHEN-BUTTON-PRESSED trigger to the following:
   ```
   call_form('contact', no_hide, do_replace);
   ```
7. Select the CONTACTS button. Then copy and paste.
8. Change the name to CUSTOMERS.
9. Change the Y position to 195.
10. Change the icon name to customer.
11. Change the WHEN-BUTTON-PRESSED trigger to the following.
    ```
    call_form('customer', no_hide, do_replace);
    ```
12. Select the CONTACTS button. Then copy and paste.
13. Change the name to EMPLOYEES.
14. Change the Y position to 230.
15. Change the icon name to employee.
16. Change the WHEN-BUTTON-PRESSED trigger to the following:
    ```
    call_form('dept_emp', no_hide, do_replace);
    set_window_property (FORMS_MDI_WINDOW, TITLE, 'Developing Oracle
    ➥Applications');
    ```

ClipArt

Now we will add an OLE2 container to display a picture from the MS ClipArt Gallery.

1. Create an OLE2 Object in the layout, under the Management Information System boilerplate text.
2. Change the item name to OLE_CLIPART.
3. Set the X position to 70 and the y Position to 140.
4. Set the width to 185 and the height to 135.
5. Set Bevel to None.
6. Set Base Table Item to False.
7. Set OLE In-place Activation to True.
8. Set OLE Resize Style to Scale.
9. From the Layout Editor, select the OLE2 item, then right-click to invoke the pop-up menu.
10. Select Insert Object from the pop-up menu to invoke the Insert Object dialog box.
11. Select Microsoft ClipArt Gallery from the Insert Object dialog box, then select the picture Three People Shaking Hands from the People category.

Color the Canvas

The final thing we want to do is add some color the welcome screen. We set the background color of some of the objects earlier, and now we will set the entire canvas to match.

1. Select the canvas, and set Background Color to r50g75b75.

   The welcome screen and each of the objects it contains should now appear in the Layout Editor and Object Navigator as shown in Figure 15.6.
2. Save, generate, and run the form. Then close the form module.

Now that we have completed the CMIS application, we will move on to review deployment, setting up the environment, and other Windows topics.

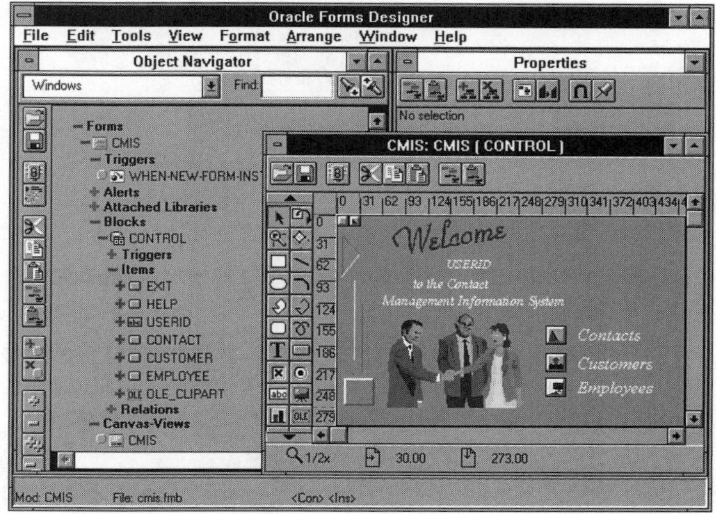

FIGURE 15.6.
The welcome screen in Oracle Forms Designer.

Application Deployment

Once you have developed applications using Oracle Developer/2000, these applications must be deployed to the end user. The successful deployment of your applications is a process that is dependent on many factors. These factors will be reviewed in the subsequent sections. They include setting up the environment, testing, installation, GUI standards, and performance.

At a minimum, each user must have a workstation running Windows with access to the Oracle runtime environment, an ORACLE.INI file in their \WINDOWS directory, and an entry point to launch the applications from.

When you run the Oracle install program ORAINST.EXE, it creates an \ORAWIN\BIN directory that contains the executable and library files, as well as the ORACLE.INI file. Each product that is installed creates it own directory that contains message files and various resource files, as well as subdirectories for samples and demonstrations. The product installations will update the ORACLE.INI as appropriate.

You will need to create and maintain your own application directory structure for your application executables as well as changes to the ORACLE.INI file. The application executables become part of the Oracle runtime environment for the end user.

The ORACLE.INI file is shown in Figure 15.7 with some of the settings highlighted.

Notice in Figure 15.7 that some of the entries in the ORACLE.INI file refer to the \DEV2000 directories from this book, like C:\DEV2000\ICONS, C:\DEV2000\GRAPHICS, C:\DEV2000\FORMS, and C:\DEV2000\REPORTS.

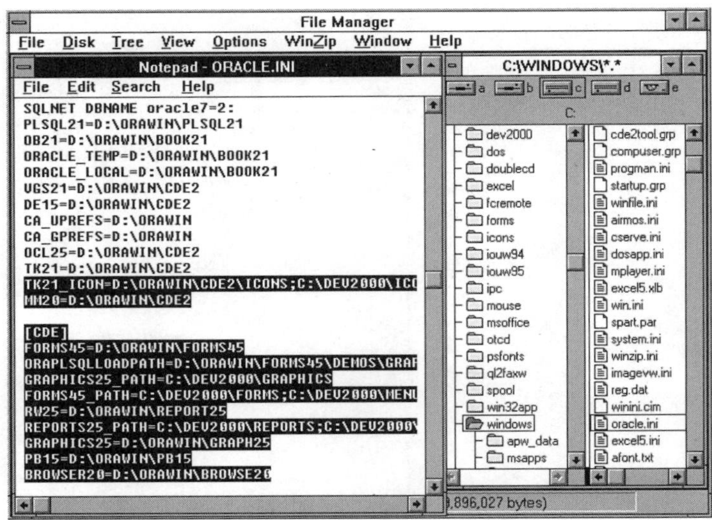

FIGURE 15.7.
File Manager showing the ORACLE.INI file.

Forms, menus, icons, libraries, reports, and graphics files are located by the Oracle tools by searching the current working directory or the paths in the ORACLE.INI file. You should append the additional directory paths to the existing ones in the ORACLE.INI file. This can be done using Notepad.

The following are examples of path setting for the ORACLE.INI file:

```
TK21_ICON=D:\ORAWIN\CDE2\ICONS;D:\ORAWIN\FORMS45\DEMOS\ICONS;D:\ORAWIN\GRAPH25\D
➥EMOS\FORMS;C:\DEV2000\ICONS

GRAPHICS25_PATH=D:\ORAWIN\FORMS45\DEMOS\GRAPHICS;D:\ORAWIN\GRAPH25\DEMOS\FORMS;D
➥:\ORAWIN\FORMS45\DEMOS\DYNCHART;C:\DEV2000\GRAPHICS

FORMS45_PATH=D:\ORAWIN\FORMS45\PLSQLLIB;D:\ORAWIN\GRAPH25\DEMOS\FORMS;C:\DEV2000
➥\FORMS;C:\DEV2000\MENUS;C:\DEV2000\LIBS;C:\DEV2000\BITMAPS;C:\DEV2000\GRAPHICS

REPORTS25_PATH=D:\ORAWIN\REPORT25\DEMO;D:\ORAWIN\REPORT25\DEMO\REQFILES;D:\ORAWIN
➥\REPORT25\DEMO\BITMAP;C:\DEV2000\REPORTS;C:\DEV2000\GRAPHICS
```

CAUTION

The search paths are a contiguous string of characters and sometimes hard to read. Also, each path is separated with a semicolon.

Setting up the Application Environment

Whether your applications are going to be running on a network or as stand-alone applications, setting up and maintaining the application environment will be one of the most important things you do.

One of the key ingredients to success in this area is to create standard and consistent directory structures. Create a directory for the project and subdirectories for each of the different types of objects you must manage. For example, you might create a CMIS directory for this project. Then create subdirectories as shown in Figure 15.8.

FIGURE 15.8.
File Manager with the CMIS directories.

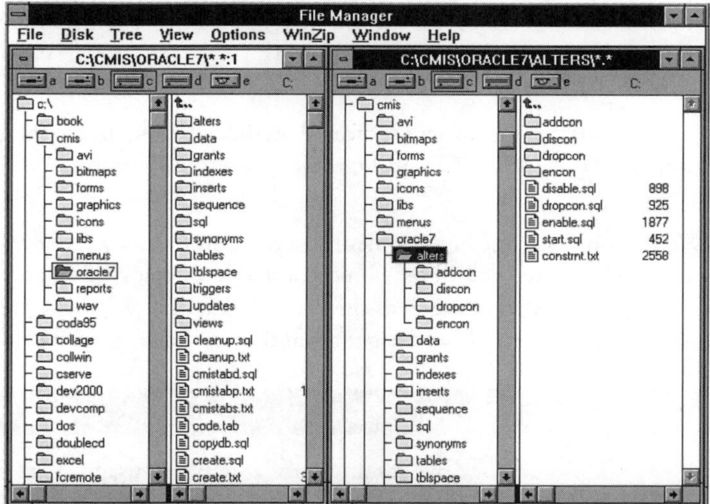

TIP

Associate each ASCII file type with Notepad in File Manager, so that you can easily open them by double-clicking.

Notice in Figure 15.8, that we have subdirectories for each of our application and database object types. Once we have the directory structure in place, we need to consider the management of all of these objects. In the next several sections that's what we will review.

Multiple Environments

An application system generally goes through various phases from development to production. To support this process, we will create separate environments for development, testing, demonstration, training, and production.

We will create separate environments by duplicating our standard directory structure. It is important to note that we are duplicating the directory structure, not creating different ones. Our directory structure is generic and supports each phase of the project.

If you are doing a small project on a stand-alone system, you may not need five phases. But at a minimum, you should create a development and a production environment. If you have a PC with two disk drives, the structure can be duplicated by dragging and dropping the project directory in File Manager from the C: drive to the D: drive. Use one for development and the other for production. If you only have one disk drive, create a DEV and a PRD directory. Then create the project directories under them.

For larger projects where you have a network and the multiple phases are needed, you should create shared directories for the different application environments. Create the shared directories with meaningful names such as \\CMIS\DEV, \\CMIS\TST, \\CMIS\DEM, \\CMIS\TNG, and \\CMIS\PRD.

Once the shared directories are created on the network, link to them just as we did on the stand-alone system with the C: and D: drives. Again, duplicate the structure on each shared directory.

We will only use one environment at a time, unless we are performing or reviewing an installation. Therefore, we will only link to a shared directory if we are using that environment. For our examples, we will use P: as the drive designator. When we are doing installations, we will use O: as the source drive designator and P: as the target drive designator.

CAUTION

Do not use the O: drive for any normal network usage. That way it will always be available for installations, without conflict.

By using this method, the ORACLE.INI file and anything else that needs to reference directory paths will only have to reference the P: drive and the standard directory structure for our project.

Now that we have created a standard directory structure, let's simplify the access to any application environment. We accomplish this by creating batch files that will set the shared directory drive designations for each environment or installation scenario we have. Then when we execute one of the files, we have instant access to the associated environment(s). The command to execute the file can be referenced from an icon on our desktop, as shown in Figure 15.9.

Notice in Figure 15.9 that the Oracle Environment program group contains icons for DEV, TST, DEM, TNG, and PRD. These icons execute the commands to set our P: drive to the appropriate shared directory on the network. Also notice the icons for DEV2TST, TST2DEM, TST2TNG, TNG2DEM, TST2PRD, and PRD2DEM. These icons execute the commands to set our O: and P: drives to the appropriate shared directories for installations.

FIGURE 15.9.
Program Manager with program groups.

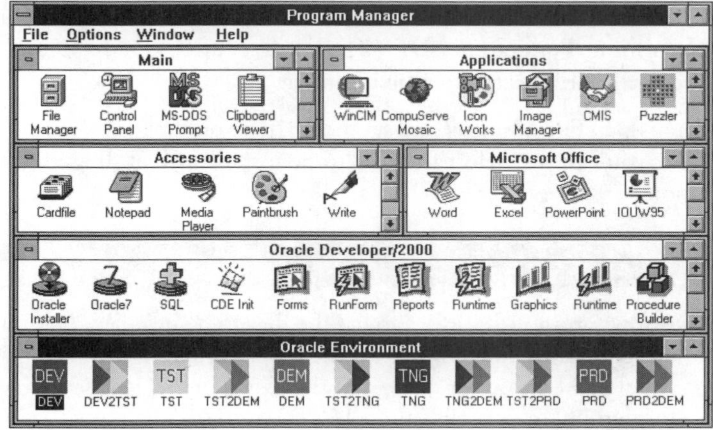

A Database for Each Environment

Now that we have multiple environments, let's associate a different default database with each one. The WIN.INI file in the \WINDOWS directory will contain a reference to the ORACLE.INI file as follows:

```
[Oracle]
ORA_CONFIG=C:\WINDOWS\ORACLE.INI
```

Copy the ORACLE.INI file to the project directories of each environment. Then change the path for the ORACLE.INI file to P:\CMIS in everyone's WIN.INI file. Having done that, we can specify the LOCAL database in each ORACLE.INI file for its environment.

This method enables us to use different databases and not have to specify which one we are connecting to, because we are always connecting to the LOCAL database, as defined in the ORACLE.INI file.

CAUTION

This process may at first seem confusing, because we are always using the P: drive yet we have different ORACLE.INI files for each environment. If you do not understand this at first, take some time to understand it, because it is an important concept.

Application Installation

Now that we've organized our project files and created support for multiple environments, let's make installing our applications as simple as possible.

If you have created the installation icons, just click on the installation scenario that you are performing. For example, DEV2TST will set up the O: drive as the development environment and the P: drive as the test environment.

Then open File Manager and set the O: drive on the left side and the P: drive on the right side. Now you can just select the files to be installed, then drag and drop to complete the installation.

TIP

Always create ASCII files to list the files to be installed, and save them in the project directories. Include in the text the requester name and request date. The installer should add his or her name and the install date. Use the following numeric convention for naming the install list: *YYMMDDSQ*.TXT, where *YY* is the year, *MM* is the month, *DD* is the day, and *SQ* is a sequential number that will accommodate 100 installations on the same day. With this method you can sort by name in File Manager, and the most recent request will be on the bottom. Also, if you change the file by adding the installer name and date, then you can sort by date, and the most recent installations will be at the top.

Windows Topics

Because our applications are being developed and implemented in a Windows environment, there are several topics that we need to consider. In the next several sections we will review GUI standards, performance considerations, and the use of OLE2.

GUI Styles and Standards

The early establishment and documentation of graphical user interface (GUI) standards and their associated style components will go a long way to improving the quality, consistency, and timeliness of your development projects.

In addition to documenting the GUI styles and standards, it is equally important to enforce them. As was stated in Chapter 1, "The Project Foundation," leadership and support from management is essential.

CAUTION

Do not allow the establishment of the GUI styles and standards to become a free-for-all in which every programmer on the project "becomes an artist." A lot of time can be wasted dabbing at the color palettes and moving GUI widgets all over the screens.

TIP

Create a separate enforcing body to establish the standards and monitor compliance.

TIP

Using standard templates for Oracle Forms and Oracle Reports can address a large part of this issue.

To establish the standards, many decisions will need to be made. For example, do you want to remove the default block label and border contained in the application shown in Figure 15.10?

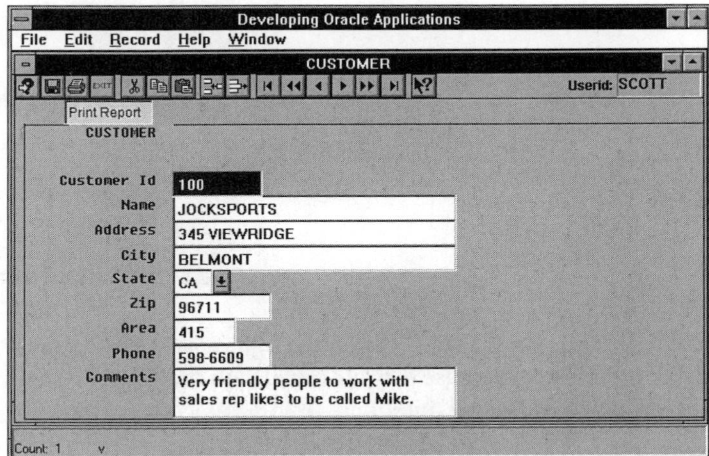

FIGURE 15.10.
The Customer application.

I think removing the default block label and border would be a good idea, but that means editing the layout each time a block is defaulted. The application in Figure 15.10, raises the following other questions as well:

- Do you want a standard size MDI window?
- Do you want a custom menu?
- What do you want in the window title?
- Do you want a standard toolbar?
- Do you want to display the current user?
- Do you want bubble help?
- Do you want field highlighting?

- Do you want iconic LOV buttons?
- What font should be used for labels and fields?

Each of these questions should be answered, and guidelines should be available for the developers. It is useful to review some different types of applications while defining and reviewing your standards.

The multi-record block applications raise additional questions. For instance, which side should the scroll bar be on? I would suggest that the scroll bar should be on the right side, as shown in Figure 15.11.

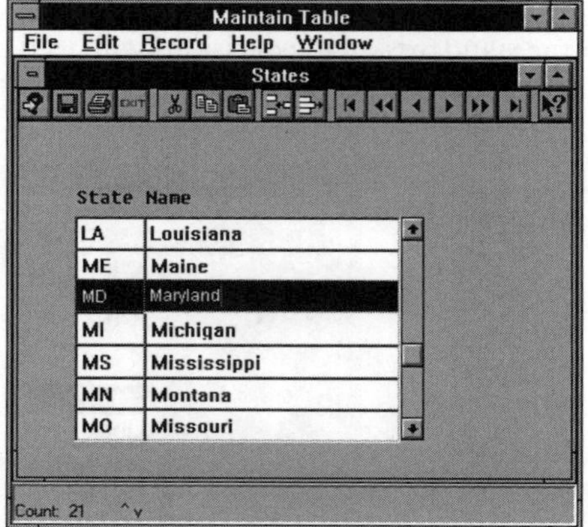

FIGURE 15.11.
The Maintain States application.

But again, placing the scroll bar on the right means editing the layout each time a multi-row block is defaulted, because they are initially on the left. The application in Figure 15.11 raises the following additional questions:

- Do you want a standard form for code tables?
- How many rows should be displayed?
- Do you want row highlighting?
- Do you want to auto-query?

Each of these questions needs to be answered as well. Keep in mind that not everyone will agree with every choice, and the choices still must be made. The templates created in this book serve to suggest some style standards. Here are some other style points to consider, along with my suggestions:

- Do you want a standard video resolution?

Yes, if possible. Using 800×600 is often an acceptable compromise. It is difficult to run and support applications in a different resolution than they were designed in. The applications in this book were all done at 640×480, as directed.

- What about color?

Avoid using color as much as possible. Windows applications adapt to the color scheme defined in the Control Panel.

- What font(s) should be used?

I like Arial; but be consistent, and keep it basic.

- What about labels, case, borders, and alignment?

Again, be consistent. Right-align labels, use uppercase for acronyms and mixed case for all others, use 3-D borders for grouping objects, and align objects to create sight lines.

Memory, Disk Space, and Performance

Let me begin this section by saying that when it comes to memory and its impact on performance, a lot is good, and more is better. Having said that, I should add that everything in this book—including the OLE2 applications, multimedia, and running an Oracle database—was done with fairly modest hardware, and a simple configuration. There was a fair amount of memory and disk swapping, but it all worked.

All of the applications, and exercises in this book were completed using a 486/50 with 12MB of RAM, a single 420MB hard disk, and a permanent swap file of 35,000KB.

The development of this book was completed using a 486/66 with 16MB of RAM, two 345MB hard disks, and a permanent swap file of 35,000KB. Since I had two hard disks, I put the swap file on one and the database on the other.

> **TIP**
>
> I would recommend more RAM and a faster processor than the configurations I just described. A Pentium with 32MB of RAM and another 1 or 2MB of video RAM should do nicely for a development machine. Also, it will help performance if you have access to an Oracle database on a server, leveraging the power of the two CPUs with their own memory and disk drives.

On both of the systems, HIMEM.SYS and EMM386.EXE were loaded in the CONFIG.SYS file, and SMARTDRV.EXE was loaded in the AUTOEXEC.BAT file. I was running Microsoft Windows 3.1, Personal Oracle7, Developer/2000, and Microsoft Office.

The icons were created using a Visual Basic application called ICONWORKS that is shipped with Visual Basic as one of the demonstration applications. The bitmaps where created using Paintbrush, and the SQL script files were created via Notepad.

TIP

Oracle Developer/2000 includes a handy utility called CDEINIT.EXE. If you run this program before running your Oracle applications, many of the common DLLs will be loaded up-front, providing better overall performance.

At times I also used a client/server configuration where the server was the 486/50 workstation running OracleWare. OracleWare is Oracle7 bundled with Novell 3.12. The client was a 486/33 with 12MB of RAM and a single 210MB hard disk. The server was used as a database, application, and file server. The Oracle tools, applications, and various support files resided on the server. Windows, an ORACLE.INI, and a program group were on the client to run the Oracle tools and applications.

TIP

Here is a simple and easy way to get better performance from your Windows environment if you're not using a swap file or your haven't defragmented your disk drive(s) lately. Launch Windows and remove your temporary or permanent swap file, if you have one. Exit Windows, free as much disk space as you can, and run DEFRAG. Return to Windows, and create a permanent swap file using the recommended settings.

OLE2 Options

There are various choices associated with using OLE2 in your applications: linking versus embedding; in-place or external activation; iconic, thumbnail, or content representation; clipping, or scaling the image of the object; and restricting the object class or leaving it open.

Linking Versus Embedding

You've seen several examples in this book of both object linking and embedding. In the upcoming sections, we cover even more. Embedded objects may be activated in-place, as we have done. Linked objects may not be activated in-place, but they can have their contents updated automatically or manually.

The Visual Aspect

Thus far, we have mostly used the content aspect. But we can use iconic and thumbnail as well. We use content to show the actual contents of the objects, iconic to represent the container as the application icon, and thumbnail preview to show a reduced view of the container.

Use scale if you want the entire image of the OLE2 object to be scaled to fit into the container, or clip to see only the portion of the object that fits within the area defined.

The OLE Pop-Up Menu

You can enable the right-click to pop up an OLE menu containing Cut, Copy, Paste, Paste Special, Insert Object, Delete Object, Links, and object-specific items. Or you can disable the right-click and prevent the OLE pop-up menu from displaying.

Advanced Topics

Now we will discuss some of the advanced topics that can be incorporated into your Oracle Forms applications. Then we will add some of these features to our applications.

Oracle Forms supports programmatic control over mouse activities. This means that you can add bubble help, right-click, double-click, and drag-and-drop functionality. In the next section, we will add bubble help to the toolbar.

Oracle Forms enables you to create user-defined triggers, and we created one in Chapter 12, "Developing Oracle Forms Applications." With these triggers, you can associate two or more different methods of executing the same code. For example, we execute the PRINT_DOC trigger from the Print menu item as well as from the Printer tool button. Thereafter, in each Oracle Forms application the PRINT_DOC trigger responds with the appropriate action. After creating the bubble help, we will modify the PRINT_DOC trigger in a form to run a report.

Oracle Forms includes the Open_Form procedure to enable two or more active form modules within the same MDI window.

> **CAUTION**
>
> You cannot use Open_Form with the `SESSION` parameter if you are using Personal Oracle7.

You may want to use the Open_Form procedure in an application where multiple instances of the same form could be used. Familiar examples of this would be having multiple documents open in Word or having multiple spreadsheets open in Excel.

Mouse-Aware Applications

By using the mouse triggers in Oracle Forms, we can add bubble help to the toolbar that will appear whenever the mouse points to one of the tool buttons. We will add the bubble help to the toolbar by creating a canvas, a text item, and mouse triggers at the block level. We will also display the label of the button to describe the function.

1. Open the CONTACT form module.
2. Create a canvas-view and change the name to HINT.
3. Change Canvas-view Type to Stacked.
4. Change Displayed to False.
5. Set the width and view width to 68.
6. Set the height and view height to 17.
7. Create a text item and change the name to HINT.
8. Set the canvas to HINT.
9. Set the width to 68 and the height to 17
10. Set the font to Arial, Regular, 9.
11. Set Background Color to yellow.
12. Set Navigable to False.

Now we will create a trigger in the CONTROL block that will check to see if the mouse is over a button, and if so, set the hint text, set the position for the stacked canvas, and then show the canvas.

1. Create a WHEN-MOUSE-ENTER trigger with the following PL/SQL text:

```
➥begin
  if get_item_property (name_in ('SYSTEM.MOUSE_ITEM'), ITEM_TYPE) = 'BUTTON'
➥then
    :control.hint := get_item_property (name_in ('SYSTEM.MOUSE_ITEM'),
➥LABEL);
    set_view_property ('HINT', DISPLAY_X_POS,
    get_item_property (name_in ('SYSTEM.MOUSE_ITEM'), X_POS));
    show_view ('HINT');
  end if;
end;
```

Next we will create a trigger in the CONTROL block that will hide the canvas.

2. Create a WHEN-MOUSE-LEAVE trigger with the following PL/SQL text:

```
hide_view ('HINT');
```

3. Set the labels for each of the buttons in the CONTROL block as follows:

Button	*Label*
ENTERQRY	Query
SAVE	Save
PRINTER	Print Screen
EXIT	Exit
CUT	Cut
COPY	Copy
PASTE	Paste
INSERT	Insert
DELETE	Delete
FIRSTREC	First Record
PREVSET	Scroll Up
PREVREC	Prev Record
NEXTREC	Next Record
NEXTSET	Scroll Down
LASTREC	Last Record
HELP	Help

4. Save and run the form.

Figure 15.12 shows the toolbar with the bubble help displayed.

FIGURE 15.12.
The toolbar with bubble help displayed.

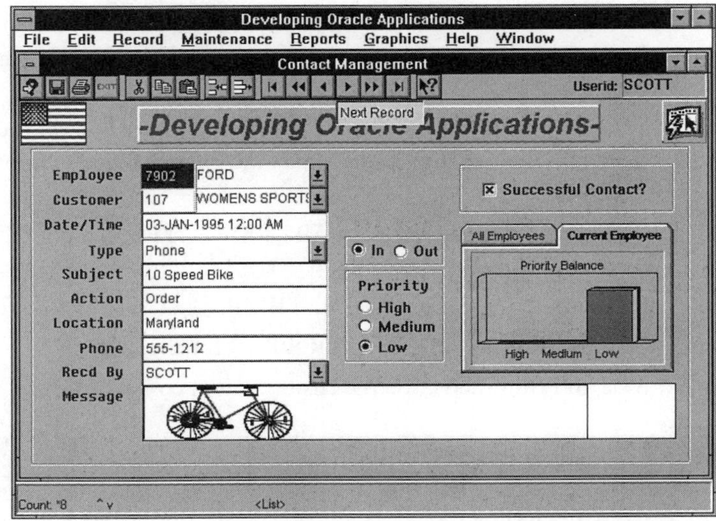

Customized Interface Elements

In Chapter 8, "Introducing Oracle Forms," we created the standard menu that included a Print menu item. In Chapter 12, we created the toolbar and placed a printer button on it. Both of those interface elements executed the same user-defined trigger. Now we will change that trigger to associate the contact-management application with a default report.

1. Open the PRINT_DOC trigger, and change the PL/SQL to run a report as follows:

```
run_product (REPORTS, 'contacts',
             ASYNCHRONOUS, RUNTIME,
             FILESYSTEM, NULL, NULL);
```

2. Change the label for the Print button from Print Screen to Report.
3. Save and run the form.

Drag and Drop Code Reuse

In Chapter 8, we created the customer application without the template form that included the standard toolbar. Now we will copy the toolbar and the form level triggers from the contact-management application into the customer application.

1. Open the form module CUSTOMER.
2. Drag and drop in the Object Navigator to copy the WHEN-NEW-FORM-INSTANCE and the PRINT_DOC triggers.
3. Invoke the Program Unit Editor for the WHEN-NEW-FORM-INSTANCE, and remove the read_image_file, and go_block statements.
4. Invoke the Program Unit Editor for the PRINT_DOC trigger, and change contact to customer.
5. Drag and drop to copy the CONTROL block. Then, in the Copy Object Options dialog box, select the Canvases tab and change Copy window to Replace with <NULL>.
6. Select ALL_EMPLOYEES, CUR_EMPLOYEES, and CONTACT canvases, and delete.
7. Select the chart, VBX, OLE, and BMP items, then delete.
8. Set Horizontal Toolbar to TOOLBAR for the window.
9. Save and run, then close the customer and contact forms.

> **NOTE**
>
> To copy the toolbar, we actually copied the control block, which is a higher-level object. Then we deleted the additional objects that we did not need.

Modifying OLE2 Containers at Runtime

One of the most interesting things about OLE2 containers is that they can be modified at runtime. Not just the contents, but the type of object itself may be changed to something completely different from what was originally defined. In the next several sections we will explore many examples of this using the Contact Management Information System we have created.

Edit the Object

In this example we will change the country represented by the flag in the upper-left corner of the Contact Management application.

1. Run the Contact Management Information System.
2. Click on the Contacts launch button to invoke the Contact Management application.
3. Right-click on the flag, and select Edit from the Microsoft ClipArt Gallery Object menu.
4. Select the Flags category and Australia.
5. Notice that in this example, we only change the content of the object and not the object type.

Figure 15.13 shows the Contact Management application with the Australian flag replacing Old Glory.

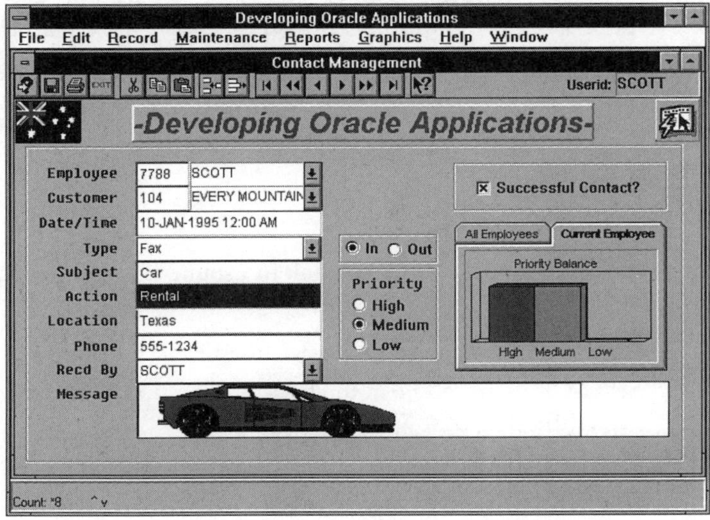

FIGURE 15.13.
The Australian flag and a sports car.

CAUTION

The OLE2 container displaying the flag is a control field and was defined at design time. Therefore if you want to make a permanent change to the contents of this OLE2 object, do it from Oracle Forms Designer.

Insert a Picture into a Database Column

Now we will insert a bitmap of a car into the contact message. Using this method, pictures can be stored in the Oracle database.

1. Execute a query, then right-click on the message and select Insert Object from the pop-up menu.
2. Select Create from File in the Insert Object dialog box, then enter \DEV2000 \BITMAPS\CAR.BMP.
3. Click the Save button on the toolbar to store the image in the Oracle database.
4. Notice that in this example, we inserted a bitmap where we had previously stored an MS Word document. This is an example of changing the object type.

Figure 15.13 shows the Contact Management application with a picture of a sports car in the message item.

NOTE

The contact message is a LONG RAW column in the Oracle database and is capable of storing any type of OLE2 object.

Link to a Sound File

Next we will change the flag into a link to a sound file, and we will listen to the music via MS Media Clip.

1. Right-click on the flag, and select Insert Object from the pop-up menu.
2. Select Create from File in the Insert Object dialog box, then enter \DEV2000 \WAV\BLUZJAZZ.WAV.
3. Check the Link checkbox.
4. Check the Display as Icon check box.
5. Click the Change Icon button.
6. Select From File, and enter \DEV2000\ICONS\BLUZMUSIC.ICO in the Change Icon dialog box.

7. Double-click the icon to listen to the music.
8. Notice that in this example we changed the content and the type of object from a static object to a multimedia object. We also used our own icon to represent the content of the linked file. Then we activated the object in-place by clicking on it.

Figure 15.14 shows the Contact Management application, with the music icon inside of the linked border of the OLE2 container in place of the flag.

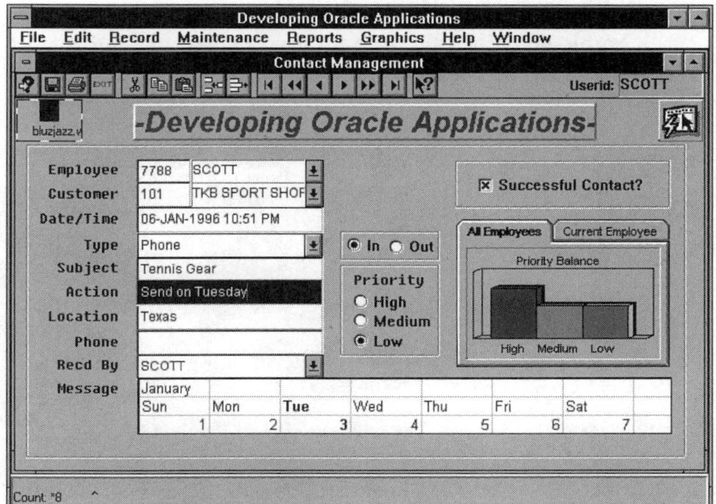

FIGURE 15.14.
The blues icon and a calendar from Excel.

Insert a Spreadsheet into a Database Column

Now we will create a calendar in MS Excel and insert it into the contact message. With this kind of flexibility, almost anything can be stored in the Oracle database.

1. Use the toolbar to scroll to another record, then right-click on the message and select Insert Object from the pop-up menu.
2. Select Microsoft Excel 5.0 Worksheet from the Insert Object dialog box.
3. Double-click the worksheet to activate MS Excel in-place. Then enter January in cell A1, Sun in A2, and 1 in A3.
4. Select A2 and A3. Then drag to the right to automatically create the rest of the week.
5. Select Tuesday and cells C2 and C3. Then set the font to Blue and Bold. Click in the form to return.
6. Click the Save button on the toolbar to store the calendar in the Oracle database.

The Contact Management application is shown in Figure 15.14 with the calendar in the message item.

A Few Moments with Larry Ellison on Video

Let's conclude the exercises in this book by running a video clip. Here we can watch and listen to Oracle CEO Larry Ellison discuss Oracle and the World Wide Web.

1. Use the toolbar to exit, and return to CMIS. Then right-click on the ClipArt and select Insert Object from the pop-up menu.
2. Select Create from File in the Insert Object dialog box, then enter \DEV2000\AVI\BUNTING.AVI.
3. Double-click the OLE2 container to see what Ellison has to say.

Larry Ellison appears in the video clip as shown in Figure 15.15.

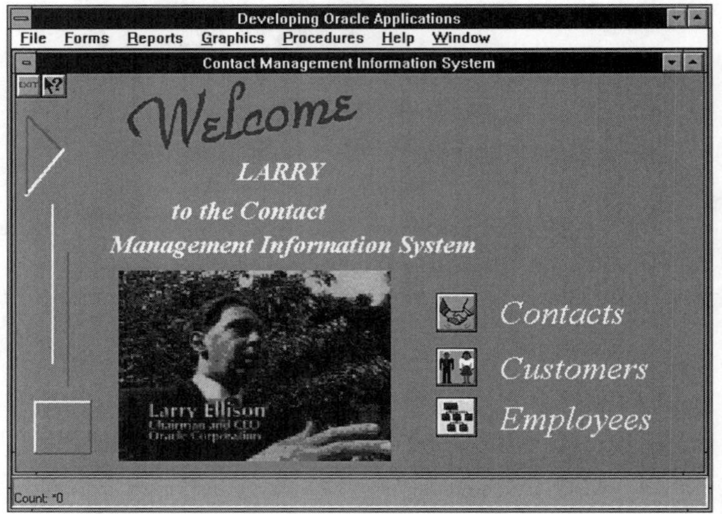

FIGURE 15.15.
Larry Ellison appears in a video clip.

Summary

This chapter concluded the development of applications with Oracle Developer/2000. During this chapter, we did the following:

- Created the CMIS menu
- Created the CMIS welcome screen

Then we reviewed deployment and configuration issues in the Windows environment, including:

- Setting up an application environment
- Creating environments for development, test, demonstration, training, and production

- Referencing a database for each environment
- Application installation
- GUI styles and standards
- Memory, disk space, and performance
- OLE2 options
- Advanced topics for application enhancements

And we explored the power of OLE2, including:

- Editing OLE2 objects
- Inserting OLE2 objects into the database
- Linking to sound files
- Running a video clip

Now that you have completed this book on Oracle Developer/2000 and developed several applications with it, I hope you enjoyed the experience and will continue to develop applications with Oracle Developer/2000 as well as the other Oracle products.

In working through this book, you have developed an application system that meets all the requirements and accomplishes all the goals set for the project in Chapter 2, "Analysis." In addition, you met and exceeded expectations set by management and staff by completing each of the bonus items for the project. You should now be well prepared for the development of your next Oracle application system.

V

Appendixes

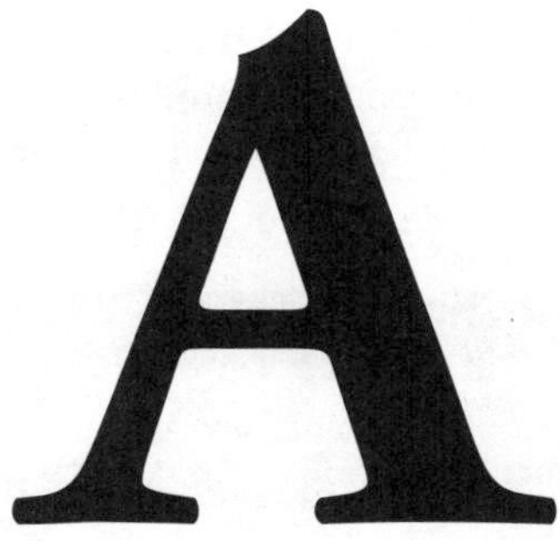

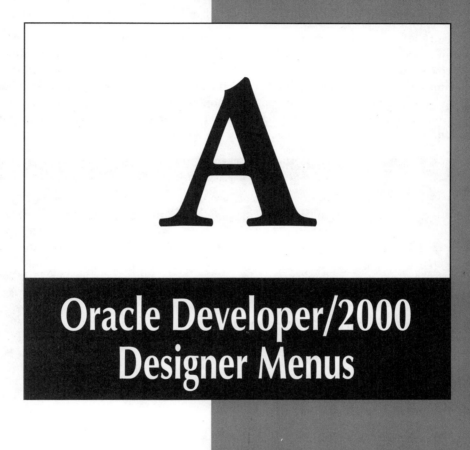

Oracle Developer/2000 Designer Menus

The Oracle Developer/2000 menus are listed here as they appear in the designers. As the focus changes in the Designer, the current menu changes to support the functionality of the object in focus. The menu items are listed as seen from left to right at the top of the Designer window. The primary menus are listed first with their items, and the supporting menus follow.

All of the menu items from the designers contain submenus. Some of the submenus also contain submenus of their own. The hierarchy of the subordinate menus is shown with the menu items separated by commas from left to right. The function of each menu item is described immediately following the heading for that menu item. Many of the menu items invoke a dialog box—particularly the menu items that are followed by three dots. The menu items that invoke dialog boxes will appear in figures, which will show the dialogs and describe their function.

TIP

Menus and menu items may be selected by using the mouse or by using the keyboard. Some menu items even have "hot" keys to directly execute the actions without requiring you to navigate the menu. You will find the hot keys for menu items referenced on the label. Most hot keys are activated by holding the Ctrl key and pressing the associated letter.

Object Navigator Menu

The Object Navigator menu contains the following items:

File
Edit
Tools
Navigator
Window
Help

Layout Menu

The Layout menu contains the following items:

File
Edit
Tools
View
Format

Arrange
Window
Help

File Menu

The File menu appears on each of the main menus in the designers. It supports tasks such as creating new objects, opening, saving, closing, compiling, and connecting to the database. The File menu contains the following items:

New
Open…
Close
Save
Save As…
Revert
Run
Compile…
Compile All…
Connect…
Disconnect
Print…
Print Setup…
Exit

File, New Menu

The File, New menu supports the creation of new modules. The creation of these modules from the menu is identical to creating them from within the Object Navigator. The File, New menu contains items that can be created in the respective designers.

File, Open…

The File, Open… menu item may invoke a filter dialog box to determine whether the module to be opened is in the database or on the file system. However, the module access may be set in the Designer options to specify the database or file system as the default preference. When the file system is selected, the standard MS Windows Open dialog box is presented with a list of available file extensions for the current module types. When the database is selected, a dialog box appears listing all of the modules that have been saved to the database.

The result of selecting the File, Open… menu item is identical to clicking on the Open icon from the Object Navigator or Layout Editor toolbars.

File, Close

The File, Close menu item closes the current module or file.

File, Save

The File, Save menu item saves the current module or file to the file system. The selection of the File, Save menu item from the menu is identical to clicking on the Save icon from the Object Navigator or Layout Editor toolbars.

File, Save As...

Like the File, Open... menu item, the File, Save As... menu item is also dependent on the module access settings in the Designer options. It will either display the Filter, Save As, or Database dialog box.

File, Revert

The File, Revert menu item reverts the current module or file back to its original state, prior to any modifications made in the designer.

File, Run

The File, Run menu item runs the current module. Depending on the setting in the Designer options, the module may be saved and generated automatically prior to running. The selection of File, Run from the menu is identical to selecting it from the Object Navigator or Layout Editor toolbars.

File, Compile...

The File, Compile... menu item compiles the current PL/SQL code and invokes the Compile dialog box (as shown in Figure A.1) to allow for the review of the compilation process.

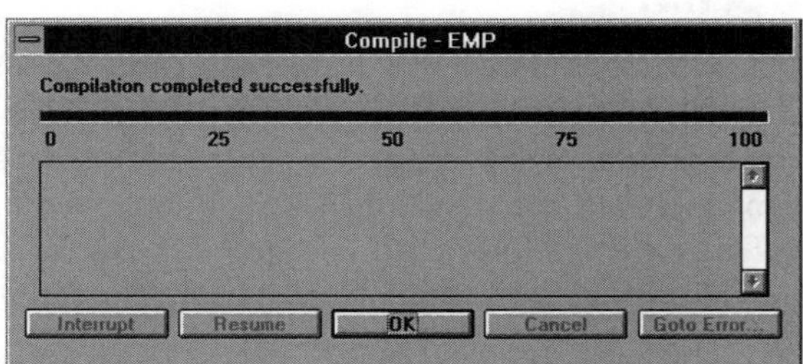

FIGURE A.1.
The Compile dialog box.

File, Compile All...

The File, Compile All... menu item compiles all of the PL/SQL code in the current module and invokes the same Compile dialog box that is shown in Figure A.1.

File, Connect...

The File, Connect... menu item invokes the Connect dialog box (as shown in Figure A.2) to enable the user to log on to the Oracle database.

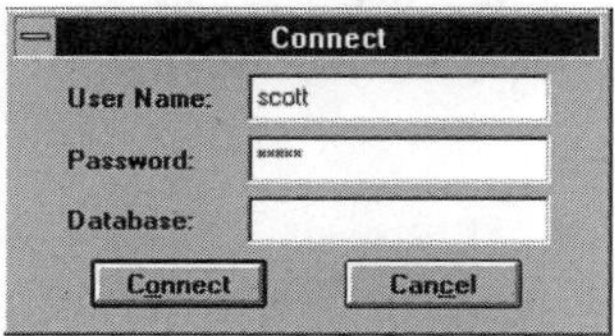

FIGURE A.2.
The Connect dialog box.

The Connect dialog box is automatically invoked whenever a database operation is to be performed and there is no current connection to the database.

File, Disconnect

The File, Disconnect menu item disconnects the current user from the Oracle database.

File, Print...

The File, Print... menu item invokes the standard MS Windows Print dialog box and provides for the capture and printing of the current screen. The screen can be printed in other ways as well. The Print Screen key on the keyboard will copy the screen image to the Clipboard, where it can be pasted into any paint utility and saved or printed.

File, Print Setup...

The File, Print Setup... menu item invokes the standard MS Windows Print Setup dialog box to allow modification to the printer settings.

File, Exit

The File, Exit menu item closes any open modules, disconnects the current user from the Oracle database, and exits the Designer.

Edit Menu

The Edit Menu appears on each of the main menus in the designers and supports tasks such as editing, searching, importing, and exporting. The Edit menu contains the following items:

Undo
Cut
Copy
Paste
Clear
Duplicate
Select All
Search/Replace...
Import
Export

Edit, Undo

The Edit, Undo menu item reverses the most recent editing change that was made.

Edit, Cut

The Edit, Cut menu item removes the currently highlighted item and places it on the Clipboard. Items may be cut to remove them or to move them. Items may be cut using the Object Navigator or Layout Editor toolbars or moved by dragging and dropping in the Object Navigator.

The Edit, Cut menu item can be selected from the Edit Menu, from the pop-up menu in the Object Navigator, or from Layout Editor by right-mouse clicking.

Edit, Copy

The Edit, Copy menu item places a copy of the currently highlighted item on the Clipboard. Items are copied by copy-and-paste actions. Items may be copied using the Object Navigator or Layout Editor toolbars or by holding down the control key and dragging and dropping in the Object Navigator.

The Edit, Copy menu item can be selected from the Edit Menu, from the pop-up menu in the Object Navigator, or from the Layout Editor by right-clicking.

Edit, Paste

The Edit, Paste menu item inserts a copy of the contents of the Clipboard into the currently highlighted item. Items may be pasted using the Object Navigator or Layout Editor toolbars.

The Edit, Paste menu item can be selected from the Edit Menu, or from the pop-up menu in the Object Navigator, or from the Layout Editor by right-clicking.

Edit, Clear

The Edit, Clear menu item deletes the current item. Items may also be deleted using the Object Navigator toolbar.

Edit, Duplicate

The Edit, Duplicate menu item copies and pastes the current item. Duplicate combines the copy and paste actions into one action.

Edit, Select All

The Edit, Select All menu item selects all of the items in the layout, whether they are visible or not, and is only available from the Layout Editor.

Edit, Search/Replace...

The Edit, Search/Replace... menu item invokes the Search/Replace dialog box (as shown in Figure A.3) to allow for the search of text strings in the current trigger, program unit, or multiline text field.

FIGURE A.3.
The Search/Replace dialog box.

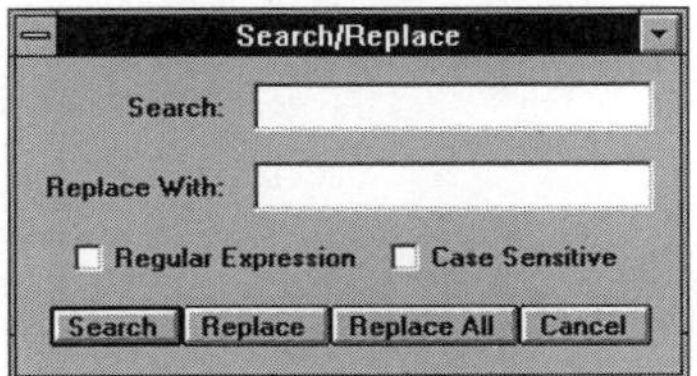

Text can be found via the Search button or it can be searched and replaced with other text by using the Replace or Replace All buttons.

Edit, Import Menu

The Edit, Import menu supports the importing of objects into the layout. The Edit, Import menu contains the following items:

Drawing...
Image...
Color Palette...
Text...

Edit, Import, Drawing...

The Edit, Import, Drawing... menu item invokes the Import dialog box (as shown in Figure A.4) to enable the importing of line drawings into the Layout Editor.

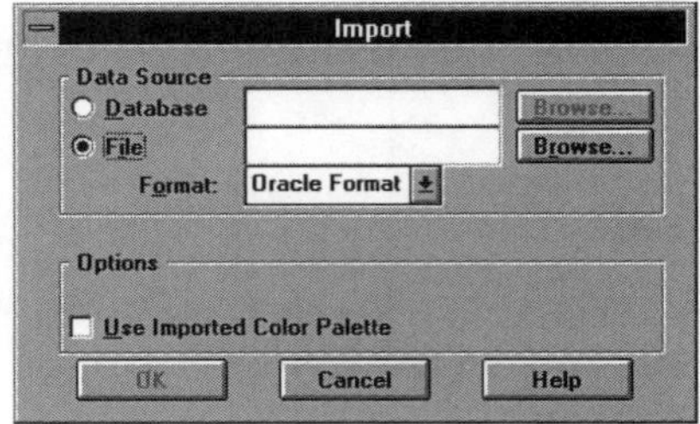

FIGURE A.4.
The Import dialog box for drawings.

A drawing may be imported from the database or the file system by using the Data Source radio buttons in the Import dialog box.

Edit, Import, Image...

The Edit, Import, Image... menu item invokes the Import Image dialog box (as shown in Figure A.5) to enable the importing of images into the Layout Editor.

FIGURE A.5.
The Import Image dialog box.

An image may be imported from the database or the file system by using the radio buttons in the Import Image dialog box. In addition, you can specify the image format and image quality.

Edit, Import, Color Palette...

The Edit, Import, Color Palette... menu item invokes the Import dialog box (as shown in Figure A.6) to enable the importing of color palettes into the Layout Editor.

A color palette may be imported from the database or the file system by using the Data Source radio buttons in the Import dialog box.

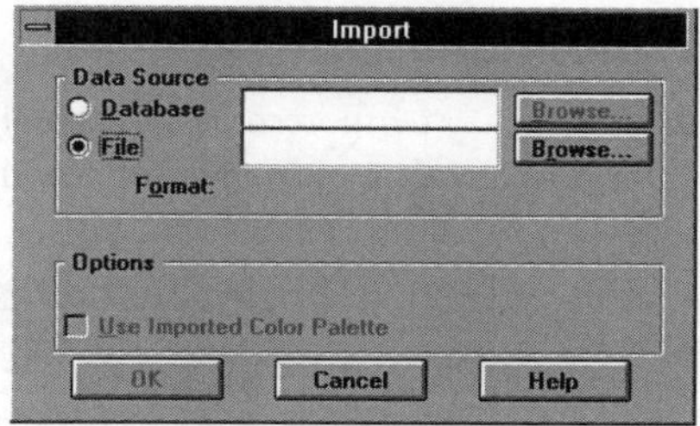

FIGURE A.6.
The Import dialog box for Color Palettes.

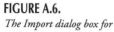

Edit, Import, Text...

The Edit, Import, Text… menu item invokes the Open dialog box to enable the importing of text strings into any of the triggers, program units or multiline text fields within the module. The text strings are imported from ASCII files on the file system.

Edit, Export Menu

The Edit, Export menu supports the exporting of objects from the layout. The Edit, Export menu contains the following items:

Drawing…
Image…
Color Palette…
Text…

Edit, Export, Drawing...

The Edit, Export, Drawing… menu item invokes the Export dialog box (as shown in Figure A.7) to enable the exporting of line drawings from the Layout Editor.

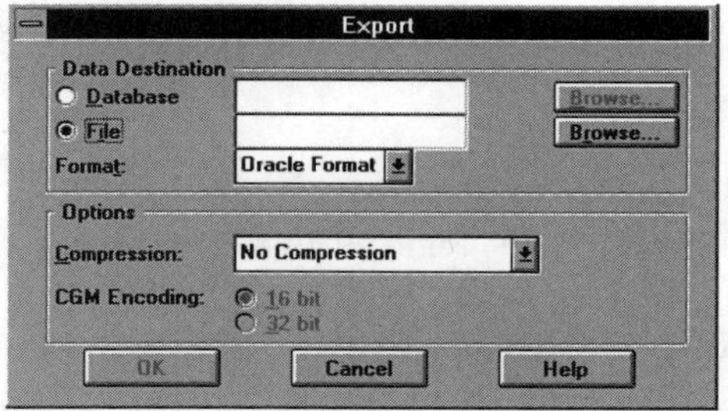

FIGURE A.7.
The Export dialog box for Drawings.

A drawing may be exported to the database or the file system by using the Data Destination radio buttons in the Export dialog box.

Edit, Export, Image...

The Edit, Export, Image... menu item invokes the Export Image dialog box (as shown in Figure A.8) to enable the exporting of image items from the Layout Editor.

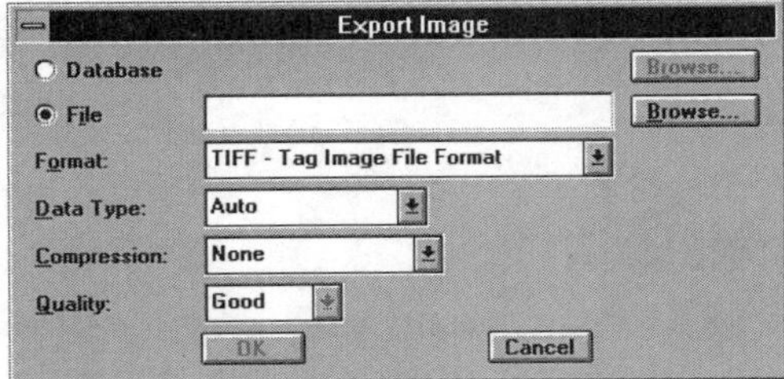

FIGURE A.8.
The Export Image dialog box.

An image may be exported to the database or the file system by using the radio buttons in the Export Image dialog box. In addition, you can use the drop-down lists to specify the image format as well as the data type, compression, and image quality.

Edit, Export, Color Palette...

The Edit, Export, Color Palette... menu item invokes the Export dialog box (as shown in Figure A.9) to enable the exporting of color palettes from the Layout Editor.

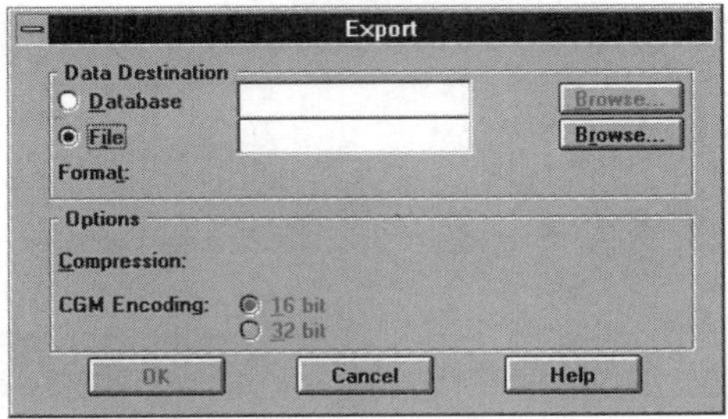

FIGURE A.9.
The Export dialog box for color palettes.

A color palette may be exported to the database or the file system by using the Data Destination radio buttons in the Export dialog box.

Edit, Export, Text...

The Edit, Export, Text... menu item invokes the standard MS Windows Save As dialog box to enable the exporting of text strings from any of the triggers, program units, or multiline text fields within the module. The text strings are exported as ASCII files on the file system.

Tools Menu

The Tools menu appears on each of the main menus in the designers and supports tasks such as navigating to different windows and editors, reviewing tables and columns, and setting options. The Tools menu contains the following items:

Properties
PL/SQL Editor or Program Unit Editor
Stored Program Unit Editor
Database Trigger Editor…
PL/SQL Interpreter

Tools, Properties

In Oracle Forms Designer, the Tools, Properties menu item invokes or sets the focus to the Properties window; in Oracle Reports and Oracle Graphics, it invokes the dialog box containing the properties of the selected item. The Tools, Properties menu item can be selected from the Tools menu or from the pop-up menu in the Object Navigator, or one of the editors by right-clicking.

Tools, PL/SQL Editor or Program Unit Editor

The Tools, PL/SQL Editor or Program Unit Editor menu items open or set the focus to the editor window. The PL/SQL and Program Unit editors are used to create and maintain local procedures, functions, and packages. If the current focus is on a PL/SQL object when the editor is invoked, then that object automatically appears in the editor window. The Tools, PL/SQL Editor or Program Unit Editor menu items can be selected from the Tools menu or from the pop-up menu in the Object Navigator by right-clicking.

Tools, Stored Program Unit Editor

The Tools, Stored Program Unit Editor menu item opens or sets the focus to the Stored Program Unit window. The Stored Program Unit Editor is used to create and maintain database procedures, functions, and packages. Each stored program unit is organized according to the Oracle userid that owns the object. The Stored Program Unit Editor can be invoked by double-clicking a program unit under the Database Objects node in the Object Navigator.

Tools, Database Trigger Editor…

The Tools, Database Trigger Editor… menu item opens or sets the focus to the Database Trigger window. The Database Trigger window is shown in Figure A.10 defining an audit trigger for the EMP table owned by SCOTT.

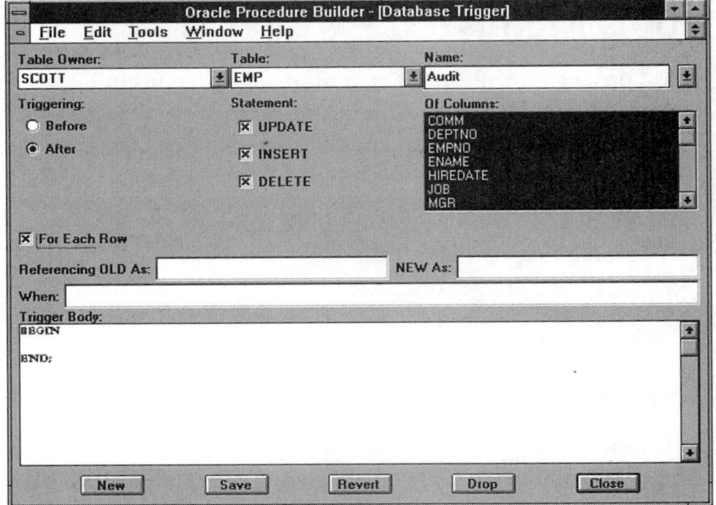

FIGURE A.10.
The Database Trigger Editor.

The Database Trigger Editor is used to create and maintain database triggers. Each database trigger is organized by the Oracle userid and table. Notice the fields with drop-down lists that identify the owner, table, and trigger name. The database trigger is constructed from the selection of options in the editor and the addition of the trigger body containing PL/SQL. The Database Trigger Editor can be invoked by double-clicking a database trigger under the Database Objects node in the Object Navigator or from the Tools menu.

Tools, PL/SQL Interpreter...

The Tools, PL/SQL Interpreter menu item opens or sets the focus to the PL/SQL Interpreter window. The PL/SQL Interpreter is used to review and debug PL/SQL code. The PL/SQL Interpreter is shown in Figure A.11.

Notice the PL/SQL Interpreter window contains panes for the source code, its own Object Navigator, and the PL/SQL command line.

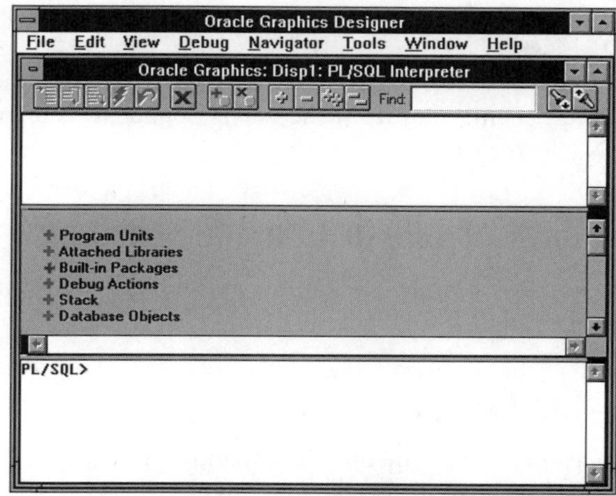

FIGURE A.11.
The PL/SQL Interpreter window.

Navigator Menu

The Navigator menu only appears on the Object Navigator menus in the designers. It supports the changing of views, as well as the creating, deleting, compiling, marking, and pasting of objects. The Navigator menu contains the following items:

Create
Delete
Compile or Compile Selection
Expand
Collapse
Expand All
Collapse All
Mark
Goto Mark
Paste Name
Paste Arguments

Navigator, Create

The Navigator, Create menu item creates an item of the type selected. The selection of the Navigator, Create menu item from the Navigator menu is identical to selecting Create from the Object Navigator toolbar.

Navigator, Delete

The Navigator, Delete menu item deletes the item or items selected. The selection of the Navigator, Delete menu item from the Navigator menu is identical to selecting Delete from the Object Navigator toolbar.

Navigator, Compile or Compile Selection

The Navigator, Compile or Compile Selection menu items invoke the Compile dialog box and compile the PL/SQL code that is selected.

Navigator, Expand

The Navigator, Expand menu item expands the current branch of the object hierarchy by one level. The selection of the Navigator, Expand menu item from the Navigator menu is the same as clicking on the plus sign in the Object Navigator or pressing the right arrow on the keyboard.

Navigator, Collapse

The Navigator, Collapse menu item collapses the current branch of the object hierarchy by one level. The selection of the Navigator, Collapse menu item from the Navigator menu is the same as clicking on the minus sign in the Object Navigator or pressing the left arrow on the keyboard.

Navigator, Expand All

The Navigator, Expand All menu item expands all of the nodes under the current branch of the object hierarchy. The selection of the Navigator, Expand All menu item from the Navigator menu is identical to selecting Expand All from the Object Navigator toolbar.

Navigator, Collapse All

The Navigator, Collapse All menu item collapses all of the nodes under the current branch of the object hierarchy. The selection of the Navigator, Collapse All menu item from the Navigator menu is identical to selecting Collapse All from the Object Navigator toolbar.

Navigator, Mark

The Navigator, Mark menu item marks the current item so that it may be returned to with Goto Mark.

Navigator, Goto Mark

The Navigator, Goto Mark menu item goes to the previously marked item.

Navigator, Paste Name

The Navigator, Paste Name menu item will paste the name of the current procedure or function into the current program unit editor or interpreter. This capability makes it easier for you to write code to call functions and procedures during development and debugging. To enable the Navigator, Paste Name menu item, select the Specification node for a program unit in the Object Navigator.

Navigator, Paste Arguments

The Navigator, Paste Arguments menu item works like the Paste Name menu item but adds the argument list to the name.

View Menu

The View menu only appears when you are working with a layout in one of the designers. It enables you to change the visual aspects of the editor. The View menu contains the following items:

Zoom In
Zoom Out
Normal Size
Fit to Window
Rulers
Ruler Guides
Grid
Grid Snap
Page Breaks
Tool Palette
Status Bar or Status Line

View, Zoom In

The View, Zoom In menu item multiplies the current magnification in the layout by two. By zooming in, the objects in the layout appear larger. The selection of the View, Zoom In menu item from the View menu is identical to clicking on the Magnify icon from the tool palette and clicking in the layout.

View, Zoom Out

The View, Zoom Out menu item divides the current magnification in the layout by two. By zooming out, the objects in the layout appear smaller. The selection of the View, Zoom Out menu item from the View menu is identical to clicking on the Magnify icon from the tool palette and shift-clicking in the layout.

View, Normal Size

The View, Normal Size menu item sets the current magnification in the layout to a power of one. By using normal size, you can quickly return the objects in the layout to their standard appearance.

View, Fit to Window

The View, Fit to Window menu item adjusts the current magnification in the layout to fit all the objects into the view of the current window.

View, Rulers

The View, Rulers menu item is a check-style menu item. It turns the rulers in the layout on and off. The rulers appear on the top and left side of the editor.

View, Ruler Guides

The View, Ruler Guides menu item is a check-style menu item. It turns the display of ruler guides in the layout on and off. Ruler guides are created by clicking on a ruler and dragging into the layout.

View, Grid

The View, Grid menu item is a check-style menu item. It turns the grid in the layout on and off. The grid appears as horizontal and vertical lines in the background of the layout. The grid spacing can be changed using the Ruler Settings dialog box.

View, Grid Snap

The View, Grid Snap menu item is a check-style menu item. It turns the snap-to-grid feature on and off. The grid snap automatically adjusts the position of objects in the layout to align with the grid.

View, Page Breaks

The View, Page Breaks menu item is a check-style menu item. It turns the display of the page breaks on and off in the layout. The page breaks show what will be contained on which pages during printing.

View, Tool Palette

The View, Tool Palette menu item is a check-style menu item. It turns the display of the tool palette on and off in the layout. The tool palette appears on the left side of the layout.

View, Status Bar or Status Line

The View, Status Bar or Status Line menu items are check-style menu items. They turn the display of the status area on and off in the editor. The status information appears at the bottom of the layout and contains the level of magnification and the current X and Y coordinates of the cursor.

Format Menu

The Format menu appears when you are in a layout. It enables you to change the visual aspects of the objects within the layout. The Format menu contains the following items:

Font...
Spacing
Alignment
Line
Bevel
Dash
Arrow
Drawing Options
Color Palette...

Format, Font...

The Format, Font... menu item invokes the Font dialog box, as shown in Figure A.12.

The Font dialog box enables the selection of a font, style, size, and effect for a text, display, button, or boilerplate text item. The dialog box also provides a sample view of the font options chosen.

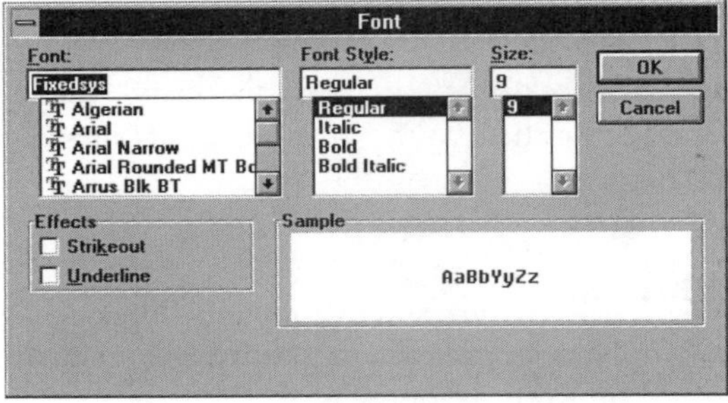

FIGURE A.12.
The Font dialog box.

Format, Spacing Menu

The Format, Spacing menu enables boilerplate text items to be set to various spacing settings. The menu style of the subordinate menu is radio group, which means that only one of the spacing styles may be selected. The Format, Spacing menu contains the following items:

Single
1 1/2
Double
Custom…

Format, Spacing, Single

The Format, Spacing, Single menu item sets the boilerplate text to single spaced.

Format, Spacing, 1 1/2

The Format, Spacing, 1 1/2 menu item sets the boilerplate text to a space and a half.

Format, Spacing, Double

The Format, Spacing, Double menu item sets the boilerplate text to double spaced.

Format, Spacing, Custom…

The Format, Spacing, Custom… menu item invokes the Custom Spacing dialog box, as shown in Figure A.13.

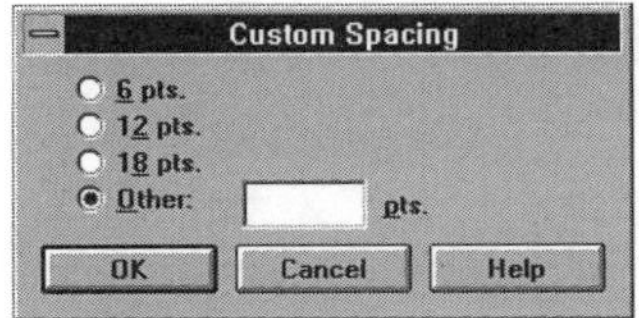

FIGURE A.13.
The Custom Spacing dialog box.

The Custom Spacing dialog box enables you to select a standard point size or a user-specified size.

Format, Alignment Menu

The Format, Alignment menu enables you to set the justification for a text item, display item, or boilerplate text item. The menu style of the subordinate menu is radio group, so only one of the alignment styles may be selected. The Format, Alignment menu contains the following items:

Left
Center
Right

Format, Alignment, Left

The Format, Alignment, Left menu item sets the justification of the selected item or items to left.

Format, Alignment, Center

The Format, Alignment, Center menu item sets the justification of the selected item or items to centered.

Format, Alignment, Right

The Format, Alignment, Right menu item sets the justification of the selected item or items to right.

Format, Line Menu

The Format, Line menu enables you to set the point size for lines that are used in the boilerplate items, including rectangles, ellipses, arcs, polygons, polylines, rounded rectangles, freehand, and text. The menu style of the subordinate menu is radio group, which means that only one of the line sizes may be selected. The Format, Line menu contains the following items:

0
1 pt.
2 pt.
4 pt.
8 pt.
16 pt.
Custom…

Format, Line, 0 through 16 pt.

The Format, Line, 0, 1 pt., 2 pt., 4 pt., 8 pt., and 16 pt. menu items set the line point size for the boilerplate item(s) selected to the chosen value.

Format, Line, Custom...

The Format, Line, Custom... menu item invokes the Custom Line Width dialog box, as shown in Figure A.14.

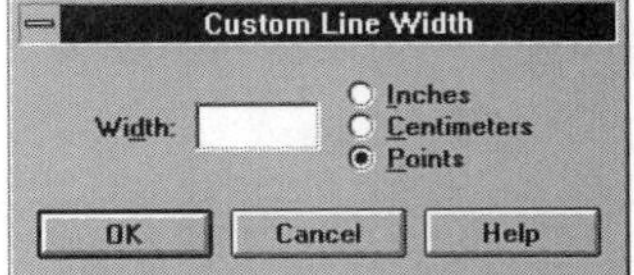

FIGURE A.14.
The Custom Line Width dialog box.

The Custom Line Width dialog box allows the entry of the line width as well as a selection for the coordinate system.

Format, Bevel Menu

The Format, Bevel menu enables you to select a three-dimensional appearance for boilerplate rectangles and text items. The menu style of the subordinate menu is radio group, which means that only one of the bevel styles may be selected. The Format, Bevel menu contains the following items:

None
Inset
Outset
Raised
Lowered

Format, Bevel, None

The Format, Bevel, None menu item turns off the 3-D appearance.

Format, Bevel, Inset

The Format, Bevel, Inset menu item makes the border surrounding the item look lower and the area inside of the border appear to be on the same level as the background.

Format, Bevel, Outset

The Format, Bevel, Outset menu item makes the border surrounding the item look higher and the area inside of the border appear to be on the same level as the background.

Format, Bevel, Raised

The Format, Bevel, Raised menu item makes the area inside of the border appear to be higher than the background.

Format, Bevel, Lowered

The Format, Bevel, Lowered menu item makes the area inside of the border appear to be lower than the background.

Format, Dash Menu

The Format, Dash menu allows for the selection of a dash style to be set for borders and lines found in boilerplate items. The menu style of the subordinate menu is radio group, so only one of the dash styles may be selected.

The subordinate menu contains visual examples of the dash styles that may be selected for each menu item. The line point size must be set to either 0 or 1 for the dash appearance to have an affect.

Format, Arrow Menu

The Format, Arrow menu allows for the selection of an arrow style to be set for boilerplate lines. The menu style of the subordinate menu is radio group, which means that only one of the arrow styles may be selected.

The subordinate menu contains visual examples of the arrow styles that may be selected for each menu item. The examples include no arrow, an arrow pointing to the right, an arrow pointing to the left, an arrow pointing to the right in the middle of the line, an arrow pointing to the left in the middle of the line, and an arrow on each end of the line.

Format, Drawing Options Menu

The Format, Drawing Options menu enables you to modify the default settings for boilerplate items in the layout. The Format, Drawing Options menu contains the following items:

General…
Arc…
Text…
Rounded Rectangle…
Image…

Format, Drawing Options, General…

The Format, Drawing Options, General… menu item invokes the General Drawing Options dialog box, as shown in Figure A.15.

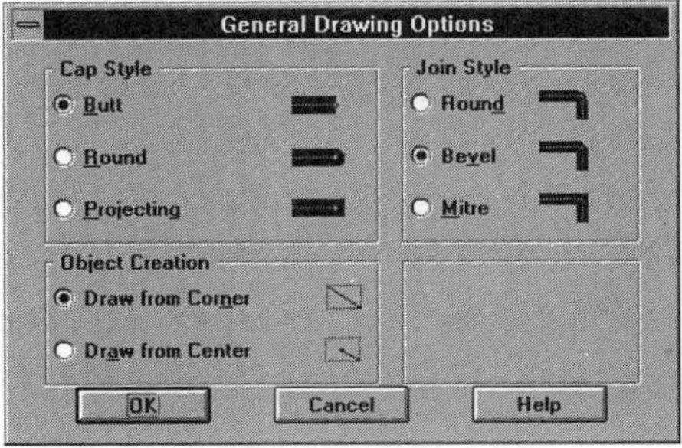

FIGURE A.15.
The General Drawing Options dialog box.

The General Drawing Options dialog box enables you to select the cap style, join style, and object-creation method. Only the object-creation options have any effect in MS Windows.

Format, Drawing Options, Arc...

The Format, Drawing Options, Arc… menu item invokes the Arc Drawing Options dialog box, as shown in Figure A.16.

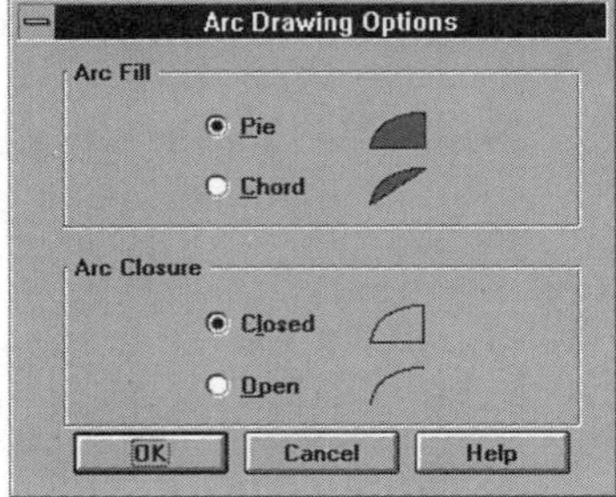

FIGURE A.16.
The Arc Drawing Options dialog box.

The Arc Drawing Options dialog box enables you to select the fill style as well as the closure method, and it provides visual examples of the options.

Format, Drawing Options, Text...

The Format, Drawing Options, Text… menu item invokes the Text Drawing Options dialog box, as shown in Figure A.17.

The Text Drawing Options dialog box provides the selection of the horizontal and vertical justification of boilerplate text items. In addition, there are options for font scaling and word wrapping.

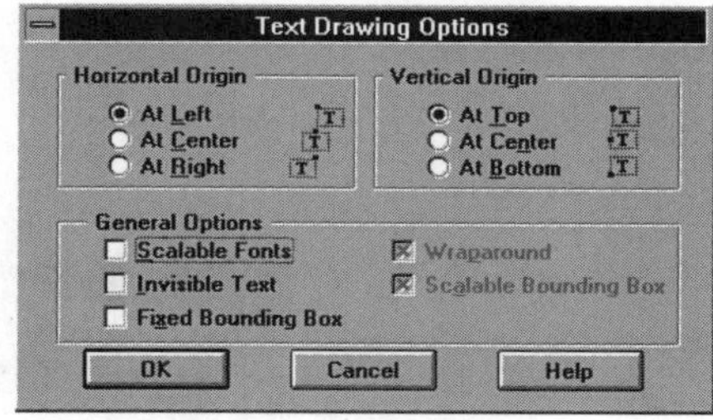

FIGURE A.17.
The Text Drawing Options dialog box.

Format, Drawing Options, Rounded Rectangle...

The Format, Drawing Options, Rounded Rectangle... menu item invokes the Rounded Rectangle Drawing Options dialog box, as shown in Figure A.18.

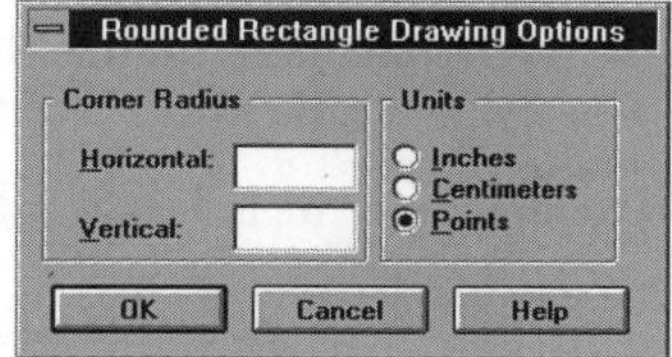

FIGURE A.18.
The Rounded Rectangle Drawing Options dialog box.

The Rounded Rectangle Drawing Options dialog box enables you to set the degree of curvature for the corners and to select the coordinate system that is used. The larger the number of the radius, the rounder the corner.

Format, Drawing Options, Image...

The Format, Drawing Options, Image... menu item invokes the Image Drawing Options dialog box, as shown in Figure A.19.

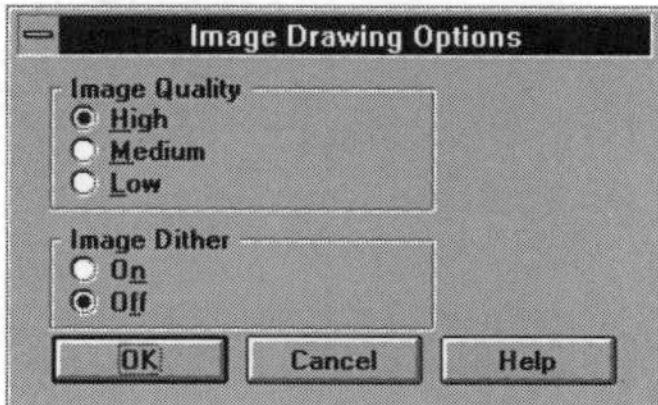

FIGURE A.19.
The Image Drawing Options dialog box.

The Image Drawing Options dialog box enables you to set the image quality and to select whether dithering will be used.

Format, Color Palette...

The Format, Color Palette... menu item invokes the Color Palette dialog box, as shown in Figure A.20.

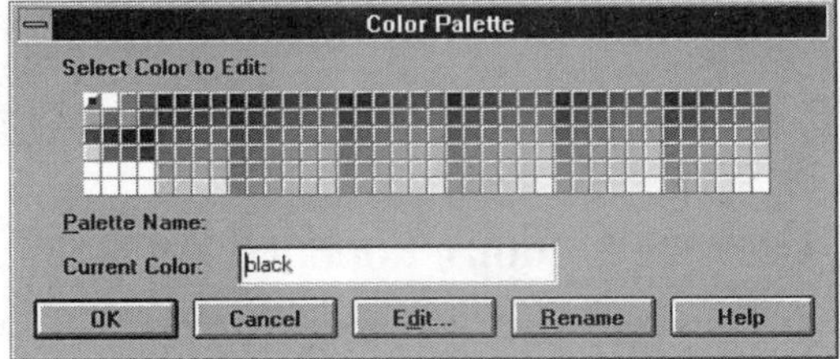

FIGURE A.20.
The Color Palette dialog box.

The color mode must be set to editable in the Designer options to enable the Format, Color Palette... menu item. The Color Palette shows the 256 colors in the current palette and allows any of them to be selected for editing.

After you select a color and press the Edit button, the Color dialog box in Figure A.21 appears.

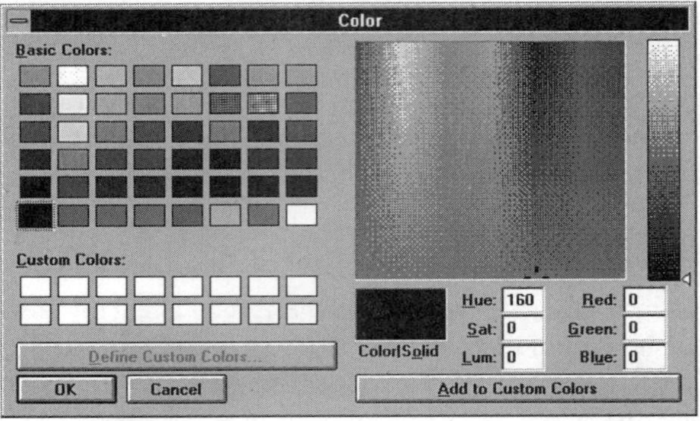

FIGURE A.21.
The Color dialog box.

The Color dialog box shows the current color, the basic colors, and any custom colors that have been defined. In addition, the current color may be modified and saved as a custom color.

Arrange Menu

The Arrange menu appears on the editor menus in the designers. It supports the layering, aligning, sizing, and grouping of objects in the layout. The Arrange menu contains the following items:

Bring to Front
Send to Back

Move Forward
Move Backward
Align Objects…
Repeat Alignment
Size Objects…
Repeat Sizing
Group
Ungroup
Group Operations

Arrange, Bring to Front

The Arrange, Bring to Front menu item moves the selected item or items to the top level in the layout. It is only necessary to arrange items to front and back when they are overlapping.

Arrange, Send to Back

The Arrange, Send to Back menu item moves the selected item or items to the bottom level in the layout.

Arrange, Move Forward

The Arrange, Move Forward menu item moves the selected item or items up one level in the layout.

Arrange, Move Backward

The Arrange, Move Backward menu item moves the selected item or items down one level in the layout.

Arrange, Align Objects…

The Arrange, Align Objects… menu item invokes the Alignment Settings dialog box, as shown in Figure A.22.

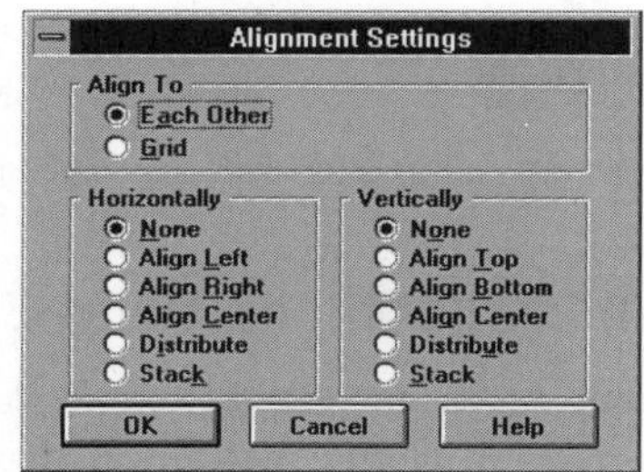

FIGURE A.22.
The Alignment Settings dialog box.

The Alignment Settings dialog box enables the selected items to be aligned to each other or to the grid. The dialog box also provides horizontal and vertical options for alignment of the items.

Arrange, Repeat Alignment

The Arrange, Repeat Alignment menu item applies the same alignment method to the currently selected items as was performed on the previous set.

Arrange, Size Objects...

The Arrange, Size Objects… menu item invokes the Size Objects dialog box as shown in Figure A.23.

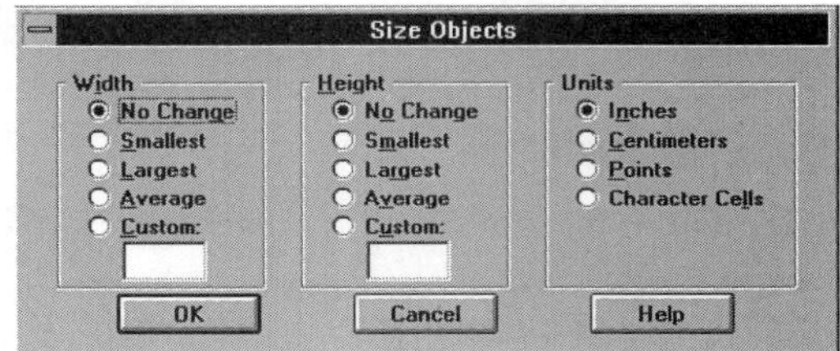

FIGURE A.23.
The Size Objects dialog box.

The Size Objects dialog box enables the selected items to be sized to each other. The items may be adjusted using width and height options. The dialog box also enables you to change the coordinate system.

Arrange, Repeat Sizing

The Arrange, Repeat Sizing menu item applies the same sizing method to the currently selected items as was applied to the previous set.

Arrange, Group

The Arrange, Group menu item combines the currently selected items into one selectable group. When items are grouped, they can be moved, sized, copied, or selected in a single action.

Arrange, Ungroup

The Arrange, Ungroup menu item removes the currently selected items from the group.

Arrange, Group Operations Menu

The Arrange, Group Operations menu enables you to manage the items in a group. The Arrange, Group Operations menu contains the following items:

Select Parent
Select Children
Add to Group
Remove from Group

Arrange, Group Operations, Select Parent

The Arrange, Group Operations, Select Parent menu item selects the single object group that includes each of the individual items.

Arrange, Group Operations, Select Children

The Arrange, Group Operations, Select Children menu item selects each of the individual items that are contained within the current parent group.

Arrange, Group Operations, Add to Group

The Arrange, Group Operations, Add to Group menu item adds the currently selected individual item or items to the group that is also selected.

Arrange, Group Operations, Remove from Group

The Arrange, Group Operations, Remove from Group menu item deletes the currently selected individual item or items from the parent group.

Window Menu

The Window menu appears on each of the main menus in the designers and is the standard MS Windows Window menu. The organization and selection of open windows is supported from this menu. The Window menu contains the following items:

Cascade
Tile
Arrange Icons
1. Object Navigator

Window, Cascade

The Window, Cascade menu item arranges the open windows in the Designer in a cascading style, on top of each other.

Window, Tile

The Window, Tile menu item arranges the open windows in the Designer in a tile fashion, next to each other, without covering any of the windows.

Window, Arrange Icons

The Window, Arrange Icons menu item organizes the minimized windows in the lower-left corner of the designer.

Window, 1. Object Navigator

The Window, 1. Object Navigator menu item is always present and is followed by a list of all of the other open windows.

Help Menu

The Help menu appears on each of the main menus in the designers, and provides access to the Microsoft Help facility, module info, and product version information. The Help menu contains the following items:

Contents
Module Info…
About…

Help, Contents

The Help, Contents menu item invokes the Microsoft Help facility. All of the Oracle products reference information is available from the Microsoft Help facility.

Help, Module Info...

The Help, Module Info… menu item displays information about the creation and modification of the current module in a dialog box.

Help, About...

The Help, About… menu item displays information about the current Designer tool and information about supporting products with version numbers.

B

Oracle Forms Designer Menus

The Oracle Forms menus are listed here as they appear in the Designer. All of the Designer menu items are listed and the items unique to Oracle Forms are described.

Object Navigator Menu

The Object Navigator menu contains the following items:

File
Edit
Tools
Navigator
Window
Help

Layout Menu

The Layout menu contains the following items:

File
Edit
Tools
View
Format
Arrange
Window
Help

The Properties and PL/SQL Editor Menus

The Properties and PL/SQL Editor menus contain the following items:

File
Edit
Tools
Window
Help

Menu Editor Menu

The Menu Editor menu contains the following items:

File

Edit
Tools
Menu
Window
Help

File Menu

The File menu contains the following items:

New
Open…
Close
Save
Save As…
Revert
Run
Compile…
Compile All…
Connect…
Disconnect
Administration
Print…
Print Setup…
Exit

File, New Menu

The File, New menu supports the creation of new form, menu, and library modules. The creation of these modules from the menu is identical to creating them from within the Object Navigator. The File, New menu contains the following menu items:

Form
Menu
Library

File, New, Form

The File, New, Form menu item creates a new form module.

File, New, Menu

The File, New, Form menu item creates a new menu module.

File, New, Library

The File, New, Library menu item creates a new library.

File, Administration Menu

The File, Administration menu supports the access, documentation, generation, conversion, and source control of modules in the Designer. The File, Administration menu contains the following items:

Module Access…
Database Roles…
Delete…
Rename…
Forms Doc…
Generate
Convert…
Check-In
Check-Out
Source Control Options

File, Administration, Module Access…

The File, Administration, Module Access… menu item invokes the Grant Module dialog box (as shown in Figure B.1) to enable the granting or revoking of access to forms modules for Oracle developers.

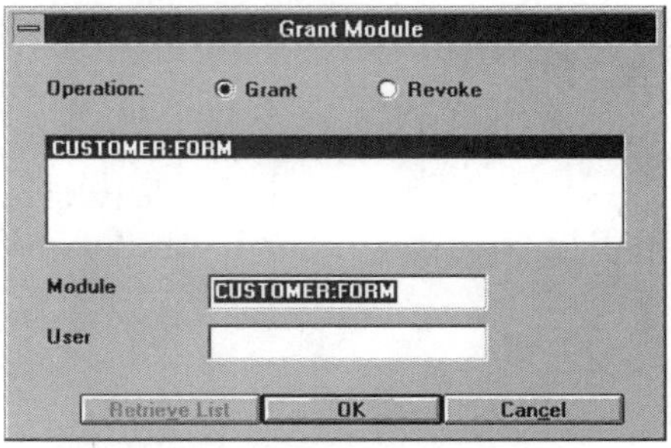

FIGURE B.1.
The Grant Module dialog box.

The modules that have been saved to the database can be listed for selection by pressing the Retrieve List button. The module name is followed by a colon and the module type in the list.

File, Administration, Database Roles…

The File, Administration, Database Roles… menu item invokes the Role List dialog box (as shown in Figure B.2) to enable the creation, modification, or deletion of roles in the Oracle database.

FIGURE B.2.
The Role List dialog box.

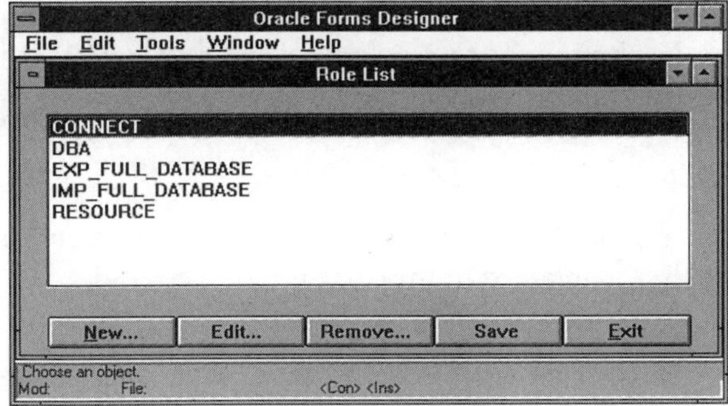

The list of roles for the current user is automatically presented in the Role List dialog box.

File, Administration, Delete...

The File, Administration, Delete… menu item invokes the Delete from Database dialog box (as shown in Figure B.3), which enables you to delete modules that have been saved to the Oracle database.

FIGURE B.3.
The Delete from Database dialog box.

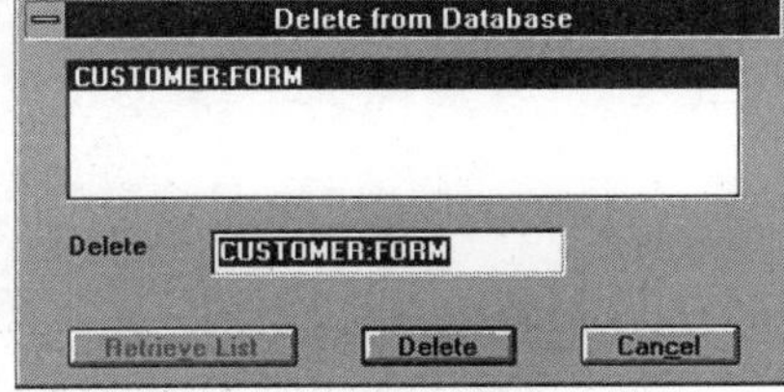

The modules that have been saved to the database can be listed for selection by pressing the Retrieve List button.

File, Administration, Rename...

The File, Administration, Rename… menu item invokes the Rename in Database dialog box, which enables you to give different names to modules that have been saved to the Oracle database. (See Figure B.4.)

FIGURE B.4.
The Rename in Database dialog box.

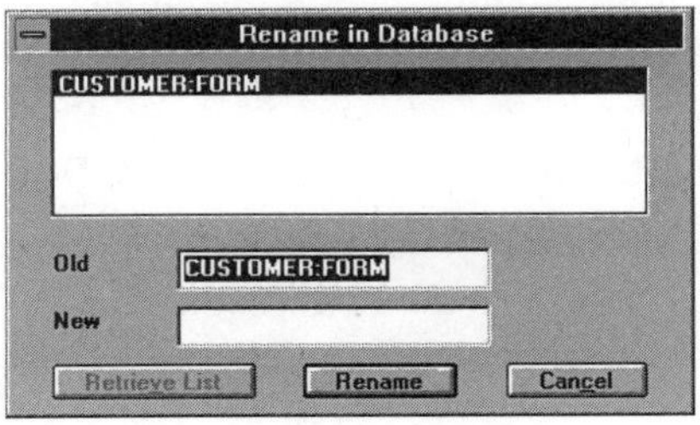

The modules that have been saved to the database can be listed for selection by pressing the Retrieve List button. The module that is selected appears in the Old field and the new name is entered in the New field.

File, Administration, Forms Doc...

The File, Administration, Forms Doc… menu item creates an ASCII text file documenting all of the objects contained in the current module.

File, Administration, Generate

The File, Administration, Generate menu item creates an executable file for the current module. The file type is FMX for forms, MMX for menus, and PLL for libraries.

File, Administration, Convert...

The File, Administration, Convert… menu item invokes the Convert dialog box, which allows form, menu, or library modules to be converted from binary format to an ASCII text file. (See Figure B.5.)

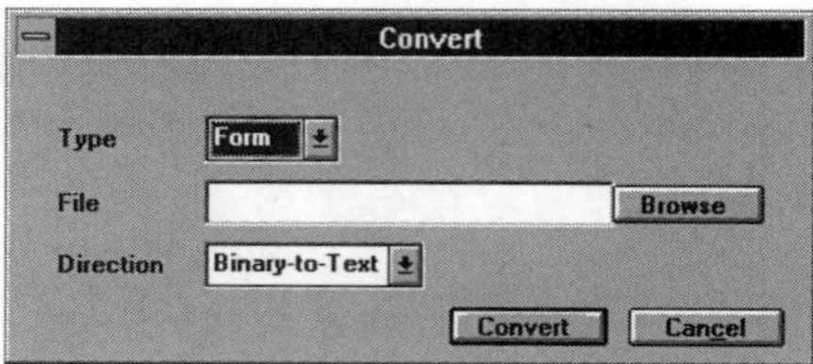

FIGURE B.5.
The Convert dialog box.

The module to be converted can be listed for selection by selecting a type from the Type drop-down list and pressing the Browse button.

File, Administration, Check-In

The File, Administration, Check-In menu item enables you to place a form, menu, or library into a PVCS (Polytron Version Control System) source archive.

File, Administration, Check-Out

The File, Administration, Check-Out menu item enables you to retrieve a form, menu, or library file from a PVCS source archive.

File, Administration, Source Control Options

The File, Administration, Source Control Options menu item enables you to change the options associated with using the PVCS source control features. To use any of the source-control options, you must have Intersolv's Polytron Version Control System installed.

Edit Menu

The Edit menu appears on each of the main menus in the Forms Designer. It supports tasks such as editing, searching, importing, and exporting. The Edit menu contains the following items:

Undo
Cut
Copy
Paste
Clear
Duplicate
Select All
Search/Replace...
Search/Replace PL/SQL...
Import
Export
Copy Properties
Paste Properties
Editor

Edit, Search/Replace PL/SQL...

The Edit, Search/Replace PL/SQL... menu item invokes the Search/Replace All Program Units dialog box to you to search for text strings in all of the triggers and program units in the current module. You can search for text by using the Search Button, or you can search and replace with other text by using the Replace or Replace All Buttons.

Edit, Copy Properties

The Edit, Copy Properties menu item places a copy of the currently highlighted item's properties on the Clipboard. Item properties are copied via Copy Properties and Paste Properties actions. Item properties may also be copied using the Object Navigator or the Layout Editor toolbars.

Edit, Paste Properties

The Edit, Paste Properties menu item inserts a copy of the contents of the Clipboard into the currently highlighted item's properties. Item properties may also be pasted using the Object Navigator or Layout Editor toolbars.

Edit, Editor

The Edit, Editor menu item invokes the built-in editor for Oracle Forms Designer. Only multi-line text items may be edited in the Designer.

Tools Menu

The Tools menu appears on each of the main menus in the Designer and supports tasks such as navigating to the different Designer windows, creating new blocks, reviewing tables and columns, and setting options. The Tools menu contains the following items:

Properties…
Layout Editor…
Menu Editor…
PL/SQL Editor…
Object Navigator…
New Block…
Tables/Columns…
Debug Mode
Options…

Tools, Layout Editor…

A forms module must first be created before the Tools, Layout Editor… menu item is enabled. Selecting the Layout Editor when no canvas-view exists automatically creates a canvas-view. The Tools, Layout Editor… menu item opens, or sets the focus to the Layout Editor. Figure B.6 shows the Layout Editor maximized in the Oracle Forms Designer window.

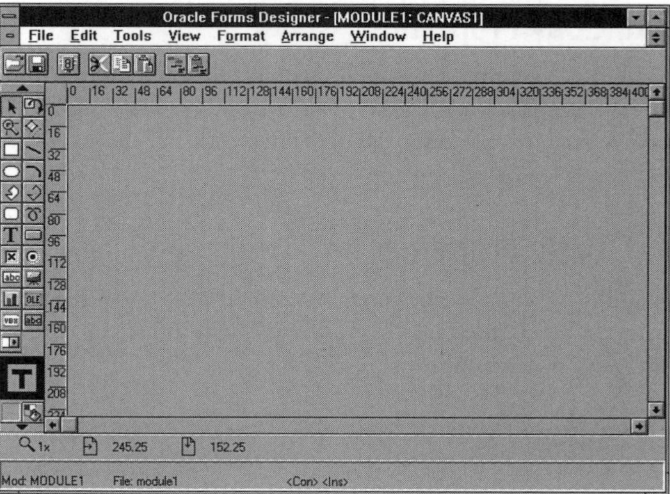

FIGURE B.6.
The Layout Editor.

The Tools, Layout Editor… menu item can be selected from the Tools menu or from the pop-up menu in the Object Navigator, or Layout Editor by right-clicking.

Tools, Menu Editor…

The Tools, Menu Editor… menu item opens, or sets the focus to the Menu Editor. Figure B.7 shows the Menu Editor with the Object Navigator.

FIGURE B.7.
The Menu Editor.

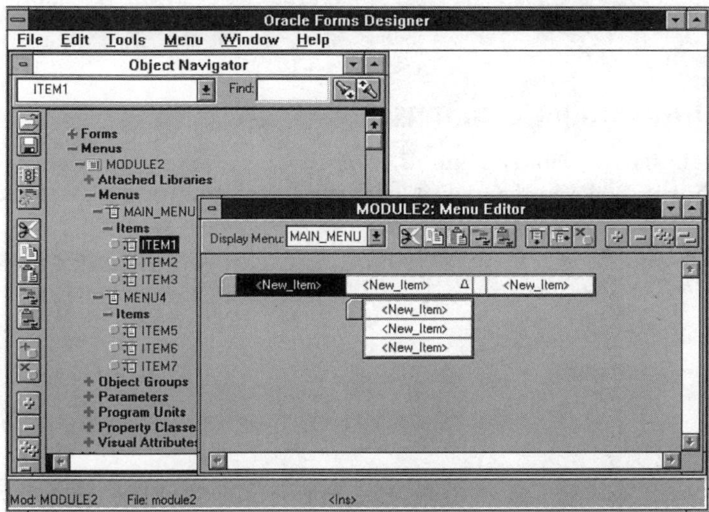

A menu module must first be created before the Tools, Menu Editor… menu item is enabled. The Tools, Menu Editor… menu item can be selected from the pop-up menu in the Object Navigator by right-clicking on Layout Editor. Notice the pop-up menu selection for the Menu Editor is Layout Editor.

Tools, Object Navigator…

The Tools, Object Navigator… menu item sets the focus to the Object Navigator. The Object Navigator window cannot be closed in the designer.

Tools, New Block…

The Tools, New Block… menu item invokes the New Block Options dialog box. Figure B.8 shows the New Block Options dialog box creating a block with emp as the base table.

The New Block Options dialog box is a tab-controlled dialog box that provides options for items, layout, and master/detail relationships.

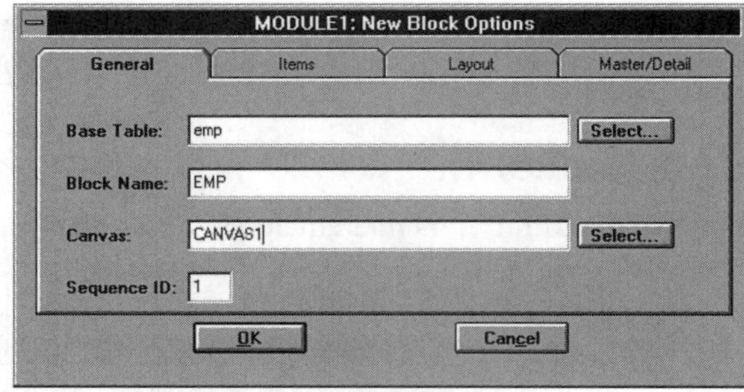

FIGURE B.8.
The New Block Options dialog box.

Tools, Table/Columns...

The Tools, Tables/Columns... menu item invokes the Tables dialog box. The Tables dialog box is shown in Figure B.9, selecting the current users tables to be displayed.

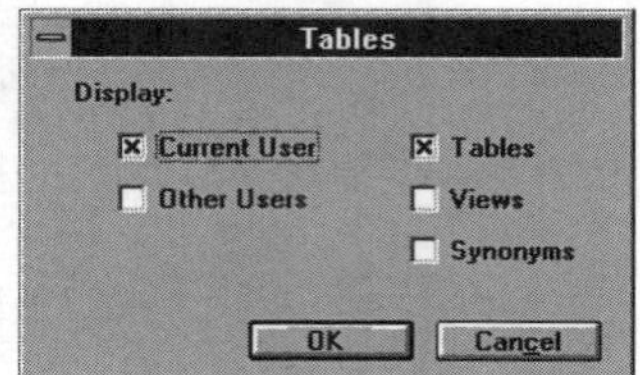

FIGURE B.9.
The Tables dialog box.

Once the user and type are selected from the Tables dialog box, the Tables/Columns dialog box is presented. The Tables/Columns dialog box is shown in Figure B.10, with the EMP table and all columns selected.

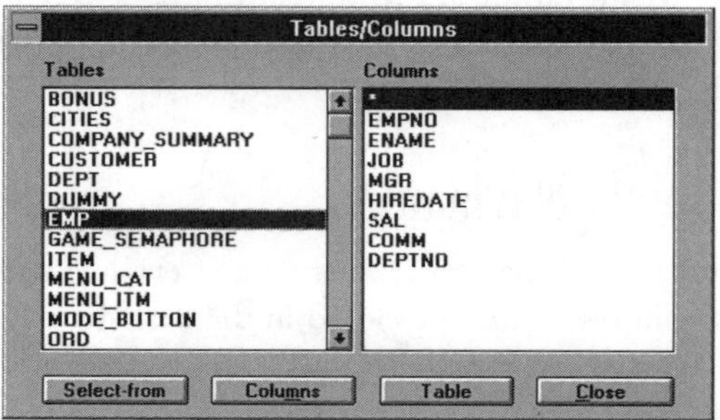

FIGURE B.10.
The Tables/Columns dialog box.

A SQL select statement can be created and returned to the PL/SQL Editor by pressing the Select-from button. The Columns and Table buttons return the selected column and table names.

Tools, Debug Mode

The Tools, Debug Mode menu item indicates whether the form will be run in debug mode. The Debug Mode menu type is check, meaning that a check mark is shown to indicate if it is selected. The Debug Mode menu item on the Tools menu provides the same function as it does on the Object Navigator toolbar. When Debug Mode is disabled, the button on the toolbar is grayed out.

Tools, Options...

The Tools, Options... menu item invokes the Options dialog box. The Options dialog box is a tab-controlled dialog box that allows the review and modification of Designer and Runtime options. Figure B.11 shows the Options dialog box with the Designer Options tab.

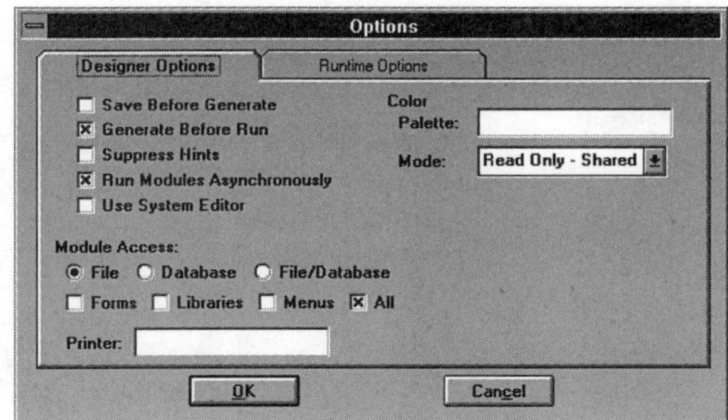

FIGURE B.11.
The Options dialog box with Designer Options.

The Designer Options include instructions to the Designer that can combine selections for you and streamline the development process. Figure B.12 shows the Options dialog box with the Runtime Options.

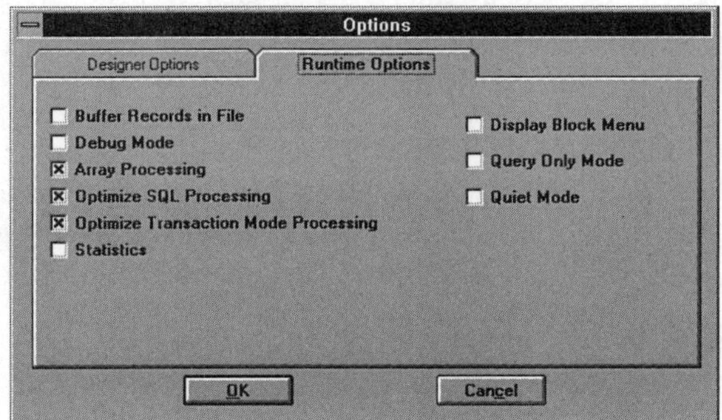

FIGURE B.12.
The Options dialog box with Runtime Options.

Notice that the Runtime Options also include a check box for debug mode.

Navigator Menu

The Navigator menu only appears on the Object Navigator menu in Oracle Forms Designer. It supports the changing of views, as well as the creation, deletion, compiling, marking, and pasting of objects. The Navigator menu contains the following items:

Ownership View
Visual View
Create
Delete
Compile Selection
Expand
Collapse
Expand All
Collapse All
Mark
Goto Mark
Synchronize
Only Objects with PL/SQL
Paste Name
Paste Arguments

Navigator, Ownership View

The Navigator, Ownership View menu item allows all of the objects in the Object Navigator to be displayed. The objects are arranged in a hierarchy showing which objects belong to each other. The Ownership View menu type is radio, and the other item in the radio group is Visual View. The objects in the Navigator are either shown in Ownership View or Visual view.

Navigator, Visual View

The Navigator, Visual View menu item allows only the visual objects in the Object Navigator to be displayed. The objects displayed are only those that the user will see. The Visual View menu item is the second item in the Navigator View radio group.

Navigator, Synchronize

The Navigator, Synchronize menu item turns on and off the synchronization between the Object Navigator and the Properties window. The Synchronize menu type is check, meaning that a check mark is shown to indicate whether it has been selected.

Navigator, Only Objects with PL/SQL

The Navigator, Only Objects with PL/SQL menu item toggles the display in the Object Navigator between just the PL/SQL objects and all objects. The Only Objects with PL/SQL menu type is check, meaning that a check mark is shown to indicate if it has been selected. The PL/SQL objects displayed are triggers, libraries, and program units.

View Menu

The View menu only appears on the Layout menu in Oracle Forms Designer. It enables you to change the visual aspects of the Layout Editor. The View menu contains the following items:

Zoom In
Zoom Out
Normal Size
Fit to Window
Rulers
Ruler Guides
Grid
Grid Snap
Page Breaks
Tool Palette
Status Bar
Settings
Show View
Show Canvas
Stacked Views...

View, Settings Menu

The View, Settings menu enables you to adjust the settings for the layout, ruler, and grid spacing. The View, Settings menu contains the following items:

Layout...
Ruler...

View, Settings, Layout...

The View, Settings, Layout... menu item invokes the Layout Settings dialog box, which enables you to adjust the horizontal and vertical settings. (See Figure B.13.)

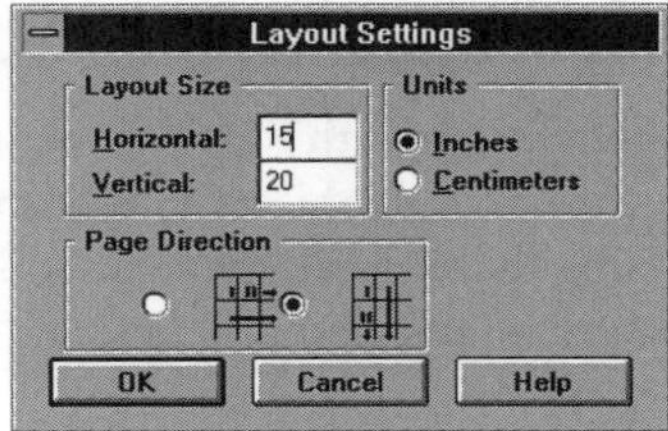

FIGURE B.13.
The Layout Settings dialog box.

The height and width are set here, as are the coordinate system and the page print direction.

View, Settings, Ruler...

The View, Settings, Ruler... menu item invokes the Ruler Settings dialog box and enables the adjustment of the coordinate system and grid spacing. (See Figure B.14.)

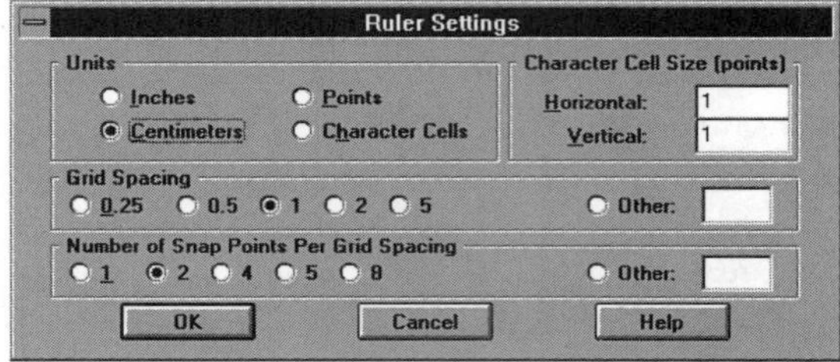

FIGURE B.14.
The Ruler Settings dialog box.

View, Show View

The View, Show View menu item is a check-style menu item that turns the display of the view area in the Layout Editor on and off. The view appears as a rectangular line in the layout. You can change the view size and location in the layout by clicking and dragging the handles of the view.

View, Show Canvas

The View, Show Canvas menu item is a check-style menu item that turns the display of the canvas area in the Layout Editor on and off. The canvas appears as a gray rectangular area in the layout. The size can be changed in the layout by clicking and dragging the handles of the canvas. For content canvases the location is fixed, but stacked canvases can be moved in the layout by clicking and dragging the edge of the canvas.

View, Stacked Views...

The View, Stacked Views... menu item invokes the Stacked Canvas-Views dialog box, which enables you to select a stacked canvas to be displayed in the Layout Editor. (See Figure B.15.)

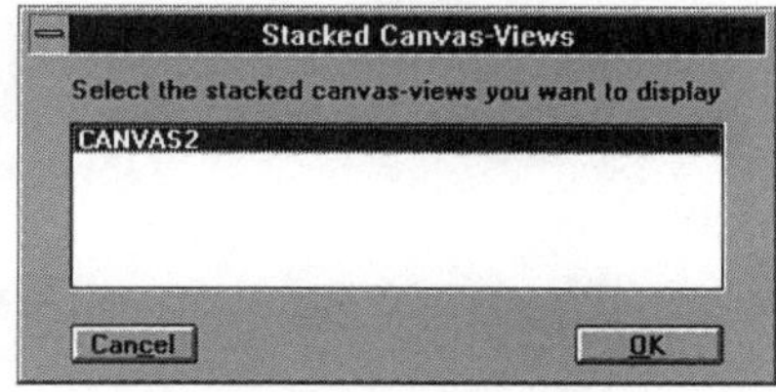

FIGURE B.15.
The Stacked Canvas-Views dialog box.

Format Menu

The Format menu only appears on the Layout menu in Oracle Forms Designer. it enables you to change the visual aspects of the objects within the layout. The Format menu contains the following items:

Font...
Spacing
Alignment
Line
Dash
Bevel
Arrow
Reduce Resolution
Drawing Options
Color Palette...

Format, Reduce Resolution

The Format, Reduce Resolution menu item lowers the quality of image resolution for the item selected. Only image items will be affected by this action.

Arrange Menu

The Arrange menu only appears on the Layout menu in Oracle Forms Designer. It supports the layering, aligning, sizing, and grouping of objects in the Layout Editor. The Arrange menu contains the following items:

Bring to Front
Send to Back
Move Forward
Move Backward
Align Objects...
Repeat Alignment
Size Objects...

Repeat Sizing
Group
Ungroup
Group Operations
Set Block
Switch

Arrange, Set Block...

The Arrange, Set Block... menu item invokes the Blocks dialog box. (See Figure B.16.)

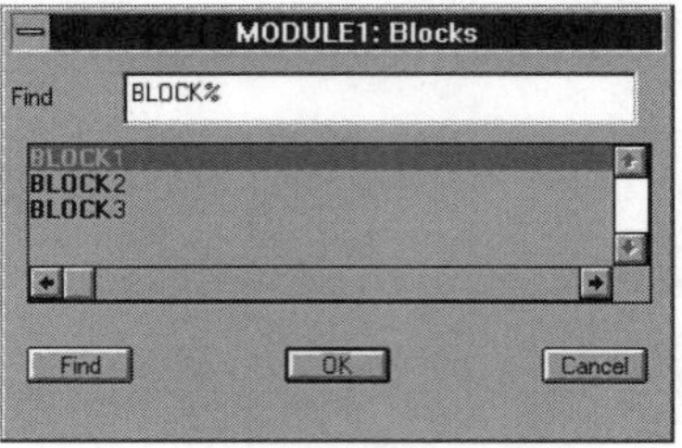

FIGURE B.16.
The Blocks dialog box.

The Blocks dialog box provides a list of the blocks in the current form module. The dialog box includes a Find field to help select the block to switch to. The selection of an item from the list sets the current block to that item.

Arrange, Switch...

The Arrange, Switch... menu item invokes the Canvas-Views dialog box. (See Figure B.17.)

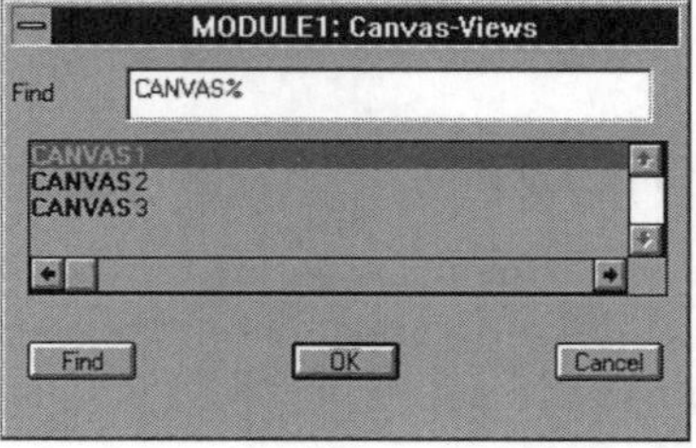

FIGURE B.17.
The Canvas-Views dialog box.

The Canvas-Views dialog box provides a list of the canvas-views in the current form module. The dialog box includes a Find field to help select the canvas-view to switch to. The selection of an item from the list sets the current canvas-view to that item.

The Menu Menu

The Menu menu only appears on the Menu Editor menu in Oracle Forms Designer. It supports the development of menu modules. The Menu menu contains the following items:

Create Down
Create Right
Delete
Expand
Collapse
Expand All
Collapse All
Next Instance
Switch Orientation

Menu, Create Down

The Menu, Create Down menu item adds a new menu item to the menu, directly under the current menu item. The selection of the Menu, Create Down menu item from the menu is identical to selecting Create Down from the Menu Editor toolbar.

Menu, Create Right

The Menu, Create Right menu item adds a new menu item to the menu, immediately to the right of the current menu item. The Create Right menu item provides the same function as selecting Create Right from the Menu Editor toolbar.

Menu, Delete

The Menu, Delete menu item deletes the item or items selected. The selection of the Menu, Delete menu item from the menu is identical to selecting Delete from the Object Navigator toolbar; however, only one item may be deleted at a time by selecting Delete from the Menu Editor toolbar.

Menu, Expand

The Menu, Expand menu item expands the current branch of the menu hierarchy by one level. The selection of the Menu, Expand menu item provides the same function as selecting Expand from the Menu Editor toolbar.

Menu, Collapse

The Menu, Collapse menu item collapses the current branch of the menu hierarchy by one level. The selection of the Menu, Collapse menu item from the menu is identical to selecting Collapse from the Menu Editor toolbar.

Menu, Expand All

The Menu, Expand All menu item expands the current branch of the menu hierarchy from the item selected downward. The Expand All menu item provides the same function as selecting Expand All from the Menu Editor toolbar.

Menu, Collapse All

The Menu, Collapse All menu item collapses the current branch of the menu hierarchy from the item selected downward. The selection of the Menu, Collapse All menu item from the menu is identical to selecting Collapse All from the Menu Editor toolbar.

Menu, Next Instance

The Menu, Next Instance menu item is used to when a menu is copied within the same menu module. To select the menu that is a copy, use the Menu, Next Instance menu item.

Menu, Switch Orientation

The Menu, Switch Orientation menu item changes the view of the menu in the Menu Editor from horizontal to vertical, or from vertical to horizontal.

Help Menu

The Help menu appears on each of the main menus in Oracle Forms Designer and provides access to the Microsoft Help facility, the keyboard mapping, and Oracle Forms reference information. The Help menu contains the following items:

Contents
Keyboard Help
Module Info…
About Oracle Forms…

Help, Keyboard Help

The Help, Keyboard Help menu item displays the keyboard mapping for Oracle Forms.

C

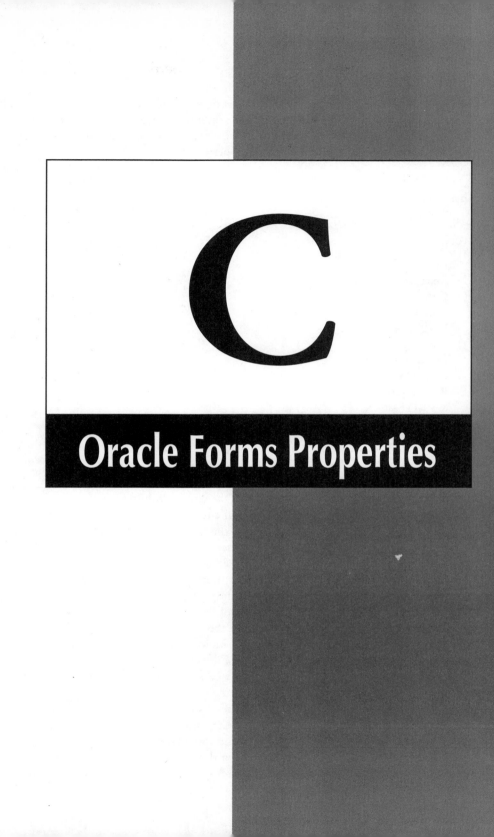

Oracle Forms Properties

The Oracle Forms properties are listed by object type, as found in the Object Navigator. Each property is listed showing the property name, a brief description of the property, and the default and optional values for the property. The properties are grouped by topic for each object type. The topics appear in bold text in the property-name column.

The properties for the following object types are described:

Form module
Trigger
Alert
Block
Item
Relation
Canvas-view
Editor
LOV
Object group
Parameter
Property class
Record group
Visual attribute
Window

The Display topic often includes the following visual attribute properties:

Display	*Description/Property Values*
Visual Attribute Name	Name of the visual attribute/ Default or custom
Font Name	Name of the font/ NULL uses system default or a font from the list
Font Size	Size of the font, in points/ 10 or any number
Font Style	Style of the font/ Plain or a font style in the drop-down list
Font Width	Width of the font/ Normal or a font width in the drop-down list
Font Weight	Weight of the font/ Medium or a font weight in the drop-down list
Foreground Color	Color of the font/ NULL uses system default or a color from the list
Background Color	Color of the background/ NULL uses system default or a color from the list
Fill Pattern	Pattern for the background/ NULL uses system default or a pattern from the list

Charmode Logical Attribute	Name of Oracle Terminal attribute/ NULL for use in character mode
White on Black	For use on monochrome displays/ False or true

These properties are described here, and later they are only referenced in the list of properties for the object type.

The Miscellaneous topic often includes the following properties:

Miscellaneous	*Description/Property Values*
Comment	For internal documentation/ Default to blank
Reference Information	Used for referenced objects/ NULL; or source module, type, and source object

Again, these properties are described here, and later only referenced.

Form Module Properties

Property Name	*Description/Property Values*
Name	A unique name for the form module/ MODULE1, assigned by default, should be changed
Class	A reference to a property class/ NULL or a property class from the drop-down list

Display	*Description/Property Values*
Coordinate Information	Defines the coordinate system/ Real or character, via Coordinate Info dialog box
Title	Title of the form module/ NULL; may be set by developer
Current Record Attribute	Visual attribute for the current row/ NULL or as defined by the developer
Horiz. MDI Toolbar	Name of the horizontal toolbar canvas-view/ NULL or a toolbar from the drop-down list
Vert. MDI Toolbar	Name of the vertical toolbar canvas-view/ NULL or a toolbar from the drop-down list
Use 3D Controls	Applies 3-D look/ True or false

Functional	*Description/Property Values*
Cursor Mode	Cursor status after a commit/ Open or close
Savepoint Mode	Create savepoints for rolling back transactions/ True or false
Mouse Navigation Limit	Determines scope of mouse use/ Form, block, record, or item
Validation Unit	Specifies when form validates an item/ Default is item; form, block, record, or item
First Navigation Block	Specifies where the cursor appears first/ NULL defaults to the first block; or a block from the drop-down list
Console Window	Name of the window to place the status line on/ WINDOW0 or a window from the drop-down list

Menu	*Description/Property Values*
Menu Module	Name of menu/ DEFAULT, assigned, or NULL
Menu Style	Style of menu to display/ Pull-down, bar, or full-screen
Use File	Specifies use of a .MMX file/ True or false
Starting Menu	Name of the top level of the menu/ NULL; defaults to the main menu
Menu Role	For backward compatibility/ Do not use

Miscellaneous
Comment

Trigger Properties

Property Name	*Description/Property Values*
Name	A unique name for the trigger/ No default; must be assigned
Class	A reference to a property class/ NULL or a property class from the drop-down list

Functional	*Description/Property Values*
Trigger Text	PL/SQL associated with the trigger/ No default; required, via PL/SQL Editor
Trigger Type	The type of trigger/ Built-in or user-named
Trigger Style	The style of the trigger/ PL/SQL or V2 (V2 for backward compatibility)
Fire in Enter Query Mode	Fire during enter query mode/ True or false
Show Keys	For key triggers, list in help keys/ False or true
Show Keys Description	A hint for the hot key/ Blank by default
Execution Style	Determines when the trigger will fire/ Override, before, or after

Miscellaneous
Comment
Reference Information

Alert Properties

Property Name	*Description/Property Values*
Name	A unique name for the alert/ ALERT1, assigned by default, should be changed
Class	A reference to a property class/ NULL or a property class from the drop-down list

Display	*Description/Property Values*
Title	Title of the alert/ NULL; may be set by developer
Visual Attribute Name	
Font Name	
Font Size	
Font Style	
Font Width	
Font Weight	
Foreground Color	
Background Color	

continues

Display	*Description/Property Values*
Fill Pattern	
Charmode Logical Attribute	
White on Black	

Functional	*Description/Property Values*
Alert Style	Style of alert/ Warning, caution, or informational
Button 1	Label for the button/ OK or any text
Button 2	Label for the button/ Cancel or any text
Button 3	Label for the button/ NULL or any text
Default Alert Button	The button selected by default/ Button 1 or any button
Message	Message text for the alert/ NULL or any text

Miscellaneous	
Comment	
Reference Information	

Block Properties

Property Name	*Description/Property Values*
Name	A unique name for the block/ BLOCK1, assigned by default, should be changed
Class	A reference to a property class/ NULL or a property class from the drop-down list

Display	*Description/Property Values*
Scroll Bar	Indicates that the block has a scroll bar/ False or true
Scroll Bar Canvas	Name of the canvas the scroll bar will appear on/ NULL or any canvas in the drop-down list
Scroll Bar Orientation	The direction for the scroll bar/ Vertical or horizontal
Scroll Bar X Position	X coordinate of the scroll bar/ 0 or any number

Scroll Bar Y Position	Y coordinate of the scroll bar/ 0 or any number
Scroll Bar Width	The width of the scroll bar/ Default width or any number
Scroll Bar Height	The height of the scroll bar/ Default height or any number
Reverse Direction	Specifies whether the block will scroll in reverse/ False or true
Visual Attribute Name Font Name Font Size Font Style Font Width Font Weight Foreground Color Background Color Fill Pattern Charmode Logical Attribute White on Black	
Current Record Attribute	Visual Attribute for the current row/ NULL or as defined by the developer

Records	*Description/Property Values*
Records Displayed	Number of records displayed in the block/ 1; can be set by the developer
Record Orientation	Determines direction of a multi-record block/ Vertical or horizontal

Navigation	*Description/Property Values*
Navigation Style	How a next or previous item is processed/ Same record, change record, or change block
Next Navigation Block	Name of the next block to go to/ Name of the next block in the Object Navigator
Previous Navigation Block	Name of the previous block to go to/ Name of the previous block in the Object Navigator

Database	*Description/Property Values*
Base Table	Name of a table or view/ NULL or any table or view

continues

Database	*Description/Property Values*
Primary Key	Determines if block must contain unique key/ False or true
Column Security	Specifies whether Runform should check the database column security/ False or true
Delete Allowed	Specifies whether Runform should allow deletes/ True or false
Insert Allowed	Specifies whether Runform should allow inserts/ True or false
Query Allowed	Specifies whether Runform should allow queries/ True or false
WHERE Clause	A default WHERE clause/ NULL or as defined by the developer
ORDER BY Clause	A default ORDER BY clause/ NULL or as defined by the developer
Optimizer Hint	A hint to be passed to the database/ NULL or as defined by the developer
Records Buffered	Specifies the number of records read into memory/ NULL or as defined by the developer
Records Fetched	The number of records fetched from the database/ Records displayed or any number greater
Update Allowed	Specifies whether Runform should allow updates/ True or False
Update Changed Columns	Include only changed columns in update SQL/ False or True
Key Mode	For use with non-Oracle databases/ Unique, updateable, or non-updateable
Locking Mode	Specifies when the database should lock the row/ Immediate or Delayed
Transactional Triggers	For use with non-Oracle databases/ False or true

Miscellaneous	*Description/Property Values*
In Menu	Show this block in the block menu/ True or false
Block Description	A description of the block/ NULL or as defined by the developer
Comment	
Reference Information	

Item Properties

Property Name	*Description/Property Values*
Name	A unique name for the item/ ITEM1, assigned by default, should be changed
Class	A reference to a property class/ NULL or a property class from the drop-down list

Type	*Description/Property Values*
Item Type	Type of item/ Text item or an item from the drop-down list

Display	*Description/Property Values*
Canvas	Name of the canvas the item will appear on/ NULL or any canvas in the drop-down list
Displayed	Specifies whether this item should be displayed by default/ True or false
X Position	The X coordinate of the item on the canvas/ 0 or any number
Y Position	The Y coordinate of the item on the canvas/ 0 or any number
Width	The width of the item/ 10 * character cell width, or any number
Height	The height of the item/ Character cell height or any number
Space Between Records	Space between rows in a multi-row block/ 0 or any number
Bevel	Describes 3-D appearance/ Lowered, raised, or none
Rendered	Screen management of the display/ True or false
Visual Attribute Name	
Font Name	
Font Size	
Font Style	
Font Width	
Font Weight	
Foreground Color	
Background Color	
Fill Pattern	

continues

Display	*Description/Property Values*
Charmode Logical Attribute White on Black	
Current Record Attribute	Visual attribute for the current row/ NULL or as defined by the developer

Data	*Description/Property Values*
Mirror Item	Item name of any other item in the block to mirror/ NULL or any item from the drop-down list
Data Type	Specifies the type of values for the item/ Char or any type from the drop-down list
Maximum Length	Specifies maximum length of the value/ Database length or any number
Fixed Length	Specifies whether the maximum length is also the required length/ False or true
Required	Specifies whether a value is required/ False or true
Format Mask	Oracle format mask for display and validation/ NULL or any Oracle format mask
Range Low Value	Specifies a low value to validate against/ NULL, a constant, an item, a global, or a parameter
Range High Value	Specifies a high value to validate against/ NULL, a constant, an item, a global, or a parameter
Default Value	Specifies an initial value to use for a new row/ NULL, a constant, an item, a global, a parameter, or a sequence
Copy Value from Item	Specifies name of an item to copy value from/ NULL or the foreign key in a master-detail block

Records	*Description/Property Values*
Items Displayed	Number of items shown for a multi-row block/ 0 defaults to records displayed; or any number

Navigation	*Description/Property Values*
Enabled	Specifies whether the item is active/ True or false
Navigable	Specifies whether the user can focus on the item/ True or false
Next Navigation Item	Name of the next item to go to/ Name of the next item in the Object Navigator

Previous Navigation Item	Name of the previous item to go to/ Name of the previous item in the Object Navigator

Database	*Description/Property Values*
Base Table Item	Represents a column in the database/ True or false
Primary Key	Represents a primary key column in the database/ False or true
Insert Allowed	Specifies whether the user can change the value in a new row/ True or false
Query Allowed	Specifies whether the user can use this item in a query/ True or false
Query Length	The maximum length of the query value/ Maximum length or any number
Case Insensitive Query	Specifies whether the user can issue a case-insensitive query/ False or true
Update Allowed	Specifies whether the user can change the value in an existing row/ True or false
Update Only if Null	Specifies whether the user can change only a null/ False or true
Lock Record	Locks the row for non-base table items/ False or true

Functional (for Display Items)	*Description/Property Values*
Alignment	Forms automatically justifies/ Left, center, or right

Functional (for Button Items)	*Description/Property Values*
Access Key	A control key on the keyboard to select the button/ NULL or any key on the keyboard
Label	Label displayed for the button/ NULL or any text
Iconic	Specifies whether this is an iconic button/ False or true
Icon Name	Name of an icon/ NULL or any icon
Default Button	Specifies whether this is the default button/ False or true

Functional (for Radio Group Items)	*Description/Property Values*
Access Key	A control key on the keyboard to select the button/ NULL or any key on the keyboard
Other Values	The value to use for any other values/ Blank defaults to no other values allowed, or any value

Functional (for Radio Button Items)	*Description/Property Values*
Access Key	A control key on the keyboard to select the button/ NULL or any key on the keyboard
Label	Label displayed for the radio button/ NULL or any text
Value	The value for the radio button/ NULL or any text

Functional (for List Items)	*Description/Property Values*
Access Key	A control key on the keyboard to select the button/ NULL or any key on the keyboard
List Elements	The list of labels and values/ NULL or any text
List Style	The display style/ Poplist, tlist, or combo box
Other Values	The value to use for any other values/ Blank defaults to no other values allowed, or any value

Functional (for Check Box Items)	*Description/Property Values*
Access Key	A control key on the keyboard to select the button/ NULL or any key on the keyboard
Label	Label displayed for the check box/ NULL or any text
Checked Value	The value for the check box when selected/ NULL or any text
Unchecked Value	The value for the check box when not selected/ NULL or any text
Check Box Other Values	The value to use for any other values/ Checked, unchecked, or not allowed

Functional (for Text Items)	*Description/Property Values*
Case Restriction	Forms automatically converts the case/ None, upper, or lower
Alignment	Forms automatically justifies/ Left, center, or right
Multi-Line	Is this a multi-line text item/ False or true
Wrap Style	How should the text item wrap/ Word, character, or none
Secure	Hide the text entered/ False or true
Keep Position	Return cursor to the location left from/ False or true
Auto Skip	Automatically move from last character to the next item/ False or true
Vertical Scroll Bar	Show a scroll bar on multi-line text items/ True or false

Functional (for Image Items)	*Description/Property Values*
Compression	Determines whether Forms automatically compresses the image/ True or false
Quality	Specifies the resource utilization for image quality/ High, medium, or low
Sizing Style	Specifies what to do with an image that does not fit/ Crop or adjust
Horizontal Scroll Bar	Shows a horizontal scroll bar/ False or true
Vertical Scroll Bar	Shows a vertical scroll bar/ False or true

Functional (for Custom Items)	*Description/Property Values*
Custom Item Type	Specifies the type of custom item/ OLE container, VBX control, or user area
OLE In-place Activation	Activates application within Oracle Forms/ False or true
OLE Activation Style	Specifies the action that will activate the application/ Double click, manual, or focus-in

continues

Functional (for Custom Items)	*Description/Property Values*
OLE Resize Style	Specifies the way the OLE item is sized for display/ Clip, scale, initial, or dynamic
OLE Tenant Types	Specifies which types of OLE objects can be in the container/ Any, none, static, linked, or embedded
Show OLE Popup Menu	Shows menu via right-mouse-click/ True or false
OLE Popup Menu Items	Specifies which menu items will appear on the menu/ NULL, or select display and enable from the list
Show OLE Tenant Type	Shows a border around the OLE item/ True or false
OLE Class	Specifies which OLE objects can be used in the container/ NULL defaults to any, or select from the list
OLE Do In Out	Allows more than one OLE object in the container/ True or false
OLE Tenant Aspect	Specifies how the OLE object appears in the container/ Content, icon, or thumbnail preview

Miscellaneous	*Description/Property Values*
LOV	List of values name/ NULL or any LOV from the drop-down list
LOV X Position	The X coordinate of the LOV on the canvas/ 0 defaults to X position of LOV, or any number
LOV Y Position	The Y coordinate of the LOV on the canvas/ 0 defaults to Y position of LOV, or any number
LOV For Validation	Should Runform use the LOV for validation/ False or true
Editor	Editor name/ Blank is default editor, or any editor from the drop-down list
Editor X Position	The X coordinate of the editor on the canvas/ 0 defaults to X position of editor, or any number
Editor Y Position	The Y coordinate of the editor on the canvas/ 0 defaults to Y position of editor; or any number
Hint	Hint text for display/ Enter value for: `<item>`, or as defined by the developer
Auto Hint	Should Runform show the hint/ False or true
Comment	

Relation Properties

Property Name	*Description/Property Values*
Name	A unique name for the relation/ RELATION1, assigned by default, should be changed
Class	A reference to a property class/ NULL or a property class from the drop-down list

Functional	*Description/Property Values*
Detail Block	Name of the detail block/ NULL or any block from the drop-down list
Join Condition	The relationship that joins the blocks/ NULL or any join condition
Master Deletes	How should master deletes relate to detail rows/ Non-isolated, isolated, or cascading
Prevent Masterless Operations	Is insert or query allowed from detail/ False or true

Coordination	*Description/Property Values*
Deferred	Defers the query of detail rows False or true/
Auto Query	Specifies whether Forms automatically queries detail/ False or true

Miscellaneous
Comment
Reference Information

Canvas-View Properties

Property Name	*Description/Property Values*
Name	A unique name for the canvas-view/ CANVAS1, assigned by default, should be changed
Class	A reference to a property class/ NULL or a property class from the drop-down list

Type	*Description/Property Values*
Canvas-view Type	Describes the type of canvas/ Content, stacked, vertical toolbar, or horizontal toolbar

Display	*Description/Property Values*
Displayed	Specifies whether the stacked canvas is initially displayed/ True or false
Width	The width of the canvas/ Default width or any number
Height	The height of the canvas/ Default height or any number
Bevel	Describes three-dimensional appearance/ Lowered, raised, or none
Visual Attribute Name	
Font Name	
Font Size	
Font Style	
Font Width	
Font Weight	
Foreground Color	
Background Color	
Fill Pattern	
Charmode Logical Attribute	
White on Black	

Functional	*Description/Property Values*
Window	The name of the window the canvas will be displayed in/ The first window in the Object Navigator; may be changed
Raise on Entry	Makes the canvas appear in front of other canvases/ False or true
X Position on Canvas	The X coordinate of the view on the canvas/ 0 or any number
Y Position on Canvas	The Y coordinate of the view on the canvas/ 0 or any number

Stacked View	*Description/Property Values*
View Width	The width of the view/ Default width or any number

View Height	The height of the view/ Default height or any number
Display X Position	The X coordinate of the stacked view/ 0 or any number
Display Y Position	The Y coordinate of the stacked view/ 0 or any number
View Horiz. Scroll Bar	The view contains a horizontal scroll bar/ False or true
View Vert. Scroll Bar	The view contains a vertical scroll bar/ False or true

Miscellaneous
Comment
Reference Information

Editor Properties

Property Name	*Description/Property Values*
Name	A unique name for the editor/ EDITOR1, assigned by default, should be changed
Class	A reference to a property class/ NULL or a property class from the drop-down list

Display	*Description/Property Values*
X Position	The X coordinate of the editor/ 0 or any number
Y Position	The Y coordinate of the editor/ 0 or any number
Width	The width of the editor/ Default width or any number
Height	The height of the editor/ Default height or any number
Title	The title to appear in the top of the editor window/ NULL or any text
Bottom Title	The title to appear in the bottom of the editor window/ NULL or any text
Visual Attribute Name	
Font Name	
Font Size	

continues

Display	*Description/Property Values*
Font Style	
Font Width	
Font Weight	
Foreground Color	
Background Color	
Fill Pattern	
Charmode Logical Attribute	
White on Black	

Functional	*Description/Property Values*
Wrap Style	Specifies how the editor performs word wrap/ Word, Character, or None
Horizontal Scroll Bar	Specifies whether the editor contains a horizontal scroll bar/ False or true
Vertical Scroll Bar	Specifies whether the editor contains a vertical scroll bar/ False or true

Miscellaneous
Comment
Reference Information

LOV Properties

Property Name	*Description/Property Values*
Name	A unique name for the list of values/ LOV1, assigned by default, should be changed
Class	A reference to a property class/ NULL or a property class from the drop-down list

Display	*Description/Property Values*
X Position	The X coordinate of the LOV/ 0 or any number
Y Position	The Y coordinate of the LOV/ 0 or any number
Width	The width of the LOV/ Default width or any number
Height	The height of the LOV/ Default height or any number

Title	The title to appear in the top of the LOV window/ NULL or any text

Visual Attribute Name
Font Name
Font Size
Font Style
Font Width
Font Weight
Foreground Color
Background Color
Fill Pattern
Charmode Logical Attribute
White on Black

Functional	*Description/Property Values*
LOV Type	Describes the type of LOV/ Record group or old
Record Group	The name of the record group that the LOV uses/ NULL or any record group in the drop-down list
Column Mapping	The columns that the LOV is mapped to/ The columns in the record group or any columns in query and form
Auto Confirm	Determines whether to select and return when list auto-reduces to one entry/ False or true
Auto Display	Determines whether to display the LOV when the user goes to the text item/ False or true
Auto Refresh	Determines whether to requery the database each time/ True or false
Long List	Determines whether to limit a long list of items with a where expression/ False or true
Auto Skip	Determines whether to go to the next item after selection from the LOV/ False or true

Miscellaneous

Comment
Reference Information

Object Group Properties

Property Name	*Description/Property Values*
Name	A unique name for the object group/ OBJECT_GROUP1, assigned by default, should be changed

Miscellaneous
Reference Information

Parameter Properties

Property Name	*Description/Property Values*
Name	A unique name for the parameter/ PARAMETER1, assigned by default, should be changed
Class	A reference to a property class/ NULL or a property class from the drop-down list

Data	*Description/Property Values*
Data Type	Specifies the type of values for the parameter/ Char or any type from the drop-down list
Maximum Length	Maximum length of the value/ 30 or as defined by the developer
Default Value	An initial value to use for a new row/ NULL or a constant

Miscellaneous
Comment
Reference Information

Property Class Properties

Property Name	*Description/Property Values*
Name	A unique name for the property class/ PROPERTY_CLASS1, assigned by default, should be changed
Class	A reference to a property class/ NULL or a property class from the drop-down list

Miscellaneous	
Reference Information	

Record Group Properties

Property Name	*Description/Property Values*
Name	A unique name for the record group/ PROPERTY_CLASS1, assigned by default, should be changed
Class	A reference to a property class/ NULL or a property class from the drop-down list

Functional	*Description/Property Values*
Record Group Type	Describes the type of record group/ Query or static
Record Group Query	The query that the record group uses/ NULL or any record group in the drop-down list
Column Specification	The columns that the record group uses/ The columns in the query or any column specification

Miscellaneous	
Comment	
Reference Information	

Visual Attribute Properties

Property Name	*Description/Property Values*
Name	A unique name for the visual attribute/ VISUAL_ATTRIBUTE1, assigned by default, should be changed
Class	A reference to a property class/ NULL or a property class from the drop-down list

Display	
Visual Attribute Name	
Font Name	
Font Size	
Font Style	

continues

Display
Font Width
Font Weight
Foreground Color
Background Color
Fill Pattern
Charmode Logical Attribute
White on Black

Miscellaneous
Reference Information

Window Properties

Property Name	*Description/Property Values*
Name	A unique name for the window/ WINDOW0, assigned by default, should be changed
Class	A reference to a property class/ NULL or a property class from the drop-down list

Display	*Description/Property Values*
X Position	The X coordinate of the window/ 0 or any number
Y Position	The Y coordinate of the window/ 0 or any number
Width	The width of the window/ Default width or any number
Height	The height of the window/ Default height or any number
Bevel	Describes three-dimensional appearance/ Lowered, raised, or none
Title	Title to appear in the top of the window/ NULL or any text
Visual Attribute Name	
Font Name	
Font Size	
Font Style	
Font Width	
Font Weight	

Foreground Color
Background Color
Fill Pattern
Charmode Logical Attribute
White on Black

Functional	*Description/Property Values*
View	Name of the primary content canvas/ NULL or any canvas-view in the drop-down list
Vertical Toolbar	Name of the vertical toolbar canvas/ NULL or any canvas-view in the drop-down list
Horizontal Toolbar	Name of the horizontal toolbar canvas/ NULL or any canvas-view in the drop-down list
Window Style	Describes the type of window/ Document or dialog box
Modal	Specifies that this window must be dismissed to continue/ False or true
Remove on Exit	Hides the document window when focus goes to another/ False or true
Icon Name	Name of an icon to show for the minimized window/ NULL or any icon
Icon Title	Title for the icon when the window is minimized/ NULL or any text
Horizontal Scroll Bar	Specifies whether the editor contains a horizontal scroll bar/ False or true
Vertical Scroll Bar	Specifies whether the editor contains a vertical scroll bar/ False or true

GUI Hints	*Description/Property Values*
Closeable	Specifies whether the window can be closed/ True or false
Fixed Size	Specifies whether the window is resizable/ False or true
Iconifiable	Specifies whether the window can be minimized/ True or false
Inherit Menu	Identifies a non-MS Windows property/ True or false
Moveable	Specifies whether the window can be moved/ True or false
Zoomable	Specifies whether the window is resizable via zoom/ True or false

Miscellaneous
Comment
Reference Information

Oracle Menu Properties

The Oracle Menu properties are listed by object type, as found in the Object Navigator. Each property is listed showing the property name, a brief description of the property, as well as the default and optional values for the property. The properties are grouped by topic for each object type. The topics appear in bold text in the property-name column.

The following Oracle Menu properties are described here:

Menu module
Menu
Menu item

Menu Module Properties

Property Name	*Description/Property Values*
Name	A unique name for the menu module/ MODULE1, assigned by default, should be changed
Class	A reference to a property class/ NULL or a property class from the drop-down list

Functional	*Description/Property Values*
Main Menu	The name of the menu to start with/ Blank; defaults to the first menu or a menu in the drop-down list
Startup Code	PL/SQL to execute when the menu is loaded/ NULL; may be set by developer via PL/SQL Editor

Security	*Description/Property Values*
Menu Module Roles	List of database roles with access to this menu/ NULL; may be set by developer from Menu Module Roles dialog box
Use Security	Should Oracle Forms enforce menu security/ False or true

Miscellaneous	*Description/Property Values*
Identification	Description of menu when in character mode/ Module name; may be set by developer
Directory	Directory location of .MMX file/ Blank; may be set by developer
File	Name of .MMX file/ Module name; may be set by developer
Comment	

Menu Properties

Property Name	*Description/Property Values*
Name	A unique name for the menu/ MAIN_MENU, assigned by default, should be changed
Class	A reference to a property class/ NULL or a property class from the drop-down list

Display	*Description/Property Values*
Title	Title, used for full-screen menus/ NULL or any text
Sub Title	Second title line, used for full-screen menus/ NULL or any text
Bottom Title	Bottom title, used for full-screen menus/ NULL or any text

Miscellaneous	*Description/Property Values*
Tear Off	Identifies a tear-off style menu/ False or true
Comment	
Reference Information	

Menu Item Properties

Property Name	*Description/Property Values*
Name	A unique name for the menu item/ ITEM1, assigned by default, should be changed
Class	A reference to a property class/ NULL or a property class from the drop-down list

Display	*Description/Property Values*
Visual Attribute Name	Name of the visual attribute/ Default or custom
Font Name	Name of the font/ NULL uses system default, or a font from the list
Font Size	Size of the font, in points/ 10 or any number
Font Style	Style of the font/ Plain or a font style in the drop-down list
Font Width	Width of the font/ Normal or a font width in the drop-down list
Font Weight	Weight of the font/ Medium or a font weight in the drop-down list

Functional	*Description/Property Values*
Menu Item Type	Identifies the type of menu item/ Plain, check, radio, separator, or magic from the drop-down list
Command Type	Identifies the type of text/ PL/SQL, NULL, menu, plus, form, or macro
Command Text	Text to execute when menu is selected/ NULL, PL/SQL via PL/SQL Editor, or a menu name
Accelerator	Name of an accelerator key for the menu item/ NULL or an accelerator name
Magic Item	Identifies the magic item/ Cut, copy, paste, and so on from the drop-down list
Menu Item Radio Group	Name of the radio group for a radio menu item/ Blank; may be set by developer
Label	Label displayed for the menu item/ NULL or any text
Icon Name	Name of an icon to show for an iconic menu item/ NULL or any icon

Security	*Description/Property Values*
Menu Item Roles	List of database roles with access to this menu item/ NULL; may be set by developer from Menu Item Roles dialog box
Display w/o Privilege	Specifies whether to display if not in role list/ True or false

Miscellaneous	*Description/Property Values*
Hint	Description of menu item when in character mode/ NULL defaults to menu-item name, or any text
Help	Help text for menu item when in character mode/ NULL or any text
Comment	
Reference Information	

D

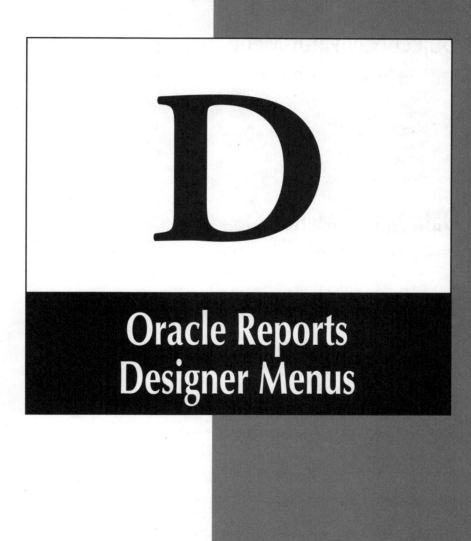

Oracle Reports Designer Menus

The Oracle Reports menus are listed in this appendix as they appear in the Designer. All menu items are listed, and the items unique to Oracle Reports are described.

Object Navigator Menu

The Object Navigator menu contains the following items:

File
Edit
Navigator
Tools
Window
Help

Data Model Menu

The Data Model menu contains the following items:

File
Edit
View
Tools
Window
Help

Layout *and&* Parameter Form Menus

The Layout and& Parameter Form menus contain the following items:

File
Edit
View
Format
Arrange
Tools
Window
Help

Program Unit Menu

The Program Unit menu contains the following items:

File
Edit
Window
Help

PL/SQL Interpreter Menu

The PL/SQL Interpreter menu contains the following items:

File
Edit
View
Debug
Navigator
Tools
Window
Help

File Menu

The File menu contains the following items:

New
Open...
Close
Save
Save As...
Revert
Run...
Compile
Compile All
Connect...
Disconnect
Administration
Print...
Print Setup...
Exit

File, New Menu

The File, New menu supports the creation of new reports, queries, and libraries. The creation of these objects from the menu is identical to creating them from within the Object Navigator. The File, New menu contains the following items:

Report
External Query
External PL/SQL Library

File, New, Report

The File, New, Report menu item creates a new report.

File, New, External Query

The File, New, External Query menu item creates a new external query. External queries are saved as ASCII files.

File, New, External PL/SQL Library

The File, New, External PL/SQL Library menu item creates a new library.

File, Administration Menu

The File, Administration menu supports the access, documentation, generation, and conversion of report modules. The File, Administration menu contains the following items:

Module Access…
Delete…
Rename…
Report Doc
Generate…
Convert…

File, Administration, Module Access…

The File, Administration, Module Access… menu item invokes the Module Access dialog box. (See Figure D.1.) The dialog box lists the users who have access to the current report module. Users may be added to or removed from this list.

The Oracle users who have access to the current report module are listed in the Access List. The current report module name is in the window title.

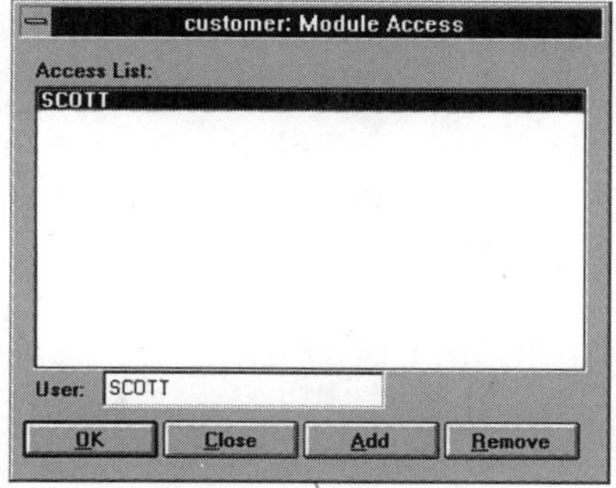

FIGURE D.1.
The Module Access dialog box.

File, Administration, Delete...

The File, Administration, Delete... menu item invokes the Delete dialog box and provides a list of display types to be selected. After the display type is selected, click OK to invoke the Database dialog box. The objects that have been saved to the database can be listed for selection in the Database dialog box by pressing the Retrieve List button.

File, Administration, Rename...

The File, Administration, Rename... menu item invokes the Rename dialog box and allows reports that have been saved to the Oracle database to be assigned a different name. The modules that have been saved to the database can be listed by pressing the Retrieve List button. The module selected appears in the Old Name field, and the new name is entered in the New Name field.

File, Administration, Report Doc Menu

The File, Administration, Report Doc menu supports the creation of reports that document the current report module. The File, Administration, Report Doc menu contains the following items:

Portrait
Landscape

File, Administration, Report Doc, Portrait

The File, Administration, Report Doc, Portrait menu item runs a report that documents the current report module. The report is SRWDOCPB.RDF and is formatted for portrait orientation.

File, Administration, Report Doc, Landscape

The File, Administration, Report Doc, Landscape menu item runs a report that documents the current report module. The report is 'srwdoclb' and is formatted for landscape orientation.

File, Administration, Generate...

The File, Administration, Generate… menu item creates an executable file for the current report module. The file type is REP for reports. The File, Administration, Generate… menu item invokes the Generate dialog box to allow the report module name and location to be entered, or selected, from the file system.

File, Administration, Convert...

The File, Administration, Convert… menu item invokes the Convert dialog box, which enables you to convert reports or PL/SQL libraries from their current format to a new format. (See Figure D.2.)

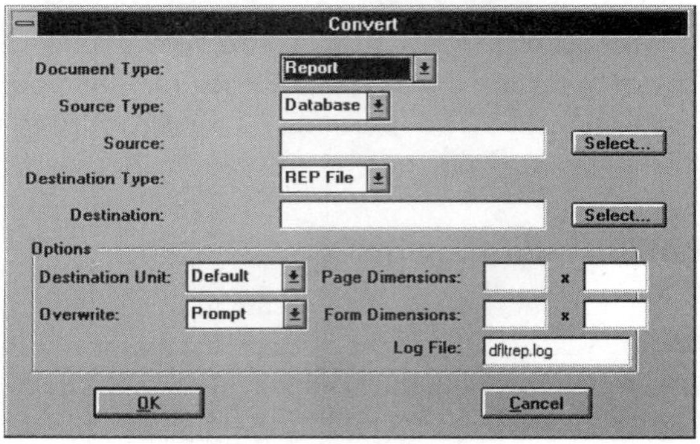

FIGURE D.2.
The Convert dialog box.

The document type is either Report or PL/SQL library, and it can be selected from the drop-down list. The source type is either Database, RDF File, or REX File and is also available from a drop-down list. Once the type is entered, the source can be entered or listed for selection by pressing the Select button. You would then select the destination type and location as well as any conversion options.

Edit Menu

The Edit menu contains the following items:

- Undo
- Cut
- Copy
- Paste
- Clear
- Duplicate
- Select All
- Search/Replace…

Import
Export
Insert Object...
Links...
Object

Edit, Insert Object...

The Edit, Insert Object... menu item enables you to create an OLE2 container object. The result of selecting this menu item is the same as selecting the OLE button on the tool palette in the Layout Editor. When a new OLE2 container object is to be created, the Insert Object dialog box appears. (See Figure D.3.)

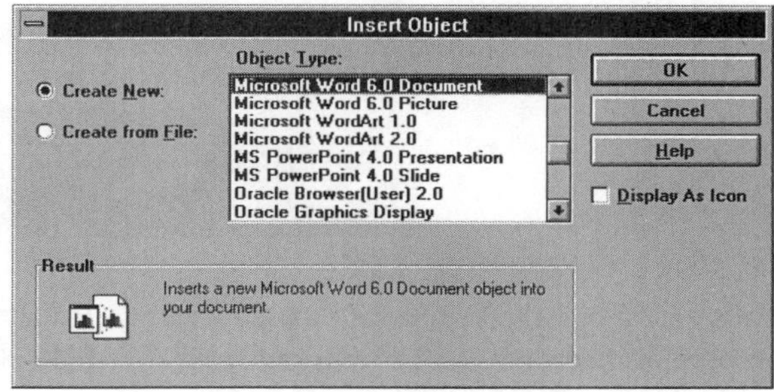

FIGURE D.3.
The Insert Object dialog box showing the object types.

The Insert Object dialog box shows the list of registered OLE servers that can be selected to create a new OLE object.

To create an OLE2 object from an existing file, select the radio button for Create from File in the Insert Object dialog box, as shown in Figure D.4.

FIGURE D.4.
The Insert Object dialog box specifying a file.

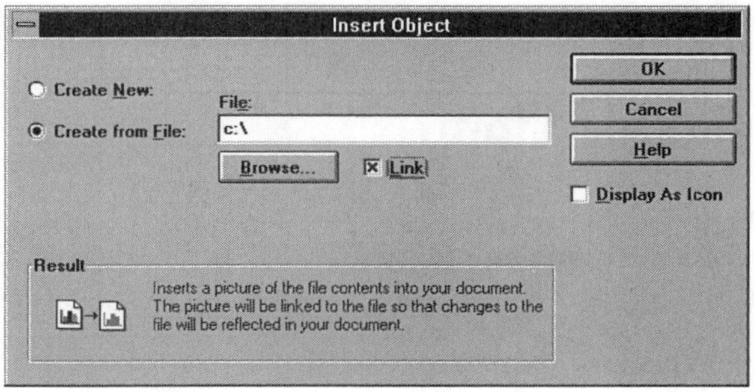

The Insert Object dialog box now enables you to enter a filename and to select whether the object is to be linked.

Edit, Links...

The Edit, Links... menu item provides a list of all the linked objects in the report and is only enabled when linked objects exist in the report. From the Links dialog box, any of the linked objects can be modified. (See Figure D.5.)

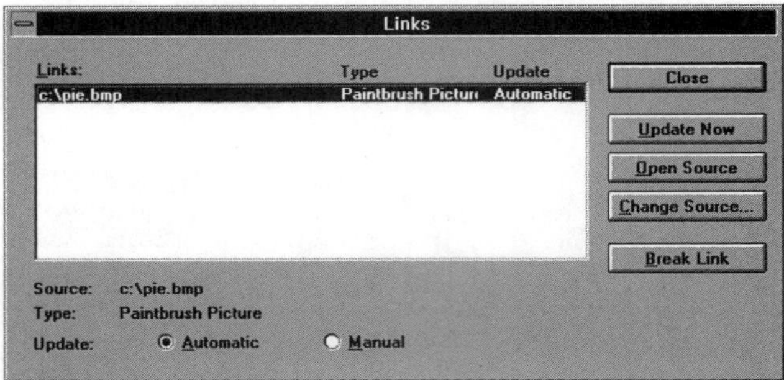

FIGURE D.5.
The Links dialog box showing a linked bitmap.

The Links dialog box shows the absolute pathname, type, and update mode for the link. The link can be modified or it can be removed from this dialog box.

Edit, Object

The Edit, Object menu item is only enabled when an OLE object is selected. The menu name is changed to reflect the type of OLE object selected. The Edit, Object menu supports the modification of OLE objects within a report. The Edit, Object menu may contain subordinate menu items for Edit, Open, Convert, and others and is dependent on the type of OLE server for the types of actions that can be performed on the OLE object.

Navigator Menu

The Navigator menu only appears on the Object Navigator menu in Oracle Reports Designer. It supports the changing of views, as well as the creation, deletion, compiling, marking, and pasting of objects. The Navigator menu contains the following items:

Toolbar
Expand
Collapse
Expand All
Collapse All

Create
Delete
Compile Selection
Set Mark
Go to Mark
Navigator Options...

Navigator, Toolbar

The Navigator, Toolbar menu item is a check-style menu item that turns the display of the toolbar on and off in the Object Navigator. The toolbar appears on the left side of the Object Navigator.

Navigator, Navigator Options...

The Navigator, Navigator Options... menu item invokes the Object Navigator Options dialog box. The Object Navigator Options dialog box is a tab-controlled dialog box that enables you to review and modify the general, group, and layout options. Figure D.6 shows the Object Navigator Options dialog box with general options.

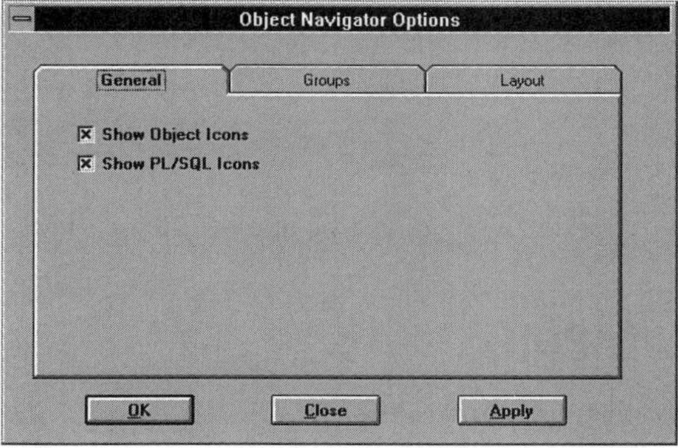

FIGURE D.6.
The Object Navigator Options General tab.

The general options determine whether iconic symbols are shown in the Object Navigator to visually identify the objects. Figure D.7 shows the Object Navigator Options dialog box with group options.

The group options organize the object groups and their columns in the hierarchy. Figure D.8 shows the Object Navigator Options dialog box with layout options.

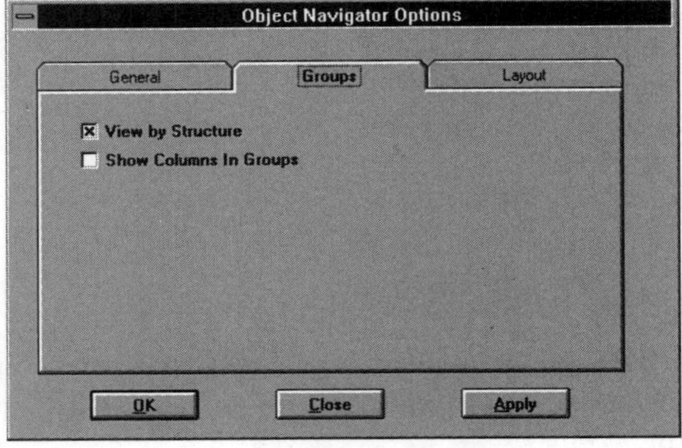

FIGURE D.7.
The Object Navigator Options Groups tab.

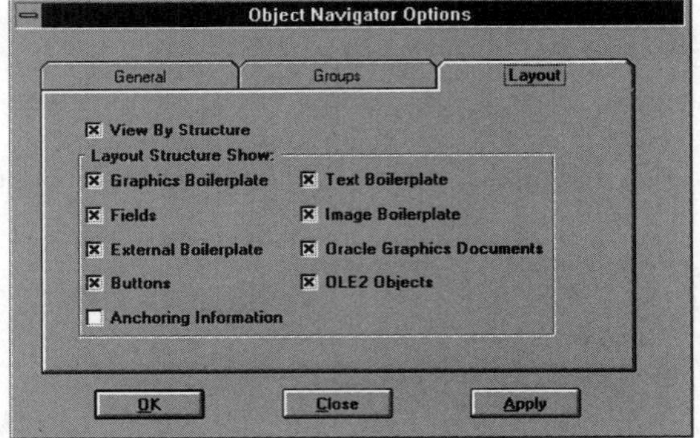

FIGURE D.8.
The Object Navigator Options Layout tab.

The layout options allow each type of object to be shown or not shown in the hierarchy.

View Menu

The View menu appears in the Data Model, Layout, and Parameter Form menus in Oracle Reports Designer. It provides the ability to change the visual aspects of these editors. The View menu contains the following items:

Zoom In
Zoom Out
Normal Size
Fit to Window
Rulers
Ruler Guides
Grid
Grid Snap

Page Breaks
Tool Palette
Status Line
Toolbar
View Options

View, Toolbar

The View, Toolbar menu item is a check-style menu item that turns the display of the toolbar on and off in the selected editor. The toolbar appears on the top of the layout.

View, View Options Menu

The View, Options menu enables you to adjust the settings for the ruler, grid spacing, and layout. The View, Options menu contains the following items:

Rulers…
Layout…

View, Options, Rulers…

The View, Options, Rulers… menu item invokes the Ruler Settings dialog box, which enables you to adjust the coordinate system and grid spacing.

View, Options, Layout…

The View, Options, Layout… menu item invokes the Layout Options dialog box. The Layout Options dialog box is a tab-controlled dialog box that enables you to review and set the options within the layout. Figure D.9 shows the Layout Options dialog box.

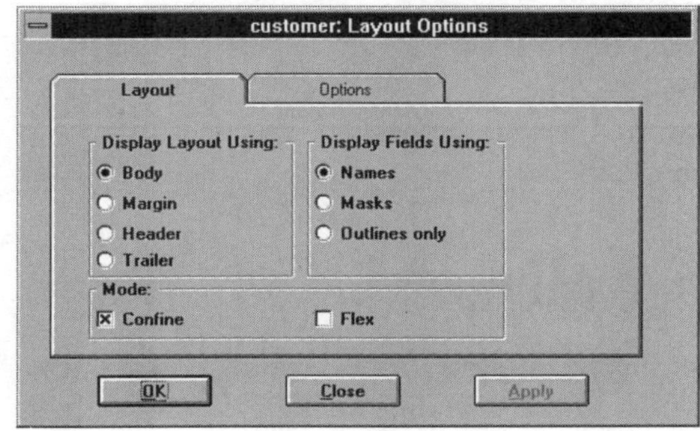

FIGURE D.9.
The Layout Options dialog box showing display options.

There is a radio group indicating which part of the report is displayed and another radio group indicating how to display fields in the layout. Lastly, there are check boxes for selecting confine and/or flex mode for the layout.

Within the Options tab there are check boxes for selecting whether each object type is shown in the layout. Figure D.10 shows the Options tab of the Layout Options dialog box.

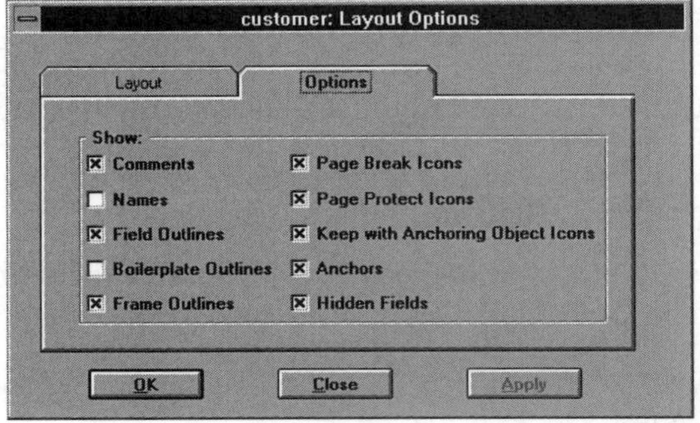

FIGURE D.10.
The Layout Options dialog box with the object types to be shown.

Format Menu

The Format menu appears on the Layout and Parameter Form menus in Oracle Reports Designer. It enables you to change the visual aspects of the objects within the editors. The Format menu contains the following items:

Font...
Spacing
Alignment
Line
Dash
Bevel
Arrow
Drawing Options
Color Palette...

Arrange Menu

The Arrange menu appears on the Layout and Parameter Form menus in Oracle Reports Designer. It supports the layering, aligning, sizing, and grouping of objects in the editors. The Arrange menu contains the following items:

Bring to Front
Send to Back

Move Forward
Move Backward
Align Objects...
Repeat Alignment
Size Objects...
Repeat Sizing
Group
Ungroup
Group Operations

Tools Menu

The Tools menu appears on each of the main menus in Oracle Reports Designer and supports tasks such as opening to the different editors, defaulting layouts, reviewing tables and columns, and setting options. The Tools menu contains the following items:

Properties...
Common Properties...
Data Model Editor
Layout Editor
Parameter Form Editor
External Query Editor
Program Unit Editor
Stored Program Unit Editor
Interpreter
Default Layout...
Default Parameter Form...
Create Matrix
Trace...
Tables/Columns...
Tools Options...

Tools, Common Properties...

Two or more objects must be selected before the Tools, Common Properties... menu item is enabled. When selected, the Tools, Common Properties... menu item invokes the Common Properties dialog box. The Common Properties dialog box is a tab-controlled dialog box that enables you to review and modify properties that are common to each of the objects selected. Properties that are not the same are displayed as null or undefined. The Common Properties dialog box is shown in figures D.11 through D.13.

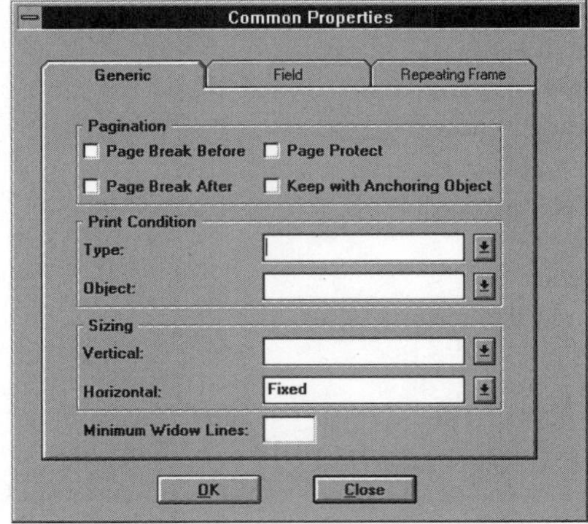

FIGURE D.11.
The Common Properties dialog box showing generic properties.

The Generic tab in the Common Properties dialog box contains information on pagination, printing conditions, sizing, and the minimum number of window lines permitted. The Field tab is also in the Common Properties dialog box, as shown in Figure D.12.

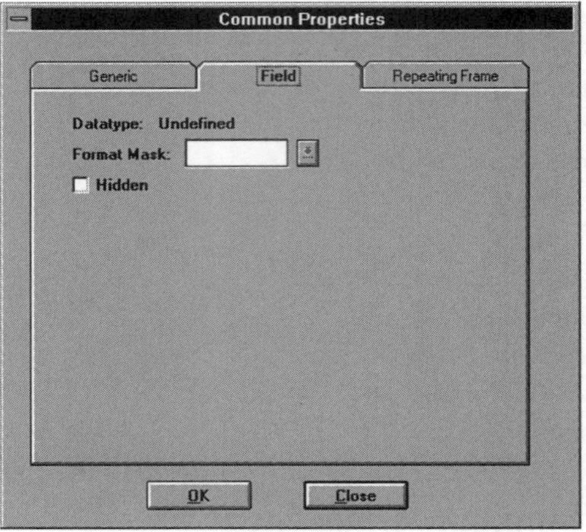

FIGURE D.12.
The Common Properties dialog box showing field properties.

The Field tab in the Common Properties dialog box only appears when one or more of the objects selected is a field. It contains the data type, format mask, and a check box indicating whether the selected fields are hidden. The Repeating Frame tab is the last tab in the Common Properties dialog box, as shown in Figure D.13.

The Repeating Frame tab in the Common Properties only appears when one or more of the objects selected is a repeating frame. It contains the direction, spacing, and maximum and minimum records per page for the repeating frame(s).

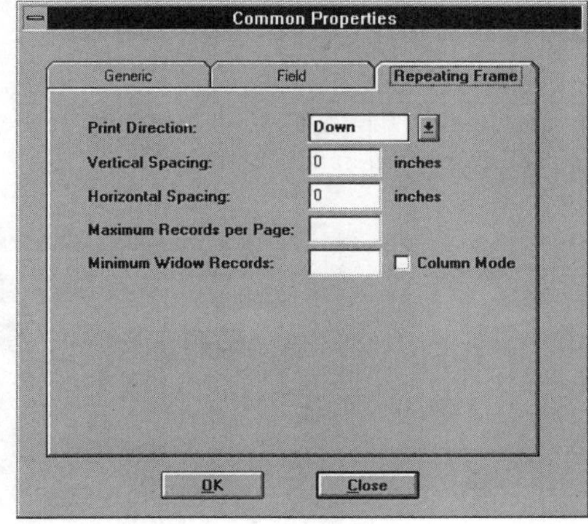

FIGURE D.13.
The Common Properties dialog box with repeating frame properties.

Tools, Data Model Editor

The Tools, Data Model Editor menu item opens or sets the focus to the Data Model window. The Data Model window is shown in Figure D.14, to the right of the Object Navigator, containing a query, a group, and columns.

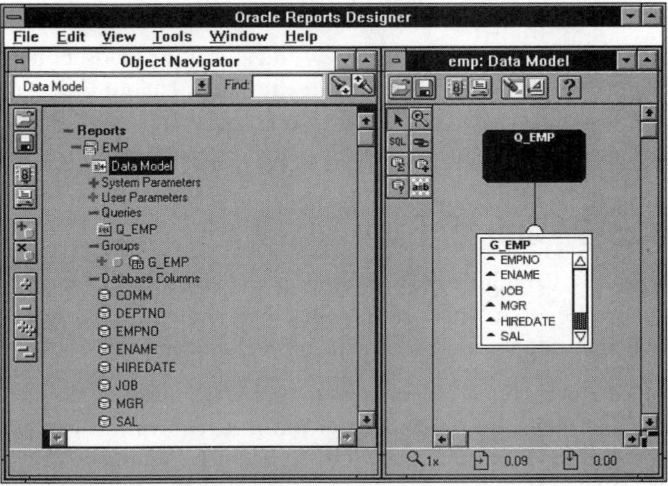

FIGURE D.14.
The Data Model window with the Object Navigator.

The Data Model Editor is used to define the queries, groups, and columns for the report. A report must first be created before the Tools, Data Model Editor menu item is enabled. The Data Model Editor can be selected from the Tools menu or invoked from the pop-up menu in the Object Navigator by right-clicking when a data model object has been selected.

Tools, Layout Editor

The Tools, Layout Editor menu item opens or sets the focus to the Layout window. The Layout window is shown in Figure D.15, to the right of the Object Navigator, with a report layout containing frames, boilerplate, and fields.

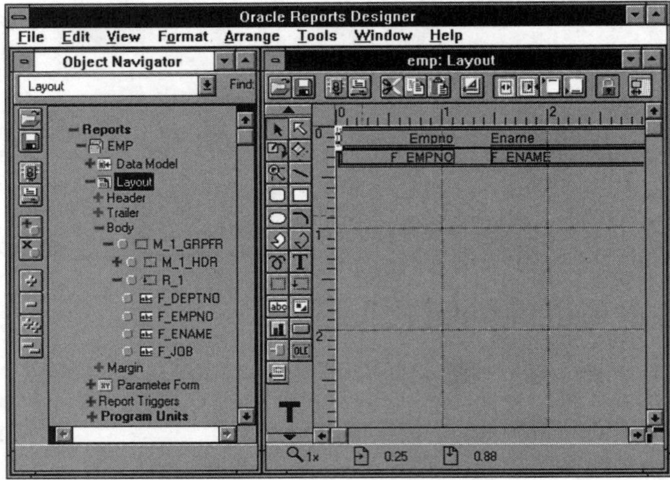

FIGURE D.15.
The Layout Editor window with the Object Navigator.

The Layout Editor is used to review and adjust the fields, boilerplate, and frames in the report. A report must first be created before the Tools, Layout Editor menu item is enabled. The Layout Editor can be selected from the Tools menu or invoked from the pop-up menu in the Object Navigator by right-clicking when a layout object has been selected.

Tools, Parameter Form Editor

The Tools, Parameter Form Editor menu item opens, or sets the focus, to the Parameter Form window. The Parameter Form window is shown in Figure D.16, to the right of the Object Navigator, containing boilerplate and parameter fields.

The Parameter Form Editor is used to review and adjust the layout of the boilerplate items and parameter fields, in the parameter form. A report must first be created before the Tools, Parameter Form Editor menu item is enabled. The Parameter Form can be selected from the Tools menu or invoked from the pop-up menu in the Object Navigator by right-clicking when a parameter form object has been selected.

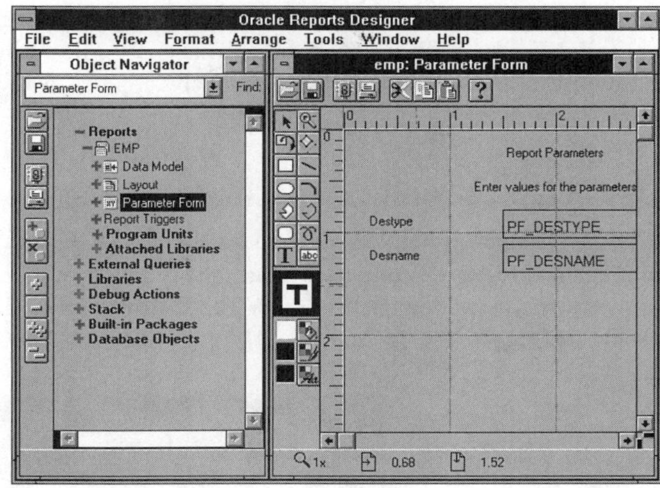

FIGURE D.16.
The Parameter Form window with the Object Navigator.

Tools, External Query Editor

The Tools, External Query Editor menu item opens or sets the focus to the External Query Definition window. The External Query Definition window is shown in Figure D.17, to the right of the Object Navigator, containing a SQL `select` statement.

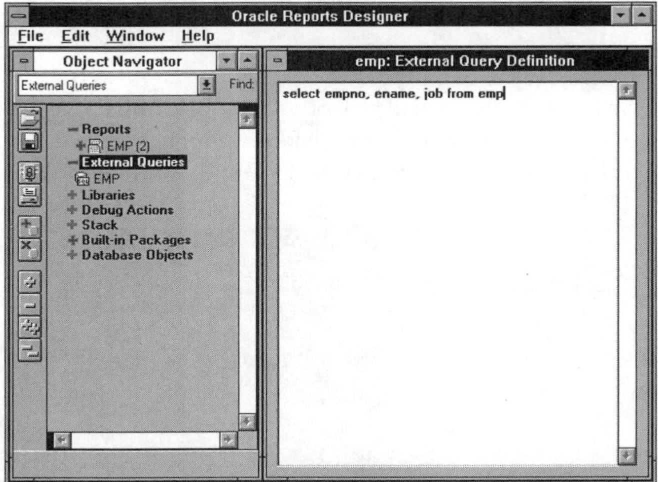

FIGURE D.17.
The External Query Definition windows containing a SQL statement.

The External Query Editor is used to define or reference queries that exist outside of the current report. If the current focus is on an external query object when the External Query Editor menu item is selected, that query automatically appears in the External Query Definition window.

Tools, Default Layout...

The Tools, Default Layout... menu item invokes the Default Layout dialog box. The Default Layout dialog box is a tab-controlled dialog box providing a selection of report styles and a list of columns to be included in the report. The Default Layout dialog box is shown in figures D.18 and D.19.

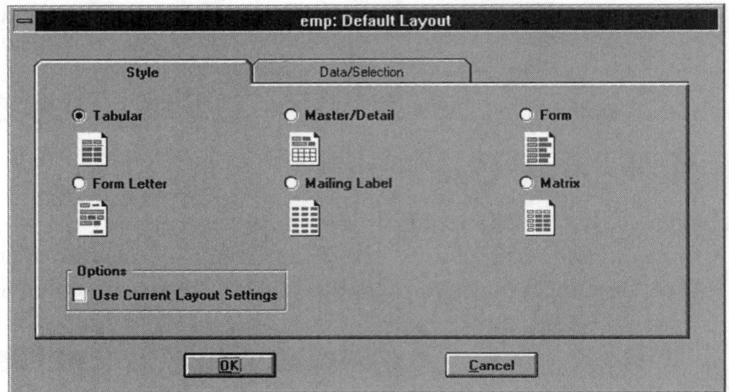

FIGURE D.18.
The Default Layout showing various report styles.

The Style tab in the Default Layout dialog box contains a radio group for selecting a report style and a check box to indicate whether or not to use the current layout settings. Figure D.19 shows the Data/Selection tab in the Default Layout dialog box.

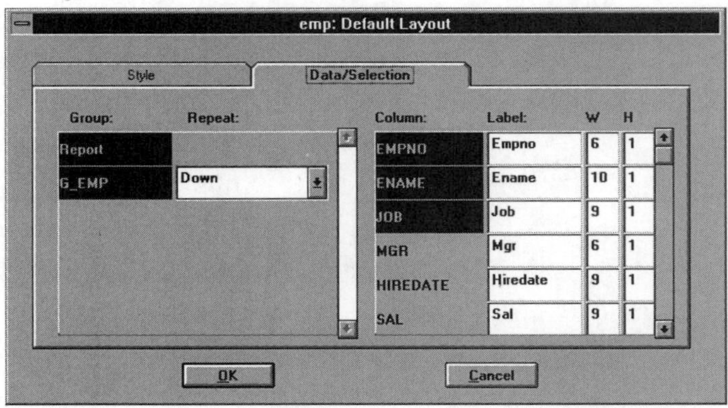

FIGURE D.19.
The Default Layout showing the Data/Selection sheet.

The Data/Selection tab in the Default Layout dialog box displays the groups and columns available to be included in the default layout of the report.

Tools, Default Parameter Form...

The Tools, Default Parameter Form... menu item invokes the Default Parameter Form dialog box, which enables you to review and select parameters and boilerplate to be included in the default parameter form. See Figure D.20 for the Default Parameter Form dialog box.

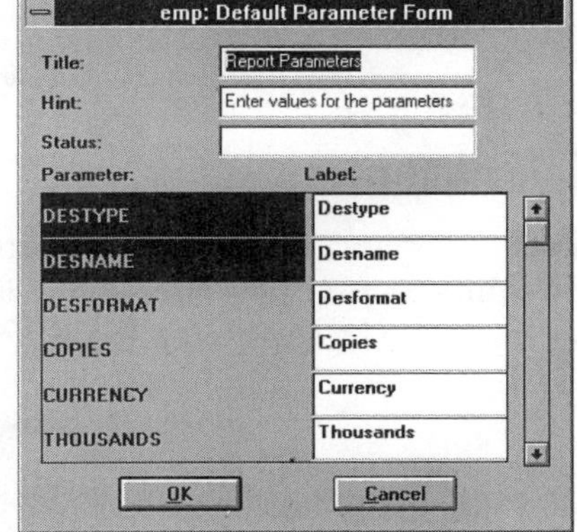

FIGURE D.20.
The Default Parameter Form dialog box.

The Default Parameter Form dialog box includes fields for creating boilerplate for the form heading, as well as a list of all the available parameters in the report.

Tools, Create Matrix

The Tools, Create Matrix menu item enables you to create a matrix from the Layout Editor manually. The Create Matrix menu item is only enabled when two intersecting, repeating frames have been selected in the Layout Editor.

Tools, Trace...

The Tools, Trace... menu item invokes the Trace Setting dialog box so the trace file can be named and the options may be set. Tracing a report writes information about the report to a log file during execution. Figure D.21 shows the Trace Setting dialog box.

The Trace Setting dialog box includes fields for naming the trace file and trace mode. Trace options may also be selected from the list of check boxes.

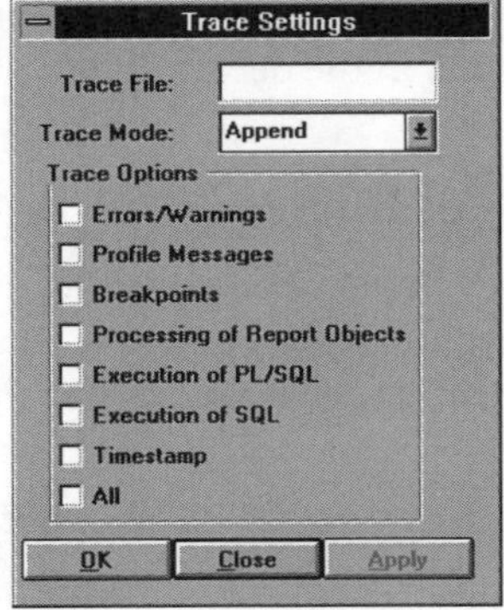

FIGURE D.21.
The Trace Settings dialog box.

Tools, Table/Columns...

The Tools, Tables/Columns... menu item invokes the Table and Column Names dialog box. The Table and Column Names dialog box is shown in Figure D.22, selecting the current user's tables and views that are to be displayed with the EMP table and columns that are selected.

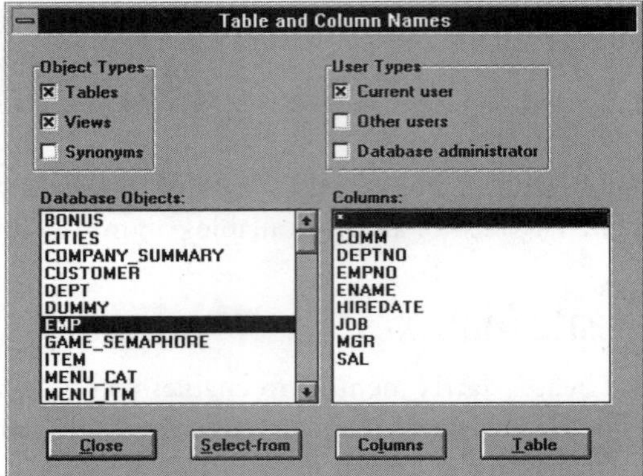

FIGURE D.22.
The Table and Column Names dialog box.

As the Object Types and User Types are selected with the check boxes, the list of database objects changes. When an object is selected from the list of database objects, the columns are displayed. A SQL select statement can be created and returned to the editor by pressing the Select-from button. The Columns and Table buttons return the selected column and table names.

Tools, Tools Options...

The Tools, Tools Options... menu item invokes the Tools Options dialog box. The Tools Options dialog box is a tab-controlled dialog box that enables you to review and modify preferences, runtime parameters, and runtime settings. Figure D.23 shows the Tools Options dialog box with the Preferences tab.

FIGURE D.23.
The Tools Options dialog box with Preferences.

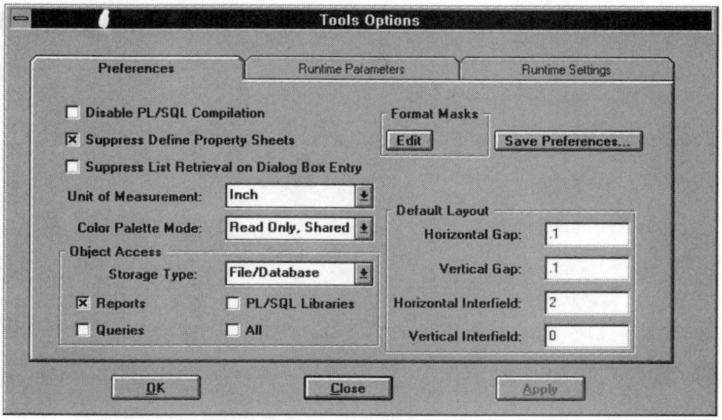

The preferences include instructions on operation, format masks, object access, and layout that are sent to the Designer to streamline the development process. Options can also be set for runtime. Figure D.24 shows the Tools Options dialog box with the Runtime Parameters tab.

FIGURE D.24.
The Tools Options dialog box with runtime parameters.

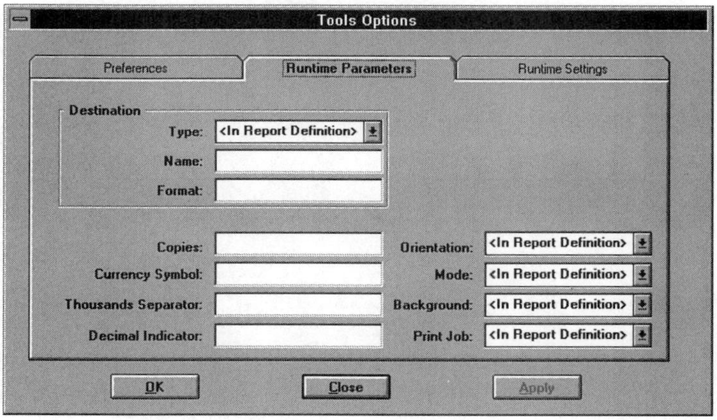

The runtime parameters include instructions to the runtime engine that can modify the output location, copies, and presentation of the report. While runtime parameters influence the appearance of the report, the runtime settings address the operation and execution of the report. Figure D.25 shows the Tools Options dialog box with the Runtime Settings tab.

Use the runtime settings to turn off the parameter form or run the report in debug mode. Notice that the non-blocking SQL is checked by default; this option enables the report to run in the background.

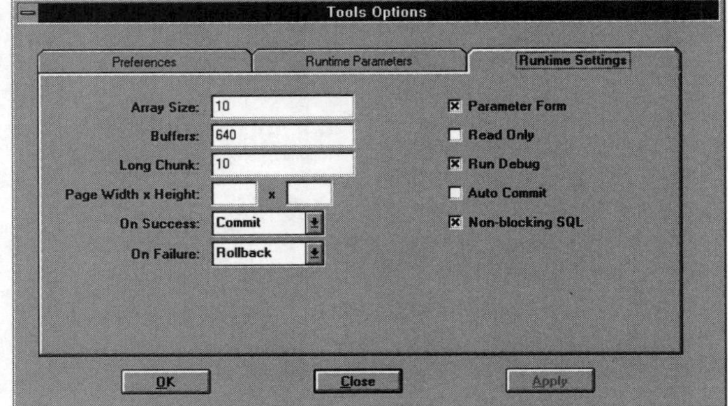

FIGURE D.25.
The Tools Options dialog box with runtime settings.

E

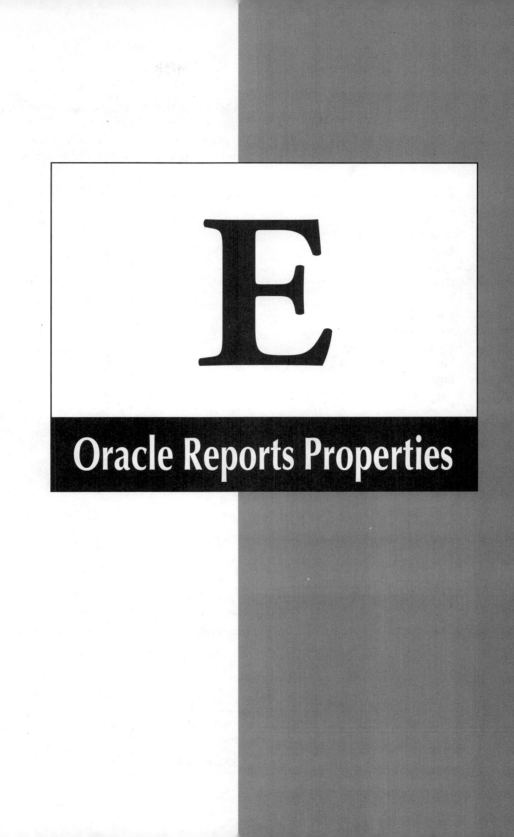

Oracle Reports Properties

The Oracle Reports properties are listed here by object type, as they appear in the Object Navigator. Each property is listed showing the property name, a brief description of the property, and the default and optional values for the property. The properties are grouped by topic for each object type. Most properties are presented in tab-style dialog boxes with the topics appearing as the tab label.

The properties for the following object types are described:

Report
System Parameter
User Parameter
Query
Group
Database Column
Formula Column
Summary Column
Placeholder Column
Link
Frame
Repeating Frame
Layout Field
Boilerplate
Anchor
Matrix
Oracle Graphics
Button
OLE2 Object
Parameter Form Field
Parameter Form Boilerplate

Common Properties

The properties dialog boxes often include a comment tab and a printer codes tab. Almost all of the properties dialog boxes have a Comment tab as described in the following sections.

Comment Tab

Property Name	*Description/Property Values*
Comment	For internal documentation/ Defaults to blank; or any text

Many of the properties dialog boxes also contain a printer codes tab with the following properties.

Printer Codes Tab

Property Name	*Description/Property Values*
Before	Oracle Reports prints this code prior to printing the object/ Blank; or any valid printer code in the printer definition file
After	Oracle Reports prints this code after printing the object/ Blank; or any valid printer code in the printer definition file

The comment and printer code properties are described here; later they are only referenced in the list of properties for that object type.

Report Properties

Report properties are presented in the Report Properties dialog box. (See Figure E.1.)

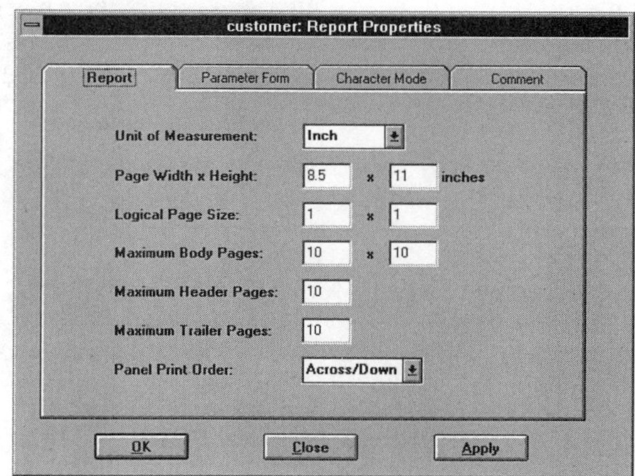

FIGURE E.1.
The Report Properties dialog box with the Report tab.

Report Tab

Property Name	*Description/Property Values*
Unit of Measurement	Coordinate system used for measurement/ Inch, Centimeter, or Point from the drop-down list
Page Width	The width of the page/ 8.5 in.; maximum 512 in., 1,312 cm., or 36,864 pts.
Page Height	The height of the page/ 11 in.; maximum 512 in., 1,312 cm., or 36,864 pts.

continues

Property Name	Description/Property Values
Logical Page Size	The number of physical pages in logical page/ 1 × 1; or any numbers from 1 to 50
Maximum Body Pages	The maximum pages in the body of the report/ 10 × 10; or any numbers from 1 to 999
Maximum Header Pages	The maximum pages in the front of the report/ 10; or any number from 1 to 999
Maximum Trailer Pages	The maximum pages in the back of the report/ 10; or any number from 1 to 999
Panel Print Order	The direction to print for multi-logical pages/ Across/Down or Down/Across

Parameter Form properties are available in the Parameter Form tab of the Report Properties dialog box. (See Figure E.2.)

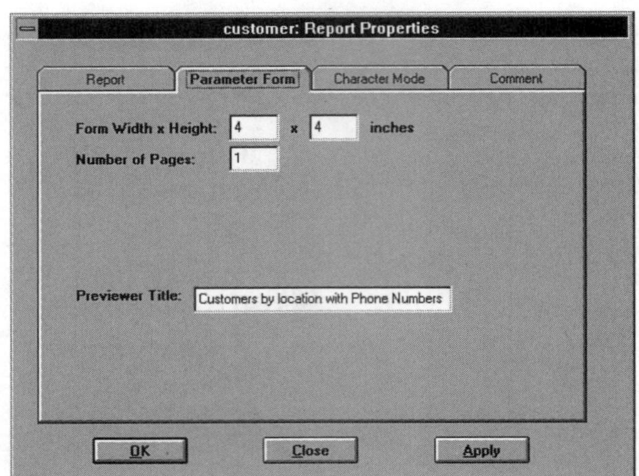

FIGURE E.2.
The Report Properties dialog box with the Parameter Form tab.

Parameter Form Tab

Property Name	Description/Property Values
Form Width	The width of the parameter form/ 4 in.; maximum 512 in., 1,312 cm., or 36,864 pts.
Form Height	The height of the parameter form/ 4 in.; maximum 512 in., 1,312 cm., or 36,864 pts.
Number of Pages	The total pages in the parameter form/ 1; or any number from 1 to 9,999
Previewer Title	The title of the report shown in the Previewer/ Report Name or any text string

Character mode properties are available in the Character Mode tab of the Report Properties dialog box. (See Figure E.3.)

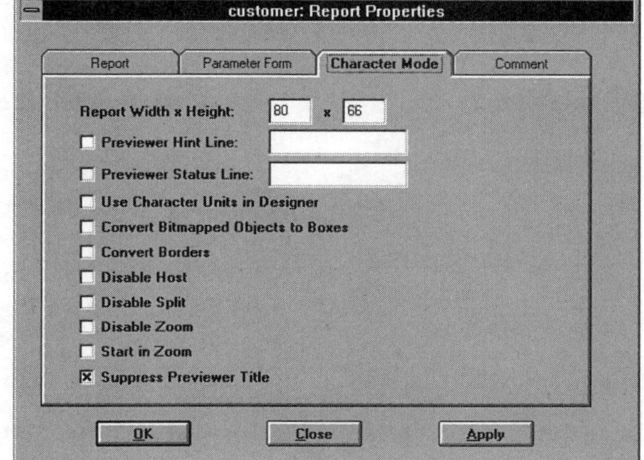

FIGURE E.3.
The Report Properties dialog box with the Character Mode tab.

Character Mode Tab

Property Name	*Description/Property Values*
Report Width	The width of the report, in characters/ 80 characters; or any number from 1 to 9,999
Report Height	The height of the report, in characters/ 66 characters; or any number from 1 to 9,999
Previewer Hint Line	Text line before the bottom of the Previewer/ Unchecked and blank; or checked and any text, 80 characters max
Previewer Status Line	Text line at the bottom of the Previewer/ Unchecked and blank; or checked and any text, 80 characters max
Use Character Units in Designer	Specifies whether to set grid in Designer to character/ Unchecked means no; or checked for yes
Convert Bit-Mapped Objects to Boxes	Specifies whether to show GUI objects as boxes/ Unchecked means no; or checked for yes
Convert Borders	Specifies whether to show GUI borders as lines/ Unchecked means no; or checked for yes
Disable Host	Specifies whether the File, Host menu item should be disabled/

continues

Property Name	*Description/Property Values*
	Unchecked means no, or checked for yes
Disable Split	Specifies whether the Previewer split feature should be disabled/ Unchecked means no; or checked for yes
Disable Zoom	Specifies whether the Previewer zoom feature should be disabled/ Unchecked means no; or checked for yes
Start in Zoom	Specifies whether the Previewer should start in a zoomed state/ Unchecked means no, or checked for yes
Suppress Previewer Title	Specifies whether the Previewer Title should be suppressed/ Unchecked means no; or checked for yes

Documentation for the application is recorded in the Comments tab of the Report Properties dialog box. (See Figure E.4.)

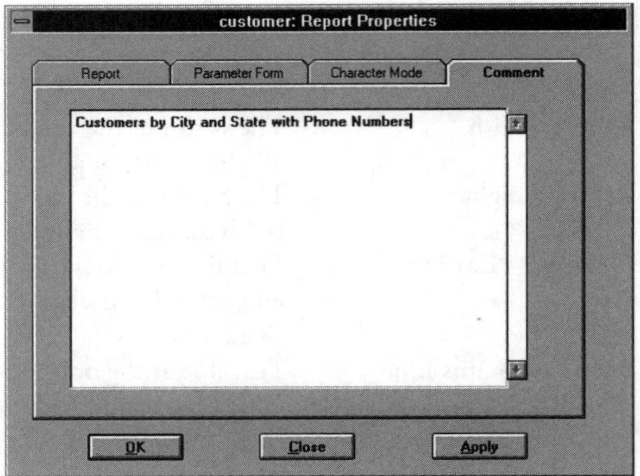

FIGURE E.4.
The Report Properties dialog box with the Comment tab.

Comment Tab

The Report Properties dialog box uses the standard Comment tab. This tab control will be found on most of the other properties dialog boxes as well.

System Parameter Properties

System parameter properties are presented in the Parameter dialog box as shown in Figure E.5.

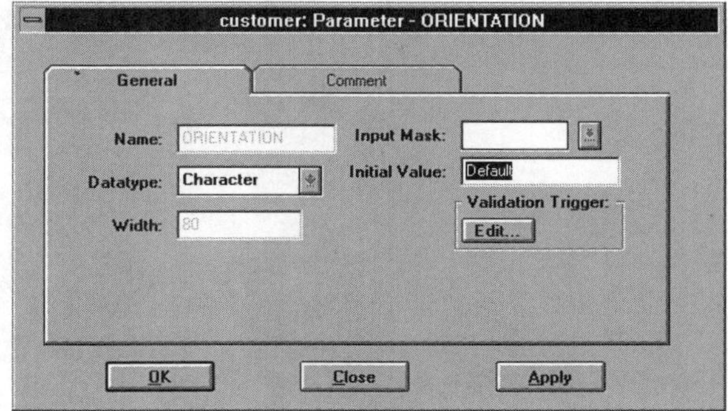

FIGURE E.5.
The Parameter dialog box with the General tab.

Notice the Parameter dialog box also contains a Comment tab.

General Tab

Property Name	*Description/Property Values*
Name	The unique name of the system parameter/ System parameters are predefined and cannot be changed
Datatype	The type of data contained in this parameter/ Character, Date, or Number
Width	The number of characters for the parameter/ 40; or any number from 1 to 64,000
Input Mask	A format mask for dates and numbers/ Blank; or any mask from the drop-down list; maximum length is 128
Initial Value	A value to substitute when no parameter is given/ Blank means no value; or any text
Edit	Invokes the Program Unit Editor for a validation trigger/ Null; or any PL/SQL

Comment Tab

The Parameter dialog box uses the standard Comment tab for accessing the comment property.

User Parameter Properties

User parameter properties are presented in the Parameter dialog box. (See Figure E.6.)

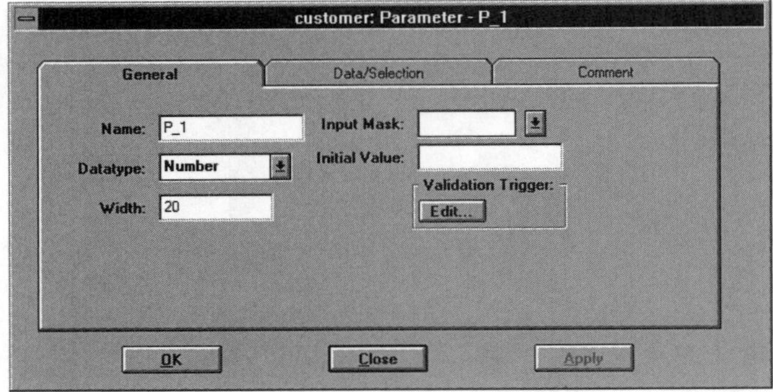

FIGURE E.6.
The Parameter dialog box with the General tab.

Notice the Parameter dialog box also has a Data/Selection and Comment tab.

General Tab

Property Name	*Description/Property Values*
Name	The unique name of the user parameter/ P_1, assigned by default, should be changed to a meaningful name
Datatype	The type of data contained in this parameter/ Character, Date, or Number
Width	The number of characters for the parameter/ 40; or any number from 1 to 64,000
Input Mask	A format mask for dates and numbers/ Blank; or any mask from the drop-down list; maximum length is 128
Initial Value	A value to substitute when no parameter is given/ Blank means no value; or any text
Edit	Invokes the Program Unit Editor for a validation trigger/ Null; or any PL/SQL

You can assign a static list of values for the parameter data in the Data/Selection tab in the Parameter dialog box. (See Figure E.7.)

The values are added in the Value field and displayed to the right of the Add button.

The data for the list of values can come from a SQL select statement as shown in Figure E.8.

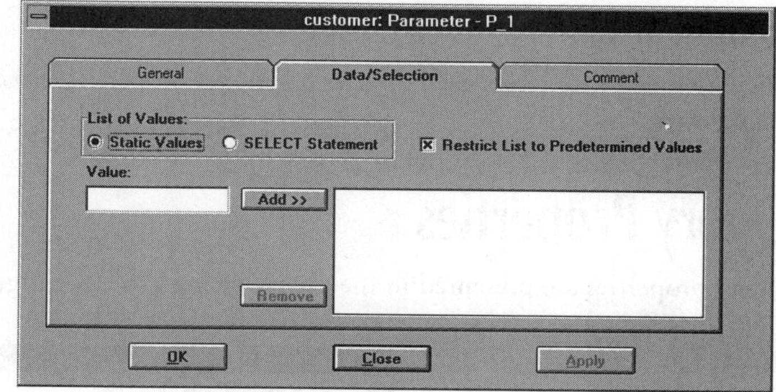

FIGURE E.7.
The Parameter dialog box with static Data values.

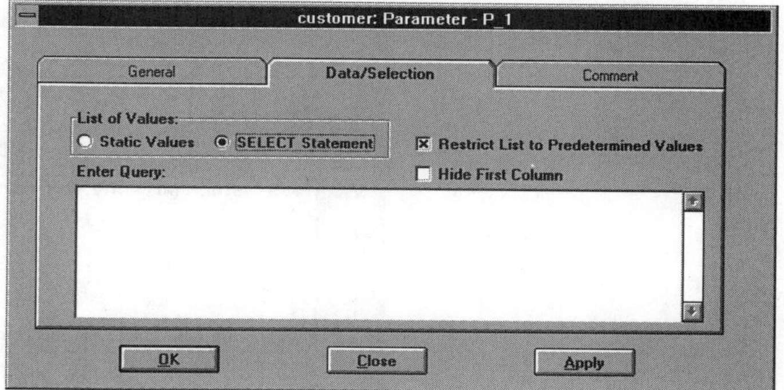

FIGURE E.8.
The Parameter dialog box with a SQL select statement.

Data/Selection Tab

Property Name	*Description/Property Values*
Static Values/ SELECT Statement	A radio group to choose the list type/ Static Values or SELECT Statement
Restrict List to Predetermined Values	Refuses other values/ Checked means yes; or unchecked for no
Value	A value to be added to the Static Values list/ Null; or any text
Add	Button used to add the value to the Static Values list/ A value must be entered
Remove	Button used to delete the value from the Static Values list/ Only enabled when an item is selected from the list
Hide First Column	Specifies whether to hide the first column in the list/ Unchecked means no; or checked for yes, used for a SELECT Statement

Comment Tab

The Parameter dialog box used for user parameter properties also contains the standard Comment tab.

Query Properties

Query properties are presented in the Query dialog box. (See Figure E.9.)

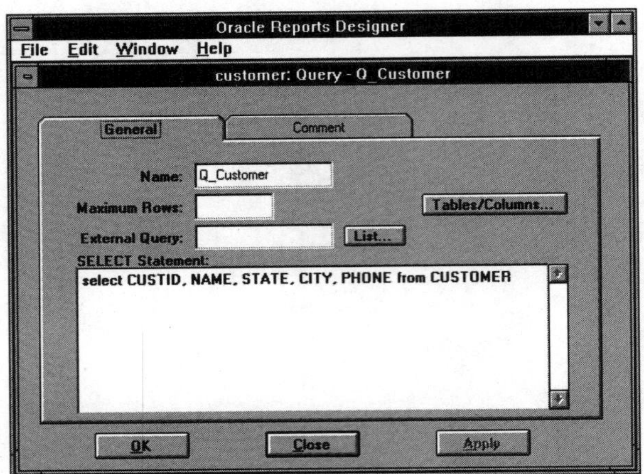

FIGURE E.9.
The Query dialog box with the General tab.

General Tab

Property Name	*Description/Property Values*
Name	A unique name of the query/ Q_1, assigned by default, should be changed to a meaningful name
Maximum Rows	The maximum number of records that will be returned/ Blank for all rows; or any number from 1 to 32,000
External Query	The name of a file in the file system or database/ Blank; or any file name
List	Invokes a dialog box for finding the external query/ Defaults to filter, file system, or database
SELECT Statement	A SQL select statement/ Blank; must be entered
Tables/Columns	Invokes a dialog box for creating a query/ Defaults to tables for the current user

Comment Tab

The Query dialog box also contains the standard Comment tab.

Group Properties

Group properties are presented in the Group dialog box. (See Figure E.10.)

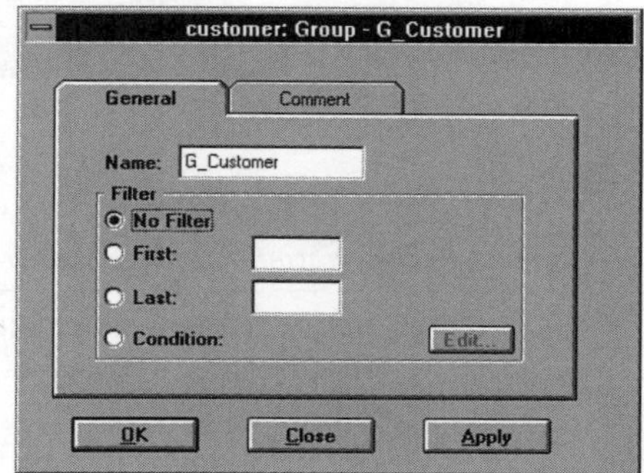

FIGURE E.10.
The Group dialog box with the General tab.

General Tab

Property Name	*Description/Property Values*
Name	A unique name of the group/ G_1, assigned by default, should be changed to a meaningful name
Filter	Defines the type of filter and number of rows/ No Filter, First, Last, or Condition
Edit	Invokes the Program Unit Editor/ Only enabled for the condition filter type

Comment Tab

The Group dialog box also contains the standard Comment tab.

Database Column Properties

Database Column properties are presented in the Database Column dialog box. (See Figure E.11.)

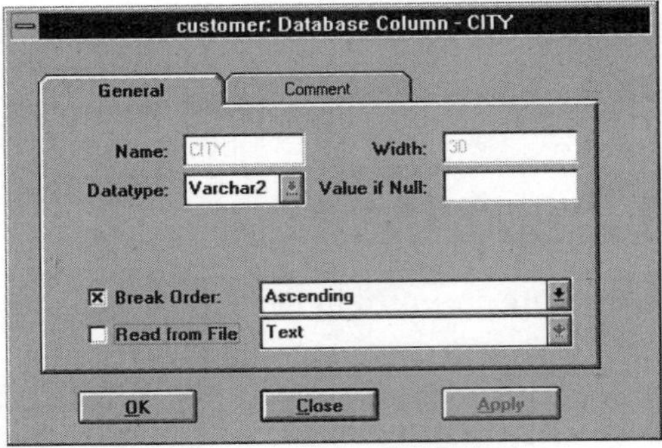

FIGURE E.11.
The Database Column dialog box with the General tab.

General Tab

Property Name	*Description/Property Values*
Name	A unique name for the database column/ Column name from the SQL select statement; or any valid column name
Datatype	The type of data contained in this column/ Varchar2, Character, Date, Long, Long Raw, Number, Raw, or Varchar
Width	The number of characters for the column/ As in the database; or any number from 1 to 64,000
Value If Null	A value to substitute for a null value/ Blank means no substitution; or any text
Break Order	Specifies whether this is a break column/ Unchecked or checked
Sort Direction	Specifies the direction to sort for a break/ Ascending or Descending
Read from File	Specifies whether the value is to be read from a file/ Unchecked means no; or checked for yes
Format	Specifies the format of the file to be read/ Text, Image, or any format from the drop-down list

Comment Tab

Notice the Database Column dialog box in Figure E.11 also contains a Comment tab.

Formula Column Properties

Formula Column properties are presented in the Formula Column dialog box as shown in Figure E.12.

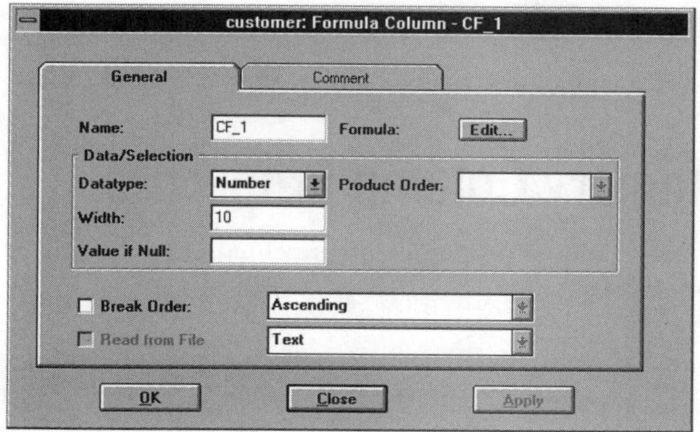

FIGURE E.12.
The Formula Column dialog box with the General tab.

General Tab

Property Name	*Description/Property Values*
Name	A unique name for the formula column/ CF_1, assigned by default, should be changed to a meaningful name
Formula	The PL/SQL function to execute for the formula/ Defaults to a function outline; must be completed
Edit	Invokes the Program Unit Editor/ Use the Edit button to enter the formula in the function outline
Datatype	The type of data contained in this column/ Varchar2, Character, Date, Long, Long Raw, Number, Raw, or Varchar
Width	The number of characters for the column/ 10; or any number from 1 to 64,000
Value If Null	A value to substitute for a null value/ Blank means no substitution; or any text
Product Order	Used to determine order of cross product groups/ The parent group; or any group from the drop-down list
Break Order	Specifies whether this is a break column/ Unchecked or checked
Sort Direction	Specifies the direction to sort for a break/ Ascending or Descending
Read from File	Specifies whether the value is to be read from a file/ Unchecked means no; or checked for yes
Format	Specifies the format of the file to be read/ Text, Image, or any format from the drop-down list

Comment Tab

The Formula Column dialog box also contains the standard Comment tab.

Summary Column Properties

Summary Column properties are presented in the Summary Column dialog box. (See Figure E.13.)

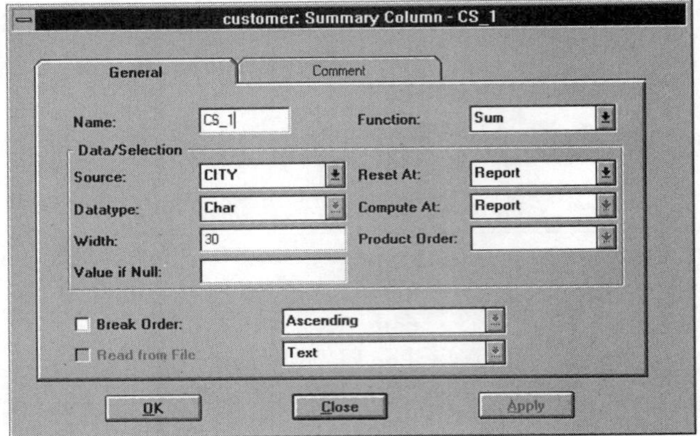

FIGURE E.13.
The Summary Column dialog box with the General tab.

General Tab

Property Name	*Description/Property Values*
Name	A unique name for the summary column/ CS_1, assigned by default, should be changed to a meaningful name
Function	Specifies the computation type for the column/ Sum; or any function from the drop-down list
Source	The name of the column to be summarized/ Blank; or any column name from the drop-down list
Datatype	The type of data contained in this column/ Varchar2, Character, Date, Long, Long Raw, Number, Raw, or Varchar
Width	The number of characters for the column/ 10; or any number from 1 to 64,000
Value If Null	A value to substitute for a null value/ Blank means no substitution; or any text

Reset At	Specifies when to reset the summary count/ Report or page from the drop-down list
Compute At	Specifies when to compute percent of total/ Report or page from the drop-down list
Product Order	Used to determine order of cross product groups/ The parent group; or any group from the drop-down list
Break Order	Specifies whether this is a break column/ Unchecked or checked
Sort Direction	Specifies the direction to sort for a break/ Ascending or Descending
Read from File	Specifies whether the value is to be read from a file/ Unchecked means no; or checked for yes
Format	Specifies the format of the file to be read/ Text, Image, or any format from the drop-down list

Comment Tab

The Summary Column dialog box also contains the standard Comment tab.

Placeholder Column Properties

Placeholder Column properties are found in the Placeholder Column dialog box. (See Figure E.14.)

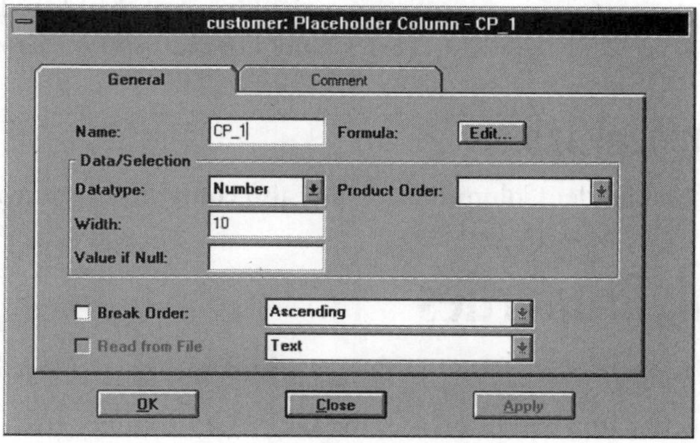

FIGURE E.14.
The Placeholder Column dialog box with the General tab.

General Tab

Property Name	*Description/Property Values*
Name	A unique name for the placeholder column/ CP_1, assigned by default, should be changed to a meaningful name
Formula	The PL/SQL function to execute for the formula/ Defaults to a function outline; must be completed
Edit	Invokes the Program Unit Editor/ Use the Edit button to enter the formula in the function outline
Datatype	The type of data contained in this column/ Character, Date, or Number
Width	The number of characters for the column/ 10; or any number from 1 to 64,000
Value If Null	A value to substitute for a null value/ Blank means no substitution; or any text
Product Order	Used to determine the order of cross product groups/ The parent group; or any group from the drop-down list
Break Order	Specifies whether this is a break column/ Unchecked or checked
Sort Direction	Specifies the direction to sort for a break/ Ascending or Descending
Read from File	Specifies whether the value is to be read from a file/ Unchecked means no; or checked for yes
Format	Specifies the format of the file to be read/ Text, or any Format from the drop-down list

Comment Tab

The Placeholder Column dialog box also contains the standard Comment tab.

Link Properties

Link properties are found in the Data Link dialog box. (See Figure E.15.)

Notice the join condition uses the DEPTNO columns from the EMP and DEPT tables.

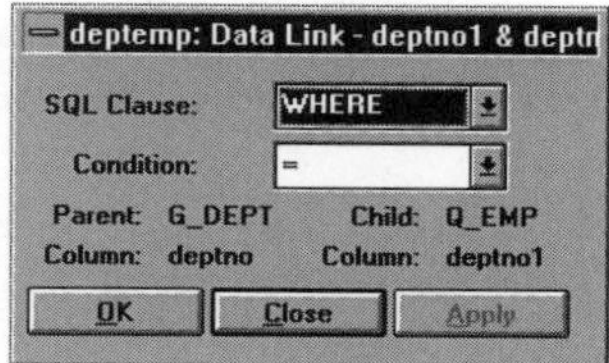

FIGURE E.15.
The Data Link dialog box with a `WHERE` *clause.*

Property Name	*Description/Property Values*
SQL Clause	The SQL clause that connects the queries/ `WHERE`, `HAVING`, or `START WITH`
Condition	The operator used to compare the columns/ =, <, <=, <>, >, or >=
Parent Group	The name of the group in the parent query/ Defaults to parent group name; cannot be modified
Parent Column	The name of the join column from the parent group/ Defaults to parent join column name; cannot be modified
Child Query	The name of the child query in the link/ Defaults to child query name; cannot be modified
Child Column	The name of the join column from the child group/ Defaults to child join column name; cannot be modified

Frame Properties

Frame properties are found in the Frame dialog box. (See Figure E.16.)

FIGURE E.16.
The Frame dialog box with the General Layout tab.

Notice the Frame dialog box contains a General Layout, Printer Code, and Comment tab as well as an Edit button that invokes the Program Unit Editor for creating format triggers.

General Layout Tab

Property Name	*Description/Property Values*
Name	A unique name for the frame/ M_1, assigned by default, should be changed to a meaningful name
Page Break Before	Specifies whether the report page should break prior to formatting/ Unchecked means no; or checked for yes
Page Break After	Specifies whether the report page should break after formatting/ Unchecked means no; or checked for yes
Page Protect	Keeps all of the objects in the frame on the same page/ Unchecked means no; or checked for yes
Keep with Anchoring Object	Keeps on same page as the object anchored/ Unchecked means no; or checked for yes
Edit	Invokes the Program Unit Editor for a format trigger/ Null; or any PL/SQL
Print Condition Type	Specifies when the frame will be printed/ Default; or any Type from the drop-down list
Print Condition Object	Specifies the object on which the printing is based/ Anchoring Object or Enclosing Object
Vertical Sizing	Specifies how the frame should be sized vertically/ Contract, Expand, Fixed, or Variable
Horizontal Sizing	Specifies how the frame should be sized horizontally/ Contract, Expand, Fixed, or Variable

You can set printer codes before and/or after the frame using the Printer Codes tab in the Frame dialog box. (See Figure E.17.)

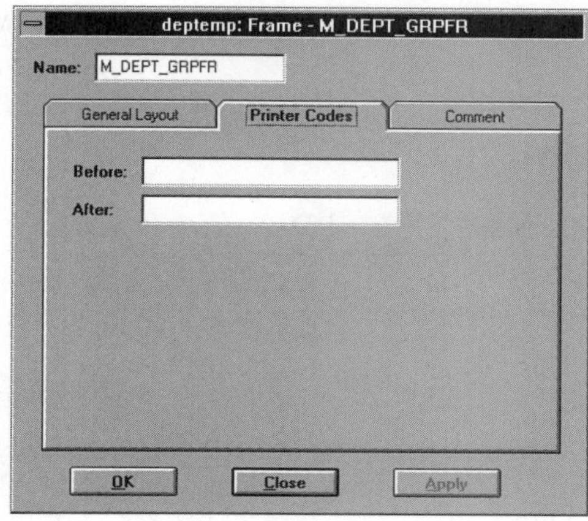

FIGURE E.17.
The Frame dialog box with the Printer Codes tab.

Printer Codes Tab

The Frame dialog box uses the standard Printer Codes tab. This tab control will be found on the other layout object properties dialog boxes as well.

Comment Tab

The Frame dialog box also contains the standard Comment tab.

Repeating Frame Properties

Repeating Frame properties appear in the Repeating Frame dialog box. (See Figure E.18.)

FIGURE E.18.
The Repeating Frame dialog box with the Object tab.

The Repeating Frame dialog box contains an Object, General Layout, Printer Code, and Comment tab.

Object Tab

Property Name	*Description/Property Values*
Name	A unique name for the repeating frame/ R_1, assigned by default, should be changed to a meaningful name
Source	Specifies the name of the Group the items in the frame belong to/ The parent group; or any group from the drop-down list
Print Direction	Specifies where to print the subsequent frames on the page/ Down, Across, Across/Down, or Down/Across from the drop-down list
Maximum Records per Page	Specifies the number of frames that may be on a page/ Blank for all that will fit; or any number from 1 to 32,000
Minimum Widow Records	Specifies the number of frames that must be on a page/ Blank for no minimum; or any number from 1 to 32,000
Column Mode	Maintains relative column position across pages/ Unchecked means no; or checked for yes
Vertical Spacing	Specifies how much vertical space is between repeating frames/ 0; maximum 512 in., 1,312 cm., or 36,864 picas
Horizontal Spacing	Specifies how much horizontal space is between repeating frames/ 0; maximum 512 in., 1,312 cm., or 36,864 picas

General Layout Tab

Property Name	*Description/Property Values*
Page Break Before	Specifies whether the report page should break prior to formatting/ Unchecked means no; or checked for yes
Page Break After	Specifies whether the report page should break after formatting/ Unchecked means no; or checked for yes
Page Protect	Keeps all of the objects in the frame on the same page/ Unchecked means no; or checked for yes
Keep with Anchoring Object	Keeps on same page as the object anchored/ Unchecked means no; or checked for yes

Edit	Invokes the Program Unit Editor for a format trigger/ Null; or any PL/SQL
Print Condition Type	Specifies when the frame will be printed/ Default; or any Type from the drop-down list
Print Condition Object	Specifies the object on which the printing is based/ Anchoring Object or Enclosing Object
Vertical Sizing	Specifies how the frame should be sized vertically/ Contract, Expand, Fixed, or Variable
Horizontal Sizing	Specifies how the frame should be sized horizontally/ Contract, Expand, Fixed, or Variable

Printer Codes Tab

The Repeating Frame dialog box contains the standard Printer Codes tab.

Comment Tab

The Repeating Frame dialog box also contains the standard Comment tab.

Layout Field Properties

Layout Field properties are found in the Layout Field dialog box as shown in Figure E.19.

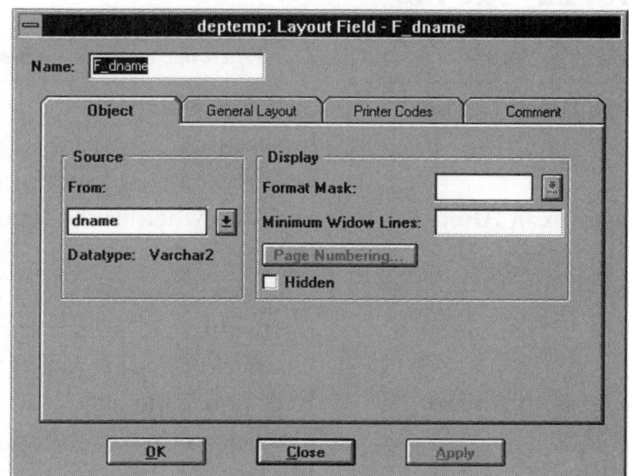

FIGURE E.19.
The Layout Field dialog box with the Object tab.

The Frame dialog box contains an Object, General Layout, Printer Code, and Comment tab as well as a button to set the page numbers.

Object Tab

Property Name	*Description/Property Values*
Name	A unique name for the field/ F_1, assigned by default, should be changed to a meaningful name
Source	Specifies the name of the column this field is associated with/ The default column; or any column from the drop-down list
Datatype	The type of data contained in the source/ Varchar2, Character, Date, Long, Long Raw, Number, Raw, or Varchar
Format Mask	A format mask for dates and numbers/ Blank; or any format mask from the drop-down list
Minimum Widow Lines	Number of fields that must be on a page/ Blank means 1; or any number from 1 to 32,000
Page Numbering	Invokes the Page Numbering dialog box for page fields/ Only enabled for fields with a page source
Hidden	Specifies whether this field should be hidden/ Unchecked means no; or checked for yes

General Layout Tab

Property Name	*Description/Property Values*
Page Break Before	Specifies whether the report page should break prior to formatting/ Unchecked means no; or checked for yes
Page Break After	Specifies whether the report page should break after formatting/ Unchecked means no; or checked for yes
Page Protect	Keeps the field on the same page/ Unchecked means no; or checked for yes
Keep with Anchoring Object	Keeps on same page as the object anchored/ Unchecked means no; or checked for yes
Edit	Invokes the Program Unit Editor for a format trigger/ Null; or any PL/SQL
Print Condition Type	Specifies when the field will be printed/ Default; or any Type from the drop-down list
Print Condition Object	Specifies the object on which the printing is based/ Anchoring Object or Enclosing Object

Vertical Sizing	Specifies how the field should be sized vertically/ Contract, Expand, Fixed, or Variable
Horizontal Sizing	Specifies how the field should be sized horizontally/ Contract, Expand, Fixed, or Variable

Printer Codes Tab

The Layout Field dialog box contains the standard Printer Codes tab.

Comment Tab

The Layout Field dialog box also contains the standard Comment tab.

Boilerplate Properties

The Boilerplate properties for line, rounded rectangle, rectangle, ellipse, arc, polygon, polyline, freehand, and text are all presented in the Boilerplate dialog box with the boilerplate type in the window title.

General Layout Tab

Property Name	*Description/Property Values*
Page Break Before	Specifies whether the report page should break prior to formatting/ Unchecked means no; or checked for yes
Page Break After	Specifies whether the report page should break after formatting/ Unchecked means no; or checked for yes
Page Protect	Keeps the item on the same page/ Unchecked means no; or checked for yes
Keep with Anchoring Object	Keeps on same page as the object anchored/ Unchecked means no; or checked for yes
Edit	Invokes the Program Unit Editor for a format trigger/ Null; or any PL/SQL
Print Condition Type	Specifies when the item will be printed/ Default; or any Type from the drop-down list
Print Condition Object	The object on which the printing is based/ Anchoring Object or Enclosing Object
Vertical Sizing	Specifies how the item should be sized vertically/ Contract, Expand, Fixed, or Variable

continues

Property Name	Description/Property Values
Horizontal Sizing	Specifies how the item should be sized horizontally/ Contract, Expand, Fixed, or Variable

Printer Codes Tab

The Boilerplate dialog box contains the standard Printer Codes tab.

Comment Tab

The Boilerplate dialog box also contains the standard Comment tab.

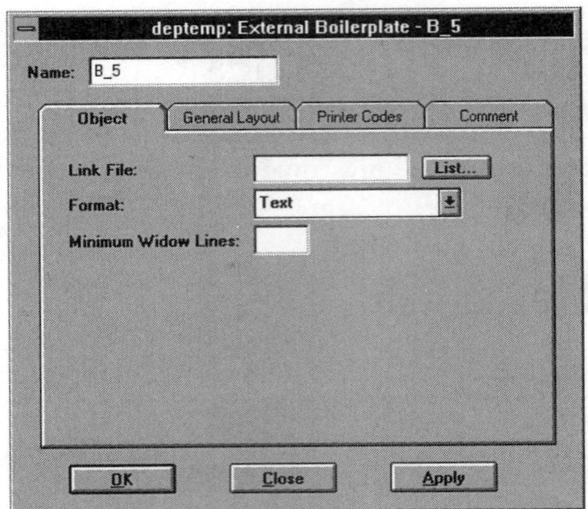

FIGURE E.20.
The External Boilerplate dialog box with the Object tab.

External Boilerplate Properties

External Boilerplate properties are found in the External Boilerplate dialog box. (See Figure E.20.)

Notice the External Boilerplate dialog box contains an Object, General Layout, Printer Code, and Comment tab as well as a button to search the file system for an external file to link.

Object Tab

Property Name	Description/Property Values
Name	A unique name for the boilerplate/ B_1, assigned by default, should be changed to a meaningful name

Link File	The absolute pathname of a file from the file system/ Blank; or any valid file in the file system
List	Invokes the File Open dialog box/ Defaults to current working directory
Format	Specifies the format of the file to be read/ Text, Image, CGM, or Oracle Drawing Format from the drop-down list
Minimum Widow Lines	Specifies the number of items that must be on a page/ Blank means 1; or any number from 1 to 32,000

General Layout Tab

Property Name	*Description/Property Values*
Page Break Before	Specifies whether the report page should break prior to formatting/ Unchecked means no; or checked for yes
Page Break After	Specifies whether the report page should break after formatting/ Unchecked means no; or checked for yes
Page Protect	Keeps the item on the same page/ Unchecked means no; or checked for yes
Keep with Anchoring Object	Keeps on same page as the object anchored/ Unchecked means no; or checked for yes
Edit	Invokes the Program Unit Editor for a format trigger/ Null; or any PL/SQL
Print Condition Type	Specifies when the item will be printed/ Default or any Type from the drop-down list
Print Condition Object	The object on which the printing is based/ Anchoring Object or Enclosing Object
Vertical Sizing	Specifies how the item should be sized vertically/ Contract, Expand, Fixed, or Variable
Horizontal Sizing	Specifies how the item should be sized horizontally/ Contract, Expand, Fixed, or Variable

Printer Codes Tab

The External Boilerplate dialog box contains the standard Printer Codes tab.

Comment Tab

The External Boilerplate dialog box also contains the standard Comment tab.

Anchor Properties

Anchor properties are found in the Anchor dialog box. (See Figure E.21.)

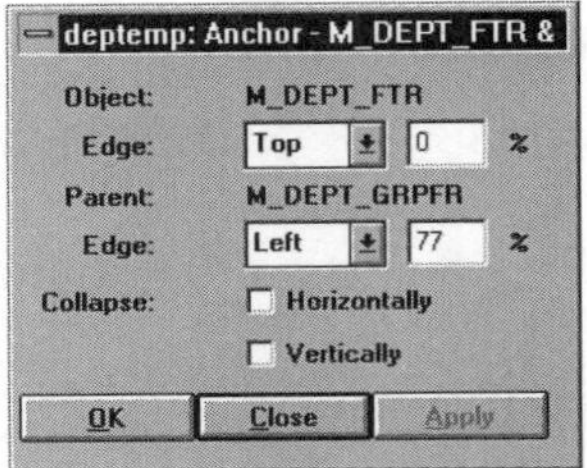

FIGURE E.21.
The Anchor dialog box showing a frame anchored to a group frame.

Property Name	*Description/Property Values*
Object	Specifies the name of the object that is anchored from/ Any object; can only be changed via the Layout Editor
Object Edge	Specifies which side of the object the anchor is attached from/ Bottom, Left, Right, or Top
Object %	The anchor location as a percentage from the top or left/ Any number from 0 to 100
Parent	Specifies the name of the object that is anchored to/ Any object; can only be changed via the Layout Editor
Parent Edge	Specifies which side of the object the anchor is attached to/ Bottom, Left, Right, or Top
Parent %	The anchor location as a percentage from the top or left/ Any number from 0 to 100
Collapse Horizontally	Moves the object over if parent is not printed/ Unchecked means no; or checked for yes
Collapse Vertically	Moves the object up if parent is not printed/ Unchecked means no; or checked for yes

Matrix Properties

Matrix properties are found in the Matrix dialog box. (See Figure E.22.)

FIGURE E.22.
The Matrix dialog box with the General tab.

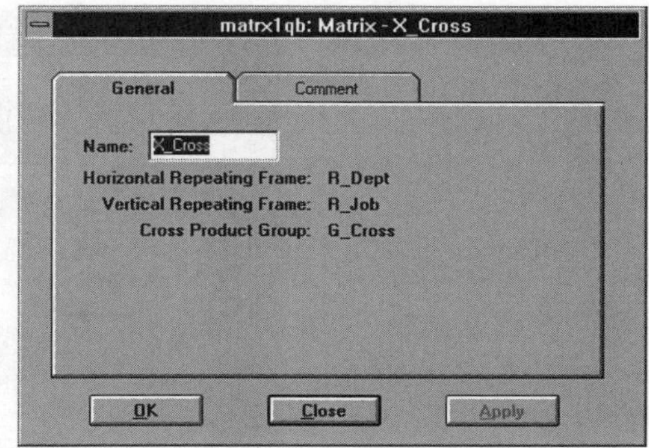

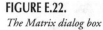

General Tab

Property Name	*Description/Property Values*
Name	A unique name for the matrix/ X_1, assigned by default, should be changed to a meaningful name
Horizontal Repeating Frame	Specifies the name of the horizontal frame/ For the row heading, display only
Vertical Repeating Frame	Specifies the name of the vertical frame/ For the column heading, display only
Cross Product Group	Specifies the group that contains the source groups/ Display only

Comment Tab

The Matrix dialog box contains the standard Comment tab.

Oracle Graphics Properties

Oracle Graphics properties are found in the Oracle Graphics Display dialog box as shown in Figure E.23.

The Oracle Graphics Display dialog box contains a Display, Query, General Layout, Printer Code, and Comment tab.

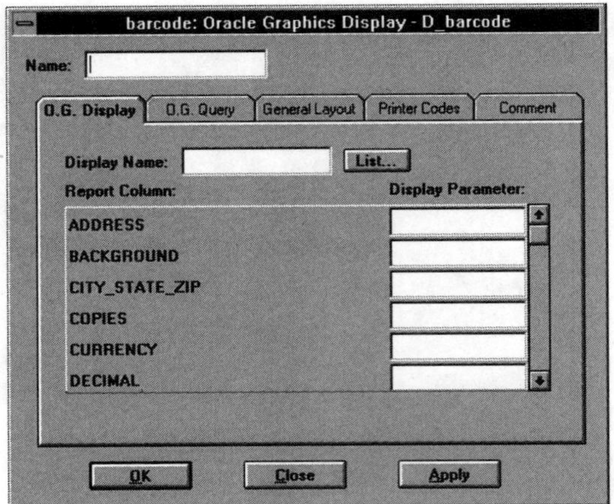

FIGURE E.23.
The Oracle Graphics Display dialog box with the Display tab.

O.G. Display Tab

Property Name	*Description/Property Values*
Name	A unique name for the Oracle Graphics display/ D_1, assigned by default, should be changed to a meaningful name
Display Name	Specifies the filename for the .OGD file/ Null; or any Oracle Graphics display
List	Invokes the File Open dialog box/ Defaults to current working directory
Report Column	A list of parameter names/ All the system and user parameters in the report
Display Parameter	A list of display names for each parameter/ Null; or any parameter name from the display

The query and columns used in the display are located in the Oracle Graphics Query tab of the Oracle Graphics Display dialog box. (See Figure E.24.)

FIGURE E.24.
The Oracle Graphics Display dialog box showing the Query tab.

O.G. Query Tab

Property Name	*Description/Property Values*
Display Query	Specifies the name of the display query to replace/ Null; or any query in the display
Source	Specifies the group that contains the data for the display/ Null; or any group from the drop-down list
Report Column	A list of parameter and column names/ All the system and user parameters and columns in the report
Display Column	A list of display columns for each report column/ Null; or any column name from the display

General Layout Tab

Property Name	*Description/Property Values*
Page Break Before	Specifies whether the report page should break prior to formatting/ Unchecked means no; or checked for yes
Page Break After	Specifies whether the report page should break after formatting/ Unchecked means no; or checked for yes
Page Protect	Keeps the display on the same page/ Unchecked means no; or checked for yes
Keep with Anchoring Object	Keeps on same page as the object anchored/ Unchecked means no; or checked for yes

continues

Property Name	Description/Property Values
Edit	Invokes the Program Unit Editor for a format trigger/ Null; or any PL/SQL
Print Condition Type	Specifies when the display will be printed/ Default; or any Type from the drop-down list
Print Condition Object	The object on which the printing is based/ Anchoring Object or Enclosing Object
Vertical Sizing	Specifies how the display should be sized vertically/ Contract, Expand, Fixed, or Variable
Horizontal Sizing	Specifies how the display should be sized horizontally/ Contract, Expand, Fixed, or Variable

Printer Codes Tab

The Oracle Graphics Display dialog box contains the standard Printer Codes tab.

Comment Tab

The Oracle Graphics Display dialog box also contains the standard Comment tab.

Button Properties

Button properties are found in the Button dialog box. (See Figure E.25.)

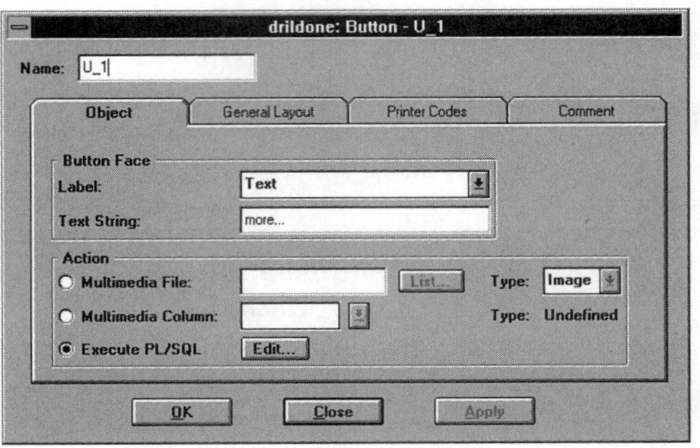

FIGURE E.25.
The Button dialog box with the Object tab selected.

The Button dialog box contains an Object, General Layout, Printer Code, and Comment tab as well as buttons to search the file system for a multimedia file and to execute the PL/SQL of the button trigger.

Object Tab

Property Name	*Description/Property Values*
Name	A unique name for the button/ U_1, assigned by default, should be changed to a meaningful name
Label	The type of label for the button/ Text or Icon from the drop-down list
Text String	Specifies what will appear as the label on the button/ Null; or any text
Icon Name	Specifies the name of the icon for the button/ Null; or any icon name
Action	Specifies what to execute when the button is pressed/ Multimedia File, Multimedia Column, or Execute PL/SQL
Multimedia File	Specifies the name of a multimedia file to execute/ Null; or any file on the file system
List	Invokes the File Open dialog box/ Defaults to current working directory
Type	Specifies the type of multimedia file/ Image, Sound, or Video
Multimedia Column	Specifies the name of a multimedia column/ Null; or any source column in the database from the drop-down list
Edit	Invokes the Program Unit Editor for Executing PL/SQL/ Null; or any PL/SQL

General Layout Tab

Property Name	*Description/Property Values*
Page Break Before	Specifies whether the report page should break prior to formatting/ Unchecked means no; or checked for yes
Page Break After	Specifies whether the report page should break after formatting/ Unchecked means no; or checked for yes
Page Protect	Keeps the display on the same page/ Unchecked means no; or checked for yes
Keep with Anchoring Object	Keeps on same page as the object anchored/ Unchecked means no; or checked for yes

continues

Property Name	*Description/Property Values*
Edit	Invokes the Program Unit Editor for a format trigger/ Null; or any PL/SQL
Print Condition Type	Specifies when the button will be printed/ Default; or any Type from the drop-down list
Print Condition Object	The object on which the printing is based/ Anchoring Object or Enclosing Object

Printer Codes Tab

The Button dialog box contains the standard Printer Codes tab.

Comment Tab

The Button dialog box also contains the standard Comment tab.

OLE2 Object Properties

Property Name	*Description/Property Values*
Name	A unique name for the OLE2 object/ B_1, assigned by default, should be changed to a meaningful name
Object Type	Specifies the type of OLE2 object/ Display only

General Layout Tab

Property Name	*Description/Property Values*
Page Break Before	Specifies whether the report page should break prior to formatting/ Unchecked means no; or checked for yes
Page Break After	Specifies whether the report page should break after formatting/ Unchecked means no; or checked for yes
Page Protect	Keeps all of the objects in the frame on the same page/ Unchecked means no; or checked for yes
Keep with Anchoring Object	Keeps on same page as the object anchored/ Unchecked means no; or checked for yes
Edit	Invokes the Program Unit Editor for a format trigger/ Null; or any PL/SQL

Print Condition Type	Specifies when the OLE2 object will be printed/ Default; or any Type from the drop-down list
Print Condition Object	The object on which the printing is based/ Anchoring Object or Enclosing Object
Vertical Sizing	Specifies how the OLE2 object should be sized vertically/ Contract, Expand, Fixed, or Variable
Horizontal Sizing	Specifies how the OLE2 object should be sized horizon-tally/ Contract, Expand, Fixed, or Variable

Printer Codes Tab

The OLE Object dialog box contains the standard Printer Codes tab.

Comment Tab

The OLE2 Object dialog box also contains the standard Comment tab.

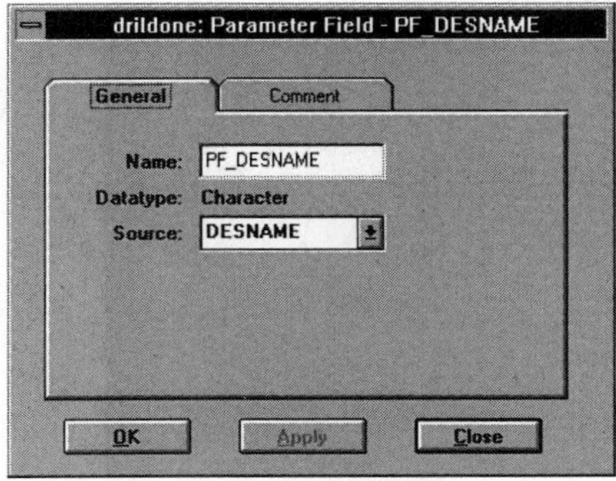

FIGURE E.26.
The Parameter Field dialog box with the General tab.

Parameter Form Field Properties

Parameter form field properties are found in the Parameter Field dialog box. (See Figure E.26.)

General Tab

Property Name	*Description/Property Values*
Name	The unique name of the parameter form field/ PF_1, assigned by default, should be changed to a meaningful name

continues

Property Name	*Description/Property Values*
Datatype	Specifies the type of data contained in the source/ Character, Date, or Number
Source	Specifies the name of a data model parameter to populate the field/ Blank; or any parameter from the drop-down list

Comment Tab

The Parameter Field dialog box contains the standard Comment tab.

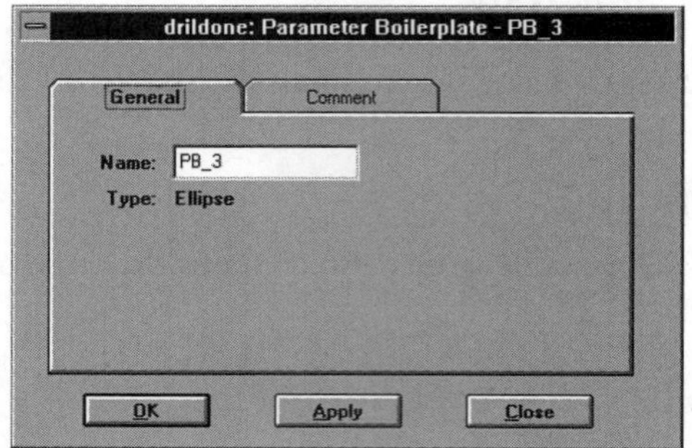

FIGURE E.27.
The Parameter Boilerplate dialog box showing an ellipse.

Parameter Form Boilerplate Properties

Parameter form boilerplate properties for graphics and text are found in the Parameter Boilerplate dialog box. (See Figure E.27.)

General Tab

Property Name	*Description/Property Values*
Name	The unique name of the parameter form boilerplate/ PB_1, assigned by default, should be changed
Type	Specifies the type of boilerplate/ Text, Rectangle, Line, or any boilerplate type

Comment Tab

The Parameter Boilerplate dialog box contains the standard Comment tab.

F

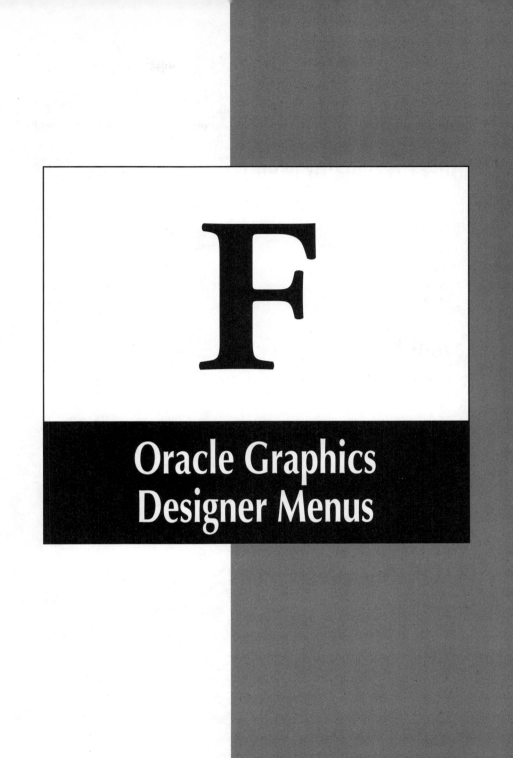

Oracle Graphics Designer Menus

The Oracle Graphics menus are listed here as they appear in the Designer. All of the Designer menu items are listed, and the items that are unique to Oracle Graphics are described.

Object Navigator Menu

The Object Navigator menu contains the following items:

File
Edit
Navigator
Tools
Window
Help

Layout Menu

The Layout menu contains the following items:

File
Edit
View
Chart
Format
Arrange
Tools
Window
Help

PL/SQL Interpreter Menu

The PL/SQL Interpreter menu contains the following items:

File
Edit
View
Debug
Navigator
Tools
Window
Help

The PL/SQL Interpreter menu contains the View and Navigator menus from Oracle Procedure Builder. The View and Navigator menus are different from the Layout, View and the Object Navigator, Navigator menus. See Appendix H, "Oracle Procedure Builder Menus," for more information on these menus.

Program Unit Menu

The Program Unit menu contains the following items:

File
Edit
Tools
Window
Help

Chart Template Menu

The Chart Template menu contains the following items:

File
Edit
Template
Type
Format
Window
Help

File Menu

The File menu appears on each of the main menus in Oracle Graphics Designer. It supports tasks such as creating new display objects, opening, saving, closing, connecting to the database, and administration. The File menu contains the following items:

New
Open...
Close
Save
Save As
Revert
Run...
Compile...

Compile All…
Check Consistency…
Connect…
Disconnect
Administration
Print…
Print Setup…
Exit

File, New Menu

The File, New menu supports the creation of new Graphics displays and libraries. The result of creating these objects from the menu is identical to creating them from within the Object Navigator. The File, New menu contains the following items:

Display
Library

File, New, Display

The File, New, Display menu item creates a new Graphics display.

File, New, Library

The File, New, Library menu item creates a new library.

File, Check Consistency...

The File, Check Consistency… menu item checks procedures and arguments for consistency in the way they are referenced in program units and triggers. If any inconsistencies are found, they are displayed for review.

File, Administration Menu

The File, Administration menu supports the access, deletion, renaming, and generation of Graphics displays. It contains the following items:

Access
Delete
Rename
Generate

File, Administration, Access Menu

The File, Administration, Access menu enables the adminstrator to grant Oracle users access to Graphics displays and other modules that are saved in the database. You must be connected to the database for this menu item to be enabled. The File, Administration, Access menu contains the following items:

Display...
Drawing...
Template...
Color Palette...
Image...
Sound...
Library...

File, Administration, Access, Display...

The File, Administration, Access, Display... menu item invokes the Module Access In Database dialog box (as shown in Figure F.1) and lists the displays that have been saved in the Oracle database.

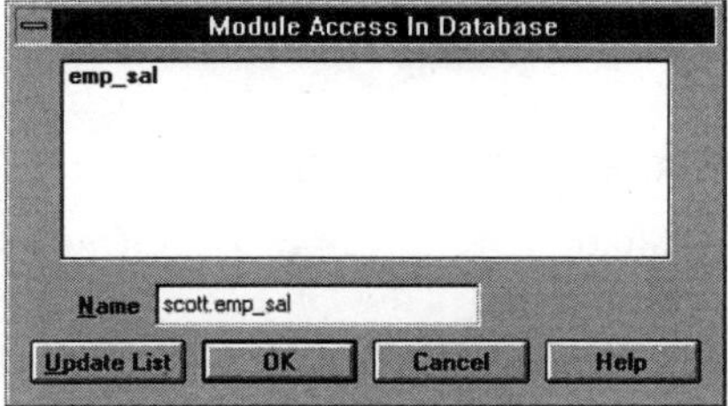

FIGURE F.1.
The Module Access In Database dialog box with a saved display.

From the list of displays, select one, or enter the name in the Name field, then click OK. The Module Access dialog box appears as seen in Figure F.2, listing all of the Oracle users who have access to the selected display.

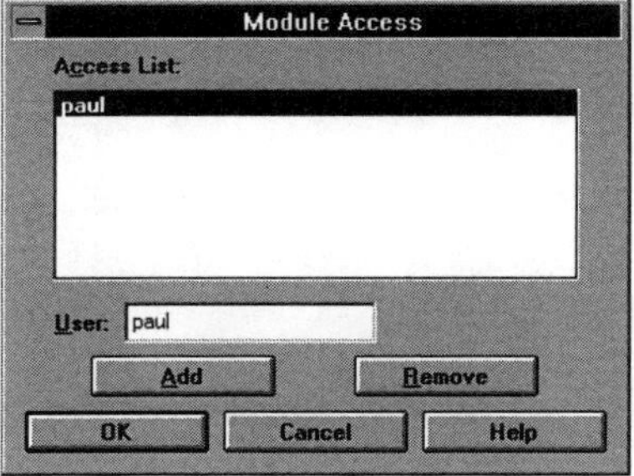

FIGURE F.2.
The Module Access dialog box listing Oracle users.

Users may be selected and removed or added by entering a new name in the User field.

File, Administration, Access, Drawing...

The File, Administration, Access, Drawing… menu item enables the administrator to assign access for drawings using the same method as is used for displays.

File, Administration, Access, Template...

The File, Administration, Access, Template… menu item enables the administrator to assign access for templates using the same method as is used for displays.

File, Administration, Access, Color Palette...

The File, Administration, Access, Color Palette… menu item enables the administrator to assign access for color palettes using the same method as is used for displays.

File, Administration, Access, Image...

The File, Administration, Access, Image… menu item allows enables the administrator to assign access for images using the same method as is used for displays.

File, Administration, Access, Sound...

The File, Administration, Access, Sound… menu item allows enables the administrator to assign access for sounds using the same method as is used for displays.

File, Administration, Access, Library...

The File, Administration, Access, Library… menu item enables the administrator to assign access for the selected library under the Database Objects node of the Object Navigator. When selected, the File, Administration, Access, Library… menu item invokes the Grant Access List dialog box (as shown in Figure F.3), which lists all of the Oracle users who have access to the selected library.

Users may be selected and removed, or added by entering a new name in the User field as shown.

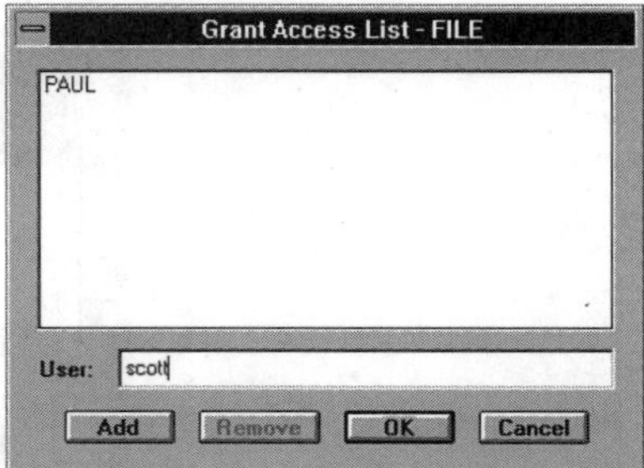

FIGURE F.3.
The Grant Access List dialog box adding a user.

File, Administration, Delete Menu

The File, Administration, Delete menu removes Graphics displays and other modules that are saved in the Oracle database. You must be connected to database for this menu item to be enabled. The File, Administration, Delete menu contains the following items:

Display…
Drawing…
Template…
Color Palette…
Image…
Sound…

File, Administration, Delete, Display…

The File, Administration, Delete, Display… menu item invokes the Delete From Database dialog box and lists the displays that have been saved in the Oracle database. (See Figure F.4.)

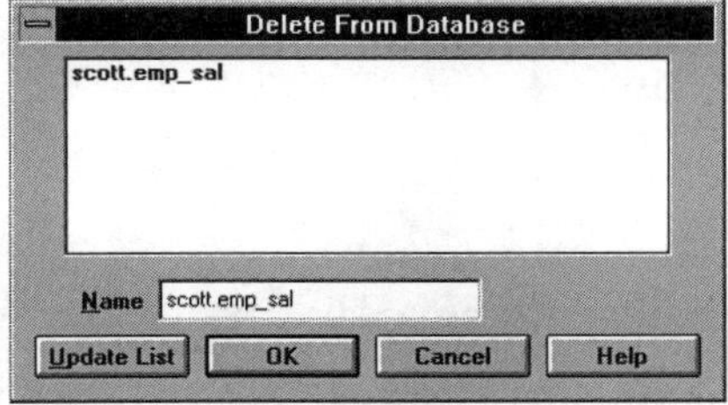

FIGURE F.4.
The Delete From Database dialog box listing a display.

Select a display from the list, or enter a display name. Once a display has been selected, click OK to delete.

File, Administration, Delete, Drawing…

The File, Administration, Delete, Drawing… menu item allows drawings to be deleted using the same method as is used for displays.

File, Administration, Delete, Template…

The File, Administration, Delete, Template… menu item allows templates to be deleted using the same method as is used for displays.

File, Administration, Delete, Color Palette…

The File, Administration, Delete, Color Palette… menu item allows color palettes to be deleted using the same method as is used for displays.

File, Administration, Delete, Image...

The File, Administration, Delete, Image… menu item allows images to be deleted using the same method as is used for displays.

File, Administration, Delete, Sound...

The File, Administration, Delete, Sound… menu item allows sounds to be deleted using the same method as is used for displays.

File, Administration, Rename Menu

The File, Administration, Rename menu enables you to change the name that Graphics displays and other modules that are saved in the Oracle database. You must be connected to the database for this menu item to be enabled. The File, Administration, Rename menu contains the following items:

Display…
Drawing…
Template…
Color Palette…
Image…
Sound…

File, Administration, Rename, Display...

The File, Administration, Rename, Display… menu item invokes the Rename dialog box and lists the displays that have been saved in the Oracle database. (See Figure F.5.)

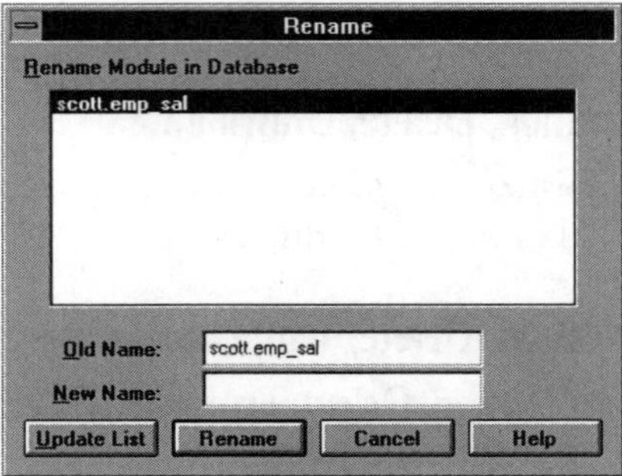

FIGURE F.5.
The Rename dialog box.

The display selected appears in the Old Name field and the new name is entered in the New Name field.

File, Administration, Rename, Drawing...

The File, Administration, Rename, Drawing… menu item allows drawings to be renamed using the same method as is used for displays.

File, Administration, Rename, Template...

The File, Administration, Rename, Template… menu item allows templates to be renamed using the same method as is used for displays.

File, Administration, Rename, Color Palette...

The File, Administration, Rename, Color Palette… menu item allows color palettes to be renamed using the same method as is used for displays.

File, Administration, Rename, Image...

The File, Administration, Rename, Image… menu item allows images to be renamed using the same method as is used for displays.

File, Administration, Rename, Sound...

The File, Administration, Rename, Sound… menu item allows sounds to be renamed using the same method as is used for displays.

File, Administration, Generate Menu

The File, Administration, Generate menu enables you to create a runtime executable file for a Graphics display. The File, Administration, Generate menu contains the following items:

Database…
File System…

File, Administration, Generate, Database...

The File, Administration, Generate, Database… menu item invokes the Save to Database dialog box and allows a display name to be selected or entered. You must be connected to the database for this menu item to be enabled. From the Save to Database dialog box, the executable file for the current display may be saved to the database.

File, Administration, Generate, File System...

The File, Administration, Generate, File System… menu item invokes the Save As dialog box to allow the display name to be selected or entered. From the Save As dialog box, the executable file for the current display may be saved to the file system. The file type for Oracle Graphics Runtime executable files is .OGR.

Edit Menu

The Edit menu appears on each of the main menus in Oracle Graphics Designer. It supports tasks such as editing, searching, importing, and exporting. The Edit menu contains the following items:

Undo
Cut
Copy
Paste
Clear
Duplicate
Select All
Select Object…
Reduce Resolution
Synchronize Program Units
Search/Replace…
Import
Export

Edit, Select Object...

The Edit, Select Object menu item invokes the Select Object dialog box (as shown in Figure F.6), which enables you to enter the name of an object that is to be selected or deselected.

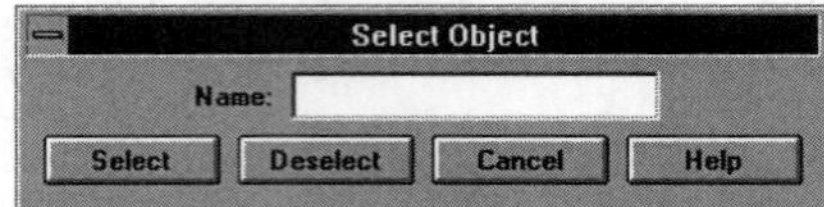

FIGURE F.6.
The Select Object dialog box.

From the Select Object dialog box, enter the name in the Name field, then click Select to select an object or Deselect to deselect an object already selected.

Edit, Reduce Resolution

The Edit, Reduce Resolution menu item requires that a single image be selected to be functional. When an image is selected and the Edit, Reduce Resolution menu item is selected, any image resolution information that is not required to support the current presentation of the image is removed. This may result in a smaller and more efficient application; however, it may not be possible to enlarge the image to its original size without losing image quality.

Edit, Synchronize Program Units

The Edit, Synchronize Program Units menu item is used after debugging to replace the original source code with the code that was edited during the debugging process.

Edit, Import Menu

The Edit, Import menu supports the importing of displays and supporting objects. It contains the following items:

Display...
Drawing...
Image...
Sound...
Text...
Template...
Color Palette...

Edit, Import, Display...

The Edit, Import, Display... menu item invokes the Import Display dialog box, which enables the display name to be entered or browsed in the database or file system. (See Figure F.7.)

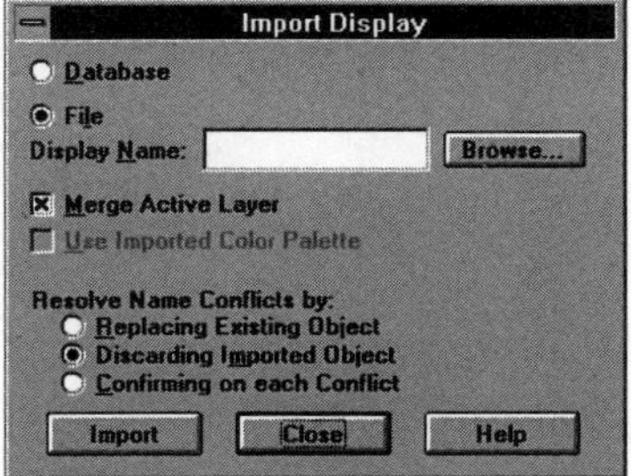

FIGURE F.7.
The Import Display dialog box.

When the Database radio button is selected, the Browse button invokes the Open From Database dialog box containing a list of all saved displays. When the File radio button is selected, the Browse button invokes the Open dialog box to search the file system for .OGD files.

Edit, Import, Sound...

The Edit, Import, Sound... menu item invokes the Import Sound dialog box, which supports the importing of sound files into the display. (See Figure F.8.)

FIGURE F.8.
The Import Sound dialog box.

A drawing may be imported from the database or a file, using the radio buttons in the Import Sound dialog box. When the Database radio button is selected, the Browse button invokes the Import From Database dialog box containing a list of all saved sounds. When the File radio button is selected, the Browse button invokes the Open dialog box search the file system for various sound file types including .WAV, .AFF, .AFC, and .AU.

Edit, Import, Template...

The Edit, Import, Template... menu item invokes the Import dialog box to enable the importing of chart templates into the Chart Template Editor. A chart template may be imported from the database or a file, using the Data Source radio button in the Import dialog box. When the Database radio button is selected, the Browse button invokes the Import From Database dialog box containing a list of all saved chart templates. When the File radio button is selected, the Browse button invokes the Open dialog box to search the file system for .CHT files.

Edit, Export Menu

The Edit, Export menu supports the exporting of display objects and contains the following items:

Drawing...
Image...
Sound...
Text...
Template...
Color Palette...

Edit, Export, Sound...

The Edit, Export, Sound... menu item invokes the Export Sound dialog box to enable the exporting of sound files from the display. A sound file may be exported to the database or a file, using the radio button in the Export Sound dialog box. In addition, the sound format may be specified as well as the encoding method, data type, compression method, and sample rate.

Edit, Export, Template...

The Edit, Export, Template... menu item invokes the Export dialog box to enable the exporting of chart templates from the Chart Template Editor. A chart template may be exported to the database or a file, using the Data Destination radio button in the Export dialog box. When the Database radio button is selected, the Browse button invokes the Export to Database dialog box containing a list of all saved chart templates. When the File radio button is selected, the Browse button invokes the Save As dialog box and a list of .CHT files.

View Menu

The View menu only appears in the Layout Editor menu in Oracle Graphics Designer. It enables you to change the visual aspects of the editor. The View menu contains the following items:

- Normal Size
- Fit to Window
- Zoom In
- Zoom Out
- Rulers
- Ruler Guides
- Grid
- Grid Snap
- Page Breaks
- Tool Palette
- Status Bar
- View Options

View, View Options

The View, View Options menu enables the adjustment of the settings for the ruler, grid spacing, and layout. The View, View Options menu contains the following items:

- Ruler...
- Layout...

View, View Options, Rulers...

The View, View Options, Rulers... menu item invokes the Ruler Settings dialog box to enable you to adjust the coordinate system and grid spacing.

View, View Options, Layout...

The View, View Options, Layout... menu item invokes the Layout Options dialog box. It enables you to adjust the layout size, coordinate system, and page direction.

Chart Menu

The Chart menu only appears in the Layout Editor menu in Oracle Graphics Designer. It enables you to manage charts in the layout. Charts may be created, modified, refreshed, and converted. The Chart menu contains the following items:

Create Chart…
Frame…
Axes…
Field Templates…
Reference Lines…
Update Chart
Convert to Artwork

Chart, Create Chart…

The Chart, Create Chart… menu invokes the Chart Genie dialog box when queries exist in the current display. The dialog box enables you to select a query to be used for the chart. (See Figure F.9.)

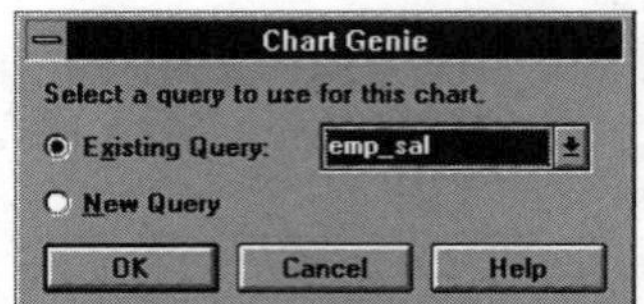

FIGURE F.9.
The Chart Genie dialog box.

You may use an existing query or create a new one. If you use an existing query, the Chart Genie takes you to the Chart Properties tab–controlled dialog box to further define the chart. You will find more on Chart Properties in Appendix G, "Oracle Graphics Properties." If no queries exist in the current display, or you select a new query from the Chart Genie dialog box the Chart Genie—New Query dialog box appears as shown in Figure F.10.

From the Query tab you enter the name of the query and the type. Based on the type of query, you may enter a SQL statement, choose an external file, or create a custom query. You can review the data returned from the query in the Data tab as shown in Figure F.11.

From the Data tab, the data may be cleared using the Clear Data button or re-queried using the Execute button. If you create a custom query, an additional tab appears for defining the schema for the query. (See Figure F.12.)

Select the New Column button and define the columns for the custom query.

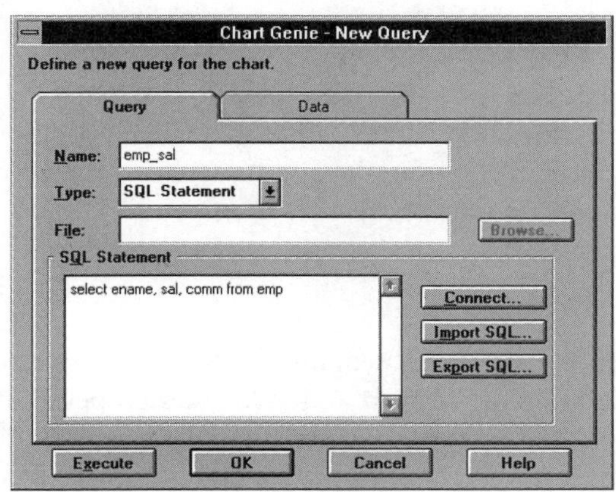

FIGURE F.10.
The Chart Genie – New Query dialog box with a SQL statement.

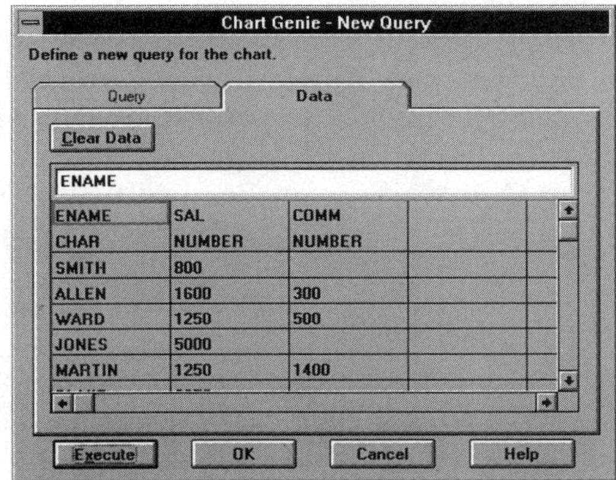

FIGURE F.11.
The Chart Genie – New Query dialog box showing queried data.

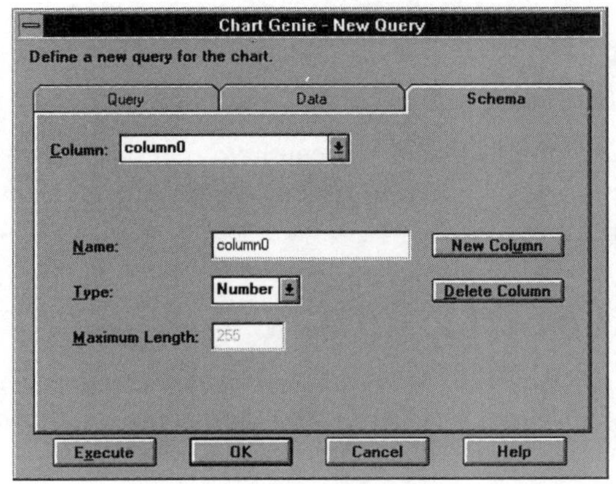

FIGURE F.12.
The Chart Genie – New Query dialog box with schema information.

Chart, Frame...

The Chart, Frame... menu item invokes the Frame Properties tab–controlled dialog box to allow for modification of the chart frame. The Frame Properties dialog box can also be invoked by selecting Frame... from the pop-up menu in the Layout Editor or Object Navigator. You will find more on frame properties in Appendix G.

Chart, Axes...

The Chart, Axes... menu item invokes the Axes Properties tab-controlled dialog box to allow for modification of the chart axes. The Axes Properties dialog box can also be invoked by selecting Axes... from the pop-up menu in the Layout Editor or Object Navigator. You will find more on axes properties in Appendix G.

Chart, Field Templates...

The Chart, Field Templates... menu item invokes the Field Template Properties tab–controlled dialog box to allow for modification of the field templates. The Field Template Properties dialog box can also be invoked by selecting Field Templates... from the pop-up menu in the Layout Editor or Object Navigator. You will find more on field template properties in Appendix G.

Chart, Reference Lines...

The Chart, Reference Lines... menu item invokes the Reference Line Properties tab-controlled dialog box to allow for modification of the reference lines on the chart. The Reference Line Properties dialog box can also be invoked by selecting Reference Lines... from the pop-up menu in the Layout Editor or Object Navigator. You will find more on reference line properties in Appendix G.

Chart, Update Chart

The Chart, Update Chart... menu item refreshes the chart with current data. The chart can also be updated by selecting Update from the pop-up menu in the Layout Editor or Object Navigator.

Chart, Convert to Artwork

The Chart, Convert to Artwork... menu item converts the current chart to a static image. Once a chart is converted to artwork, no other changes can be made to it.

Format Menu

The Format menu only appears on the Layout Editor menu in Oracle Graphics Designer. It enables you to change the visual aspects of the objects within the display. The Format menu contains the following items:

Font...
Spacing
Alignment
Line
Dash
Bevel
Arrow
Symbol
Drawing Options
Color Palette...
Number...
Date...

Format, Symbol Menu

The Format, Symbol menu item enables you to change the current symbol size. The menu style of the subordinate menu is radio group, which means that only one of the sizes may be selected. The Format, Symbol menu contains the following items:

Large
Medium
Small

Format, Symbol, Large

The Format, Symbol, Large menu item sets the size of the selected symbol to large.

Format, Symbol, Medium

The Format, Symbol, Medium menu item sets the size of the selected symbol to medium.

Format, Symbol, Small

The Format, Symbol, Small menu item sets the size of the selected symbol to small.

Format, Number...

The Format, Number… menu item invokes the Number Format dialog box, which provides a list of numeric-format masks as well as the capability to add or remove format masks from the list. (See Figure F.13.)

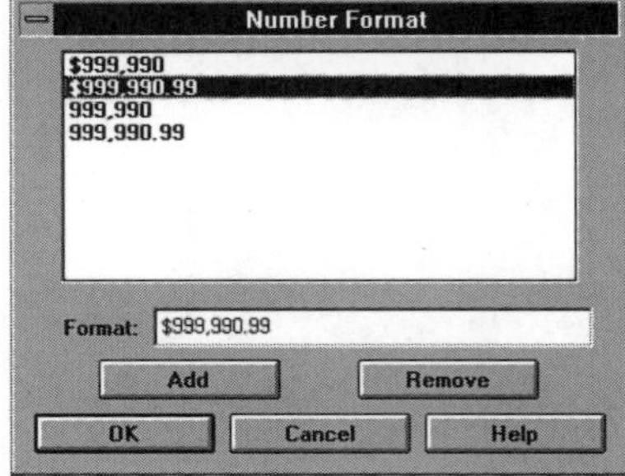

FIGURE F.13.
The Number Format dialog box listing numeric format masks.

The format mask selected from the list appears in the Format field and can be edited to create a new mask. The Number Format dialog box can also be invoked by selecting Number… from the pop-up menu in the Layout Editor or Object Navigator.

Format, Date...

The Format, Date… menu item invokes the Date Format dialog box, which provides a list of date format masks as well as the ability to add or remove format masks from the list. (See Figure F.14.)

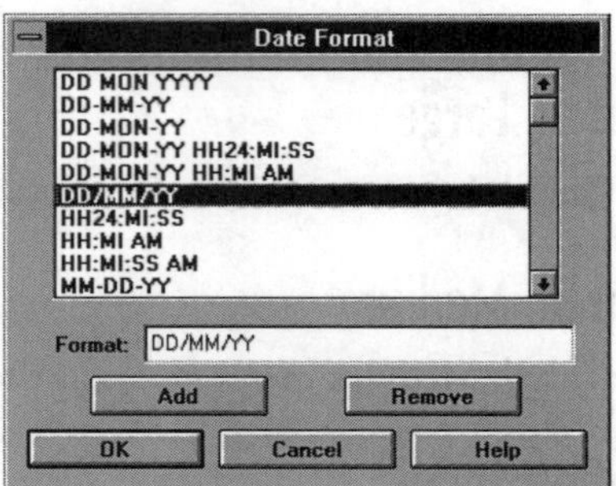

FIGURE F.14.
The Date Format dialog box listing date format masks.

The format mask selected from the list appears in the Format field and can be edited to create a new mask. The Date Format dialog box can also be invoked by selecting Date… from the pop-up menu in the Layout Editor or Object Navigator.

Arrange Menu

The Arrange menu appears on the Layout menu in Oracle Graphics Designer. It supports the layering, aligning, sizing, and grouping of objects in the display. The Arrange menu contains the following items:

Bring to Front
Send to Back
Move Forward
Move Backward
Align Objects...
Repeat Alignment
Size Objects...
Repeat Sizing
Group
Ungroup
Group Operations

Debug Menu

The Debug menu appears only in the PL/SQL Interpreter menu in Oracle Graphics Designer. It enables you to load program units and debug scripts, log the session, set breaks and triggers in program units, and navigate through the source code during debugging. The Debug menu contains the following items:

Load...
Interpret...
Log...
Break...
Trigger...
Edit...
Step...
Go
Reset
Interpreter Log...

Debug, Load...

The Debug, Load... menu item enables you to load PL/SQL program units. Once a source file is loaded, all of the PL/SQL objects in that source file may be referenced. When the Debug, Load... menu item is selected, the Load Program Unit dialog box is invoked. From the

Load Program Unit dialog box, you may enter the name of a PL/SQL source file or search for the file by clicking the Find… button. When the Find… button is selected, the Open dialog box appears.

Debug, Interpret...

The Debug, Interpret… menu item enables you to load and execute script files in the PL/SQL Interpreter. The script file is loaded and each of the PL/SQL or Oracle Procedure Builder commands in that script file are executed. When the Debug, Interpret… menu item is selected, the Interpret Debug Script dialog box is invoked. There are three check boxes in the Interpret Debug Script dialog box. When the Echo check box is selected, the contents of the script file are displayed in the PL/SQL Interpreter pane as the script is executed. When the Silent check box is selected, no status information is displayed. And, to prevent the confirmation dialogs from appearing, select Suppress Confirmation. From the Interpret Debug Script dialog box, you may enter the name of a PL/SQL debug script file, or search for the file by clicking the Find… button. When the Find… button is selected, the PL/SQL Debug Script File dialog box appears.

Debug, Log...

The Debug, Log… menu item enables you to save the results of the session to a log file. When the Debug, Log… menu item is selected the Log Interpreter dialog box is invoked. There are three check boxes in the Log Interpreter dialog box. Selecting Append will add the current session's results to the existing log file. Checking Disabled suspends the entry into the log file. When Show Log… is selected, the PL/SQL Interpreter Log window is displayed. From the Log Interpreter dialog box, you may enter the name of a log file, or search for a file by clicking the Find… button. When the Find… button is selected, the Open dialog box appears.

Debug, Break...

The Debug, Break menu item invokes the PL/SQL Breakpoint dialog box to create breaks for a given line number and can include a break trigger. The PL/SQL Breakpoint dialog box can be invoked from the source pane of the PL/SQL Interpreter window by double-clicking a line of source code or right-clicking and selecting Break… from the pop-up menu.

Debug, Trigger...

The Debug, Trigger menu item invokes the PL/SQL Trigger dialog box to create conditional breakpoints. The PL/SQL Trigger dialog box can be invoked from the source pane of the PL/SQL Interpreter window by right-clicking and selecting Trigger… from the pop-up menu.

Debug, Edit...

The Debug, Edit menu item opens the Program Unit window, or if the Program Unit Editor has already been opened, it sets the focus to the Program Unit window. The Program Unit Editor is used to modify or create procedures, functions, and packages during debugging. The Program Unit Editor can be also be invoked by double-clicking a program unit under a Program Units node in the Object Navigator or from the source pane of the PL/SQL Interpreter window by right-clicking and selecting Edit… from the pop-up menu.

Debug, Step...

The Debug, Step menu item invokes the PL/SQL Step dialog box. The PL/SQL Step dialog box provides a radio group indicating step mode. There are corresponding buttons on the PL/SQL Interpreter toolbar for the STEP command modes INTO, OVER, and OUT. When mode TO is selected, fields for a program unit name and line number are enabled.

Debug, Go

The Debug, Go menu item executes the Oracle Procedure Builder GO command. When the Debug, Go menu item is selected, the execution of the current program unit resumes. There is a corresponding button on the PL/SQL Interpreter toolbar for the GO command.

Debug, Reset

The Debug, Reset menu item executes the Oracle Procedure Builder RESET command. When the Debug, Reset menu item is selected the execution of the current process is terminated. There is a corresponding button on the PL/SQL Interpreter toolbar for the RESET command.

Debug, Interpreter Log...

The Debug, Interpreter Log… menu item opens the PL/SQL Interpreter Log window, or if the PL/SQL Interpreter Log has already been opened, it sets the focus to the PL/SQL Interpreter Log window. A log file must be open for the Debug, Interpreter Log… menu item to be enabled. The PL/SQL Interpreter Log is used to review the current log file during debugging. The PL/SQL Interpreter Log window can be activated by selecting Show Log… from the Log Interpreter dialog box.

Template Menu

The Template menu only appears in the Chart Template menu in Oracle Graphics Designer, and provides the ability to create and modify templates for the current display. The Template menu contains the following items:

Create...
Rename...
Delete...
Frame...
Axes...
Field Templates...
Reference Lines...

Template, Create...

The Template, Create... menu item invokes the New Template dialog box, which enables you to select the chart type and to assign a chart template name. (See Figure F.15.)

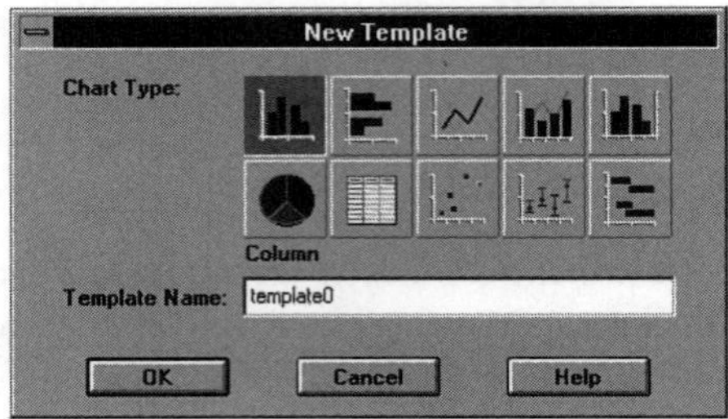

FIGURE F.15.
The New Template dialog box.

Notice the convenient visual display of chart types.

Template, Rename...

The Template, Rename... menu item invokes the Rename Template dialog box, which enables you to assign a new name to the current chart template. (See Figure F.16.)

FIGURE F.16.
The Rename Template dialog box.

Template, Delete

The Template, Delete menu item deletes the current chart template from the display.

Template, Frame...

The Template, Frame... menu item invokes the Frame Properties tab–controlled dialog box, which enables you to modify the chart template frame. You will find more on frame properties in Appendix G.

Template, Axes...

The Template, Axes... menu item invokes the Axes Properties tab–controlled dialog box, which enables you to modify the chart template axes. You will find more on axes properties in Appendix G.

Template, Field Templates...

The Template, Field Templates... menu item invokes the Field Template Properties tab–controlled dialog box, which enables you to modify the field templates. You will find more on field template properties in Appendix G.

Template, Reference Lines...

The Template, Reference Lines... menu item invokes the Reference Line Properties tab–controlled dialog box, which enables you to modify the reference lines on the chart template. You will find more on reference line properties in Appendix G.

Type Menu

The Type menu appears only in the Chart Template menu in Oracle Graphics Designer. It enables you modify the chart type for the current chart template. The menu style of each of the subordinate menus is iconic, which provides an easy visual selection of the chart type. Only one of the chart types may be selected. The Type menu contains the following items:

- Column
- Bar
- Line
- Mixed
- Pie
- Double-Y
- High-Low

Gantt
Scatter
Table

Type, Column Menu

The Type, Column menu enables you to select a column-style chart to be set for the current chart template. The column styles include plain column, column with stacked bars, column with overlapping, column with percent scaling, column with baseline at zero, column with shadows, column with depth, and column with connecting lines.

Type, Bar Menu

The Type, Bar menu enables you to select a bar-style chart to be set for the current chart template. The bar styles include plain bar, bar with stacked bars, bar with overlapping, bar with percent scaling, bar with baseline at zero, bar with shadows, bar with depth, and bar with connecting lines.

Type, Line Menu

The Type, Line menu enables you to select a line-style chart to be set for the current chart template. The line styles include plain line, line with symbols, stacked lines, stacked lines with fill, step, step with symbols, stacked step, stacked step with fill, curved line, curved line with symbols, stacked curved lines, and stacked curved lines with fill.

Type, Mixed Menu

The Type, Mixed menu enables you to select a mixed column- and line-styles chart to be set for the current chart template. The mixed styles include plain column and line mixed, mixed column and filled line, mixed column and curved line, and mixed column and curved filled line.

Type, Pie Menu

The Type, Pie menu enables you to select a pie-style chart to be set for the current chart template. The pie styles include plain pie, pie with shadow, and pie with depth.

Type, Double-Y Menu

The Type, Double-Y menu enables you to select a chart with two Y axes to be set for the current chart template. The chart styles include double-Y column, double-Y column with overlapping bars, double-Y line, and double-Y line with symbols.

Type, High-Low Menu

The Type, High-Low menu enables you to select a high- and low-value styles chart to be set for the current chart template. The high-low styles include plain high-low, high-low spikes with close symbols, high-low close symbols with spikes, high-low close with connecting lines, and high-low close with fill.

Type, Gantt Menu

The Type, Gantt menu enables you to select a Gantt-style chart to be set for the current chart template. The Gantt styles include plain Gantt, Gantt with shadow, and Gantt with depth.

Type, Scatter Menu

The Type, Scatter menu enables you to select a scatter-style chart to be set for the current chart template. The scatter styles include plain scatter, scatter with regression line, scatter with grid, logarithmic scatter, log-log scatter, and scatter with connecting lines.

Type, Table Menu

The Type, Table menu enables you to select a table-style chart to be set for the current chart template. The Table styles include plain table, table with shadow, and table with depth.

Navigator Menu

The Navigator menu appears on the Object Navigator menu in Oracle Graphics Designer. It supports the changing of views, as well as the creation, deletion, compiling, and marking of objects. The Navigator menu contains the following items:

Create
Delete
Expand
Collapse
Expand All
Collapse All
Set Mark
Go to Mark
Navigator Options…

Navigator, Navigator Options...

The Navigator, Navigator Options... menu item invokes the Navigator Options dialog box. The Navigator Options dialog box enables you to change the way objects are displayed in the Object Navigator. The Object Navigator Options dialog box is shown in Figure F.17.

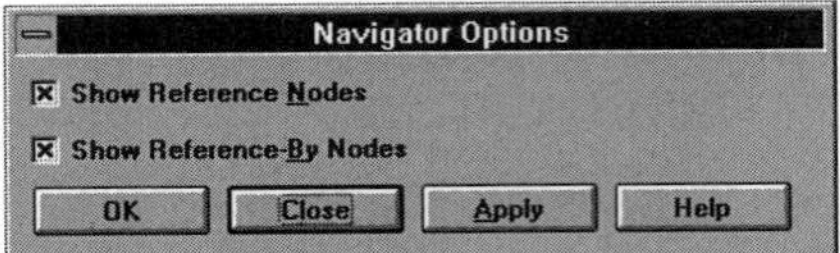

FIGURE F.17.
The Navigator Options dialog box.

The Show Reference Nodes checkbox will include all of the objects that are—or may be—referenced by the parent object in the display of the Object Navigator hierarchy. The Show Reference By Nodes check box will include a Reference By node under each object in the display of the Object Navigator hierarchy.

Tools Menu

The Tools menu appears on each of the main menus in Oracle Graphics Designer. It supports tasks such as reviewing and modifying properties, opening the different editors, managing display objects, and setting options. The Tools menu contains the following items:

- Properties...
- PL/SQL Interpreter...
- Program Units...
- Stored Program Units...
- Database Triggers...
- Display...
- Layers...
- Parameters...
- Queries...
- Templates...
- Timers...
- Tools Options...

Tools, Display...

The Tools, Display... menu item invokes the Display Properties dialog box. (See Figure F.18.)

The Display Properties dialog box enables you to select open and close triggers for the display or to create new ones. In addition, you may reference a format mask for the date parameter or create new date format masks using the List... button to invoke the Date Format dialog box.

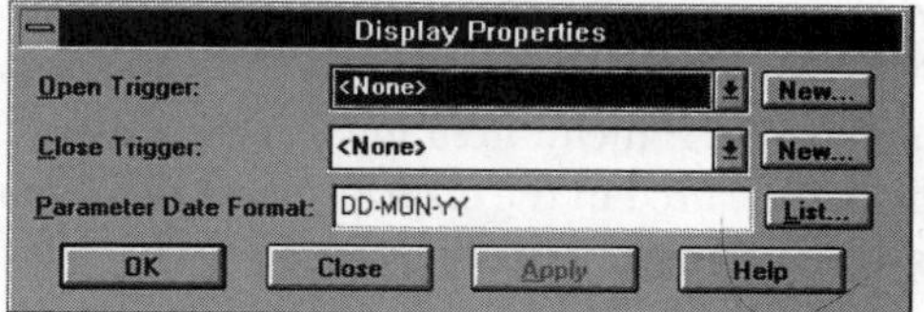

FIGURE F.18.
The Display Properties dialog box.

Tools, Layers...

The Tools, Layers... menu item invokes the Layer Settings dialog box, which enables you to manage the layers in the layout. (See Figure F.19.)

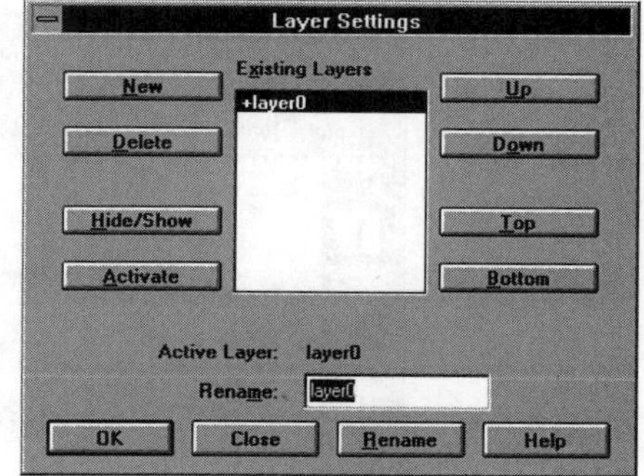

FIGURE F.19.
The Layer Settings dialog box.

The Layer Settings dialog box enables you to create, delete, display, rename, or rearrange the order of layers. Layers are used to provide multiple charts in the same layout.

Tools, Parameters...

The Tools, Parameters... menu item invokes the Parameters dialog box, which enables you to defne and modify display parameters. (See Figure F.20.)

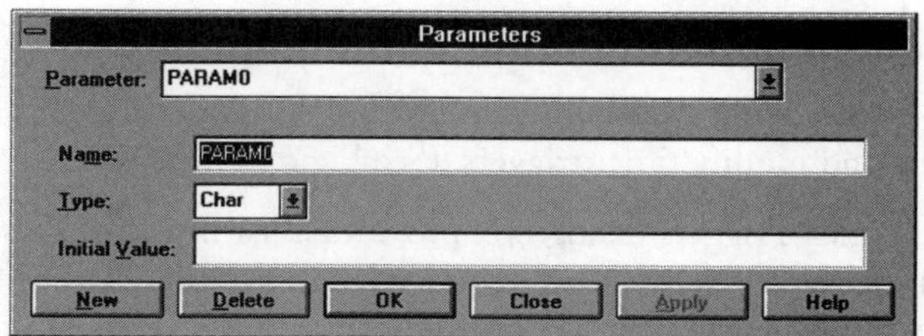

FIGURE F.20.
The Parameters dialog box.

The Parameters dialog box provides a list of existing parameters, as well as fields for defining the name, data type, and initial value for each parameter. You can create or delete parameters using the buttons on the bottom of the dialog box.

Tools, Queries...

The Tools, Queries... menu item invokes the Query Properties tab–controlled dialog box to manage the queries used in the display. You will find more on query properties and the Query Properties dialog box in Appendix G.

Tools, Templates...

The Tools, Templates... menu item opens the Chart Template Editor, or if the Chart Template Editor has already been opened, sets the focus to the Chart Template Editor window. The Chart Template Editor is shown in Figure F.21 creating a frame template for the display.

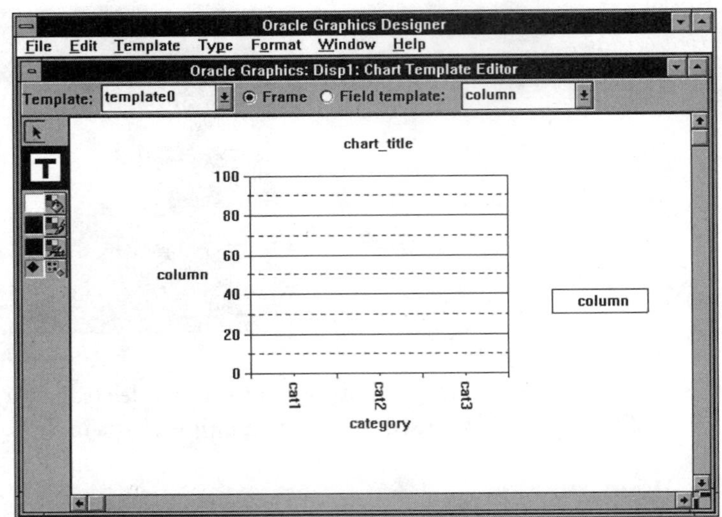

FIGURE F.21.
The Chart Template Editor creating a frame template.

The Chart Template Editor is used to create frame and field templates.

Tools, Timers...

The Tools, Timers... menu item invokes the Timer Triggers dialog box, which enables you to define and modify timer triggers. (See Figure F.22.)

The Timer Triggers dialog box provides a list of existing timer triggers, as well as fields for defining the name, procedure, interval, and status of each timer. You can create or delete timers using the buttons on the bottom of the dialog box.

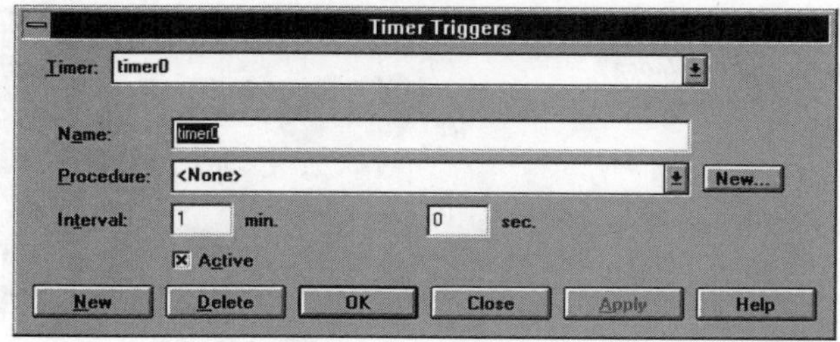

FIGURE F.22.
The Timer Triggers dialog box.

Tools, Tools Options...

The Tools, Tools Options... menu item invokes the Tools Options dialog box. The Tools Options dialog box is a tab-controlled dialog box that enables you to review and modify defaults and preferences. Figure F.23 shows the Tools Options dialog box, showing the Defaults tab.

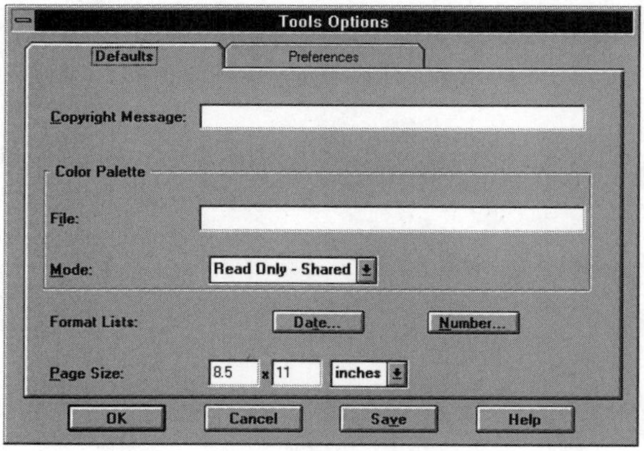

FIGURE F.23.
The Tools Options dialog box with Defaults tab.

The default copyright message, color palette, and page size can be set here. This dialog box also provides access to the format masks for dates and numbers. Additional options may be set using the Preferences tab as shown in Figure F.24. The Designer startup options and other general options may also be set here.

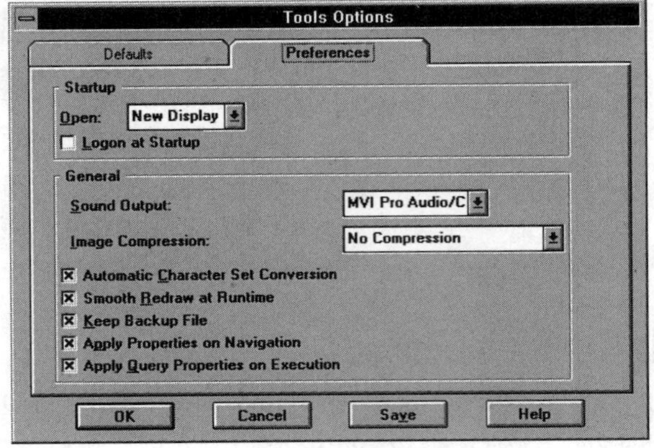

FIGURE F.24.
The Tools Options dialog box with Preferences tab.

G

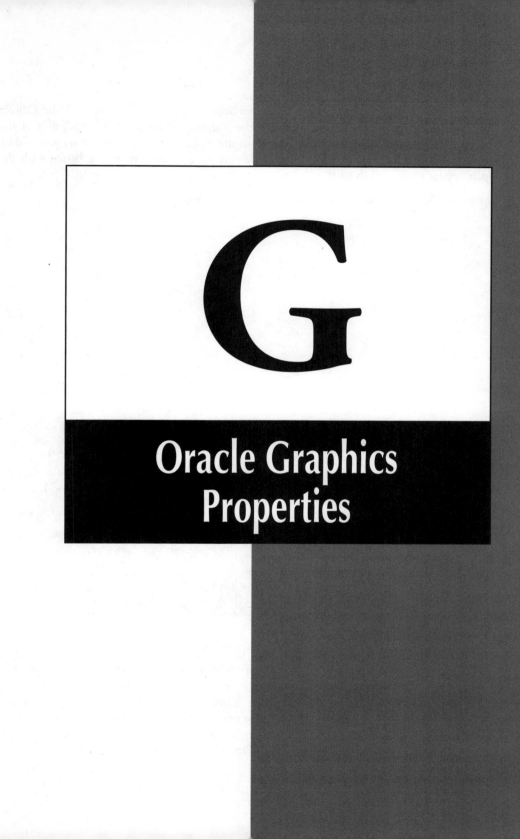

Oracle Graphics Properties

The Oracle Graphics properties are listed by object type, as they appear in the Object Navigator. Each property is listed showing the property name, a brief description of the property, and the default and optional values for the property. The properties are grouped by topic for each object type. Most properties are presented in tab-style dialog boxes, with the topics appearing as the tab label.

The properties for the following object types are described:

Display
Layer
Chart
Frame
Axis
Field Template
Reference Line
Object
Query
Parameter
Sound
Timer

Display Properties

The major node in the object hierarchy for Oracle Graphics is Display. Each graphics application is a display. Display properties are presented in the Display Properties dialog box. (See Figure G.1.)

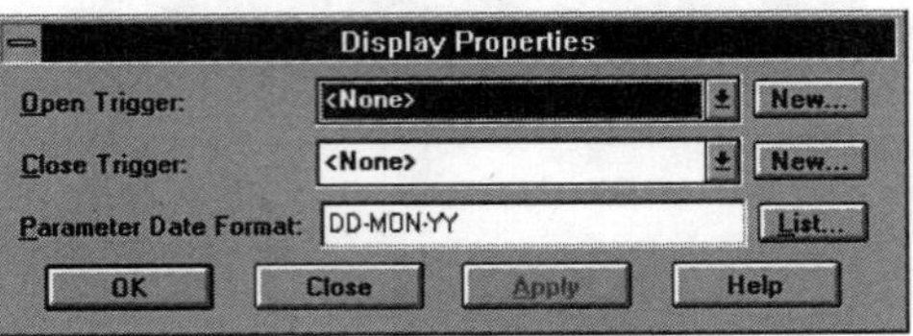

FIGURE G.1.
The Display Properties dialog box.

Property Name	*Description/Property Values*
Open Trigger	The procedure to execute when the display is opened/ None; or any procedure from the drop-down list
Close Trigger	The procedure to execute when the display is closed/ None; or any procedure from the drop-down list
Parameter Date Format	The format mask used for date parameters/ DD-MON-YY; or any mask from the list

New open and close triggers can be created in the Program Unit Editor by clicking one of the New buttons to the right of the trigger name fields. The List button invokes the Date Format dialog box, which enables you to select an existing format or create new format masks for dates.

Layer Settings

Displays contain one or more layers, and layers contain one or more charts. Multiple layers are used for graphic displays that contain several levels of charts. Layer settings are presented in the Layer settings dialog box. (See Figure G.2.)

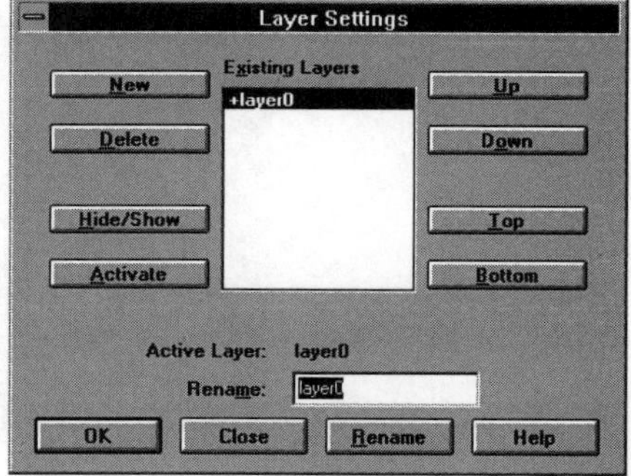

FIGURE G.2.
The Layer Settings dialog box.

Property Name	*Description/Property Values*
Existing Layers	List of layers, in order, showing status/ +layer0; or all layers in the current display
New	Creates a new layer/ +layer1; or a layer with the next sequential number
Delete	Deletes the selected layer
Hide/Show	Changes the visibility of the selected layer
Activate	Activates the selected layer
Up	Moves the selected layer up one in the list
Down	Moves the selected layer down one in the list
Top	Moves the selected layer to the first layer in the list
Bottom	Moves the selected layer to the last layer in the list
Rename	Used to change the name of the selected layer/ Current layer name, or any new name

The plus and minus symbols preceding the layer name indicate whether or not the layer is shown or hidden.

Chart Properties

Charts graph data onto a graphical display. Each layer in the display will contain one or more charts. There are a wide variety of chart types available in Oracle Graphics. Chart properties are presented in the Chart Properties dialog box. (See Figure G.3.)

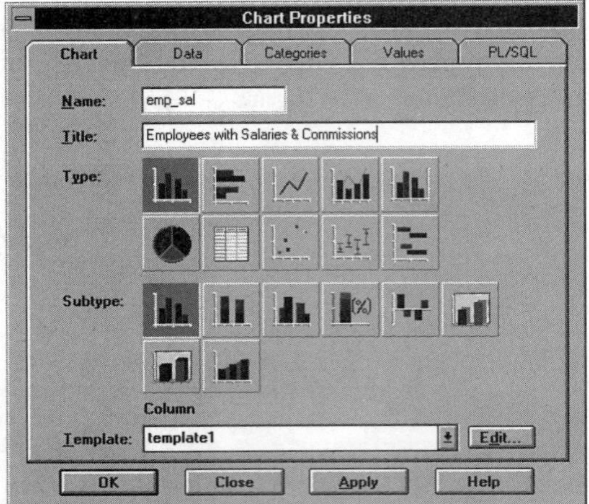

FIGURE G.3.
The Chart Properties dialog box with the Chart tab.

Notice that the chart types and subtypes are displayed as iconic buttons and provide a simple and visual selection list.

Chart Tab

Property Name	*Description/Property Values*
Name	The name of the chart
Title	The title to be used for the chart
Type	The primary chart type/ column; or any chart from the iconic buttons
Subtype	The secondary chart type/ basic; or any chart from the iconic buttons
Template	The template to use for the chart/ template1; or any template from the drop-down list

The Chart Template Editor can be invoked using the Edit… button to the right of the Template field.

Data properties are available in the Data tab of the Chart Properties dialog box as shown in Figure G.4.

FIGURE G.4.
The Chart Properties dialog box with the Data tab.

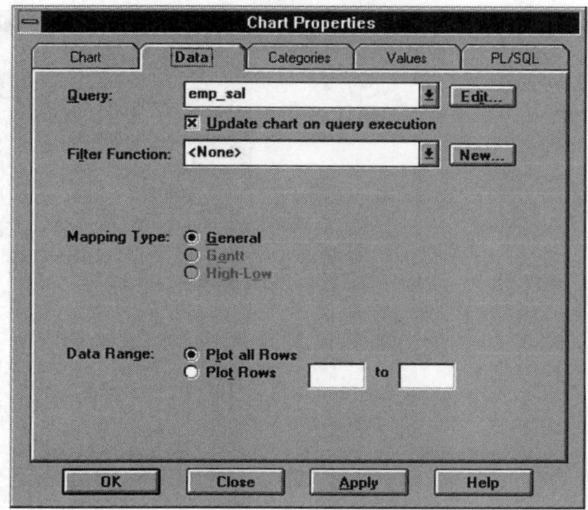

Data Tab

Property Name	*Description/Property Values*
Query	The query used to populate the current chart/ The current query; or any from the drop-down list
Update Chart on Query Execution	Refreshes the chart with new data/ Checked for yes, or unchecked for no
Filter Function	A PL/SQL program unit used to filter out rows/ The current filter; or any function from the drop-down list
Mapping Type	The type of mapping to use in the chart/ General, Gantt, or High-Low
Data Range	Specifies which rows of data should be used for the chart/ Plot all Rows, or Plot Rows as specified

The Query Properties dialog box can be invoked using the Edit… button to the right of the Query field, and the Program Unit Editor can be invoked by clicking the New… button to the right of the Filter Function field.

Category columns for the X axis are available in the Categories tab of the Chart Properties dialog box. (See Figure G.5.)

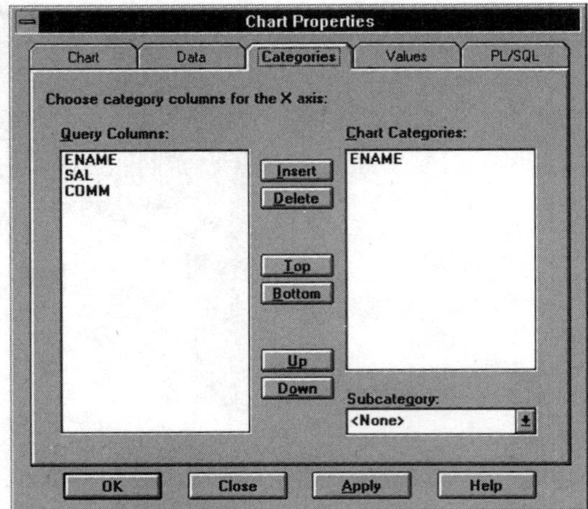

FIGURE G.5.
The Chart Properties dialog box with the Categories tab.

Categories Tab

Property Name	*Description/Property Values*
Query Columns	List of columns from the query/ all the columns in the query
Chart Categories	The column used for the X axis/ first column; or any column from the list of query columns
Insert	Inserts the selected query column as a category
Delete	Deletes the selected category
Top	Moves the selected category to the first column in the list
Bottom	Moves the selected category to the last column in the list
Up	Moves the selected category up one in the list
Down	Moves the selected category down one in the list
Subcategory	Category used for break charts/ None; or any category from the drop-down list

Value columns for the Y axis are available in the Values tab of the Chart Properties dialog box. (See Figure G.6.)

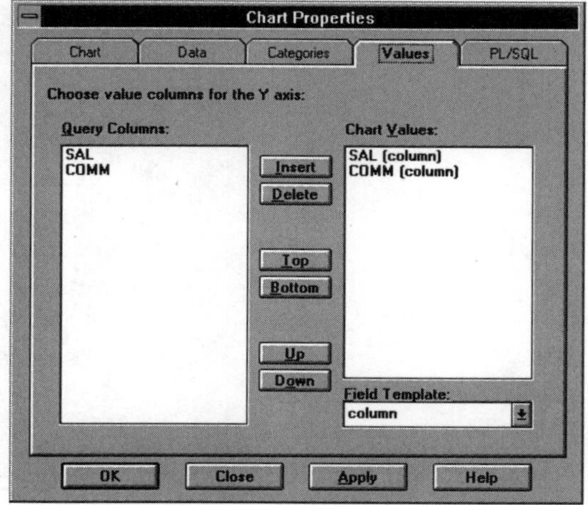

FIGURE G.6.
The Chart Properties dialog box with the Values tab.

Values Tab

Property Name	*Description/Property Values*
Query Columns	List of columns from the query/ all the columns in the query
Chart Values	The columns used for the Y axis/ second and subsequent columns; or any from the list of query columns
Insert	Inserts the selected query column as a value
Delete	Deletes the selected value
Top	Moves the selected value to the first column in the list
Bottom	Moves the selected value to the last column in the list
Up	Moves the selected value up one in the list
Down	Moves the selected value down one in the list
Field Template	Specifies the field template to be used for the chart values/ None; or any field template from the drop-down list

PL/SQL procedures for mouse events may be defined or edited using the PL/SQL tab of the Chart Properties dialog box as shown in Figure G.7.

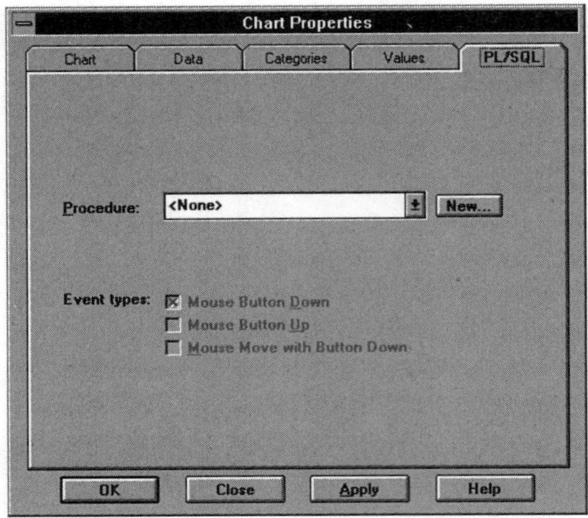

FIGURE G.7.
The Chart Properties dialog box with the PL/SQL tab.

PL/SQL Tab

Property Name	*Description/Property Values*
Procedure	Specifies the procedure to execute for the mouse event/ None; or any procedure from the drop-down list
Mouse Button Down	Specifies whether to execute the procedure on mouse down/ Checked for yes, or unchecked for no
Mouse Button Up	Specifies whether to execute the procedure on mouse up/ Unchecked for no, or checked for yes
Mouse Move with Button Down	Specifies whether to execute the procedure on mouse drag/ Unchecked for no, or checked for yes

Mouse triggers can be created in the Program Unit Editor by clicking the New… button to the right of the procedure field.

Frame Properties

Each chart has frame properties that define the visual aspects of the chart. Depending on the chart type, different tabs will appear in the Frame Properties dialog box. All chart types include the Frame tab in the Frame Properties dialog box. (See Figure G.8.)

FIGURE G.8.
The Frame Properties dialog box with the Frame tab.

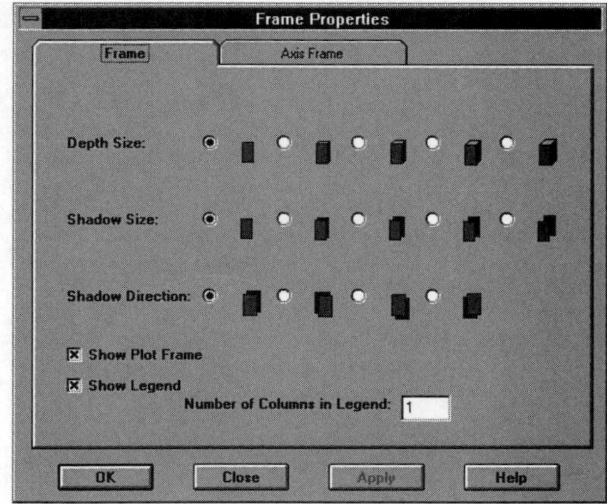

Notice the visual aids to the right of the radio buttons for depth and shadow effects.

Frame Tab

Property Name	*Description/Property Values*
Depth Size	Depth for 3-D display/ none, small, medium, large, or extra-large
Shadow Size	Shadow size for 3-D display/ none, small, medium, large, or x-large
Shadow Direction	Shadow direction for 3-D display/ upper right, upper left, lower right, or lower left
Show Plot Frame	Specifies whether to include the rectangular line around the chart/ Checked for yes, or unchecked for no
Show Legend	Specifies whether to include the legend on the display/ Checked for yes, or unchecked for no
Number of Columns in Legend	The size of the legend in columns/ 1; or any number

Axis Frame Tab

All chart types except pie and table include the Axis Frame tab in the Frame Properties dialog box. (See Figure G.9.)

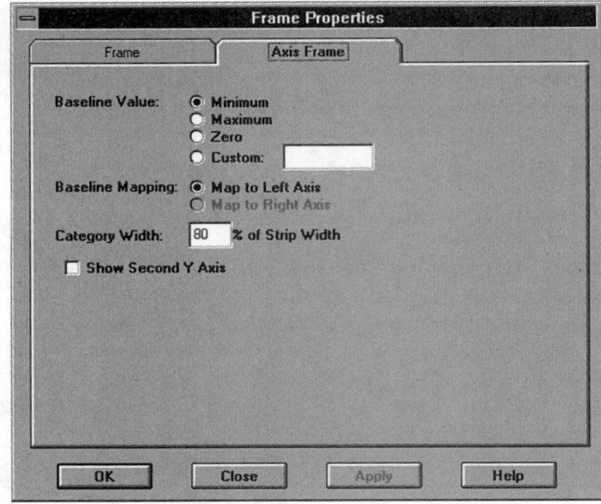

FIGURE G.9.
The Frame Properties dialog box with the Axis Frame tab.

Property Name	*Description/Property Values*
Baseline Value	The value from which the plotting begins/ Minimum, Maximum, Zero, or Custom
Baseline Mapping	The axis used to map the baseline Map to/ Left Axis, or Map to Right Axis
Category Width	The percentage of space between the categories/ 80 percent; or any percentage
Show Second Y Axis	Determines whether a second Y axis should be displayed/ Unchecked for no, or checked for yes

Pie Frame Tab

Pie charts contain a Pie Frame tab instead of an Axis Frame tab in the Frame Properties dialog box as shown in Figure G.10.

Property Name	*Description/Property Values*
Pie Usage	The amount of the pie shown/ 100 percent, any percentage, or Total Value greater than sum
Plotting Order	The direction the pie graph is plotted/ Counter-Clockwise, or Clockwise
Show Category Labels	Specifies whether the categories are to be labeled/ Checked for yes, or unchecked for no
Show Data Values	Specifies whether to display the values/ Unchecked for no, or checked for yes

Show Percent Values	Specifies whether to display the values as a percentage of the sum/ Unchecked for no, or checked for yes
Show Ticks	Specifies whether to display lines from pie to labels/ Checked for yes, or unchecked for no
Put Slices Smaller than % as Other	Specifies whether to group small values in other/ Unchecked for no, or checked for yes
Slice percentage for Other	The percentage threshold for other values/ 0; or any percentage number
Prevent Label Overlap	Specifies whether to organize labels without overlapping/ Checked for yes, or unchecked for no

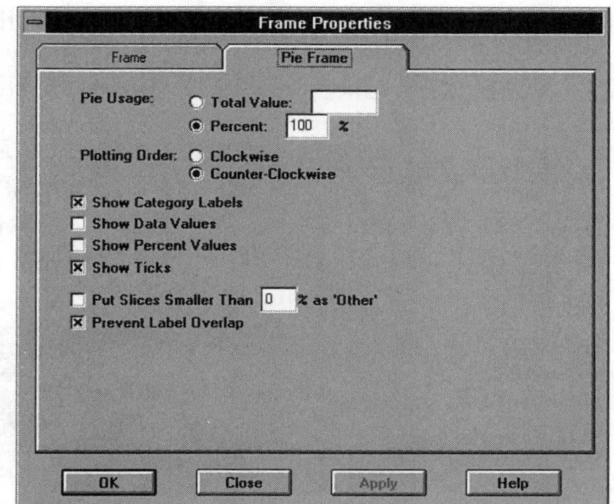

FIGURE G.10.
The Frame Properties dialog box with the Pie Frame tab.

Table Frame Tab

Tabular charts contain a Table Frame tab instead of an Axis Frame tab in the Frame Properties dialog box. (See Figure G.11.)

Notice the visual aids for the Table Direction radio group.

Property Name	*Description/Property Values*
Table Direction	Specifies the direction for the labels and data/ labels across and data down, or labels down and data across

continues

Property Name	*Description/Property Values*
Minimum Number of Rows	Specifies the required number of rows to be displayed/ Null; or any number
Minimum Number of Rows Auto	Specifies whether Oracle Graphics will set the minimum number of rows/ Checked for yes, or unchecked for no
Maximum Number of Rows	A number restricting the rows displayed/ Null; or any number
Maximum Number of Rows Auto	Specifies whether Oracle Graphics will set the maximum number of rows/ Checked for yes, or unchecked for no
Show Column Names	Specifies whether to include column labels/ Checked for yes, or unchecked for no
Show Vertical Grid Lines	Specifies whether to include lines in the table/ Checked for yes, or unchecked for no
Show Horizontal Grid Lines	Specifies whether to include lines in the table/ Checked for yes, or unchecked for no
Rows per Horizontal Line	Specifies how many rows between grid lines/ 5; or any number

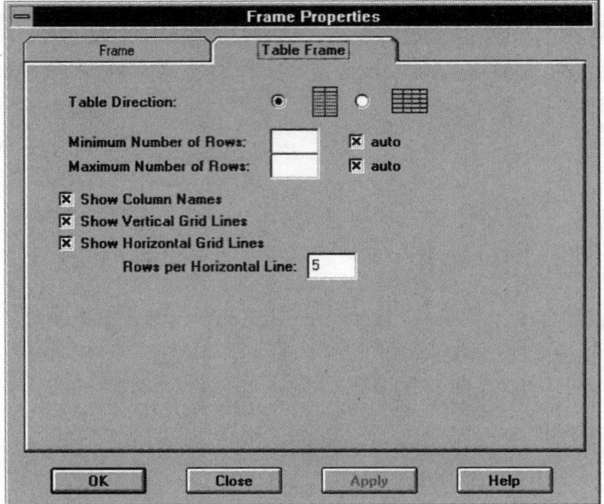

FIGURE G.11.
The Frame Properties dialog box with the Table Frame tab.

Axis Properties

Axis properties are presented in the Axis Properties dialog box as shown in Figure G.12.

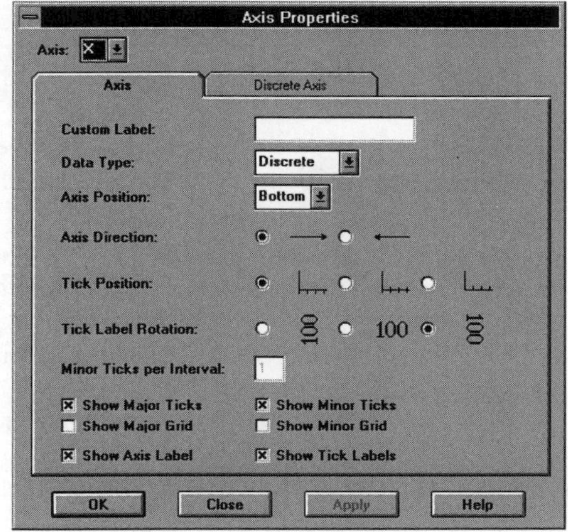

FIGURE G.12.
The Axis Properties dialog box.

Notice the visual aids for the Axis Direction, Tick Position, and Tick Label Rotation radio groups.

Axis Tab

Property Name	*Description/Property Values*
Custom Label	To replace the default category or value column name/ Null; or any text string
Data Type	Specifies the type of calculation applied to the data values/ Discrete, Continuous, or Date
Axis Position	Specifies where on the graph to display the axis information/ Bottom, Top, Left, or Right
Axis Direction	Specifies the direction the data is plotted/ Right, or Left
Tick Position	Specifies the style of tick marks used in the display/ Bottom, Center, or Top
Tick Label Rotation	Specifies the direction to display the tick labels/ Top to Bottom, Flat, or Bottom to Top
Minor Ticks per Interval	The number of ticks between reference intervals/ 1; or any number

continues

Property Name	Description/Property Values
Show Major Ticks	Specifies whether to display tick marks for major intervals/ Checked for yes, or unchecked for no
Show Minor Ticks	Specifies whether to display tick marks for minor intervals/ Checked for yes, or unchecked for no
Show Major Grid	Specifies whether to display gridlines for the major intervals/ Unchecked for no, or checked for yes
Show Minor Grid	Specifies whether to display gridlines for the minor intervals/ Unchecked for no, or checked for yes
Show Axis Label	Specifies whether to display the default or custom label/ Checked for yes, or unchecked for no
Show Tick Labels	Specifies whether to display the category or data values/ Checked for yes, or unchecked for no

The major and minor intervals for ticks and grid lines are automatically calculated for the discrete axis based on the number of categories in the graph.

Discrete Axis Tab

Categories are charted using an axis data type of discrete. The number of categories displayed may be limited using the Discrete Axis tab in the Axis Properties dialog box. (See Figure G.13.)

Property Name	Description/Property Values
Minimum Number of Categories	Specifies the required number of categories/ Null; or any number
Minimum Number of Categories Auto	Specifies whether to automatically calculate minimum/ Checked for yes, or unchecked for no
Maximum Number of Categories	Restricting number of categories/ Null; or any number
Maximum Number of Categories Auto	Specifies whether to automatically calculate maximum/ Checked for yes, or unchecked for no

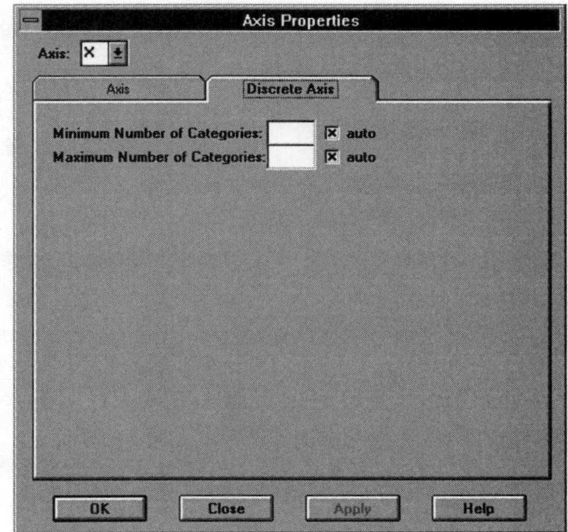

FIGURE G.13.
The Axis Properties dialog box with the Discrete Axis tab.

Continuous Axis Tab

Values may be charted using an axis data type of continuous. The range and interval of data values plotted as well as the scaling method used may be modified via the Continuous Axis tab in the Axis dialog box. (See Figure G.14.)

Property Name	*Description/Property Values*
Maximum	Specifies the largest value on the axis/ Null; or any number
Maximum Auto	Specifies whether to automatically calculate largest value/ Checked for yes, or unchecked for no
Step Size	The value used to determine intervals/ Null; or any number
Step Size Auto	Specifies whether to automatically calculate interval value/ Checked for yes, or unchecked for no
Minimum	The smallest value on the axis/ Null; or any number
Minimum Auto	Specifies whether to automatically calculate the smallest value/ Checked for yes, or unchecked for no
Scale	The calculation method used for scaling/ Linear, Logarithmic, or Percent of

continues

Property Name	*Description/Property Values*
Percent of	For Percentage scaling, percent of what/ Sum, Minimum, or Maximum
Percent by	For Percentage scaling, percent by what/ Field, or Category

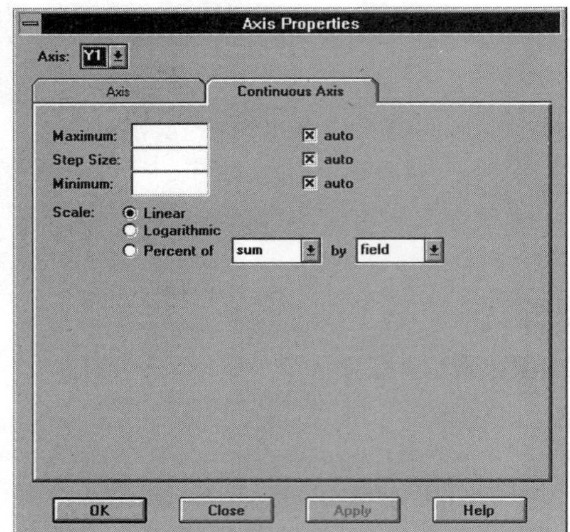

FIGURE G.14.
The Axis Properties dialog box with the Continuous Axis tab.

Date Axis Tab

Values that are dates may be charted using an axis data type of date. The range and interval of data values plotted, as well as the labeling method used, may be modified via the Date Axis tab in the Axis dialog box. (See Figure G.15.)

Property Name	*Description/Property Values*
Maximum	The largest value on the axis/ Null; or any number
Maximum Auto	Specifies whether to automatically calculate the largest value/ Checked for yes, or unchecked for no
Step Size	The incremental value for the intervals/ second, minute, hour, day, week, month, quarter, or year
Step Size Auto	Specifies whether to automatically calculate interval value/ Checked for yes, or unchecked for no

Minimum	The smallest value on the axis/ Null; or any number
Minimum Auto	Specifies whether to automatically calculate smallest value/ Checked for yes, or unchecked for no
First month	The month to start the axis with/ January, February, March, and so on.
Skip weekends	Specifies whether to ignore Sunday and Saturday/ Unchecked for no, or checked for yes
Seconds	Specifies whether to include seconds on the axis label/ Unchecked for no, or checked for yes
Minutes	Specifies whether to include minutes on the axis label/ Unchecked for no, or checked for yes
Hours	Specifies whether to include hours on the axis label/ Unchecked for no, or checked for yes
A.M./P.M.	Specifies whether to include AM or PM on the axis label/ Unchecked for no, or checked for yes
Day	Specifies whether to include days on the axis label/ Unchecked for no, or checked for yes
Week	Specifies whether to include weeks on the axis label/ Unchecked for no, or checked for yes
Day of Week	Specifies whether to include days of the week on the axis label/ Unchecked for no, or checked for yes
Day of Week Format	A drop-down list of days-of-the-week formats/ Sun/Mon/Tue…, or S/M/T…
Month	Specifies whether to include months on the axis label/ Unchecked for no, or checked for yes
Month Format	A drop-down list of month formats/ Jan/Feb/Mar…, or J/F/M…
Quarter	Specifies whether to include quarters on the axis label/ Unchecked for no, or checked for yes
Quarter Format	A drop-down list of quarter formats/ I/II/III/IV…, or 1/2/3/4…
Year	Specifies whether to include years on the axis label/ Unchecked for no, or checked for yes
Year Format	A drop-down list of year formats/ 1994/1995/1996…, or 94/95/96…
Custom	Specifies a custom format mask for the date values/ DD-MON-YY; or any date format mask

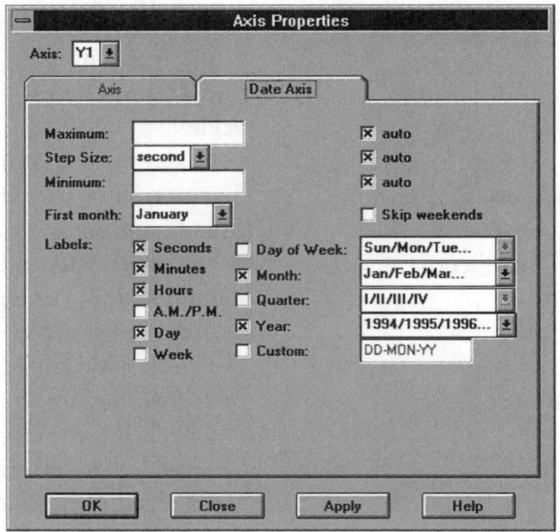

FIGURE G.15.
The Axis Properties dialog box with the Date Axis tab.

Field Template Properties

Field templates are created by default based on the chart type. You must have a chart before you can define a field template. Field templates may be created and maintained via the Field Template Properties dialog box. (See Figure G.16.)

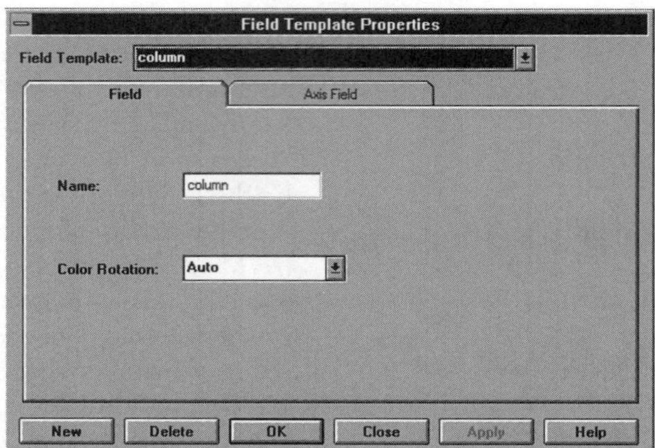

FIGURE G.16.
The Field Template Properties dialog box.

Field Tab

Property Name	*Description/Property Values*
Name	The name of the field template/ ftemp1, a default based on chart type, or any text

Color Rotation	Specifies the method of coloring the chart categories/ Auto, None, Colors only, Patterns only, or Colors and Patterns

The following table lists the default field templates that are created for each chart type.

Chart Type	*Field Template Name*
Column	Column
Bar	Bar
Line	Line
Mixed	Column
	Line
Double-Y	Y1
	Y2
Pie	Default
Table	Default
Scatter	Symbol
High-Low	Low
	Close
	High
Gantt	Begin
	End

Axis Field Tab

The Field Template dialog box includes an Axis Field tab for each of the chart types except table. The Axis Field tab in the Field Template dialog box is shown in Figure G.17.

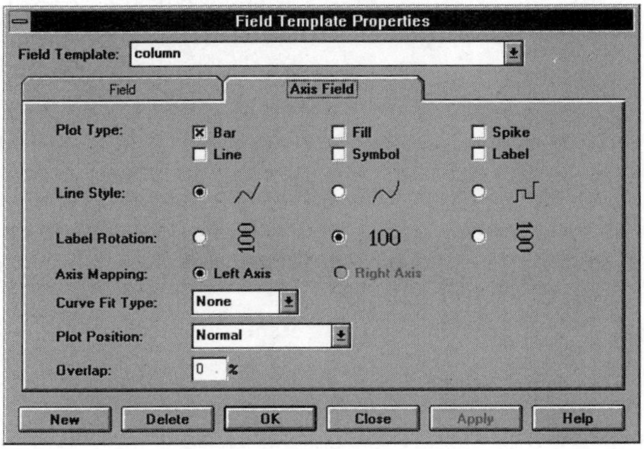

FIGURE G.17.
The Field Template Properties dialog box with the Axis Field tab.

Notice the visual aids for the Line Style and Label Rotation radio groups.

Property Name	*Description/Property Values*
Bar	Specifies whether to format data as bars in the field template/ Checked for yes, or unchecked for no
Line	Specifies whether to format data as lines in the field template/ Unchecked for no, or checked for yes
Fill	Specifies whether to format data as the fill area in the field template/ Unchecked for no, or checked for yes
Symbol	Specifies whether to format data as symbols in the field template/ Unchecked for no, or checked for yes
Spike	Specifies whether to format data as spikes in the field template/ Unchecked for no, or checked for yes
Label	Specifies whether to format data as labels in the field template/ Unchecked for no, or checked for yes
Line Style	Specifies the line style for Line Plot Types/ straight, curved, or step
Label Rotation	Specifies the direction to display the labels/ Flat, Bottom to Top, or Top to Bottom
Axis Mapping	Specifies which axis the data values are mapped to/ Left Axis, or Right Axis
Curve Fit Type	The curve type for curved lines/ None, Linear, Logarithmic, Exponential, or Power
Plot Position	Specifies the method of positioning the next field/ Normal, From Previous Field, or Stacked
Overlap	The percentage of overlap for column and bar charts/ 0; or any percentage

Reference Line Properties

Reference lines provide a static reference on the chart and are created and maintained via the Reference Line Properties dialog box. (See Figure G.18.)

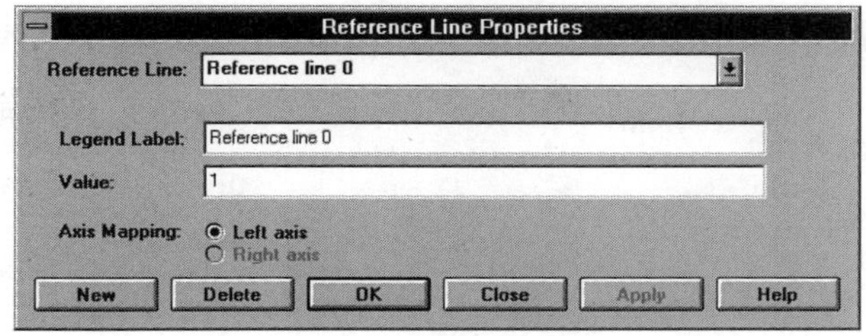

FIGURE G.18.
The Reference Line Properties dialog box.

Property Name	*Description/Property Values*
Reference Line	The name of the reference line/ Reference line 0; or any reference line in the drop-down list
Legend Label	The label for the reference line in the legend/ Reference line 0; or any text
Value	The data value for the reference line/ 1; or any number
Axis Mapping	Specifies which axis the reference line is mapped to/ Left Axis, or Right Axis

Object Properties

Many layout objects use the Object Properties dialog box to access their associated mouse-event procedures and format triggers, as shown in Figure G.19.

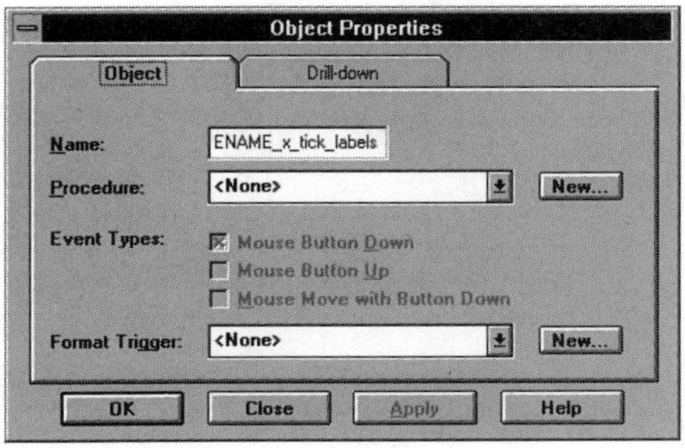

FIGURE G.19.
The Object Properties dialog box.

Object Tab

Property Name	*Description/Property Values*
Name	The name of the object
Procedure	The procedure to execute for the mouse event/ None; or any procedure from the drop-down list
Mouse Button Down	Specifies whether to execute the procedure on mouse down/ Checked for yes, or unchecked for no
Mouse Button Up	Specifies whether to execute the procedure on mouse up/ Unchecked for no, or checked for yes
Mouse Move with Button Down	Specifies whether to execute the procedure on mouse drag/ Unchecked for no, or checked for yes
Format Trigger	The trigger used to format chart objects/ None; or any trigger from the drop-down list

Mouse procedures and format triggers can be created in the Program Unit Editor by clicking the New… button to the right of the Procedure field and Format Trigger field, respectively.

Drill-Down Tab

Chart objects can be used to drill-down to another chart. This is done by defining a parameter, assigning a value to the parameter, and executing the associated query. The parameter, value, and query is assigned via the Drill-down tab in the Object Properties dialog box. (See Figure G.20.)

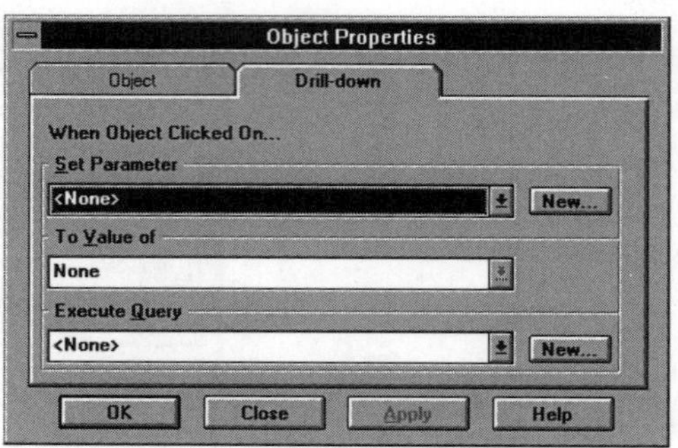

FIGURE G.20.
The Object Properties dialog box with the Drill-down tab.

Property Name	Description/Property Values
Set Parameter	The parameter to set when the object is clicked on/ None; or any parameter in the drop-down list
To Value of	The value to set when the object is clicked on/ None; or any value in the drop-down list
Execute Query	The query to execute when the object is clicked on/ None; or any query in the drop-down list

Parameters and queries can be created via the Parameter and Query Properties dialog boxes by clicking the New… button to the right of the Set Parameter or Execute Query fields.

Query Properties

All charts are based on queries. To define or modify a query, use the Query Properties dialog box. (See Figure G.21.)

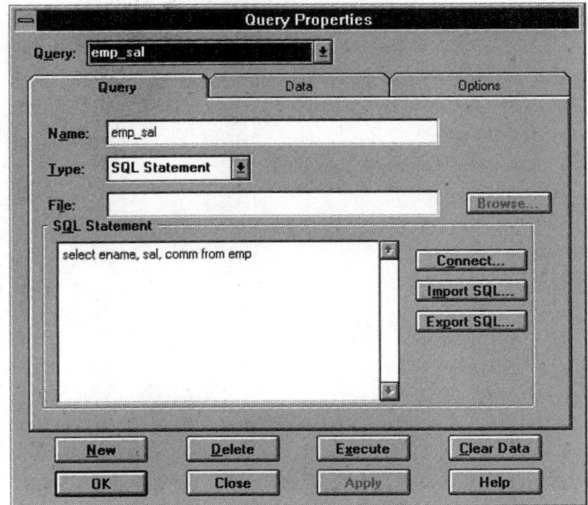

FIGURE G.21.
The Query Properties dialog box.

Query Tab

Property Name	Description/Property Values
Name	The name of the query/ query0; or any name assigned
Type	The type of query SQL/ Statement, SYLK, WKS, PRN, External SQL File, or Custom

continues

Property Name	Description/Property Values
File	The path and/or filename for the query/ Null; or any valid file from the file system
SQL Statement	The text of the SQL select statement/ Blank; or any SQL select statement

SQL statements can be imported or exported from and to the file system via the File Open and File Save As dialog boxes by clicking the Import... and Export... buttons to the right of the SQL Statement fields.

Data Tab

Once the query has been executed, the data can be reviewed in the Data tab of the Query Properties dialog box. (See Figure G.22.)

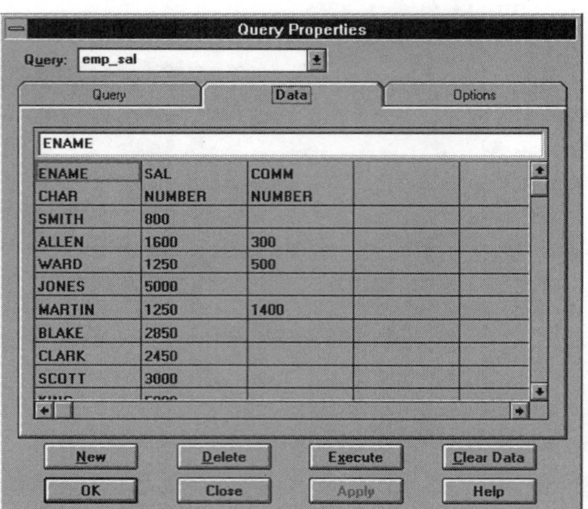

FIGURE G.22.
The Query Properties dialog box with the Data tab.

Property Name	Description/Property Values
Column Name	The name of the column from the query
Column Data Type	The data type of the column from the query
Column Data	The data values returned from the query/ Defaults to blank

Options Tab

Using the Options tab of the Query Properties dialog box, you can set options for when to execute the query, data management, and PL/SQL. (See Figure G.23.)

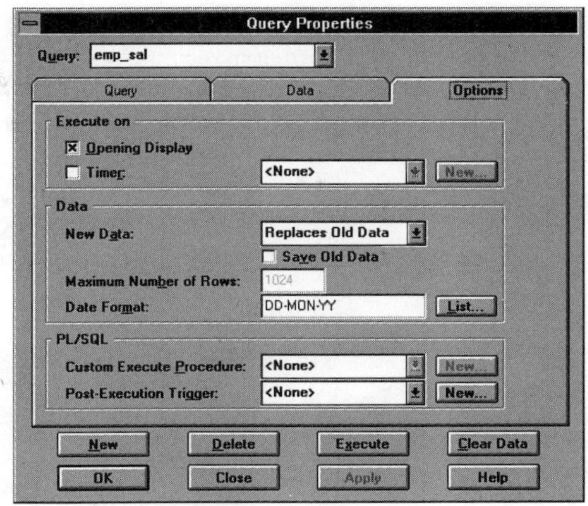

FIGURE G.23.
The Query Properties dialog box with the Options tab.

Property Name	*Description/Property Values*
Opening Display	Specifies whether to execute the query when the display is opened/ Checked for yes, or unchecked for no
Timer	Specifies whether to execute the query when timer expires/ Unchecked for no, or checked for yes
Timer list	Specifies the timer that will execute the query/ None; or any timer in the drop-down list
New Data	Specifies what to do with the new and old data that is queried/ Replaces Old Data, or Appends to Old Data
Save Old Data	Specifies whether to save the old data prior to replacing it with new data/ Unchecked for no, or checked for yes
Maximum Number of Rows	Specifies the largest number of rows used by the query/ 1024; or any number
Date Format	Specifies a format mask for date values/ D-MON-YY; or any date format mask
Custom Execute Procedure	Specifies the procedure to execute for a custom query/ None; or any procedure in the drop-down list
Post-Execution Trigger	Specifies the trigger to execute after the query/ None; or any trigger in the drop-down list

Timers can be created via the Timer Triggers dialog box by clicking the New… button to the right of the Timer field. New format masks can be created for the date using the Date Format dialog box by selecting the List… button to the right of the Data Format field. And both PL/SQL objects have a New… button that invokes the Program Unit Editor.

Schema Tab

If you have defined a custom query type, the Schema tab is also presented with the Query Properties dialog box. (See Figure G.24.)

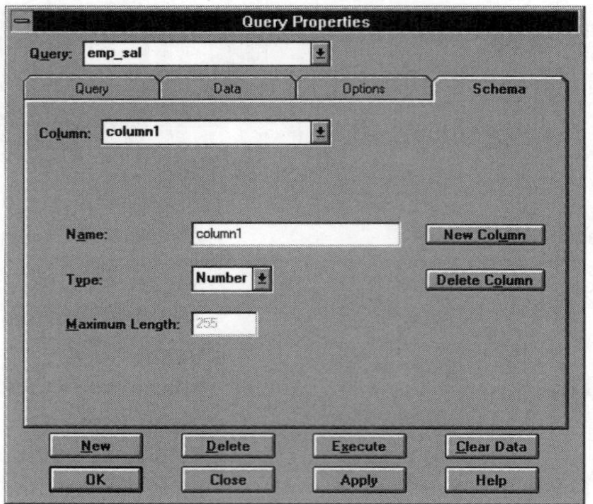

FIGURE G.24.
The Query Properties dialog box with the Schema tab.

Property Name	*Description/Property Values*
Column	The list of custom columns/ Null; or any column from the drop-down list
Name	The name of the column/ fcolumn0; or any text
Type	The data type for the column/ Number, Char, or Date
Maximum Length	The length of a Char column/ 255; or any number from 1 to 255

Custom columns are created by clicking the New Column button. They are removed by clicking the Delete Column button.

Parameters

Display properties are presented in the Display Properties dialog box. (See Figure G.25.)

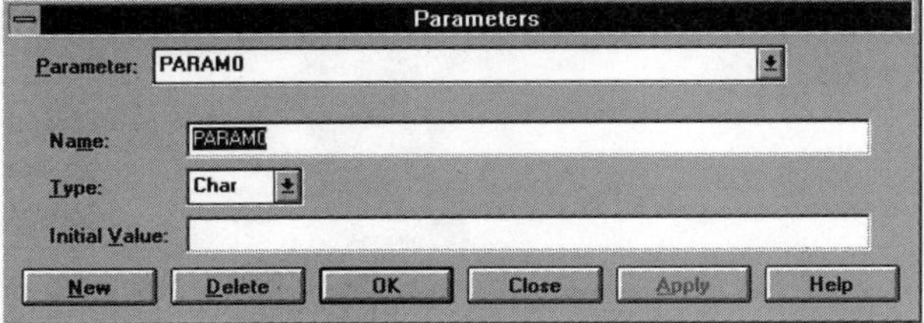

FIGURE G.25.
The Parameters dialog box.

Property Name	*Description/Property Values*
Parameter	Specifies the existing parameters/ PARAM0; or any parameter from the drop-down list
Name	The name of the parameter/ PARAM0; or any text
Type	The data type for the parameter/ Char, Number, or Date
Initial Value	The initial values of the parameter/ Null; or any value

Sounds

Selecting properties for sounds invokes the Sound Player dialog box. (See Figure G.26.)

FIGURE G.26.
The Sounds dialog box.

Property Name	*Description/Property Values*
Name	The name of the sound/ sound0; or any text

The name is the only property for sounds; however, the Sound Player dialog box enables you to record and play sounds. Sounds may be recorded or imported from the file system or the database.

Timer Triggers

Display properties are presented in the Display Properties dialog box. (See Figure G.27.)

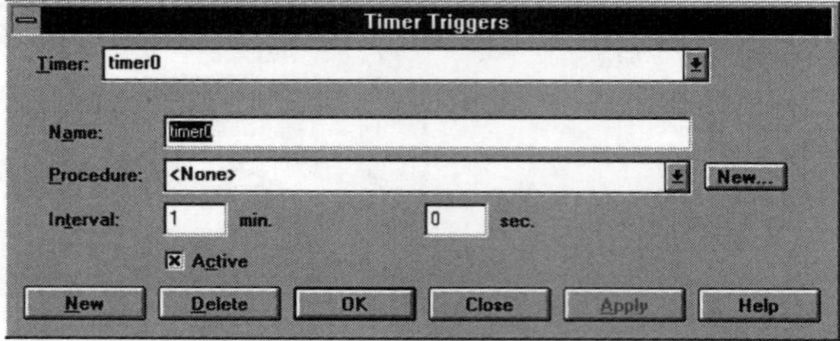

FIGURE G.27.
The Timer Triggers dialog box.

Property Name	*Description/Property Values*
Timer	Specifies the existing timers/ timer0; or any timer from the drop-down list
Name	The name of the timer/ timer0; or any text
Procedure	Specifies the procedure to execute for the timer/ None; or any procedure in the drop-down list
Interval	Specifies the time interval for the timer to fire/ 1 min. 0 sec.; or any interval in minutes and/or seconds
Active	Specifies whether the timer is active or deactivated/ Checked for active, or unchecked for deactivated

H

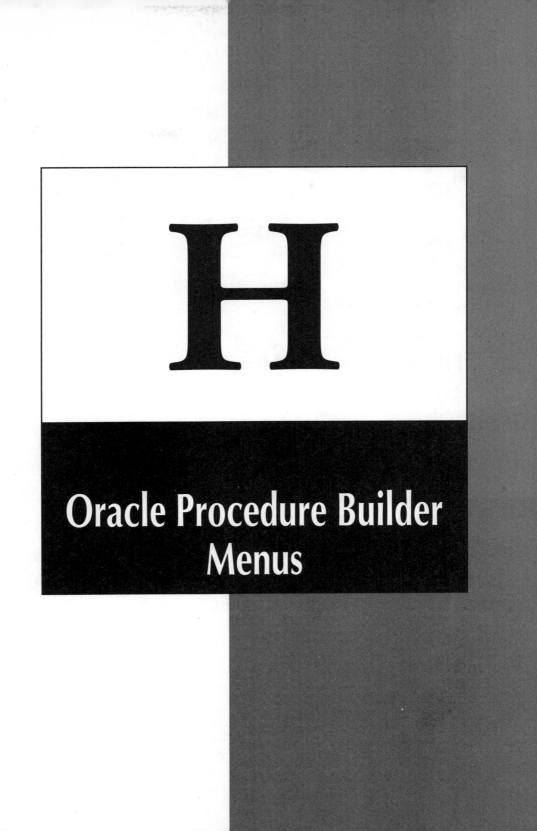

Oracle Procedure Builder Menus

The Oracle Procedure Builder menus are listed in this appendix as they appear for each tool. This appendix lists all menu items, and describes the items that are unique to the Oracle Procedure Builder.

Object Navigator Menu

The Object Navigator menu contains the following items:

File
Edit
Tools
Navigator
Window
Help

PL/SQL Interpreter Menu

The PL/SQL Interpreter menu contains the following items:

File
Edit
Tools
View
Debug
Navigator
Window
Help

Editor Menu

The Editor menu contains the following items:

File
Edit
Tools
Window
Help

File Menu

The File menu appears on each of the main menus in Oracle Procedure Builder and supports tasks like creating new libraries, opening interpreter files, saving log files, connecting to the database, and managing access. The File menu contains the following items:

New
Open…
Close
Save
Save As…
Revert
Attach…
Compile…
Load…
Interpret…
Log…
Connect…
Disconnect
Library Access…
Exit

File, New

The File, New menu item supports the creation of new libraries. The creation of a library from the menu is identical to creating it from within the Object Navigator.

File, Attach…

The File, Attach… menu item enables you to attach external libraries to your application. Once a library is attached to your application, all of the PL/SQL objects in that library may be referenced. A library is attached in read-only mode. You must open a library to make changes to it. When the File, Attach… menu item is selected, the Attach Library dialog box is invoked. The Attach Library dialog box is shown in Figure H.1.

FIGURE H.1.
The Attach Library dialog box.

From the Attach Library dialog box, you may enter the library name, or you can search for a library file by specifying where to search from and clicking the Find… button. When the File System is chosen and the Find… button is selected, the PL/SQL Library File dialog box appears. When the Database is chosen and the Find… button is selected, the Database Libraries dialog box appears.

File, Load…

The File, Load… menu item enables you to load PL/SQL program units into Oracle Procedure Builder. Once a source file is loaded, all of the PL/SQL objects in that source file may be referenced. When the File, Load… menu item is selected, the Load Program Unit dialog box is invoked. Figure H.2 shows the Load Program Unit dialog box.

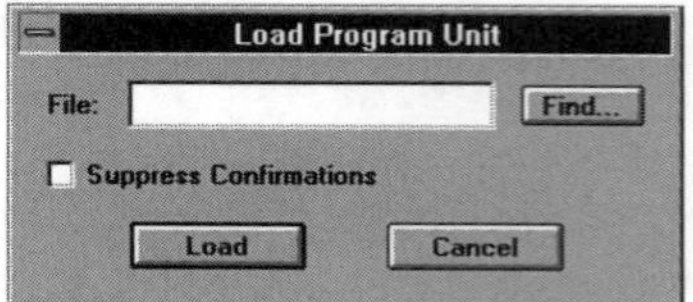

FIGURE H.2.
The Load Program Unit dialog box.

From the Load Program Unit dialog box, you may enter the name of a PL/SQL source file, or search for the file by clicking the Find… button. When the Find… button is selected, the PL/SQL Source File dialog box appears. The file extensions for source files—or all file types—are available from the List Files of Type drop-down list. The file extension for PL/SQL source files is .PLS. Loading a PL/SQL source file is similar to opening a library file.

File, Interpret…

The File, Interpret… menu item enables you to load and execute script files in the PL/SQL Interpreter. The script file is loaded, and each of the PL/SQL or Oracle Procedure Builder commands in that script file are executed. When the File, Interpret… menu item is selected, the Interpret Debug Script dialog box is invoked. Figure H.3 shows the Interpret Debug Script dialog box.

FIGURE H.3.
The Interpret Debug Script dialog box.

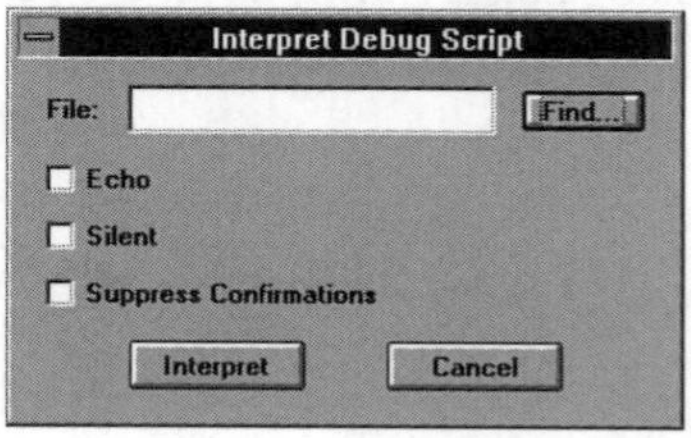

Notice the three check boxes in the Interpret Debug Script dialog box. When the Echo check box is selected, the contents of the script file are displayed in the PL/SQL Interpreter pane as the script is executed. When the Silent check box is selected, no status information is displayed. To prevent the confirmation dialog boxes from appearing, select Suppress Confirmation.

From the Interpret Debug Script dialog box, you may enter the name of a PL/SQL debug script file, or search for the file by clicking the Find... button. When the Find... button is selected, the PL/SQL Debug Script File dialog box appears. The file extensions for PL/SQL debug script files—or all file types—are available from the List Files of Type drop-down list. The file extension for PL/SQL debug script files is .PLD.

File, Log...

The File, Log... menu item enables you to save the results of the session to a log file. When the File, Log... menu item is selected, the Log Interpreter dialog box is invoked. Figure H.4 shows the Log Interpreter dialog box.

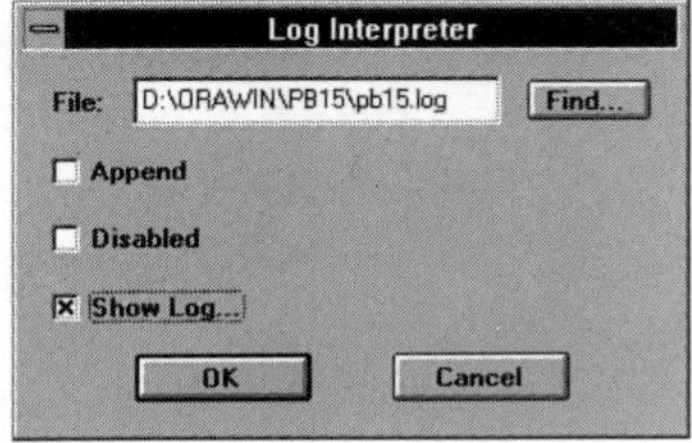

FIGURE H.4.
The Log Interpreter dialog box.

Notice the three check boxes in the Log Interpreter dialog box. Selecting Append will add the results from the current session to the existing log file. Checking Disabled suspends the entry into the log file. When Show Log... is selected, the PL/SQL Interpreter Log window is displayed.

From the Log Interpreter dialog box, you may enter the name of a log file or search for a file by clicking the Find... button. When the Find... button is selected, the Open dialog box appears. The file extensions for log files—or all file types—are available from the List Files of Type drop-down list. The file extension for PL/SQL Interpreter log files is .LOG.

File, Library Access...

The File, Library Access... menu item enables you to manage the user access to libraries saved in the Oracle database. Once a library is saved in the Oracle database, you can grant or remove access for any Oracle user. When the File, Library Access... menu item is selected, the Grant Access List dialog box is invoked. (See Figure H.5.)

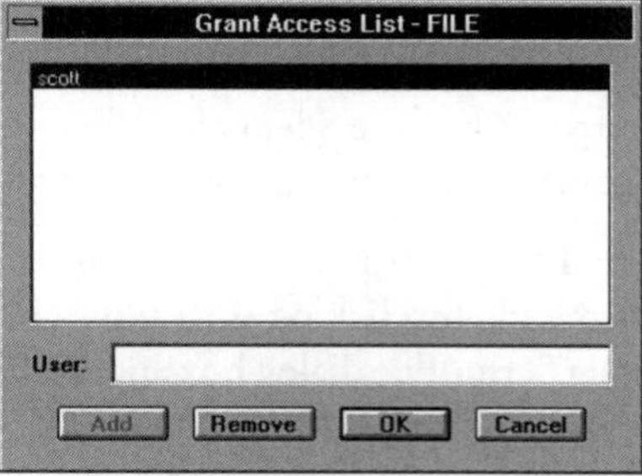

FIGURE H.5.
The Grant Access List dialog box.

The Grant Access List dialog box automatically queries the Oracle database and lists all users who have been granted access to the current library. You may enter a new userid in the User file and click the Add button, or you can select a user from the list and click the Remove button.

Edit Menu

The Edit menu appears on each of the main menus in Oracle Procedure Builder. It supports tasks such as editing, searching, importing, and exporting. The Edit menu contains the following items:

Undo
Cut
Copy
Paste
Clear
Duplicate
Search/Replace…
Search/Replace All…
Import…
Export…

Edit, Search/Replace All…

The Edit, Search/Replace All… menu item invokes the Search/Replace All Program Units dialog box to provide the search and optional replacement of text strings using the Object Navigator. The Program Unit Editor or the Stored Program Unit Editor is automatically invoked when a search is successful. Text may be searched for using the Search button, or it may be searched and replaced with other text using the Replace or Replace All buttons.

Tools Menu

The Tools menu appears on each of the main menus in Oracle Procedure Builder and supports the opening and activation of the various editors. The Tools menu contains the following items:

Program Unit Editor
PL/SQL Interpreter
Stored Program Unit Editor
Database Trigger Editor

View Menu

The View menu only appears in the PL/SQL Interpreter menu in Oracle Procedure Builder. It contains check-style menu items that define which window panes are presented in the PL/SQL Interpreter. The View menu contains the following items:

Source Pane
Navigator Pane
Interpreter Pane

View, Source Pane

The View, Source Pane menu item is a check-style menu item that turns the display of the source pane on and off. The source pane is where the source code is displayed for the current program unit. It appears at the top of the PL/SQL Interpreter window. To edit the source code, use the Program Unit Editor.

View, Navigator Pane

The View, Navigator Pane menu item is a check-style menu item that turns the display of the Object Navigator on and off within the PL/SQL Interpreter window. The Object Navigator pane enables you to review and modify variables during debugging. It is located in the center of the PL/SQL Interpreter window.

View, Interpreter Pane

The View, Interpreter Pane menu item is a check-style menu item that turns the display of the PL/SQL command-line interpreter pane on and off. The interpreter pane is where the Oracle Procedure Builder commands and the PL/SQL statements are displayed and/or entered. It appears at the bottom of the PL/SQL Interpreter window.

Debug Menu

The Debug menu only appears in the PL/SQL Interpreter menu in Oracle Procedure Builder. It enables you to set breaks and triggers in program units as well as navigate through the source code during debugging. The Debug menu contains the following items:

Break…
Trigger…
Edit…
Step…
Go
Reset
Interpreter Log…

Debug, Break…

The Debug, Break menu item provides a graphical interface to the Oracle Procedure Builder `BREAK` command. When the Debug, Break menu item is selected, the PL/SQL Breakpoint dialog box is invoked. Figure H.6 shows the PL/SQL Breakpoint dialog box, indicating a break on line 7 of procedure `MAIN`.

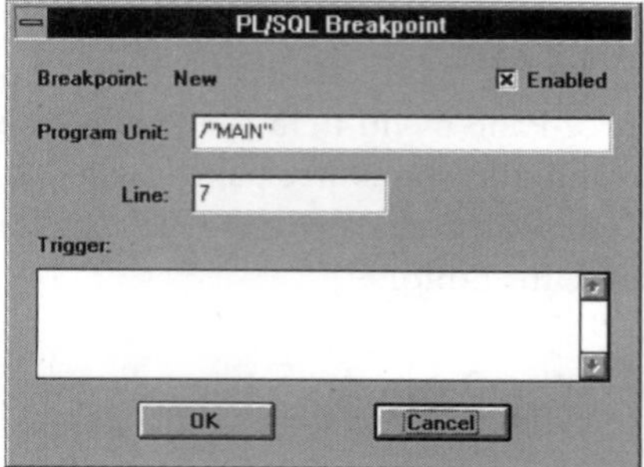

FIGURE H.6.
The PL/SQL Breakpoint dialog box setting a break.

The PL/SQL Breakpoint dialog box can be used to create breaks for a given line number and can include a break trigger. The PL/SQL Breakpoint dialog box can be invoked from the source pane of the PL/SQL Interpreter window by double-clicking a line of source code or by right-clicking and selecting Break… from the pop-up menu.

Debug, Trigger…

The Debug, Trigger menu item provides a graphical interface to the Oracle Procedure Builder `TRIGGER` command. When the Debug, Trigger menu item is selected, the PL/SQL Trigger dialog box is invoked. (See Figure H.7.)

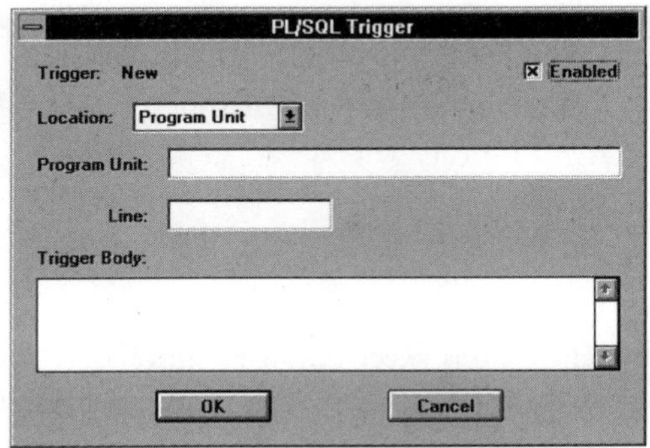

FIGURE H.7.
The PL/SQL Trigger dialog box.

The PL/SQL Trigger dialog box is used to create conditional breakpoints by including `if…then…else` logic in the break trigger. The PL/SQL Trigger dialog box can be invoked from the source pane of the PL/SQL Interpreter window by right-clicking and selecting Trigger… from the pop-up menu.

Debug, Edit…

The Debug, Edit… menu item opens the Program Unit window, or if the Program Unit Editor has already been opened, it sets the focus to the Program Unit window. The Program Unit Editor is used to modify or create procedures, functions, and packages during debugging. The Program Unit Editor can be invoked by double-clicking a program unit under a Program Units node in the Object Navigator, or from the source pane of the PL/SQL Interpreter window by right-clicking and selecting Edit… from the pop-up menu.

Debug, Step…

The Debug, Step… menu item provides a graphical interface to the Oracle Procedure Builder `STEP` command. When the Debug, Step… menu item is selected, the PL/SQL Step dialog box is invoked. (See Figure H.8.)

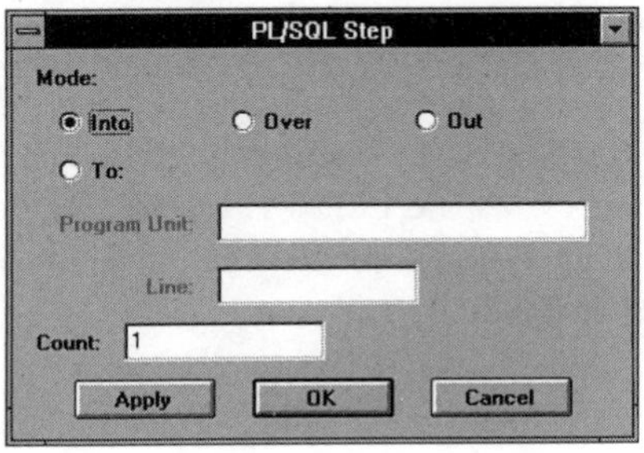

FIGURE H.8.
The PL/SQL Step dialog box.

Notice the PL/SQL Step dialog box provides a radio group indicating step mode. There are corresponding buttons on the PL/SQL Interpreter toolbar for the `STEP` command modes `INTO`, `OVER`, and `OUT`. When mode `TO` is selected, fields for a program unit name and line number are enabled.

Debug, Go

The Debug, Go menu item executes the Oracle Procedure Builder `GO` command. When the Debug, Go menu item is selected, the execution of the current program unit resumes. There is a corresponding button on the PL/SQL Interpreter toolbar for the `GO` command.

Debug, Reset

The Debug, Reset menu item executes the Oracle Procedure Builder `RESET` command. When the Debug, Reset menu item is selected, the execution of the current process is terminated. There is a corresponding button on the PL/SQL Interpreter toolbar for the `RESET` command.

Debug, Interpreter Log...

The Debug, Interpreter Log… menu item opens the PL/SQL Interpreter Log window, or if the PL/SQL Interpreter Log has already been opened, it sets the focus to the PL/SQL Interpreter Log window. A log file must be open for the Debug, Interpreter Log… menu item to be enabled. The PL/SQL Interpreter Log is used to review the current log file during debugging, as shown in Figure H.9.

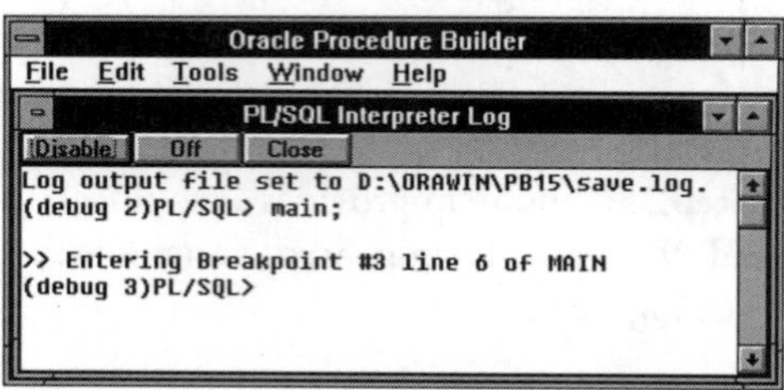

FIGURE H.9.
The PL/SQL Interpreter Log window.

Notice the buttons under the PL/SQL Interpreter Log window title bar. The Disable button stops the entry into the log file and changes to Enable. The Off button closes the log file, and the Close button closes the PL/SQL Interpreter Log window. The PL/SQL Interpreter Log window can be activated from the Debug menu or by selecting Show Log… from the Log Interpreter dialog box.

Navigator Menu

The Navigator menu appears on the Object Navigator and PL/SQL Interpreter menus in Oracle Procedure Builder. It supports the display and management of objects in the Object Navigator. The Navigator menu contains the following items:

- Create
- Delete
- Compile
- Expand
- Collapse
- Expand All
- Collapse All
- Mark
- Go to Mark
- Disable
- Enable
- Paste Name
- Paste Arguments

Navigator, Disable

The Navigator, Disable menu item temporarily disables the current break point or break action during debugging.

Navigator, Enable

The Navigator, Enable menu item turns on the currently disabled break point or break action during debugging.

I

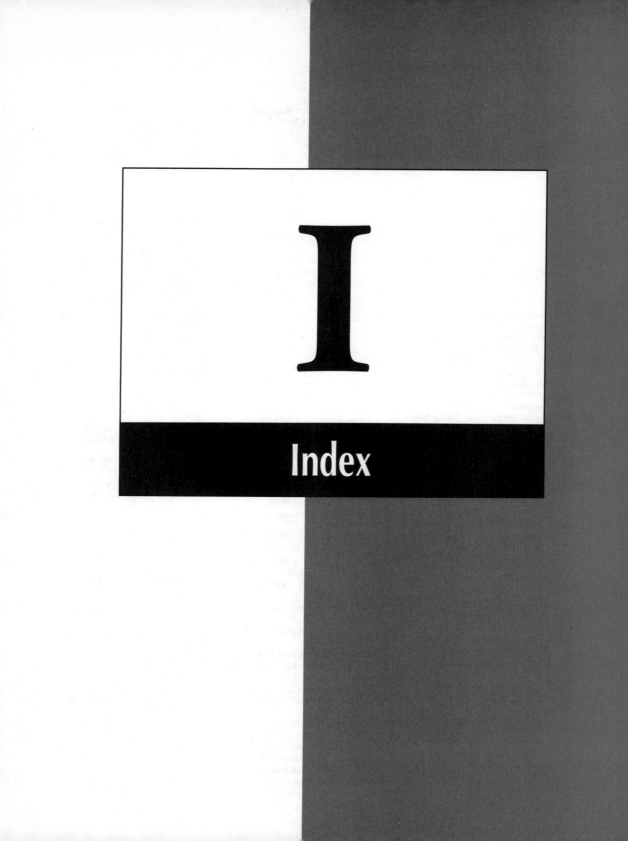

Index

Symbols

A

B

D

G

H

I

M

N

O

P

S

Book ISBN 0-672-30852-5

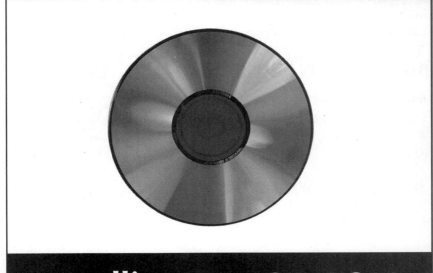

Installing Your CD-ROM

Installing the CD-ROM

The companion CD-ROM contains sample programs developed by the author, plus an assortment of third-party tools and product demos. The disc is designed to be explored using a browser program. Using Sams' Guide to the CD-ROM browser, you can view information concerning products and companies, and install programs with a single click of the mouse. To install the browser, here's what to do:

Windows 3.*x*/NT Installation Instructions

1. Insert the CD-ROM disc into your CD-ROM drive.
2. From File Manager or Program Manager, choose Run from the File menu.
3. Type `<drive>\setup` and press Enter, where `<drive>` corresponds to the drive letter of your CD-ROM. For example, if your CD-ROM is drive D:, type `D:\SETUP` and press Enter.
4. The installation creates a program manager group named Oracle Developer/2000. To browse the CD-ROM, double-click on the Guide to the CD-ROM icon inside this Program Manager group.

Windows 95 Installation Instructions

1. Insert the CD-ROM disc into your CD-ROM drive. If the AutoPlay feature of your Windows 95 system is enabled, the setup program will start automatically.
2. If the setup program does not start automatically, double-click on the My Computer icon.
3. Double-click on the icon representing your CD-ROM drive.
4. Double-click on the icon titled Setup.exe to run the installation program. Follow the onscreen instructions that appear. When setup ends, double-click on the Guide to the CD-ROM icon to begin exploring the disc.

Following installation, you can restart the Guide to the CD-ROM program by pressing the Start button, selecting Programs, then Oracle Developer/2000 and Guide to the CD-ROM.

NOTE

The Guide to the CD-ROM program requires at least 256 colors. For best results, set your monitor to display between 256 and 64,000 colors. A screen resolution of 640×480 pixels is also recommended. If necessary, adjust your monitor settings before using the CD-ROM.